PEOPLE
From Impoverishment to Empowerment

People

From Impoverishment to Empowerment

Edited by
Üner Kırdar and Leonard Silk

Thinkers from many countries address the
relationship between prosperity and peace.

NEW YORK UNIVERSITY PRESS
New York and London

Library of Congress Cataloging-in-Publication Data

People : from impoverishment to empowerment / edited by Üner Kıdar and
    Leonard Silk
    p. cm.
  ISBN 0-8147-4670-5 (alk. paper)
  1. Social policy. 2. Social problems. 3. Poverty. 4. Peace.
  5. Economic development. I. Kırdar, Üner, 1933-   . II. Silk,
  Leonard, 1918-   .
  HN17.5.P445 1995
  361.6'1--dc20   94-39338
                                                        CIP

The content of this book does not necessarily reflect the views of the
United Nations Development Programme. The papers in this volume were
contributed by the authors in their personal capacities and they are solely
responsible for their views.

New York University Press books are printed on acid-free paper,
and their binding materials are chosen for their strength and durability.

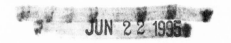

Contents

Foreword

This book is about people. How to end their impoverishment and how to empower them? Today, the challenge before us is twofold: to comprehend and analyze the nature of the social, economic, and political changes happening in the world; and to understand their implications for the management of the international system and its institutions.

The international community will be considering some of these issues in March, when Heads of State and of Government convene at Copenhagen for the first ever World Summit for Social Development. I see this book as a valuable contribution to the preparation being made for the Summit meeting.

The capacity of States to maintain social peace, and to provide an environment in which their citizens are able to fulfill their full potential as human beings, is being challenged from above—by new forces of a supranational nature, which no State, acting on its own, can control—and from below—by societies which are losing their cohesion and, in some places, are affected by a crisis of values.

New global understandings, involving many actors other than States themselves, may be needed if States are to retain the capacity to determine how their societies evolve. New dimensions of international cooperation have to be imagined, defined, and implemented.

New global economic and social issues are now challenging the very stability and good governance of States. They cannot be effectively tackled except at a global level. They include the environment and sustainable development, disease, such as the AIDS pandemic, and transnational migration. Some illegal groups, such as drug traffickers and mafias dealing in the trade of arms, precious metals, and other commodities are now a major subversive threat to many States. Some criminal "empires" are richer than many poorer States.

How, then, can the international community work together, and help

States protect their integrity and sovereignty against new threats?

The global economy itself brings new challenges for the international community. Competition is inevitable and beneficial; but it must take place within an agreed framework. If there is not an agreed set of international economic rules and accepted international standards of behavior, States will be tempted to opt out of the global economy by attempting to introduce bilateral controls and regulations. If all countries do not subject themselves to the same disciplines and systems of surveillance, the global economy will not function to the mutual advantage of all.

One paradox of economic globalization is that, while individual governments are increasingly relinquishing economic power to the forces of the market, there is a need for concerted intergovernmental action in the economic sphere: should States not therefore consider, for example, what action should be taken by them collectively to safeguard fairness and discipline in the global economy?

While new roles for concerted action by States at the global level still need to be defined and discussed, it is accepted that an important function of any State is to provide social services and to make social provision for its citizens.

Alongside the global challenges faced by the international system of States is the crisis of adjustment faced by human society generally. This crisis is unprecedented both in its nature and in its impact. It raises key issues for national communities, as well as for the global community.

Three major issues are affecting human society today: poverty, employment and the reduction of unemployment, and social integration. Of all these issues, action to combat poverty is perhaps the key. More than one billion people in the world live in poverty; even more do not have access to drinking water and sanitation. At least 500 million children do not have access to primary education and about one billion adults remain illiterate. Most people who are poor are born into poverty.

Because the poor often live among the affluent, and, through modern systems of communications, are aware of their situation and of their inequality and therefore, of the injustice which they suffer, the existence of many millions of poor and deprived people in the world is a likely cause of social unrest, and therefore, a potential threat to international peace and security. Such a situation is a moral affront in a world which has all the necessary resources to remedy the situation; it is a denial of dignity to those affected; and it is a waste of productive resources.

If the argument that poverty should be eliminated is morally and politically unassailable, what needs to be done politically to ensure that the appropriate action is taken?

Social integration is also an important ingredient to empower the people. The sense of belonging which is essential in any fair and tolerant society is under attack in many parts of the world. Global economic and cultural forces are bringing cultural homogenization and materialism to societies which previously stressed the values of community and solidarity. Those who feel threatened by such forces sometimes turn to extreme and exclusivist doctrines, which stress cultural identity but which are further polarizing and fragmenting many societies.

There is a need, therefore, to consider what action the international community can take to encourage and assist States and their societies to foster a spirit of pluralism, inclusion, and tolerance of diversity. Within States, a major underlying cause of social tension and disintegration is unemployment. Unemployment is clearly linked with the other themes of the Social Summit agenda: it makes poverty almost inevitable, and it feeds the forces of social disintegration. It threatens the social fabric and political stability of States. Conversely, work helps to give dignity and a sense of worth to individual human beings.

But as one of the sections of this book makes clear, demographic trends in many countries make it extremely unlikely that unemployment will be appreciably reduced. What can be done globally to help create jobs, now that the role of the State in national economic management has been so drastically reduced in many countries?

Today there is a new awareness that the social, economic, and military aspects of security are indivisible. In a sense, we can return to the original vision of the framers of the Charter. The interrelationship among elements previously regarded as separate and compartmentalized—such as peace, the environment, social justice, democracy, and development—is now both understood, and, increasingly, accepted by the international community.

Action on all fronts should proceed simultaneously and in coordinated fashion:

- Without peace, human energies cannot be productively employed.
- Without economic growth, there can be no sustained, broad-based improvement in material well-being.
- Without protection of the environment, the basis of human survival will be eroded.
- Without societal justice, mounting inequalities will threaten social cohesion.
- Without political participation in freedom, development will remain fragile and perpetually at risk.

Can the international community, half a century after the United Nations Charter was signed, now evolve ways of ensuring an international social and economic order which contributes to the overriding goal of a peaceful and stable world?

I see this book as an important undertaking to share international knowledge, insight, and experience at a critical time for the international community. Studies of this type are indispensable prerequisites if we are to rise to the conceptual and political challenges the world now faces.

I congratulate the United Nations Development programme and the editors of the book, Dr. Üner Kırdar and Dr. Leonard Silk, for their foresight, energy, and skill both in the selection of the topics for the book, and also for assembling such a distinguished group of experts and practitioners to contribute to it.

January 1995   Boutros Boutros-Ghali
                                                Secretary-General
                                                United Nations

Introduction

This book is the result of a collaborative international effort of more than fifty global citizens of different backgrounds committed to improving the state of humanity. It addresses some of the world's most compelling social problems by offering ideas for empowering people and lifting them out of poverty.

No book could be more timely. With depressing frequency, we learn about another society that has disintegrated into conflict, another 10,000 people who have lost their jobs, and worsening living standards in many countries.

We live in a world where one-fifth of the world's population goes hungry every night, where one-quarter lacks even the most basic necessities, such as safe drinking water, where one-third lives in a state of poverty—below any recognizable level of human dignity. Poverty and its handmaidens—joblessness and social disintegration—stand with environmental decay as the four horsemen of the modern apocalypse.

From the perspective of someone working at the United Nations, one cannot help but feel that the world as constituted today can be appropriately described as a disaster machine, producing crises with distressing regularity—civil conflicts, floods of refugees, famine and environmental disasters, even failed states.

These events have complex causes, but one of the fuels for the disaster machine is underdevelopment. Underdevelopment means human deprivation, wide disparities in opportunities, social disintegration, and marginalization. Underdevelopment means chronic widespread joblessness and chronic environmental decline.

It means low resilience and ability to cope with destructive change. Moreover, however large the role of underdevelopment as a *cause* of today's crises, development is surely a major ingredient of the *cure—*

at least if development is people-centered and sustainable, what we call "sustainable human development."

Development empowers people. It gives them a sense of personal security. Development means safety from chronic threats such as hunger, disease, and repression. And it means protection from sudden and destructive disruptions in our daily lives, the sudden violence that can attack individuals, communities, and entire nations.

In short, development means providing people with a sense of security in their homes, at their jobs, and in their communities.

People will not be secure unless they have a job that will earn them enough money to feed their families and provide them with shelter. They will not be secure unless they have escaped the worst of poverty and have some hope for the future. And they will not be secure if they are in danger because of ethnic strife or drug violence or violence against women, or terrorism or other aspects of social disintegration.

Development is necessary, but not the same type of development that the international community supported while the Cold War raged. Now that the Cold War is over, we need a new vision of development, one that can turn off the world's disaster machine, and one that recognizes that even where there is peace, there is poverty.

What we need to respond to the challenges ahead is a new approach to development, one that not only generates economic growth but distributes its benefits equitably, that regenerates the environment rather than destroying it, that empowers people rather than marginalizing them, and that gives priority to the poor, enlarging their choices and opportunities and providing for their participation in decisions affecting them. We need development that is pro-poor, pro-nature, pro-jobs, and pro-women and pro-children. In short, we need sustainable human development.

None of the great goals our societies seek today — peace, jobs, environmental protection, human rights, population stabilization, democracy, social integration — can be achieved except in the context of this new approach to development.

The founders of the United Nations recognized nearly fifty years ago that the battle of peace — within and among countries–has to be fought on two fronts.

The first front was described as "the security front where victory spells freedom from fear." The second front was the "economic and social front, where victory means freedom from want. Only victory on both fronts can assure the world of an enduring peace.... No provisions that can be written into the Charter will enable the Security Council to make the world secure from war if men and women have no security in their homes or jobs."

The United Nations' fiftieth anniversary is taking place this year. This is therefore an ideal time to start waging the second battle with renewed determination.

Also in 1995, heads of state, development experts, members of the business community, the press, academia, and others will converge on Copenhagen for a summit to address three of the most compelling issues of our time: widespread poverty, growing unemployment, and the disintegration of societies. The World Summit for Social Development will be the first time that so many leaders and representatives of hundreds of institutions will come together to seek common solutions to these problems that are now so common to virtually every country.

The so-called "Social Summit" will be an extremely important event for individuals, communities, and governments. And, the "programme of action" that is drawn up during the summit will be extremely important to the United Nations because it will guide much of the organization's work after it marks its fiftieth anniversary.

The Social Summit must breathe new life into the part of the United Nations' Charter that calls on the organization to promote higher standards of living, full employment, and economic and social progress. The United Nations cannot be a strong force for peace unless it is also a strong force for development.

I hope that the Social Summit will result in a new mandate for the United Nations, one that will guide it through the institution's next fifty years. I hope it will set a global goal backed by an international compact to eliminate the worst aspects of world poverty within a definite time frame. About 150 years ago, the world began a global crusade against slavery. The Social Summit must launch a similar crusade against poverty. I am confident that *People: From Impoverishment to Empowerment* will make a tremendous intellectual contribution to meeting this challenge. Each section of this volume provides unique insights into the complexities of poverty and other vexing social problems and offers innovative strategies for confronting them.

Time is short—not just the time to prepare for next year's events, but the time to address the world's escalating challenges. Everything that must be done should have been done yesterday. Tomorrow it will be more costly. Time is the most important variable in the equation of the future. A sense of urgency is merely common sense. That is probably what we are most in need of: a sense of urgency.

This book brings fresh, independent, and cutting-edge ideas from some of the world's greatest thinkers into a dialogue on the future of humanity. I thank all the contributors to this book for offering their expertise, views, and intellectual leadership to this project. Their work will help chart a new course for all of us intent on empowering people and eliminating poverty in the decades ahead.

January 1995

James Gustave Speth
Administrator
United Nations Development Programme

Overview

Üner Kırdar and Leonard Silk

Despite advances over the past fifty years in the quest for "empowering people," a large unfinished agenda to combat human deprivation challenges humanity in the twenty-first century. Global poverty is worsening, unemployment is on the rise, and social disintegration is becoming an ill that plagues all countries. People are increasingly turning against their neighbors in brutal ethnic conflict. With these, come other social problems: crime, violence, disease, pollution, environmental destruction, and the total breakdown of governments and institutions such as the family. In brief, social time bombs are ticking under each society.

Never before have people had so much knowledge and information at their disposal. But unfortunately, the international community has so far failed to use this knowledge to transform the people from impoverishment to empowerment. Meanwhile, each day, another piece of the planet sinks into chaos, despair, and desperation, and behind every failed state there is a failed process of the development of people.

The international community must reverse this trend before any more societies collapse. We must make better use of our knowledge and other resources to prevent social problems from occurring and to fix the problems that have already erupted.

The United Nations is sponsoring a World Summit for Social Development, which will take place in March 1995 in Copenhagen. There, delegates from all countries and major international institutions will join forces to formulate an urgently needed strategy for curing some of the world's major social ills.

To help the global community prepare for this "People's Summit," the UNDP Development Study Programme convened a roundtable meeting in Stockholm, Sweden, from 22 to 24 July 1994, titled "Change: Social Conflict or Harmony?" The Stockholm Roundtable was the third in a conference series on "Global Changes." The meeting gathered together more than 160 eminent statesmen, leading international thinkers, development practitioners, representatives of academia, the business world, and media, who participated in their personal capacities, to examine current global transformations and to suggest policy priorities and action initiatives.

The first roundtable, which was held in Antalya, Turkey, in September 1990, considered whether the changes of the post-Cold War era would bring the fresh impetus needed to meet global development challenges. Thus, this constituted not a threat but a true opportunity for human progress. Its findings and proceedings were published in a five-volume set entitled *Change: Threat or Opportunity?*

The second roundtable in the series, held in Bucharest, Romania, in September 1992, examined the political, economic, and social aspects of ongoing changes and their impact on the lives of people. Its outcomes were the subject of the book *A World Fit for People.*

The overview of the present volume reflects the different views expressed at the Stockholm Roundtable. It is a collection of abbreviated and edited versions of a select number of papers presented at the meeting. The volume covers a broad range of issues affecting the lives of people today. The last section of the book offers proposals for "An Agenda for People," which emanating from the Stockholm Roundtable discussions and the different sections of this volume.

In the view of Ambassador Juan Somavia, Permanent Representative of Chile to the United Nations and a main architect of the World Summit for Social Development, one of the most important prerequisites for the summit's preparatory process is a well-grounded intellectual framework and engaging vision. Traditional thinking and recipes are not enough and are not working; new concepts and policy approaches are needed. We hope that this book will be considered as a contribution in that respect.

Swings of Thought

The 1970s

A major root of many of today's problems is impoverishment. Observers in the 1970s agreed that to eradicate poverty and underdevelopment, the international community needed to promote economic growth and social reform. But in the 1980s, development thinking changed. Many experts believed that economic growth should be not only a prerequisite for social development, but that once growth was under way, social progress would follow naturally. The results of this approach were gravely disappointing: many countries are worse off today than they were decades earlier, and social problems are intensifying.

Thus the pendulum of development thinking swings back and forth. But now most development experts are returning to the beliefs of the 1970s. Development requires a balanced and integrated set of economic, financial, and social policies.

Before the 1980s, the development community generally accepted the view that high rates of economic growth are necessary for achieving social goals, such as poverty reduction and the generation of jobs. But growth by itself is not enough.

Research has shown that high rates of economic growth were not solely responsible for East Asia's attainment of full employment in the early 1970s. Instead, government emphasis on the full use of the factors of production–especially labor–was the cornerstone of the region's high-growth rate. Without development policies geared toward employment, the region would not have experienced 8 to 10 percent growth rates. The lesson drawn from East Asia is that the pattern of growth is just as important as the rate of growth.

This pattern depends on governments' choices–choices about which economic sectors should receive support and which population groups should receive special attention. The pattern of growth also depends on the quality of human resources in a country, the degree of balance between regions, and the extent to which people have an opportunity to participate in the decisions that affect their future.

Experience taught the development community in the 1970s that economic growth is effective for achieving social objectives and tackling poverty, but this might take three to five generations. Such a long period would be humanly unacceptable and politically irresponsible.

The 1980s

The lessons learned in the 1970s were all but forgotten in the 1980s. The global recession in the first part of the decade and the debt crisis that began in 1982 resulted in the return to an older development paradigm: first economic growth, then everything else would follow. Gone was the idea that economic and social goals were one. Gone was the belief that attaining one goal without the other would lead to disaster. Development experts seemed to have forgotten that too much emphasis on social goals without sufficient attention to economic goals leads to bankruptcy. They also seemed to have forgotten that too much attention to economic goals without enough attention to social goals leads to unrest and an end to economic growth.

The results of the policies pursued during the 1980s can be seen everywhere. Employment has become a universal problem, unmanaged urban development has reduced standards of living, and education quality has deteriorated. Health services everywhere need restructuring, social security and pension funds (where they exist) are faltering, and economic migrants are coming in increasing numbers to many industrialized countries.

It is more appropriate than ever to say that "poverty anywhere is a threat to prosperity everywhere."

The Challenge

The economic and social problems that emerged in the late 1980s and early 1990s present the development community with a new challenge and require a new development vision. This vision can be captured by the phrase, put people first, or perhaps, poor people first. The big challenge for the World

Summit for Social Development is to have the foresight and courage to make "Poor People First" the underlying theme for its commitments.

Poverty

In Part 1 on poverty, the contributors consider the patterns and nature of poverty and the political, economic, social, and environmental impacts of poverty. They ask, what could be learned from experience and what are the best means for reducing and alleviating poverty.

The Nature of Poverty

More than one billion people live in absolute poverty. Half of these people live in Asia, and about one-quarter of them live in Sub-Saharan Africa. The largest part of the poor population lives in rural areas, but the ranks of the urban poor are growing steadily. Most of the poor are female.

Poverty is usually defined in terms of income. But this is only one dimension of poverty. The criterion for poverty should be broadened to include more than income. It should include social status, physical strength, and power. The poor suffer from their inferiority, isolation, vulnerability to abuse, powerlessness, and humiliation.

In the view of one of our distinguished contributors, Princess Basma Bint Talal of Jordan, "the poor know the issues affecting them and what the development experts say. But they express them differently. It is time that policy makers learned their language."

Thus, a key approach to reducing poverty and deprivation is enabling the poor to freely express their needs. Part of that approach includes encouraging the rest of society to respect and support poor people's efforts to change their living conditions. Enabling them to be better off in their own terms will require actions on both micro- and macrolevels. The reduction of poverty and deprivation must be sought through changes in national policies, through the tapping of new resources, and through institutional, professional, and other changes that will help reach the poor and improve their lives.

National Policies

The poor are everywhere, but most live in the developing world. Global economic shocks, sudden environmental changes, and other factors make them more vulnerable to worsening poverty, as reflected in sickness, disability, or loss of assets and livelihoods.

Governments must take a close look at how national policies affect the poor and devise ways to reduce the poor's vulnerability to worsening poverty.

Some forms of structural adjustment are necessary. But too often, structural adjustment has penalized the poor–especially women–in a variety of ways, including declining resources for education and health and the elimination of some subsidies. Governments should provide the poor with safety nets to cushion the shocks of economic transition.

National investments should seek to empower the poor. This means investments that respond to the poor's own vision of their opportunities and their own analyses of their problems. Governments should turn the ownership of these investments over to the poor. This would help ensure that the poor's labor is more productive and would give them a greater chance to improve their own well-being in the long run.

National governance structures make it difficult for the poor to influence decisions that affect their lives. For example, national legal systems often discriminate against the poor because they are unfamiliar with their rights and lack access to legal support.

Unemployment

In Part 2, the contributors look into the issue of unemployment and under-employment. They search to pinpoint the causes of these problems, which afflict practically every rich and poor country, and to propose solutions.

As the world's economies have grown increasingly interdependent, global unemployment has risen. Because of this interdependence, we need a global solution to the problem.

Unemployment in the 1990s

The employment situation varies by region. In East and Southeast Asia, including China, output and employment have been growing dramatically. In South Asia, absolute poverty is on the decline, but the growth in employment has been precarious; much valuable work pays workers barely enough to survive. These regions have been relatively successful at boosting employment, but the success is fragile.

For people in much of the rest of the world, having a productive, remunerative and reasonably secure job is only a dream. Societies that fail to offer the prospect of this type of job are bound to be socially unstable and economically insecure.

In the relatively rich nations that belong to the Organization for Economic Cooperation and Development, economic growth has resumed. But jobs are growing more slowly than production. And even where unemployment has fallen (as in the United States), new jobs pay less and are less secure than in previous periods.

Eastern Europe's rapid economic transformation has wiped out many jobs. Subsidies to cushion the impact of job losses require massive government spending, which contributes to inflation and makes the new poor even poorer.

In Latin America, the workforce is changing. The working-age population is increasing, more women are entering the job market, and growing numbers of people are moving to urban areas in search of work. Meanwhile, governments are cutting back on the public sector, resulting in fewer jobs. Most new jobs are found in the informal sector.

In the Middle East and North Africa, the population has been growing at a time when oil revenues have been shrinking. Reduced oil revenues mean that governments are no longer able to be the employer of last resort, especially for university graduates. This situation is resulting in instability that prevents governments from implementing economic reforms.

The unemployment crisis is greatest in Sub-Saharan Africa, where the population is growing at an unprecedented pace. More than half of all nonfarm workers have found jobs in government, but governments in the region cannot afford to hire any more people or raise wages. In addition, structural adjustment programs have failed to result in increased employment.

Employment and economic activity are on the rise in East and Southeast Asia. Here, the state sector is small, labor markets are only lightly regulated, and government policies favor private-sector employers. Manipulated exchange rates have promoted exports. Protectionism — especially in imports like rice — have supported social stability and quality of incomes. Governments in the region have assigned human rights a low priority, but there are signs that social progress is following economic progress in some countries.

Because of its large size, China is a special case. A rush toward economic liberalization has contributed to astonishing and probably unsustainable rates of economic growth and a quick decline in poverty. This progress has been achieved under tight political control, with no concessions to human rights or to the rights of workers.

The countries of South Asia have generally survived the shocks of the oil and debt crises. Nevertheless, they still need to create huge numbers of jobs because more and more women are joining the labor force. Even though many workers in rural areas are moving to cities, employment in agriculture may grow. Meanwhile, governments are reducing restrictions on labor markets to enable many enterprises to become more competitive.

The employment crises in some regions are often the result of government incentives that have distorted the job market and of inadequate government institutions. Some countries, for example, have promoted capital investment, when labor-intensive investments would have been more appropriate.

Monetary restraints in the industrial countries have brought growth to a halt. When growth stopped, the industrial countries cut back on imports, thereby hurting the economies of many countries, particularly ones that export commodities. In an attempt to limit domestic borrowing, governments of the OECD countries raised their interest rates. As a result, interest rates rose everywhere, putting a particularly great burden on the heavily indebted developing countries.

Impact of Unemployment

The painful experience of the Great Depression and the economic decline that led to World War II caused the founders of the United Nations to identify full employment as one of the main pillars of international peace, stability, and well-being. But today, the goal of full employment seems to be all but forgotten.

"Jobless growth" has been a disturbing phenomenon in recent years. Elimination of jobs is now considered an important measure to increase competitiveness. In some of the richest countries, structural unemployment has recently reached record levels. Three and four decades ago, a normal unemployment rate was between 3 and 4 percent. Today, a normal rate may exceed 6 to 10 percent.

In the past, economists considered unemployment a temporary problem that would be resolved by market forces. But this is no longer the case. Instead, market forces are leading to permanent job cuts. The profit-making philosophy of today is that workers should be fired if their termination has no effect on production and sales. Because new technologies enable companies to produce more goods with fewer workers, businesses are posting gains by cutting down the workforce.

The growing impact of job cutting is becoming more evident in national economic statistics. Although wages are falling as a percentage of national incomes, corporate profits are rising. In industrial countries, most of the new jobs are being created in the service sector, such as in banking, tourism, insurance, retailing, health care, and restaurants, while jobs are being shed in such areas as manufacturing and mining. What is happening in these sectors, at present, is very similar to the transformation of the agricultural sector at the beginning of this century. The increased mechanization of farming displaced and forced farmers to migrate to urban areas in order to find new jobs in the industrial sector.

The link between "full employment" and the fear of "rising inflation" is also inhibiting the growth of jobs. A different choice needs to be made in the trade-off between job growth and low inflation. In the view of many market-oriented economists and policy makers, the safeguarding of the value of currencies and low interest rates seems more important than job security and economic growth.

The employment problems of developing countries have other dimensions as well. The number of jobs that must be created to accommodate new entrants into the labor market is reaching the insurmountable number of nearly one billion. On the other hand, each day the powerful role of corporations in the globalization of the world economy and in the channeling of capital, according to their own policies and priorities, is becoming more apparent. Capital and goods are moving freely from one country to another. However, the same freedom does not exist for the labor force, and strict regulations govern the movements of workers. This has led to a flood of illegal immigrants. Also, the moment that a developing country learns to produce something that is labor intensive, restrictions are immediately applied to those very products. Trade must be open to the products of developing countries; completion of the GATT treaty is essential for their well-being.

In summary, the world economy is operating far below its potential, and that is the main reason for persistent high unemployment. Policy makers use the structural argument as an excuse for not trying hard enough to get their own and the world economy moving again. As Professor Lawrence R. Klein states in his contribution to this book, "single minded attachment to orthodox monetary policy to deal with inflation is used instead and, all too often, has been pursued so vigorously that it has inevitably generated high values of unemployment. This is particularly the case when policy makers have pursued zero-inflation; they achieved these goals in a practical sense, but also placed prominently in tables as countries with high unemployment. Not only this, they have the dubious distinction of being the world leaders who led the world into the last recession."

Social Integration

In Part 3, the contributors consider issues of social disintegration and ethnic conflicts and discuss strategies for making societies more cohesive.

The social fabric of most countries—rich or poor—is weakening. As a result, some nation-states are falling apart. People are increasingly abandoning established social values, and a highly materialistic global culture is evolving. The value of competition is replacing values of sharing and cooperation. The pursuit of happiness is more and more defined in terms of money and consumerism.

Ethnic, tribal, religious, and cultural differences are polarizing groups within nations. The list of causes and effects of growing social instability is long. It includes discrimination against minorities, the inferior status of women, increasing numbers of single-parent households, poorly educated children, juvenile delinquency, drug addiction, disease, and crime. These social ills are both the main causes, as well as the results of, growing social instabilities. They are no longer isolated events, confined within specific national borders. They and their consequences are global.

Patterns of Social Integration

In a normative sense, social integration refers to improved living standards, social justice, and harmonious relations among people. In an analytical sense, social integration refers to patterns of interaction between individuals and groups (these patterns may be unjust or equitable, conflictual or harmonious). But however defined, social integration takes place in a framework of institutions, such as families, communities, the workplace, or states. Furthermore, it is deeply embedded in the social, political, and economic processes and structures of societies, nations, and global systems.

Put simply, social integration is the degree of real harmony (real means freely chosen, not imposed) that exists between groups in a society. Social disintegration is the degree of negative tension between groups. These groups can be workers and employers, men and women, poor and rich, old and young, black and white, or the governed and the governing.

Many forces have influenced social integration. These include the spread of liberal democracy, the dominance of markets, the acceleration of economic globalization, the change in productions systems and labor markets, technological progress, and the revolution in the mass media and communications.

The past decade has been characterized by widespread slow growth, economic stagnation or debt crises, and sharp declines in production, incomes, employment, and living standards. These changes have deeply influenced integration through their impact on the role, responsibilities, and capacities of institutions ranging from the family to the state.

Social fabrics are under stress. Families and communities are disintegrating, crime and violence are spreading, drugs and alcohol are being consumed by an increasing number of people, and homelessness, child labor, and prostitution are becoming commonplace. Fundamentalism, xenophobia, and racism are on the rise. Ethnic conflicts are growing. Organized crime is taking over many markets. The extreme cases of social disintegration are in a growing number of countries that are suffering from prolonged civil strife. In these countries, infrastructure is collapsing and millions of people are losing their livelihoods. Entire populations are being uprooted. Communities and other institutions are disappearing. The ultimate tragedy is the total collapse of the state and all established institutional authority. The result is an environment of chaos and misery.

According to one contributor, Wangari Maathai, the decolonization of territories in Africa has only been the first step. A more difficult challenge is the mental and cultural decolonization that has been completely ignored to the detriment of the social cohesion of people in this region.

Building Blocks of Security for People

In Part 4, the concluding section of the book, the contributors examine the issues of the changing concept of security from political to personal, Poor People First policies will require strengthening international cooperation through the United Nations and moving towards an "Agenda for People."

One of the main goals of *People: From Impoverishment to Empowerment* is to contribute ideas and recommendations to the World Summit for Social Development, which will address all of the topics covered in this book. These issues also include the multiple dimensions of security for people and a new paradigm for development and policies to put people first.

The ineffectiveness of the League of Nations after World War I and the eruption of World War II only two decades later highlighted the necessity for an international organization that could ensure international security.

When the United Nations was established in 1945, its Charter noted that international peace could be achieved only if security for people could be guaranteed for all. Therefore, one of the major goals of the United Nations was to foster peace by promoting social progress and higher standards of living in an environment of freedom. The world cannot be secure unless people are secure in their homes, their jobs, and their communities.

During the Cold War, security meant mainly military and political security. The threat of armed conflict between East and West shaped this concept during that period. States sought weapons to protect their security.

Now that the Cold War is over, there is a pressing need for the international community to return to the basic and original aims of the United Nations Charter. The preamble of the Charter begins with the words, "We the peoples." We must put people at the center of all our concerns for the future. People's capacities and capabilities must be better utilized.   The release of the people's energies must be encouraged in accordance with their aspirations.

Lasting peace and security depend on a new paradigm, "People's Development," a development process that not only generates economic growth but distributes its benefits equitably. It regenerates the environment instead of destroying it. It empowers people rather than marginalizing them. It give priority to the poor, enlarging their choices and opportunities and providing for their participation in decisions that affect them. As James Gustave Speth, Administrator of the United Nations Development Programme, has put it, people will not be secure unless they have a job that will earn them enough money to feed their families and provide them with shelter. They will not be secure unless they have some hope for the future.

New Role of Governments

Up to the middle of the twentieth century, most development experts believed that development required an active role for government in boosting the productive sectors, establishing enterprises, subsidizing the private sector, and protecting some industries. These policies resulted in economic growth, but failed to improve living standards.

Today, most experts believe that governments should intervene less in areas where markets work efficiently and intervene more where markets cannot be relied on. This shift does not necessarily mean less governance. It means better governance. In a market-driven economy, governments have the role of creatively and sensitively facilitating, regulating, and monitoring growth.

Government plays a catalytic role in strengthening the knowledge base of a country by improving education and training and stimulating research and development. Government also has an important role in encouraging the growth of small businesses, diffusing entrepreneurial skills throughout an economy, and supporting people's participation in the economy. In the area of international trade, governments have to improve access for their countries' exports. Meanwhile, emerging social problems require action by governments — nationally, regionally, and internationally.

Finally, governments are responsible for helping their citizens reach their full potential. In the view of Helle Degn, the former Minister for Development Co-operation of Denmark, political leadership is crucial for future global social change and political commitment of the leaders of the world is necessary to sustain results.

Role of the People

The public's participation is necessary for finding policies that encourage global sharing and reduce inequities between groups.

When people feel that governments are responding to their needs, the establishment of a more effective system of global governance that will be in a position to take on the challenge of achieving a balance between growth and the fair distribution of wealth will be more likely.

People are expecting and demanding a more direct role in development decisions and in the international, regional, and national institutions in charge of development. In fact, nongovernmental organizations are already playing a greater role in the United Nations.

The quest for social innovation presents enormous challenges to development Organizations and "knowledge-based institutions." How can they build a global partnership of knowledge and increase developing countries' capacity to participate in decisions? Using knowledge requires people to assume ownership and direction of knowledge – knowledge that they have learned the hard way.

Reorientation of Policies

An important lesson learned from East Asia's success is that lower inequality is not only a corollary, but an important contributor to economic growth. Higher incomes for the poor means they can afford to save and invest, leading to greater human development and higher productivity and growth.

Lowering inequality can stimulate growth by improving social mobility, increase domestic multiplier effects, promote macroeconomic stability, and increase political stability.

A New Framework for Development Cooperation

Now that the Cold War is over, governments have an opportunity to replace ideological competition with a new spirit of solidarity and cooperation. Thus, we must be careful to avoid a new global divide – between North and South.

Instead of approaching international relations in terms of conflicts between states, we should see them in terms of resolving global problems as people, not as citizens of states. A new framework should be based on the mutual interests of people.

Lessons of Experience

Countries performing the best are the ones that have given priority to the development of human resources: education and health care for both men and women and policies to assist the disadvantaged.

Development requires investments. These can only be ensured by savings at the national level, which are supplemented by foreign aid and private investment. Welfare can be extended and maintained only where there is economic growth. And if economic growth is to result in increased welfare for all groups, the resulting higher income must be widely redistributed. Aid is no substitute for economic growth in eliminating poverty or improving welfare.

Aid can be extremely important for some countries. But aid – except in emergency situations – should focus on long-term development goals and be supplemented by a country's public and private resources which could be raised through domestic savings. Sufficient capital flows can be created only if resource mobilization is mutual and if private investment is stimulated.

Resource flows to developing countries are inadequate. Donors need to make an unambiguous commitment to human development and economic transformation. Part of this commitment might involve earmarking 20 percent of official development assistance for human development programs.

UNDP and UNICEF have recently proposed a "20:20" proposal, which calls for 20 percent of official development assistance and 20 percent of developing countries' budgets to be allocated to "human priority needs." These needs include primary education, primary health care, basic water and sanitation, nutrition, and family planning. This proposal is still being developed.

Some proponents of the proposal believe that it should be seen as only as one important part of a renewed commitment to social development. Others say that the 20 percent target should be only a baseline for assistance, not a minimum expenditure.

Redirection of Aid Policies

A fundamental reassessment of aid policies to support human development is overdue. "Tying" aid to structural adjustment has been counterproductive.

External resources would have a greater impact on development if they supported improvements in human conditions and national efforts aimed at democratization, popular participation, and transparency and accountability in governance. Donors should begin channeling resources directly to the people and their organizations, educational institutions, "watchdog" groups, and other institutions.

Reinforcing International Cooperation

The present system of international cooperation is a patchwork of disparate actions dominated by humanitarian and emergency relief. Monetary cooperation has been handed over to an unregulated market that has no responsibility for a stable world economy.

The North–South axis of wealth and poverty is changing. Indeed, the entire concept of North and South obscures the true meaning of development. A more accurate description of the world today would be a geographically heterogeneous axis of the "included" and the "excluded."

International development organizations will become irrelevant unless they move quickly beyond their current and narrow preoccupation with demonstrating their own effectiveness.

United Nations: Back to Basics

Reforming and renewing major international development organizations—the United Nations and the Bretton Woods institutions—must be a priority for the World Summit for Social Development.

According to Ambassador Samuel R. Insanally, the President of the 48th session of the General Assembly of the United Nations, the malaise that exists in the United Nations' developmental activities is not due to the fact that development has fallen off the political agenda, but rather because the development agenda is discussed outside the United Nations system. The international community, therefore, must sharpen, clarify and establish priorities for the United Nations' socioeconomic agenda (other regional and specialized agencies may be better-situated to handle some issues). Coordination of multilateral field activities is essential, and the growth and involvement of non-governmental organizations in development is also important. These organizations are a vehicle for the United Nations to build constituencies in many parts of the world.

An equally important goal for change is to have the major economic powers assume the burden of helping the world's less fortunate people. The United States demonstrated its ability to mobilize international cooperation at the time of the Gulf War. The United States must now show equal resolve to mobilize the North to resolve the problems that plague both North and South. The United Nations has fallen into disarray and needs stronger leadership.

Role of the Media

A set of new players has appeared on the stage of global action. One of the most powerful is the media. At the Stockholm Roundtable we considered the role of the mass media in aiding development and promoting social cohesion. We are critical of the media's role for succumbing to commercial and entertainment values and for their growing addiction to sensationalism and violence. Distortions in communication can slow down, block, or even scuttle economic and social reform programs.

Policy makers, however, particularly in democratic developing countries, must understand the importance of open and clear communication. Similarly, the media must understand the need to observe higher professional standards in the exercise of their craft.

Still, journalists play an important role in alerting the world to such crises as starvation and genocide. The central mission of the media should be to discover and publish the news, no matter who may find it unpleasant or threatening to their own interests. Journalists must remain independent and critical of all special interests in order to serve the public interest.

Promises of the Future: The Youth

The youth of today are the most promising foundation for our common future. Therefore, including youth in decision making is critical in reaching our goal of people's security. "When the winds of change blow, the youth are the first to stir" says Thales. We must understand their "hopes and fears" and act accordingly.

Youth are vulnerable to instability and conflict. They are the first to suffer the effects of poverty, unemployment, and social conflict. Yet they often lack the opportunities, representation, jobs, and rights to remedy this situation. Consequently, in societies around the world youth are acting out in increasingly destructive ways instead of working for positive change.

International organizations, governments, and communities have a responsibility to face the challenges posed by today's younger generations. Yet, youth themselves must be agents of positive change by promoting concrete innovative grassroots solutions to the world's problems and by leading by example.

Managing social change requires that the international community tap the energy, idealism, entrepreneurial spirit, and intellectual contributions of youth. In this context, part of a poem of commitment written by the late Turkish poet Nazim Hikmet, which was translated and read at the concluding session of the Stockholm Roundatable by Professor Talat H. Halman of New York University, is appropriate:

> *Let's give the world to the children so that even if it's just for one day*
> *It will learn what friendship is*
> *The Children will take the world out of our hands and they will plant*
> *immortal trees....*

Conclusion

We hope that strategies to put Poor People First will provide new direction for the world leaders and policy makers at the World Summit for Social Development and kindle commitment to a fairer world. These three words should pave the way for a new "People's Agenda" at the Copenhagen summit. We urge that it be kept in mind that the future of political freedom is closely linked to economic prosperity and social progress. Today, the poverty of opportunity, as well as poverty itself, causes widespread suffering and discontent. Individual political freedom in the long run depends on the well-being of people. True economic development must therefore become a peace-building process to alleviate the present poverty of opportunity. It should become a process through which human capabilities can expand, people's energies can be freely released, and individual initiative and innovation encouraged. Growing personal economic strength is the key to empowering people. This basic message is the guiding framework for this book.

We cannot conclude our overview without expressing our heartfelt thanks to our host country Sweden for its generous support to the Stockholm Roundtable. Our gratitude also goes to His Excellency Boutros Boutros-Ghali, Secretary-General of the United Nations, for writing the foreword, and James Gustave Speth, Administrator of the United Nations Development Programme, for his introduction. We are deeply indebted to the participants in the Stockholm Roundtable and the contributors to this book for grasping the central theme that the concerns of people have the most vital role to play in their own development. The authors have given their personal views, which should not necessarily be attributed to the institutions with which they are affiliated. Final responsibility for the selection, abbreviation, and editing of the papers rests with the editors. This volume owes much to the commitments of Colin Jones and Niko Pfund of New York University Press, the most valuable professional help of Barbara A. Chernow and George A. Vallasi of Chernow Editorial Services, Inc., and of Maria Figueroa who has assisted us most efficiently in every phase of this project.

Part 1

Reduction of Poverty

Poverty and Livelihoods: Whose Reality Counts?

Robert Chambers

This section is a challenge to all development professionals. It asks: Whose reality counts? The reality of the those few at the centers of power? Or the reality of the many poor at the periphery? It argues that these realities differ more than most people recognize. Insights into these differences and their implications are generating a new paradigm, with a new and hopeful agenda. To recognize, accept, act on, and evolve that new agenda is a personal, professional, and institutional challenge, demanding deep change in the way we think and behave. The Social Development Summit provides an opportunity for this change—for putting first the reality of the poor. Will the opportunity be recognized and seized?

The Context and the Record

Any balance sheet of development has to acknowledge achievements, and some indicators of human well-being have shown aggregate percentage improvements in recent decades.[1] For example, smallpox has been largely eradicated; polio and Guinea worm disease greatly reduced. In little more than a generation, the proportion of rural families with access to safe water rose from fewer than 10 percent to more than 60 percent, and the proportion of children in primary school from fewer than 50 percent to more than 75 percent. Such facts and figures can lull one into an impression of laudable achievement.

The record, however, is appalling. Although conditions would be much worse without the efforts of many organizations and individuals, the downside, particularly as the population increases, is dreadful. Income averaging often conceals adverse income distribution and the condition of underclasses. Some economies, particularly in countries where there are civil wars, are on a downward slide. In some countries, life expectancy has fallen, with internal strife, famine, and breakdown in government services. Malaria and tuberculosis, in particular, are on the increase worldwide. HIV is a time bomb that menaces whole peoples and economies. Nearly one billion people remain illiterate, and the primary school drop-out rate has reached 30 percent. Perhaps as many as 40 million people are refugees or displaced within their countries. Globally the number of people conventionally defined as in absolute poverty is more than one billion, or one person out of every four or five.[2]

Scholarly argument about statistics will never end. The danger is that debate distracts us from seeing what needs to be done. It is both tempting and difficult to generalize about these problems, but certain trends seem evident. The nature of poverty, suffering, and other deprivations is growing increasingly diverse, because living conditions are changing in different ways in different countries and for different groups of people. These problems are becoming more regional, as with the three Indian states of Uttar Pradesh, Bihar, and Madhya Pradesh with their combined 1994 population of more than 300 million, or are concentrating in countries that are least able to improve conditions, as in many nations of Sub-Saharan Africa.

As the scourge of HIV spreads, its hitherto localized impact will become regional. Eight million AIDS-related deaths are projected by the year 2000,[3] the target year of "Health for All." In the longer term, HIV mocks development programs. With AIDS, as with other problems, the South is more exposed and vulnerable, will suffer more, and will be far more devastated than the North.

Illness and early death take many forms. Some, because of their sensational impact, are regularly in the news. Examples include genocide and civil wars in Rwanda, Angola, and the former Yugoslavia, as well as the denial of human rights in Myanmar and Tibet. But less conspicuous forms have much greater long-range impact. Many of them are hidden or taboo, such as the selective elimination, persecution, and plight of women. The enormity of the abuse, sexual and otherwise, of girls, is often concealed by the family. Worldwide, with a concentration in South Asia, 110 million females are missing. This number is almost the total population of Pakistan; four times the population of Canada; twice the population of France, Iran, Italy, Turkey, or the United Kingdom; and the combined populations of Sudan, Kenya, Uganda, Tanzania, Malawi, and Zambia. The scale of discrimination, deprivation, and suffering that underlies these figures beggars the imagination.

The scope of human suffering is underscored by the fact that never before have the powerful been able to witness what is happening. The nightmare foreseen by C. P. Snow in 1959 has come about. The communications and technology revolutions, which have brought us all closer together, also enable the powerful to watch the poor die on television, turning them on and off at will. Frequent viewing inoculates people against compassion. Although there is more insight on how to help poor people than ever before, more wealth with which to achieve these goals, and the dividend of relative peace, aid is declining and hundreds of millions of the world's poorest people continue on a downward slide.

For many who read this section, this information is familiar, maybe even boring. One wonders about the diverse and different realities behind the statistics. The excitement comes when we ask whether our insights have changed and if new possibilities have opened up for positive action. People in positions of influence have the power to improve the world, but to grasp and use that power, they must question fundamental realities and concepts, explore and embrace a new paradigm, adopt a new professionalism, empower the poor to analyze and express themselves, and put the reality of the poor first.

Professional Reality: Rhetoric and Concepts

We are all part of a world system that perpetuates poverty and deprivation. Although people believe that poverty should be reduced or eliminated, it proves robustly sustainable. Why?

The usual answer involves analyzing poverty and deprivation themselves. Papers on the poor proliferate. One may speculate on what topics the poor and powerless would commission papers if they could convene conferences and summits—perhaps on greed, hypocrisy, and exploitation. But the poor remain powerless; those papers are rarely written. It is not surprising. We do not like to examine ourselves. To salve our consciences, we rationalize. Neoliberalism paints greed as inadvertent altruism. The objects of development are the poor, not we. It is they who are the problem, not we. We are the solution. So we hold the spotlight on them (from a safe distance). The poor have no spotlight to hold on us.

But poverty and deprivation are functions of polarization, of power and powerlessness. Any practical analysis has to examine the whole system "we" the powerful, as well as "they" the powerless. Since we have greater power to act, it is hard to evade the imperative to turn the spotlight round and look at ourselves.

In doing this, rhetoric and concepts provide a starting point. Our views on the realities of the poor and on what should be done, are constructed mainly from a distance and for our convenience. We embody those views in the very words and concepts we use. Two that receive much prominence are poverty and employment.

Thinking about Income-Poverty

"Poverty" is used in two main senses. In the first, which is common in development, it is a blanket word referring to the whole spectrum of deprivation and suffering; in the second, it has a narrow technical definition for purposes of measurement and comparison. Poverty is then defined as low income or often as low consumption, which is easier to measure. This meaning of poverty, common among economists, is used to measure poverty lines, for comparing groups and regions, and often for assessing progress or backsliding in development. In this section, it is described as income-poverty.

In professional discourse, the technical definition colonizes the common usage. Income-poverty starts as a proxy or correlate for other deprivations, but then subsumes them. What is recorded as having been measured—usually low consumption—then masquerades in speech and prose as the much larger reality. It is then but a short step to treating what has not been measured as not real. Patterns of dominance are then reinforced: of the material over the experiential; of the physical over the social; of the measured and measurable over the unmeasured and unmeasurable; of economic over social values; of economists over disciplines concerned with people as people. It then becomes the reductionism of normal economics, not the experience of the poor, that defines poverty. The preeminence of income-poverty seems wrong. But it is understandable. Four reasons can be given for its widespread acceptance and use.

First, economists and their concepts still dominate the development discourse. In most multilateral or bilateral aid agencies and ministries of planning, economists (and accountants) are the most numerous professions. Economic concepts, measures, and methods are the norm in much development practice and policy making. This is not to undervalue the utility of economic concepts and methods, but to illustrate that poverty, as defined by economists, tends to become the norm for other disciplines and professions.

Second, income-poverty is generated and sustained in the centers of power, reflecting and reinforced by conditions in the rich industrial North. Poor people in the North are mainly urban. They live in an industrial milieu and rely on cash income, whether wages or social security payments. As a result, much of their economic status can be captured in cash income or on cash-based consumption. Projecting and applying this Northern concept of poverty to the South assumes that similar conditions prevail.

Third, poverty defined as income-poverty or consumption-poverty is measurable. Nonmonetary flows for subsistence or consumption can in principle be given monetary values and conflated into a single scale. This permits comparisons worldwide between the income, or more usually consumption, levels of different households, regions, and nations. It also makes possible the measurement and assessment of poverty lines (meaning income-poverty or consumption-poverty lines). These provide time series measurements to show how income-poverty or consumption-poverty are changing, and how well a government is doing in its efforts to reduce poverty in these senses. The utility of these measures for centrally placed professionals gives them a primacy that tends to go unquestioned. What is measurable and measured then becomes what is real, standardizing the diverse and excluding the divergent and different.

Fourth, it is generally assumed that the poorer people are, the more they are preoccupied with income and consumption, with the need to gain subsistence food and basic goods in order to survive. In a recent article, Martin Greeley argued for an income-based concept of welfare, and that "…only when absolute poverty [meaning absolute income-poverty] is no longer the core issue should our measure of development encompass a broader agenda of human need."[4]

Given these four factors, it is not surprising to find that income-poverty has some primacy as a measure in the World Bank. In a widely quoted statement, Lewis Preston, President of the World Bank, wrote in the *Poverty Reduction Handbook*: "Sustainable poverty reduction is the overarching objective of the World Bank. It is the benchmark by which our performance as a development institution will be measured."[5]

The overarching objective is defined as something that can be measured — sustainable poverty reduction. Thus income-poverty becomes the end or objective of development. During the 1990s, the World Development Report's approach to sustainable poverty reduction will be two-pronged, consisting of "broadly based economic growth, to generate efficient income-earning opportunities for the poor, and improved access to education, health care, and other social services, so the poor can take advantage of these opportunities." In this thinking, income is the end; improved access to education, health care, and other social services are justified as means to that economic end. They are not, as presented here, justified as ends in themselves or as means to enhance capabilities or other human values (all hard to measure). Social development is a means not an end; the end is economic development.

That the World Bank considers sustainable poverty reduction its overarching objective is a matter for celebration. The narrowness and circularity of the thinking should not cause surprise; it is an organization with many economists conditioned by normal economic thinking. But Preston's simple statement contrasts with the mission statements of other bilateral agencies. The Overseas Development Administration of the British Government, for example, includes more numerous and influential social development advisers. Its goals are "to promote sustainable economic and social development and good government, in order to improve the quality of life and reduce poverty, suffering and deprivation in developing countries."[6] By going beyond economic development to include social development and good government, and beyond reducing poverty to improving the quality of life and reducing suffering and deprivation, a much broader set of values is embodied.

Few would want to deny that measures of income-poverty have uses. They point to one dimension of inequality and inequity between and within nations. But income-poverty is only one of many measures, and it is suspect because it serves the needs of professionals in the centers of power; it does not emerge from the realities of the poor at the peripheries.

Thinking about Employment

As with poverty, the normal professional categories of employment have been applied worldwide. Employment, unemployment, job, workplace, and workforce are concepts and categories derived from the urban industrial experience in the North. Attempts have been made to impose and apply them in the South, even in rural and agricultural areas. Perhaps this will become more marked now that the North is so preoccupied with its own unemployment. Although livelihood has been proposed as a better word than employment to capture the complex and diverse reality of the poor, employment thinking remains deep rooted. Whatever happens to the poor, economists and statisticians are assured of full employment, as they continue to analyze the available data and project their categories and concerns onto the raw and rather different reality of most of the poor in the South.

Offsetting Normal Professional Biases

Efforts have been made to offset the biases toward the income measure of poverty and deprivation and to move toward an employment measure of livelihood. Since their inception, the World Bank's *World Development Reports* have ranked countries according to per capita gross domestic product (GDP).

However, the relationship between per capita GDP and human well-being is weak. The critical factor for human well-being is income distribution. Many aspects of the good life (e.g., friendship, love, self-sacrifice, laughter, music, health, and creativity) are not counted when determining GDP, but many aspects of a lower-quality life (e.g., insurance claims, security guards, fossil fuel consumption, and deforestation) are computed in GDP. Very different perspectives have been given by UNICEF's annual *State of the World's Children*, which ranks countries according to their under age five mortality; by the Physical Quality of Life Index (PQLI), which combines in a single scale life expectancy at age one year, adult literacy, and infant mortality; the human development index (HDI) of the UNDP's annual *Human Development Report*, which combines per capita GDP, life expectancy at birth, and literacy; and by the World Bank itself, with its *Social Indicators of Development, 1993*, which lists poverty indicators such as public expenditure on social services, immunization, and fertility rates.

All these reveal weaknesses in the correlations between income-poverty and other deprivations. Strikingly, the 1994 *Human Development Report* shows Sri Lanka, Nicaragua, Pakistan, and Guinea all with per capita incomes in the $400 to $500 range, but life expectancies of, respectively, 71, 65, 58, and 44, and infant mortality rates of, respectively, 24, 53, 99, and 135. Whatever the criticisms of these measures and scales, they have been useful for comparisons and critical in determining priorities.

Efforts to offset the bias toward employment measures are less developed. Because livelihood is harder to measure than mortality rates, life expectancy, or literacy, it is treated as less real. Labor-intensive growth, which is designed to increase employment — and may indeed do so — is not the same as sustainable livelihood-intensity, where livelihood depends on a multiplicity of activities and resources.

The root problem is that professionals and poor people seek, experience, and construct different realities. The view from on high seeks and sees sameness and simplifying stereotypes. The question is whether concepts and measures that are universal, standardized, measurable, and generated by and designed for conditions in the urban industrial North can be universally applied in the more rural and agricultural South, and whether they fit or distort the diverse and complex realities of most of the poor.

The Realities of the Poor

A person who is not poor, but who pronounces on what matters to those who are, is in a trap. Although self-critical analysis, sensitive rapport, and participatory methods can contribute some valid insight into the values, priorities, and preferences of poor people, there will always be distortions. The nonpoor can never fully escape from their conditioning, and the nature of interactions between the poor and the nonpoor affect what is shared and learned. Thus, in what follows, much is wrong in substance and emphasis, for I am trying to generalize about what is local (rural and urban), complex, diverse, dynamic, personal, and multidimensional. My efforts are based on scattered evidence and experience, which is perceived, filtered, and fitted together in an inevitably personal and idiosyncratic way. Error is inherent in the enterprise. There must always be doubts. But if the reality of poor people is to count more, we must try to know it better.

Help comes from field researchers, especially social anthropologists, from those facilitating new participatory methods of appraisal, and increasingly from poor people themselves. The new methods enable poor people to analyze and express what they know, experience, need, and want. They bring to light many dimensions of deprivation, ill-being, and well-being, and the values and priorities of poor people. Three sets of findings provide illustrative insights.

Jodha's Paradox: Income-Poorer But Better Off

When N. S. Jodha asked farmers and villagers in two villages in Rajasthan for their own categories and criteria of changing economic status, they named 38 criteria. Comparing data from his fieldwork in 1964 to 1966 with that of 1982 to 1984, he found that the 36 households that were more than 5 percent *worse off* in per capita real incomes were on average *better off* according to 37 out of their own 38 criteria. The one exception was consumption of milk, more of which was being sold outside the village. The improvements included quality of housing, wearing of shoes regularly, less dependence in the lean season, and not having to migrate for work. Several of the criteria reflected more independence.[7] The reality that these income-poorer villagers presented to Jodha contrasts with an economist's reality. They were income-poorer, and so in an economist's terms worse off; but in their own terms, they were on average much better off.

Findings from Participatory Analysis

Analysis by local people using participatory rural appraisal (PRA) methods have shown similar outcomes. In a PRA process in a Pakistani village in April 1994

...the local people did a matrix on their existing sources of income to determine the preferred income source. Interestingly, for me, the criterion "more income" was the 9th or 10th one listed (out of a total of about 20 criteria). "More time at home," "ability to get involved in neighbours' joys and sorrows" were listed earlier...the generally perceived-to-be-preferred source of income (high-paying skilled/manual labour in the Middle Eastern countries, particularly Dubai) did not emerge as victor..., the reason worked out by the local analysts being that it did badly on their social criteria.[8]

Diverse criteria have also emerged from well-being ranking, one of the methods of PRA. In an economic tradition, "wealth" was originally the criterion by which local people were asked to sort the households in their community. Repeatedly, when outside facilitators have tried to focus discussion and ranking on wealth, local people have insisted on using a wider range of criteria as contributing to their concepts of well-being and ill-being, of the good and bad life. Health and physical disability feature strongly.[9]

Participatory Poverty Assessments

The World Bank has been breaking new ground in its poverty assessments, which are designed "to help us to address three fundamental issues: Who is poor? Why are they poor? What needs to be done to reduce the number of the poor?" The Participatory Poverty Assessments (PPAs) conducted under the auspices of the World Bank in Ghana, Zambia, Kenya, and several other countries now have the potential to move beyond these questions to ask: Who defines poverty? Who are the poor as defined within a society by local people themselves? What criteria of poverty or deprivation do they have? What are their priorities?

The PPA sponsored by the World Bank in Zambia, using PRA techniques, gave insights about conditions, trends, and poor people's priorities with practical implications.[10] To illustrate some of the range:

- Health was repeatedly and consistently given a higher priority than education. Indeed, education was not raised as a priority need in most communities.

- Payment of school fees was found to be required at the most difficult time of the year, coinciding with food shortages, heavy work in agriculture, indebtedness, expenditures for Christmas, and high incidence of disease.

- The rudeness of health staff deterred poor people from going for treatment.

- Food-for-work at bad times was highly valued.

- All-weather roads were desired not only for marketing, but also to give access to clinics and hospitals during the rains.

- Mangoes are good because they provide food at the worst times of the year.

These insights indicate that actions such as postponing school fee payments, training health staff to be more caring, food for work for all-weather roads, improving and spreading mangoes and similar tree food crops, will provide high benefits in poor people's own terms for relatively low financial costs.

Dimensions of Deprivation

These and other examples illustrate the multidimensionality of deprivation and disadvantage as poor people experience them. Deprived people are often thought of as being uniform. The "rural masses" commonly expresses a stereotype. But, if anything, there is more diversity among the poor than among the nonpoor. Under extreme deprivation, as Viktor Frankl found in his study of inmates of concentration camps, people react in sharply different ways. Disadvantage itself takes many forms. Any list of dimensions will be provisional and personal. The eight that follow are an attempt to capture some of poor people's reality, but can surely be improved on. Of the eight, the first three are better recognized.

1. Poverty refers to the lack of physical necessities, assets, and income. It includes, but is more than, being income-poor. Poverty can be distinguished from other dimensions of deprivation, such as physical weakness, isolation, vulnerability, and powerlessness.

2. Social inferiority can be ascribed, acquired, or linked with age and life cycle. It can be socially defined as genetically inferior or disadvantaged because of gender, caste, race, and ethnic group; "lower" in terms of class, social group, or occupation; or linked with age, as with children and sometimes daughters-in-law.

3. Isolation refers to being peripheral and cut off. Poor people can be isolated geographically by living in a "remote" area, but also isolated by lack of communication, contacts, and information; the inability to read; and the lack of access to social services and markets.

The following five other dimensions that are prominent in the realities of the poor and weak have been relatively neglected by the development professions.

4. Physical weakness. Professionals, dependent as they are on their brains more than their bodies, tend to undervalue the importance of physical well-being to many of the poor. A household member who is too physically weak, sick, or handicapped to contribute to household livelihood, but requires food and care, is a common cause of income-poverty and deprivation, as is illustrated now with the spread of AIDS. The prominence of disability in the consciousness of poor people in the South is shown by the frequency with which, in participatory social mapping, village analysts spontaneously represent the disabled as a category. Those who are sick are a concern of health services; those who are otherwise disabled are numerous, but neglected. The South has perhaps 200 million disabled persons, with another 200 million who are impoverished and adversely affected by having to support the disabled. Yet, in 1993, the UNDP *Human Development Report* did not include disability in any of its tables.

The disabled are among the most unseen and politically powerless – and not only in the South.

5. Vulnerability. Vulnerable and poor are often used as synonyms. But vulnerability is not the same as income-poverty or poverty more broadly defined. It means not lack or want, but defenselessness, insecurity, and exposure to contingencies. It has two sides: the external side of exposure to risk, shocks, and stress, and the internal side of defenselessness, meaning a lack of means to cope without damaging loss. Loss can take many forms – becoming or being physically weaker, economically impoverished, socially dependent, humiliated, or psychologically harmed.

For hundreds of millions of people, vulnerability has increased, and so their livelihoods have become less securely sustainable, even when their incomes have risen. In most cultures and contexts, patron–client safety nets have weakened, the extended family gives less support, contingencies such as weddings, funerals, brideprice, and dowry have become more costly, and effective health services have become less accessible or more expensive or both. More people have moved into insecure environments. More people live exposed to risk of famine, flood, storm, and some human, crop, and animal diseases than before. War and civil disorder remain widespread. And where there have been past disasters, many are more vulnerable through the earlier loss of livelihood assets and the means to cope. It then takes less to create a famine, as in Ethiopia.

For poor people, there are often trade-offs between income and security. Income-poverty thinking can neglect vulnerability in seeking to raise incomes. On a huge scale, the Integrated Rural Development Programme in India provides subsidized loans to poor people to acquire assets aimed at raising their incomes. But as many have learned, this increases vulnerability. The loss of the asset can lead to debt and being worse off than before. At the margin, poor people often prefer a lower income with less risk of debt and dependence.

6. Seasonality. The seasonal dimensions of deprivation are inadequately perceived by professionals, who are urban-based and season-proofed. Yet many adverse factors for the poor often coincide with the rains. These include hard agricultural work, shortage of food, scarcity of money, indebtedness, sickness, the late stages of pregnancy, and diminished access to services. This is borne out by such indicators as birthweights, body weights, infant mortality, and morbidity.

7. Powerlessness. The poor are powerless. Dispersed and anxious as they are about access to resources, work, and income, it is difficult for them to organize or bargain. Often physically weak and economically vulnerable, they lack influence. Subject to the power of others, they are easy to ignore or exploit. Powerlessness is also, for the powerful, the least acceptable point of intervention to improve the lot of the poor.

8. Humiliation. Self-respect, with freedom from dependence, is the dimension most overlooked and undervalued by professionals. Indira Hirway in Gujarat found that poor people disliked acquiring debts because what followed included "abuses and insults," "helplessness, insults and pain," and "touching the feet of the lenders and swallowing insults and abuses."[11]

Deprivation and well-being have, then, many dimensions. Poor people have many priorities. What matters most to them often differs from what outsiders assume, is not always easy to measure, and may not be measurable at all. If poor people's realities are to come first, development professionals have to be sensitive, to decentralize, and to empower, enabling poor people to conduct their own analyses and express their own multiple priorities.

Sustainable Livelihoods

The knowledge of the urban North has advantages when discussing the physical universe and whatever is microscopic, macroscopic, large-scale, or distant from where poor people live. In these areas, our linked communications, instruments, and science empower us. But the knowledge of the poor has advantages with the local and the social, with whatever is continuously observed and experienced, and with whatever close to them touches their lives and livelihoods. They are the only experts on their life experiences and priorities. But our power in the past has overwhelmed their knowledge, hidden their analytical abilities, and allowed us to assume that we know what they experience and want. The problem is one of balance between two realities—ours which is powerful, and theirs which is weak. Standing back and standing down, we need to search for overlapping areas, where their realities and aspirations can give rise to practical concepts that we can then use to help empower them.

One such overlap is suggested by sustainable livelihood. For many of the poor, livelihood is a better concept than employment to capture how poor people live. "Sustainable" then refers to the longer-term, and "livelihood" to the many activities that make up a living.

In discussing sustainability, it is a common prejudice among those who are not poor that poor people inherently "live hand-to-mouth" and take the short view. But in practice, again and again, they show tenacity and self-sacrifice in trying to take the long view and safeguarding the basis of their livelihoods. Small farmers with secure rights invest their labor in land shaping, terracing, and creating fertile microenvironments; in harvesting water, silt, and nutrients; and in planting and protecting trees. It is less the poor and more the outsiders who take the short view— contractors who cut the forest, officials fixated on the financial year, and politicians who cannot see beyond the next election.

In analyzing livelihoods, the strategies of the poor are usually diverse and often complex. They can be compared to those of hedgehogs and foxes, after the saying of Archilochus that "The fox has many ideas but the hedgehog has one big idea." Full-time employees in the industrial world and industrial sectors are hedgehogs, with one big idea, a single source of support. Poor people, often powerless, desperate, or exploited, who also have only one survival strategy are the same—slaves, bonded laborers, outworkers tied to supplier-buyers, beggars, some vendors, prostitutes, and some occupational specialists. But most poor people in the South, and more now in the North, are foxes, with a portfolio of activities, with different members of the family seeking and finding different sources of food, fuel, animal fodder, cash, and support in different ways in different places at different times of the year. Their living is improvised and sustained through their livelihood capabilities, through tangible assets in the form of stores and resources, and through intangible assets in the form of claims and access. The strategies of foxes are rarely fully revealed by conventional questionnaires. Schedules construct a standardized, short, and simple reality, and investigators' incentives are to record less, not more.

The ingenuity and opportunism of poor people, and the diversity and complexity of their strategies, can be illustrated by case studies and the accounts of social anthropologists and others. Strategies and sources of food, income, support, and survival include:

- Rural and urban home gardening and exploitation of microenvironments.
- Use of common property resources, such as fishing, hunting, grazing, and gathering in lakes, ponds, rivers, seas, forests, woodlands, swamps, savannas, hills, wastelands, and roadsides. Such resources are often a major source of livelihood for the rural poor and a safety net fallback source of food and income in bad times.
- Scavenging (mainly urban) and gleaning (mainly rural), including traditional rights and access to private residues, such as buttermilk and crop residues for fuel.
- Processing, hawking, vending, and marketing, including produce from home gardens and common property resources.
- Share-rearing of livestock, where livestock are lent for herding in exchange for rights to some products and/or offspring.
- Transporting goods by horse, donkey, mule, cart, bicycle, and head or backloading.
- Mutual help, including small borrowings from relatives and neighbors.
- Contract outwork, such as weaving, rolling cigarettes, and making incense sticks.
- Casual labor and piecework, especially in agriculture.
- Specialized occupations, including barbers, blacksmiths, carpenters, prostitutes, and tailors.
- Domestic service, especially by girls and women.
- Child labor, both domestic (e.g., collecting fuel-leaves, twigs, branches, dung, and fodder; weeding; herding animals; removing stones from fields and ticks from livestock) and in factories (e.g., making matches, candles, and fireworks), restaurants, and people's houses.
- Craft work of many sorts.
- Mortgaging and selling assets, future labor, and children.
- Family splitting, including putting out children to others.
- Migration for seasonal work, in areas such as agriculture, brick-making, and urban construction.
- Remittances.

- Seasonal food-for-work, public works, and relief.
- Stinting in many ways, including food and other consumption.
- Begging.
- Theft.
- Triage, especially with girls and weaker people.

This list illustrates that often an individual or a household engages in many livelihood activities over a year. This does not fit the concept of "employment" in "a job." Individuals and families diversify and complicate their livelihood strategies in order to increase income, reduce vulnerability, and improve the quality of their lives.

A similar pattern is shown by "the third agriculture." The first or industrial agriculture is standardized and simple; the second, or green revolution, agriculture has high-yielding packages in controlled conditions. The third agriculture, on which perhaps 1.5 billion people depend for their livelihoods, is complex, diverse, and risk-prone (CDR). CDR farmers seek to reduce risk and increase food and income by complicating, diversifying and, where labor is available, intensifying their farming systems, adding to their enterprises. They multiply the internal links and flows within their farming systems, for example through aquaculture, composting, cut-and-carry for stall-fed livestock, multiple cropping, agroforestry, home gardening, and the concentration of nutrients, soil, and water in such microenvironments such as silt deposition fields and other protected pockets of fertility.

For these realities, the strategies of most of the rural—and many of the urban—poor, sustainable livelihood is therefore a better concept than employment. Employment, in the sense of having an employer, a job, a workplace, and a wage, is more widespread as an aspiration than a reality. Where economic crisis and structural adjustment cut urban jobs, the proportion of foxes can be expected to increase. In addition, no matter hard poor people seek employment and how much they educate their children, a secure and remunerative job is not a realistic prospect for most. Even in the North, the classic concept of a single employment is being challenged; portfolio, fox livelihoods are becoming more common. In much of the South, most livelihoods of the poor will continue to be adaptive performances that are improvised and versatile in the face of adverse conditions, sudden shocks, and unpredictable change.

In identifying actions, then, it makes sense to shift thinking from labor-intensive growth toward sustainable livelihood-intensive change. This is not to argue against growth, or against a strategy of labor-intensive growth, but to qualify and complement it. For labor-intensity and sustainable livelihood-intensity (SL-intensity), although overlapping, are not identical. As a concept, labor-intensity links with employment. A SL-intensive strategy goes beyond employment to include:

- The sustainable management of and equitable access to natural resources, especially common property resources.
- The redistribution of private and public livelihood resources to the poor.

- Prompt payment for what poor people sell, and terms of trade between what poor people sell and what they buy.
- Accessible health services for prevention of disease and for prompt and effective treatment of disabling accidents and disease.
- Abolishing restrictions and hassle on livelihood activities that are used to exploit the poor.
- Safety nets for poor people to mitigate seasonal stress, thereby enabling them to conserve their livelihood assets.

To conclude, deprivation and well-being as perceived by poor people, and sustainable livelihoods as a shared goal of outsiders and the poor, question the degree of primacy often attributed to income-poverty. The realities of the poor are many and particular. They can experience and agonize over acute trade-offs between different dimensions of deprivation and well-being. What they value and choose often differs from what professionals expect. Income does matter, but so do other aspects of the quality of life, such as health, security, self-respect, justice, access to goods and services, family and social life, ceremonies and celebrations, creativity, the pleasures of place, season and time of day, fun, spiritual experience, and love. If development means good change, it is so much more than economic growth and income; it is all aspects of the quality of life as poor people experience and wish them.

The Paradigm of Reversals

Antipoverty action has often been justified to the rich and powerful by appealing to enlightened selfishness; this has stressed mutual interests and the bad impacts of poverty, suffering, and deprivation on those who are better off and on the North as a whole. The strongest argument was perhaps that of the Brandt Commission, that the North had an economic interest in economic growth in the South. To the extent that reciprocal nonzero sums exist or can be found, they must be welcomed. But such arguments do not always hold up. Well-meaning casuistry about mutual interest, argued during the development decades to justify helping the poor, can prove to be shifting sand. To rely on arguments about mutual material interests is to risk loss of support if they do not exist. Ethical arguments are stronger, surer, and better. The prescriptions that follow are founded not on the self-interest of the rich and powerful, which may or may not be served, but on the values of common decency, compassion, and altruism.

The differences between top-down reductionist definitions and objectives, and poor people's realities present development professionals with challenges that are institutional, professional, and personal. The challenges are paradigmatic: to reverse the normal view, to upend perspectives, to see things the other way round, to soften and flatten hierarchy, to adopt downward accountability, to change behavior, attitudes, and beliefs, and to identify and implement a new agenda. In sum, to define and embrace a new professionalism. This new professionalism and its paradigm stress reversals, decentralization, local diversity and complexity, and empowerment.

The new paradigm is people-centered, participatory, empowering, and sustainable. These nice words are more deeply embedded in the reflexes of writers than in the mental frames and personal behavior of those in positions of influence. For the paradigm demands reorientation, the upending of much of the normal upper–lower, North–South dominance. It combines reversals and altruism: reversals to stand the normal on its head, to see things the other way around, to enable the poor and weak to express their reality, and to put that reality first; and then altruism, to act in the interests of the poor and powerless. This paradigm of reversals and altruism stands as a challenge for the Social Development Summit.

This reversal of logic is fundamental. Instead of starting with the analyses of professionals, the logic starts with the realities of the peripheral poor. Policy is not deduced and driven center-outwards, with distant assumptions about effects on the poor, but induced and drawn up from the experience and analyses of those who live local realities and know what happens close to them. Nor is the argument that this should be the only logic; it is complementary. But the scales are so weighted against it, that unless it is put first and kept first, a good balance and mix of logic can never be achieved.

A key point for healthy skeptics is the cost-effectiveness of this agenda. The things poor people want have low financial costs and can have high payoffs. Rights, security, the rule of law, information, access, changes in procedures, removals of restrictions, polite behavior by officials, timing actions for the right season, timely delivery, providing diverse "baskets of choices" (of crop varieties, trees, uses of credit, and so on) are examples. The key is identifying and implementing such measures.

Conclusion

In its concern with poverty and employment, the Social Development Summit may be in danger of plodding in worthy but well-worn ruts that lead nowhere new. The challenge is to go beyond the normal agenda—beyond poverty to well-being and beyond employment to sustainable livelihoods. It is to explore the new paradigm, to embrace the new professionalism, and to concern itself with whose reality counts. To justify the cost, time, and effort of the Summit, to make things better for the poor, it will have to question conventional concepts of development; to challenge us to change, personally, professionally, and institutionally; and to change the paradigm of the development enterprise. If the poor and weak are not to see the Summit as a celebration of hypocrisy, signifying not sustainable well-being for them, but sustainable privilege for us, the key is to enable them to express their reality, to put that reality first, and to make it count.

Notes

1. For a fuller balance sheet, see UNDP, *Human Development Report 1993*, pp. 12–13; Peter Adamson, *The Progress of Nations: The Nations of the World Ranked According to Their Achievements in Health, Nutrition, Education,*

Family Planning, and Progress for Women, UNICEF, 1993; and subsequent publications in these series.

2. The source is the "Worldwatch Institute's Country Estimates of Absolute Poverty and Other Social and Economic Indicators." These estimates should be viewed as midpoints in a range of plus or minus 10 percent. The figures probably refer to the late 1980s; they are presented here to indicate relative orders of magnitude by regional location.

3. *HIV/AIDS Pandemic 1993 Overview,* Global Programme on AIDS, WHO, Geneva. There is much uncertainty about projections. Locally, especially in parts of Africa, the impact is already devastating.

4. Martin Greeley, "Measurement of Poverty and Poverty of Measurement." In Susanna Davies (ed.), *Knowledge Is Power? The Use and Abuse of Information in Development.* IDS Bulletin No. 25, 1994, p. 57.

5. *Poverty Reduction Handbook.* Washington, D.C.: World Bank, 1993.

6. *Foreign and Commonwealth Office, Including Overseas Development Administration, Departmental Report.* London: HMSO, 1992, p. 28.

7. N. S. Jodha, "Poverty Debate in India: A Minority View," *Economic and Political Weekly,* (November 1988): 2421–2428.

8. Rashida Dohad, personal communication.

9. Barbara Grandin, *Wealth Ranking in Smallholder Communities: A Field Manual.* London: Intermediate Technology Publications, 1988; Neela Mukherjee, "Villagers' Perceptions of Rural Poverty Through the Mapping Methods of PRA," *RRA Notes* 15 (May 1992): 21–26; Stephanie S. Schaefer, "The 'Beans Game' – Experiences with a Variation of Wealth Ranking in the Kivu Region, Eastern Zaire," *RRA Notes* 15 (May 1992): 27–28; Marie-Therese Sarch, "Wealth Ranking in the Gambia: Which Households Participating in the FITT Programme?," *RRA Notes* 15 (May 1992): 14–20; A and J Rajaratnam, personal communication.

10. Andy Norton, Dan Owen, and J. T. Milimo, *Zambia Participatory Poverty Assessment.* Vol 4 in *Zambia Poverty Assessment.* Washington, D.C.: World Bank, 1994.

11. Indira Hirwaym, *Abolition of Poverty in India with Special Reference to Target Group Approach in Gujarat.* New Delhi: Vikas, 1986, pp. 142, 144, 147.

Chapter 1

Impacts of Poverty: Political, Economic, Social, and Environmental

Section 1

The Poverty–Growth Dichotomy

Donald Brown

Today, there is an emerging consensus that the reduction and eventual elimination of poverty should be a major priority for the agenda of international development assistance. But there still remain many differing views on how poverty reduction should be pursued. This section offers basic insights into the nature and dynamics of rural poverty and proposes effective approaches to its alleviation.

Evolution of Concepts for Dealing with Poverty

Overcoming poverty has been the professed objective of many development strategies for the last forty years, but the results are not very encouraging. Of the world's population of some five billion, more than one billion in the developing world live below the poverty line – the great majority in rural areas. Although the percentage of the poor among the rural population has decreased, their absolute number has increased. In too many countries, there has emerged a relatively more sophisticated urban-based modern sector surrounded by an economically depressed countryside that, failing to support its own population, pushes its surplus people into the mushrooming slums of the larger cities. What went wrong?

The way development programs have addressed poverty issues over the years has changed considerably. Initially, poverty and development were analyzed in terms of the poverty of nations, and the objective of growing international assistance was national economic growth. Relatively little attention was paid to the needs of the poor themselves.

The assumption that the poor would benefit from general economic growth changed somewhat in the late 1960s, when it was perceived that the number of the poor was not declining and that their participation in economic advancement was necessary to assure the social stability needed for overall economic growth. From this reasoning, there emerged a specific line of "antipoverty" thinking that emphasized activities aimed at assuring the basic needs of the poor. However, this approach had less to do with what the poor could offer to the growth process than with what they should receive from that process. The "basic needs" strategy and the social "safety net" approach that followed basically emphasized the consumption needs of the poor. As a consequence, poverty alleviation was all too often thought of as an alternative to, or distraction from, accelerated growth. Discussions were therefore framed in terms of trade-offs between poverty reduction and increased investment/output, between helping the poor today and helping more of them tomorrow.

Recently, in the context of structural adjustments programs, experience has again demonstrated that macroeconomic changes will not automatically work as incentives for the poor to produce more. Price liberalization, for example, is not automatically translated into advantageous effective prices received by farmers at the farm level. A reduced governmental role in providing credit or inputs or marketing outlets has not necessarily been followed by the development of market structures that respond to the concerns of the poor. Investments in health and education have been promoted to improve the long-term productive capacity of the people. Important as such programs may be in helping to empower poor people, they will produce the desired results only if the poor are also given the resources and means to respond to, and take advantage of, the new incentive framework.

Poverty Alleviation and Economic Growth

Thus, although there has emerged over the years an increasingly strong consensus on the need to support the process of poverty alleviation, there still remain some ambiguities with regard to the relation between poverty alleviation and the long-standing priority objective of most international development assistance and national development policies—that is, economic growth. These ambiguities relate largely to the perceptions that poverty alleviation is the result of growth of economic activities outside the production systems of the poor and that poverty alleviation is a social sector concern.

Poverty and Growth

It should not be assumed that poverty alleviation and economic growth are incompatible or antithetical. If poverty is not addressed effectively and a substantial part of the population is left behind in absolute poverty, then growth is likely to be narrowly based and vulnerable to disruption.

With regard to the growth-poverty nexus, economic expansion can undeniably, under certain circumstances, help reduce poverty. An example is expanded employment opportunities for the poor. More to the point, however, is that when the poor, particularly the rural poor, have access to the resources they need, they become not simply the objects of development, but can contribute to it substantially through their own productive efforts.

It is also often the case, and this is certainly substantiated by some of experiences of the International Fund for Agricultural Development (IFAD), that support to production by the poor can contribute more to the overall growth process than equivalent investments in larger scale and apparently more prosperous sectors—and often at a lower cost, and certainly a lower foreign exchange cost, than those more "modern" sectors.

The right large- and medium-scale productive activities certainly have an important role in long-term economic growth. But optimal growth strategies must also involve major support to small-scale rural producers, among whom poverty is concentrated. The question, then, is not either growth or poverty alleviation, as if the one is somehow an obstacle to the other, but the elaboration of growth strategies through poverty alleviation defined as improving the productivity and income of poor, small-scale producers.

Poverty as an "Economic" Rather Than a "Social" Issue

Poverty alleviation is not simply a "social" issue; it is primarily an economic one. The answer to poverty does not lie only in transfers to improve consumption nor solely in the improvement of social services, but primarily in strengthening the position of the poor as economic agents, preferably within an economic environment that provides the poor with incentives to tap their production potential. This is much more an issue of economic policy and productive resource allocation than it is of social policy and social expenditure. Poverty alleviation is no more, and no less, a social issue than overall development.

To reformulate the position: poverty alleviation certainly does not involve a major change in focus away from growth, nor does it involve abandonment of economic criteria in investment. In effect, what it does involve is recognizing the productive role and potential of the poor and reflecting these in the development of investment portfolios and economic policy. A dichotomy between projects oriented to overall growth and those relating to poverty alleviation may, therefore, lead to quite wrong operational conclusions.

Poverty Is Not a State of Being, But a State of Activity

In sum, although recognizing the need for attention to poverty alleviation is a precondition to effective action, it must be accompanied by full recognition of the poor as producers, of poverty as a production problem, and poverty reduction as an investment—an investment in creating the conditions within which the poor are allowed to produce and earn more, thereby contributing not only to the well-being of their families but also to that of the nation.

These conditions are necessarily specific. One of the obstacles to effective understanding of how to deal with poverty is the very concept of "the poor." They are not homogeneous, and the word "poor" is best used as an adjective rather than a noun. There are poor farmers, poor herders, poor artisans, poor traders, and so on. This means that poverty itself should not be addressed per se, but through the activities associated with poverty. Effective reduction of poverty, therefore, involves identification of who the poor actually are, the economic activities in which they are engaged, specification of the means of realizing their potential, and elaboration of a suitably supportive structure of policy, services, and investment to reverse the particular conditions facing poor people.

Such an approach recognizes the basic truth that the problem of poverty is less the "imperfection" of the producers and much more the imperfection of the markets, institutions, and services on which they depend. Overcoming this implies, primarily, two things: targeted delivery of relevant assistance to help the poor overcome the concrete obstacles they face, and help in the development of the institutional framework through which the poor can better organize and interface with macromarkets and public and private institutions.

The Need for Targeted Interventions

Targeting means designating resources for the poor according to rigorous and explicit criteria of eligibility. The rationale is quite simple. In most developing countries, resources are scarce and subject to vigorous competition. Under normal conditions, this competition is won by the most socially influential members of the community, who are not typically the poor nor necessarily the most productive. The absence of specific targeting and targeting mechanisms, therefore, frequently means that the poor do not receive the resources they need to become more productive, even those resources nominally destined for them. Unequal local, social, political, and economic power, therefore, necessitates that external resources for the poor be provided within a framework that ensures minimum "leakage." This does not mean subsidization; in fact, subsidization is likely to divert from the poor those resources specifically intended to help them. What is needed is to determine the real needs of the poor and how these can be met in ways most likely to have the most direct beneficial impact on their needs. In this regard, it is not entirely sufficient that poor areas be targeted. For example, in poor areas there is also inequality in social power. Thus targeting resources to such regions by no means ensures that the poor will receive all, or indeed, any of the resources provided.

Targeting has become a highly important issue, particularly because macroeconomic theory looks principally to the role of the market in resource allocation and assumes that liberal policies will benefit all levels of society. Although it is clear that a major cause of poverty is the lack of access by the poor to many facilities critical to economic improvement, such as credit, inputs, and marketing facilities, there is nothing inherent in current macroeconomic policy approaches likely to overcome this deprivation. Because unequal social power gives rise to important "market failures" by both public and private institutions, poverty alleviation projects and programs must contain specific means for overcoming those distortions. Targeting is such a means. It should be stressed that targeting is not inherently contradictory to a proper conceptual view of market forces.

The point to be stressed is that targeting, rather than introducing market distortions, aims at correcting existing ones. Even in the context of structural adjustments, targeted support is necessary to ensure that the poor have equitable access to newly established markets.

Whom to Target and How

The first step in targeting is to define the poorest groups. Smallholder farmers constitute, numerically, the most important group of the rural poor. The landless and near landless come next, followed by such groups as artisanal fishermen, nomadic pastoralists, indigenous ethnic populations, and refugees. Across all these groups, the position of women requires special attention, particularly in view of the complexity of relations between their productive and reproductive roles as well as their contributions to household food security. The percentage of female-headed households is high and is rising, as is the number of women living below the poverty line. Notwithstanding their increasing responsibility for agricultural production and income generation in rural areas, women have the least access to means of production, receive the lowest wages, and are the least educated. In a sense, the poverty question has thus become inseparable from the gender question.

Targeting can be achieved through the establishment of a number of criteria. For certain investment goods, such as roads, the poverty of the area may be an adequate criterion. For other investments, household wealth or signs of that wealth may be taken into consideration. Indicators of wealth vary according to the nature of the local economy. In some cases it is extent of land ownership; in others size of cattle herds; and in yet others ownership of draught animals. The principle, however, remains the same: investment in those with the least assets. Targeting may involve direct systems of allocation of resources, such as placing eligibility criteria on the availability of credit. More often, however, targeting can be accomplished by other means, including the choice of technology to be promoted in accordance with the traditions and farming systems of the poor; packaging inputs in amounts related to the actual needs of the poor; structuring institutions so that they reach out to the poor rather than require the poor to seek them out; or developing environmental protection programs that promote rather than detract from current production. Finding the right means for targeting is essential to making the process work.

People's Participation

Targeting by itself, however, is not enough. A high level of people's participation is critical and fundamental in enhancing the relevance of services and investments to the requirements of the poor. Further, it is vital to the establishment of services at a reasonable cost in contexts where governments have withdrawn their activities and investments, and where the limited development of the private sector frequently involves inadequate competition and the persistence of monopoly/monopsony situations. In its broadest sense, perhaps, people's participation signifies the articulation of previously marginalized sections of society with modern economic, political, and social institutions on viable and equitable terms.

In the context of development projects, people's participation can promote sustainability and replicability; take advantage of traditional practices and indigenous technologies, especially suited to the environment and the capacities of the people; facilitate training, extension, input delivery, credit and services; enhance community cohesion and consciousness; and in some cases reduce project development and implementation costs.

True participatory development must transcend the artificial bounds of the externally aided project and find its root in the existing social structure, in its inherent democratic values. Only through the development of grassroots-based democratic institutions, be they cooperatives or peasant associations, formal or informal, can participation take root.

Even in their isolation, the rural poor are seldom without basic forms of organization. Where village councils, women's clubs, associations of smallholders and the landless, or cooperatives exist, such groups can be entry points for project participation, provided concrete and immediate benefits are apparent as a result of their involvement. Where no basic organization exists, it can be fostered around tangible benefits and through the use of trained group animators.

It should be noted, however, that success in establishing viable and enduring forms of people's participation has been neither automatic nor uniform. In particular, the ability of any organization to provide a stable basis for an activity or a service relies critically on the degree to which the activity concretely contributes to attainment of individual and collective interests, as well as the degree to which it has become a vehicle for mobilization of the resources and investments of the poor themselves. Satisfaction of this requirement places a premium on involvement of the beneficiary population in project development from the design stage through implementation. Only then do people commit to a particular project, because it is their project, because it expresses their own interests and understandings, and because it is not something imposed on them from the top. Such early and continuous involvement can lead to effective maintenance and follow-up and thus enhance the chances for sustainability of project benefits. Many interventions have failed because they have formed groups of, for example, women on the basis of external definitions of women's social and economic interest. The response must be a more demand-driven approach that does not try to second guess the interests of the target group, but seeks to articulate the demands of the poor on both projects and the larger social system.

Since its establishment, IFAD has promoted people participation mainly in rural areas; there have been two objectives. The first corresponds to raising participation at the design and implementation stage for the promotion of economic activities in line with people's felt needs, opportunities, and aspirations, and for which they will take full responsibility. The second corresponds to strengthening the long-term capabilities of the rural poor in their relations with the larger environment within which they function.

In the long-term the second set of issues is of the greater importance, involving what the poor can do for themselves. The importance of people's participation in rural areas has risen, partly in response to declining direct public activities. People's participation in self-organized groups has been promoted to establish more equitable and enduring interface between the rural poor and larger economic and political systems. This is notably the case in associations of the poor dealing with sales of rural products and distribution of inputs, as well as with productive credits, as in the case of the relation between local savings groups and national credit institutions. In essence, the objective of the participatory approach should be the creation of an independent social fabric among the poor capable of enhancing, individually and collectively, their ability to respond to the demands of their environment and providing them with the capacity for empowerment that they have lacked.

Participatory Approaches to the Alleviation of Rural Poverty

The participatory approach is particularly important in some key areas of intervention, two of the most important are credit and the preservation of the environment.

Credits

The importance of mobilization of participant resources at the grassroots level has been well demonstrated in credit operations. Institutions that have been used, or groups that have been formed "from above," to function simply as channels for the distribution of credit provided by external agencies, have had difficulty in maintaining their role beyond the period of the flow of external assistance. More enduring credit programs have been based on both group savings and group credit recycling, and this implies direct participation of the beneficiaries, usually through organized groups.

Given the vital long-term need for viable local savings and credit institutions in rural areas, the local development of independent savings and loan operations among the poor is equally, if not more, important than the provision of credit from the outside. In this regard, it must be noted that the difficulties encountered by the poor are not exclusively problems of absolute lack of resources, but often result from the lack of stable institutions through which existing resources can be put to work. Thus, while traditional institutions and groups do have an important role to play, the demands faced by the poor are often untraditional, requiring effective institutional redirection and reformation. In this sense, people's participation is not only a means of integrating the poor into development processes, but also a means of identifying the essential institutional structures that are needed and that derive from the experience and knowledge of the participants themselves.

Increasing the availability of credit targeted to small producers is a major field of operation of IFAD, and it has been one in which there have emerged differences in perception with some other donors. IFAD's position is that there must be substantial support to the development of low-level informal and formal savings and credit institutions; that credit should be made available to the poor without necessary recourse to land as collateral (relying more on group joint responsibility and internal group discipline); that external supplies of credit should be tightly targeted to those who otherwise would not have access to it; that the discipline of saving is critical to effective credit systems; that the availability of credit is more important than its cost; and that subsidized credit is more likely to be hijacked by the wealthier and less available to the poor.

Like all other producers, the poor require credit as a normal element of the framework of production and commercialization; this necessitates the creation of an enduring financial system to serve them.

Environment and Poverty Alleviation

The focus on poverty necessarily involves confronting the issue of sustainable livelihoods for small-scale producers on the basis of more sustainable patterns of natural resource use. For the vulnerable rural poor, the degradation of the environment poses a constant threat to survival. Therefore, special attention is needed to the preservation and rehabilitation of the natural resources (especially soil and water conservation) on which the long-term future of its beneficiaries is vitally dependent.

A large number of soil and water conservation programs have failed in developing countries. These failures result in part from poor government incentive policies, which have in some cases favored land and water consumption. But part of the problem, perhaps the major part, has come from how governments—and donors—have approached the issues involved. They have tended to define the problem without reference to the farmers; top-down plans that frequently prohibit the farmer from using valuable resources have been enforced; and organization, technologies, and materials completely alien to the local community have been mobilized. The results have tended to be very low levels of success, farmer hostility, and limited areas treated; all the benefits of which have disappeared once the external programs ended.

There is a need to profit from these lessons of the international experience in resource conservation and pursue a different strategy. The basic postulate of such a strategy should be that it is the farmers themselves who are on the frontline against environmental degradation, and that the objective is to support their efforts rather than supplant them.

Conclusion

It is the content of poverty that dictates the form of poverty alleviation. Understanding this should characterize all projects and programs attacking poverty, irrespective of their particular institutional sponsor.

Whatever the particular requirements of each case, however, three objectives have to be observed: identification of the concrete obstacles faced by the poor producer; targeted delivery of relevant assistance; and help in the development of the organizational framework through which the poor can better organize the interface between themselves and macromarkets and institutions. These have worked on the microlevel. The challenge now is to build them into the overall structure of national policy and development assistance. This is what needs to be promoted: a framework for the most efficient use of the poor's own resources and for the maximum impact of the limited additional resources brought to bear by governments and aid agencies so that the poor will have the means to serve themselves.

Section 2

The Effects of Agricultural Modernization

Anthony W. Pereira

> "Mtaua jembe sie mkulima."
> *The one who chooses the hoe is not the digger.*
> —Swahili proverb[1]

As the proverb above suggests, agricultural activity is shaped by the social and political environment in which it takes place. Reciprocally, forms of agricultural production influence social and political outcomes, although how they do so is debated. For example, the effects of agricultural modernization have been analyzed in opposite ways. One perspective sees modernization as the salvation of developing countries, staving off catastrophic food shortages by using science and capital to increase output. In this technocratic vision, the high-technology, capital-intensive, large-scale farming of countries such as Canada, the United States, and Australia is a model that can be approximated by unleashing market competition. Such competition should be allowed to push the productivity of land and labor inexorably upwards, no matter what the social costs.

The second perspective is a reaction to the first. It sees modernization as part of a hegemonic discourse of development that invariably threatens the local knowledge, solidarity, and livelihood of peasant smallholders. In such a view, which tends to romanticize peasant "tradition," sustainable development is represented by peasant resistance to any sort of change in agricultural techniques.

Both types of analysis, however, are misleading. The first reflects the perverse logic of conventional development economics, in which the expansion of total output is valued above human welfare. The second skirts absurdity by celebrating peasants' desperate struggle for subsistence, using rudimentary equipment, as a kind of postmodern victory against the forces of universalism, modernity, and the West.

This section argues that agricultural modernization often imposes unconscionably high social and political costs on the rural poor. While not intrinsically undesirable — the world's urban population would not have an adequate food supply without it — such modernization needs to be supplemented by greater support for peasant smallholders. This can be seen most vividly in the case of newly industrializing countries, where agricultural output and productivity have often been increased at the same time that peasant smallholders and rural workers have suffered decreased access to land and food security, in addition to lower levels of employment and income.

How can the social benefits of the developing countries' agriculture be widened, and farming made more productive, without large numbers of poor peasants being coerced into the ranks of a rural or urban lumpenproletariat? This section explores that challenge. The first part examines the global context in which developing countries' farming currently takes place. The second looks at changes in agricultural production, showing that the negative impacts of modernization are often due to an environment characterized by marked social inequality and weak states. The third part briefly reviews some of the proposals to ameliorate those impacts, arguing that institutional reform within the state is the foundation upon which all the other suggestions rest.

The Global Context

Agricultural modernization is not just a "discourse" employed by the powerful; rather, it is a measurable process that directly transforms the lives of hundreds of millions of rural people in developing countries. It is the application of scientific knowledge and capitalist rationality to the ancient art of farming. The process involves transforming agriculture from a productive system in which profits derive primarily from land and labor, to one in which profits accrue mainly from capital investment, and in which land or labor productivity — or both — is increased.

The last fifty years have seen an unprecedented broadening and deepening of agricultural modernization. Its most significant and specific features have been the introduction of chemical fertilizers and pesticides, mechanization, and high-yield varieties (HYV), or "Green Revolution" seeds. These changes have been most extensive in the industrializing countries of Asia and Latin America. While ancient practices such as slash-and-burn cultivation and nomadic pastoralism are the local, relatively self-sufficient activities of small groups, modern farming relies on extensive markets and a division of labor, usually extending across national borders. It therefore must be analyzed in a global context.

Agricultural modernization is part of a world economy where inequalities between countries have widened, and world trade has increased faster than growth.[2] Trade relations are asymmetric, with control residing largely in the most powerful capitalist nation-states, transnational corporations, and multilateral agencies. In world agricultural trade, which is largely in food, asymmetries are also noticeable; while trade in food accounts from 15 to 35 percent of the GDP in developing countries, any individual state has little influence on markets. Developed countries, where most new agricultural technology is developed and where two-fifths of the world's cereals are produced, have also used their preeminent position to block competition from other agricultural exporters. Thus although developed countries protect their farmers through quotas and tariffs and subsidize them through price supports, they have successfully pressed for the opening of developing countries' markets to their agricultural exports.

The result of industrial world policies has been that global food prices are lower and more volatile than they otherwise would be, hurting developing world food exporters (and potential exporters). Food price variability also seems to have increased over time, accompanied by overall declines in real prices, particularly in the 1980s. This picture has discouraged developing world governments from greater investment in agricultural infrastructure, research, and development. Developing countries' share in world agricultural exports has declined steadily over the last twenty years, and several countries that were formerly self-sufficient in food, such as Nigeria, have now become net importers.

Prior to the Uruguay Round of the General Agreement on Tariffs and Trade (GATT) negotiations, concluded in December 1993, agriculture was not covered by GATT clauses XI and XVI, which banned quantitative import restrictions and export subsidies. As an indirect result of the clash between the United States and the Economic Community, North–South agricultural trade was liberalized in the agreement that goes into effect in 1995. This change, as with most cases of trade liberalization, is likely to help the strong and hurt the weak in the developing world. Food exporters, such as Argentina and Thailand, are likely to benefit, while importers will lose. Regionally, Asia is likely to gain most and Latin America less, but Africa may lose income as a result.

Because most agricultural output is not internationally traded, global impacts on most farmers are indirect rather than direct. For example, industrialized countries' subsidies to their agricultural producers, along with practices of unloading surplus grain via foreign aid programs or "dumping" food on world markets, have often crowded out local food production for the market in developing countries. In addition, the developing countries' debt crisis seriously affected their agriculture. Because of austerity measures adopted to facilitate debt repayment, many governments cut back on extension services and other infrastructural support for farmers. Structural adjustment programs, for their part, have had an ambiguous impact on agriculture. These programs often depress domestic demand, reducing the size of the market for agricultural producers. Although freeing prices from government control may bring higher returns to some farmers, especially large-scale farmers who market a substantial share of their produce, smaller farmers may be hit by parallel increases in transport and input costs.

Not all agricultural problems in the developing countries can be attributed to relations of power in the global economy. These countries have also adopted policies that discourage food production. Import-substitution industrialization (ISI) policies, for example, often forced farmers to pay higher than world market prices for inputs, while reducing the incomes of agricultural exporters by maintaining high exchange rates. Since ISI has been largely abandoned in the developing world, some farmers may benefit. Similarly, the elimination of monopolies on the part of state-controlled marketing boards has begun where they were most a problem—in Sub-Saharan Africa—with positive results for farmers engaged in export production.

Some Effects of Agricultural Modernization

The phrase "agricultural modernization" should not suggest that new techniques in agricultural production are always more "rational" than those they replace, nor that these innovations clearly and unambiguously represent "progress" in social terms. The changes associated with modernization are neither inevitable nor irreversible, nor are they occurring everywhere. They are consciously adopted by landowners, sometimes for noneconomic reasons: labor-saving machinery, for example, may be abandoned when labor costs decline significantly enough.[3]

Several corollaries spring from this conception of modernization. Modern agriculture usually entails the private ownership of land as opposed to customary and communal forms of land use. It tends to result in production for markets rather than for subsistence, and, because of economies of scale, in large estates rather than small family farms.[4] It favors high technology over low technology, nonrenewable energy sources over renewable sources, and has the potential for being more destructive of the environment than labor-intensive agriculture.

These dichotomies are meant to be suggestive rather than definitive. They should not be thought of in terms of rigid polarities, but rather, in terms of a series of changes that often, but do not always, go together. For example, highly commercial and market-oriented production is carried out by small family farms in certain places, such as the coffee regions of Venezuela. Similarly, smallholders can be environmentally destructive, as in the rain forests of the Amazon region. Despite these anomalies and the existence of substantial numbers of small farmers in countries such as France and Japan, it is possible to identify a type of farming cultivated most extensively in developed countries as a result of the industrial revolution; it is large-scale, capital-intensive, high-technology, specialized, and market driven.

This model was consolidated in the advanced capitalist countries after World War II, when rural labor became relatively scarce because of the growth of urban industry. This forced agricultural producers to adopt capital-intensive forms of production; the new technologies caused relatively little social dislocation, because they were introduced in societies whose rural labor force had already become largely urban.[5] In the developing countries, however, the new technologies were adopted in very different social environments. For various reasons, including transnational pressures and incentives, state subsidies to large estates, highly unequal distributions of land, large farmers' desire to insulate themselves from rural union organizing, and the prestige associated with "modern" forms of agriculture, the new technology spread despite the relative scarcity of capital and the abundance of labor. Unlike advanced capitalist countries, the labor surplus often produced by high-technology, capital-intensive agriculture in the developing world could not be absorbed by the industrial and service sectors. The agricultural revolution in these countries has thus made a less positive contribution to development than it did in the industrialized countries.

Agricultural modernization has been spread in the developing countries through the expansion of markets and the influence of multilateral international institutions, transnational corporations, and bilateral aid bureaucracies. The way in which the results of agricultural research, the bulk of which is still done in North America and Northern Europe, are disseminated throughout the world through agricultural-extension services is an example of how the industrial countries' model of agriculture is exported.

It is not clear that this model of agriculture is sustainable in its countries of origin. Modern agriculture's overspecialization of production has accelerated soil erosion, leading to a decline in the growth of yields. Extensive irrigation has depleted water tables, while chemical fertilizers have contaminated them. Similarly, chemical pesticides have sickened agricultural workers and endangered consumers, while at the same time forcing farmers to use larger amounts of poison due to insect resistance. Just as TNCs have shifted a considerable portion of world manufacturing to the developing world because of low wages, agribusinesses may shift more production there because of its undepleted soil and low wages.

In any case, agricultural modernization is likely to increase in the developing countries, and evidence suggests that its impact on peasant smallholders is often negative. For example, modernization in South Korean agriculture—in the form of the use of machinery, fertilizers, and high-yielding seed varieties—has led to broad improvements in rural welfare due to the relatively egalitarian distribution of land in the country.[6] However, South Korea is exceptional for many reasons. The more common pattern in the developing countries is for modernization to be introduced into highly inegalitarian social structures. The result is to widen the gap between rich and poor, creating a landless group of peasants who are marginalized from productive activity in both country and town.

An example of this is the introduction of Green Revolution varieties of seeds in various parts of the world in the 1960s. Large farmers able to buy and adapt to the Green Revolution technology were able to increase yields, but often by consolidating their holdings, displacing small farmers, and contributing to an overall drop in the demand for labor. There are exceptions to this general pattern. In Thanjavur, in the south Indian state of Tamil Nadu, the introduction of high-yielding rice (ADT.27) and mechanized irrigation pumps in the late 1960s increased rather than decreased demand for labor. This occurred because it allowed for double cropping, expanded the total cropped area on farms, and required the use of fertilizer. But this outcome was the result of unusual circumstances: the technology was not capital intensive, and small farmers in Thanjavur had better access to inputs than small farmers in other districts. More frequently, Green Revolution prices and practices excluded small producers from its benefits.

Similarly, a common effect of mechanization—in the context of labor surplus economies—is to reduce overall demand for rural labor and to drive down wages for unskilled agricultural workers. Those workers face a seasonal demand for their labor, which leaves them with severe problems during the "dead time" after the harvest. According to the World Bank, mechanization also induces the "faster growth of incomes of landowners or those who have capital than those who have labor as their primary source of income" and tends to "favor larger farms ...[and] increase farm size." This increase in farm size pushes smallholders off the land. By one estimate, there are now more than 600 million landless peasants in the developing countries. It is significant that estimates of the number of "chronically hungry" people in the world nearly matches this figure. While these two groups are obviously not identical, they overlap to a considerable degree.

Many forms of modernization worsen the position of women in the countryside. Women produce more than half the food in the developing world, yet they tend to have the least access to means of production and education and receive the lowest wages.

In Sub-Saharan Africa, where women account for an estimated seventy percent of the agricultural labor, only eight percent of the continent's agricultural extension officers are female. Women are also marginalized by Western-style land laws that establish individual titles to land. Because titleholders are often presumed to be men, land that women previously had claims to is often privatized under exclusively male title. When women are denied land to work on, they are often forced into wage labor as temporary workers; this can lead to child care and nutritional problems. In another example, one study concluded that the introduction of centralized pump irrigation in rice production in central Gambia, although intended to incorporate women, changed the intrahousehold division of labor to the detriment of women's access to the best lands, technology, productivity, and independent income. It also elevated their workload, time constraint, and dependency on their husbands.

Gender biases are not the only biases of modernized agriculture. The transformation of communally held areas into private, individually held plots on the Western model can seriously disrupt the social and political cohesiveness of indigenous communities, accelerating class differentiation and landlessness. The requirement of most banks that land be held individually before credit can be granted also works against people who till land in some sort of communal arrangement, preventing them from selectively adopting new technologies in order to survive.

All these examples point to the conclusion that, while the technology and organization of production associated with modernization are not always harmful in themselves, their introduction often worsens the plight of peasant cultivators on the bottom rung of the rural social structure. That this exists is, to a large degree, a reflection of the nature of state power in the countryside.

States can harm peasant smallholders in at least three ways. The first is by neglecting them, thereby allowing the differentiation of the peasantry that normally accompanies capitalist development to proceed unchecked. By promoting the expansion of large estates through cheap credit, tax incentives, and export subsidies, and by doing little for small farmers, it fails to integrate these workers into the national economy. It also indirectly encourages rural–urban migration.

The second way that states can harm peasant cultivators is by serving as a direct instrument of coercion and exploitation of the peasantry. In many African countries, where agrarian relations are not synonymous with landlord–tenant relations, the state uses peasants as forced labor and taxes them exploitatively. The capital accumulation is often more important than internal differentiation within the peasantry itself in generating a surplus. In Latin America, where landlord–tenant relations are more important, the state often uses its coercive apparatus on behalf of landlords to drive peasants off the land and to repress peasant leagues and rural trade unions that attempt to oppose such expulsions.

The role of state violence, or state complicity in the private violence of dominant classes, in imposing agricultural modernization has also not been fully acknowledged. The marginalization of the rural poor that often accompanies technological change is not simply the result of market forces, but coercion and the absence of state enforcement of law. Landlessness, for example, would not be quite so harsh for the poor if states in the developing world enforced minimum wage legislation. Other political features contributing to the marginalization of the poor include the capture of local state institutions by landlords, and the latter's use of patronage to influence electoral outcomes.

The third way that a state can damage small peasant interests is to collapse, as has happened in Cambodia, Afghanistan, and the African countries of Angola, Mozambique, Somalia, Liberia, and Rwanda. In these worst-case scenarios, the state is incapable of fulfilling its basic responsibility to maintain order. The countryside becomes the natural base of operations for guerrilla armies; it remains unsafe to cultivators: peasants flee to the comparative safety of cities as agriculture collapses; and food provision becomes a task for international relief agencies. In such cases, agriculture suffers retrogression rather than modernization, and only the surpluses produced by the developed countries keeps the population alive.

Most developing states have not collapsed, but engage in both neglect and exploitation/coercion of their peasantries. The logic of state-building seems to run counter to policies in favor of smallholders. From the viewpoint of state managers, there are good reasons for this. Medium-to-large farms market the most surplus, which is helpful in providing cheap food to placate potentially restive urban populations and to underwrite industrialization. Small farmers are more likely to produce only for subsistence and not add to the total food supply. Furthermore, subsistence producers are difficult to tax. Large estates, on the other hand, provide exports, which are easy to tax and provide foreign exchange. Large farmers and landlords also control votes in the countryside, if the regime is forced to contest elections. Moreover, they can make campaign contributions and are better equipped to acquire new agricultural technology and make production more efficient. Ignoring the peasant smallholder sector results in what Paul Streeten has called the "stark and growing dualism" produced by economic growth, in which the fruits of growth are concentrated in the hands of a minority. The majority are made worse off or left in the same position, and employment generation lags behind growth in output. In many newly industrializing countries, agricultural exports have risen, while per capita food production has declined. Production on large farms using state-of-the-art machinery has expanded notably, while the inequality of landholding and the imparity between regions have increased. A lack of incentives for small farmers has also contributed to massive rural–urban migrations.

In Latin America, for example, the Food and Agriculture Organization found that the number of rural poor in 10 Latin American countries increased between 1960 and 1980, despite considerable economic expansion. A major factor in the increase in rural poverty was the decline of small-farm tenancies and the creation of a large category of temporary wage laborers unable to gain adequate, year-round incomes. This evidence points to the urgent need to prioritize small-scale peasant agriculture in development projects, not just for economic reasons, but to sustain and consolidate democratic regimes.

The Case of Mexico

When agricultural modernization widens inequalities and marginalizes the rural poor, a political backlash often results. The most dramatic, recent example of this has occurred in Mexico, where large agroexport concerns were favored over peasant agriculture, especially after the 1982 debt crisis and the resulting closer integration with the U.S. economy. Agriculture in Mexico was dualistic, not only between peasant smallholders and large enterprises, but between the relatively prosperous, mestizo, market-oriented, and modernized north and the less affluent, indigenous, peasant south. Thousands of peasants from the south migrated to vegetable-growing regions serving the U.S. market in the north, such as Culiacán, sometimes moving across the border to work on farms in the United States on a seasonal basis.

Mexico's peasant agriculture is organized into *ejidos*, communal holdings established after the revolution of 1910–1920, especially under the government of Lázaro Cardenas (1928–1940). *Ejidos* are usually composed of a village — common land — including woods and grazing land, and plots tilled by individual families. In the early 1990s, there were 28,000 *ejidos* and about 3.5 million *ejidatários* (*ejido* members) in Mexico, covering half of the country's 253 million acres.

Productivity on the *ejidos* is low: 50 percent of the plots are less than 2 acres, and only about 12 percent of *ejido* land is arable. Little bank credit has been extended to the *ejidos*. The Mexican government responded to this problem in 1992 by altering the Agrarian Reform Law (Article 27 of the Constitution) to allow the privatization of the *ejidos*. The government is using Japanese satellite technology that transmits aerial maps from the field to the National Statistics Institute headquarters in Aguascalientes. Eventually, the government hopes to give all of the nation's *ejidatarios* titles to their individual parcels of land. According to one scholar, "the reforms of Article 27 may have a more far-reaching and enduring impact than any other of the economic reforms introduced in Mexico by technocratic governments since 1982."[7] The best historical analogy to what is occurring in Mexico is the Stolypin reform in Russia (1906–1911), which attempted to individualize and privatize collectively held land. Peasant reaction against these reforms contributed to the 1917 Bolshevik revolution.

The privatization of Mexico's *ejido* land, along with the North American Free Trade Agreement (NAFTA), which went into effect at the beginning of 1994, is likely to result in the buying up of *ejido* land by both U.S. and Mexican agribusinesses. At the same time, the inflow of cheap U.S. grain as a result of Mexico's tariff reductions in conformance with NAFTA will drive many small Mexican corn producers (most of whom are *ejidatarios*) out of business. These two forces will push hundreds of thousands of former *ejidatarios* (more than 1 million in the next 10 years, according to one estimate) out of the Mexican countryside; many of these will move into U.S. agriculture. The illegal status of Mexican workers in the United States will be used by landowners to drive down wages and roll back gains in both working conditions and unionization, which are already becoming fragile in the sluggish U.S. economy.

Resistance to Mexico's agricultural policies surfaced dramatically on January 1, 1994, the first day of NAFTA's implementation. The Zapatista National Liberation Army (EZLN) engaged in armed actions in Chiapas, southern Mexico, on that day. The insurgency was avowedly anti-NAFTA, but was also fueled by local conditions. Contributing to the revolt was a government colonization scheme that was established in Chiapas (as were Amazonian colonization schemes in Brazil) to avoid land conflict in other parts of the country. This program settled peasants and set up *ejidos* (cooperatives) on the poor-quality soils of the Lacandon rain forest. The land on these soils was quickly depleted, and the government refused to authorize the enlargement of the size of the *ejidos*. Furthermore, the state government, dominated by large farmers and ranchers, used violence to repress protests by indigenous people – Mayan Indians who identify themselves as Tzotzil, Tzeltal, Tojolabal, Chol, and Mam.[8] The drop in coffee prices and the intensification of logging and livestock enterprises that drove peasants off their land in the 1980s were also forces squeezing the Chiapas peasantry and contributing to the revolt.[9]

The revolt in Chiapas does not seem to be part of an atavistic defense of peasant traditions. Marcos, the spokesperson for the Zapatista army, has indicated in interviews that land seizures are not permitted in rebel territory and not supported by the EZLN. "Farmers in the United States have tractors and machinery, and we are planting our corn with a stick and using slash-and-burn methods," he has said. "The way out is to raise productivity, and for that we need investment," as well as better markets, roads, information, and education.[10]

Agricultural modernization on its own, of course, does not cause peasant insurrection. Scholars have shown that such insurrections do not arise spontaneously; they are the result of patient recruiting, training, and mobilization of peasants by leaders with a strategy for seizing state power. Nevertheless, agrarian conditions are the parameters within which such leaders do their recruiting. Agricultural modernization can disconnect the rural poor from the production process, making them more available to recruitment by guerrilla armies.

Possible Solutions

Ending the marginalization of peasant smallholders is no easy task. Their situation is the result of long-term structural and historical changes whose direction can only partly be altered by new policies. It also arises from global inequalities in exchange relations – in trade, finance, and aid – that are unlikely to disappear. Where policies can make a difference, it seems preferable to try to unleash the productive potential of the rural poor by directly affecting the production process itself, rather than by attempting post-facto redistributive measures. Supporting small cultivators engaged in subsistence or market-oriented farming – by granting them access to assets such as land, credit, machinery, and education – is probably easier than trying to alleviate their poverty after they have been removed from the land.

Excessive population growth clearly worsens the effects of agricultural modernization, because as it decreases the number of workers per hectare, population growth increases pressure on the land. Although rich countries clearly advocate population control programs, the poor pay much of the costs of population growth. For individual families, it may be rational to have as many children as possible, but for the poor increased competition for jobs, land, and other resources can only be negative. However, population programs that emphasize female education and expand women's choices seem preferable to top-down programs that concentrate exclusively on contraception. Population control cannot be a substitute for development itself, because chronic poverty is not caused by an inadequate global food supply, but by the poor distribution of food.

Land reform, in conjunction with credit and infrastructural support for small farmers, could be an excellent way to ameliorate the inequalities generated by agricultural modernization. Economic growth alone is not capable of raising the incomes of the rural poor when land ownership is highly concentrated. Land reforms in South Korea and Taiwan point to the beneficial welfare effects of a more equitable distribution of land; however, they also show how politically difficult land reform is to achieve. These reforms were implemented after major wars and were backed by occupying armies (U.S. forces in South Korea, the Guomindang in Taiwan). But, in the absence of war or revolution, in political systems in which large landowners have a disproportionate share of political power, land reform is very unlikely.

A more viable set of policy recommendations would consist of both reform of agricultural policies and more general changes in the rural environment. The former would include changing credit policies to favor small and medium cultivators producing food for the domestic market, maintaining minimum prices for staple food items and providing marketing assistance and better infrastructure. In addition, tax burdens on small and medium producers could be lifted, while improved agricultural equipment could be made available to smallholders.

Another suggestion would be to widen the nature and reach of rural extension programs so that they more fully reflect and affect the needs of the rural poor. David Leonard showed in the late 1970s how rural extension in Kenya was biased towards large farmers and suggested how the benefits of government agricultural programs could be spread more evenly.[11] However, the collapse of many public sector programs in Africa in the 1980s means that the present situation is probably worse than when Leonard researched it.

A second set of policy recommendations is indirect, in that it concerns rural society in general rather than agriculture alone. One of these is rural employment schemes, designed to supplement incomes of smallholders and the landless. Public works projects that hire rural people to engage in road building, repair, and other projects raise the incomes of the rural poor.[12] Because of the fiscal pressures on the governments of developing countries, such public works programs may be limited in scope. An alternative, less state-centric solution would be to allow for the formation of rural cooperatives, which could bid for labor contracts in the countryside. This would cost the state money, but less than under the previous proposal, because it would leave organization and management of the projects in the hands of the cooperatives.

Much has also been made in recent years of informal lending arrangements that have proved effective in generating employment in the countryside. Cooperatives that pool financial resources and lend it to members on a rotating basis promise to rid the rural poor of dependence on village moneylenders and help to finance grassroots initiatives. The *assusu* in the Gambia, the *cheetu* in Sri Lanka, and the *samabaya* in Bangladesh are all examples of this kind of cooperation; the Grameen Bank in Bangladesh, while part of the formal sector, works on similar principles. Yet, some questions persist as to how effective these lending schemes are. Patron–client ties are pervasive in many rural areas in the developing world, and they might easily absorb these new networks. Another problem is that of raising sufficient capital in poor societies. A third drawback is that even if the capital is sufficient to enable members to start small enterprises, local purchasing power may not be sufficient enough to sustain them. Nevertheless, these schemes do seem capable of allowing participants to plan purchases over the long term, and if their independence is maintained, nurturing a sense of self-sufficiency.

Not all proposals for enabling peasant smallholders to boost incomes and welfare need be directly concerned with agricultural production itself. One study from Malawi suggests that there is a strong link between agricultural productivity and nutrition and health. Higher public expenditures on health, especially in periods of greatest agricultural activity, might have a large positive effect on production.[13] The provision of clean water, a relatively cheap infrastructural expense, might have a similar effect.

All of the ideas mentioned so far—rural employment schemes, informal lending arrangements, expanding the reach of rural extension agencies, and the building of health and water infrastructure—depend on state policies to some extent. Although all except rural extension could be done by either the state or private organizations, the situation requires a minimum of autonomy from social classes that expropriate surplus or labor from the poor peasantry, the provision of essential services, and a consistent regulatory environment throughout a territory.

The importance of capable, coherent, and accountable state institutions to development is generally recognized. A lack of awareness of this connection has hobbled previous approaches to development, such as basic human needs. A body of interdisciplinary literature concerned with the operations and effects of certain state institutions exists for development practitioners and theorists to draw on.

This literature suggests that the project of making state institutions more capable and democratically accountable is not identical to that of economic liberalization. The example of Russia shows how free-market shock therapy may enervate public authority to such an extent that a flourishing civil society is no longer possible.[14] Similarly, democratizing the local and quotidian forms of state power cannot be equated with multiparty elections. Neither is democratization synonymous with decentralization. As the authors of the UNDP's 1993 *Human Development Report* acknowledge, decentralization may merely devolve branches of the local state to the control of landed elites. While the decentralization of state power seems a necessary ingredient in any process of democratization, especially in societies where large numbers of peasants exercise limited citizenship rights, it is not commensurate with the creation of autonomous forms of state power outside the direct control of landed elites.

Democratic and organizational reforms of state institutions is indeed a contradictory process. In the absence of a revolutionary rupture, reforms designed to reduce the power and privileges of those who control the central state must be managed by that state itself. State managers can be expected to resist such reforms. Where they are constrained by multiparty elections, they may want to construct the so-called "two-track political systems," in which democracy exists in the electoral arena, but not in the government.

A state capable of mitigating the effects of agricultural modernization outlined here would be a democratized and more capable state than is common in the developing world. It would combine enhanced participation from below with improved managerial skills and technical knowledge from above. It would possess embedded autonomy, in which institutions with bureaucratic cohesiveness and skilled management develop close links with civil society. Decisions made within the state can be enforced beyond it, because private-sector actors are knowledgeable and responsive about state policies. The power states have to construct, manage, and guide social projects by enforcing rules distinct from their despotic, arbitrary power over individual subjects. As with embedded autonomy, the development of infrastructural power requires bargaining with civil society.

Rebuilding and democratizing states in the rural areas of the developing world, if and where it occurs, will vary according to local conditions. In some places, unions may be the most prominent vehicles of rural popular expression and democratization; in others, it will be peasant leagues; in still others, political parties. A blueprint for such a project cannot exist because local conditions are so variable.

Conclusion

Agricultural modernization in the context of inequality exacerbates poverty and marginalizes the poorest part of the rural population. Strict adherence to market forces alone will not address these problems. Governments of both industrialized and developing countries could cheaply promote the efforts of small farmers to produce food more efficiently and manage their resources more carefully, even though, judged by a technocratic calculus, most small farmers are less efficient than large farmers. Because of their major contribution to rural employment, small farms should not be neglected or used as an easy source of revenue and labor-power by government officials. Modest programs to reach smallholders, more politically feasible now that the worst of the debt crisis seems to be over, could result in major increases in food output and avoid the "jobless growth" that typically results from the expansion of large estates.

Informal credit networks, enhanced extension services, and seasonal public works projects seem to be three of the best ways to prevent small farmers' loss of access to land and to boost their output. These proposals, however, presume a level of political stability and state autonomy that does not exist in many parts of the developing world. No doubt they are nothing more than empty moral exhortations when applied to the worst cases, where states have literally been torn apart by violence. It is well known that world arms expenditures overshadow the resources devoted to agricultural research, that the science of death attracts more money than the science of life. Millions of land mines will pose an obstacle to farming in places like Cambodia, Angola, Nicaragua, and Afghanistan for a generation to come, even if state support for smallholders exists. In other places, however, the situation is not so bleak.

Agricultural modernization need not be an implacable enemy of human development. It can play an important role in producing food, but its attractions should not lead to the neglect of peasant smallholders, whose skills, knowledge, and willingness to work have often been wasted. Returning to the proverb that began this section, the world needs political change that allows the digger to choose his own hoe, instead of having one chosen for him, or taken away as he is expelled from the land.

Notes

1. From Jan Knappert, *Proverbs from the Lamu Archipelago and the Central Kenya Coast.* Berlin: Dietrich Reimer Verlag, 1986, p. 91.
2. In 1950 the average per capita income (in 1980 US$) of low-income countries was $164, whereas the per capita income of the industrialized countries averaged $3,841, yielding an absolute income gap of $3,677. In 1990, high-income countries had a per capita GNP of $20,173, versus $353

in the low-income countries, a gap of $19,820 (1990 US$). In terms of ratio, the rich countries were 23 times richer in 1950, but 57 times richer in 1990. From Mitchell Seligson, "The Dual Gaps: An Overview of Theory and Research." In Mitchell A. Seligson and John T. Passé-Smith (eds.), *Development and Underdevelopment: The Political Economy of Inequality.* Boulder, CO: Lynne Rienner, 1993, p. 3.

3. However, in some socialist countries, modern agriculture was based on state ownership of farms. Cuba's highly mechanized and productive sugar estates were an example of this, at least before the fall of the Soviet Union. See Andrew Zimbalist (ed.), *Cuba's Socialist Economy: Toward the 1990s.* Boulder, CO: Lynne Rienner, 1987.

4. Wallerstein argues that the concentration of "decision-making procedures in production" are crucial to modernized agriculture, rather than the concentration of ownership per se. See Immanuel Wallerstein, *The Modern World-System*, vol. 3, San Diego: Academic Press, 1989, p. 138. This is probably correct, but in those crops where economies of scale exist, modernization does usually result in concentration of land ownership as well. In the United States, for example, average farm size has risen steadily in the twentieth century. See Daniel B. Suits, "Agriculture." In Walter Adams (ed.), *The Structure of American Industry.* New York: Macmillan, 1990, pp. 1–2.

5. For example, in the United States today, fewer than 4 percent of the labor force works in agriculture, while fewer than 10 percent of workers are on farms in Western Europe. From Suits, "Agriculture," p. 1.

6. At the end of World War II, 51.6 percent of rural households in South Korea did not own any land. But during this time, land belonging to Japanese landlords was distributed to Koreans, and after 1950, a land reform distributed land from large estates held by Koreans to tenants. By 1964, 71.6 percent of rural households owned land. Later, industrialization helped to raise wage levels in agriculture, which rose 151 percent, on average, between 1971 and 1979. International Labor Office, *World Labor Report,* pp. 78, 80.

7. Wayne A. Cornelius, "The Politics and Economics of Reforming the *Ejido* Sector in Mexico: An Overview and Research Agenda," *LASA Forum,* 23, no. 3 (1992): 3. See also Jonathan Fox, "Agriculture and the Politics of the North American Free Trade Debate," *LASA Forum,* 23, no. 1 (1992): pp. 3–9; Ted Bardacke, "Nuevo Giro en Política Agrícola," *Este País,* (September 1992) 3–7; and Gerardo Román Ruenes, "El Agro: Los Sectores Social y Privado," *Este País,* (September 1992): 9–21.

8. Tim Golden, "In Remote Mexican Village, Roots of Rebellion Are Bared," *The New York Times,* January 17, 1994, A8.

9. Jeffrey Rubin, "Mexico—A Tale of Two States," *New York Times,* Jan. 7, 1994; Tim Golden, "Left Behind, Mexico's Indians Fight the Future," *New York Times,* January 9, 1994: 6; and Andrew Reding, "Chiápas is Mexico," *World Policy Journal,* 11 (1994): pp. 11–25.

10. Quotes from "Mexico: Promised Land," *The Economist,* May 14, 1994, 47, and Alma Guillermoprieto, "Zapata's Heirs," *The New Yorker,* May 16, 1994: 61.

11. David K. Leonard, *Reaching the Peasant Farmer.* Chicago: University of Chicago Press, 1977.
12. Amartya Sen, "The Economics of Life and Death," *Scientific American,* May 1993: 43. Such programs were initiated by the Brazilian government in March 1993 after hungry peasants raided markets in dozens of towns in the interior of the arid northeast, then suffering from a drought.
13. This observation is taken from Agnès Callamard, "Populations Under Fire, Populations Under Stress: Mozambican Refugees and Malawian Villagers in the District of Mwanza, Malawi: A Study of Resistance, Interaction, and Change." Ph.D. dissertation (draft), New School for Social Research, 1994, pp. 117–118, 257.
14. See Alice H. Amsden, "From Pseudo-Socialism to Pseudo-Capitalism," *New School Commentator* 5, no. 3 (1994) for an insightful critique of free-market shock therapy in Russia and Eastern and Central Europe. For an article that questions liberalization in Latin America, see Guillermo O'Donnell, "The Browning of Latin America," *New Perspectives Quarterly* 10, no. 4 (1993): 50–53.

Reducing Poverty: "Horizontal Flows" Instead of "Trickle Down"

Gustav Ranis

The notion, current some years ago, that per capital income growth, if sufficiently sustained, would automatically eliminate poverty is clearly wrong— just as wrong as the notion that poverty can be reduced by some form of direct attack via the provision of basic needs goods to target groups, thus avoiding traditional "trickle-down" problems. The answer is to rely neither on growth percolating down to those below the poverty line nor on public sector provision alone to do the trick. Indeed, the experience of the mixed economies of developing countries, leaving the exsocialist countries aside, is to select a middle road between these two positions. The answer is not to reject growth, but to insist on a better way in which it is routinely generated. In brief, growth need not be identified, as it all too often has been, with the relatively narrow urban-biased variety, which led to its association with "trickle down." Instead, it should be identified with vigorous "horizontal flows," breaking down compartments, and thus helping to solve the poverty problem at the same time.

What Kind of Growth?

There are essentially two reasons why we need the "right" kind of growth in order to simultaneously reduce poverty. In a mixed economy, the way incomes are generated through the production process (before taxes and transfers) has to carry a heavy part of the burden of poverty reduction. The political as well as technical obstacles to significantly adjusting disposable incomes through taxes and transfers are likely to be beyond the capacity of most developing countries to overcome. Thus, if what has sometimes been called primary income generation is highly inequitable, it would take unreasonably high overall growth rates to make any dent on poverty in the face of a worsening distribution of income. On the other hand, even modest rates of growth are consistent with poverty reduction if growth proceeds through vigorous horizontal flows, that is, broadly based, employment-intensive, and not compartmentalized. Latin America represents an example of the former, and Asia, especially East Asia, an example of the latter.

A second reason why the right kind of growth is necessary is that the provision of public goods, which are an essential part of poverty and poverty reduction, requires resources, largely domestic, and provided to a greater extent via taxes and/or fees paid out of growing incomes. This includes access to schools, health care, potable water, and so on, encompassing the monetary value of public spending or the access of the population to social services.

Because we have two kinds of incomes (i.e., disposable private income and social income) and two kinds of poverty (private and public goods poverty), it would make sense to draw separate poverty lines with respect to primary incomes (or consumption) of families and their social incomes based on public goods that determine such basic quality of life indicators as literacy, infant mortality, and life expectancy. It would be even more sensible, although more difficult, to attempt to consolidate the two poverty lines by placing monetary values on the public goods reaching different income groups.

East Asian Versus Latin American Growth

For growth to be both necessary and sufficient to reduce poverty, policy changes from what might roughly be called the Latin American pattern of growth in the direction of the East Asian pattern of growth may be required. Certainly, contrasting these two patterns leads one to observe more trickle down in Latin America and more horizontal flows in Asia. In both of these types of developing countries, the initial development phase, characterized by the well-known import substitution syndrome, entailed a relatively segmented, narrowly based growth process, with employment generation, even in Asia, barely keeping up with labor force growth. However, once this early, consumer-goods type of import substitution regime had run its course by the early 1960s in both regions, there was a parting of the ways.

While Latin America continued to pursue an increasingly narrow, increasingly urban, and increasingly capital-intensive, industry-oriented development path, focused now more on durables, capital goods, and the processing of raw materials, Asia now moved toward a more participatory, employment-intensive growth path, emphasizing, if to a varying degree, a balanced rural growth pattern and labor-intensive industrial exports interacting in a mutually reinforcing, complementary fashion. It is interesting to note that, as a consequence, poverty in Latin America shifted from a predominantly rural to a predominantly urban phenomenon. This was clearly the result of unbalanced growth, a lack of agricultural mobilization, and the movement of people into the cities looking for the relatively few high paying organized sector jobs, shifting the relative incidence of poverty to the urban areas, but increasing its absolute total incidence.

The Role of Dynamic Agriculture

The Latin American experience needs to be contrasted with the Asian experience, which entailed a relatively more dynamic agriculture, with relatively much more rural nonagricultural activities growing in a balanced fashion in tandem with agricultural productivity change. This means a greater chance to hold their populations in rural areas and, at the same time, through a participatory process involving both rural and urban activities, to reduce poverty via the horizontal flow of incomes, as compartmentalization breaks down and the previously disenfranchised in both the rural and urban sectors find remunerative employment opportunities. Ideally, this means both a vigorous agriculture, as labor-intensive in terms of output and technology choices as possible and, most importantly, a dynamic set of rural nonagricultural activities in both industry and services. These work in tandem with agricultural output change and may be substantially complementary to the larger-scale urban industrial activities.

Labor-Intensive Industrial Exports

A second important feature of such a horizontal flow mechanism that renders growth and poverty reduction highly complementary is, of course, the well-known labor-intensive industrial export pattern. This may benefit from export processing zones as transition devices, but is basically focused on the access of medium- and small-scale firms, either directly to export markets or indirectly through their complementary activities with larger-scale urban activities. To the extent that the poor are producers of tradable goods, this, of course, is very helpful; to the extent that the poor are mainly consumers of tradables, this may be less helpful, especially if real devaluations are required to make the country internationally competitive.

Share of Wages

The contrasting experience, at least until recently, of Latin America and Asia in this context points to certain policy conclusions as well, which have facilitated the breakdown of compartmentalization in Asia and a more mixed experience in Latin America. There is little point in rehearsing the pros and cons of continued import substitution in Latin America versus the shift toward export orientation in East Asia. But, with respect to our particular issue of poverty reduction through the primary income channel, it is important to avoid the premature ossification of labor markets through government unions and minimum wage legislation. To ensure that the horizontal flow mechanism is at full strength, the focus should be on the relative share of wages, not on the unskilled wage rate, at least until the labor surplus condition has been eliminated and wage rates can rise as a result of increased unskilled labor scarcity. It is clearly more advantageous to a typical working class family to have three of its members employed at moderate wages than to have one working at a high wage, because of one kind or another of government intervention on behalf of the elite 5 to 10 percent of the labor force.

Land Reform, Credits, and Technology

With respect to the capital side, of course, much can also be accomplished in making growth more complementary with poverty reduction. For example, something can be done about initial asset distribution. Land reform is a case in point, and Asia has generally done much better than Latin America on this front. A similar observation can be made about the credit market, which is often biased in favor of the rich, while such examples as supervised credit through the Grameen Bank and the Farmers' Association-related cooperative banks represent mainly Asian examples of institutional mechanisms that assist in strengthening the horizontal flow mechanism.

Needless to add, the contribution of an enhanced technological capacity on a broad front with respect to both output mix and technique changes is but part and parcel of this horizontal primary income generation process. It is here that government action to overcome the common experience of market failure with respect to information on markets, on alternative technologies, and the legal structure, encouraging broad-based research and development activities are in order. A good example is the so-called utility model of patents that has been deployed in Asia, encouraged broad-based local blue-collar innovations as an alternative to the traditional Western-style frontier patents invoked in Latin America, basically the province of the large-scale multinational and domestic firms.

Tax and Transfer Systems

Although disposable income poverty reduction must be achieved largely through changes in the way primary incomes are generated through the productive system, some progress, even if limited, can also be made through the tax and transfer system. The empirical evidence unfortunately indicates that, even in the Asian case, transfers are likely to be nonprogressive, while the progressivity of taxes differs widely across countries. The most we can realistically hope for is that the poverty problem is not made worse through the tax/expenditure efforts of government. Undoubtedly, to the extent that there is more devolution of fiscal powers from the center to local governments, the chances for a larger total tax as well as more progressivity in the tax system are substantially enhanced.

We do not mean to ignore lower-end poverty families that are not likely to be able to participate in the primary income generation process and need a welfare or safety net; however, help to them should be carefully targeted, perhaps in a geographic fashion to avoid the normal problems of high jacking, but also in a fashion not so narrow as to miss a substantial number of unemployable poor, on the one hand, or to lose the political support of the lower middle class on the other.

Social Poverty Reduction

Turning to social income poverty, we are dealing with public goods delivered by the government, or possibly NGOs, in such areas as education, health, and potable water. Not only are resources drawn from the growth required for public expenditures of any kind, but the allocation of those public expenditures as between household, military, and so on, on the one hand, and public goods, on the other, is, of course, crucial. Moreover, within the various social income categories, the extent to which the consumption of the poor relative to that of the rich is favored in another critical component. Thus, the volume of financial resources available for public goods to the poor depends very much on the revenue capability of government, on the proportion of these revenues preserved for public goods allocation, as well as on the extent to which people below the social poverty line are likely to benefit.

Clearly, overall resource availability, reflected in the growth of GDP, is necessary, if not sufficient, for social poverty reduction. For example, South Korea increased its investment per head in education by 1300 percent and in health by 1800 percent between 1975 and 1990 partly because its GDP grew by about 9 percent annually. How much of this went to people under the social poverty line also depends, however, on the allocation within the social sectors, as between goods focused on the socially poor versus those who are nonpoor; there are the well-known examples of primary education relative to university education, preventive health relative to hospital expansion, and, generally, rural versus urban water supplies. One interesting contrast is between Bangladesh, which subsidizes tertiary education to the tune of 250 percent of per capita income and primary to the tune of 5 percent, and South Korea, where the relevant magnitudes are 12 percent and 17 percent, respectively. It is clear that both health and educational deficits, which can be calculated as the difference between actual and "normal" levels of health and school attendance, are usually much larger for the poor than for the nonpoor in developing societies, and that these deficits are moreover much larger in Latin America than in Asia. For example, in Brazil, education deficits approach 60 percent for the lowest quintile, and are only at 20 percent for the highest; and even in Costa Rica, which has done much better on primary income generation and primary income poverty reduction, these educational deficit numbers by quintile are 44 percent, as opposed to 26 percent. Thus, even though health and educational expenditures add up to 17 percent of total government expenditures in Paraguay and to 44 percent in Costa Rica, we need to look at every component of the above relation to ensure maximum complementarity between GDP growth and social poverty reduction. Once again, experience indicates that the extent to which government is decentralized, especially if decentralization takes the form of actual devolution, this is bound to lead to a larger allocation to the social sectors and, within the social sectors, to a more accurate reflection of local preferences and an enhanced ability to curb elite demands for social sector products and services.

A similar analysis can be carried out in the realm of economic overheads, representing public goods that affect the strength of the primary income horizontal flow mechanism. Infrastructural allocations that help determine where primary income generation via markets takes place can also be examined in terms of their poverty impact. A good example is the difference between mini-infrastructure farm-to-market roads, on the one hand, and superhighways, on the other. Once again, the arguments we made earlier on behalf of the possible devolution of central government functions to local governments would be relevant. Although the subject is controversial, most of the evidence indicates that real devolution serves to enhance the complementarity between overall resource generation (i.e., growth) and the reduction of poverty, this time because of the relatively lower dominance of local relative to central elites in determining the nature and allocation of overhead capital.

Conclusion

Experiences acquired in different regions of the world in the fight against poverty show that there is no single remedy. Although growth is a prerequisite, the question becomes what type of growth. The answer is growth with horizontal flows, not just through trickle down.

Chapter 2

Learning from Experiences

Sub-Saharan Africa's Development Crisis[1]

Robert S. McNamara

Africa is heading towards an inevitable tragedy. And no one can prevent such an outcome except the African leaders themselves.

Much has been written about the growing marginalization of the region in recent years. The evidence is grim. Among all the areas of the world, Sub-Saharan Africa has the lowest life expectancy, the lowest literacy rate, the highest infant mortality, and the highest population growth rate. Nearly one-half of the region's population lives below the poverty line. The story of the area's growing economic marginalization has been told so often – and in such graphic detail – that I need not belabor the point.

What is more disturbing, however, is the fact that the situation is getting worse. Over the last three decades, the Sub-Saharan Africa's global share of GNP has fallen from around 2 percent in 1960 to around 1 percent in 1990; in global trade, the share declined from 4 percent to 1 percent during the same period. Throughout the 1980s, per capita income declined in 19 African countries.[2] In several countries, including Côte d'Ivoire, Gabon, Niger, and Nigeria, per capita income in 1990 was only one-half to three-quarters of what it was ten years earlier. Can one imagine the depths of human despair when wholly inadequate incomes fall to about half of their previous levels and when there is little prospect of a significant increase during the next decade? In fact, the latest estimates from the World Bank show that, even on fairly optimistic assumptions, in the year 2000 Sub-Saharan Africa will not have reached its per capita income level of 1980, and that was totally insufficient.

We are already witnessing the slow descent of the region into social confusion and political anarchy. Several countries are beginning to disintegrate from within. Ethnic and regional conflicts are erupting as fierce battles develop over declining incomes, diminishing jobs, and reduced socioeconomic opportunities. In the last three years, there were at least ten domestic conflicts within Africa, each leading to more than 1,000 deaths. Somalia and Rwanda are only an early warning of the events yet to unfold—unless we act in time.

And the real action lies in the hands of the African leadership. It is convenient to find an external alibi for every internal problem confronting Africa today. It is tempting to recall the injustices of colonialism, the brutality of the slave trade, and the dark shadows of a receding past. It is easy to suggest that more liberal doses of foreign assistance will turn around the continent's economic destiny. But let me say as a friend of Africa, as someone who feels the African tragedy deep in his bones, none of this will be determinative. African problems are structural ones. And they require African solutions.

The first task facing African policy makers is to recognize that only they can rescue Africa from its current dilemmas. It would be courageous to admit that no one from outside obliges Angola, Somalia, and Ethiopia to spend twice as much on arms as on the education and health of their people. They do it themselves. No one from outside forces Cameroon to lose more budgetary resources every year from the losses of its inefficient public enterprises than its total oil revenues. This is its own choice. And no one from outside orders Mali and Sierra Leone—two of the poorest nations of Africa—to spend more than 80 percent of their limited health budgets on urban hospitals rather than on primary health care. The decision is theirs.

It is time to be brutally frank with ourselves. African problems require courageous decisions within Africa. External alibis will not help. We are all anxious to mobilize worldwide financial support for African development. No one can deliver an African turnaround from the outside. It requires fundamental reforms within the region.

Population Growth

The rapid population growth rate in Sub-Saharan Africa must be slowed down. This growth rate, which was 2.8 percent from 1960 to 1992, is expected to accelerate to 3.4 percent between 1992 and 2000. A demanding target is to reduce the average population growth rate to 2.2 percent per year over the next 30 years. Even then, the population of Sub-Saharan Africa would more than double to over 1.2 billion by 2020, and it would not level off much below 3 billion. Admittedly, a population growth rate of 2.2 percent per year for the next three decades is ambitious. It would require a reduction in the total fertility rate from about 6.7 children per woman to 3.6 by 2025. This means that the number of African married couples using effective contraception would grow from the current rate of 15 percent to nearly 50 percent. It also means that all African leaders must quickly commit to effective family planning programs. And they must recognize that population growth is a development issue, as well as a clinical problem. Any effective policy must create the underlying conditions for fertility decline—expansion of basic education, especially for girls; economic independence of women; and rising income and employment levels.

Human Development

Sub-Saharan Africa needs substantial investment in human development. Of the 47 countries in the region, 41 are in the bottom half of the low human-development category according to the UNDP's 1994 *Human Development Report.* About one-half of the adult population of Sub-Saharan Africa is illiterate. The mean years of schooling for adults above 25 years of age are only 1.6 years. The average life expectancy is only 51 years — 24 years lower than in the industrial world. Most social indicators are a shocking reflection of the diminished value of human life.

No magic formulas exist to reverse this situation. It will take great patience, major financial investments, and time. Overall, investment in social services must increase, must be spent more efficiently, and must be earmarked for such basic services as primary health care, basic education, safe drinking water, essential family planning services, and nutrition programs for the severely malnourished. Such expenditures are small at present. For instance, they are only $2 per person per year in Tanzania and $6 in Nigeria. All Sub-Saharan African countries should formulate long-term human development strategies and commit their political energies and financial resources to implementing those strategies.

Economic Growth

None of these investments, on the scale required, will be possible and no reforms will ever succeed unless the pace of economic growth is accelerated and the process of economic policy reform and adjustment continued. In everything from exchange rate management through investment in education and agriculture, the lessons of failed or inadequate policies in Africa stand out. One of the most telling indications of poor policy frameworks has been Africa's declining competitiveness in world markets. Certainly, the external environment has not been kind to Africa with the fall in commodity prices, oil shocks, and high interest rates. But a hostile external environment is not the main reason for Africa's poor economic performance. The region's disappointing GDP growth compared, for example, with growth in East Asia, has been associated with very low levels of domestic saving and investment.

The Need for Domestic Savings

In recent years, South Asian economies have been growing at nearly 2 percent per capita per year, compared to Africa's -0.2 percent. A major factor contributing to the higher Asian growth rate has been a rate of investment, as a percent of GDP, nearly twice that of Africa's. It is often said that Africa's low rate of investment is a function of inadequate flows of external financial assistance. But Africa, as a percent of GDP, has been receiving seven times as much external aid as Asia. Africa's investment problem can be traced to a totally inadequate domestic savings rate and inefficient use of its financial resources. India's domestic savings, as a percent of GDP, are about 50 percent higher than the level in Africa. Even more disturbing, the incremental output generated by Africa's investment has dropped dramatically from 31 percent of investment in the 1960s to 2.5 percent in the 1980s.

To increase domestic savings, Africa must further reduce fiscal deficits. There is a contentious debate going on about the nature and content of structural adjustment programs in Africa and about the harsh conditionality of World Bank and IMF loans. Certainly, there is considerable room for improvement on all sides. Why, after all, should budgets be balanced on the backs of the poor rather than on the backs of the rich? Why must food subsidies to the poor be cut ahead of interest and credit subsidies to rich landlords and industrialists? Why must education and health expenditures be slashed in preference to military expenditures? Who makes the final decisions? And when there is so much waste and corruption and inefficiency, does it require a genius to figure out how to move toward balancing national budgets without unbalancing the lives of poor people or future generations?

However, the waste of scarce resources in many of the countries of Sub-Saharan Africa on high levels of military expenditure is also a fact. This military spending has increased steadily from 0.7 percent of their combined GNP in 1960 to 3.5 percent by 1990. This is the only region where, during the last 30 years, the ratio of military spending to social spending has not declined but risen: from 27 percent in 1960 to 43 percent in 1990. Many of the poorer nations are spending large amounts on their armies rather than on their people. Three countries in the region—Angola (20 percent), Ethiopia (13.5 percent), and Mozambique (13 percent)—devote more than 10 percent of their GDP to military expenditures, at a time when 3 million people face starvation in Angola, when 50 percent of the population in Mozambique lives below the poverty line, and when nearly two-thirds of the population in Ethiopia does not have access to the simple basic necessity of safe drinking water. They are not alone in diverting funds from the poor to military establishments. According to the 1994 Human Development Report, Nigeria purchased 80 battle tanks from the United Kingdom in 1992 at a cost that could have immunized all of its 2 million nonimmunized children and provided family planning services to nearly 17 million out of the 20 million couples who lack such services.

The Responsibility Belongs to Africa's Leaders

It is for African leadership to decide what are the legitimate needs of their national security and what are the competing claims for their human security. The evidence from the past is clear. Those nations that spent too much on arms and too little on human development were neither able to protect their territorial security nor the welfare of their people. Somalia spent five times as much on its military as on education and health in 1980; the international community added to the problem with external supplies of arms. On the other hand, Botswana invested only one-fifth as much in arms as in the education and health of its people. Today, its adult literacy rate is 75 percent, its life expectancy 60 years, and its average GNP growth rate was over 6 percent from 1980 to 1992.

This is a time to move away from excessive expenditures on military establishments. In the post-Cold War era, global military spending has been declining by nearly 4 percent per year (i.e., since 1987). But the poorest region of the world, Sub-Saharan Africa, continues to spend over $8 billion a year on defense. A few years ago, an international study commission, chaired by Helmut Schmidt and including such senior officials as Pierre Trudeau and General Obasanjo, suggested that any poor country spending more than 2 percent of its GNP on the military should be penalized in aid allocations. Based on published data, such a policy would immediately affect 21 countries in Sub-Saharan Africa. It may be necessary to start with a more moderate goal and at a more gradual pace, but a start should be made.

In Africa, a spreading new menace does require defense spending, although of a different kind. That menace is HIV/AIDS. According to the latest estimates, the cumulative number of HIV-infected people in the world is now around 15 million, of which 9 million (60 percent) are in Sub-Saharan Africa. The rate at which AIDS is spreading in Africa can frustrate all well-laid development plans. At this stage, it is receiving little effective attention. This is an avoidable tragedy, if national and international policy makers devote sufficient attention to it.

External Assistance

In focusing so much attention on the domestic agenda of reform in Africa, it is not meant to imply that continued external assistance is irrelevant. It is essential. But it will not be justified unless internal reforms are carried out simultaneously. In fact, in 13 Sub-Saharan countries, aid already represents more than 20 percent of their GNP—namely, in Mozambique (115 percent), São Tomé and Principe (108 percent), Guinea-Bissau (59 percent), Equatorial Guinea (51 percent), Tanzania (48 percent), Cape Verde (42 percent), Gambia (36 percent), Zambia (30 percent), Burundi (26 percent), Uganda (23 percent), Malawi (22 percent), Ethiopia (20 percent), and Chad (20 percent). But in none of these countries has it made a decisive difference. What has been decisive are the domestic policies.

Although we must continue to ensure that the poor countries of Africa receive liberal amounts of concessional flows, along with appropriate debt rescheduling, two fundamental points must be emphasized. First, aid is no substitute for trade: Sub-Saharan Africa is almost falling out of the world markets. With 10 percent of the world population, Sub-Saharan Africa has less than a 1 percent share in global trade. Sub-Saharan Africa must diversify its exports and improve its export competitiveness. At the same time, world markets must accommodate more of Africa's exports. Second, aid money must be more intelligently allocated and more efficiently spent. Donors should question whether it is wise to continue to allocate less than 10 percent of their aid to human development in Sub-Saharan Africa when resources for human development constitute the region's greatest need. They should consider, as well, whether it makes much sense to support, through technical assistance, 100,000 foreign experts in a region which in a 5-year period (1985-1990) lost an estimated 60,000 of its own technicians by emigration, for want of adequate opportunities at home.

Conclusion

There is no dearth of analysis today on what ails Africa. Many scholarly treatises have been written. Many professional reports have been prepared. What is missing is a political commitment on the part of many of the leaders of Africa — a recognition that it is their responsibility to turn their countries around to move them from a specter of impending tragedy to a story of hopeful change. If they step forward with courage and decisiveness, it is our sincere belief that the international community will support their every step.

Notes

1. I am grateful to Mahbub ul Haq, Special Adviser to the Administrator of UNDP, for assistance in preparing this section.
2. Africa and Sub-Saharan Africa are used interchangeably in this section.

Section 2

How Can Poverty and Inequality Be Avoided in Eastern Europe?

Arvo Kuddo

The whole transformation process from socialism to the market economy is an economic and social experience unique in the history of humanity. Radical changes in all spheres of society have taken place in an extremely short period of some two to three years. A great number of unexpected social consequences, contradictions, and conflicts have occurred that were not predictable at the initial stage of the reforms. However, it will take a generation or more for the new social structures and relationship of the new market economies to become established.

One of the biggest areas of concern and disappointment is the living standard and insufficient income policy in the transitory countries. The dual hardship of poverty and prolonged unemployment are the most vulnerable aspect of the whole process of transformation. The aim of this section is to analyze some of the key aspects of the income policy in Eastern Europe, in the former Soviet Union (FSU), and especially in Estonia.

The living and cultural standards, incomes, and consumption – the whole way of life of people in the former socialist system are well-known and have been analyzed in numerous publications. In spite of official slogans and tutelage by party and state, the well-being of the population was not the first priority of the system.

Nonetheless, the old system had its own values and realities. It had created a pattern of well-being and a way of life in which many generations grew up. It was the only one they knew. From the human point of view, it is not fair to look at only the negative aspects of socialism. The paternalistic dependence of people and the administrative control over the whole social life during two to three generations created a new mental climate for a large part of the nation. For the elderly, in particular, reforms have meant not only the loss of their habitual way of life, but also of their incomes and savings. Instead of security and stability, which many of them regard as the most important values of the previous system, they are experiencing hopelessness, fear, and an inability to solve even the simplest problems of everyday life.

The same situation and feelings are shared by many families with several children, single parents, the unemployed, and even school graduates who are discovering that their knowledge is, to a great extent, useless in the labor market. It would be a mistake to underestimate this factor in analyzing the future development of society. Many people still regard family welfare entirely as a state responsibility. One of the aims of the reform, therefore, is to create a new psychological climate and to strengthen the self-help mentality of individuals.

In the new market economies, the social determinants of reforms are having different effects on the transformation process. In Russia and in most of the other republics of the FSU, reformers need to focus on social factors and adopt a policy of gradual development rather than shock therapy. The latter has caused more painful disorder and collapse in many countries. But in other FSU republics, especially in the Baltic countries where the people were massively repressed, humiliated, and depressed during the Soviet period, the "silent majority" has accepted more radical measures at a faster pace to achieve the market economy.

So far, the transition experience has shown that the countries and regions with higher levels of economic development and living standards are better prepared for and more successful in carrying out reforms. The same is true of people who, through education and culture, have a higher social position. As a rule, they are not among the winners in the transformation process. From an economic point of view, their relative well-being is declining. This phenomenon illustrates the historical rule that revolutions tend to devour their children.

In some countries and regions, where some traditional private entrepreneurship survived, there is a better psychological environment for the restoration of a market economy. During Soviet rule, the private sector, especially in agriculture, was permitted in some former socialist countries. In Poland, for example, the ratio of the private to public sector was close to one fifth of national income at the end of 1980s; in former Yugoslavia, it was 13 to 14 percent; and in Hungary, 7 percent.[1] In the Baltic republics, the tradition of private entrepreneurship also survived in spite of Soviet suppression.

The Reform Process

There are fairly substantial national differences in the implementation and acceptance of reforms in Central and Eastern Europe. In different republics, the transformation process has different time schedules, patterns, conditions, and finally, results.

For example, in Estonia, special investigations were conducted to determine the support of different national groups for the 1988 price reform. While the majority of Estonians accepted the idea of converting huge state subsidies into direct compensations, most of the so-called Russian-speaking population rejected the proposal. This can be explained by the fact that most non-Estonians live in the cities, where they work in industry and so-called former "all-union" enterprises. These jobs offered certain economic advantages, such as housing supplements, heavily subsided food, and separate distribution of consumer goods. The loss of these advantages was the major cause of their resistance to the reforms. According to the 1989 census, 87 percent of Estonia's rural population were Estonian nationals; their percentage in urban areas was 51. They understood better the "real value" of food.

The Baltic republics were among the first to begin political and economic liberalization; they have achieved positive results from the reforms. In 1990, when rapid economic reforms first began, these republics were completely dependent on the central authorities and the rest of the FSU. In Estonia, for example, the ratio of industrial enterprises under the direct control of republican ministries was less than 25 percent. Having declared their intention to regain political independence, however, these countries were not in a position to receive aid from the rest of the FSU or the West. Comparatively, the Baltic countries have a very open economy; the average ratio of exports and imports exceeded half of their GDP—in Latvia and Lithuania, 55 percent, and in Estonia, 64 percent.[2] As late as 1991, some 85 to 95 percent of exports and imports were composed of ruble zone. The Baltic countries were completely dependent on the currency emission and monetary policy of the Central Bank of the Soviet Union (later Russia) until the monetary reforms in 1992 and 1993.

Subsidies and Price Distortions

One of the key issues and a starting point for reformers was the dismantling of huge state subsidies on consumer goods and services. These subsidies distorted price structures, disorientated producers and consumers, and generated financial deficits. These subsidies had always created social tensions, largely because of unequal accessibility to them. Urban dwellers, who were closer to the points of distribution of these goods and services, and higher-income people benefited more from artificially low prices and tariffs on some primary commodities and social services than did the rural population. This meant that reforms affected different groups unequally.

In planning reforms, one had to consider the artificiality of these subsidies. For example, the agricultural sector covered its own substantial expenditures on education, medical care, postal services, preschool education, road construction, and other infrastructure projects. In many cases, former collective or state farms paid partly or fully the salaries of state employees working in the country villages. Otherwise, nobody would work there. In contrast, the state covered these expenditures in the cities. Thus, reform required a redistribution of some revenues and incomes. In the new economic circumstances, the state had assume all of these costs, which resulted in extra expenditures not directly related to price subsidies.

For a long time, prices on some foodstuffs, which were regulated by the state, were frozen. In the FSU, for example, tea, sugar, macaroni, and sunflower oil prices had remained basically unchanged since 1956; prices on milk and meat products since 1962; and tariffs on rent, water, and heating since 1920s. At that time by a special decree, "the working proletariat" had to pay no more than 10 percent of his salary for housing. These tariffs remained at the same levels until the 1980s.

The beginning of reform in the FSU was complicated by the fact that prices on industrial goods, especially agricultural machinery, were decontrolled at an earlier stage than agricultural products. Because this widened the price gap even more, the state was forced to pay huge subsidies to the agricultural sector. In 1988, these subsidies, which exceeded 79 billion rubles in the former USSR, were covered by an increasing budget deficit. In 1989, the deficit of the state budget reached 9.9 percent of GDP in the USSR.[3] Economic shortages led to price distortions and repressed inflation, and parallel markets and prices developed. Before price reform, huge amounts of food—estimated at about 40 percent—were distributed through means other than state retail outlets. These included enterprises' own or other special canteens, shops, and "under-the-counter" businesses. Many retailers made illegal profits from the shortages.

The system of artificially low prices distorted food distribution between the republics and the regions. In 1990 and 1991, it posed a serious problem for the local authorities, who had to safeguard local markets from illegal food flows to other regions. At that time, efforts to establish economic borders between the republics of FSU resulted in the creation of state borders between the independent countries.

One factor considered in planning price reform was the rapid increase in nominal wages, which in the 1980s exceeded the growth in productivity. This caused a huge monetary overhang, forced demand-pull inflation, created excess demand, and resulted in even more acute shortages.

Social Amenities

During the socialist period, the majority of social services were free of charge or very inexpensive. Even at the enterprise level, a variety of social services were available to enhance the welfare of the employees and their families. These advantages exist even today in many regions of FSU, such as Russia and Ukraine.

Social security was guaranteed for everybody from birth in a state hospital to a state-supplied funeral, if necessary. The system was well developed quantitatively and, to some extent, qualitatively. Notwithstanding its many negative aspects, such as bureaucratic rationing, coupon schemes, rationed products and services, and parallel markets, the totalitarian system guaranteed a relatively poor life without fear. Before the reforms, the primary form of social insurance was guaranteed full employment. Thus, people must learn to distinguish between social benefits and employment remuneration in order to make the transition to a market economy.

Another factor affecting income policy reform is that during Soviet rule, people could not convert their savings or salaries into hard currency or to protect their savings in Western banks. The legal framework of private property was also restricted. As a result, during the initial period of reform, living standards were completely dependent on the dynamics of inflation and nominal increase in incomes.

One important factor that eases the tensions caused by rapid inflation and helps families manage their budgets is the kitchen-garden, which results in a high ratio of self-produced food. For example, in Estonia more than 60 percent of the families have a plot of land with a vegetable garden or some other extra source of food, such as support from relatives. Because of limited recreational opportunities, gardening also became a popular way to spend one's leisure time. To encourage this "plot economy," the Russian government subsidized fare reductions on local trains.

One serious problem for the reformers was the demographic structure of the population. There is a growing number of retired people in need of social support and patronage. As elsewhere in the world, the percentage of the senior population is growing. In addition, the pension age in most of the former socialist countries is still low (55 for women and 60 for men); some people who work under dangerous or in stressful conditions are eligible for early retirement, and the ten year difference in life expectancy between men and women has created a large number of single elderly women. As a result, in Estonia, for example, the ratio of pensioners is more than 25 percent of the population.

During the Soviet period, the average pension in the FSU was relatively low. At the end of 1980s, it was less than 40 percent of the average salary. The pension ceiling was 120 rubles per month, with a maximum 10 percent increment for the length of service. However, the Soviet system offered pensioners other advantages, such as heavily subsidized housing, food, and public transport, which enabled people to survive even on an average pension. Many pensioners—60 percent in Estonia and 30 percent overall—continued to work after retirement. Now they are among the first to be dismissed. Thus, those people who suffered most directly from the massive repression of the 1940s and 1950s are now suffering most from the reforms.

Another demographic feature of the last decades is the rapid growth of single-parent families. More than 30 percent of the births in Estonia are to single mothers. One-parent families are among the most vulnerable groups in the population.

Society is now divided into polar social groups. Some would like to restore "socialism with a human face and without the rule of the communist party." Others would like to build a society of entrepreneurs regardless of the needs of pensioners, the unemployed, families with many children, or other dependent groups. Yet others want to build capitalism without capitalists.[4] All must be taken into account in planning the reforms.

Implementation of Price Reform and Income Policy

The most complicated part of economic reform was price liberalization and the reduction of subsidies. These were also the key components of a broader program of economic reform and macrostabilization.

Stanislaw Gomulka has pointed out that true shock therapy was, in fact, applied only in East Germany. Although real wages and benefits were increased sharply, Western prices were imposed without protection for local producers.[5] In other countries and regions, price reform has been more gradual. Prices reform could not be imposed independently; other economic processes had to be analyzed. These included structural adjustment, privatization, and property reform, all of which promote a competitive economic environment.

Another key issue is the effect of price reform on energy resources. If this stage of reform is delayed, it will seriously affect further progress in other areas requiring reform. In Russia and many other FSU republics, energy prices were frozen but still subsidized for a long period after the reforms were initiated.

At first, most of the countries went through a short period hyperinflation, during which prices increased more than 50 percent per month. It was a misconception to argue that establishing free market clearing prices and free competition would stop inflation. For example, in Estonia the inflation rate was 36 percent in 1993 compared with 1,076 percent in the previous year. However, price increases sped up again early in 1994.

A main aspect of price reform and a key element of its success was a proper and adequate mechanism of social protection for the population. In the new market economies, every possible means of social support was used, including cash benefits and supplements, benefits in kind, and institutional care for those unable to manage by themselves. To a great extent, the first difficulties in implementing social protection were technical.

Three different social security systems existed in FSU republics in the Soviet period: social security by the state, by trade unions, and by collective farms. Benefits were more or less stable for many years, and a vast majority of them were paid through state-owned enterprises—a situation that does occur in a free market society. Obviously, such a scattered mechanism could not work quickly and efficiently, and one of the first tasks was to integrate these separate social security systems into one.

A second key aspect of reform was the amount and level of compensation. Especially at the initial stage of reform, many voices demanded full compensation and indexing of all incomes. The "reformed" trade unions—a new version of the old ones—were very active in this regard. However, the demands were unrealistic.

Of the FSU countries, Estonia was the first to start preparation for and implementation of radical price reform at the beginning of 1988. The proposal for price reform was made public in May 1988.[6] The idea was to reduce the huge subsidies on agriculture, but to pay people the same amount in cash. However, the central authorities rejected the idea because the Price Committee of the USSR was preparing its own price reforms. When it became apparent that the central authorities would reject the basic idea of a transformation to free market prices and would retain administratively controlled prices all over the Soviet Union, Estonia and other Baltic republics moved ahead with the implementation of independent price reform.

For countries in transition, the actual social security system had to be quickly and simply adjusted to reduce the time lag between price increases and compensation payments. In Estonia, a simplified system of flat rate benefits reduced this lag to less than one month. The government compensated only so-called risk groups and public employees for price increases. Risk groups were defined as those dependent on the state or families: children and students, mothers on maternity leave, disabled people, pensioners, and unemployed persons. All other groups of the population and enterprises, in particular, (including state-owned firms) had to compensate their workers for inflation at their own cost.

To finance the reforms, Estonia established very restrictive budget constraints. Of the countries in transition, Estonia is one of the few to recognize that fiscal balance is a key element for monetary restraint, moderate inflation, and exchange rate stability. The budget has been balanced for the past three years, and the parliament has approved a balanced budget for 1994.

What kind of measures and income support programs were implemented to compensate for rapid inflation? From October 1990 through the first quarter of 1992, a special monthly price compensation payment, which was regulated according to inflation and budget constraints, was introduced for risk groups. Flat-rate compensations calculated in accordance with the age of children, type of pension, and similar factors, were used. In April 1991, a special cash compensation for the price increase in industrial goods was introduced throughout the FSU. Since the second quarter of 1992, these price compensations have formed either the basis for new family benefits or became part of the pensions that would be regularly adjusted later. In 1992, special food coupons (stamps) were given to low-income families. This helped to introduce a more selective income policy and reduced the shortage of bank notes. By 1994, family benefits were no linked longer to minimum salaries. In Estonia, as in most of the other FSU republics, flat rate pensions were introduced; this helped to regulate pensions quickly.

The Baltic countries remained in the ruble zone until the first half of 1992. Unfortunately, during this period, there were no regular deliveries of ruble bank notes from Russia. This necessitated the temporary use of other surrogate money (e.g., coupons and checks) or other forms of compensation. At the local level, some benefits for low-income families were paid in kind—as special food packages. School canteens as well as kindergartens were partly subsidized. In the cities, communal kitchens were opened to serve the poor despite the protests of many pensioners for whom they were mostly intended.

An important measure to protect the lowest income households was the establishment of an economic poverty line and its periodic adjustment according to price increases. There are different experiences and recommendations concerning the level of poverty line. Sometimes the poverty line is calculated as the level of incomes equal to 35 to 50 percent of the average wage or 50 percent of the average consumption. In some cases, families are classified as poor if their expenditure on food, housing, and transportation exceeds 60 percent of their disposable incomes. For the most part, a minimum subsistence based mainly on nutritional requirements (consumption-based poverty line) is determined, and the cost of this minimum level is regularly surveyed.

In all transition countries, the definition of a realistic level of minimal consumption or a socially guaranteed minimum requirement is an important instrument of income policy. However, it should be determined for what purposes this poverty line is established. Is it to calculate the dynamics of families living below the poverty line or to render these families additional and real support? This poverty line must be realistic in order to provide adequate support for those living below this level.

Although taxation is also used for redistribution policies, there is a danger of erosion in government revenues and expenditures in the new market economies that are experiencing high rates of inflation. To redistribute budget revenues to lower income brackets, many politicians wanted to increase the tax burden beyond the economically acceptable level. Such an action would reduce entrepreneurship activities, decrease resources for new investments that are urgently needed in these economies, and enlarge the part of hidden incomes not covered by taxation.

There are also discussions on whether a progressive or proportional tax system is more effective and what kinds of taxes should be imposed. Should they be direct taxes, such as an income tax, or indirect taxes, mainly consumer taxes. Until 1994, Estonia had three tax scales for personal income tax: 16, 24, and 33 percent of taxable income. After the monetary reform in 1992, a 50 percent tax bracket was introduced for a short period to reduce wage push inflation. Since nominal incomes are rapidly increasing, the government has had to adjust the income brackets regularly, making technical implementation complex. Such high tax rates force employers to use informal labor or to by-pass the tax system in other ways.

The effectiveness and actual amount of economic support to the low-income population depends to a great extent on social security or payroll taxes. These taxes also effect the cost of labor; low labor cost is one of the most important economic advantages in this region.

The highest payroll taxes (including health insurance) are in Hungary at 60 percent in total (49 percent paid by employers and 11 percent by employees), in the Czech Republic at 49.5 percent (36 and 13.5 percent correspondingly), in Slovakia at 50 percent (38 and 12 percent correspondingly). In Latvia this tax is equal to 38 percent and in Lithuania 31 percent. However, the state subsidies to the social funds and measures financed through these taxes are not the same in all countries. Therefore, comparison is not feasible.

The ratio of average pension in comparison with the average wage is highest in Poland—86 percent; in Hungary, this ratio is equal to 61 percent, whereas in Russia it is close to 31 percent, and in Ukraine even less than 20 percent.[7] For a true picture of comparison not only the level of taxes, but the real value of social benefits should be used in the different countries.

One of the criticisms of the compensation mechanism in Eastern Europe is that these payments are not means-tested and targeted and, as a rule, are flat-rate amounts. To some extent, the flat-rate system lowers the cost-effectiveness of income policy.

Management of Social Programs

The management of social programs needs to be improved to increase their capacity to adjust to rapidly changing economic and social conditions. Sufficient technical support is needed to create proper registry of families who need extra assistance and to train social workers.

Criticism has also been directed toward the fact that there is no linkage between past contributions and current benefits. Today, it is not even possible to convert prereform salaries (not including previous state-paid social security contributions) into new income or salary levels. Moreover, salaries before the reform were extremely disproportional, and semiskilled employees with less education were often paid much better than more qualified and well-educated workers. Education was considered a gift of the state; it did not give you the right to a higher salary. The labor shortage among the less-educated workers was also more severe than in the skilled groups.

Many countries in transition are implementing an insurance type of social security system. However, it will take decades to establish different and effective systems of compulsory, voluntary, private and/or other types of social insurance.

New Consumption Patterns

The transformation has substantially affected the living standard of the ordinary family. Price distortions, differences in cash and in-kind sources of incomes, and the huge share of free public services makes it quite difficult to evaluate and compare the previous living standards in the Eastern European countries with current conditions. At present, income levels in the Eastern European region are incomparably low, not only by Western standards but when compared to previous levels of consumption and living standards.

As a rule, national currencies are. heavily undervalued on a purchase power parity basis. Therefore it is not feasible to directly convert current salaries and incomes into Western currencies.

How should the dynamics of incomes and living standards in the transition period be measured and analyzed? Nominally, the average disposal income per family member of workers and employees has increased in Estonia from 197 rubles in 1989, and 233 rubles in the families of collective farmers, to 747 kroons per family member in 1993.

On the basis of exchange ratio of monetary reform, nominal incomes have increased 32 to 38 times on average. When compared to the price index for that period, the increase in family incomes is almost 3 to 4 times less. However, these average figures should be analyzed more exactly to characterize the real changes in living standards.

The first is the rapid changes in income structure. According to the 1989 family survey, salaries were the main source of family income. In total, 76 percent of disposable cash income came from salaries. Other social benefits accounted for 7.7 percent of the average gross income. By

1993, in an average family, only 60 percent of disposable income came from salaries. The ratio of different social benefits (e.g., pensions, family supplements, unemployment benefits, and social assistance), increased on an average to 15 percent of disposable income. Although people now have more opportunities to work hard and to earn more or they have other source of income, severe inequality in income is a new phenomenon in the region.

Traditional indicators of income evaluation in the new market economies need to be carefully examined. Not only disposable incomes, but salaries and other incomes in cash and in-kind of different social groups are fluctuating heavily. These indicators cover, as a rule, only current cash incomes; they do not adequately reflect changes in other sources of income or in taxation or in consumption patterns. In addition to current incomes, many other factors determine a family's living standard. For example, real estate purchased in the prereform economy also influences family welfare today.

One of the most painful aspects of inflation is the loss of real savings and the high inflation tax that was the price of transformation. From an economic viewpoint, inflation has eliminated monetary overhang. But for families, it has often meant a real economic tragedy. At the beginning of 1990, there were 1,145 thousand saving accounts in Estonia out of a total population of 1,506 thousand. An average account contained 2,038 rubles, which equaled more than the average salary for five months. At the beginning of 1993, this average savings amount dropped to one-third of the average monthly salary; while at the beginning of 1994, it had increased to three fifths.

Of course, savings were unequally distributed even before the reforms. However, the latest surveys show that 48 percent of the families now have no savings at all, and 31 percent of the families have savings amounting to less than one month's salary. In 1993 only 2 percent of the families were able to put aside savings.

One of the reactions to rapid inflation was excessive demand for consumer goods, especially at the beginning of 1992. After being paid, people hurried to the shops and bought everything available. In every family, the stock of household goods was and remains significant. Money was not used for privatization of housing or for buying stocks, but for consumption. Consumption patterns have changed in both volume and structure.

Formally there seem to be no significant changes in the consumption and structure of the family budget. The only exemption is the increased cost of housing. Nevertheless, changes are substantial. Families have much less to spend on household equipment, clothes, and textiles. For example, in 1993, the average family spent only 0.3 percent of its disposable income on textiles and 7.1 percent on clothes and shoes.

Different income groups have distinct patterns of consumption. In comparing the consumption of the lowest income group (where income constitutes less than one minimum salary per person) with the highest income group (where income constitutes more than 3 minimum salaries per capita), the latter group spends 2.5 times more money on food and almost 7 times more money on consumer goods and services than the former. There are also considerable regional differences in incomes and consumption. In Tallinn, the average net income per family member was 1.6 times higher than in the rural areas (in the fourth quarter of 1993).

Social Consequences of Poverty and Inequality

In April 1993, a sociological survey identified the three most acute problems in Estonia. A second survey was taken one year later. During that year, reforms solved or alleviated some problems, such as property issues or unemployment for non-Estonians, especially for those living in the northeast. However, the main social problems were the same: inadequate social protection, a fall in the living standard, a high crime rate, and for non-Estonians, the uncertainty regarding the citizenship question. Recently, demands for the state to solve or alleviate the problems of falling living standards by means of social protection are being quoted more often. A large number of people are still unable to manage on their own and expect the state to redistribute revenues to support them more adequately.

In the lowest income brackets, three groups are most vulnerable because of the reforms. The first group are those families where one or even two breadwinners are unemployed. The combination of unemployment and poverty has numerous variations and patterns. Many unemployed are not covered by any kind of social support nor are they participating in training or job creation programs. The number of discouraged unemployed people is growing. Some potential unemployment is apparent in the form of underemployment and declining real wages. In addition, long-term unemployment is growing. Therefore, the creation or enhancement of job opportunities and active employment policy measures are one of the key elements of an antipoverty program as well.

The second vulnerable group consists of families with many children or single-parent families (as a rule, single mothers). In spite of the fact that family benefits were increased and new benefits introduced, it was not enough to cover the growth in outlays. Also, one of the largest social groups that lives poorly consists of old-age pensioners. In 1993, family benefits constituted 4.8 percent of the disposable income of an average family. By 1994, 2.3 percent of the estimated GDP was allocated in the state budget for family benefits. It has some redistribution effect, but not enough.

Most of the countries recently extended maternity leave until the child reached the age of three years. But, simultaneously, state subsidies for kindergartens were sharply cut. As a rule, the average cost to a family to place one child in a kindergarten was nearly one minimum salary. Therefore, in Estonia, the preprimary enrollment rate had decreased from 69 percent in the 1980s to 46 percent in 1992 (as percentage of relevant population). Families have to choose between sending a child to kindergarten at the cost of one parent's salary or having the mother stay at home. According to calculations, more than one-tenth of the women in the working age bracket are now at home with their children. This factor has reduced pressure in the labor market.

There is also a new class of the working poor. During the reforms, salaries of workers differed substantially. The highest salaries are usually in industries and enterprises oriented toward the export of goods and services. Fields with closer ties to the international labor market, such as shipping, and joint-venture enterprises with foreign capital pay higher salaries. In private enterprises, salaries do not exceed the average by much. Many companies are just establishing themselves and need money for investment.

Although the minimum salary is established by law, some employees are paid less because the control mechanism does not function properly. Trade unions are too weak or have disappeared altogether, especially in new branches and enterprises. Collective salary agreements are not very common, and workers, especially in rural areas, have to agree to lower salaries in order not to lose their jobs.

The Role of International Institutions

The role of the international community in the implementation of reforms should also be evaluated. There is an increasing criticism of some international institutions whose recommendations the new market economy countries are supposedly following.[8] The economic reforms in Eastern Europe began at a time when Western countries were experiencing a deep depression that affected the amount of support they could provide.

Possibly, it was also the fault of the FSU countries, which were unable to attract more international economic aid to support their reforms. Political and economic instability in the region often scared off potential investors, who could have helped with the necessary structural adjustments. In some cases, these countries were not able to use effectively those financial resources offered by the international community. In Estonia, for example, at the beginning of 1994, the total amount of state foreign loans, including balance of payments support, exceeded US$167 million, but only 45 percent, or US$50 per capita was paid out to the investors.

One criticism of Western consultants is that foreign experts concentrated on "shock" treatment at a time when "therapy" was the concern of national and regional leaders. For Western experts and researchers, these reforms constituted a unique and interesting economic experiment. But for Eastern Europeans, the priority was to find concrete and immediate solutions to real social problems. Western social policies cannot be quickly implemented in Eastern Europe. The process has been delayed by such factors as lack of infrastructure, resources, and legislation, as well as by different backgrounds, living conditions, and ways of life. Unfortunately, Western experts often undervalue these aspects.

The sharp decline in living standards in the region has affected all facets of the everyday life, but none more than the institution of the family. For example, rapid changes have occurred in fertility rates. In Estonia alone, the number of live births declined from 25.1 thousand in 1988 to 15.3 thousand in 1993, or by nearly 40 percent. The death rates from alcohol poisoning, suicide, and homicide have increased from 39.2 in 1988 to 84.0 in 1993 (per 100,000 population). Crime has interfered so deeply with the economic structure that some of the new market economies (particularly that of Russia) have been characterized as gangster economies. This rapid increase in crime is to a large extent the result of growing inequality of property and income and the greater number of poor and unemployed families. It is one of the most acute social problems.

Conclusion

In summary, price shock, in connection with many other economic and social aspects of the transition, has meant real tragedy for many families. Hardest hit are large families; the disabled; the unemployed; pensioners; families of low paid workers; and individuals who have no access to land or other alternative sources of incomes. The entire population has been forced to completely change their way of life and consumption patterns, adapt to new economic conditions, and to lower their living standards. The social class which has benefited in terms of income from the transition constitutes less than 10 percent of the population.

The growth of inequality is also a factor in these societies. The less developed the society is, the greater the inequality in the dispersion of incomes, consumption, and well-being. The state has a difficult task. One the one hand, it must create a favorable environment for further development by lowering taxes, limiting redistribution measures, and economizing manpower and other resources for social policy. On the other hand, the state has to provide support to the most vulnerable part of population, whose needs cannot be ignored. The only solution to this dilemma is to increase the efficiency of income policy. Limited resources must be spent on more targeted and means-tested support and assistance programs must focus on those social groups that really need them.

The social cost of reforms is very high. Nevertheless, people are trying to adapt to a new situation. They understand that liberating the country from its past is a painful process and requires sacrifices from everybody. It is obvious that any improvement in the living conditions requires economic growth. The way to fight the poverty is to create productive income-earning opportunities.

Notes

1. Janos Kornai. *The Socialist System: The Political Economy of Communism.* Princeton, NJ: Princeton University Press, p. 72.
2. *Macroeconomic Policies and Financial Programming.* Washington, D.C.: IMF Institute, 1992, p. 37.
3. Blanchard, R. Dornbusch, P. Krugman, R. Layard, and L. Summers. *Reform in Eastern Europe.* Cambridge, MA: MIT Press, p. 13.
4. See, for example, *Transforming the Polish Economy.* Warsaw: Warsaw School of Economics, 1992, pp. 32, 33.

5. S. Gomulka. *Lessons from Economic Transformation and the Road Forward.* Warsaw: Center for Social and Economic Research, 1994.
6. R. Otsason, J. Sillaste, A. Sirendi, M. Habakuk, A. Kuddo. "Ettepanek: Maksta dotatsioon sularahas kätte." *Rahva Hääl,* May 11, 1988.
7. *Public Policy and Social Conditions.* Regional Monitoring Report, No. 1, Florence: UNICEF, 1993, p. 79.
8. See Andre Gunder Frank, "Soviet and East European Socialism: A Review of International Political Economy on What Went Wrong." *Economic Review,* 19 (1993).

Section 3

Reducing Poverty: Lessons from Taiwan[1]

Deborah Brautigam

The past generation (1965–1990) has seen real progress in the struggle for a better life in low-income countries. On average, real incomes have at least doubled; infant mortality rates have been nearly cut in half; and the percentage of children enrolled in primary education has risen by fifty percent. Yet while providing compelling evidence that the quality of life can and has been significantly improved in low-income countries, these figures mask the great variety of experiences among regions and between countries, and they tell us nothing about the strategies that lie behind the impressive results in the more successful countries.

This section considers the experience of Taiwan in alleviating poverty. Taiwan's GNP per capita grew from $143 in 1953 to $7,284 in 1990.[2] This sustained growth has been widely shared by all income groups: the share of income held by the top 20 percent is only 4.5 times as much as the bottom 20 percent of households. In Brazil, by contrast, the top fifth holds almost 32 times the share of the bottom fifth; in Botswana, the share of the top is almost 47 times the share of the bottom.[3]

Many have examined the reasons for Taiwan's extraordinary economic growth. This section explores the comparable increases in family welfare in Taiwan, focusing primarily on the period between 1952 and 1972, a period when Taiwan was able to raise its per capita GNP from levels comparable with many countries that remain much less developed today, to levels comparable with the countries of southern Europe.

Climbing Out of Poverty

Taiwan was colonized by the Japanese between 1895 and 1945. Within the first decade of Japanese rule, the colonizers implemented a partial land reform that eliminated the large landlord system and distributed land to smallholders. Building up the island's physical infrastructure and productive capacity as an offshore base for Japanese agriculture and, later, industry, the Japanese also invested in social services. This led to a better educated, healthier population. By the start of World War II, approximately 27 percent of the population was literate (in Japanese) as a result of free and compulsory primary education programs; 79 percent of primary school-aged children were attending school. Investments in sewage systems, sanitation services, and vaccination programs had cut the death rate in half. After the war, Taiwan emerged from Japan's colonization with a stronger base for broad-based growth than many, if not most, former colonies elsewhere in the world.

Building on the comparatively favorable conditions provided by Japanese colonialism, the Nationalist government in Taiwan continued to invest in infrastructure, education, primary health care, and sanitation. As is well-known now, the government shifted from import-substitution to export-promotion in the early 1960s, and the economy, which had already been growing at a sustained rate of 7.5 percent (1952–1961), accelerated to 10.2 percent (1961–1971). Real wages grew very slowly until the labor market reached the turning point in 1968, when wages started to rise. Since the late 1960s, unemployment has averaged only 1 or 2 percent annually. Real wages for manufacturing workers are currently 600 percent higher than 1961 levels; since 1970, average real wages have increased by more than 8 percent annually.

This rapid, sustained growth was accompanied by continued, broad-based improvements in the standard of living for Taiwan's people. In 1987, Taiwan's Gini coefficient, a measure of income inequality, stood at 0.30, one of the lowest levels in the world.[4] By comparison, the Gini coefficient for Mexico is approximately 0.54, Brazil 0.60, and Jamaica, 0.66.

Alternative Explanations

Poverty wears many faces and can be measured and combated in many ways. Public policies and foreign assistance can address poverty at the policy level and at the program and project level. For low-income countries, economic growth is necessary for poverty alleviation, but not sufficient. Economic growth that also alleviates poverty requires "particular kinds" of policies. One set of strategies many governments use to address poverty problems involves consumption-raising transfers directly to the poor. Whether devised as a safety net to help support the poorest of the poor during periods of economic stress, or developed as a more general government policy during good times and bad, these strategies include targeted food subsidies and nutrition support, public works programs and employment guarantee schemes, public housing for low-income families, and minimum wage rates that raise the cost of unskilled labor above market levels.

Another set of policies and programs focus on raising the productivity of and demand for labor (the major asset of the poor) and increasing the access of the poor to information, as well as land, capital, and other factors of production. These include land reform, universal primary education and primary health care programs, business credit programs targeted to low-income people or labor-intensive industries that employ low-income people, communication and transport infrastructure in low-income (particularly rural) areas, child-care programs, and policies that raise the price of commodities and goods produced by the poor.

Policies to Reduce Poverty

Taiwan's experience of poverty alleviation largely follows the second set of strategies. Policy makers focused on raising the productivity of and demand for labor through education and vocational training and through relatively high interest rates and low wage rates that kept the price of capital high and the price of labor low, encouraging labor-intensive industrialization. Just as importantly, in the early 1950s, Taiwan implemented a major land reform that equalized the access of most rural families to land, while contributing to increased land and labor productivity. Finally, economic policies and government investments provided roads, rail, and electricity in rural areas, enabling the decentralization of industry and the growth of small and medium sized firms in rural areas, providing full and part-time employment for members of farm families.

Land Reform

Taiwan benefited from the irrigation construction, research, and agroindustries developed by the Japanese, but the improvements in income and asset distribution are a function of a comprehensive, three-phased land reforms imposed by the Kuomintang (KMT) government after the war. The reforms first reduced rents to a maximum of 37.5 percent of the harvest, then sold public lands to smallholders, and finally, imposed a maximum acreage ceiling for larger landowners. The government's appropriation of Japanese lands and investments after the end of the war supported the land reform by providing extensive public land (25 percent of the arable land in Taiwan) to sell to smallholders on easy terms, and by allowing landowners to be compensated by industrial bonds based on confiscated Japanese factories.

In the year the land reforms were completed, the Gini coefficient was 0.56; within 10 years, it had fallen to 0.33. By setting a ceiling on landholdings and redistributing land to smallholders and tenant farmers, the poorest of Taiwan's population, the land reform underwrote the remarkable income equality still felt today in Taiwan, an important lesson for other developing countries, many of which are affected by the pressures of unequal access to land.[5]

Investment in Agriculture

The land reform also enabled the government to better squeeze resources from agriculture, without the need to compensate a politically powerful landlord class. Net capital outflows from agriculture averaged almost four percent under the Japanese, and rose to ten percent under the KMT.[6] As one of its first economic policy decisions after arriving in Taiwan, the KMT government set the terms of trade between the main staple — rice — and fertilizer, with fertilizer sold on a barter basis. Rice production received an implicit tax, with fertilizer overpriced in rice terms. Rice prices under the compulsory barter system and land taxes, which were paid in kind, were lower than market or international rice prices (rice exports were under a government monopoly). Although farmers lost from the price squeeze, they benefited from stability, from the lower transaction costs afforded by fixed prices, and assured and timely fertilizer delivery. Indeed, despite low prices, rice output increased steadily at about 3 percent per year from 1952 to 1964, when farmers began diversifying into higher value export crops such as asparagus and mushrooms. The fertilizer–rice barter system was discontinued in 1973.

Although the net transfer from the agricultural sector to the rest of the economy amounted to some 15 to 22 percent of total agricultural production between 1952 and 1969, the sector itself received considerable investment and recurrent resources from the government, enabling it to increase productivity and serve as the basis for economic transformation.[7] The government invested in institutional capacity and agricultural research. In 1948, the Chinese–American Joint Commission on Rural Reconstruction (JCRR) was established, with U.S. funding, as an insulated, semipublic "de facto superministry of agriculture."[8] By 1960, Taiwan had 79 agricultural research workers per 100,000 farmers, compared with Japan (60 workers) and India (1.2 workers).[9]

In Taiwan, land reform, investment in research, protecting farmers from risk, and assuring fertilizer supply all supported agriculture, enabling farmers to increase output and eventually to diversify production. This also increased the productivity of farm labor to the point where families could release their members to work in the proliferation of decentralized industries. Although farmers received lower prices for their rice than those available in international markets, the lower prices benefited those households that had to purchase some or all of their rice consumption and enabled wages to be lower, thereby underwriting the expansion of labor-intensive growth.

Education and Human Development

Taiwan's industrial growth was fueled in part by government investments in universal literacy and in vocational and science-based learning. Funding, social values, and legal compulsion brought Taiwan's literacy rates to almost 87 percent by 1972. As a percentage of total government expenditure, spending on education in Taiwan rose from 7.8 percent in 1952 to 17.6 percent in 1972. In low-income countries across Africa, by comparison, the average has remained close to 17 percent since 1970. However, two additional factors affect the outcome of government spending and help explain why performance in African countries generally remains far below that in Taiwan.

First, in the grim economic climate of the 1980s, most African countries have had to reduce their overall spending, meaning that education spending may remain the same percentage of the total, but be lower in real terms. Sierra Leone cut per capita spending by 62 percent between 1980 and 1988, and Tanzania by 73 percent. Overall, spending on education per student in Africa's low-income countries declined from $32 in 1980 to $15 in 1987.[10] Second, the higher population growth rate in much of the developing world, particularly Africa, means that spending must increase at least at the rate of population increase merely to stay even with past spending. In countries where the overall population increase is stabilized, spending increases can lead to improved programs.

Taiwan's government invested heavily in planned, vocational education. Vocational training in Taiwan as a percentage of all senior high school enrollments rose from 37 percent in 1950 to 66 percent in 1980.[11] Like most African parents and students today, Taiwan's families in the 1950s and 1960s did not envision their educated children becoming blue collar laborers, but rather as white collar workers and government employees. Yet the government did not provide the education demanded by society. Instead it channeled students into educational streams needed by the economy. By 1985, Taiwan had 767 enrollments in engineering per 100,000 population;[12] African countries for which similar data existed had an average of 9 engineering enrollments per 100,000 population.

Finally, Taiwan's primary school enrollment rates for girls were significantly higher than the average for its income level in the 1952–1972 period. Women's education levels are linked to lower fertility rates, lower infant mortality levels, and higher family incomes. This reduction of the "gender gap" helped make the opportunities more equal for the children of both higher- and lower-income families.

Labor Policies

Labor policies in Taiwan kept employment high, urban-rural wage differentials low, and real wages rising at or below average productivity. Taiwan maintained a fairly competitive (or repressed) labor market: strikes were generally prohibited, unions weak, and there was effectively no minimum wage. Real wages grew at a slightly slower rate than the consumer price index and slightly under the growth rate for labor productivity; by 1972, at the point when real wages in Taiwan started to turn upward, they still averaged only US$.20 per hour.[13]

The fairly flexible and undistorted labor market, without the common interventions of minimum wages, high public sector pay policies, and strong unions, supported labor-intensive industrialization. By the 1980s, as might be expected from a well-working labor market, manufacturing wages were only 20 percent higher than wages in agriculture, compared with differentials of some 100 percent in many Latin American countries. The low differential between rural and urban wages reinforces the income equality experienced in Taiwan.

Decentralization of Industry

In a major study of Taiwan's development path, *Growth with Equity* (1979), Fei, Ranis, and Kuo attribute Taiwan's success in part to policies that allowed the decentralization of industry as opposed to its concentration in urban areas. With an excellent network of roads and railroads and ports, with industrial energy and fuel prices equalized across the country, and with a ready supply of farm-based labor, rural-based entrepreneurs had incentives to start small businesses in their rural locations. New employment and investment opportunities in rural industries provided a larger and larger share of family income, eventually outpacing agricultural income in rural families.[14] With more family members employed for wages, family incomes rose. This helped ensured that the pattern of rural poverty and lack of rural-based employment so pervasive in the low-income countries did not characterize Taiwan's development.

Social Welfare and Redistribution Policies

The government in Taiwan provided only limited social security, health, and welfare to offset the low wages, investing three times as much in education as in health over the two decades of this study. Public health rose from 1.5 percent of government expenditures in 1951–1955 to only 1.7 percent in 1971–1973, very low figures compared with 1972 average figures of 5.5 percent for low-income countries (excluding China and India), 6.1 percent for middle-income countries, and 11.1 percent for high income countries. No unemployment compensation existed, but there was a labor insurance scheme, which by 1976 covered some 50 percent of all employees, and by 1988, 75 percent. Although other of the NICS—Singapore, for instance—invested in public housing, Taiwan provided very little public housing, but the national government has subsidized twenty-year home mortgages at 3 percent for government employees.[15]

A minimal income support program exists for poor families. However, it applied (in the 1980s) only to the approximately 1.5 percent of households that have annual income levels below US $360 for a family of four.[16] The government in Taiwan appears to have disaggregated human resource development into investment in education as a public good and investment in other forms of social welfare as primarily private goods.

Although small enterprises provided the bulk of Taiwan's employment and have been pointed to as important mechanisms for broad-based growth on the island, the government gave little if any direct support to small businesses during the 1952–1972 period.[17]

Finally, Taiwan has not used the tax system as an instrument to further the redistribution of incomes. As one study found, "the distribution of the total tax burden was neutral with respect to its impact on the equity of distribution of family income. In other words, the degree of inequality of family income before and after taxes was about the same."[18]

Conclusion

Without the extraordinary growth Taiwan experienced over the past two generations, the high standard of living enjoyed by most people on the island would not be possible. Yet growth alone would not have ensured the general prosperity that accompanied growth in Taiwan, and indeed, that growth would likely not have been as successful as it was, without government policies that provided the foundation for the broad distribution of the fruits of growth.

First among these was the land reform, which contributed greatly toward equalizing the most important capital asset of the island's families. Second, investment in agriculture and maintenance of stable prices ensured that agriculture could grow and thus be taxed to support industry without impoverishing rural dwellers. Third, investment in education and, in particular, in female education, gave the country the labor base for industrial transformation, while lowering the birthrate and spreading the benefits of skilled employment throughout the population. Fourth, labor policies ensured that real wages kept pace with production increases. The subsequent tightening of the labor market pushed wages up through the actions of supply and demand. This allowed the economy to use labor-intensive technologies which stimulated employment. Finally, Taiwan's policy decisions on infrastructure and energy eased the decentralization of industry, allowing families to find employment in rural areas close to their farms.

By contrast, social welfare policies in Taiwan tended to be fairly limited. Low government prices for rice were undoubtedly helpful for poorer families and implied a government-mandated transfer from producers to consumers. But public health spending was relatively low, and public housing almost nonexistent. Income transfers through taxation were almost nil, and income support programs were minimal. The government offered little if any specialized support to small businesses, which, nonetheless, grew at a remarkable rate in Taiwan.

It is impossible to generalize, let alone to prescribe, based on Taiwan's experience. Yet Taiwan's experience of poverty alleviation suggests that some aspects bear further scrutiny. In particular, it suggests that land reform may be essential to provide initial conditions of equitable asset distribution. Then, concentrating on education and infrastructure investments, and on employment-generating industrial policies, can provide the basis for rapid, broad-based growth.

Notes

1. This section draws heavily on a forthcoming article, Deborah Brautigam, "What Can Africa Learn from Taiwan?" *Journal of Modern African Studies.*
2. Economic Planning Council (EPC), *Taiwan Statistical Data Book.* Taipei, Taiwan, 1975 (current prices); Economist Intelligence Unit, *Country Report: Taiwan No. 1,* 1993.
3. For Taiwan, see K. T. Li, *The Evolution of Policy Behind Taiwan's Development Success.* New Haven: Yale University Press, 1988, p. 161. Figures for Brazil and Botswana are from World Bank, *World Development Report 1993.* New York: Oxford University Press, pp. 296–297.
4. A Gini coefficient of "0.0" would be perfect equality; "1.0" would represent perfect inequality.

5. The privatization programs being undertaken by many low-income countries under structural adjustment and liberalization have some potential to play a similar role.

6. Alice Amsden, "Taiwan's Economic History: A Case of Etatisme and a Challenge to Dependency Theory," *Modern China* 5, no. 3 (1979): 353.

7. Erik Thorbecke, "Agricultural Development." In Walter Galenson (ed.), *Economic Growth and Structural Change in Taiwan*. Ithaca, NY: Cornell University Press, 1979, p. 203.

8. Thorbecke, "Agricultural Development," pp. 172, 184, 203.

9. U.S. Department of Agriculture, "Changes in Agriculture in 26 Developing Nations, 1948 to 1963," cited in Samuel Ho, *Small-Scale Enterprises in Korea and Taiwan*. World Bank Staff Working Paper, No. 384. Washington, D.C.: World Bank, 1980, p. 178.

10. World Bank, *Education in Sub-Saharan Africa*, p. 138; EPC, *Taiwan Statistical Data Book*, 1975; United Nations, *Statistical Yearbook, 1990;* UNESCO, 1990.

11. Jennie Hay Woo. "Education and Industrial Growth in Taiwan: A Case of Planning," Harvard Institute for International Development, E.E.P.A. Discussion Paper No. 18, August 1988.

12. Woo, "Education and Industrial Growth," p. 33; Manuel Zymelman, *Science, Education, and Development in Sub-Saharan Africa*. World Bank Technical Paper No. 124. Washington, D.C.: World Bank, 1990, p. 27.

13. Maurice Scott. "Foreign Trade." In Galenson, *Economic Growth and Structural Change in Taiwan*, p. 360.

14. John C. H. Fei, Gustav Ramis, and S. W. Y. Kuo, *Growth with Equity: The Taiwan Case*. New York: Oxford University Press, 1979, p. 315.

15. This may vary by government unit. For example, the tobacco monopoly offered its employees subsidized loans at four percent covering up to 40 percent of a house purchase. In 1975, beyond the period under discussion, the national government started a housing program for workers. See Galenson, *Economic Growth and Structural Change*, pp. 421, 440.

16. This is the official level below which a family qualifies for public assistance: NT $3000 per household member, per month. See Gary Fields, "Living Standards, Labor Markets, and Human Resources in Taiwan." In Gustav Ranis (ed.), *Taiwan: From Developing to Mature Economy*. Boulder, CO: Westview, 1992, p. 398.

17. A Small and Medium Industries Bank was created in 1976. See Ho, "Small-Scale Enterprises in Korea and Taiwan," p. 96.

18. See Fei, Ranis, and Kuo, *Growth with Equity*, p. 321.

Chapter 3

Measures for the Reduction of Poverty

Section 1

The Role of the State and Market in Addressing Inequality and Growth

Carl Tham and Dag Ehrenpreis

In classical Athens, according to Plutarch, the disparity of fortune between the rich and the poor had reached its height, so that the city seemed to be in a dangerous condition, and no other means for freeing it from disturbances seemed possible but despotic power. The poor began to talk of violent revolt. The rich prepared to defend themselves by force.

However, good sense prevailed; a new leader was elected, who introduced policy reforms with currency devaluation that eased the burden of the debtors, a progressive income tax, popular courts, and arrangements for the sons of those who had died in war for Athens to be brought up and educated at the government's expense.

The rich protested that these measures were outright confiscation; the radicals complained that land had not been redivided; but within a generation almost all agreed that the reforms had saved Athens from revolution.

In England in the 1750s, severe food riots increased the pressures on the government to intervene in the grain market. As a result, both local and national governments gradually shifted towards more vigorous interventions during the next century. By the mid-1800s, famines had become a scourge of the past—not because of improved climate or improved technology, but as a result of government policy.

When a famine was developing in India in 1812, the Governor of Bombay, quoting Adam Smith, turned down a proposal for moving food into an affected area by asserting the advisability of leaving such matters to the market mechanism. The basically noninterventionist famine policy in India lasted until late into the nineteenth century, when Famine Codes were adopted as a result of conspicuous and tragic market failures. Massive public works programs were then introduced, as well as social relief for those unable to work.

However, in the Great Bengal Famine of 1943, which is estimated to have killed nearly three million people even though there was no overall food shortage, the Famine Codes were deliberately ignored for political reasons.

UNU/WIDER studies of the Ethiopian famines of 1972–1974 and 1982–1985 strongly indicate that the absence of public intervention to redress a situation of drought-induced rural mass unemployment was a dominant feature of both major famines. Although adverse natural conditions caused the destitution and food shortages, it was the governance failure of the imperial and revolutionary regimes, respectively, that caused the development of the actual disasters. They also contributed significantly to the downfall of these regimes.

Lessons to Be Learned

What lessons can we learn from these historical experiences? Famines have been the result of market failures and of policy failures to predict and prevent the consequences of market failures. The problems of poverty cannot be solved by the market alone – nor by the state alone.

The issue is not whether the state should intervene to prevent famines and destitution and promote social and economic development, but how to shape socially efficient government intervention. It is not the size of the public sector, but the quality of public policies and administration in relation to the particular conditions and challenges in each country that are important for efficient economic and social development.

Neoliberal doctrines have dominated economic policy reforms throughout the world for more than a decade. They have in many cases correctly emphasized weaknesses and failures of state intervention. In addition, market reforms have removed some obstacles to economic growth.

But neoliberal reform programs have failed to solve both immediate and long-term economic and social problems. It has failed to contribute constructively to defining the proper role of the state as an agent of transformation and economic development.

There is now increasing demand for a less doctrinaire and more pragmatic approach to the governance issue. This is evident from recent developments in Eastern Europe, where democratic elections have resulted in the departure from power of the extreme economic liberals and "market romantics."

Douglass North, 1993 Nobel laureate in Economic Sciences, in his Prize Lecture stated that "neoclassical theory is simply an inappropriate tool to analyze and prescribe policies that will induce development. It is concerned with the operation of markets not with how markets develop. How can one prescribe policies when one doesn't understand how economies develop?"[1] North also pointed out that "transferring the formal political and economic rules of successful western market economies to third world and eastern European economies is not a sufficient condition for good economic performance. Privatization is not a panacea for solving poor economic performance."

The Role of Institutions

The main message from Douglass North and the New Institutional Economics is that institutions form the incentive structure of a society. Political and economic institutions are therefore the underlying determinant of economic performance. Successful political and economic systems have evolved flexible institutional structures that can adapt to the shocks and changes that are a part of successful evolution.

Institutions are products of long gestation. They continue to develop along a path dependent on the historical, cultural, social, political, and economical factors specific for each country. They are generally not deliberately created as a framework for an efficient economy but rather the result of history and an intensive struggle for power. Institutions-building is power-building.

There is no generally accepted theory of how to change the economic and political institutional structure and promote sustainable human and economic development. In the epoch of the East Asian Miracle, there are several examples of successful countries, and innumerable opinions about the causes of their transformation. But there is no consensus among development economists about this, nor about the reasons why most African and other low-income countries are lagging ever further behind.

What we do know is that development and policy are results of numerous and complex factors, many of which are beyond the scope of economic theory. There is also an increasing understanding and convergence towards the view that a functioning and legitimate government is a prerequisite for the evolution of efficient markets and for the social and economic environment and institutions that are conducive to growth.

Economic growth is a necessary condition for sustainable human development and poverty reduction, but to create growth you need not only entrepreneurs and "sound economic policy," but also an appropriate public policy with respect to the creation and distribution of jobs, assets, incomes, infrastructures, redistribution, and social services.

Inequality

The 1992 Human Development Report (HDR) from the UNDP highlighted the increasing disparities between the rich and the poor in the world. The income gap between rich and poor is immense, and widening. Between 1960 and 1989, economic growth in countries with the 20 percent of world population that had the highest per capita incomes was 2.7 times faster than the lowest 20 percent. Thus, the richest group of countries increased their share of global GNP from some 70 percent to nearly 83 percent, while the share of the poorest group fell from 2.3 percent to 1.4 percent.

The consequences for income disparities have been dramatic. In 1960, the national incomes of the top 20 percent countries were 30 times higher than the bottom 20 percent. By 1991 they were more than 60 times higher.

The poorest half of the bottom 20 percent are the least developed countries (LDCs, mostly African), which now contain more than 10 percent of the world population. Their share of global GNP shrank from only 1 percent to a miserable 0.5 percent. In other words, the LDC share of global GNP is only 1/20th of their population share, whereas for all developing countries the ratio is one-fifth. For industrial countries, the GNP share is four times their share of world population.

The skewed income distribution within each country is concealed by the average national incomes above. HDR 92 calculated that the inequality ratio between the 20 percent richest and poorest people in the world, respectively, may well be over 150 to 1.

Calculating real purchasing power rather than nominal GNP figures reduces the disparities, but it is still greater than 50 to 1. There is probably no country in the world with such large disparities, but the extreme case of Botswana comes close with 47 to 1. The income gap of Brazil, the most unequal of major countries, is now estimated to have increased to 32 to 1. Global income inequalities are much larger than even the most glaring national disparities. But inequalities within nations are politically more disturbing and destabilizing than inequalities between nations.

One more complication is important to add to such estimates of income inequalities. The above figures are all based on national income statistics, that is, on transactions that are registered in the national accounts. That excludes by definition the informal sector, which according to many estimates is large and growing in many countries, especially in low-income countries.

Recent calculations of the informal sector in Tanzania indicate that it has grown to some 60 percent of the official GDP. Poverty has actually been reduced from, approximately, 70 to 50 percent of the population during the economic crisis and subsequent structural adjustment, because of the dynamism of the informal sector.

But the informal sector also includes the unpaid production of goods and services within the households, that is, the gender aspects of the intra-household income distribution of work and benefits. Most data on income distribution are based on household surveys. Development economics has customarily assumed government policies to be directed at resource allocation between, not within, households. Recent studies have been made of resource and work allocation mechanisms within households, looking at inequalities in food and health care allocations, and in education and workload — between men and women, young and old, boys and girls (by gender as well as by birth order). Needless to say, the women are in almost all countries worse off than men. They work harder, they are generally oppressed by tradition and legal systems and they are poorer.

Data that do not penetrate the household are incapable of exposing this kind of inequality and therefore display less than actual inequality. The resulting bias can be quite large. In many parts of the world, inequality among people would be some 30 to 40 percent higher were household inequality to be included.

Notwithstanding the large and widening income disparities in the world, the inequalities of human social welfare are much less. That follows naturally from the fact that the rich can earn unlimited amounts of money but there are limits to longevity, literacy, schooling, access to water, and other basic social needs. The poor countries are also improving their average levels of most basic human development indicators.

UNDP's Human Development Index (HDI) is a composite index of human development, combining indicators of life expectancy, educational attainment and real income per capita based on purchasing power parities. HDR 94 has modified the HDI calculations so that meaningful comparisons across countries and over time can now be made. Thus, it is estimated that the majority of the world population has shifted from low to medium and high human development over the period from 1960 to 1992.

In 1960, nearly three-fourths of the world population lived in countries with low average human development levels. In 1992 this proportion had fallen to just above one-third of the population. The proportion in the medium human development category had quadrupled to 42 percent, and in high human development from 16 to 22 percent.

All countries made substantial progress in human development. The overall HDI value for developing countries more than doubled. Even the least developed countries and those in Sub-Saharan Africa made clear progress. They started from very low levels, but managed as a group to increase their HDI values by approximately 80 percent. East Asia had the largest increase both absolutely and relatively; HDI grew more than 2.5 times. This shows that the fast pace of economic growth in East Asia was built on a broad and solid foundation of human development.

There is no automatic link between economic growth and the level of human development. That link is determined by policy, by the extent to which a country's resources are shared between different social strata of its population, and by the extent to which the government is mobilizing and devoting resources to the task of raising the levels of human development for all its population. That extent is highly variable. Some governments have overextended their commitment to public sector support for social development far beyond its economic sustainability, so that economic crisis has led to a collapse of the quality of social services, and unplanned de facto privatization and petty corruption. Others have given low priority to human development and spent their resources elsewhere.

Yet other countries, mainly in East Asia, have managed to strike a sustainable social balance between the growth of resources and their allocation for social and human development purposes. Whether that balance also can be ecologically sustained, however, remains an open issue and a challenge for development studies.

Sustainable Growth with Equity

Twenty years ago, the Chief Economist of the World Bank and perhaps the most influential development economist at the time wrote: "It is now clear that more than a decade of rapid growth in underdeveloped countries has been of little or no benefit to perhaps a third of their population.... While growth policies have succeeded beyond their expectations... the very idea of aggregate growth as a social objective has increasingly been called into question."[2] Today, it is no longer very clear whether economic growth is of little or large benefit to the poor. Sometimes it is large, and sometimes it is not even little. A lot of research is going on to explore the strategic factors behind these crucially different outcomes.

Sustainable growth with equity is a fundamental objective of a welfare-oriented development strategy. A key issue has been whether this objective itself is feasible, or to what extent there is a trade-off between augmenting growth and reducing inequality.

According to conventional economic wisdom regarding the nature of the development process, unequal distribution of income is both necessary for and an inevitable result of economic growth for two reasons.

The first reason is connected to the necessary mobilization of savings: the rich were assumed to have higher marginal propensity to save, so increased concentration of incomes should bring about higher savings, which lead to higher investments and growth. However, the role of savings for economic growth in developing countries has not been found to be a crucial factor, as long as there is financial repression and lack of credit market institutions to channel savings into productive investments. The state has in many cases been more efficient than the markets to invest productively, for example, in physical and social infrastructure.

The studies of long-term economic growth in industrial countries by Simon Kuznets did not find any significant correlation between rates of capital formation, rates of saving, and level of income, in spite of growth theory expectations.[3] What he did find was the second reason above: a U-shaped curve for income distribution during long-term growth (based on time-series data for Britain, Germany, and the United States): first decreasing equality in income distribution, followed later by an upturn in equality, as labor shifts from lower to higher productivity sectors.[4]

However later statistical analysis based on cross-country data has rejected these results. Anand and Kanbur have shown that the functional form with the closest fit to the best available consistent data set displays a reversal of the U-curve.[5] In other words, in poor countries, growth and equity tend to be complementary; in richer countries, there is a tendency for income inequalities to increase with economic growth.

Similar results emerge from new econometric studies of the impact of the distribution of income on subsequent economic growth.[6] They show a robust negative relationship between income inequality and average annual growth in per capita GDP for 1970–1988. In a modified version for 74 countries in 1960–1985, significant correlations were found between growth and, respectively, education variables (positive) and inequality (negative).

Although the impact of a change in income inequality is smaller than for education (primary education in particular), the growth effect of reducing income inequality is still substantial. After 25 years, one statistical unit (standard deviation) of decrease in inequality would raise GDP per capita 82 percent higher in a country with low inequality than in a country with high inequality. The income difference for the poor in the two countries would be much larger, as the effects of lower inequality—higher share of incomes to the poor—are combined with the effect of higher average incomes.

There is considerable evidence that the statistical correlation between economic growth and human development tends to work through the impact of GNP expansion on higher public expenditure and lower poverty, that is, through the expanded ability to undertake public action to improve living conditions, and the share of the additional income that accrues to the poor.

The relation between growth and equity is not automatic. It depends on the pattern of growth, the degree of labor-intensity and popular participation, the prevailing economic, political, and social structure, and other institutional conditions.

In Latin America, where the distribution of political power, land, and other assets is extremely skewed, economic growth has in general led to increased inequalities and poverty. The share of the total population living in poverty increased from 41 percent in 1980 to 46 percent in 1990, that is, nearly 200 million people. The absolute numbers living in poverty in the urban areas doubled during the 1980s and reached 116 million in 1990. The few exceptions were the result of deliberate and persistent care for equity in economic policy design and implementation.

In Africa, there is a mixed picture. There are cases of extreme income inequality with extreme growth records, both positive (Botswana) and negative (Zambia). Many African countries seem to have as high degrees of income inequality as in Latin America, with either higher growth rates per capita (Gabon and Mauritius), or lower (Ghana and the Ivory Coast), or about the same (Kenya). Some African countries have both low growth and low inequality (Malawi and Tanzania).

In response to economic crisis and structural adjustment, there has been a vigorous growth of informal sector activities, which in some cases has reduced poverty. But it is also a reflection of increased destitution and loss of formal employment. The rural poor have sometimes benefited from the realignment of exchange rates and some market liberalization, but the rural rich always, and more.

Structural adjustment in Africa remains a dilemma, since sometimes necessary donor-imposed policy reforms are ineffective and undermine both the credibility of the reforms and the legitimacy of the governments. This is clearly counterproductive in the long run and may contribute significantly to the political crisis in Africa.

East Asia: Equitable Growth and the Role of the State

In East Asia, eight countries have grown at rates higher than the industrial countries experienced during their earlier periods of most rapid growth. These record high economic growth rates, sustained over three decades, have been associated with low and decreasing degrees of income inequality. Among the East Asian countries, the distribution of income is substantially more equal in those with the fastest growth.

New research indicates that one of the strongest lessons from East Asia is that lower inequality is not only a corollary, but an important contributing factor to economic growth. Public policies aimed at improving human developing conditions for all groups can have a direct effect in stimulating growth as well, in the following ways:

- If the poor receive higher incomes, they can afford real savings and investment that improve human development, and thus productivity and growth. Researchers have often overlooked that poor people save by devoting more of their families' resources to children, feeding them better, taking them to the clinic, and sending them to school. Such human investment may be as important to economic growth as investment in physical infrastructure, machinery, and plants. In unequal low-income countries, the poor cannot afford those "investments" in their children, even if they understand their payoffs.

- Education has been emphasized as a particularly important factor that stimulates both increased growth and decreased inequality. As the general level of education improves, productivity and wages rise. Educational expansion can reduce total income inequality by reducing the inequalities of pay. Lower income inequality increases household demand for education and probably increases public supply. Thus, productivity and growth are enhanced.

- Lower inequality can stimulate growth by improving social mobility, and thus the incentives and rewards for longer and better education, harder work in the fields or factories, and greater risk-taking in new ventures.

- Land reform is the most straightforward example of a major development policy measure, implemented in Korea and Taiwan, that both reduced inequality and increased productivity. Reduction of inequality of land holdings, and of the average size of farms increased both labor intensity, yields, and incomes.

- Lower inequality can increase the domestic multiplier effects. Smaller rural–urban income gaps and less rural poverty means higher demand for agricultural inputs and consumer goods that are produced and traded by urban workers and small businesses. In contrast, when the incomes of the urban elite increase, the tradables on which they spend them tend to be capital- and import-intensive goods, such as cars and stereos. A strong domestic demand for labor-intensive goods may have given East Asia's early manufacturers a competitive advantage in international markets.

- Trade and industrial policies, especially the strong export promotion policies, also combined growth and equity objectives. They increased employment of unskilled factory workers, thus relieving pressure on the land.

- Lower inequality can help promote macroeconomic stability, which is generally agreed to have been one of the crucial factors in East Asia. Keeping inflation under control and the real exchange rate at a realistic level is easier if there is broad social participation in the growth process rather than elite and special interest groups diverting resources to their own ends. Low-income groups are more likely to be willing to share the burden of adjustment to a negative shock if better-off groups also adjust, and if the benefits of resumed growth are perceived to be equitably shared. If the burden of adjustment is much heavier on the poor, it is likely to provoke strong negative reactions that could lead to political and economic disruption.

• Lower inequality can stimulate growth by increasing overall political stability. A stable political environment is conducive to economic growth: investment is likely to be higher where the risk of a shift toward populist policies, which may even include the expropriation of private assets, is reduced. When there are rapid increases in income for selected groups and for the elite, while the incomes of the poor and middle class stagnate, the risk is that the latter groups become politically alienated. By contrast, a pattern of economic growth with wide sharing of the benefits reduces the political risks and legitimizes the government in the eyes of the mass of the population. It also helps to build broad-based political support. Thus, the risk of economically disruptive political upheaval is reduced.

The East Asian experience is in general one of shared growth policies carried out by strong, developmental states on a trial-and-error basis, led by the example of Japan. Errors have no doubt been committed, but they are of small significance in comparison with the success achieved. What is important is the adaptive skills of the governments, the capacity to learn from experience and adjust policies when necessary.

The East Asian success certainly is no vindication of the efficacy of laissez-faire policies, as some have argued. On the contrary, it proves the importance of a synergetic interaction between the state and the actors on the market. Policy makers fulfilled an important developmental function by carrying out necessary policy reforms, which created and maintained a macroeconomic environment conducive to rapid economic growth.

The state also made necessary investments in physical infrastructure and in human development. In contrast to many other countries, policies explicitly aimed at the inclusion of girls in education, which had great significance for the success of family planning policies.

But the role of the state was much more important than that. The state actively intervened in the development of markets (except in the very special case of Hong Kong) by direct industrial policy with guided investments, subsidized and targeted credits, low interest-rate policies, protection of domestic markets from imports, and active support of exports. They managed to both protect their infant industries and make them grow strong for world market competitiveness.

It is "social engineering" at its best, with adaptive efficiency based on close(d) institutional contacts between captains of industry, politicians and state administrators – normally a bogeyman of economists. But they succeeded where others have failed.

The Political Economy of Equity-Based Growth

The relation between economic growth, inequality, and the development of democracy is far from unambiguous. Democratic governments have not been very successful when it comes to structural reforms which may be to the disadvantage of important interest groups, or when it comes to welfare and reduced inequality.

The East Asian miracle countries have achieved tremendous success in reducing inequalities and increasing economic growth, but they are no models of democracy. On the contrary, they all have more or less authoritarian systems, and their success is linked to sometimes severe repression of political opposition and trade union activity. Both the carrot and the stick have been used to adapt the institutional structure to the perceived needs of development. An important factor has also been the vibrant nationalism of all "miracle" countries, as well as the massive political and economic support of the United States. Economic success and increasing welfare have gradually led to increased legitimacy for the regimes.

Many political scientists and philosophers have tried to find some systematic connection between the political system and the achievement of welfare-oriented development strategies, but no one has clearly succeeded. One of the best comparative studies have been done by Georg Sorensen, who stressed "that the abstract distinction between democracy and authoritarianism does not provide sufficient guidance for deciding about the effects on economic development and welfare."[7]

It is perhaps more relevant to ask what economic development can do for democracy than the reverse. Aid donors should consider the consequences for the political legitimacy of aid-recipient governments, of far-reaching policy conditionality for economic and social reforms as well as democracy and human rights. Can policy reforms in developing countries deemed to be essential by aid donors be achieved in a sustainable way by their intervention? Is there not a considerable risk of a counterproductive backlash effect? But, on the other hand, will the public opinion in donor democracies permit continued aid without such reforms? This is a true dilemma for aid donors.

One of several prerequisites for economic growth and development is legitimate and reasonably well-functioning governments that will define and implement rules of good governance as well as adequate development policies. In the words of the UN World Economic Survey: "Both historical and contemporary experience suggest that the State has indispensable functions in defining legal frameworks, providing infrastructure, establishing monetary and financial stability, ensuring education and health, maintaining an acceptable distribution of income and social justice, safeguarding the environment and providing a vision of the future role of the country in the world economy."

Basic development policy choices to be made relate to the scope and pace of integration in the world economy and to the national political context for development strategies. There are two crucial dimensions here. One concerns what the state can do, its political and administrative capabilities. The other what it will do, the political will to promote economic development based on popular participation and equitable distribution.

The effectiveness of a new institutional set-up for state and civil society interactions will depend on a mutually agreed new role definition and the capacity of the different actors involved to assume these new roles. The whole process of democratization which is going on in many parts of the world will remain an empty shell in the absence of a state that has the basic capacity to fulfill its role and in the absence of organized interest groups in civil society that have the capacity to influence the policy process.

The East Asian miracle countries managed to establish strong developmental states by skillfully building on historical experience and traditions, regional models, aggressive nationalism, and anticommunism that could subdue special interests and mobilize powerful external economic and political support, and by mutual spillover effects within the region, led by the growth engine of Japan. In contrast with Latin America, the power elite was wise enough to understand that the system and their own privileged positions could not be maintained if the benefits of economic growth were not shared on a wider basis.

The conclusions of this experience are evident, but not very easy to implement for other countries. The decisive role of the political structures stands out. In order to create efficient and growing economies, legitimate and effective political systems, and institutions are required. They may emerge from the internal or external power struggles. Historical evidence indicates that only a strong state power can move the economy in the right direction.

But adequate external conditions are also necessary. Economic, military, and political support and, not least, an ability both to interact with the world markets to take advantage of their dynamic potential and to protect internal markets from their competitive dangers. Not only East Asian countries, but also Latin America in the 1960s and Arab countries, such as Jordan and Tunisia, have achieved rapid industrialization with a battery of interventionist policies.

It should be noted, however, that many of the policies behind the East Asian miracle would not have been accepted today by the World Bank or GATT. Today, the financial markets are moving billions of dollars every day at the touch of a button, which severely limits the prospects of nationally independent finance policies, as Sweden knows from recent painful experience.

The proposal for a tax on international currency transactions by James Tobin, Nobel Prize Laureate in Economics, is against this background worth the renewed interest it has received recently. It is important both for limiting the speculative and disruptive capital flows and for raising revenues for international development purposes at the same time.

The political and cultural conditions behind the immense efficiency of the interactions between the state and the market in East Asia cannot be copied by countries in political and economic crises. But it should be noted that their success is hardly compatible with the proclaimed superiority of the predominant neoclassical doctrine of development. On the contrary, their policies have been characterized by the kind of national mercantilism that was used by the industrial countries to develop their economic strength.

Conclusion

The conclusion from historical experience is this: no country has been able to develop without a strong state that has managed to protect and promote the national economy. The challenge lies in the need to strengthen the capacity of the public sector to design and implement development policies, in education, health, labor training, regulation of private monopolies and the financial sector, and investment in infrastructure. There will be no reduction of poverty or reduced inequality without growth and redistribution.

Today, however, it seems as if most governments are not interested in such policies. The governments of the South talk a lot about the injustice in the world and specifically about the gap between rich and poor countries. When it comes to poverty alleviation policy and redistribution in their own societies the same governments are generally more cautious and even reluctant to act. That is also in the line with the conventional advice they get from international institutions and the business and finance community: first growth then – maybe – poverty alleviation.

The governments of the rich countries are almost all of them more or less ideologically committed to a policy of nonintervention and nonredistribution. The slogan and praxis of the 1980s was that rich must be richer to get the market to move. Now, when that policy has been tried, the idea seems to be that poor must be poorer to get the necessary flexibility and dynamics. With current world policy the future prospects are bleak.

Notes

1. Douglass C. North, Economic Performance through Time. Prize Lecture in Economic Science in memory of Alfred Nobel, Stockholm, December 9, 1993.
2. Hollis Chenery, et al., *Redistribution with Growth*. Oxford: Oxford University Press, 1974.
3. Simon Kuznets, *Quantitative Aspects of the Economic Growth of Nations*. 1960.
4. Simon Kuznets, *Modern Economic Growth: Rate, Structure, and Spread*. New Haven: Yale University Press, 1966.
5. Sudhir Anand and Ravi Kanbur, "Inequality and Development – A Critique." *Journal of Development Economics* 41 (1993).
6. Nancy Birdsall, David Ross, and Richard Sabot, "Inequality and Growth Reconsidered." Paper presented at the annual meeting of the American Economic Association, Boston, 1994.
7. Georg Sorensen, *Democracy and Democratization: Processes and Prospects in a Changing World*. Boulder, CO: Westview, 1993.

Section 2

Burst with Indignation Against Poverty

Maria de Lourdes Pintasilgo

In December 1993, the Independent Commission on Population and Quality of Life initiated a series of eight Regional Consultations with Public Hearings of groups and individuals. The first one was in Harare, with the English-speaking countries of the African continent, anticipated the testimony of some 400 people from all the NGOs of Zimbabwe, from regional associations, and state, academic, and private institutions. Would it be possible to find a common language among such diversified groups? Would any message come out of it? But as the hearings progressed, there was no doubt.

On the wall, in huge red letters, was their message: "We deserve a better Quality of Life" Then, one after the other, the groups explained, mimed, talked, sketched, and sang scenes of their lives (the old wondering why the land is not yielding as it used to; the women plotting ways to cope with violence in the street and at home; and the young without jobs, referring to sex as an escape, so eager to live a different life). Experts provided context, and civil servants described their efforts. All the time, there was a cry, as the young repeated their questions: "Is there anybody listening? Is there an echo? To whom shall I speak who will listen to me?" The questions were haunting.

Change and Complexity

This is not rhetoric. It is affirming the first precondition for change—that people will take things in their own hands and speak up, that they will refuse the fatalism and resignation of a magic thinking, and that they will start imagining how things could be, searching for partners who will listen to them in this interconnected world.

After the experts and international leaders listened, they must reexamine obsolete tools, programs, and mechanisms; grope for new concepts; and propose new modes of operation, Indeed, a map of still unchartered landscapes needs to be drawn up.

What will happen next? Of course, international conferences are part, but not all, of the answer. If what is said is to be implemented, it must be transformed with determination and imagination into political action. The question is: How ready is political action for change, for the jump needed?

At present, as the need for action grows more urgent, the political system seems less able to cope. Again and again in the last 20 years leaders have met at the highest levels in different fora and made important decisions from The Hague Declaration to Agenda 21. What has happened to their decisions?   Which mechanisms stopped the process of implementation? Why is it that enforcement in the social and economic area does not seem viable?

One striking example of the apparent powerlessness of the powerful was described publicly last June by a member of the G7. There he was, theoretically one of the seven men at the highest level of political power, saying to an international audience: "We cannot anymore entrust the evolution of the world to the monetary regulations." He went on to say: "We have to refuse the disappearance of development aid from the agenda of the rich countries Summit."

The questions then become: Who is deciding that agenda if not he? Who is deciding? Who is responsible for implementation? Where is the authority for enforcement?

These are not new questions. They gain momentum as we are witnessing the exponential complexity of the interwoven fabrics of ideas/events/ institutions. Indeed in a situation defined by complexity, there are multiple causes and effects interacting in unceasing movement. Each fact, event, sector of activity, and institution (national or international administration) is at the same time autonomous and interdependent. This is why any expression of conceptual and programmatic inconsistency has its counterpart in institutional anarchy. Governance is at stake there. But the governance needed today cannot bypass the complexity of reality.

Political Leadership

To cope with complexity, leaders have to know and interrelate the facts. They have to look at reality through different types of knowledge and from different sectors of society.   Such are the conditions for the much needed political vision. It is only then, in the interplay between a guiding vision and multifaceted reality, that true leadership can be exercised—a leadership that will bring about answers not only for the problems of today, but also—and maybe most of all—for the problems of the coming decades.

Indeed, demographers, among others, are pretty rigorous in establishing scenarios for tomorrow.   Among their questions: How many young people will there be, so that adequate educational facilities and jobs can be created? Equally, how many people will require old-age protection from the community? In what circumstances and for how long? It is not only

"numbers" the political leaders are compelled to see; it is also the modification of population structures, the speed of the urbanization processes,
the types of infrastructures needed, and the big migratory movements. Too
often, political action confines itself to macroeconomic management, while
the accumulation of pressing problems is much nearer and requires another
type of action.

It is time for leaders to hear what people are feeling and saying in very
diverse social, economic, and cultural situations. They do want the fabrics
of their lives—what really matters to them—to be of concern to politicians.
One man, in a public hearing in South Asia, denounced with indignation
the too easy replacement of real problems living people by indicators. For
him, this was a scandal—what he called a "Numbergate" scandal.

There are however other questions at the core of today's governance.
A fundamental one is can democracy in its present form contribute to the
guiding vision needed? Is our contemporary democratic culture able to
encompass the questions of today's complex society? Indeed, a long period
of time is needed to formulate and implement a vision that requires a
profound transformation of accepted concepts and institutions. And yet
democratic rule can only tackle the long-term through discreet, fragmented
units that correspond to the electoral cycles. In this context, is there a
way in which democratic rule may also be vision-oriented? Can democracy
contemplate the expected trends of the future, or is it bound and tied to
the unexpected events of the present? How can the two be combined?
These questions are decisive for the future, particularly for the wide array
of public policies connected with population.

Population policies should embody a vision—whether implicit or explicit. Indeed, a vision through which society, like the atom, may live in
harmony because of a continuous process of "conflicts and exchanges" in its
population composition. Such a harmony is rooted in the culture of each
society and in the values it cherishes. There the vision is one of a dynamic
population balance in the relationship between men and women; between
young and old; between those who are autonomous, actively earning their
living and those who are entrusted to the care of the community; and
between society and nature.

If vision is to be embodied in the short term, integrated policies in
social and economic areas are essential, particularly in health and education
policies. No population program can be carried out effectively without an
education program for both men and women and a network of primary
health care services. In the short term, these are preconditions for efficient
and humane programs.

If population policies are part and parcel of an integrated approach
to society's well-being, government itself must redirect public policy and
balance the conflicting demands. Let us be clear about our aspiration. If
we mean strong political action, this means more state intervention, state
regulation, and public initiative. These must be made compatible with the
current trends toward deregulation and a free market. To translate new
ideas into feasible policies and operational measures, it is impossible to
count on the market as an initiator or regulator. Whatever "natural laws"

may be guiding the market, its instincts are not enough to address the need for more jobs, for a direct fight against poverty, for stopping the degradation of the environment, and for developing the basic infrastructure needed for health and education. In order to take social development seriously, the economy must be regulated.

One important element of political action is that no leader can work democratically in isolation or only within a circle of colleagues and friends. Industrial society provided the concept and practice of social partners in questions of production, namely the trade unions. No policy of social development can be elaborated or made effective without the participation of those who are the main actors. The concept of social partner should be expanded to involve in the decision making those who are directly concerned with the questions at stake.

Thus, comprehensive population policies require dialogue with those who will live by them. By treating family planning as mere technology, we miss the boat. What we need are packages of development with family planning. At the national level, we must pursue the dialogue with all interested parties. This dialogue is indispensable. It is also the sign that political leadership is contributing to the empowerment of people, particularly of women.

Concerted International Action

In many different ways, we need concerted international action. But with the array of different organizations, institutes, organs, and agencies, how can one ensure integrated international policies?

The radical changes, which have taken place in technology in the last 50 years, are encompassed by changes in international institutions, which came into being through successive adjustments after World War II and which had nothing of the same radical zest. The split in institutions within the international machinery has led to serious inconsistencies in problems addressed, in strategies defined, and in actions undertaken.

This is notorious, for example, in the so much claimed concern with population matters. In all regions, but especially in countries with structural adjustment programs, the inconsistencies reach the level of the absurd. Indeed, how is it possible to carry on any population policy when the structural adjustment programs demand a reduction or control of public expenses? This automatically means a substantial cut in health and education. Even with the best intentions, different international agencies and representatives of bilateral agreements have different perspectives. The situation is totally unmanageable.

Today, what we need is a truly integrated approach to the field in both substance and machinery? International organizations and bilateral cooperation should work toward that end. As we look for new resources, it is clear that a new rationale will be needed to manage them. But it is also true that international institutions are modern tools of governance, and they must submit to democratic control by organs with political legitimacy.

Conceptual Breakthroughs

Important as they are, institutional reforms do not solve all problems. They must be accompanied by conceptual breakthroughs into new theoretical perspectives. The most important one concerns the end of the limitless horizon. It is easy to verify that the 1960s and 1970s were the climax of a vertiginous "always more." It is easy to demonstrate that resources are limited, that the planet, the land, the cities, the organization of society cannot proceed anymore with the expectation of endless growth. It is even easy to acknowledge that life is process of learning to accept personal limits.

But it is difficult to establish a paradigm that includes limits, which has entropy at its core. We need to formulate a new paradigm that we are dealing in the most acute way with the question of production and consumption patterns.

At the Cairo Conference on Population and Development, as well as in all the related literature, it was an acknowledged fact that in terms of the threat to the ecosystem and to future generations, population and consumption go together.

Apparently this is only a North–South divide. Twenty years ago, the community of nations was voting the new international economic order declaration, which was based culturally on the concept of endogenous development. What a change since then!

Conclusion

At present, all countries are following the same path, whether by choice of necessity, using the same pattern: the need to tackle scientifically this overwhelming tendency toward consumption scientifically.

The open question on production and consumption patterns illustrates a basic fact. For new ideas and concepts on social development to be effective, there is an urgent need for new economic tools, for new economic theories that incorporate a factor of flexibility. Paradoxically, at the moment when freedom in the economic field is the line of the day, economic science itself is still caught in the monolithic economic perceptions that characterized the Cold War period. Liberalism has become ever more dogmatic, unable to adjust itself to different sociological situations. Flexibility in economic theories is particularly in demand when the social development agenda assumes as its own the fight against poverty, a whole set of actions through which "freedom from want" is pursued. Running contrary to the monolithic perception of economies, the fight against poverty implies specific economic and social strategies aimed at the eradication of extreme poverty. This is a field where the contributions of all disciplines will be necessary. But most of all, this can only come about if, having burst with indignation against colonialism, against dictatorship, and against apartheid, we are sensitive enough to burst with indignation against poverty.

Section 3

The People Fix

Margaret Catley-Carlson

We who have lived in the second half of the twentieth century have had the privileged paradox of working in a field that was as unthinkable 100 years ago as it may seem archaic 100 years from now. We are workers, thinkers, advocates, and analysts of international development. This idea stems from the concept that people should reach across national borders to help each other.

It was not always so. The idea that people within nations should help each other has only taken hold imperfectly around the world; that taxation of the relatively rich should be used to help the relatively poor dates back only to that enormously productive period following World War II.

It is worth recalling that the 1943 Bengal famine, in which probably 3 million people died, did not call forth much of an international outcry. That the government did not observe the Famine Codes has made it into the history books, but state assistance did not exist. No international agencies or aid organizations were called to account—for none existed.

International development is constantly evolving. The development process that has undoubtedly helped to produce some remarkable progress in the world probably now needs to begin to be supplanted by new forms of international action. These should be based on different categories, different forms of resource flow, changing concepts of personal security, and heavy demands for emergency and civil stabilization assistance. There are forces affecting poor people in rich societies and rich people in poor societies; these have not yet been touched. There are many places in the world, many groups of people, and many needs that development assistance has not reached.

Some would say that international developers succeeded missionaries. Although missionaries are sometimes viewed as people whose beliefs so prohibited them from enjoying life in their own countries that they traveled abroad to convert others, they may well have been sincere people suffering from the meddler's itch.

That is what infects and inspires—the itch to see processes go faster. We want to see birthrates decline faster, food productivity increase faster, people living longer, more people in school, better transportation, and an improved capacity to seize the world's possibilities. We use investments to try to accelerate the pace of these positive developments.

Population: Nightmares and Visions

Most people do not need to be told why population worries us; it is seen as a problem on the global agenda. The issue is, of course, some rather incredible numbers and very worrying trends. There are a lot of people around. As of January 1994, the world population is 5.7 billion people. The growth is far from finished. Depending on what we do in the next 10 years, it will continue to grow until some number between 8.5 billion and—an almost unimaginable worse-case scenario—15 billion. The fastest growth is occurring now. It took 1 million years—until the nineteenth century—for the world population to reach 1 billion. Now, this growth happens in a decade, and it will indeed happen over the next two decades.

Why is this a concern? It is not because of some celestial adding machine producing numbers that only demographers can see. It is the impact that this population growth will have on food availability, the struggle against poverty, the environment, water resources, political stresses and tensions, and the goals and health of individuals, particularly women.

Let us make no mistake about it. If environment is our main concern, we should not be looking in the present to the developing world. Environmental problems in this decade are largely the creation of the consumption, energy use, and waste disposal patterns of the industrialized world.

But where development is concerned, the rate of growth is the issue. The billion per decade in this decade, the next, and possibly the one following are happening in our lifetimes—for many of us in our working lifetimes. This is why the "IF" game has elements of Russian roulette.

- IF we managed world water differently, everyone would have enough to drink, floods would be controlled, and agriculture would be improved. But are there any signs of this happening?

- IF Africa accounted for more than 1 percent of global trade and had more than the same GNP as Belgium, then it could support more people. But are there any signs of the factors that will change this during this time of unprecedented population growth?

- IF we distributed food differently, everyone would have enough to eat. But are the changes in the way the world eats moving in the right direction? Or cereal production per person? Or fish catches?

- IF the world's trading regimes were more open, there would be more opportunity for the poor of any number. But are markets opening in the direction of the poor?

This population growth will also produce political stresses and tensions. Europe, with its rapidly declining population rates, has really changed. Its share of the world's population dropped from 15 percent in 1950 to 9 percent in 1991; by 2020, it will be 6 percent. In contrast, Africa now accounts for about 10 percent of the world's population. Before its population stabilizes, it will account for 25 percent; by current trends, these will be poor people.

Population is growing fastest where people are poorest. The biggest problems can be found in countries where 40 to 50 percent of the population is under 15 years of age. There is a high degree of parallelism between the 50 or so countries with per capita income under $3 per day per year and those that will double their populations in a little more than two decades.

Migration pressures are building up at enormous levels. It has always been so. When England, Scotland, Belgium, and The Netherlands were doubling their populations every 25 years, people also left in droves. In the nineteenth century, 20 million people left the United Kingdom. Now, as many as 100 million people, mostly from developing countries, are working legally or illegally in other countries.

Above all, this level of fertility brings some very staggering human implications. In the developing world alone:

- about 50 percent of conceptions are unplanned.
- research suggests that between 25 and 40 percent of all pregnancies are not wanted.
- more women die in India in one week from maternity-related conditions than in Europe in an entire year.
- 150,000 pregnancies are terminated every day by induced abortion — about two-thirds under legal conditions, which does not always mean safe; about one-third under illegal conditions, which too often means unsafe conditions.
- Every three minutes a woman dies from an unsafe abortion. In ethical terms, that is certainly bad news — for the woman, for her family, for all of us.

What Is Going On: Clarifying the Vision

This enormous growth is one of the characteristics of the demographic transition through which our global civilization is passing. It is unique. It never happened before. It will never happen again. It is a phenomenon of the last 200 years. And it will be finished in another 100 or 150 years. We are living in it.

What is it? A term used to describe the change from high birth rates and high death rates, where a very high percentage of the population dies before the normal life span. Most die in the first year or before five years of age. Thereafter, they probably die of infections diseases. They evolve to societies with low birth rates and low death rates, within which most of the death takes place in the last ten years of life expectancy. The cause of death tends to be chronic disease, genetic diseases, and diseases of lifestyle.

The transition took place in Europe in the last part of the nineteenth century, without the benefits of modern contraception. It took place in the first half of the twentieth century in North America, with some contraception. Once modern contraceptives became available, they certainly became the method of choice for 74 percent of the industrialized world and now over 50 percent of the developing world. This is in itself an extraordinary transition.

The demographic transition is underway everywhere in the world right now. The rate differs, but the phenomenon is the same. It is in all of our interests to accelerate this transition. It is in all of our interests to hasten the year in which the planet will have its peak population. The earlier this happens, the smaller this number will be.

Once traditional societies have completed this transition from subsistence and agriculturally based economies to modern industrialized economies, the desire for family size usually drops to around two children. On a global level, this is replacement fertility, or stability. But this transition may take a long time — too long a time.

Nigeria, with just under 100 million people now, will have more than 600 million if its fertility stabilizes in 2040; the number will be closer to 350 million if stability were reached in two decades — 2010. In Bangladesh, if it takes another generation after the year 2020 to reach stability, another 70 million will have been born.

If we had all the time in the world, a larger planet, and more resources, we could wait the process out. If there were not as much tangible evidence of the impact of population density and population pressures on the well-being of people alive today, on other species, and on our ecosystem, we could relax. We could assume that the secular forces of change would eventually bring about fertility decline.

Achieving the Possible

There are three demographic imperatives we can take to hasten the transition. It is easiest to discuss these by analyzing what factors are contributing to the doubling of population that the world will experience in the next century. Population in the developing countries will increase from 4.5 to 10 billion.

Unmet Need

According to reliable surveys, in country after country one finds that one-fourth of women and their families would have postponed or avoided approximately their last full-term pregnancy had methods been available to them. Thank goodness for our world that this does not mean that 25 percent of children are unwanted or unloved. But it does mean that we have a global opportunity.

In addition to those now using contraception, women around the world would have preferred to delay or avoid about 25 percent of all pregnancies that take place. About 100 million more women would use contraception if it was available and of high quality. African women are no exception. Although family size desires are very different, the lowest amount of unmet need revealed in surveys of any African country is 20 percent—and the numbers ranges up to 45 or 50 percent.

If we met the needs of these women all around the world, we might raise contraception prevalence to between 60 and 65 percent. Let us note that 75 percent is enough to reach replacement levels. In developing countries, stability would be reached at 8 billion, instead of 10 billion.

So, providing quality contraceptive services to meet this unmet need is obviously the first line of action. If this demand were met with real quality care, the demand would grow even more. The bill for this would not be exorbitant; we would need to double the $5 billion spent today on contraceptives and services, with developing countries providing about three-fourths of this amount.

Yet, even if we meet this demand, we are still less than one-third of the way to population stabilization.

Fertility

Fertility would still be well above the replacement level of two births per family because desired family size is still higher than two in virtually all of the developing countries. An extensive survey program conducted in 27 countries in Asia, Africa, and Latin America in the late 1980s found not a single country with a desired family size at or close to two children. These surveys document a preference for large numbers of children in Sub-Saharan Africa, with an average desired family size of about six children, while in most countries of Latin America, Asia, and North Africa, the average desired number of surviving children was between three and four.

These preferences for high fertility and the social and economic insecurity that underlie them are fundamental causes of high birth rates and rapid population growth. For us to achieve replacement level fertility, women, on average, will need to bear only two surviving children.

In having high desired family size, women are acting in response to their perceptions of likely survival of children, and of the need for children to help meet the needs of the family and provide care for the parents in later years. These perceptions will be affected significantly by another perception—whether comprehensive social and economic development is or is not making a tangible impact on their lives.

We have to go deeper into why most of the world's families still want more than two children. Put simply, meeting the unmet demand for family planning—although vital—is an inadequate approach. We must create conditions—through selective, creative, and ethically sound social investment—for women and couples to seek a lower number of surviving children.

Luckily, these are positive things to do. Infant survival is key. We also have to enroll girls in school. Girls with seven years of schooling on average want two children less than girls with no schooling. We will also have to take steps to eliminate gender inequality in schooling, but we have working and affordable models for this. They include lower or no school fees for girls, subsidized books, adjustable school hours and months, parental involvement, and women teachers.

We also need to eliminate legal barriers to a women's right to inherit and access to the marketplace. We have to ensure better access to credit for women and more entry into the cash economy. Small steps yield large results; it is not necessary to achieve perfection before change happens.

Not all of this is about domestic policy. If women in developing countries working in export manufacturing plants have been dismissed because those exports have encountered new protectionist barriers, how effective can family planning promotion be? These women have now been cast by distant economic forces back into nonemployment and traditional childbearing roles for their only support and security.

The necessary factors ultimately include better distribution of productive assets, including land and credit; open access to market opportunities; and social safety nets for those who are bypassed by the markets. We need a far more equitable distribution of responsibilities in the family, especially with regard to the care of children. We must continue to emphasize the reduction of infant mortality.

Population Momentum

This is the third megaforce with which we must content. Even if from 1995 on every women in the developing world had only 2.1 children, we would still increase the global population to 7.3 billion. This population momentum is a powerful demographic force. Since we are not going to move to 2.1 children right away, we will not get away with as few as 7.3 billion. But it does show a third window of opportunity.

For the sake of the planet and the health of the women on it, we have to become more serious about stopping the "too early, too often" birth pattern that still persists in many places. In Nigeria, 17 percent of 15-year-old girls give birth.

If the first birth in developing countries could be delayed by five years, global population would stabilize at 6.1 billion instead of 7.3 billion, still using our model. Later marriage in many societies could also have a significant effect—as significant as the introduction of new contraceptives. Teenage pregnancy has a demographic effect as well as an often devastating human effect. The dangers to a girl under 18 giving birth are a factor of 3 to 4 times what they are for women between 21 and 24.

Conclusion

In order to secure the future, we must improve our vision. Clearly, we must focus on meeting the unmet need for contraception around the world. There are 747 million women of reproductive age, 350 million of whom are not using contraceptives and 100 million of whom would prefer to space the next birth or to have no more children. Let us concentrate our attention and our resources on the reproductive health needs of these women and their families. In the many pages of the Cairo document, this is what emerges; this is where the money must go first. Reproductive health is the right of all the world's women, and it includes, but is not limited to, contraceptive availability.

We can demand that population programs have a higher priority in national programs around the world. Population is bigger than family planning; all those measures that reduce desired family size and promote later marriage come into play here. We must similarly demand that development assistance programs give higher priority to this issue. With only 2 percent of the official development assistance from donor countries, most contraceptive needs could be funded. With 20 percent centered on human resource development, we could go a long way to meeting the other needs as well.

We must recognize and demand—in our own societies and around the world—social and economic policies that stress the development of human resources. The countries that build up a healthy, educated, well-trained workforces experience slower population growth and faster GNP growth. What could make more ethical or economic sense?

We must become enemies of the quick fix. Whether in migration, family planning, international development, or teenage pregnancies, there are no quick fixes. We must accept and advocate patient change strategies that encompass small changes across a wide spectrum of issues.

We must reject coercion; we must understand and advocate that the best and most effective long-term way to achieve our demographic targets is by meeting the development needs of the world and the reproductive health needs of our populations. We need choice, service, privacy, follow-up, and quality. The total cost is the equivalent of days of military expenditure; we must look at it in these terms.

There are things we can do to ensure a healthier planet. We are strengthened by the vision of those who have gone before us. Stephen Wise put it well: "Vision looks inward and becomes a duty. Vision looks outward and becomes aspiration. Vision looks upward and becomes faith." Let us keep faith.

Section 4

Women's Empowerment

Khadija Haq

The worst victims of poverty and social discrimination are women. Yet most poverty elimination and social integration strategies forget women as a group. Those strategies try to be gender neutral, but they often end up as gender indifferent. In such indifference lie the seeds of their very failure.

Any successful strategy for an effective attack on global poverty must reach out to women. The liberation of women from poverty must not come about through a welfare approach that treats women as a residual of development, but through an empowerment approach that treats women as the vanguard for the elimination of poverty. Development paradigms must be newly engendered for all people first strategies. The empowerment of women must increasingly be seen as the most important strategy in any attack on poverty.

Who Are the Really Poor?

Out of the billion people who live in poverty, 80 percent are in the rural areas of the development world; women comprise a large percentage of them. The number of rural women living in absolute poverty rose by 50 percent during the last two decades according to the International Fund for Agricultural Development (IFAD).[1] them are in Asia and Sub-Saharan Africa.

Although the responsibility of women for food production is recognized, women have least access to means of production, receive the lowest wages, and are least knowledgeable about improving the productivity of land through modern inputs and technology. As a result of rural male migration to urban areas or to other countries has increased the number of female-headed households that carry the full burden of income generation and household management without any augmenting reciprocal strategies and facilities to enable women to perform these tasks.

Under the strain of the debt crisis and structural adjustment policies, unemployment of women has increased. As a result, their purchasing power has declined. Inflation and elimination of subsidies has meant that women have to work longer hours to provide food for their children. This leaves then less time to spend with their children and no time to rest. Armed conflicts, civil strife, and ethnic tensions all lead to the impoverishment of women. Strategies for fighting poverty must be clearly targeted to poor women and children. As James Grant said, "Children and women can be our Trojan horse for attacking poverty, for ungirding democracy, dramatically slowing population growth, and accelerating economic growth."[2]

Is the Welfare Approach the Answer?

The traditional approach to the alleviation of poverty has been top down. The poor are treated as victims and not as contributors to economic and social development. Special programs, such as food price subsidies and food rations, public employment schemes, and income transfers are designed to offer a safety net to the poor. Properly targeted and administered in a cost-effective manner, these can play an important role in protecting the poor from the short-term impact of the loss of income. Particularly in the case of rural women, to whom poverty is a pervasive characteristic of their existence, these programs provide a social safety net in countries with no other system of social security. But, we must ensure that by empowering women the need for welfare programs ceases to exist. We must not confuse short-term relief with long-term sustainable strategy. The only permanent solution for the poverty of women is to create an environment in which women can stand on their own, in which they can emerge out of a dependency situation, in which they can have equal access to economic and social opportunities by building up their own capabilities. In other words, empowerment of women is the only realistic and long-term strategy to liberating them from the ravages of poverty.

Why Empowerment of Women Is Critical

Poverty is both a cause and effect of high population growth, environmental degradation, and inadequate access of women to means of production. The worst forms of poverty persist because women lack status, education, and opportunities. This leads to early marriage and repeated pregnancies. To break this cycle, the empowerment of women through education, health care, family planning services, and access to means of production is a precondition.

To focus on the processes that create poverty, it is important to isolate those that are responsible for the low status ad disempowerment of women. For the long-term sustainable elimination of poverty, there can be no better approach than the empowerment of women through gender-sensitized planning and operational strategy.

What Are the Most Important Areas of Empowerment?

Three areas stand out as critical for women's empowerment. These are basic education and skills training; basic health, nutrition, and family planning; and credit to encourage self-employment and income generation.

Education

The first element in any empowerment strategy is education and skills training, which provide the foundation for better health, nutrition, and income earning capability. The principal asset of the poor is their labor. Education increases the productivity of this asset. Educating poor children greatly improves their chances of escaping poverty. Research has amply demonstrated the close link between education and poverty reduction through enhancement of economic growth, improved agricultural productivity, which contributes to income equality, and providing such noneconomic returns as reducing fertility and improving the quality of life.

Sufficient evidence has also been accumulated to show the beneficial impact of the education of women on economic productivity, family health and nutrition, and on an understanding of their political and legal rights. Many studies have shown a positive correlation between women's education and socioeconomic development. According to the World Bank's 1990 *World Development Report*, one year of schooling for mothers has been associated with a 9 percent decrease in the under five-years-of-age child mortality rate.

The Declaration of the Education Summit of the Nine High Population Countries in 1993 recognized that "the education and empowerment of girls and women are important tools themselves and are key factors in contributing to social development, well-being, and education of present and future generations." Larry Summers, a former chief economist of the World Bank, argued that "educating girls quite possibly yields a higher rate of return than any other investment available in the developing world."

Basic primary education, complemented by skills training and knowledge relevant to the various roles of women, is the most important empowerment tool for the elimination of poverty.

Health Facilities

The second element in any empowerment strategy is to liberate women from the constant fear of illness and premature death. Although this requires a comprehensive strategy for health care for women throughout their lives, two aspects are particularly important in the developing world.

First, essential family planning services must be available. Such services enable women to control the spacing of their children, to avoid the tragic risk of unwanted pregnancies and illegal abortions, and to combine their reproductive responsibilities with their economic roles. High fertility rates and low contraception rates in the least development countries of Asia and Sub-Saharan Africa make it impossible for women to break out of the poverty cycle. Because family planning programs enable women to acquire control over their own bodies, they are viewed as the programs that enable women to gain access to market opportunities. Programs for reducing child mortality and malnutrition should also be seen in this context. When child mortality rates decline, parents respond by having fewer children.

Second, one of the most disgraceful manifestations of the low status of women is the extremely high rate of maternal mortality. In developing countries, maternal mortality rates average 420 per 100,000 deliveries; in Sub-Saharan Africa, it is as high as 700. Compare this with only 24 maternal deaths per 100,000 in the industrial world. In other words, the maternal mortality rate is 18 times as high in the developing world as in the industrial world — the largest gap in any health indicator. Although all other health indicators have shown tremendous improvement in the last three decades, particularly infant and child mortality rates, the North–South gaps in maternal mortality have increased. This shows that developing societies regard the health and well-being of women as such a low priority that they are not willing to spare even small amounts for the provision of trained midwives at the time of birth. Unless maternal mortality rates are drastically lowered and women are liberated from this constant fear, their access to market opportunities will always remain limited.

Credit Facilities

The third most potent weapon for women's empowerment is the availability of credit. Even when human capabilities are improved through education and health, they need to be used effectively. Often, credit facilities are denied to women because they can offer little in the way of collateral; they are regarded as appendages to their husbands' financial and social positions and not as independent human beings.

Several credit plans have been designed to provide credit directly to poor women and to encourage self-employment and income generating activities. The most successful has been the Grameen Bank in Bangladesh, which serves as a pattern for many other developing countries. The Grameen Bank destroyed the myth that poor women, particularly in rural areas, are not creditworthy. It demonstrated that they are far more reliable and far better risks than influential industrialists in urban areas or feudal landlords in rural areas. More than 90 percent of the total credit of the Grameen Bank has been given to poor rural women. The amounts are small — $60 per person is the average. No subsidy or handout is given. In fact, the Grameen Bank charges a slightly higher interest rate than the market rate to cover the extra administrative costs of these small loans. And yet all of these loans have been used well. The recovery rate has been over 95 percent, compared with a recovery rate of less than 66 percent of the loans given to the mostly male urban rich in the developing world.

Small credit plans are certainly the most important element in any successful attack on poverty. They are also the most liberating force for poor women who realize for the first time that they are being treated as equal and respectable members of society. It is a precious gift for women's empowerment and for utilizing the latent talent of all members of society.

Of particular importance to rural women is the development of legal measures and the administrative machinery to improve their access to land. Research has shown that a rural woman's customary land rights have been increasingly threatened by agrarian reform measures. These measures have tended to redistribute land titles to men or tenancy rights to male heads of households.

Although a majority of developing countries have signed the Convention on the Elimination of All Forms of Discrimination Against Women (CEDAW), progress in eliminating discriminatory parts of civil, family, and labor laws, as well as financial regulations, has been slow. More importantly, in almost all countries, the gap between existing laws and their enforcement has limited women's access to productive resources.

Conclusion

Poverty elimination strategies should not only treat women as the worst victims of poverty, which they certainly are, but also as potential agents of change. It is the positive contributions of women to development and change that must be recognized if the world is to graduate from a welfare approach to poverty to an empowerment approach. Empowering women by improving their capacities and providing equal access to market opportunities is the only reliable strategy for liberating societies from the continuing burden of poverty. Investment in education, health, and credit is the core of women's empowerment. Such empowerment is the beginning of a more dynamic strategy for putting people first.

Notes

1. IFAD, *The State of World Rural Poverty*, 1992.
2. James Grant, Address to the International Development Conference, Washington, D.C., 1993.

Part 2

Expansion of Productive Employment

The Employment Challenge[1]

Azizur Rahman Khan

This section investigates the question: Which policies will do most to create decent jobs in sufficient numbers? In recent years, a consensus has emerged that developing countries must achieve macroeconomic stability as a precondition for growth. But stability may not ensure the expansion of employment, and may not ensure sustained and equitable growth of incomes. Not only is there a need for creative government policies and interventions, but also for a better external environment, including faster growth in OECD countries and a redirection of aid flows.

Economic policy exists to deliver social progress, which is denied where there is high and persistent unemployment. In the mid-1990s, high unemployment characterizes the economies of the world's richest and poorest countries alike. Something has gone wrong.

Unemployment has risen, and stubbornly persisted, as the world's economies grow increasingly interdependent. National economies are being ever more closely tied to each other by global pacts (such as that which concluded the Uruguay Round of the GATT) and by regional arrangements (such as the European Union and the North American Free Trade Agreement [NAFTA]).

Even without such arrangements, new technologies by their own momentum promote economic integration. The revolution in communications moves goods, services, and capital around the world at a rate never seen in history. New manufacturing techniques make possible unprecedented increases in productivity. Humankind can at last hope for a future in which poverty has been abolished.

But the immediate problem centers on too little production and too few jobs. Economic integration makes it impossible for any one country to make a dash for growth and jobs on its own. The problem is global; thus the solution must be global as well.

Of course, situations look different in different places. In East and Southeast Asia (including China), output and employment have been growing dramatically, but parts of that successful region lag sadly behind. In South Asia, absolute poverty is being reduced, but the growth of employment is precarious, and much valuable work is paid at levels barely sufficient to keep families alive. The relative success of those regions, containing almost half of the world's populace, proves there is no reason to despair. But the achievement is fragile. Even there, far more remains to be done before the unemployment crisis can be considered solved.

In the rest of the world, entire generations of people grow up believing that it is unrealistic to hope for productive, remunerative, and reasonably secure jobs. Societies that fail to offer that prospect are bound to be socially unstable and economically insecure. The likely rates of output and labor force growth point to the danger of increasing unemployment if policies do not change.

The pace of change is, in fact, overwhelming whole sectors of economic activity. Those displaced from their jobs are often not equipped to work in the new activities that emerge. When new jobs are created, they are often less well paid, less secure, and of lower quality than those that disappear.

Without concerted international action across national frontiers and occupational differences, unemployment and its attendant miseries seem bound to persist, even to worsen. The prospect is intolerable, yet techniques exist for improving it. This section offers an overview of the world employment scene and of ways in which it can be made brighter by international cooperation through a global compact for growth.

The trend toward world economic integration gathered pace in the early 1990s, promoted by international agreements and circumstances. The following are some examples:

- The completion in early 1994 of the Uruguay Round of negotiations in the GATT has set the scene for a worldwide opening of trade.
- Regional blocs (in North America, for a start) have been set up to foster free trade.
- Trade in services, although not adequately measured, seems to have grown much faster than trade in goods.
- The former centrally planned economies are being integrated (although at a low level of activity) with the rest of the world economy.
- Barriers to the international movement of capital have been reduced.
- The international migration of labor has grown fast, albeit subject to new restrictions.

These developments impose new constraints upon purely national economic policies. They limit taxation, interest rates, exchange rates, and public-sector deficits. They make protected industries unviable and unable to sustain their labor forces, however lavishly governments may support them. In particular, they make it almost impossible to increase the relative price of labor in one country. Thus solutions must be sought across national frontiers, by concerted action.

Recent history shows what happens when countries try, and fail, to escape on their own from the unemployment trap. The economic woes of the 1980s followed the economic shocks of the 1970s. The sudden rise (and subsequent fall) of energy prices after 1973 encouraged massive and unsustainable international lending. Soaring interest rates and huge government deficits in countries at all stages of development were followed by a worldwide epidemic of inflation.

In reaction, many governments suddenly retrenched, often under pressure from international lenders. Stability, not dynamism, became the watchword. World trade slowed down; the annual average rate of growth in world merchandise exports was 6.6 percent in the 1965–1980 period and 4.1 percent between 1980 and 1991. As industrial activity declined in the industrialized nations, the prices of primary commodities fell, impoverishing the producing countries.

Seeking to redress the harm done by inflation, the industrialized countries tolerated what they hoped would be temporarily high levels of unemployment. Many of them raised new protective barriers against imports: the World Bank (1991) estimated that in the previous decade, 20 of the 24 member countries of the Organization for Economic Cooperation and Development (OECD) became more protectionist, especially against competing products from developing countries.

None of these restrictive policies worked as they were meant to. True, inflation was curbed almost everywhere, and governments prophesied that monetary stability would, of its own accord, stimulate growth. But unemployment continued to increase and where (as in the United States) it eventually started to roll back, rates of pay for the new, unskilled jobs were far lower than those prevailing before the recession. Inequality increased, and so did the sense of deprivation. Meanwhile, in the poorest countries, life grew worse. If one examines region by region the world employment situation in the mid-1990s, the picture is decidedly gloomy.

Unemployment in the 1990s

Similar employment problems are faced by seven groups of countries, each of which has attempted a broadly similar solution. These geographical groups are, of course, economically diverse, and the figures relating to them may look different, depending (for example) on whether their incomes are calculated on the basis of exchange rates or of purchasing-power parities.

With those reservations, we can examine the world labor force along with growth rates and income levels.[2] These data show that rapid proportional increases in the labor force expected in the Middle East and throughout Africa, from north to south, in addition to the vast absolute increase in the labor force that will occur in South Asia.

In the relatively rich industrialized nations that belong to the OECD, economic growth has begun again. But jobs are growing more slowly than output, and even where (as in the United States) unemployment has fallen, new jobs pay less for less-skilled workers and are less secure than those that were eliminated during the latest recession.

Eastern Europe is leaping from central planning towards a market system for which its peoples and institutions are wholly unprepared. The transition has wiped away many jobs, without putting others in their place. Subsidies, intended to cushion this effect, demand massive government spending without providing government revenue. This contributes to inflation, which makes the new poor even poorer.

Latin America and the Caribbean face rapid growth in the working-age population, in the number of women in the labor force, and in the shift from rural to urban employment. At the same time, governments are reducing the size of and employment in the public sector. The new jobs that are being created are almost all in the informal sector, unregulated and uncounted.

The Middle East and North Africa confront the consequences both of recent population growth and of a sharp decline in the oil revenues upon which the region's potential prosperity depends. Governments can no longer act as the employer of last resort, especially for graduates from the vastly expanded university systems. The resulting social instability prevents governments from tackling reforms that they know to be desirable.

In Sub-Saharan Africa, the crisis is at its fiercest. With almost three-fourths of the region's people living in rural areas and their numbers increasing at an unprecedented rate, figures for employment and job creation are at best sketchy. More than half of all nonfarm employees work for governments, which clearly cannot afford to hire more or to raise the real wages of those whom they do employ. The process of structural adjustment devised for the heavily indebted African countries has not yet been translated into increases in employment, or reductions in absolute poverty.

East and Southeast Asia show rapid growth both in general economic activity and in employment. Typically, the state sector is small, labor markets are lightly regulated, and policies are devised to favor private employers. Exports have been carefully promoted by manipulated exchange rates. Social stability and equality of incomes have been shielded by protection against imports, especially of farm staples such as rice. A low priority has been given to human rights, especially to freedom for workers' associations and the promotion of opportunities for women. There are signs, in countries such as the Republic of Korea, that economic progress is being followed by social progress.

China, as befits its size, is a unique case. A headlong rush for economic liberalization has contributed to astonishing (and probably unsustainable) rates of economic growth and a rapid decline in poverty. This has been achieved under tight political control, with no concessions to human rights or the rights of workers.

South Asia consists entirely of low-income countries that export no oil. On the whole, they survived the shocks of the oil and debt crisis rather well. But they need to create huge numbers of jobs, because women are joining the labor force rapidly, just as large numbers of young people of both sexes enter the labor market. A surging flow of labor from farms into the cities has also occurred, but productive employment in agriculture may grow. Governments are reducing the labor market restrictions that make many large enterprises (especially in the state sector) uncompetitive.

"Jobless Growth" – or Benign Transition

The contrast in performance between the world's most and least successful regions is sharp and bitter. East and Southeast Asia are enjoying unprecedented growth of both real incomes and employment. Africa and the Middle East confront a potential catastrophe of demographic growth and economic failure. Meanwhile, the industrial countries of the OECD are baffled by the persistence of unemployment amid prosperity.

The facts do not support the view that the world is inexorably set on a path of "jobless growth," by which technological progress will benefit a few and disadvantage the many. New technologies have created, and made possible, many millions of jobs in most regions. Employment has grown fastest in economies that have grown fastest.

Where unemployment crisis exists, it has been created not by chance but by error – by incentives that distort and institutions that are inadequate. For example, national policies have often been mistakenly devised to promote capital investment, when labor-intensive production was what the country needed. Before the debt shock of the late 1970s, the economies of Latin America were growing fast, but they created far fewer jobs than have recently been developed in Asia's economic boom.

National governments borrowed imprudently for unproductive purposes and thus made necessary the structural adjustment programs about which their successor governments now understandably complain. Excessive borrowing fostered domestic inflation. The attempt to curb that inflation brought about recession. Today, the fight against inflation continues, even now that the battle is largely won, and the jobs crisis is more menacing than the monetary one.

External influences imposed the debt crisis and also helped to impose its successor, the employment crisis. Monetary restraint in the industrial countries brought growth there to a halt. They therefore reduced their imports from primary-producing developing countries. Those developing countries – especially the weakest of them, heavily dependent on commodity exports – in turn suffered recession.

In particular, the OECD countries limited domestic borrowing by increasing their interest rates. These rates rose everywhere, above all in the developing countries that had borrowed heavily, such as those in Latin America. Capital stopped flowing from the OECD countries to the developing world; this limited the developing countries' ability to buy goods and services from the OECD countries and made their recovery harder. It was a vicious circle that must be broken in the future.

Domestic Policies

The importance of domestic policies is self-evident. The East Asian economies that in the 1980s avoided stagnation and unemployment did so because they got their domestic policies right. Prudent borrowing, creative use of exchange rates, promotion of exports, protection of food producers, restraint of nominal wages—all these factors combined to keep the growth of employment in step with overall economic growth. Other nations and regions should look carefully at the implications.

Without sound domestic policies, no country will progress toward the goal of prosperity and full employment. A stable and noninflationary currency, a high rate of savings and investment, and prudent management of exchange rates, are necessary preconditions for sustainable growth. Yet many countries still lack civil peace, the rule of law, and the efficient delivery of public administration. In so far as the international community can help to install good governance, it should endeavor to do so.

The most important contribution that national governments can make to economic growth and the efficiency of the labor market is through education and training. Overwhelming evidence shows that the best investment countries can make is in basic education, especially of women. Women's education reduces birth rates and improves children's health. The *World Development Report* (1992) of the World Bank noted that improving girls' education contributes to environmental conservation and sustainable development.

Governments can ease the transfer of employment from declining to growing sectors by new forms of social security and temporary income supplements, and by ensuring the transferability of pensions and benefits such as health insurance.

As some economic sectors decline and others rise, the opportunities to increase employment in declining sectors should not be forgotten. For example, investment in irrigation may create new jobs in labor-intensive agriculture, while the general farm labor force continues to decline. Equally, service industries can often develop new and profitable markets, with a high potential for employment by adapting to match new forms of demand.

International Policies

Interdependence between nations has increased and will continue to increase; no solution can work unless it takes that into consideration. In the 1980s, the growth of world trade slowed markedly for most groups of countries, and where trade faltered, unemployment rose.[3]

Between 1980 and 1991:

- The OECD's share of world exports increased sharply, from 63 percent to 72 percent. Meanwhile, the OECD's trade with the developing countries fell sharply, from 30 percent to 20 percent as a share of OECD's imports. Falling oil prices speeded this decline.

- Asia's share of world exports rose, while that of the other developing countries declined. In particular, OECD imports of Asian manufactures rose sharply.

- As the developing countries' trade with the OECD countries declined, their trade among themselves increased significantly (from a low base).

This increase was wholly accounted for by Asian countries.

- The largest proportional increase in international trade took place between China and the rest of East and Southeast Asia. But the figures may be deceptive; much trade with China was not recorded, for political reasons.

- The OECD's terms of trade improved, while the terms of trade of Africa and the Middle East grew dramatically worse.

- The OECD countries reduced their imports because they were in recession, then reduced them still further by protectionist import restrictions. Non-Asian developing countries failed to increase their exports.

- Capital flowed from the developing to the developed nations. in 1985, largely because of heavy debt repayments, the reverse flow of capital towards the rich nations was as high as US$30.2 billion.

The worst may be over. Recently, there has been a general, if fragile, recovery in most commodity prices (but not in oil). Real interest rates fell dramatically in the early 1990s, but they may be heading up again. Capital is flowing toward the developing countries by US$26.8 billion in 1992 (but much of that was short-term lending, and the poorest countries of Africa felt little benefit). Several heavily indebted countries have escaped from the trap; strengthened by capital inflows, they are borrowing on international markets.

A few developing countries achieved high growth of their economies and of employment, while the OECD's recession was at its zenith. Now the OECD's recession may be ending. The World Bank has recently projected an overall annual growth rate of 2.6 percent for the OECD economies in the 1994 to 2003 period. Yet if growth is to gather pace throughout the developing world, faster OECD growth is essential.

In particular, economic expansion in the OECD countries would revive Africa's export performance and improve Africa's terms of trade. Among the main beneficiaries would be the OECD countries themselves, whose African markets would expand quickly.

Like the generals in the old story, the governments of the industrial world would have readied themselves to fight the last battle: the battle against inflation. But the real enemy in the mid-1990s is not inflation, but unemployment.

Careful monetary expansion by the OECD countries would, to be sure, entail some risk of renewing inflation. But high unemployment throughout the OECD should help to ensure that wage increases do not contribute to inflation. And the risk of inflation would be much reduced if the expanding countries kept pace with each other, and did not seek to gain a competitive advantage in the process. By increasing, in concert, domestic demand, they would put to work large numbers of their own unemployed. Soon that increased demand would translate itself into higher commodity prices enabling the poorest developing countries to increase their imports. This, in turn, would promote the noninflationary growth of exports from the OECD countries. Everybody would gain – especially the unemployed in rich and poor countries alike.

Freer Trade, Better Aid

With the conclusion (and it is to be hoped, speedy ratification) of the Uruguay Round of bargaining in the GATT, the conditions have been established for worldwide freer trade in goods and services. That was a necessary precondition for speeding the growth of economic activity. International cooperation is more than ever necessary if full advantage is to be taken of the opportunity to put more people to work.

We have seen that, in the bad years on the 1980s, many industrialized countries sought to mitigate the effects of recession by restricting imports, and thus made recovery harder for themselves. Opening borders to the flow of trade would reverse that damage. In 1993, the World Bank made the following estimate: "Total exports from China, Jamaica, Pakistan, Thailand and the Philippines would increase by at least 40 percent if OECD tariff barriers were removed. Other countries would gain even more...." In particular, several countries specializing in exports of textiles and clothing would benefit dramatically, with corresponding gains in their ability to import from the OECD itself.

Poor countries, where real wages are low, obviously have a competitive advantage in labor-intensive manufacturing. If rich countries import more low-price goods, they will obviously employ fewer of their own people in low-wage jobs. If economic growth is fast enough, the lost jobs will be replaced by new jobs demanding higher skills and paying higher wages. But this process cannot be left to chance. Governments and social partners must work together to ease the transition, especially in retraining displaced workers and in ensuring that labor markets operate humanely and efficiently.

In the industrialized countries, ill-considered protectionist measures are often called for as a response to cheap imports or against the failure of exporting countries to safeguard workers' rights. But trade restrictions defeat their own objective. They reduce the rate of economic growth, and thus in turn increase unemployment. When unemployment is high, workers' conditions rarely improve, and their rights are rarely acknowledged. In this respect, too, progress can best be made by cooperation, not confrontation. Exporting and importing countries must work together to raise standards without resorting to protectionism; only exceptional circumstances can justify restraints on the growth of trade.

Trade should grow rapidly in the coming decade, especially because of the conclusion of the Uruguay Round and the creation or strengthening of regional free trade pacts. According to the GATT secretariat, the agreement should by the year 2000 boost world merchandise trade by an extra 12 percent. The benefits could be larger still.

The GATT agreement permits some discriminatory trade barriers against developing country exports of textiles, garments, and footwear—labor-intensive products, in which low pay gives the poorest countries a competitive advantage. Even where, as is certainly the case, workers are at present exploited in such countries, the fastest way to end the exploitation is to increase the demand for labor and thus raise its price.

Special attention must furthermore be paid to the effect of the Uruguay

Round on the food-importing countries of Sub-Saharan Africa. By raising world food prices, the agreement may in the short term harm the trade balances of these countries, for which compensatory arrangements should be made.

Aid and Its Conditions

Official development assistance (ODA) is defined as net disbursement of grants and loans made on concessional financial terms. In 1991, the world total of ODA was US$58.2 billion, the vast majority of it from member countries of the OECD. Overall, this was equal to 0.33 percent of those countries' total GNP.

Private flows of capital to the developing world were much larger, at $113 billion in 1992–1993. After the low period of the 1980s, this was a return to the level seen before the debt crisis. The flow may once more prove unsustainable; in any case, most of it went to a few countries whose national incomes are already classed in the middle-income category and above. Private capital hardly benefited the poor.

A high proportion of ODA, too, flows towards relatively prosperous countries. During the days of the Cold War, aid was sent mainly to political allies, or with the aim of maintaining regional stability. With that confrontation over, it is time to focus aid deliberately upon those who most need help—say, the 48 countries (containing 72 percent of the people in the developing world) that in 1991 had a per capita income below US$1,000. The relatively successful developing countries would, in this case, rely mainly on flows of private capital, which we have seen to be larger in total than ODA. If ODA were clearly seen as an instrument of economic development, rather than of military or political manipulation, its allocation would be much simpler. Aid would go to the countries that most need it, and use it best.

A main test of performance could be the expansion of productive employment; other relevant social achievements are those analyzed in the UNDP's annual *Human Development Report.* Simply put, countries that create jobs and improve the lot of their people would be rewarded for doing so. Furthermore, ODA to genuinely poor recipients should be conceded entirely as grants, rather than as loans that have often served mainly to plunge indebted countries even deeper into debt.

Debt Reduction

Most of the world's most severely indebted countries are in Sub-Saharan Africa; these are desperately poor countries, gravely affected by recession in the OECD. The Uruguay Round will not benefit them much, and may, by raising world food prices, make their lives yet harder. Few of them were ever able to borrow much from private creditors. Their debts to individual donor countries have mostly been forgiven or deferred. Their main outstanding debts are, therefore, owed largely to the multilateral aid agencies, which at present are not allowed formally to write off debt. It would be reasonable and prudent, and a great saving of administrative time and ingenuity, if a way could be found of eliminating those debts altogether.

People come first. Governments must create the conditions in which all their citizens have the opportunity to find reasonably secure, remunerative, and productive employment. Yet it is not states but families that decide how many citizens there shall be.

Several countries in different parts of the world have dramatically reduced the rate of growth of their population. Success is most likely in economies that are growing and where educational opportunities are improving. Yet even where birth rates have fallen, the number of children born each year will continue to rise, as the many women born in past years reach the age of parenthood.

And for many nations — especially in Africa — the demographic time-bomb has already exploded. There are too few jobs for too many young people, who see almost no chance of finding secure employment. Many governments have made things worse by attempting to become the employers of last resort. For those who could not find productive work, they have created jobs with no identifiable purpose, producing no goods that people want and no useful services.

A swollen and underemployed public service imposes an inflationary burden on national exchequers; rates of pay are therefore kept very low, adding to the frustration of those intended to be the beneficiaries. The social consequences are worst when, as is often the case, government jobs are offered automatically to all those completing a specified level of education. Past policies of this kind are regarded as significant contributors to social unrest.

Without underlying economic growth, the attempt to increase state employment is unsustainable and self-defeating. The way forward must be by increasing productive activity, and offering an appropriate education to those who will work in it. The best way to strengthen labor markets — and to satisfy individuals — is by providing basic education for all.

Women and Other Disadvantaged Groups

It is of course a human and moral imperative to encourage full participation of women in all aspects of society. The practical points we make here are that female advancement has a quick and lasting effect on birth rates, and that well-educated mothers improve the educational chances of the children they bear. Improving women's educational and other opportunities, including those for entry on equal terms into the labor force, is the key both to limiting the growth of population and to improving the welfare of coming generations. It is the most significant single way to bring about general social advancement.

Yet in most regions, women suffer disadvantages. In the Middle East and in most of Africa, they are in practice largely excluded from paid employment; and almost everywhere, notably in East Asia, women's wages are discriminately low. Even in many otherwise enlightened societies, their educational opportunities are limited. Very rarely are they offered the child-care facilities they need if they are to compete on equal terms with men.

Many societies treat members of certain ethnic (and sometimes religious) groups with equal unfairness; examples are indigenous people in Latin American countries and Gypsies in Eastern Europe. Members of traditionally disadvantaged groups tend to suffer long-term unemployment, giving rise to further social disadvantage. Legislation against discrimination is only the start of a comprehensive policy for the protection of disadvantaged groups, including women. They need better access to education and to productive resources if they are to make their full contribution to society.

Labor Markets

Like all markets, the market for jobs works best when demand roughly matches supply. At times of high unemployment that is not the case, and the fault lies with governments. It means that their macroeconomic policies are failing to ensure the efficient use of resources, especially of labor.

Inappropriate government policies may also distort labor markets so badly as to contribute to mass unemployment. Especially in Western Europe, labor market policies have often been enactments of agreements between organizations of workers and of employers. Laws and regulations formalize massive social gains made over many years.

It is often argued that, as technology and the economic environment change, such policies may come to limit job creation as well as labor mobility. If so, the policies need changing. But it is extremely difficult to tell whether labor market distortions are caused by inappropriate regulation or by general market failures.

East Asia has shown in recent years that labor mobility can be compatible with increased employment and rising pay—but only in the context of rapid economic expansion. In most other developing countries, where growth is sluggish, labor mobility is also slow. Most new jobs are generated through self-employment and the informal sector. Sometimes, but too rarely, the informal sector achieves high productivity and dynamic growth; mostly, though, informal-sector work is relatively unproductive, and low paid.

Appropriate responses should be devised in light of several considerations:

- The method by which wages and conditions of work are set in any country should respect democratic traditions; growth in developing countries may be hampered by rules copied from those prevailing economies with more highly developed labor markets.

- Restricting labor mobility by employment quotas, or by guaranteeing employment in unviable enterprises, may reduce overall economic activity and deny job opportunities to new entrants in the labor market.

- If public-sector pay is disproportionately high, it can distort labor markets and contribute to unproductive public expenditure; and if public-sector employment is too high a proportion of total employment, it may lead to inefficiency in public services and further labor market distortions.

- The most effective government action to improve the working of the labor market is by promoting basic education and encouraging the retraining of workers bypassed by technical or economic change.

- Legislation and persuasion can help to ensure that members of disadvantaged groups have a fair chance to find work.

- Exceptional problems may call for special labor market policies. One example is natural disasters, where well-established public works programs can be efficiently expanded to both relieve distress and build capital assets, such as roads or dams. Another example would be economic disasters, such as those affecting much of Eastern Europe, where jobs have been eliminated by harsh but necessary reforms and savings by hyperinflation. There, as the World Bank has argued, it may be impossible to find even short-term work for those affected, and cash income supplements may be the only way to avoid distress. The overriding rule is that emergency relief be finite, offering the beneficiaries a strong incentive to return actively to the labor market as soon as possible.

Conclusion

Nations that act together can greatly increase their chances of providing remunerative and sustainable work for all their citizens. Full employment is possible only if economic growth is rapid. The world has become a global market in which trade transfers the benefits of growth and its risks—from one economy to another.

Certainly, individual countries can exclude themselves from the growth process by, for example, bad macroeconomic management, bureaucratic rigidity, or institutional corruption. Good governance and the rule of law are the domestic foundation for growth. But no one country can keep growing for long on its own. The approach to full employment in an interdependent world must start with an intentional compact.

The World Summit for Social Development in Copenhagen in March 1995 will provide the opportunity for agreement on an agenda for worldwide growth. This section has outlined some of the problems and prospects. Here we briefly offer some proposals:

- The industrial countries of the OECD must coordinate their policies for faster growth.

- The momentum toward freer trade must be sustained, with reductions in tariffs and other barriers by countries at all levels of development.

- The system of official development assistance should be entirely reformed to concentrate the resources available on the countries most in need.

- The outstanding debt of the poorest developing countries should be reduced or, better, eliminated.

- Basic education for all (especially for women) and retraining for adults are essential preconditions for increasing and upgrading employment everywhere. They should be supported by more and better technical assistance, including the transfer of educational technology.

An integrated world demands concerted action. All nations have a common interest in the growth of trade and of economic activity; so do all enterprises, national, multinational, and workers' organizations. Faster growth will put the jobless to work.

To promote world growth, a global compact is needed. No country, or sector, can on its own fulfill its full potential and provide the jobs that people need. The aims of a global compact would be to speed the growth of employment, reduce poverty, and improve the quality of the jobs provided. The subjects it would need to consider are wideranging but closely interwoven. They include trade, aid, the operation of labor markets, migration, the movement of capital, and the safeguarding of the environment.

In all these areas there are shared risks to be a avoided and mutual advantages to be gained. Global action must be defined by a global forum. It is for the World Summit for Social Development in Copenhagen in 1995 to draw up the agenda and start the process.

Notes

1. This section is based on the discussion and findings of an expert group convened by UNDP/ILO in May, 1994, in Geneva, on economic policies and employment and on the papers prepared for that meeting.
2. This data comes from the United Nations, *World Population Prospects*, 1992 revision. New York, 1993; the International Labour Office, *Economically Active Population*. Geneva, forthcoming; and the World Bank, *World Tables*. Washington, D.C., various dates.
3. Information based on the United Nations, *World Economic Survey*. New York, 1993.

Chapter 1

The Pattern and Nature of Unemployment and Underemployment

Section 1

Full Employment Revisited

Lawrence R. Klein

It might seem strange that such a commonplace term as unemployment can pose serious problems of interpretation. An edition of *Webster's* defines unemployment as "the state of being unemployed." That is not very helpful; so one moves up the page to unemployed, which is defined as "being without a job, not current in use, not productively used." Another way of looking at unemployment in a country is to measure:

1. Total population of the country;
2. Participation rate (in the paid labor force);
3. The size of the labor force, which is determined by dividing the total population by participation in the labor force;
4. Unemployment, which is determined by subtracting the number of people employed from the labor force.

Although it seems straightforward, there are treacherous technical problems in filling in all the details. Enumerating total population is difficult, but determining who is in the labor force and who is at work is even more so. Some people work part time; some work at extra jobs; some do not work productively (in *Webster's* sense).

Nearly all developing countries, where unemployment is more severe, do not generally produce regular national measurements of unemployment, because such determinations are difficult to make. The most intricate details about unemployment are available from advanced industrial countries, but even in these cases, there are vast misunderstandings and difficulties in comparing labor market situations internationally.

Difficulties of Comparability

It is because of the measurement difficulties that most detailed analyses of unemployment statistics are confined to advanced industrial countries. The consideration of unemployment and labor market conditions in developed countries provides a useful starting point because we know more, in a quantitative sense, about unemployment there, and because developed country labor market conditions affect conditions in developing countries.

More than fifty years ago, Sir William Beveridge (later Lord Beveridge) introduced his celebrated report, *Social Insurance and Allied Services,* for Great Britain, in order to lay the foundations for "cradle-to-grave" social support—a social "safety net" in present terminology.[1] Sir William had hoped that the postwar experience would be better, and indeed, it was for some time. Yet we seem to have made little progress from the pre-World War II period, because today the unemployment rate in developed countries is near the 10 percent level and is expected to remain that high for years to come. If we exclude the United States and Japan, we can see that the unemployment rate exceeds 10 percent on average. If this were just a temporary business cycle deviation, it would not be so serious; it is, in fact, a more than decade-long predicament for most of the developed-world economy. It appears to validate the influential economist John Maynard Keynes' concept of an "under-employment equilibrium."

Industrialized Countries

An examination of the statistics shows low rates of unemployment (significantly below 10 percent) for the United States, Japan, Portugal, Iceland, Norway, and Switzerland. A cyclical high point for the United States, after World War II, is about 10 percent, but the rate falls in recovery periods. That does not signify that there is no unemployment problem in the United States; however, the distribution of unemployment is very uneven, varying by region, geographical area, race, age, and other important social characteristics. Moreover, in recent years, job growth concentrated in service-producing sectors, often with slim wages, poor working conditions, and few social benefits.

Labor conditions in Norway, Iceland, and Portugal fluctuate, but generally fall well below 10 percent. A much lower barrier used to prevail for Japan and Switzerland; in the former case associated with "lifetime employment" and the dual economy, and in the latter with a well-run economy and the forced migration of labor during unproductive times. The low rates, however, may be left to the memories of Japan and Switzerland. Special circumstances that allowed these two countries to log-in with rates of 1 to 2 percent are fading as a result of structural changes in their economies.

It is interesting to note that Finland and Sweden used to maintain low rates of unemployment, not below 2 percent, but below 5 percent. In the latter case, the movement away from Sweden's celebrated "welfare state" and Finland's disrupted economic relationship with the former Soviet Union have upset labor market conditions to the point at which cyclical or temporary troubles led to significant increases in unemployment. The question of whether these two socially responsible countries can bring unemployment rates back to moderately low levels again remains to be seen.

If we examine the unemployment figures again, we find estimates for Spain well above 20 percent, often between 15 and 20 percent. Denmark, France, Ireland, and Italy are all well above 10 percent. Australia, New Zealand, and Canada carry the unemployment problem far beyond Western Europe; South Africa is something else, again, with rates near 50 percent. This discrepancy borders on the racial imbalance of wealth, which will remain a problem of grave concern for the new biracial government.

Developing Countries

In the case of the developing world and the former socialist countries that are restructuring their economies, we encounter a new set of labor market problems. In the first place, measurement is so difficult for developing countries that unemployment figures are rarely made available, and when they are published, they are generally not reliable enough to form a basis for economic analysis or policy formation.

From the UN *Report on the World Social Situation 1993*, we get some idea of the problem, along with rough indicators of unemployment's magnitude in developing countries. For example, the African figures are sparse and erratic. The extremely low figures for Ghana are hardly believable, but the preponderance of reported figures about 10 percent, and reaching as high as 56.3 percent in one case, show that unemployment poses a serious problem. The Latin American figures are more plentiful and large in most cases, but not a high as the peak figures reported for Africa. The Asian figures are much lower, mainly under 10 percent, but some appear too tiny to be accurate.

Instead of following the time paths of unemployment rates, as in the industrial countries, we simply make qualitative judgments—either the labor situation is tolerable or intolerable. Unemployment benefits rarely exist in developing countries, and even if the official statistics suggest that a low unemployment rate prevails, we can generally judge a country's situation through indirect indicators of labor market conditions. Almost always, there is a high degree of "disguised" unemployment, that is, people who cannot find urban and/or industrial employment and go back to the land, where they eke out a weak subsistence living.

Linkages Between Poverty and Unemployment

It is not only unemployment that concerns us in pointing out the social ills generated by poor economic conditions. Poverty may be a more comprehensive and meaningful concept than unemployment for judging the prevailing economic conditions in a country—developed or developing. Poverty statistics are even more difficult to prepare on a regular summary basis for each country, yet accounts of public health, sanitary conditions, nutrition, and other indirect indicators can tell us more about the country status and situation.

In metropolitan areas of poor developing countries, visitors often encounter great numbers of assistants engaged in protective security. Likewise, there are numerous street vendors, volunteer guides, and general hangers-on in urban environments. These extra persons may often be reported as being at work, no matter how low the productivity becomes.

The urge and drive for emigration, either permanent or temporary, are often indirect indicators of how weak or strong labor market conditions remain. For U.S. states such as California, Texas, and Florida, the lure of industrial or agricultural employment drives neighboring peoples to seek American jobs, no matter how menial. This, in effect, tells us a great deal about how the relative attractiveness of life in Latin America versus life in North America. The stronger the business cycle becomes in the United States, the more attractive American jobs seem, even at low rates of pay.

Advanced industrial countries are not the only ones to which workers emigrate as "guests" or as permanent residents for jobs in service and agricultural sectors. The oil-exporting countries of the Persian Gulf hire temporary workers from many Asian and North African countries to engage in service activities or other work that local citizens do not desire. Relative to the labor force or population of the host countries, the temporary work force has become quite large—almost equal to the domestic work force in some cases. The oil industry has been an important income source for people who have poor job opportunities internationally, but it meets with a great deal of trouble and dislocation when a major disturbance occurs. Consider the case of the Gulf War, where many foreign "guest" workers were located in Iraq and Kuwait. These people were forcibly removed; thus they lost their source of personal and family income.

In the agricultural sector of developing countries, the introduction of labor-saving capital equipment on a large scale would be unsettling in labor markets, opening the potential for political and/or social instability. The service sector—taxi driving, beauty parlors, fast-food outlets, tourism, waste disposal—are available and taken up at low wages. Some jobs are also available in light manufacturing, where automation and other labor-saving business practices have not been fully introduced.

In the longer term, more workers will receive training, both from the prosperous host economy and at home. However, this requires time to build up human capital and to place people; therefore, we can expect to be concerned with high unemployment in poor developing countries. If an accurate count could be made of the labor force, employment, and the prevalence of low-productivity work, we would undoubtedly find high unemployment rates of 30, 40, or 50 percent in many developing countries (like those figures reported for South Africa), or even in low-income areas of U.S. cities, where racial discrimination is practiced or felt.

The World Bank, in its comprehensive statistical report on China, has included some estimates of underemployment in 1990 and 1995 (projected). These figures, compiled by the State Planning Commission, show the under-employed to be five times the number estimated as unemployed in urban areas in 1990. The underemployed number is as large as 20 million persons and would certainly reach two-digit figures as a rate of unemployment. The projection for 1995 is also 20 million, while the number unemployment is as high as 6 million. In the rural areas, the underemployment problem is more serious. It is as high as 140 million persons in 1990; however, this figure is projected to decline to 120 million by 1995.

Former Centrally Planned Countries

A similar unemployment situation has occurred in Russia, in other republics of the former Soviet Union, and in Eastern Europe. Many people have turned to unproductive service work (i.e., selling trinkets on the streets of Moscow) or to crime in order to survive or flourish in a lawless situation. The figures are exceptionally high in many areas of the former Soviet Union. In Eastern Europe, including what was East Germany, the rates are also high by OECD standards, even if they do not match the exorbitant ones in some developing countries. At the onset of the capitalist transition, it was often forecast that unemployment would rise from its socialist rock-bottom values (of less than 2 percent in most cases) to about 5 or 6 percent. The forecast was very faulty, however, and rates have been in two-digit ranges in many of the Eastern countries.

The Economic Commission for Europe puts unemployment in Bulgaria, Poland, and Hungary at substantial two-digit rates. It is somewhat below 10 percent in Romania, although fairly high at 8.4 percent (and rising since 1990). It is only in the Czech Republic that the figures are down to rates that would be considered promising in Western Europe.

Main Causes of Unemployment

The world economy is operating far below potential, and simply speaking, that is the main reason for persistently high unemployment. There is some structural unemployment that is inevitable when major changes are being introduced, but policy makers use the structural argument as an excuse for not trying hard enough to get their own and the world economy moving again.

The most common reason heard for not pushing for higher levels of economic activity and more jobs is that prices will rise. It is true that a vigorous growth economy puts pressure on price movements to compensate for higher wage demands, short supplies of strategic inputs in the production process, and higher costs for financial capital. Policy routes for dealing with such situations exist, but they have never been tried in full. They involve varieties of incomes-policies that establish guidelines between final prices and unit costs. Single-minded attachment to orthodox monetary policy to deal with inflation is used instead and, all too often, has been pursued so vigorously that it has inevitably generated high values of unemployment. This is particularly the case when policy makers have pursued zero-inflation; they achieved these goals in a practical sense, but also placed prominently in tables as countries with high unemployment. Not only this, they have the dubious distinction of being the world leaders who led the world into the last recession.

There is a much maligned, misunderstood, and underappreciated inverse economic relationship between wage changes and unemployment. It has strong justification in abstract economic analysis and holds up quite well in a statistical sense. It is misunderstood when it is interpreted as a naive link between inflation and unemployment, but between wage change and inflation, a term that depends on productivity must operate. One cannot take account of the adverse trends in productivity during the OPEC-dominated years of the 1970s, which misled people looking for a stable, inverse relationship between inflation and unemployment. When strong supply-side shocks occur, as in the 1970s, the link between inflation and unemployment can turn from being inverse to being direct (which is precisely what happened). In addition, demographic aspects of the relation must be considered. When these relationships are put in proper perspective, both the policy and understanding of the wage-change and unemployment relationship becomes clear.

Full Employment

As demographic changes occurred in the period since World War II, it became harder to achieve the full-employment levels of activity and labor market conditions—with moderate inflation—that prevailed in the early part of the postwar period. At that time, unemployment rates of 3 or 4 percent were generally achievable. In some countries, even lower rates could prevail. But as it became harder and more demanding to achieve such levels of unemployment in a stable price environment, economic policy makers gave in too easily and kept raising the full-employment level of unemployment. They would have us believe that the 6 percent unemployment in the United States represents full employment.[2] Another dimension of labor market conditions to be construed is a job opportunity. In addition to the direct measurement of unemployment, there are also measures of job vacancies or advertising for "help wanted." A problem with the 6 percent level of U.S. unemployment is that relatively few job opportunities are available, as compared with previous situations when the unemployment rate has been at 6 percent.

In a sequel to the "Beveridge Report," Sir William provided a very interesting and useful definition of full employment with very deep implications.[3] He described a state of full employment as "... having always more vacant jobs than unemployed men, not slightly fewer jobs. It means that the jobs are at fair wages, of such a kind, and so located, that the unemployed men can reasonably be expected to take them; it means, by consequence, that the normal lag between losing one job and finding another will be very short." When modern politicians speak of having good jobs available, certain aspects should be present. With a 6-percent average figure, black unemployment can be as high as 12 percent, and in urban areas, teenage black unemployment is many times higher.

Policy makers fixed only the price level and orthodox monetary policy—looking for stability—are actually destabilizing our entire social structure. If one generalizes and extrapolates the U.S. labor market situation to a world level, we shall find poor countries with very high rates of unemployment experiencing poor output growth in the midst of high levels of living, with low unemployment in only the best neighborhoods of advanced industrial countries.   Also, there are entire countries that have high (disguised) unemployment in the interdependent international economy, side-by-side with industrial countries that have 10 percent unemployment. This is not a socially stable universe, and if the industrial countries were to embark on a bolder expansion path with lower unemployment, many of the gains would flow simultaneously to the labor markets of developing countries. There are, indeed, structural aspects of unemployment, but nothing contributes as much to improved labor market conditions as high rates of production growth.

The Case of the United States

Countries that have not done as well as the United States in job creation are looking for a model to alleviate their unemployment problem. Although some aspects of the U.S. labor market seem attractive, enough caveats exist to suggest that it is indeed not a role model.   A primary characteristic of the U.S. labor market is flexibility.   This is revealed in many ways, two significant ones being the shifts in sectors of employment, and the downward adjustment of real wages (hourly or weekly).

For the past five years, job creation has not occurred in goods-producing sectors.   Only in recent months has there been a modest, observable increase. Jobs in service-producing sectors, on the other hand, have been climbing upwards for many years, even during the recession and weak recovery periods. The decline in real earnings has continued for even more than five years.

After the second oil shock and ensuing recession (1979–1982), it was generally noted that Japan and Asia-Pacific developing countries exhibited unusual flexibility. They, too, suppressed wage growth. Moreover, they had only modest inflation, despite the fact that most of the economies involved were oil importers. Based on the low inflation rate and favorable competitive position, these countries expanded rapidly through export-led growth—providing many new manufacturing jobs, keeping unemployment from being a significant problem, and attracting world-wide attention for their economic achievements. Still, they perform well economically, but they are being challenged by the United States. In comparison to the developed country level, Japan is experiencing rising unemployment. The drawback in the case of the United States, however, is that what are traditionally called "good" jobs are quite elusive. Jobs in manufacturing and construction with high hourly wage rates and strong packages of fringe benefits (vacation, medical care, retirement) have been significantly restricted by automation and corporate "downsizing."   In many instances, employees have been dropped from regular positions on corporate payrolls, and then re-hired on a newer and more temporary basis without the usual package of fringe benefits. Corporate downsizing did not begin in the United States; but the practice grew rapidly in America, soon spreading to more companies worldwide.   On a competitive basis, taking into account wage changes, inflation, productivity gains, and exchange rate adjustments, the United States has become a much more cost-effective producer; yet these relative changes are sure to move in cycles. Our unit-labor costs will remain as low as they are currently, but will fluctuate with changing conditions. The developing countries of Asia and Latin America will stay fairly competitive, not always at the lowest values of unit-labor costs, but low enough to encourage a solid spurt of growth.

Regarding the present U.S. recovery, the Federal Reserve Authorities (Federal Open Market Committee [FOMC]) have stimulated discussion about the concept of "full employment" in the U.S. economy today by tightening monetary conditions — specifically raising short-term interest rates through intervention in the open market for U.S. Government securities. This would occur in advance of inflationary pressures not yet visible, but sighted on the horizon by the FOMC and business cycle analysis who trust in leading indicators of inflation.

In effect, the policy makers have deemed that the U.S. economy is now at full employment, with 6 percent of the labor force estimated to be unemployed (with much higher figures for some demographic groups). The policy makers do not seek economic recovery more quickly than at present, thus implicitly accepting the prevailing rate of unemployment as consistent with the overall economic situation of modest growth, low inflation, current unemployment, large-trade deficit, and still-large federal budget deficit. They think that either the U.S. economy is in "equilibrium" or approaching "equilibrium."

NAIRU

Some economic theoreticians have tried to justify these substantial, prevailing unemployment rates as indicative of full employment — in the sense that present conditions represent a nonaccelerating-inflation-rate-of-employment (NAIRU). Either (1) the monetary authorities in the United States could be satisfied with the unemployment rate because it qualifies as a NAIRU rate and thus concentrates on holding down inflation, or (2) the authorities could be concerned with the prospect of falling unemployment, below 6 percent, as leading to wage pressures causing price markups on rising wage costs.   This latter position might seem to contradict monetarist theory, which says that inflation is purely a monetary phenomenon and that only excessive growth of money supply causes demand.

Many points of criticism can be levied against the NAIRU concept. First, NAIRU theorists are now adjusting their target figures cyclically. Should not the full-employment rate of unemployment be a trend statistic rather than a fluctuating cyclical statistic?   Full-employment labor force and full-capacity output are definitely trend magnitudes.   The ratio of aggregate employment or aggregate output to their full-use trends should indeed by cyclical and generally fluctuating, but they are not meant to be measures at the full-use levels except in special periods. The trends show that full-utilization levels are not constants; they obviously grow with technology, innovation, education, and population expansion. In capacity utilization measures, I have argued that full capacity should be calculated as trends-through-peaks (or near peaks).

Full-utilization percentages are estimated at the peak points, with some allowance for trends in the length of the working week, vacations, seasonal adjustments, and so on. Of course, times change. We once had work weeks of 60 or more hours; later they were reduced to 40 hours and perhaps to 35. Vacations were allocated one week per year. Now they are as generous as one month (or more) per year. Similarly, the age, sex, and marital status composition of the work force is changing. This, very appropriately, accounts for raising the full-employment-rate-of-unemployment from 3 to 4 percent, but not to 6 percent, simply because policy makers will not try to get full employment or because they set their sights on inappropriate targets.

It makes no sense to argue, as some NAIRU exponents now do, that the rate for 1992 should be about 6.7 percent, while the 1990 figure was about 6.9 percent. Such refinements fall within the appropriate intervals of estimation. The figures and estimates derived from them are too shaky to support the cyclical adjustments being made. What has been influencing the estimated NAIRU include energy prices, food prices, and financial market conditions. Indeed, these variables influence the economy, but policy measures to neutralize their effects on activity and employment can be taken, leaving the quantitative dimensions of full employment intact, except for trend effects.

To find the unemployment rate associated with zero inflation turns the economic policy problem upside down. In 1965, Ronald Bodkin and I made that estimate for the Commission on Money and Credit, finding that unemployment would be as high as 10 percent. We knew that reference point all along, but I would not let that interfere with my notion of full employment. I would deal with finding the policies that would establish full employment—then at about 4.0 percent—without generating inflation. It was noted about that time that central bankers in countries pursuing zero-inflation targets (such as Canada and New Zealand) achieved their stated goals, but they are left with labor markets that report unemployment rates in the neighborhood of 10 percent—hardly equilibrium positions.

Conclusion

One should bear in mind that theorists extended the concept of full employment (rate of unemployment) to natural rate, and then to NAIRU. The last-mentioned extension refers to acceleration of inflation. Theorists implicitly presume that every upward adjustment of inflation will lead to a higher rate of inflation. However, this is not demonstrably so. Since the immediate postwar control of prices during the late 1940s, the U.S. economy has not experienced accelerating inflation for any significant period of time. In the aftermath of early OPEC power in raising oil prices, the yearly rate reached a figure as high as 15 percent, but that is hardly comparable with inflation rates in three- and four-digit numbers that have been typical in countries evincing acceleration. Acceleration, or even a tendency toward it, has not been characteristic of the U.S. economy in the second half of the twentieth century.

The FOMC is making a prudent projection if it perceives future inflation above 2 percent annually. Even if the inflation rate, as part of the growth process, moves to 3, 4, or 5 percent, does that indicate a stage of acceleration; does that suggest a deteriorating economic environment? It boils down to a set of preferences. Many citizens, probably most, can live very comfortable economic lives with as much as 5 percent inflation, provided that productive and diverse jobs exist. An inflation rate of 5 percent does not necessarily mean that much higher rates are in prospect, and we should not be subjected to a premature restraint of the urge for the economy to grow faster, in real terms.

Notes

1. Sir William Beveridge, *Social Insurance and Allied Services.* New York: Macmillan, 1942, p. 185.
2. For a contrasting view, see William S. Vickrey, "Why Not Chock-Full Employment?" *Atlantic Economic Journal,* 22 (March 1994): 39–45.
3. Sir William H. Beveridge, *Full Employment in a Free Society.* New York: Norton, 1945, p. 18.

Section 2

Employment Creation and Development

David Turnham

This section reviews the prospects of employment creation in developing countries, with brief references to supply-side factors (principally labor force growth) and more extensive discussion of the factors governing the demand for labor. Past experience shows some rather sharp differences among countries. The majority accommodated labor force growth through new types of higher-productivity employment and increased earning power, extended to some relatively well-educated and/or capital-rich families and workers. This was coupled with casual work and survival self-employment for many others, plus rather severe unemployment, especially among young people. Such a "muddling-through" approach to employment, however, may be more difficult to sustain in the future.

In contrast, another—albeit much smaller—group of developing countries, mostly located in Asia, achieved sustained, fast growth of productive employment. Unemployment in these places fell to very low levels, with real wages rising for all earning classes, unskilled as well as skilled. With some important, country-specific nuances, the policy package can be described as an orthodox approach to monetary and fiscal management, coupled with the vigorous promotion of exports, all in a setting friendly to and supportive of private enterprise. Other distinguishing features are exceptionally efficient government services and large outlays on education (partly privately financed), and on public-sector infrastructure.

From the late 1970s into the 1980s and 1990s, more and more countries have followed similar approaches, some much more successfully than others. This section suggests that for many countries, including many of the large countries, the systematic and consistent application of such policies offers the best prospect of a successful transition to more productive forms of employment, in addition to sustained, broad-based growth in earnings. Among the difficulties, however, are the trade policies of the Organization for Economic Cooperation and Development (OECD) countries, which could pose increasing problems. The importance of a open environment with respect to trade is stressed, and it is illustrated with regard to both global and national self-interests.

The Challenge of Employment Creation

Developing countries desperately need more productive jobs. The labor force is rising quickly—at levels of more than 2 billion presently and more than 3 billion in 20 years. It could be more—quite a few people, especially women, would probably work if suitable jobs were available. As an example, in the mid- to late-1980s in conservative Bangladesh, Korean textile factories had no difficulty finding women for their new factory jobs—mostly those who had never worked before. Similarly, the activity rate among females has risen sharply in some of the rapidly growing countries of East Asia.

The slow growth of a labor force in the OECD countries, and the fast growth in developing ones, produces some bizarre results: quite early in the next century (by the year 2015), Sub-Saharan Africa will each year add three times as many new workers to the world's labor force as all the OECD nations, Eastern European countries, and former Soviet Union combined. In the future, developing countries will account for nearly the entire increment of the world's labor force.

However, increasing the number of productive jobs is extremely difficult, as many of the OECD European countries have recently discovered. Yet productive jobs are fundamental to the achievement of social goals, such as the satisfaction of basic needs and the reduction of poverty. One cannot be sanguine about the prospect of the wealthy countries learning to care more about the poor ones; nor can one remain passive about improving the efficacy of aid that is provided.

This does not mean that social safety nets and security systems cannot work. Yet it is certainly true that they can be made to work more easily, particularly as countries attain income levels similar to those enjoyed by today's upper-middle income groups (to use World Bank terminology). In poor countries, the impoverished mostly rely on themselves, with little support from the state. Thus the exchange value of labor services is the principle determinant of the living standards of the poor.

A certain complacency about employment can be observed in the governments of many developing countries, because most have so far avoided an explosion of open unemployment, and hence the unrest likely to ensue in its wake. But, even if "muddling through" with respect to employment worked in the past, there is no guarantee of similar results in the future.

Today, a bigger proportion of the population is urbanized, with the urban informal sector significantly stretched. Governments also seem increasingly less able to handle the financial burdens of acting as employer of last resort, and thus cannot be counted upon to absorb educated, labor-market entrants as they were able and willing to do in the past. Unemployment in the urban areas—which is where most measurements have been made—is usually very high when omitting the "Asian tigers" (Hong Kong, Korea, Singapore, and

Taiwan) and the near-tigers (Thailand, Indonesia, Malaysia). With these exclusions, the unweighted average rate of urban unemployment among the remaining 30 developing countries (for which post-1985 data exist) is 11.7 percent. As is well known, in developing countries, measured youth unemployment rates are typically three to six times higher than those for older workers; in several countries they exceed 30 percent. Furthermore, youth labor force and unemployment may be substantially underreported, since many young people seem not to be included in the labor force or in school.

The unemployment data include some wide – and hard to explain – differences, with very high rates reported for most African states and states bordering the Mediterranean, counterbalanced by what seem to be very low rates for certain countries – Brazil and Mexico, for example. One should not read too much into the numbers, although it is a fascinating challenge to try to understand some of the reasons behind the differences, especially as the methodologies used in collecting data become more similar.

On the whole, survival self-employment and casual employment are the main reasons why unemployment measures need to be supplemented by information as to the real earnings of the above-employed groups. If governments were to examine closely what is happening to the incomes of those in survival employment – the small farmers and casual workers in agriculture, and the unskilled self-employed and wage workers in the informal sector – they might find more revealing evidence about the improvement or deterioration of labor market conditions than is given by open unemployment data.

Interestingly, the efforts to measure unemployment through labor-force survey methods have increased in recent years among developing countries. In quite a few, a series of unemployment data monitors a period of about two decades. Thus far, however, little effort has been focused to measure and to quantify the earnings aspect of the employment problem, or to assess changes in the magnitude of survival employment. For reasons discussed elsewhere, the difficulties posed by the collection of such information seem to have been exaggerated. Data requirements could be met by sampling no more than a narrow range of carefully chosen occupations, as part of a labor-force survey of the type now regularly carried out in many countries. Most evidence has been indirect and partial – what exists often supports the idea of a worsening trend in earnings within many countries of Africa and Latin America.

The idea of people being driven by poverty to seek out survival employment is sometimes expressed as an aphorism: developing countries are said to be full of people too poor to afford to be unemployed. But it also remains self-evident that no amount of urgency or need will guarantee that work is always available; even among the poor, where there are several earners within the family, the unemployment of one or two members can be sustained, at least for a time. Thus, despite the iron necessity of earning a living, measured unemployment rates are often high even in poor countries – as appears the case throughout urban Africa. In many instances, unemployment rates are higher among the poorer-income strata, and evidence shows considerable unemployment among casual-wage workers (Indian data are particularly helpful in this respect). Casual workers are usually among the poorest categories of worker, although this type of unemployment tends to be experienced in forms hidden under standard, labor-force survey procedures; for example, casual workers in agriculture who obtain only two or three days of work per week will not usually be counted as unemployed.

Lessons from Previous Development Experience

Indeed, lessons can be learned from observing the fortunes of developing countries and the effects of policies followed over the past two to three decades. One important, negative lesson is that policies failing to create productive jobs at a fairly rapid pace are also policies that mostly fail in their narrower objectives, including that of securing a sustainable and respectable rate of national output growth. The old gods of the 1950s and 1960s — an array of inward-looking, antimarket strategies orchestrated by would-be master planners — have all been toppled. Their last hurrah echoed during the easy-money, international lending of the 1970s' petrodollars era, and the wreckage was strewn all over the debt-ridden 1980s.

More important than the failures are the workable strategies that have, at their core, invested in people along with labor-intensive production systems. While the successes of the East Asian tigers in the form of 10 percent GDP growth or 20 percent export growth are well known, a less-publicized feature is their record in employment creation and in increasing the real wage of *unskilled* labor.

In all four of the original tigers (Hong Kong, Korea, Singapore, and Taiwan), rapid labor-force growth of between 3 and 3.5 percent per annum (partly a result of migratory flows and partly due to rising participation among women) was sustained over long periods. In all four countries, labor was both redirected into new jobs and occupations (most obviously in Taiwan and South Korea, where a large agricultural labor force was absorbed into industry and services) at real wages that have strongly increased. Of course, real-wage increase is also due to the rising education and skill levels of workers, and their absorption into jobs that utilize these strengths. But employers in agriculture and construction have also had to pay more to retain their unskilled workers. In Taiwan, for example, the real earnings of construction workers have increased by more than 8.8 percent per annum since 1975. In Korea, the real wages of agricultural laborers more than doubled in the 1980s. In addition, in all these economies, unemployment is measured at frictional levels — 2 percent or less — and the use of more immigrant labor is much debated as a means of easing labor shortages.

The Hong Kong experience proves particularly interesting. Its dramatic new challenge was posed by the combination of laissez-faire policies and the sudden, and unforeseen, early 1980s' opening to foreign capital and entrepreneurship of a giant neighbor economy — China — endowed with plentiful, cheap labor. Manufacturing jobs were drained from Hong Kong: the colony has seen its manufacturing employment decline from close to 40 percent of the total in 1980 to only 26 percent in 1992. Yet Hong Kong's workers and consumers appear to have suffered little from this change. Over the same period, GDP rose an average of 7 percent per annum, real wages increased sharply, and unemployment is currently less than 2 percent of the total labor force.

If the economy-wide impacts from macroeconomic policies are the most important influences on employment and poverty, a further lesson is the demonstrated possibility to help the poor through low-cost, programmed interventions in a variety of situations. At the community level, even where the distribution of land is not equal, investments in well-designed rural development and rural infrastructure programs are often successful in achieving output, productivity, and employment gains for a broad spectrum of the rural population. Landless and near-landless labor (often plentiful in densely populated areas) can be employed to create low-cost infrastructure through public works. This is related along the lines of Korea's Saemul Undong movement of the 1970s, Maharastra (India) State's Employment Guarantee Scheme, and Indonesia's Kabupaten programs.

Among nonfarm rural activities, cottage industries and low-productivity work are often of special importance among the poorest. It is the smallest-scale farmers and the landless households that earn the highest share of income outside agriculture—over 70 percent in parts of Asia, and 50 percent or more in Africa, where landlessness is uncommon. Thus the growth of new forms of rural, nonfarm employment is particularly important to poor households. A rising share of income from non-farm enterprise and employment is also a partial solution to the problem of an expanding, rural labor force faced with a stagnant or shrinking land base. Nonfarm work in the local area also contributes to smoothing the work and income profile of on-farm labor demand, which is often highly seasonal. The promotion and support of informal and microscale enterprise, as well as farmers, through local savings and credit institutions is another category of programming, with the Grameen Bank in Bangladesh and Indonesia's Badan Kredit Kecamatan (BKK) among the better-known examples.

While rural credit schemes and improved rural infrastructure (power and roads are particularly important) all contribute to stimulating off-farm rural employment, the demand factor is usually the most critical. Higher farm income is the main source of extra demand. More production on the farm can also create a base for local, resource-based enterprises exporting to urban areas and the outside world, and thus expanding the employment opportunities afforded by rural export industries. The spectacular success of China's agriculture during the 1980s helped to produce the remarkable expansion of rural enterprise in that country. The number of workers employed in rural enterprises almost tripled, from about 37 million in 1978 to close to 95 million in 1989. Among agricultural households, the income from production derived from nonagricultural sources grew from less than 8 percent in 1978 to 31 percent in 1989. With agricultural output growing fast, at close to 6 percent per annum, rural factories were able to expand output on the basis of greater quantities of agricultural products used as inputs (cotton, oil seeds, silk cocoons, feedgrains, tobacco). Evidently, the expansion was buoyed by demand—a combination of rapidly increasing local demands for quality foods, such as poultry and pork, and a demand for industrial raw materials, boosted in some instances by exports like silk manufacture.

While many types of programs can be used to help specific "target groups" of low productivity and income, another lesson is the vital role played by an education system that provides basic primary skills to all children, not just those from better-off families. The provision of basic education is increasingly seen as the most effective way of building up assets of the poor. Programs to deliver a better quality of primary education to a larger share of children in rural areas merits top priority, and much more could be done, notably in Sub-Saharan Africa where the systems seem to have deteriorated in recent years. How best to do this is a subject beyond the scope of this section. One can only note: (a) a critical role for educational reforms in improving the quality and cost-effectiveness of conventional systems; and (b) a surprisingly limited role of aid in the provision of primary education, especially among the bilateral donors, despite broad recognition of the importance of education and the high priority that donors place on tackling poverty.

Prospects and Development Scenarios

The developing world's new generation of well-educated and well-trained bureaucrats seems to have taken some of these lessons to heart, especially in regard to macroeconomic policies. In the 1980s, in Latin America and Asia, efforts were made to realign a wide range of domestic policies, so as to be able to follow outward-oriented development strategies. As Dani Rodrik recently put in an NBER Working Paper: "Since the early 1980s, developing countries have flocked to free trade as if it were the Holy Grail of development."

The Harvard and Chicago school Ph.Ds now running Mexico and Chile (or the ex-World Bank bureaucrats in charge of finance in India) are not necessarily pursuing Asian-style development policies just because they are sensitive to the needs of poor people. Rather, hope springs from the consideration that the pursuit of sustainable growth and development, based on Asian methods, is most likely to lead to a fast rate of job creation. And this effect is critical in a strategy to help the poor.

Taking into account the difficulties of policy reform and uncertainties about the speed and depth of impact on employment and earnings, there can be no room for complacency. The new policies have not come a moment too soon and, thus far, few countries have managed to use labor abundance as a springboard for rapid development. Perhaps for most of the countries of Sub-Saharan Africa, and for some other countries, the application of the recommended policies poses special difficulties that have frustrated progress. Nevertheless, the progress with new policies in Latin America and Asia—progress born of crisis—is remarkable given the sort of wrenching change that often involves immediate losers for little early net gain. With few exceptions (albeit China), it takes some five to 10 years before the effects of reform *begin* to show themselves in growth and other performance indicators, including employment.

What is the likelihood that those developing countries that have achieved sustained rapid growth will be able to continue it? What, too, is the prospect that countries that have not achieved rapid growth in the past will be able to do so? These questions take us well beyond the scope of this section, yet a few points can be made. Establishing and maintaining appropriate domestic policies is probably the single major influence on performance. Other largely domestic factors include savings capacities, the supply and rate of increase of skilled labor, the management of infrastructure investment and urban development, and environmental challenges and natural-resource constraints.

An agricultural failure poses two sorts of threats to labor-intensive development. In rapidly developing, low-income economies, high-income elasticities of demand for food and other agricultural produce ensure an expanding demand for agricultural products. As the experience of China shows, burgeoning consumption demand met by production increases can be an important element in higher growth of rural employment and diminished rural poverty. A supply-side failure puts such gains in jeopardy, and immensely complicates the problem of structural transformation. Such a failure also diminishes economy-wide growth prospects, since supply-side failures in domestic agriculture result in a very rapid growth of imports.

Indeed, we have heard talk of a "world food crisis," talk which has lingered for a long time. Yet international prices for main food crops and agricultural materials have been stable or falling for many years. With some major exceptions, notably in Africa, investment and new technology in agriculture has in recent decades more than kept pace with resource availability, in the global, if not always regional, setting. This, however, could change. Serious local threats to the environment frequently center around the links between agricultural potentials and performance, as well as various types of land degradation and deforestation. In China, extra demands for industrial land have led to a fall in the arable area, at the same time as the problems of ground-water pollution from industrial wastes (including wastes from China's burgeoning rural industry) and agrochemical residues are growing. Elsewhere among the developing countries are problems of soil degradation and toxicity (alkalinity and salinity), notably in the many intensively-cropped irrigation areas suffering from inadequate drainage and/or excessive pumping of the ground water (in India and Pakistan, for example). Soil erosion and other negative effects also result from the combination of unsound logging practices (clear felling without enforcement of reforestation) and the cultivation of nearly cleared but fragile uplands by impoverished settlers.

In the long term, the evolution of technology and environmental considerations seems likely to become increasingly significant, not only for agricultural prospects. Concerning agriculture, many have been predicting the onset of a new, biotechnology revolution to help improve crop yields and output and to reduce the need for harmful agrochemicals and other resources. The results, however, have been slow in coming. In large parts of Africa, the need for a better system of agricultural incentives, coupled with the generation of new techniques and methods in applying them, remains as urgent as the solutions appear distant.

The prospects of maintenance — or in some cases, the introduction — of appropriate domestic policies for broad-based development is linked to the workings of the political system. Although no single form of political system is necessary to promote economic development, experience does tend to underline the importance of stable and administratively competent government. In many developing countries, the improvement of governance must be tackled *pari passu* with the implementation of the economic-reform agenda. Again, Africa presents special problems, and many of the targeted schemes and specific programs that have seen success elsewhere have been largely ineffective in Africa, partly for want of better governance. However considering the very wide scope of the situation, as well as the inherent difficulties in dealing with political issues, in the next few years it would be surprising if quite a large number of countries — including those outside Africa — do not experience domestic turbulence, spelling little or no progress.

China, however, is of outstanding importance and interest. Observers there draw attention to many problems of a political nature: (a) the uncertainties due to an aging leadership, the unclear succession arrangements in the single party state, and the potential for unrest as part of a struggle to establish representative government; (b) the strains on national unity as the more successful provinces and regions assert an increasing degree of independence from central government and backward regions; (c) the challenge of putting market mechanisms into place and improving the legal and regulatory basis of property rights and safeguards against corruption; and (d) the uncertainties relating to the impact of reforms, such as threats to job security and income, notably regarding the unproductive parts of the state enterprise sector.

Subject to a considerable caveat on this account, the likelihood that past rates of growth can be maintained or improved upon would seem most favorable in the case of East Asia. Here, the combination of a rapidly expanding China and Indonesia, bordered by several countries that can increasingly supply technology, expertise, and capital, is especially propitious. Indeed, the combination of continued, rather sluggish growth in the major OECD countries, combined with rapid growth in East Asia, could produce a significant rebalancing of the global economy over the next 15 years. Other populous Asian countries can also gain from their regional associations, notably Vietnam and the Philippines.

South Asia might also develop fairly rapidly if reform agendas are pursued vigorously, especially by India. Savings rates, stocks of educated manpower, and infrastructure are, however, not nearly so favorable as in East Asia. Still, Pakistan's 6 percent average growth over the past 20 years seems to suggest that much can be done, despite the difficulties and shortfalls in policy. In this case, an uneven distribution of education as a factor likely to exacerbate inequality in incomes and earning power, as well as acting as a drag on growth, was somewhat offset by the opportunities for contract labor work in the Middle East.

Many countries in Latin America have also undertaken major reforms, and some are beginning to see benefits from them. However, Latin America is still exposed to high interest rates and reduced capital flows, and the composition of its exports and imports results in greater exposure to adverse impacts from terms-of-trade shifts. In this case, the risk from sluggish growth in the OECD economies is particularly pronounced, especially in the next few years, as the effects of adjustment continue to work their way through the economy.

The Role of the OECD Countries

The OECD growth rate is one of several international factors that will influence the prospects of broad-based growth among developing countries. By its nature, such growth is linkage-intensive. It involves the expansion of two-way trade, plus positive encouragement to foreign investment and capital, and the transfer and adaptation of business and other skills. In recent years, a remarkable surge has occurred in both direct foreign investment and portfolio investment—albeit a surge that is quite selective, favoring a few but bypassing the majority of developing countries. The big economies such as China, Indonesia, and increasingly India (in Asia), and Mexico and Brazil (in Latin America), are especially favored, along with smaller countries already successful in establishing orthodox, business-friendly policies and in exporting goods (i.e., Chile and the near-tigers of Asia, Thailand, and Malaysia).

Although important, such flows are no more than a small part of the savings or wealth of main source countries. From the supply perspective, there are prospects that flows could be substantially increased in the future as part of investment diversification strategies, notably on the part of big, OECD institutional investors such as pension funds. In addition, flows in recent years from the Asian tigers and Japan into China and Indonesia are a noteworthy addition. For those able to attract such flows, they constitute a valuable supplement to domestic savings, as well as a source of expertise and technology. More countries are likely to access such sources in the future, although many will not.

The dependence on official, development finance associated with the virtual exclusion from private capital markets affects most developing countries. Aid, however, has only increased in real terms by little more than 1 percent per annum since 1980. As the aid budgets of most OECD members remain tight, dilemmas about allocation are posed. Developing countries with ready access to private capital are obvious candidates for a gradual cutback in ODA, yet they may be in the best position to make effective use of the resources. Also, in some instances aid serves to complement bilateral commercial objectives; it can be an effective tool in dialogue with governments on priorities such as environmental management, sound governance, and the promotion of structural reforms. All this said, it is the least-developed countries where the financing needs are most evident, even though the obstacles for implementing successful aid projects there are often the most formidable.

Development prospects are perhaps most strongly influenced by the trade policies of the OECD members—policies which are partly determined by the impact perceptions of stronger, developing-country competition. One should not be surprised at the attention given and the depth of concerns expressed about the threat to jobs from rising imports of East Asia and China—in contrast to the lesser interest (except among the business community itself) about the significance of the new markets for OECD exports created through the rapid growth of these economies. Yet, as many of the numerous, recent studies have confirmed, it is unlikely that imports from developing countries are responsible for the OECD's employment problems. Although manufactured exports have grown, the penetration of OECD markets is still quite limited. In the 1980s, for instance, the overall share of the OECD market for manufactured goods increased by just 1 percent—from about 2.36 percent in 1980/1981 to 3.36 percent in 1990/1991. Yet this increase was, in fact, insufficient in offsetting the lost market share in primary products during the same period.

Unfortunately, the effects of imports from developing countries on employment in OECD countries, while small in themselves, may reinforce other more powerful tendencies that are likely (unless countered by new policies) to create insecurities among OECD workers. Thus the vigorous lobbying of governments by shareholders, farmers, and industrial workers who feel threatened or disadvantaged by imports is partially successful. The OECD trade policies vis-à-vis the developing world are a patchwork of compromises between conflicting impulses and interests. The positive effects of tariff liberalization have been weakened by nontariff measures designed to protect sectors perceived as threatened by low-cost imports. A considerable fraction of manufacturing imports from developing countries is affected by such opaque, nontariff barriers. The tightening in April 1994 of import quotas on a wide range of goods imported from China into the European Union is a recent illustration of such tendencies.

A variety of domestic reasons exist as to why the temptation to extend the use of trade restraints in protecting local industry should be resisted. Free trade helps to maintain the competitive pressures spurring cost-reducing and quality-enhancing innovation and productivity growth, and it extends the range of goods available to consumers and producers. As is well known from discussions of agriculture and textiles, the costs of protecting jobs and livelihoods through trade restraints are extremely onerous. Access to OECD markets will remain critically important if the developing countries are to have a chance to establish, or maintain, a rapid pace of development—with all the international benefits that flow from success in this endeavor, both for their own people and for the OECD community.

Looking towards more distant futures suggests prospects that are more and more dominated by technology and sustainability considerations. Experience shows that a long-term effect related to the success of a broad-based employment growth is a sustained decline in the rate of population growth. Higher incomes and more remunerative jobs (especially for women) favor smaller families and fewer children. A rapid growth of nonfarm jobs would also help induce a population movement out of agronomically and environmentally precarious areas. And, as incomes rise, the demand for fuelwood and other destructive uses of the natural environment should also decline

Without serious efforts to tackle pollution and respect sound, resource-management principles, fast-growth scenarios associated with a rapid growth of employment could not be indefinitely extended into the future. Thus, environmental degradation and global pollution seems to pose increasingly severe threats to solving poverty problems, especially in the long term. Experience also shows that rapid development and rising incomes would likely bring a greater consciousness of and concern about environmental and social problems, particularly on the part of a population more secure economically, that has larger resources and generates more know-how to address problems.

Conclusion

This section voices both optimistic and pessimistic views on the question of how well developing countries are likely to cope with present and future employment challenges. Of course, every country is unique in its blend of economic conditions, culture, social history, and political circumstances. There can be no ready-made policy solutions or approaches divorced from particular circumstances. Nevertheless, optimism stems from the improved knowledge and understanding of how to promote a more effective use of labor. The track record of success pertains to a growing number of cases, evidenced among many countries by the deployment of labor use that promotes policies. Many more, however, (often the smaller countries) have no such policies in place. There are also countries for which policy and governance problems are formidable, and in which no sign exists that a well-tested policy package is available or in place.

From the international perspective, reforms among the developing countries are in danger of being overturned or frustrated by the timidity and lack of vision of OECD government leaders. Thus, it is more important than ever that the developed countries find better ways of managing their economies to produce more growth and more jobs, without shutting down the job-creating prospects for a new generation of would-be developers seeking opportunity for closer economic links. It would be ironic, indeed, if the export pessimism of policy makers in developing countries in earlier times (a pessimism that was as influential as it was harmful to the cause of linkage-intensive development), is finally to triumph because of policy paralysis in the OECD countries.

Section 3

A World in Transition: Polarization or Development?

Wally N'Dow

With the end of the Cold War, the international community was able to breathe a collective sigh of relief as the bipolar nuclear rivalry between East and West subsided. Even as the hands of the atomic clock were being pushed back, however, a new and potentially more devastating and destabilizing rivalry threatens to replace that of the Cold War as an organizing principle for the international community: the polarization between rich and poor.

Indeed, as we approach the millennium, a picture of the global community — especially its urban areas — is one of growing division between rich and poor; of increased poverty; and of social inequality. Every year of the current decade has been marked by falling average world per capita income, falling employment and wages in the urban zones of developing nations, little or no increase in agricultural output, and, outside of Southeast Asia — in developing and developed countries alike — employment levels sustained at the potentially crippling cost of falling wages in real terms.

More than two decades ago, development economist Dudley Seers formulated three classic questions to measure development.

> The questions one must ask concerning a country's development are the following: What is the level of poverty? What is happening in the area of unemployment? What is the situation regarding social inequality? When all these problems have become smaller, this would without a doubt signify that the country in question has experienced a period of development. If one or two of these core problems has become more severe, or indeed if all three of these indicators have worsened, it would be absurd to speak of development even if per capita income had experienced a rise.

These questions remain as pressing and important today as they were when Seers first articulated them. They can provide valuable signposts as we attempt to articulate a "new paradigm" for understanding the multiplicity of complex development problems posed by the current era of global transformation and transition. Indeed, the very nature of these problems— the widening fissure between rich and poor, both within and between countries—threatens in the long run our very notion of a cooperative international community.

Whenever employment deteriorates, poverty, social marginalization, and instability, inevitably follow. On the human level, this dynamic is simple to understand: the risk of job loss increases the sense of personal insecurity. This is especially true for the young, who, when faced with difficulties in finding employment, can quickly become alienated, contributing to a general mood of hopelessness and foreboding. This dynamic is evident in countries large and small, although in some regions of the globe the evidence of decline is particularly unsettling. In Sub-Saharan Africa, for example, the fall in the formal urban sector unemployment has been combined with a precipitous fall in wages, with, in some cases, the latter falling some 50 to 70 percent in the past 20 years. According to a recent report compiled by the International Labor Organization, minimum wages purchase no more than a weeks supply of food in most African countries.

Equally troubling, the trends of long-term economic decline and structural change have contributed to the growth and importance of the informal sector in Sub-Saharan Africa, Latin America, parts of Asia, and, for that matter, in developed and transition countries as well. This informalization of the global economy is most marked and most evident in rapidly growing urban areas. In much of Africa, for example, where urban areas witness annual migration rates of 6 to 8 percent in combination with already high population growth rates, new job seekers are oftentimes forced into the informal sector for mere survival. Whereas three decades ago the informal sector was virtually unknown in Africa, today two-fifths of the urban labor force is employed there. At a time when smallholder farms, so typical of rural Africa, are reaching their capacity to provide for a rapidly growing population, the stresses created by the march of labor towards the informal economy calls into question that sector's ability to serve its traditional role as an economic safety net.

In Latin America, the parallels can be seen in the rapid growth of the informal sector as the recent alternative to agricultural employment. In 1992 alone, this rose from 26 to 32 percent. The share of self-employment rose from 19 to 23 percent in the same period. Most of these jobs, of course, were low-paying, low-productivity jobs in the service sector, contributing insignificantly to the reduction of the high levels of urban poverty (estimated at 46 percent by the Inter-American Development Bank) or to narrowing a continent-wide pattern of skewed, income distribution between rich and poor, estimated as among the worst in the developing world.

Problematic in themselves, these dynamics are even more worrying when viewed in the context of overall Latin American and Caribbean economic development. The year 1993 marked the third successive one of positive economic growth for the area, with regional Gross Domestic Product (GDP) growing at a healthy 3.3 percent. In light of the already high overall level of urbanization in the region—with continued growth expected in the years ahead—it is clear that most of the new employment and income-earning opportunities are to be found in urban areas, where the economically active population is already growing faster than the total population. It is important to understand that this is a consequence of increasing female participation in the labor force and of the overall age structure of the population, a phenomenon associated with all developing regions. To choose just one example, in the Arab countries, 70 percent of the population was born after 1970.

A Renewed Focus on Social Development?

The social forces unleashed by these rapid demographic and economic changes have placed new stresses on the political system and the development programs of the world's developing countries. Indeed, if these trends continue unheeded, they offer the specter of a world unable to cope with new demands of development. They have led the Inter-American Development Bank (IADB) to conclude in its 1993 annual report that economic growth and modernization are not likely to be sustainable in the region in the absence of political and social stability. Paradoxically, the political and social stability needed to ensure growth requires a more equitable distribution of the benefits of growth. Thus, while noting that "economic reform is an essential ingredient of a strategy of social development," the IADB underscored that reforms would have to be broadened to address the region's urgent social agenda. An emphasis on social reform would thus become an "imperative for growth" in such critical areas as health, nutrition, and human resource development, and serve as a central component of a policy stressing investment in people as a long-term strategy to raise productivity and lead to a sustainable reduction in poverty levels.

In large part, there is need to link human development with economic reform, thus providing a much-needed response to the fact that over the past years GDP has performed better than employment. Disturbingly, if this trend continues it threatens to act as a barrier to long-term social and economic development, particularly in the developing regions of the world. This phenomenon, however, is not associated only with developing countries. In the advanced industrialized countries, the prospect of a long-term decline in employment growth, accompanied by improvement in output, has led the G7 group of major industrialized countries to take the unusual step of convening a summit meeting on the question of employment in these countries. The potential social and political repercussions of global, regional, and national economies unable to absorb current or future labor into productive employment are worrying indeed. One can easily envisage scenarios in which desperate populations resort to radical action in an attempt to escape poverty.

In some regions, the search for solutions to pressing societal problems is leading back to the past: witness recent election results in Eastern Europe and the growing appeal of fundamentalism in Islamic social and political order in the Middle East. All this leads to the conclusion that employment and the related issues of poverty reduction, social equality, and mobility will be a primary concern for policy makers in developed and developing countries alike in years to come. How this issue will interact with other, pressing global priorities, such as environmental protection, remains to be seen. It is, nonetheless, a challenge calling for the adoption of a comprehensive and synthesizing approach to development issues on the global agenda.

A World in Transition

The trends described above are in many ways a reflection of a world undergoing a rapid and almost total transition, of a new world in the process of being born.

In many ways, twentieth-century history can be seen as an attempt to forge an international order inducing stability and predictability in international affairs. It has also been an effort to exert positive influences on the process of global economic and political development. Following World War II, these efforts increasingly took the form of international institutional structures. Today, these structures are under assault from a variety of directions. The end of the Cold War, although it removed the immediate threat of nuclear terror, has also removed the stable geopolitical balance — "the long peace," as historian John Lewis Gaddis has termed it — that had structured world affairs for close to half a century. Moreover, the increasing globalization of the world economy and the emergence of new regional centers of economic influence have thus far occurred without the formulation of new rules. The global community exists in a state of flux, in which the collapse of the old balance has yet to be replaced with a new global order that is capable of promoting peace, stability, and development.

Small wonder then that as the United Nations approaches its fiftieth anniversary, one cannot realistically speak of anything resembling the beginning of a Fourth Development Decade. Rather, one discovers a growing sense of perplexity about the future. Indeed, development experts have yet to even arrive at a common lexicon to guide discussion and debate. With the demise of the so-called "Second World," the concept of a Third World has lost its meaning. Marxism, having failed as a strategic development option not only in Eastern Europe but also in Africa, Asia, and Latin America, seems likewise to have foreclosed the option of developing a "third way" between capitalism and socialism.

In the absence of a well-articulated, global development paradigm that will equal the challenges posed by the next century, what remains is an increasing danger of growing differentiation and disparity among and within countries and regions, of increased polarization between the lucky winners — the "tigers" of East and Southeast Asia, the rich members of the Organization of Petroleum Exporting Countries (OPEC), and the skilled professional classes of every nation — and the unlucky losers. To give an idea of this growing disparity between rich and poor: in 1989, the combined GDP of all Sub-Saharan African countries (with the exception of South

Africa) stood at about $162 billion—one third less than the $212 billion GDP of the Republic of Korea.

A New Development Paradigm

In the face of this perilous trend—of the prospect of ever increasing disparities between and within countries—the question then arises as to what the international development policy response ought to be. What should be the strategy to arrest this dangerous tendency of increasing inequality within and between countries in a new world order? An urgent response is required, if only to endorse the view that equitable global socioeconomic development is a necessary precondition of building a stable and secure foundation for the future world order. In this context, few would question the urgency for the international community to arrive at a consensus on a development policy for international peace and security, and to agree on the role and relevance of global institutions in ensuring that such a policy is quickly brought under implementation.

For this to happen, two main questions remain outstanding. What attitudes and outlooks towards international development and cooperation will be compatible with a "One World" model? And how, at the national and global levels, can this development be assured sustainability in human terms? In this regard, there is a growing sense that past strategies—such as the efforts by the United Nations to reconcile the First and the Second worlds and find a third way that characterized development efforts of the Cold War—cannot be an adequate guide for the future. Given persistent poverty, chronic unemployment, and social decline even in countries with otherwise positive economic indicators, it is clear that the development crisis will not be solved by market forces alone. The way forward must include a linking of economic and financial processes with a social action strategy; of implementing policies that focus on investments in people; and of emphasizing increased human security, in the social sense, as a chief objective of international effort.

Global Trends and Global Change

Any attempt to pursue the above-stated, fundamental development goals— to which the goal of environmental protection should be added—must increasingly take into account three trends that are transforming the globe: globalization, urbanization, and democratization.

The first of these is the globalization and liberalization of the world economy. This tendency towards an ever greater and more rapid integration of national economies in a highly competitive global economy will shape and structure GDP growth and employment trends more in the future than it has in the past. Globalization essentially is about a freer flow of capital in search of a profit maximization through, inter alia, cost minimization, or more bluntly, cheap and productive labor. Its spread can be attributed to the changing nature of production processes and the lowering of trade barriers. As a rough cut in determining who will be the winners and losers, it gives the advantage to those countries with sufficient skills and quality in the labor force to attract investment and technology from the more-advanced countries. The implications for developing countries not possessing such a critical mass of technologically skilled human capital is that they will be left behind, unless they focus on human resource development.

Thus, the challenge of globalization may, in fact, require a more interventionist state if liberalization within countries is to be successful. Sustained economic growth requires more than just specific macro- and microeconomic reforms. It also requires concerted government action in technology incubation and development, in improving the quality of human capital, in building infrastructure, in resource mobilization, and in increasing investments. Likewise, policy consideration of economic factors without addressing issues such as population planning and environmental sustainability runs considerable risk of producing suboptimal results. Gauging the proper degree of government intervention and activity on these issues lies at the heart of the problem in arriving at a new development paradigm.

As noted below, democratization, which by definition can at the outset breed a certain degree of political uncertainty and even instability, may not immediately allow for optimal economic efficiency. As is well known in developed and developing countries alike, the trade-offs between economic growth and efficiency, on the one hand, and individual political and human rights, on the other, are destined to provide fuel for the development debate for the foreseeable future. Nevertheless, sound argument exists for a central role in public action during a "transitional period," in order to ensure a fair distribution of the fruits of growth. As the World Bank so perceptively noted in its seminal study on poverty in 1990, the decisive factor in reducing poverty and increasing human welfare is not growth alone, but the quality of that growth. Thus decisive governmental policy will remain critical for ensuring a coordinated pursuit of that qualitative growth, that is, growth with social equity.

The second trend that will exercise considerable impact on the elaboration of the new development paradigm is urbanization. This silent revolution has yet to enter fully into the consciousness of decision makers in either the developing or the developed world, and its implications—which touch on almost every aspect of development—may still not be sufficiently appreciated. Although it is difficult to capture with statistics the dynamics of this revolution, a few quick reference points should suffice.

By the end of the century, the percentage of the developing world population living in cities will have tripled from what it was just 50 years ago. In 1950, it stood at 13 percent. In 1980, it was 38 percent. By the year 2000, it is projected to be upwards of 40 percent. Istanbul, which will be the site of the United Nations Conference on Human Settlements (Habitat II) in 1996, has seen its population double every 15 years since 1950, providing just one example of the stresses that such rapid urbanization can create.

Another measure of the true dimensions of this trend can be seen in the fact that in 1980, most people in developing countries lived in rural areas. By the year 2015, the opposite will be the case, with 50 percent of a projected developing world population of 6.2 billion expected to be urban dwellers, a number that will increase even more rapidly in the years thereafter. Urbanization per se does not necessarily represent a destabilizing threat or impediment to development. (Indeed, the modern city is as much a result of the need to aggregate population for economic growth as any other factor.) Nevertheless, the trend towards urbanization, when combined with other factors—such as inadequate physical infrastructure to absorb new city residents, an insufficient economic base to keep pace with the rapidly rising population, and the lack of resources which can be devoted to developing the necessary social infrastructure to accommodate the stresses of urbanization—creates a potentially explosive situation.

These urban problems are not unique to the developing world. Rather, all that distinguishes the urban centers of the developed and the developing world is time. Not, as is commonly thought in the West, that New York or London are becoming more like Mexico City or Delhi. Just the opposite applies. In the problems that must be addressed and in the inability thus far in arriving at satisfactory solutions, it is the cities of the developing world that are catching up to the cities of the developed.

What compounds the situation in the developing world, however, is the size and scale of its urban poverty and the need for developing programs to meet the special needs of urban populations for housing, sanitation, education, social services, and the like. Urban centers are where the pain of adjustment are being most perceptibly felt. Moreover, the dynamic of urban poverty is one which feeds upon itself, as ever greater numbers of urban poor create a drain on resources and a stress on social and political institutions that may, in turn, create an even greater number of urban poor. Governmental preoccupation with urban policy, for example, can have the perverse effect of creating a situation in which the neglect of rural areas gives rise to increased urban migration, which in turn creates an even greater urban problem than before.

The third and final trend that will shape development policy in the coming years is democratization. Although it can be seen as a relatively recent phenomenon in developing countries, it has a potentially profound impact on development policy and the pursuit of social progress and equity. In some formulations, democracy is seen as being a necessary condition for a competent and accountable government, without which a competitive, free-market economy cannot prosper. It may thus be seen as a necessary precondition of development. As a whole, this view rests on the crucial assumption—which may or may not necessarily hold true—that although the prevailing political formula is essentially Western in origin, it has universal application and relevance for all cultures and societies in the modern world.

Whatever the ultimate reasons, the percentage of formally democratic states increased from 25 percent in 1973, to 45 percent in 1990, and to 68 percent in 1992. Although it may well be true that it was to a large extent the context of global, political events which allowed the expression of this democratic effervescence, neither the depth of feeling that produced it, nor the force of the expectations for freedom, human rights, and a better life, should be underestimated.

There can be little doubt that democratization will exercise a profound influence on the process and direction of development. Whereas throughout the 1970s and most of the 1980s community participation often appeared to be a substitute for democracy (a term considered decidedly impolite to mention in donor dialogue with many governments), democratization now opens the door to a new form of participatory development. It also means that governments will be under more political pressure from an increasingly more impatient public — especially in urban areas — to respond to its pressing needs for jobs, services, health, education, and housing. Turning this potential for confrontation into a dynamic of cooperation while taking advantage of the opportunities afforded by the growth of civil society in most developing countries (cooperatives, NGOs, community groups, private sector associations, and political parties), will certainly be a daunting task, and one which again offers a rationale for a more people-centered development strategy. It is a strategy that should be adopted with considerable caution by international and multilateral agencies. Firstly, because many governments may feel that assistance tied to democratization interferes in a sovereign political realm. Secondly, international development agencies, dominated as they are by technocrats, generally lack the expertise to deal with decidedly more political undertakings.

Sustainable Human Development

The elucidation of a new strategy primarily focused on sustainable human development will require examination of the interactions of the trends discussed above: globalization, liberalization, urbanization, and democratization. These phenomena and the interactions between them are taking place primarily in the urban centers of the world; the recognition of this fact necessitates a strategic shift in development policy that takes account of a rapidly urbanizing world.

Today, urban poverty poses one of the most explosive of sociopolitical issues, particularly in developing countries. Globally, some 300 million people have incomes inadequate to fulfill even basic nutritional and housing requirements, while another 600 million people in urban centers live in "life- and health-threatening" situations. With an additional 700 million people expected to be added to the population of the developing world's cities and towns in the next decade alone, these problems can only be expected to worsen.

As it is, up to one-third of national urban populations inhabit substandard housing in slums and squatter settlements, where physical security is poor, and people are frequent victims of crime. At least 240 million people in urban areas of developing countries are still without access to a clean and safe supply of water, and some 330 million lack adequate sanitation. The implications of such statistics go far beyond questions relating to mere urban poverty, however. The absence of adequate waste disposal and sanitation, for example, is not only a health risk to the poor, but also a major cause of ecological degradation.

What is emerging in these exploding urban areas is a vicious circle of poverty, characterized by increasing numbers, declining productivity, and insufficient human capital investment. This effect is amplified in countries undergoing adjustment. Shifts in government expenditures necessary to achieve macroeconomic adjustment often mean that key subsidies for food, water, transport, and energy are cut, simultaneous with increases in transitional unemployment. The net result is that the marginally urban poor are pushed even closer to absolute poverty. Such problems are further aggravated by the fact that agricultural subsistence, which often provides the means of survival for the rural poor, is not viable in densely populated and crowded cities, leaving the urban poor with fewer and fewer options for survival. This urbanization of poverty calls for imaginative and effective policy countermeasures.

With urban unemployment ranging from an average of 7 percent in Latin America to 25 percent in much of Africa, in many developing countries a large portion of the urban population—up to 70 percent in some cities—makes a living in what is referred to as the informal sector. This involves small-scale manufacturing, petty trading, and service activities. For many, employment in the informal sector—where levels of labor exploitation are high, and job security and wages are low—is part of a strategy for mere survival, given that all other alternatives have been foreclosed. While there is some debate on the "transitional" nature of the informal sector, its capacity to serve as a social safety net is being increasingly strained in many parts of the developing world. With an ever-greater number of people being forced to rely upon it, an ever-increasing number, as a consequence, are falling through.

As it is constituted now, the informal sector cannot be the only foundation of national economic development in an integrated global economy because of its low productivity, lack of formal labor training, and insufficient financing. In effect, the informal sector at its worst in some developing countries may act as a screen to hide what would otherwise be massive unemployment.

For all that, the informal sector does point to potential solutions for increasing economic growth and employment opportunities: small- and medium-scale private entrepreneurship, and community and cooperative enterprises. Only these, in the long term, have the capacity for labor absorption of the type and scale that is required. For it to play a significant role in the new, sustainable human development strategy, the informal sector must be invigorated with investments in human capital, technology, small-enterprise development, marketing, and appropriate finance mechanisms.

Another significant characteristic shared by the employment sector of developing countries also merits mention—the increasing feminization of the labor force. In Africa and Latin America, in particular, female labor-participation rates have increased dramatically in urban areas (in rural areas, women usually work full time on farms), with women going mostly to the informal sector to maintain family incomes above the poverty level. Given the increasing tendency towards women-headed households in urban areas, however, this feminization of the labor force may imply that increasing numbers of children are being left on their own in the care of friends and relatives.

Not to be confused with the desirable goal of an equitable distribution of political or economic power between the sexes, the issues raised by the feminization of the labor force points up the unraveling effects which urbanization, especially when combined with poverty, can exert on traditional social structure, solidarity, and customs. An example from Africa illustrates this point. In the villages of Africa, it is perfectly natural to feed in any house and perhaps lodge in many. But in cities this communal existence no longer holds true. One must pay for lodging and be invited for food. When unemployed young men find out their relations in the city cannot house and feed them, they become bewildered, join other migrants, and often slip gradually into a world of criminality in order to survive. This pattern is repeated almost everywhere in developing countries, making many of its cities increasingly unsafe. Given the rising rates of urban poverty, the relative youth of most migrants, and the age structure of urban populations, the situation appears to be worsening. Developing-country cities are cities of the young, but they are not cities of youthful hope and ambition. There simply does not appear to be enough opportunity to go around. As a result, it is all too common to find groups of idle young men, loose agents in a volatile, uncertain environment. Recent experience in Africa teaches that the expansion in urban crime can be viewed as a vivid expression of incipient civil strife, brought on by the pressures of urban existence.

Reversing the process of social disintegration that is turning cities more and more into arenas of conflict will not be easy, and this trend may in fact increase dramatically given the new, and sometimes misunderstood, political freedoms offered by democratization. Governmental indifference or a laissez-faire attitude in the face of escalating chaos will not suffice. A more interventionist role appears necessary, which once again calls for a redefinition of the state's role.

Experience suggests that the solution to the threat of social disintegration lies in a policy of concrete public action that would support the cohesion of the stable social unit, training and education, the creation of new job opportunities, the alleviation of poverty, and the encouragement of new, civil society organizations, both as vehicles for social integration within the urban setting and as vehicles for self-help and mutual reliance. These actions must be pursued in ways that respect cultural particularities, social expression, human rights, and political pluralism. It must, in brief, enhance human security in ways other than those provided by armaments.

Development Strategy for an Urbanizing World

This urban-focused development strategy must contain not only liberal macro- and microeconomic policy instruments, but also strong social and political development components. Without them, mere economic policy instruments will not succeed, nor will the social or political stability essential for economic growth be guaranteed. The strategy will need to be informed by both the catalogue of ills accumulated over the past several decades of rapid urban growth in many developing countries, as well as by an acceptance of the more prominent role that cities, with their intricate combination of social, political, and economic forces, will play in the future.

To successfully address these issues, a new development strategy needs to be structured to engage five issue clusters: building communities, building capacity, building productivity, building partnerships, and building a citizenry.

Building Communities

Despite the disintegrating impact urbanization can have on traditional forms of social cohesion, it can also be a force for the resynthesis of physical, economic, and social integration. In some countries, for example, the liberating potential of the urbanization process has created opportunities for the extension of self-organized initiatives and new forms of communitarianism that provide the social elasticity to overcome the chaos that might otherwise ensue. This is especially significant given that where this process of self-organization is denied by authorities, political tensions escalate and the development of cohesive communities is frustrated, resulting in an escalation of social crime and violence.

A number of steps can be taken by governments to facilitate the process of building cohesive and productive communities. The first would be the recognition of the informal sector as a key transformative element, and to assist it through the transition to small- and medium-scale manufacturing, service, and community enterprises. As developing countries' governments lose their resource base due to liberalization and the shedding of public enterprise, they must increasingly depend on urban residents to organize their own enterprises. Beyond serving as the necessary catalyst for this change, the less governments try to control this process, the more successful they will be. Supporting transition on the part of the informal sector not only calls on governments to revise, relax, and rescind regulations that inhibit small-business growth, as suggested by Hernando de Soto. Governments should also provide assistance in human resource development leading to a more technically skilled labor force, aid businesses in accessing new technologies and in building market networks, and help establish financing mechanisms for business development.

A second step in the direction of building cohesive, healthy, and productive communities would be a renewed emphasis on housing and the provision of basic services, especially through community-based efforts. The importance of safe and adequate housing for stable community and family life, and for giving children a positive environment to nurture their growth and development, is all too often underestimated, as is the role that the provision of housing and services can play in reducing the effects of urbanization on environmental degradation.

The third and final step towards building viable urban communities is the strengthening of political and social institutions and organizations of civil society. Yet in the final analysis, development and economic growth can only be sustained by organizations and institutions in the affected countries themselves. In many countries, and in urban areas in particular, these tend to be weak and ineffective. To provide the proper support for their development, the means to build the capacity of community groups and other social and political organizations to act as intermediaries, and to ensure their full participation in decision making at all levels, must be found.

Building Capacity

The second essential element of the new approach to development is the building of capacity, measured primarily in terms of human resource development. Such a measure builds on the more narrow focus on the informal sector suggested above, to include the whole range of human capital and skills required if developing countries are to complete the transition towards integration in the wider global economy.

Such capacity building will put a premium on the development of advanced technical skills, the absence of which in many developing countries is so evident. The roots of this deficiency can be found in the primary and secondary levels of education. Yet human resource development aimed at enhancing technical capacity is costly; it demands large investments in facilities and equipment. This suggests that the best way to address the task is through a partnership between government, private sector, voluntary and community organizations, and external support agencies, including key U.N. development agencies such as UNDP, UNICEF, UNESCO, ILO, and FAO, and of course, the World Bank and regional banks. If such an effort were launched in tandem with the expansion of those sections of the modern urban and rural sectors where skilled labor is required, the investments would be repaid in short time, as the tax base and levies derived from the resultant economic activity would increase rapidly.

Developing countries that ignore human resource development do so at their peril. Historically, countries recognizing the importance of human resource development have been able to build stable manufacturing and service sectors and focus on production improvements. It is such manufactured goods, as opposed to more primary commodity exports, for example, that may provide the key to success in the world economic order.

The second element of capacity building is in the area now referred to in development circles as "governance." Political stability, well-established central and local authorities, public-spirited leaders, and a professional and well-trained civil service are prerequisites for the success of any economic or development program. During the politically conservative 1980s, attention was often directed elsewhere; less acknowledgment was given to the positive role that governments can play in economic development.

Even if we now move to recognize the important role of sound government in implementing development, practical problems stand in the way of achieving it. The first is definitional and political. As a 1989 World Bank report on Africa argued, "Underlying the litany of Africa's development problems is a crisis in governance. The Bank then went on to define governance as...the exercise of political power to manage a nation's affairs." Good governance should include some or ideally all of the following features: an efficient public service, an independent judicial system, a legal framework to enforce contracts, an accountable administration of public funds (including an independent public auditor), respect for the law and human rights, a free press, and a pluralist institutional structure.

This adds up to a comprehensive statement of the minimal institutional, legal, and political conditions of liberal democracy. These characteristics were advanced in some quarters as largely functional and institutional prerequisites of development, although often never stated explicitly. The practicality of applying only this recipe in developing countries with their heterogeneous social, political, legal, and cultural traditions must be thought through.

Building Productivity

The third prong of the new development strategy should be the improvement of productivity, primarily through the improvement of the social and physical infrastructure in developing countries. Although productivity questions are usually approached from a purely economic standpoint, the current imperatives suggest that a strong social component must also be addressed. As a first step, this means improvements in health care, especially preventive care, to improve the productivity of workers in both rural and urban areas. It also entails improving living and working conditions through access to housing, clean water, and sanitation.

A second area of focus in building productivity needs to be on investments in physical infrastructure. This often-missing factor prevents the expansion of both rural and urban economies and retards investment from both domestic and international sources. Large and focused investments in infrastructure have been the key to success for a number of countries that have successfully reached the threshold of development, especially in urban areas where the construction and manufacturing sectors are based.

To achieve success, such investments in infrastructure require a long-term outlook on development perspectives, consistency in policy, and, perhaps most importantly, planning. Without such foresight, perseverance, and planning, inadequate infrastructure can become a bottleneck preventing further economic growth. The initial outlay of resources for such infrastructural improvement is a considerable hurdle for many developing countries, however, and will continue to be so unless solutions are found which involve collaboration between government, multilateral and bilateral lending institutions, and the private sector, as well as between developing and developed countries.

Building Partnerships

In light of all of the above, the fourth element of a more urban-oriented approach to development must be the creation and nurturing of partnerships at every level of social, political, and economic life. On the political side, it seems safe to conclude that cooperation between various important social actors in the process of development is more conducive to success than confrontation. However, this goal will be far from easy to achieve, as a more open political system will make the process of forging consensus on long-range development strategies infinitely more contentious, especially at the urban level.

Yet the opening up of the political system holds forth the possibility that once a consensus is reached, that consensus will produce better results. One can expect, therefore, that urban policy and management will have to be built on new forms of partnership and a new modus vivendi, varying from country to country and city to city, and including representatives of both state and civil society institutions. It will also have to include representatives of the private sector, particularly as the liberalization of the political process in many — if not most — developing countries has gone hand-in-hand with the opening of the domestic economy, market reform, and a greater role of the private sector as the prime agent of development.

Building a Citizenry

The final issue-cluster that must be addressed for the elaboration of a new, people-oriented approach to development is the building of a cohesive citizenry with a national identity. Divisions, whether of class, religion, or ethnicity, disrupt many urban areas. Often, large segments of the population, especially the urban poor, are alienated from those in authority. The failures of the past have created an environment lacking in the trust necessary for partnership. In part, however, this lack of trust is also a result of the very newness of the phenomenon of massive urbanization. Many urban residents, newly arrived from rural areas, have yet to be fully or properly integrated into the urban polity and community. Different groups, with different habits, have yet to grow comfortable with the idea of being in such close proximity, and working alongside, those who are different from themselves.

Paradoxically, the resultant unrest that currently characterizes so many urban centers points towards its own solution. Indeed, a window of opportunity is now open in which these recent migrants can be shaped and socialized into urban citizens. As the cities themselves mature, so too, one hopes, will the combustible mix of social forces eventually mellow. Such a process will not occur unaided, however, and will require responsive institutions and adept political leadership at every level. For it is only when all those in the urban centers feel that they have a stake in the success of the city — and that the city has a stake in their success — that urban populations will successfully interact and participate towards building a healthy, fully functioning, and productive society.

Conclusion

Although this discussion is far from a fully formulated concept of the new development agenda, it suggests the modalities that the implementation of such a policy may take in order to integrate new trends of globalization, liberalization, and democratization that are today shaping the new global environment. It also underscores, most vividly, that economic development can never be merely a technical process that excludes people; rather, it must be one that actualizes the full human potential of a given society. A main objective here has been to refute the idea that government and governance are not essential for the success of economic growth and development. Although theories advocating a heavy hand may well have been disproved, so too have we seen that hands-off policies inevitably lead to suboptimal, if not disastrous, results.

Lastly, it seeks to underline the centrality of the political aspects of development. In the final analysis, a failure to face and engage the political challenge in an appropriate fashion does not bode well for any development program. Addressing these political questions, moreover, will meet only with limited success if done from without. The modes of political intercourse must spring from within any given society.

In conclusion, it may be fair to say that what is required, in essence, is a combining of social, political, economic, and financial reform in a new form of social contract linking all—rich and poor, government and governed, private and public—in a bond of mutual obligation to achieve common social objectives. Such a social contract will also require new rules governing international political and economic affairs. The present institutional arrangements and regimes governing the world economy came into being in the wake of World War II. The dramatic changes ushered in by the end of the Cold War have opened a new window of opportunity for a global compact. A revision in the rules governing the conduct of international economic life may be the final, but critical, component of the effort if all countries are to be able to compete and prosper in a liberal and global world economy. Human development must be given a real chance of sustainability, in actions large and small.

Ironically, perhaps no better guide to the progression of this new development paradigm can be found than in the words offered more than 30 years ago by Ambassador Adlai E. Stevenson, then the U.S. Permanent Representative to the United Nations, in his address to the Thirty-second session of the Economic and Social Council, presaging the declaration of the U.N.'s First Development Decade:

> Economics must always be the servant of society. No amount of steel or cement produced, of oil wells drilled, or acres of wheat harvested is of any consequence except as it fills a human need—unless the steel and cement make decent houses and schools and hospitals, unless the oil warms and transports man and his goods, unless the wheat means bread and strength for those who hunger. The most efficient factory cannot justify a city's slums. And economic growth is of little avail if it serves only a fraction of the people. It must serve them all.

Chapter 2

Learning from Experiences

Section 1

Changing Poverty and Employment Patterns under Crisis in Africa

Vali Jamal

Given the context of falling average incomes, from levels which were already low to begin with, it seems almost axiomatic that poverty increased in Sub-Saharan African countries. While the problem is recognizable, the answer is less straightforward. For one, income declines have been unevenly spread and the vulnerable groups—farmers and wage-earners— have adopted complex survival strategies to make ends meet, straddling both the rural and urban areas, the formal as well as the informal sectors, and rendering the usual indicators of levels of living—wages and prices— inadequate to reflect changes in family welfare. The pattern of poverty and associated poverty has changed in Africa, complicating analysis but more substantively requiring a rethinking in our modeling of these economies. To cite the most prominent example, most of the "urban bias" once thought to be the hallmark of African economies—and which recently was blamed for their crises—has by now disappeared, with massive turnarounds in the rural–urban terms of trade and decline in wages.

If changing the internal terms of trade implies a redistribution of income, that redistribution is not as cataclysmic as it once was. Because the same individual may be both farmer and wage earner, the kind of reallocation of labor attendant upon changes in relative prices does not happen as predicted in theory. Thus, we may need a new paradigm to explain African economies.

This section of the book provides a basis for understanding the changes in poverty and employment that have occurred in African countries in the last two decades. It also draws upon their ramifications for policy formulation. The first part will discuss structural characteristics of African economies, particularly their engines of growth and labor-force profile. What is important are the implications of recent changes in employment patterns for income levels. The latter is specifically described in the part on poverty, based on indicators relating to agricultural output and wages. The limitations of such indicators in the face of changing employment patterns are also highlighted. The major conclusion that emerges is the huge turnaround in the rural–urban gap, perhaps even rural–urban terms of trade, in the last decade. What does this signify for "urban bias?" And how do we measure urban bias in the context of export, crop-oriented marketing controls?

Economic Structures and the Labor Force

The overriding feature of African economies that decides their employment and poverty outcomes is undoubtedly their agricultural orientation. Sectoral shares of Gross Domestic Product (GDP), labor force, and exports are all higher here than in the other developing regions. While the GDP share of agriculture has fallen since the mid-1960s, this occurred more in the context of declining agricultural incomes than in a faster growth of non-agricultural sectors. By contrast, the South Asian region, which at mid-1960s was more agriculture-oriented than Sub-Saharan Africa (46 percent of GDP from agriculture compared to 43 percent), had by 1991 seen agriculture's share fall to the same level as in the Sub-Saharan (31 percent). Even oil-rich Nigeria had 37 percent of its GDP emanating from agriculture in 1991, the same, incidentally, as from industry. Two-thirds of the African labor force is engaged in agriculture, whereas by 1985, this share in Latin America fell to 29 percent. Agricultural exports provided over one-third of total exports of Sub-Saharan Africa in 1991, or 44 percent of those exports (excluding Nigeria), whereas in Asia this share was under 15 percent.

The African economies are also more "open" than their Asian or Latin American counterparts, making them more vulnerable to external shocks. In 1991, some 23 percent of the regional GDP was exported, compared to only 10 percent for South Asia. One-third of the agricultural output of Sub-Saharan Africa (excluding Nigeria) was exported, compared to only 7 percent in South Asia. In most African countries, the two largest exports generate over one-half of export proceeds, and in some, just one commodity attains this status. For example, coffee earned 76 percent of the total exports of Burundi between 1980 and 1990; coffee earned 53 percent in Ethiopia; tobacco 66 percent in Malawi; cotton 47 percent in Mali; and live animals 44 percent in Somalia. In the mineral-based economies, one single mineral may provide upwards of four-fifths of exports.[1]

Apart from agriculture and minerals, remittances play an important role in some African countries. Botswana, Lesotho, and Swaziland are long-standing examples of remittance economies in southern Africa. Recently in Egypt, Tunisia, Sudan, and Somalia, as in some West African countries, remittances have gained importance. In Lesotho, practically one-half of the male labor force works in South African mines, contributing the same proportion of the country's national income. For Somalia, it was estimated in the late 1980s that as many people worked in the Persian Gulf countries as in the domestic modern sector, contributing about the same amount in remittances as the entire urban GDP. In West African countries, too, migration is significant, as typified by the well-publicized expulsion of 1 million Ghanaian workers from Nigeria in 1982.

Rural Labor Force

Agricultural labor force dominates. Within that, smallholders prevail, even in such countries as Zimbabwe and Kenya, which have a distinct, large-scale agricultural sector. It should be noted that the figures of smallholder population comprise the head of the family plus family members. Farms are small (1.5 hectares being the average per household), households large (six members), and hence, little labor is employed on a wage basis on the smallholdings. In the typical smallholder country – Ghana and Sierra Leone cited here – agricultural wage earners comprise no more than 5 percent of the agricultural labor force at the outset, and one-fifth of the total wage employees. Most farm laborers are employed on a seasonal basis and are likely to come from farm households.

A gender-based division of labor prevails, with food crops being women's responsibility (apart from their domestic duties) and export crops men's. Given that more food crops are grown than export crops, a great majority of labor time has to be devoted to the former. In terms of cash-income generation, however, the division could turn in favor of export crops. The implication is that women who do the bulk of work on farms receive only a fraction of the cash income. Days of 12 to 14 hours are common for women, as opposed to the typical eight for men. Moreover, a growing proportion of rural households are female-headed, because of males out searching for employment. Figures above 25 percent are recorded in at least 20 countries.

Another emerging trend is that farmers undertake diverse, nonfarm activities to ensure survival ("straddling"). They engage in side businesses in the rural areas and have family members work on neighboring farms or in towns. Appleton and Collier (1990) show that in Ghana, rural households undertake numerous activities apart from farming. In Kenya in 1981/1982, farm income provided (only) 48 percent of the income of a rural household, with wages contributing 21 percent, nonfarming activities 17 percent, and remittances and gifts 14 percent. Pinstrup-Andersen (1989) shows that in Hurungwe District of Zimbabwe, in 1985/1986, 43 percent of a farming household's cash income came from non-farming sources. Wages generated 7 percent and remittances 17 percent, the two together attesting to the direct (wages) and indirect (remittances) importance of wage employment for farm families. Business and other nonagricultural activities contributed the rest of the cash income.

Differentiation on the farms arises from the fact that larger farmers have more surplus land available for cash crops; consequently, they dominate crop sales. At the bottom of the ladder, farms are much too small to produce sufficient calories for their families. Higher producer prices do not mean higher incomes for them; in fact, they mean higher expenditures, since they are net purchasers of food. Unacknowledged until now, some 30 to 40 percent of African farmers most likely fall in this category.

Increasing landlessness also contributes to rural differentiation.   In densely populated countries, such as Rwanda and Burundi, the proportion easily reaches 20 percent.   Landlessness is also present in countries such· as Kenya and Zimbabwe, where significant tracts of fertile land have been appropriated by large-scale farmers.

Urban Labor Force

The urban labor market has changed even more than the rural in the last 15 years.   It has become practically informalized, with the informal sector easily providing the bulk of employment in towns.

In both Kenya and Tanzania, the informal sector was a rarity at independence.[2] Even a decade later, when the International Labor Organization (ILO) first put the informal sector on the map (1972), Kenya's urban economy was quite formal, with four-fifths of the urban labor force still in wage employment.   At the same time, because of stagnating employment, Tanzania's urban sector was already 40 percent informalized. During the rest of the 1970s and 1980s, Tanzania went through even faster informalization, due to its much higher rate of urbanization compared to Kenya (10 to 12 percent versus 6 to 8 percent).

Situations were different at the start of the 1970s.   At that time, four types of African economies, based on the role of the informal sector, distinguished themselves: (1) informal sector traditional: North Africa; (2) informal sector dominant: West Africa; (3) informal sector emergent: East Africa; (4) informal sector negligible: southern Africa.   The first category signals the fact that in North African countries, small-scale activities have always been the norm on which a modern sector was imposed, whereas elsewhere, the modern sector first fostered growth in the informal sector. The contrast between the second and the third categories arises because urban-zoning laws were much stricter in East Africa during the colonial days than in West Africa.   The same situation pertained to the southern African countries, where the mines in South Africa siphoned off excess labor that could not find productive employment on land.

By now, a definite escalation has occurred with southern African countries in the "informal sector emergent" category and eastern African ones in the "informal sector dominant" group.   For both, zoning laws have eroded in the face of rapid urbanization.   Informalization has continued in West Africa, and even in the north.   One could now be talking more appropriately of the informal sector, as opposed to the traditional sector, since newcomers to towns have been pushed into nontraditional, small-scale activities.

The informal sector has not only managed to create employment but has also provided a source of income to newly pauperized urban families. However the sector is famous for its heterogeneity, and for "disguising" underemployment.   Moreover, recent increases in unemployment in African cities show limits to the absorptive capacity of this increasingly ubiquitous sector.

Poverty Trends

What happened to poverty levels during the African crisis? The presumption should be that poverty increased: average incomes fell in most countries from levels that were never high, hence the incomes of a significant proportion of the population must have fallen below poverty levels. By and large, this reasoning is correct; spot indicators confirm the situation. Yet the whole issue must be approached quite gingerly, since the composition of household incomes has changed drastically in recent years. The broad picture shows that income declines were indeed uneven between rural and urban areas—the urban areas lost more, as did the wage earners.

Rural Areas

Agricultural output is an appropriate indicator to use when a majority of the agricultural population are subsistence-oriented (consuming what they produce), and where wage labor is of marginal importance. Agricultural production doubled between 1961 and 1992, translating to a decline of 13 percent on per capita terms, and, because of massive migration from rural areas, an increase of 16 percent in per agricultural capita terms. Most of the increase occurred between 1961 and 1970. During the two decades of the crisis itself (1970–1992), agricultural productivity stagnated. Food production fared better than export production, which rather neatly coincides with the generally held belief that African farmers withdrew from export crops because of unattractive prices, yet still maintained their food production.

One should relax some of the implicit assumptions in the above, broad-based picture to take account of the distributional angle. At the lower end of the scale, an increasing number of farmers are net purchasers of food, as opposed to being self-sufficient. To them, higher food prices mean higher expenditures. The middle third should be self-sufficient in food, and the top one-third should serve as sellers of food and export crops.[3]

The cash position of the top farmers probably remained stable in the 1975–1985 period, with declines in export incomes being counterbalanced by increases in food income. Since 1985, their position should have improved with the turnaround in export-crop prices and the continued increases in food prices. The position of self-sufficient farmers, too, should have improved, since average food production increased. Concern centers on the bottom third. Not only have they been faced with higher food prices, their food production may have declined more than that of the average farmer, due to poor weather conditions. These farmers also depend on remittances from urban family members to make ends meet, and, as we shall see, urban wages fell even more than agricultural incomes.

Altogether, the point that emerges is that agricultural incomes (or output) fell much less than average incomes (GDP per capita). The impact, however, was on the whole regressive due to the deteriorating position of the bottom third of farmers. While not all farmers fell into poverty, the implied decline in cash incomes in the 1975–1985 period visibly translated into a decline in housing standards and a reduction of durable goods (bicycles, utensils, agricultural implements). Since the late 1980s, export volumes have begun to recover—as have producer prices—but both remain far below their levels in the early 1970s.

The picture thus painted is incomplete, since farmers are much more than farmers, and since their extra-farm sources of income have been changing. As stated earlier, agricultural smallholders obtain a large part of their total income from wages, remittances, and nonfarm activities. It is difficult to gage precisely how these changed, or how the different levels of farmers were affected. Zimbabwe data indicates that the wage sources of income (wages and remittances) contribute proportionately more to family income at the lower end of the distribution than at the upper end. Farm wages have been failing, as have urban wages; congruently, the bottom end of the farmers are most affected by these trends. As for nonfarm activities, the better-off farmers dominate these, since they have savings to carry on trade and production. The increasing attention to rural, nonfarm sectors in Africa signifies a genuine expansion: the collapse of the infrastructure has pushed rural areas to their own resources, while at the same time providing them with natural protection against town products.

Urban Areas

The most visible impact of the crisis lies in urban areas. As noted, rural incomes fell much less than total GDP—that is, *ipso facto* urban incomes fell more than total GDP. At the same time, urban areas have been growing much faster than rural areas (5 to 6 percent a year compared to 2 percent); hence average urban incomes have fallen sharply, declines of 30 to 40 percent being registered in countries such as Ghana, Uganda, Tanzania, and Zambia. One could say that urban incomes above subsistence needs could afford to fall, whereas farm incomes were too near bare sufficiency to countenance any decline. Moreover, urban production requires a host of inputs and supporting infrastructure and services, all of which disappeared under the crisis, whereas the average farmer self-sufficient in input usage could maintain at least his food production, despite the widespread collapse.

Within the urban areas, wages fell the most. On average, wages have fallen by 50 to 60 percent in most African countries, with much greater declines if comparison is made against 1975, when wages were generally at their highest in Africa. Thus in Kenya, wages fell by 50 percent compared to 1975, and in Ghana and Tanzania, by 70 percent.

Such enormous wage declines obviously mean a cut in living standards, but what do they mean for poverty? We need a poverty yardstick. In this case Tanzania is appropriate, since it largely corresponds to most other African countries. Let us examine some comparisons. One is what the minimum wage would purchase in maize meal, while the others set the minimum wage against a food- and total-poverty line. The first comparison needs a measurement to be meaningful: two-thirds of a kilogram of maize meal provide 2,200 calories, the absolute minimum for an average person. On this basis, by 1991 the minimum wage would feed only three persons—on maize meal alone, and *uncooked* at that.

Estimates of the food and total poverty line allow for other essential needs. The poverty lines (for a family of five members) were originally calculated at March 1984 prices and extrapolated to other years by applying the consumer-price index. Very simple baskets were chosen. In the case of food, maize meal was given a weight of 75 percent of daily per capita calories (set at 2,200), beans 15 percent, fats 5 percent, and sugar 5 percent. In the nonfood basket, only core items such as clothing, rent, transport, fuel, and water were included. School fees, medicines, and entertainment were deliberately omitted as were tea, spices, milk, meat, etc. Obviously, those falling below such austere poverty lines are to be considered in extreme poverty.

At its maximum (1974), 40 percent of the minimum wage would have sufficed to purchase the minimum needs poverty basket; in other words, 60 percent of the income would be available to purchase more discretionary items. By 1984, the minimum wage had fallen below the minimum basket, and by 1988, below even the minimum food basket. Since then, the real wage measured against the consumer price index has improved (though not against maize meal price), and by 1991, the minimum wage would purchase 20 days' worth of basic goods. If we were to add the other essential items — medicines, transport, and the like–the minimum wage would be exhausted within 12 to 15 days.

The question arises as to how wage earners survive? The issue is worth pursuing because ultimately it yields vital information about the changes that have occurred in African countries. For example, a calculation of minimum wage in terms of its purchasing power would imply starvation for the urban wage earners, yet nowhere do we see such a dire situation. First of all, the average wage in most countries is higher than the minimum wage. In Tanzania, the average wage at the start of the 1990s was one-and-a-half times the minimum wage. This means that while the minimum wage could only buy 20 days' supply of goods, the average wage managed to buy a month's supply. Yet even the average wage would buy only a most austere basket, and to date, only half the wage earners earn just minimum wage.

The answer to the "wage/poverty puzzle" is provided by "straddling." Urban households have reestablished their links with the countryside, reversing the labor-force stabilization process of the 1960s. Compared to when they regularly remitted a part of their wages back to rural areas, now they are as likely to be recipients of remittances from rural areas — in the form of food collected from family farms. Urban dwellers have begun to grow their own food in towns, something that was always practiced in Africa but had declined because of increasing urban specialization.

These kinds of fusions have managed to keep urban families above absolute poverty. Certainly, the type of declines depicted by wage figures do not translate to declines in family incomes. Wage is no longer a reliable indicator of family welfare, since the composition of family incomes has changed. Whereas up to the mid-1970s wages comprised nearly three-quarters of a wage-earner family's income, now they provide less than two-fifths. What has most likely happened is that compared to the 60 to

80 percent decline in wages shown by the statistics, total family income probably declined by only half as much. This should not be scoffed at. In the context of generally low incomes, it means the loss of command over all except the most basic goods. It would mean food absorbing three-fourths of the family income, compared to only half as much in the early 1970s.

The "topping" has disappeared from urban incomes. We have only to look at import figures to see how far living standards have fallen. Most Sub-Saharan countries are now importing less than one-third as much in per capita terms as 15 years ago, and this in a context of a virtual collapse of local industries. Income for the majority of urban dwellers now effectively means 2,200 calories per day, plus basic necessities and emergency funds for health care.

Moreover, just as in rural areas, differentiation has increased in the towns since the straddling solutions are not equally available to all wage earners. Growing food in urban areas is only possible for those with a plot of land in the vicinity; this effectively means long-term residents and migrants with ethnic ties to the city. Making forays to the rural areas to tap on family farms is only possible for those who have migrated from nearby areas. On both counts, migrants from outlying districts lose out, and it is not unknown for these non-native migrants to move back to rural areas.

A quick summation on the trends in rural and urban poverty will provide a transition to the next section. Urban incomes have fallen much more than rural incomes, and poverty has increased in the urban areas to the extent that we now speak of an "urbanization of poverty" in Africa, whereas at the start of the 1970s it was rare to speak of urban poverty.[4] The great decline in urban wages has been the contributing factor. Two famous casualties have been the wage-farm gap and the rural-urban gap. Insofar as these were taken to be manifestations of "urban bias," that bias has been reduced; in fact, based on discussion to follow, urban bias has disappeared.

The Urban Bias

As understood up to now, urban bias implied a redistribution of income: farm prices were held low and urban wages high, and the former fed the latter (literally). The bias mostly derived from the case of Asian countries where "farm prices" meant food prices, and where holding down farm prices could be taken to imply a subsidization of urban consumers. However, when the African case came to be considered in the World Bank's 1981 report, urban bias was almost exclusively applied to export crops, since these comprised the bulk of crop marketing in Africa and since their prices were controlled by the state. Grain prices too were nominally controlled, but evasion was common; nongrain staple prices were almost never controlled.

By the start of the 1980s, urban wages had been declining for at least five years, and the income gap between farmers and wage earners had begun to turn in favor of the former. The wage declines became an Africa-wide phenomenon, applicable even to the Francophone countries.

Trends after 1980 should be emphasized, since they tell the common tale of disappearing urban bias in agriculture-pricing policies in Africa. Between 1972 and 1980, producer prices declined by a staggering 85 percent, whereas external prices more or less held their own. The difference between the country's purchasing power and the farmers' came mostly from the maintenance of an overvalued exchange rate: farmers' real income was simply allowed to erode away, the difference pocketed by those who had access to imports at the official exchange rate. After 1980, devaluations enabled farm prices to rise in the face of falling external prices. For a while, these opposing trends could be accommodated by reducing overt taxation; with the surplus exhausted, additional increases in real prices have effectively been financed by income transfers from other groups.

Similar trends are shown by most other African countries applying standard-structural adjustment programs — and that means a majority of the African countries. "Rural bias" is now well ensconced in Africa. To cite two other examples, by 1991–1992 the Tanzanian cotton farmers were getting the full international price, and the coffee farmers were subsidized as in Uganda, while in Ghana the trends for cocoa were running counter to international trends after the mid-1980s. By now, the attempt to maintain internal prices in real terms means effective subsidization.

A final comment brings us back to the question of poverty. The average African farmer has never risen above a position where food constitutes less than two-thirds of a total income. It is a comment on international price trends that farmers obtained much more from their produce in the distant past. Their accumulated savings had enabled them to build a stock of durable goods through the mid-1970s, but much of this has disappeared in the last 15 years.

Challenge of New Policies

In a situation where whole economies have collapsed and infrastructure has decayed, the problem is to revive economies onward to growth. The unpalatable truth is that although export-crop prices are on a falling trend, export crops remain the main growth engine of most African countries; hence they must be rejuvenated. Simultaneously, all efforts must be made to diversify into nontraditional exports. The direct beneficiaries will initially be the large-scale farmers who dominate export production, but exports have indirect benefits by increasing government revenues. These could then be used to increase sorely needed social services and rebuild the infrastructure.

Increasing export production will require changing agricultural technology and rehabilitating the supporting infrastructure. The task was always difficult, and became even more so given the intensification of the "vicious circles of poverty" as a result of the persistent crisis. At the household level, this has meant that farm incomes have fallen even below their already low thresholds, and farmers have no surplus to invest in tools, fertilizers, bags, etc. At the national level, given the contraction in revenues, the government is in no position to supply any of these, let alone repair the infrastructure and import the medicines and books.

The vicious circle has to be broken—the best bet is by increasing agricultural incomes. The onus falls on the government to marshal all resources in a major effort to revive the agricultural sector. At the international level, aid should be increased with this specific objective in view. The truth is that African economies need to be jump-started. Without this, gains from minor increases from export production may not be sufficient to stop the cumulative decline.

Once the economies begin to achieve 5 to 6 percent growth based on the agricultural sector, all efforts must be made to diversify the economies. Except for windfall gains, prices of traditional exports will remain weak, perhaps forever. The first avenue for diversification could be nontraditional export crops, such as fruits, vegetables, and flowers, but even here the markets are beginning to soften as other developing countries attempt to compete.

Diversification may reduce the reliance of the economies on agricultural exports. Initially, the rural nonfarm sector should be targeted to ease the pressure of land population, as well as stop the drift to towns. Nonfarm activities have burgeoned spontaneously as a coping mechanism under the crisis, but now they must be explicitly incorporated in the growth process. They not only have a vast potential for labor absorption, they also have the great advantage of being linked with the agricultural sector. The rural informal sector— for that is what the rural nonfarm activities amount to—utilizes agricultural product as inputs; its own outputs are used for agriculture. Thus growth in agriculture would stimulate nonfarm activities, which would in turn stimulate agriculture.

In the past, great emphasis was placed on the urban informal sector as the answer to the employment problem in Africa. This should be guarded against. The informal sector is simply the embodiment of a coping mechanism, and it is often dysfunctional. Much of the increase in informal sector employment simply signifies an increase in underemployment. The rural-based, recommended strategy is to help stem the tide of migration to towns, giving the urban economy a chance to clear the backlog of unemployment. At the same time, informal sector skills should be improved to ensure growth.

Skill enhancement is the sine qua non of African growth. In all sectors, production technology remains rudimentary. African countries achieved success in spreading primary and secondary education, but the weak link was that university education was seen as the culmination of the learning cycle. Vocational training, which can start mid-way through secondary school, should be the focus of educational attention. Even the rudimentary vocational training that once existed has virtually disappeared with the breakdown of equipment and the brain drain of teachers to foreign countries.

Major constraints need to be lifted to break the downward spiral. Africa resembles a war-torn continent—ravaged by famine, civil war, and falling commodity prices. Like any region emerging from destruction, it faces a crumbling infrastructure, as Africa's depredations are continuing and its basic skills are disappearing.

Conclusion

The list of factors responsible for Africa's decline should include "bad governance." In fact, it should be put at the top. This envelops policies that favored the urban sector at the expense of the farmers. In the nature of things, this debate (the relative contributions of external and internal factors to the crisis) is indeterminate: economics is like that, everything is interconnected and no economic models are yet available to disentangle the impacts of myriad exogenous and endogenous factors. In a way, the debate was won by the internalists; everywhere in Africa the major distortions in factor and product markets have been corrected.

Most African countries are now also going through a process of democratization. These positive developments should be recognized, at the same time, there should be an acknowledgement that results have been lacking. The real threat is that withdrawal of the state from social and economic functions is leaving an utter vacuum in the Sub-Saharan countries which privatization is not yet able to fill. There should be a recognition that free-market dictates at the international level are tying up the African countries to declining markets. There should be a recognition that the debt burden is eating away at Africa's only source of foreign exchange and savings. There should be a recognition that the African countries have fulfilled their part of the bargain by accepting strict, structural-adjustment programs. Now is the time to set that ideological debate aside to ensure that some visible results are forthcoming.

Notes

1. Petroleum provided 96 percent of Nigeria's exports in 1989 and 1990, 91 percent in Angola, 80 percent in Congo, and 77 percent in Gabon; in Niger, uranium contributed 80 percent of total exports in 1989 and 1990, the same as did copper in Zambia and Zaire.
2. In fact, calculations show that the nonagricultural wage employees exceeded the nonagricultural labor force at the start of the 1960s in both countries. This should not be considered a negation of the estimating procedure. It could simply mean that some of the "nonagricultural" wage employees were, in fact, not located in urban areas. They could be in rural transportation, mines, etc.
3. Obviously, this is another stylized picture. Both export-crop and food-crop sales are made by many more farmers than just the top one-third. In terms of concentration, however, the top group controls upwards of three-fourths of the marketing. Kenya (3,000 or so large-scale farmers contribute more than one-half of the crops marketed) and Zimbabwe (6,000 or so large-scale farmers contribute two-thirds) may seem like exceptions because of

the legacy of large-scale farming. They are actually not too far from the pattern in other African countries.

4. For example, for Kenya in 1976, I (and other researchers) estimated urban poverty at under 10 percent, whereas for 1990, I estimated it at one-third.

Section 2

Employment Patterns in Russia: Between Socialism and the Market

Vladmir Gimpelson

Suffering from enormous pain, Russia is trying radically to transform its entire economic and social system. State socialism is to be replaced by social relations embedded in market and democracy. This transition has to be performed in a very short time, and it concerns all systemic features of the society and economy. Labor and employment are also shifting from the state-socialist pattern towards the market model. The main purpose of this section is to look at labor market transformation and to display some of the key changes taking place in this area.

What I call the "state-socialist model of employment" was created in the 1930s under Stalinist-forced industrialization. It has since gone through many changes and mutations; however, its main systemic features survived until the late 1980s. They are full and obligatory employment guaranteed by the state and accompanied by a permanent labor shortage; very rigid employment; low and deliberately limited labor and social mobility; the absence of open unemployment and high excessive employment with inefficient utilization of labor; use of compulsory labor; the total domination of employment in the state-run sector; and the absence of a private sector.

On the contrary, the market economy supposes voluntary employment and open unemployment with relatively high labor mobility. The labor market is much more deregulated and flexible than the employment determined by the state, and the bulk of jobs is created in the private sector.

The awkward attempts of Soviet leader Mikhail Gorbachev's reforms in the late 1980s gave initial impulse to this transformation. The total collapse of Soviet political and economic institutions in 1991, and the economic policy pursued by the Yeltsin-Gaidar government in 1992, speeded up the systemic changes and made them irreversible. It brought spontaneity and contradictions into this transformation. Thus we are witnessing a flamboyant mixture of various elements of socialism and market economy on what is largely a "no-man's land." Like other aspects of social and economic life in Russia, employment is in deep crisis. Although open unemployment is still moderate by any standards, the possibilities to sustain jobs are shrinking rapidly. Growing, hidden unemployment may soon burst into considerable, open unemployment.

Let us examine more concretely the changes in nature and features of employment in Russia.

Employment in General

The number of employees in the Soviet economy, which for much of the twentieth century consisted of only state-owned enterprises, continued to grow until 1987. At that point, an absolute decline began in the state sector, concurrent with a relatively rapid rise of new private firms. Total employment fell from 75.2 million in 1987 to 71 million by the end of 1993. This drop reflects three major tendencies: inflow into open unemployment, inflow into the informal sector, and movement out of the labor force, particularly for women and elderly people whose involvement in the economy had been extremely high. Decreased total employment occurred at the same time that the public sector, which had previously dominated labor, was losing its monopoly status.

Employment in the public sector had shrunk from almost 100 percent to about 60 percent by the beginning of 1994. This decrease occurred as a result of the privatization of state enterprises, the intersectoral labor (voluntary) mobility, and lay-offs from the state sector. New businesses, which started to grow from scratch in 1987, now employ about 6 to 8 percent of the total labor force, or around 5 million people (the lack of reliable statistics makes these numbers only estimates). Operating mostly in trade and services, they provide employees with insecure but well-paid jobs.

Privatization creates another segment of nonstate employment, which embraces not only small, but medium-size and large enterprises as well. It employs one-third of the total, economically active population. Since the beginning of the mass privatization campaign in 1992, some 86,000 Russian enterprises (or one in three) have changed their type of ownership. Among them are about 12,000 medium-sized and large firms that have been converted into joint-stock companies. Employment patterns within this segment of the economy were similar to those of the traditional state enterprises, becoming different over time after privatization. Evidence show that enterprise needs two to three years on average to change the type of labor-management relations, to overcome paternalism, and to shed excessive employment.

Part-Time Employment and Hidden Unemployment

Employment conditions in the Soviet economy have been particularly rigid — any fluctuation from the standard, working-day option was usually not allowed. Numerous restrictions corresponded to part-time work, changes in work schedules, and unpaid leave (even in the case of personal emergency). Due to labor shortages, personnel managers resisted any reductions in working hours. Even if workers' demands were accepted, administrative rules constituted additional constraints. The rigid employment conditions were accompanied by equally rigid wages, the elasticity of which was restricted by administratively set tariffs.

In 1992, employment and wage policies were notably deregulated. At the same time, Russian enterprises, challenged by a lack of funds, a drop in output, and undue financial arrears, started searching for adjustment mechanisms. Many of them introduced part-time work, unpaid leaves, early retirement, and the like. In August of 1992, about 2 million employees from 5,500 enterprises worked under these conditions. In mid-1993, 2.8 million were on involuntary vacations; in industry, this statistic reached 11.9 percent. The average duration of the involuntary vacations was 18 days per employee. Indeed, this policy helped prevent mass labor-force reductions.

The phenomenon of part-time employment is key in understanding what is happening in the Russian labor market. It is often considered as a component of unemployment—hidden or open—and interpreted as misleading managers' motivations (they prefer to keep collectives instead of dismissing excessive employees). The lack of comprehensive and reliable data makes any final conclusions on this issue difficult. In fact, growing levels of part-time employment create new problems and may soon turn into considerable open joblessness. Nevertheless, part-time employment hides divergent patterns, and in the current Russian context, it can be considered a positive rather than negative element.

The movement to a more-flexible labor market and employment options is certainly optimistic. First, it displays the considerable adjustment capacity of both managers and workers. Given the undeveloped labor-market institutions and the restraints on interregional and interindustry mobility, intra-enterprise labor flexibility becomes important. Second, part-time employment (compared with joblessness) sustains a minimum of social stability. Taking into account the social and political tensions in Russia between 1992–1993, one can acknowledge that open unemployment could create additional impediments for a peaceful and democratic transition.

Vulnerable Employment

The Soviet state declared full employment—and guaranteed it—through labor legislation and through overly dependent managers and trade unions. However, the most efficient guarantee was provided by the acute and chronic shortage of labor, for this gave considerable bargaining power to workers and secured them from dismissals. Once hired, an employee had few chances to be fired, either in a major economic downturn or due to poor personal performance.

Although 1992–1993 did not bring mass joblessness, the nature of employment clearly changed; in fact, it became much more vulnerable and fragile. First, the legal rights of employers to fire excessive workers were considerably enlarged. Second, the Russian trade unions demonstrated helplessness, weakness, and the complete loss of orientation. Lastly, the labor shortage disappeared, and open unemployment began to rise.

Although many employees move to part-time jobs voluntarily, for others this shift means a short pause before being fired. The use of short-term labor contracts (compared with life-long hiring) is of particular interest, for this practice had been limited by Soviet labor law, and restrictions still exist. Nevertheless, short-term hiring is becoming ever more popular. Technicians and low-level managers were the first ones who found their employment status had changed; later, many rank-and-file workers joined them. The management of privatizing enterprises often uses formal symbols of restructuring (such as changing the name of the enterprise) to introduce short-term contracts. When the term of the contract finishes—usually it lasts from three to five years—employees will automatically be fired, and managers will be free to choose those to be rehired. The weakness of trade unions (the old, official ones are demoralized, while the new, independent ones are frail and few) makes this policy feasible. Thus, short-term contracts postpone mass redundancies, making it easier to fire workers in the future. Moreover, the management will greatly benefit from these conditions, obtaining valuable privileges in buying shares from displaced employees.

The increasing vulnerability of jobs is illuminated by public opinion. At the end of 1991, about half of those polled considered a loss of job in the near future quite probable; by mid-1993, this share rose to 60 percent.

Mobility of Labor

Today, the capacity for labor mobility becomes one of the principal preconditions for radical reforms. Under the planned economy, labor mobility used to be quite limited. The aim was to provide workers with stability and job security. In the beginning of the 1980s, mobility started to grow, although it still remains insufficient.

In 1992, about 20 percent of the labor force changed jobs. Similar processes were observed in 1993. In both those years, voluntary quits remained the principal means of mobility: 90 percent of those who moved to new jobs were not fired (at least officially, though many of them were forced to quit). The flow of those who quit previous jobs is divided between new, private businesses and state enterprises, which still had vacancies.

The inflow in the state sector resulted in the growth of employment in mining, the fuel and energy sector, and metallurgy. These industries, even in the case of output decreases, had opportunities to raise wages and hire new employees, although most vacancies were low-skilled jobs with deficient working conditions. On the contrary, machine building, the research and development sector, education, and health care head the list of areas in which employment and real wages dropped drastically.

Another portion of labor mobility is caused by mass dismissals. Huge layoffs, which were expected as a key source for labor reallocation, so far have not played a significant role in this process. In 1991, about 0.5 million people were displaced; in 1992, this number rose by 2.7 times to

1.3 million. These facts are much less than was predicted. The first wave of displacements came as a reaction to the collapse of the Soviet Union and the breakdown of economic links. By the end of 1992, the scale of dismissals slowed. The rate of increase in unemployment also fell, while the number of vacancies grew. In the first half of 1993, about 430,000 people were fired. Nevertheless, voluntary quits in industry were 8.5 times more frequent than involuntary ones. Even given the significant drop in industrial output, and given considerably enlarged employers' rights, layoffs have not been widespread, and managers do not seem in a hurry to use their new power.

Although the mobility of those who were laid-off comprises a rather small portion of the total flow, it displays the social cost of economic adjustment under the most unfavorable conditions. In 1992–1993, those who persisted in searching for a new job managed to find one rather easily. Nevertheless, employees with relatively high social status had to pay for reemployment by accepting the lower positions and less-skilled jobs. Social status became the price that job seekers paid for rapid reemployment. The higher the previous status was, the shorter was the spell of joblessness and the lower were the chances to retain previous position. On the contrary, those who were fired from jobs with lower social status usually retained their position, but spent more time job seeking. Despite the dismissal and losses in status, work satisfaction at the new job seemed higher than at the previous one.

Mass dismissals stimulated the reallocation of labor to private firms. One-fourth of those who managed to restore permanent employment found a new job in the private sector. Moreover, higher outgoing status helped to get a job in a private firm, providing necessary social resources and networks.

At the same time, geographical mobility remained low, reflecting the absence of a developed housing market. While the real-estate market in the largest cities is being rapidly developed, in general it remains rudimentary. The total economic downturn has not passed by housing construction, which also decreased. Housing prices are kept at high levels; in Moscow, they are approaching Western European levels (while population incomes remain extremely low). Limited geographical mobility will also create difficulties in restructuring factory towns and mono-industry areas, which are likely to be threatened by chronic unemployment.

Secondary Employment

Various surveys indicate a rise in secondary employment. The share of those holding a second job fluctuates from between 18 and 20 percent of the labor force. The secondary employment significantly increases total work load and emotional burden, but partially absorbs the shock caused by drops in real income and living standards. This means that 12 to 14 million people (or 36 to 42 million including their family members) have additional incomes that often are de-facto tax exempt and not shown by statistics. For many, the second job provides the main family income and becomes the principal way of adjusting to the hardships of transition. Different social and occupational groups vary in their access to secondary employment. For example, young, male professionals and those working in education and health care have several jobs — one-and-a-half to two times more than average. Two other social categories are relatively more involved in secondary employment — unskilled blue-collar workers in state-run enterprises and high-paid employees from the private sector. Thus, secondary employment prevents impoverishment for one group while raising wealth for another.

Unemployment

In all post-Communist countries, a sharp increase in unemployment is considered an unavoidable price to be paid for the restoration of market economies. The employment crisis is a result of excessive labor in enterprises, its low efficiency, and the uncompetitiveness of domestically produced goods. This expectation has been born out in the majority of cases, despite considerable divergence in economic policies during the transition to a market economy. For example, Bulgaria, Romania, Poland, Hungary, and the Slovak Republic are all experiencing unemployment rates at 10 to 16 percent.

Until 1991, Russia had no legal regulations related to unemployment issues. As a result, it also had no unemployment statistics. The Federal Employment Service — the state agency in charge of employment policy — was reorganized and started registration of the unemployed only at the end of 1991.

Unemployment in Russia has been expected for several years. Already in the late 1980s, during the last years of Gorbachev, a sharp rise in unemployment was predicted if a more radical approach toward economic reform were to be adopted. The fear of unemployment became a popular tool in the rhetorical arsenal of those supporting a more gradualist approach. Yet even the most radical versions of reform under discussion during that period are, at best, moderate in comparison to current changes.

The attempt, in the beginning of 1992 by then acting Prime Minister Yegor Gaidar, to introduce macroeconomic stabilization induced forecasts of coming catastrophe on the labor front. Discussion of this became increasingly popular not only among hard-line opponents of economic change, but also among government experts at various ministries, including the Ministry of Labor or Federal Employment Service (FES). In the two last years, FES experts have consistently predicted unemployment rates several times higher than actual levels.

Despite the drastic drop in Gross Domestic Product (GDP) and industrial production in 1992–1994, the unemployment rate had only reached 0.7 percent by the end of 1992, and 1 percent by the end of 1993. From the beginning of 1994 it tends to rise more quickly, but according to official data does not exceed 1.5 percent. Such information debates catastrophe, and one can thus recognize that the current unemployment rate is much lower than the expected level.

What Affects Dismissals and Unemployment?

In all postsocialist Eastern European countries, the growth in the unemployment rate correlates strongly with the dismissal rate. Dismissals from functioning enterprises – the most significant source of unemployment – comprise 85 to 90 percent of all unemployment in these countries. Nominally, the contribution of mass layoffs to overall unemployment in Russia is less than in these countries. In 1992, dismissed employees constituted about 40 percent of all the unemployed; their share reached 60 percent in some regions. The same picture was repeated in 1993. More than one-third of the unemployed left their previous jobs voluntarily, however, these figures conceal the large number of workers who involuntarily quit due to direct or indirect pressure from managers. This means that in Russia, the unemployment rate depends first of all on dismissals as well. Yet nine out of 10 employees are employed by state-owned or newly privatized enterprises, which can and have to cut jobs (the new private sector, on the other hand, creates jobs). Thus the unemployment issue is to a considerable extent a problem of redundancies at state-owned or newly privatized establishments.

Statistics show insignificant numbers of those fired, and most managers seem reluctant to launch mass dismissals. The analysis allows one to conclude that the refusal of managers to lay off employees is motivated and amplified by their own privatization schemes, embedded in the general framework of Russian privatization. It supposes that property rights are redistributed between three, main contesting actors: the managers, the workers' collectives, and outsiders possessing different sets of economic, political, and social resources. Since no single actor has enough available resources to control the enterprise, cooperation between them results. At the first stage of privatization, a "management–workers partnership" is likely due to the previously established structure and pattern of relationships, as well as the distribution of power and privileges.

For all these reasons, the policy of maintaining overemployment becomes, on the one hand, a sort of remuneration to the employees in exchange for management-directed privatization and, on the other hand, an instrument of political pressure. This social exchange modifies the mechanisms and substance of informal bargaining, which has always been typical for Soviet industrial relations.

Thus, within enterprises, preconditions exist for helping management avoid mass displacements. The policy of "keeping the work collective together" is maintained by soft-budget constraint. Nevertheless, other factors help finance excess labor in spite of shrinking funds – among them are diminishing labor costs and the selling or leasing of surplus assets. Another way is to increase labor flexibility. One should also mention voluntary and semi-voluntary labor mobility, which in part results in labor inflows into the new private sector.

Despite the circumstances blocking mass displacements and postponing a burst in unemployment, the general labor market situation remains unstable and highly dynamic. The factors that in the past have blocked mass dismissals (like management–workers bargaining) are losing their influence.

fluence. Due to privatization, control over enterprises shifts from workers to managers, and the former lose their bargaining power. This undermines the implicit management-labor pact to maintain employment in exchange for support during privatization.

The economic space for maintaining overemployment is also shrinking. Monetary policy is becoming tighter, and financing excessive labor at the expense of decapitalization of the enterprise has obvious limits. The cumulative impact of these factors may dramatically increase the scale of Russian dismissals, generating a sharp burst in unemployment.

Employment and Poverty

In Soviet years, the government exercised centralized control over employment and wages, using this as a means to regulate incomes, keeping them close to subsistence levels. The average income of Soviet citizens was not much higher than the minimum amount necessary to cover basic needs. Roughly speaking, the entire population was poor — but not too poor. At the same time, the level of income differentiation was rather insignificant. Those who suffered from poverty included pensioners, the disabled, and large families with only one wage earner.

With price liberalization, wages and salaries have risen, but by nowhere near as much as prices have increased. The top 10 percent now earn 11 times as much as the poorest 10 percent. A year ago, the equivalent figure was eight times; two years ago, it was five times as much. Open income disparity is still a new phenomena for Russian society. In December of 1993, the Gini coefficient measuring the extent of income differentiation reached 0.346, against 0.256 in 1991. It is lower than in the United States, but the speed of change is extremely high.

About one-third of the Russian population found themselves below the minimum subsistence level, allowing them only basic provisions. Hence the problem of poverty became acute, not only for those out of the labor force, but for a number of economically active and skilled employees as well.

Living standards are largely determined by the dynamics of wages as a principal source of income for the majority of population. Two factors mainly affected the wage dynamics in 1992–1993. First was the opportunity for enterprises to increase prices for their products. Second was workers' and managers' capacity to reinforce their claims by collective action (strikes or threats of strikes, for instance), or by lobbyist pressure. This explains the leading position of the coal and oil industries. Accounting for less than 10 percent of the total industrial employment in 1992, these sectors received more than 21 percent of the total wages fund. In contrast, machine-building enterprises take up less than 27 percent of the total wages fund and have about 39 percent of all employed. The highest losses fell on many of the previous beneficiaries, such as military industrial enterprises devoid of guaranteed state financing and support.

The deregulation of wage policy was accompanied by the introduction of a minimum-wage level and a universal tariff system for budget-financed organizations. The average salary in education, research, and the health sector is about two-thirds the average wage in industry. Facing opposition to its monetary policy from various industrial and agrarian pressure groups, the government attempted to compensate for its weakness by tough measures in the budget-financed sector, where the resistance power is much weaker. As a result, a considerable part of intellectuals and white-collar employees found themselves below the poverty level, having lost both in current incomes and savings. The social group that generated reform is thereby in danger of turning into marginals and lumpens.

Conclusion

In the years between 1992 and 1994, radical transformation of the Russian society started. Employment patterns that obviously corresponded with the prevailing economic and social model began to be alter. These changes meant that the previously dominated, socialist type of employment was being eroded and replaced by market-oriented patterns. Although Russian society has passed a considerable way from state socialism, it is still "finding itself" within mixed components of both systems.

Positive changes include the disappearance of compulsive labor, the weakening of state domination on labor markets, and growth in the private sector. Negative tendencies include growing unemployment, low geographical mobility, and the extremely rapid process of social differentiation, which is often accompanied by the growth of poverty. As in other countries, poverty becomes more and more a problem for those who have jobs and in particular, for professionals.

The anticipated burst of unemployment in 1992–1993 did not happen. To a considerable extent, this is explained by the lack of bankruptcies and slack firings. The Russian managers' reluctance to lay off employees is motivated and amplified by their own privatization strategies. Managers, workers' collectives, and outsiders competing for control over enterprises possess different sets of economic, political, and social resources. No one has enough resources to gain, however, without cooperation among the others.

Despite the circumstances blocking mass displacements and postponing a burst in unemployment, the general labor-market situation remains wobbly. The possibilities to delay mass firings are shrinking rapidly; firms' external sources of finance are lessening due to the tightening of monetary policy and because of internal reasons, such as the decapitalization of enterprise. This temporary period of calm is just that — temporary — and may be regarded as an ephemeral gift to the Russian government, giving it time to formulate sound policy.

Section 3

Lessons to Be Learned from East Asian Economies

Yue Chim Richard Wong

The post-war development experiences of many East Asian economies illustrate that the right type of economic development can reduce poverty and create employment in poor, developing countries. The most important lesson is that economic development should be market driven. This allows the economy to grow on a broad base and maintain high rates of growth, so that benefits can be widely shared within the population to avoid social divisiveness.

Most East Asian economies followed market-oriented development strategies. In doing so, they by and large developed economic activities in which they had a comparative advantage. This is not to claim that the state did not intervene in the market, but that most of those interventions did not try to pursue grand strategies that were in conflict with market signals. Most of those interventions were piecemeal in nature, and seldom implemented on either a massive scale or were maintained for prolonged periods of time—unless they were successful. Grand strategies required the state to suppress market forces, distort the price structure, and impose regulatory constraints that generate huge economic losses. Imbalances between supply and demand created by such intervention have to be rationed by costly administrative measures. Efforts to circumvent controls beget further controls and lead to even greater distortions and higher costs.

Distortionary regulations create formidable barriers to economic entry, retard economic growth, and lead to a narrow base of economic activities that benefit the privileged. Income and wealth disparities that stem from such discriminatory regulations are socially divisive; they foster a deep sense of envy, frustration, and alienation. On the other hand, dispersions in income and wealth that result from equal competition in the marketplace provide incentives for participants to seek to advance oneself and one's family through work and savings, to respect the fruits of others' labor, and to make for a more cohesive and self-assured society. A broad base of economic activities also creates a more resilient economy, makes high growth rates sustainable, and speeds up the trickle-down process.

Dangers of Grandiose Strategies

Many developing countries try to achieve economic progress by pursuing various grand strategies and development plans based on specific goals. These strategies and plans often entailed the adoption of policies that suppressed market forces and resulted in a huge loss of economic efficiency, lower growth rates, and a narrow and precarious economic base. This allowed scarce resources, especially human resources, to become unemployed or underemployed. The poor invariably become the worst victims of these unfortunate policies.

It is useful to consider the following, stylized example to examine the logical implications of what took place in many developing and socialist economies. Many labor-abundant agricultural economies pursued rapid industrialization through promoting capital-intensive industries at the expense of more labor-intensive industries, services, and agriculture. Such a developmental strategy required resources to be allocated to capital-intensive industries through a variety of administrative means. The price structure was severely distorted, and extensive rationing had to be relied upon. Control measures proliferated as market forces tried to circumvent earlier imposed controls. Sometimes, widespread nationalization and the adoption of national economic planning became necessary tools for the state to achieve its purposes.

In impoverished economies, promoting capital-intensive industries meant working against market forces. Since the return from investing in capital-intensive industries can only be realized after a long period of time, a rapid rate of capital accumulation has to be secured by artificially boosting profits through the manipulation of price and cost structures. The cost of using capital was lowered by suppressing interest rates. The cost of foreign exchange was depressed to protect these industries from foreign competition and to lower the cost of importing essential facilities and equipment used to develop capital-intensive industries.

Wage rates were kept down by providing basic necessities consumed by urban workers at very low prices by exploiting the rural sectors; for example, food prices had to be depressed. Monopoly state-marketing boards were relied upon to compel raw material and agricultural suppliers to sell to the state at administered low prices. The state-marketing boards practically eliminated agricultural and primary-commodity markets. As incentives were curtailed, productivity sagged. Many poor peasants fell heavily into debt, some sold or abandoned their land, and others migrated to the cities and became urban squatters. In some places, urban to rural migration was resisted by denying services to immigrants. Even more draconian and coercive measures were also employed from time to time.

Flow of Resources

Nevertheless, these controls could not always guarantee that resources would voluntarily flow toward the capital-intensive industries that the state favored. Competitive private enterprises have little incentive to reinvest their earnings in low-profit industries. To encourage their development, many enterprises were granted subsidies, monopoly rights, or became outright, state-run monopolies. In the extreme case, a highly coercive, administered system of managing resource flows became imperative. National economic planning was also pursued in some instances and became an indispensable tool for pursuing policy goals that had to work against market forces.

Within the urban sector, employment opportunities were few for dwellers in the shanty towns, because most resources were invested in heavy industries that created few jobs. Regulatory restrictions that discriminated against light industries and services made it difficult to set up legitimate practices within the formal economy.

Investment in residential and other structures was severely hampered by the absence of property titles that provided security of ownership and tenure. The absence of significant housing investments, provided through the market, prevented the housing industry from becoming a major competitor for resources that could be used for industrialization. In a sense, the housing market could not be allowed to function.

The result of many of these grand strategies was to generate severe imbalances in various markets, such as credit markets, foreign-exchange markets, commodity and raw material markets, and agricultural markets. Foreign-exchange controls, credit rationing, and state-marketing boards had to be maintained, and this had economy-wide, resource misallocation effects. A narrow-based modern sector was manufactured by siphoning off resources from the rest of the economy. But few benefited from such a development, and the population as a whole remained in poverty. The narrow economic base was also vulnerable to shocks emanating from domestic and foreign sources; such economic development was often found to be unsustainable. Moreover, to add insult to injury, the manufactured modern sector often found itself unable to survive international competition.

Outside the modern sector, economic conditions failed to improve, partly because it was starved of resources. More importantly, the choices of people outside the modern sector often were severely limited by the myriad of discriminatory barriers and regulatory controls established to facilitate the growth of the modern sector.

Incentives Versus Public Programming

The East Asian economies did not seek to reduce poverty through massive transfer programs. Public programs transferring substantial amounts of resources to provide for the poor have had limited success in eliminating or reducing poverty in most economies. Although programs that seek to enhance the productive capacities of the poor — like investments in education and health — and to extend the mobility of resources — like investments in transportation and communication—have proven invaluable. But public provision of many services are seldom efficient and often beset by corruption. The political and financial sustainability of many transfer programs are doubtful. Large-scale transfer programs are often too expensive to be affordable in poor societies, where large sections of the population remain in poverty or near poverty. More focused programs aimed at targeted groups often fail to help the poor because of their limited reach. More importantly, the poor lack political access to mobilize the state for their interests.

People stay in poverty because they do not command sufficient resources for economic well-being; they are deprived of the choice to deploy their meager resources effectively; and they lack the incentives to accumulate more resources over time and pass them on to the next generation. It is useful to think of these resources as taking many forms: human, natural, physical, financial, family, social, and political. From this perspective, helping the poor involves enhancing their command over resources, removing barriers to a more efficient utilization of the resources they have at their disposal, and providing incentives for them to accumulate more resources.

The poor typically have few resources aside from their own, largely unskilled human resources and those of their families and close relatives. In agriculture, they may own small plots of land. For this reason, policies and measures that limit the choices of the poor to deploy their meager resources and apply them to their most productive uses have severe, adverse effects on those in poverty. Consider a poor peasant household. Often, their economic circumstances would improve greatly if they had secure and transferable land ownership rights, credit facilities, insurance to manage risk, access to markets unfettered by state marketing boards, provisions for infrastructure investments in transportation and irrigation systems, and extension services. Although the provision of these services at affordable prices depends on a number of factors, one major stumbling block in developing economies is the high cost imposed by regulatory barriers.

As agricultural productivity grows, surplus agricultural labor has to be absorbed in labor-intensive manufacturing and service enterprises. The cost of starting new enterprises or becoming self-employed depends critically on entry barriers and the regulatory environment. Improved access to education will improve the employment opportunities of rural workers, while transferable rights in land will improve access to credit facilities for setting up new businesses. Significant rural to urban migration can be avoided if nonagricultural rural enterprises could emerge without too many hurdles. The rapid growth in China in the recent reform decade was due to the rise of rural collective enterprises, supported by rural credit cooperatives and a more relaxed regulatory environment.

Migrants who arrive in urban areas will also benefit enormously from a less-regulated environment. Hernando de Soto, in his important study *The Other Path,* clearly shows why the absence of secure property rights and a highly regulated economic environment have suffocated economic growth in Peru. Self-employment and small family businesses in the development process in many East Asian urban economies are not only important for economic growth; these situations have been instrumental in helping poor families increase their income and savings.

Shifting Resumes to Productive Activities

Economic growth in developing nations is to a large extent concerned with shifting resources from less-productive into more-productive activities. Unlike developed nations, economic growth in developing nations are derived primarily from a more efficient allocation of resources, rather than from the development and application of new technologies. Arguments about alleged market failures are therefore less relevant to growth issues in developing nations. The importance of allocative efficiency in promoting growth in developing nations has also been emphasized in a study by Alwyn Young, entitled "Lessons from East Asian NICS: A Contrarian View" (NBER Working Paper No. 4482, 1993). Economic growth and sectoral (or structural) shifts should therefore be more closely related in developing, rather than developed, nations.

Sectoral shifts in employment are often believed to be a source of unemployment. While this may be true, the relationship is likely to be weaker in developing nations, where sectoral employment shifts are associated with greater gains in allocative efficiency that foster faster economic growth and create more and better job opportunities.

Conclusion

While it is generally correct to observe that economic development in poor nations entails shifting resources away from agriculture into manufacturing, and subsequently into services, it is not obvious that this is best done through state intervention. Markets are the preferred mechanism for achieving allocative efficiency, fostering economic growth, and creating employment opportunities. The East Asian experience demonstrates this in the clearest of terms.

Chapter 3

Measures for the Expansion of Productive Employment

A Global Employment Strategy

John Langmore

> *"...the United Nations shall promote...full employment...."*
> Article 55, United Nations Charter

The world is at an economic watershed. For the last 20 years, since the collapse of fixed exchange rates and the increases in oil prices in the early 1970s, the central preoccupation of Western governments has been with reducing inflation. The growth rate of consumer prices peaked at an Organization for Economic Cooperation and Development (OECD) average of 12.5 percent in 1974, and by 1993 it was down to just over 3 percent.[1] At the same time, unemployment has risen from an OECD average of 3.9 percent in 1974 to 8.5 percent in 1993. By the end of 1993, 36 million people were unemployed in the OECD area.

Thus, goals must be changed from "inflation first" to a more balanced approach involving commitment to full employment and low inflation. The international goal of full employment was first adopted in 1945, in the UN Charter. The readoption of this goal has begun: the communiqué from the June 1993 OECD ministerial meeting began with the heading "Reducing Unemployment: A Central Goal." In reality, though, many governments have not adopted employment growth as a central goal, or implemented such a goal rigorously by applying policies that are consistent with it.

Industrialized Countries' Concern: Inflation Versus Unemployment

The Western preoccupation with inflation is exemplified clearly in the Maastricht Treaty signed in February 1992. Jacques Delors, then president of the European Commission, said that the two driving forces towards European unity are a single currency and a single defense. The main feature of the treaty provides for economic and monetary union (EMU) for member states that meet convergence criteria with regard to inflation, interest rates, exchange rates, public sector debt, and deficits. A forerunner of a European Central Bank is to be established, the main function of which is to achieve price stability. When the European Central Bank is established, its "primary objective...shall be to obtain price stability."[2] Targets are also set for government deficits, which should not exceed 3 percent of Gross Domestic Product (GDP), and for general government debt, which should not exceed 60 percent of GDP. Not only is no mention made of the importance of employment growth, but fiscal policy is constrained, in some countries severely.

This is a deflationary framework. A summary of the Treaty concludes that: "The path to monetary union will therefore mean sustained high unemployment in many countries unless labor market intervention can be made effective." Thus implementation of this package will increase unemployment at exactly the time when unemployment has become a central economic and social issue.

European leaders increasingly recognize this inconsistency. Delors went to the European Community Summit in June 1993 with an extensive paper proposing more spending on training and re-training, advice for the unemployed, sharply increased spending on infrastructure and on research and development, increased taxing of energy, and reduced employment taxes. There is already limited, informal discussion about the need for a new treaty in the mid-1990s that would reflect current issues such as employment and investment, rather than inflation. Fortunately, the collapse of the exchange-rate mechanism (ERM) in September of 1992 gives member countries greater freedom for action, at least temporarily.

Countries outside Europe and Germany have considerable scope for independent action. Several of the group of the seven (G7), major industrial countries (Canada, France, Germany, Italy, Japan, the United Kingdom, and the United States), which together account for about 60 percent of gross global product, could readily adopt a more stimulatory stance. An international employment conference held by U.S. President Bill Clinton in 1994 symbolized the end of the two decades when Western macroeconomic policy was dominated by the anti-inflationary goal.

In hindsight, three long stages in the post-World War II era can be perceived: recovery and steady growth from 1945 to 1973, which enabled strong growth of employment and low unemployment; a disorderly, turbulent period from 1973 to the beginning of the 1990s, when inflation was the principal preoccupation, real interest rates were high, and unemployment increased; and the post-Cold War era since 1989, in which military expenditure can be cut, outlays redirected towards productive economic and social programs, inflation and interest rates can be maintained at low levels, and small and large enterprise, formal and informal, can be encouraged.

This era offers opportunities unimagined for the last 50 years. Hope can be realistically high, provided that goals and policies are directed at sustainable human development. A global employment strategy could provide a valuable framework for such progress.

With commitment to the goal of sustainable human development and a global employment strategy, important changes to macroeconomic policies would follow. The first would be to complete the movement away from overreliance on monetary policy, towards the balanced use of both monetary and fiscal policy. With such balance, the scope for reducing real interest rates, and maintaining them at lower real levels throughout the 1990s than they were in the 1980s, would be greater. The capacity to lower real interest rates would be greatly increased if major economies coordinated such action. High real interest rates may well turn out to have been the most powerful factor constraining economic development throughout the world since 1980, for not only did they retard investment in industrialized countries, they were the principal cause of the developing country debt crisis.

Second, Japan in particular and other countries to a more limited extent, have potential for fiscal expansion, and international pressure must be maintained to encourage that. Japan's current account surplus of well over US$100 billion is forcing an enormous loss of jobs on to its trading partners. Japanese budget outlays should therefore be increased more than in the packages announced by Prime Ministers Miyazawa and Hosokawa during 1993, for despite the recession in Japan, there is little net fiscal stimulus. Japan's astonishingly strong protection should also be reduced. Other current account surplus countries such as Switzerland, the Netherlands, Taiwan, Denmark, Norway, and Singapore also have some capacity to adopt more expansionary fiscal policies. As Lester Thurow recently wrote: "The right answer from the United States' and the world's perspective is an aggressive coordinated fiscal monetary expansion with the three big economies (Germany, Japan and the United States) acting as a joint locomotive."

Third, all countries should introduce some form of incomes policy suitable to their institutional framework, so as to address directly the struggle for shares of income, which is the principal force driving inflation. The adoption of this neglected instrument of national economic policy would enable many countries to maintain more expansionary fiscal and monetary policies than would otherwise be possible. Australia has conclusively demonstrated the benefit of this approach through the success of the Accord during the 1980s. Other countries such as Japan, Germany, Austria, and Sweden, which also use consensual approaches to income negotiation, demonstrate the value of this approach.

Fourth, all countries, developed and developing, have an opportunity for cutting wasteful military expenditure to release funds for more urgently needed and more productive economic and social programs. Empirical research shows that military expenditure generates fewer jobs than do equivalent amounts of expenditure on education, health, and other economic and social programs. Moreover, military expenditure is economically wasteful, for it diverts funds away from investment and civilian research. It also weakens the current account of weapons importers and tends to be inflationary. Hence, reducing military expenditure and replacing it with outlays on education, infrastructure, and civilian research would increase the level of economic activity, and thus the level of employment. More weapons make countries poorer, not safer; strategic security is better achieved by strengthening international, dispute-settling mechanisms through the UN and regional security arrangements. Progress at both those levels since the end of the Cold War increases the hope that these tools can become even more effective.

Fifth, completion of the General Agreement on Tariffs and Trade (GATT) Uruguay Round should put an end to the creeping protectionism spreading across the industrialized world, and lead to the progressive opening up of major markets. Restrictions on the flow of goods through tariff and non-tariff barriers cost developing countries, for example, about as much as the total amount of development assistance they receive each year — about US$50 billion. Thus, it seems likely that a steady, global reduction in protection will increase global employment.

Developing Countries' Choices

The tragedy of absolute poverty and deprivation in developing countries offers enormous opportunities for sustainable development that would increase employment everywhere. Faster economic growth in developing countries would allow them to increase their imports, and also increase employment in richer exporting countries.

The desperate needs were powerfully described in the United Nations Development Programme's (UNDP) *Human Development Report, 1993:*

> More than a billion of the world's people still languish in absolute poverty, and the poorest fifth find that the richest fifth enjoy more than one hundred and fifty times their income. Women still earn only half as much as men.... Rural people in developing countries still receive less than half the income opportunities and social services available to their urban counterparts. Many ethnic minorities still live like a separate nation within their own countries.

Sustainable human development strategies are used to some extent in many developing countries; they could be adopted in the rest and applied more rigorously everywhere. There are, however, no panaceas for ending jobless growth in the developing world any more, than there are in the developed. The range of constructive policies that should be adopted, all of which would contribute to stimulating employment, include:

- investing generously in basic and vocational education and worker re-training;

- improving basic health services, women's education, and the availability of family planning information and techniques, so as to reduce the rate of population growth;

- support for small-scale enterprises and informal employment, particularly through increasing access to credit and by maintaining low interest rates;

- extending the national infrastructure, particularly using labor-intensive techniques for public works construction;
- expanding research and development and seeking appropriate new labor-intensive technologies internationally;
- concentrating on a regulatory framework that offsets market failure by increasing opportunities for new indigenous enterprises, and, where appropriate, for foreign investors; and
- reducing military expenditure, and reallocating funds and personnel to more productive economic and social programs.

There are also important ways in which developed countries could increase economic opportunities for those that are developing. Increasing development assistance is fundamental. Western governments are averaging aid of only 0.49 percent of GDP, well below the UN target of 0.7 percent; in fact, Australia's aid is only 0.36 percent of our GDP. Both humanity and long-term self-interest require that those levels be increased, for both developing and the former Eastern bloc countries require aid and credit on a massive scale. Whatever increase is achieved by Western governments recent experience suggests that aid alone will be insufficient to meet the financing needs of developing countries. Funds made available by the World Bank and the regional development banks must be increased, and debts need to be slashed.

A simple, readily available change could double the lending capacity of the World Bank. In view of increased demands for Bank funds from the economies in transition, and of the difficulty of increasing budget aid to these and developing countries, the one-to-one link between the Bank's capital base and its lending could be broken. The extent to which lending could exceed the Bank's capital base would thus be set by the financial market responses to this move. At a time when the Bank is barely a net lender (the repayments and interest it receives from borrowers is only slightly less than new lending), it is essential that new loans be increased Such expansion, however, would only be warranted if the Bank's lending conditions continue to become less doctrinaire. Conditionality must move beyond the contractionary, inequitable, simplistically free-marketeering, and gender- and environment-insensitive policies of much of the 1980s. Bank rhetoric has now been changed; thus all policy must follow. Establishment of an international parliamentary monitoring assembly to review both the Bank and Fund would increase accountability and could well improve the humanity of policies.[3]

The enormous debts of developing countries must also be swiftly reduced. The debt crisis has been the cause of irreparable damage to indebted countries during the 1980s. For example, compared with the GDP growth rate in sub-Saharan Africa between 1965 and 1980 this, the poorest continent, lost a cumulative 40 percent of income during the next decade. Moreover, the debt crisis is far from over. About 60 countries in Africa, Latin America, the Middle East, and Asia have arrears of interest on debts totaling about US$300 billion. These deeply indebted countries have populations totaling 770 million, and income averaging about $600 a year per person. Certainly, it should be considered that the official debt of low-income countries be forgiven.

Such dismissals have, in fact, occurred many times before. After World War I, the United States effectively wrote off billions of dollars of British debt. After World War II, West Germany was given debt relief estimated to be 70 percent of prewar German debts. If Western nations can write off debts for each other, then they can do the same for deeply impoverished developing countries, particularly when the relative size of those debts is low. The IMF should sell gold and use the proceeds for reducing developing-world debt to the Fund. These policies are essential to stop the perverse, destructive net transfer of funds from the impoverished South to the rich North. Ending the debt overhang would also remove a major impediment to private investment in developing countries. For today, experience in administering foreign investment can be used to ensure net benefits to recipient countries.

A new global employment strategy should also be prepared and implemented. The World Summit for Social Development, to be held in Copenhagen in 1995, has expansion of productive employment as one major theme, thus providing the opportunity for strategical preparation. Unfortunately, the conference of industrialized countries on employment initiated by President Clinton did not result in a global strategy. In fact, initiative was proposed over a decade ago by the late Nobel Laureate Jan Tinbergen and his associates.

Global Economic Reform

Widespread disarray is prevalent in the international economic system. First, the bipolarity of the Cold War has been replaced by a multipolar global economy. The 1980s fashion for deregulation allows more than 2 trillion dollars a day to slosh unimpeded in international financial markets. In the transitional economies in Eastern Europe and Asia, it looks as though the dash for the market is causing chaos and destruction, whereas a more gradual transition might have allowed sustained economic activity without the injustice of corruption and exploitation (which is occurring). Second, the remedies of the 1980s have caused reductions in living standards for the impoverished in developing countries, as much as for the poor and unemployed in the industrialized countries where they originated.

One step towards reform is already on the official agenda – a new issue of Special Drawing Rights (SDRs), the international money created through the International Monetary Fund (IMF). Michel Camdessus, managing director of the IMF, pointing to the low-reserve positions of small, low-income countries and of former Soviet bloc countries, is advocating a new allocation of SDRs. These countries compensate for lack of international reserves by lowering imports, causing an undesirable brake on international trade. An increase in the reserves of these low-income, balance-of-payments deficit countries would therefore enable the world to make better use of available, underutilized productive capacity without risking an inflationary impulse. A new issue of, say, 100 billion SDRs spread over three years, reallocated by recipient countries to low-income countries and those in transition, could make a significant difference in their import capacity. This reform has been resisted in the past by the United States and Germany, because it was claimed that it would be inflationary. Such a criticism could not credibly be made now, when the proposed addition to global reserves would be relatively small, and when average inflation rates are so low.

A far more valuable reform would be the global introduction of a uniform tax on foreign-exchange transactions, as proposed by American economist James Tobin. This tax would be applied by governments on foreign-exchange transactions in their countries. It would be an effective response to widespread concerns about the turbulence of international financial markets, the damage this does to trade, and the powerful influence exerted over governments by private dealers' views about policy. The real problem is that governments are often unable to do what they judge in the national interest, for fear of upsetting financial markets and causing a run on the currency.

The Tobin tax would have at least five important benefits. First, it would reduce the turbulence of exchange-rate fluctuations by increasing the cost of short-term speculative transactions, in turn increasing the attention given to longer-range fundamentals. If the tax were imposed at the 0.5 percent rate proposed by Tobin, it would be too small to deter trade or long-term capital commitments; however, it would penalize speculation.

Second, a small speculators' tax would allow greater autonomy in national macroeconomic policies by making possible wider differences between short-term interest rates in different currencies. Currently, interest rates are being used to target exchange rates and domestic, economic activity levels, yet it is impossible to achieve goals relating to both with only one instrument. The international capital markets have, in effect, been imposing a charge on all other borrowers by requiring a higher real interest rate as the price governments pay for avoiding a flight of capital or unwanted inflationary depreciation. Short-term capital markets have become a destructive monster. A tax on speculation would reduce their power—a power that has been used in Australia throughout the last decade to exert deflationary pressure on economic policy, thereby reducing pecuniary activity and increasing unemployment.

Third, the tax would be a useful addition to a system aimed at greater international financial stability. Other measures could include increasing the amount of capital banks are required to hold in support of their foreign-exchange transactions and strengthening supervisory regulations. Fourth, by reducing the potential return to foreign-exchange speculation, the tax would discourage the wasteful application of skilled personnel and a scarcity of capital. And fifth, the tax would generate revenue without damaging side effects. If the present level of foreign-exchange dealing in Australia continued, the revenue would be $170 million a day—though the tax's impact would be to reduce significantly the value of such transactions, and hence revenue. Tobin suggests that the proceeds go to the World Bank; national treasuries might also be allocated funds.

The principal criticism of the proposal relates to the difficulty of achieving agreement about the tax among all major countries involved in foreign-exchange dealing. Yet in the late 1980s, the Bank for International Settlements succeeded in persuading countries to introduce increased prudential reserve ratios for commercial banks. Since the Tobin proposal would be of benefit to everyone except foreign-exchange dealers, such agreement could well be possible. The major difficulty would be evasion of the tax through use of tax havens. Even if some small countries refused to collect the tax, much would be achieved for all participating countries by the greater stability of their currency, the increase in macroeconomic independence, and the growth of revenue.

Risks to the global financial system and for individual investors have been increased by financial deregulation, thus pressure is growing for reform. The more deregulated a financial system, the stronger and more detailed central banks supervision must be.

Reform of the Bretton Woods Institutions

The fundamental reform required in the international economic system pertains to the Bretton Woods institutions. The IMF has been the subject of criticism on behalf of the developing nations from such sources as development economist and former Pakistan Finance Minister Mahbub ul-Haq who has pointed out that the Fund is not *truly* international if it only polices the transactions of the poorer nations—a mere ten percent of global liquidity. The IMF is crippled and marginalized and, to the extent it has influence, asymmetrical and deflationary. Central bankers in the United States and Germany are far more powerful than Fund managers, while all are dwarfed by the daily transactions of the financial markets. The Fund is limited to trying to discipline low-income, current account deficit countries, while making no significant impact on the surplus countries—notably Japan in recent years—causing a deflationary effect that soaks up global purchasing power and retards employment growth everywhere.

It is time to reexamine American economist John Maynard Keynes' proposal for a Clearing Union. A Clearing Union would issue a currency, which Keynes called "Bancor," to debtor countries. These countries would use it to pay surplus countries, which would in turn deposit the Bancor into the Clearing Union. The Clearing Union would not create liquidity, it would simply facilitate the transactions of debtor and surplus countries. Keynes also proposed that interest be charged on the use of Bancor, so as to punish, symmetrically, both deficit and surplus countries. These interest rates would create pressure for exchange-rate adjustment, as for structural adjustment to reduce current account deficits and surpluses.

This system would eliminate the deflationary bias of current, international financial arrangements. If countries expanded demand unilaterally to increase employment, thereby going into deficit (as France did in the early 1980s), pressure would be put on the surplus countries both to increase their demand and appreciate their currencies. Similarly, the system would assist developing countries that increased its deficits to finance investment. This would overcome much of the current account constraint on the developing countries.

This proposal is remarkably simple. It would be cost free in the sense that countries would not have to allocate funds for its establishment.

Resistance would come from those countries fortunate enough to issue currencies desired as reserve assets, notably the United States, Japan, and Germany. Nevertheless, the proposal is not radical. Despite the enormous benefits, negotiating such a system would be difficult. Yet now is the time to begin such discussion, for the global financial disorder is overwhelmingly apparent. The international economic system is at a watershed, allowing new possibilities for serious consideration. The fiftieth anniversary of the Bretton Woods institutions will provide a forum for such discussion, and an International Monetary Conference would be timely to consider reform of the international monetary system. Whether this opportunity is seized depends on the strength of commitment to global economic development and to full employment.

Even more broadly, the institutional framework for international economic decision making is quite inadequate. The G7 represents only seven of the largest and richest economies, neglecting both developing countries and economies in transition. The UN is powerless, and the Bretton Woods institutions powerful, only with developing countries. A new representative, a new powerful institution, is required, one that is equivalent to the UN Security Council. One possibility would be a UN Economic Security Council, with permanent and temporary membership reflecting economic size (so that China, which is second largest, and India, which is fifth largest on a purchasing-power parity basis, might be permanent members). Such a body could have powers and responsibilities equivalent to those of the enhanced Security Council, which is now being discussed.

Conclusion

To conclude, the goal of global security has moved from the military focus of much of the postwar period to an economic and environmental imperative. The end of the Cold War, the conquering of inflation, and the erosion of the doctrinaire ideologies of communism, monetarism, and libertarianism all offer opportunities for formulation and implementation of new strategies for sustainable human development. This section advocates a global reflation program which would increase the rate and equity of economic development in both rich and poor countries. Major reforms to reduce the destructive dominance of the international financial system are also proposed. Finally, regional and global cooperation must be strengthened in order to enhance prospects for equitable economic development and the growth of employment everywhere.

Notes

1. All figures from OECD, 1993.
2. Article 2 of the Protocol.
3. Joint Parliamentary Committee on Foreign Affairs, Defence and Trade, 1993.

Section 2

Toward a Global Workforce Policy

Mihály Simai

Regardless of political ideologies, systemic factors, or cultural differences, in defining the sources of social conflicts, or in the efforts for achieving social harmony, employment is considered a fundamental issue in all societies. Work and gainful employment has many "faces" and dimensions in the global system. The issues and policies related to employment are centrally important in shaping the global development process. As the January 1994 Report of the Secretary General of the United Nations to the Preparatory Committee for the World Summit for Social Development states:

> Employment is the result of a number of interlinked factors. On the supply side, population growth, labour force participation rates, migration, and education and skills development affect the growth and pattern of employment. On the demand side, while expansion of output is, in general the major determinant of employment creation, it is also influenced by the labour intensity of technology used, productivity increase, various structural factors and the way available work is distributed.

The politics and economics of employment directly connect the factors mentioned in the above report, with the decision-making process in governments and business, as with other main issues of economic development.

According to UN, estimates, the world labor force was comprised of 2.8 billion people in the early 1990s. This represented about half of the total population of the globe. Out of this large reservoir of people, the number of those who were not productively employed was close to 800 million, a little over 30 percent. The number of registered unemployed was 120 million (about one-fourth of them in the industrialized world). More than 700 million were underemployed. Agriculture was still the main source of employment for about half of the global labor force (reflecting the situation in South and East Asia, China, Africa, and Latin America). The share of the nonagricultural sector in the total labor force is, however, growing fast.

The high level of unemployment and underemployment in the mid-1990s is a signal of major structural problems and policy deficiencies in the world economy. Employment creation and the reduction of unemployment will probably be one of the most important socioeconomic issues of the next 20 to 25 years for the majority of the countries. The wasting of human resources in the forms of unemployment and underemployment is a major loss for the global community in general, and particularly for certain countries. It is not just the loss of important investments made in health and education; it is a source of dissatisfaction, tension, and human suffering. Exclusion from the category of employed people is a source of poverty and declining standards of living for hundreds of millions, in large parts of the world. The politics and economics of global employment became issues of crucial importance related also to the future of global stability. While discussions of the first, global ministerial meeting of the seven, major industrialized countries on employment (March 1994) concentrated on the industrial world, it has also recognized the global character of the problems.

Employment as a Global Concern

People are employed or unemployed within a national economic framework. The individual governments formulate and implement their employment policies in response to the domestic political, social, and economic pressures and conditions. These domestic policies may also have important, international implications. Most of the world labor force is working or looking for jobs within the frontiers of their nations; indeed, the labor market institutions are fundamentally national. Such macroeconomics category, as the definition of full employment or the natural rate of unemployment cannot accurately be given at the global level. Employment has its dominant demographic, technological, macro- and microeconomic, political, and institutional dimensions at the national level.

First of all, while most dimensions of the national employment problem have their international aspects or consequences, the institutions and policies related to the labor markets are predominantly national. Second, while international economic interactions through trade, capital, and technology flow interconnected with changes in national employment and unemployment trends at a historically unprecedented scale, the international mobility of labor is still rather limited. Third, a few specific issues in the labor markets, are, by definition, of international nature, yet the level of cooperation on those issues is rather limited or nonexistent.

In the mid-1990s, the problems of unemployment and the creation of employment opportunities became a global concern for the following main reasons:

Recession

The first half of the 1990s has seen the most widespread and longest global recession of the post-World War II period. It has been distinctive because its factors were not just the "regular" cyclical economic components. The recession has been connected or coincided with some the longer-term problems of the world economy. Certain branches of manufacturing industries in the industrialized countries have stood at a depressed state, due to sharpening global competition, shifts in demand, and a decline in the defense sector. The developing countries (with the exception of Southeast Asia) did not have any real recovery in the 1980s. Moreover, the collapse of the European Communist regimes and the beginnings of the transition to the market system resulted in a major, 30 to 40 percent decline in Gross Domestic Product (GDP), along with mass unemployment in those countries.

In addition, a certain degree of synchronization of the recession has lasted in the industrialized world. The recession influenced the functioning of the labor markets not only directly, but also by increasing unemployment and shrinking employment opportunities. It has weakened the capacity of many governments to deal with human development issues and has diverted resources from productive investments to unemployment benefits — the principal macroeconomics aim being blocking the fall of consumption.

The Structural Causes of Unemployment

The recession accentuated and deepened some of the longer-term problems present in the labor market of industrialized countries for some time. Unemployment became a reality for more widespread groups in societies. For the first two years of the U.S. recession, about 20 percent of the labor force was temporarily unemployed — this also reflects the greater mobility of labor there than in other countries. Long-term unemployment also became part of the new reality, especially in Europe. These trends in the labor market reflected the deceleration of employment opportunities in the manufacturing sector, and the constraints in the service sector for creating new jobs and absorbing those squeezed out from the industry. There has also been a trend toward temporary and part-time jobs. Thus the high level of unemployment, together with the large number of part-time and lower-wage jobs, made a strong and durable recovery more difficult to achieve through their implications on the consumer market. As a result, job security was reduced, which undermined the confidence of consumers, widened income inequalities, and increased poverty in many countries.

Jobless Growth

A large part of long-term unemployment and the emergence of the dangers of "jobless recovery" are connected with the new interrelations between demand patterns, competition, production, employment, and technological change. Excessive labor-market regulations and wage rigidities were already being blamed in the 1980s in Western Europe for the reluctance of entrepreneurs to add to their workforce. The 1990s is characterized by a new wave of rationalization of the production process, a number of important characteristics being based on technological change.

First, the technologies involved are much more labor saving than earlier technologies. Second, the technological transformation is now confined to industry—it includes all sectors. The computer-based and telecommunications-related processes revolutionized the service sectors as well, which in the past could absorb a large number of people released by industry. Moreover, job creation is increasingly confined to low-paid traditional services. Third, the process is spreading to developing countries mainly by the transnational corporations. Their investments create fewer new jobs than previously, when a key attraction for their investments had been inexpensive, semiskilled labor. Yet today, low-wage competition involves increasingly skilled, low-wage labor working with highly productive technology. Fourth, two other areas of the technological transformation do not receive sufficient attention at present, but already have or will have major influences on global employment.

One of them, the more efficient use of metals, minerals, and fuel along with the further growth of the "knowledge" or information content of GDP will certainly continue. The other is the increasing role of biotechnology in agriculture. Due to the fact that in the mid-1990s, agriculture still employs the bulk of the world labor force, the spread of biogenetically produced plants may have a major influence on them. According to historical experiences, technology not only saves but also creates new jobs; some are related to the needs of producing and using the new technologies, others are the sources of the related growth of income. At this stage, however, the job-saving tasks are in the center of research and consulting work related to new technologies, or to the reorganization of the production processes.

The Gender Dimension of Labor Markets

Another important general trend influencing employment problems has been the increase of the participation of women, particularly of married women, in the economically active population. Country- or region-specific sources of this trend exist. In general, the educational level of women has increased, boosting their productivity in employment. The lowering of the fertility rate also increased the amount of time women have for activities outside the home; in addition, urbanization moved a large number of women from the rural informal sector to the labor market.

Income also forced many women to find jobs. In many industrialized countries in earlier decades, women were the "secondary participants" in the labor force, with the principal aim of increasing household income. In the mid-1990s, a large proportion of the working women are "primary participants," as heads of households or independent persons. In industrial countries, the participation rate of women increased from 48.3 percent in 1973 to 60 percent by 1990; the share of women increased to 42 percent in the economically active population by 1990 in these countries. In the developing countries, the share of women is also growing in the economically active population, beyond those sectors to the informal sector, where the share of women has been traditionally high. In export-processing zones, for example, 70 to 90 percent of the labor force is accounted for by women.

The increasing participation rate and share of women raises a number of employment issues, and also influences in many ways the functioning of labor markets. First, the large influx of women into the labor force may be cushioning the impact of falling fertility rates on the labor markets at a given stage of development. Second, in general more jobs will have to be created to satisfy the increasing demand for female employment. Third, in spite of achievements in the struggle for equality and against discrimination in the labor market, women are still much more vulnerable and exposed to changing, especially deteriorating, economic conditions. This been has manifested very strongly in the countries of Central and Eastern Europe during the early 1990s.

Consequences of Population Growth

Employment problems in the long term are closely interrelated with demographic issues; however they are rather complex. Historical evidence from late eighteenth-century England shows that the interaction of population explosion and rapid technological change could be favorable. The population growth stimulated the demand for food and encouraged investments in agriculture, while industrialization increased employment and demand. The post-World War II baby boom in the United States also boosted investments, demand, and employment. Yet this happened within one country. In the economy of the late twentieth century, those favorable interactions are not present on global level. While the rise in industrial employment has been quite rapid in developing countries (around 4 to 4.5 percent during the past 25 years), it was able to absorb only 22 to 24 percent of those in the working-age group. By the end of 1993, the world population had reached about 5.4 billion, and according to UN projections, it will surpass 6.2 billion by the year 2000, and 7.2 billion by 2010. The 25 years between 1975 and 2000 will have experienced the largest absolute growth in global population of any quarter century in all of human history to date — more than 2.2 billion people.

There has, however, been an important difference in the population trends of the developed and developing countries, and also within the group of the developing countries. The diverse growth rates have resulted in major changes in the territorial and age distributions of the population throughout many regions of the world; their continuation will further accentuate the role of demographic factors in the future employment problems. Most directly, however, is the number and proportion of people in the working-age groups, those between the ages of 15 and 64, which indicate how many new jobs are or will be required globally. This number has increased on a global level from 57 percent in 1970, to 62 percent in 1990, and will reach 64 percent by 2000.

In the industrialized countries, it has remained relatively high (close to two-thirds of the population); in the developing countries, however, it will increase from 54.4 percent in 1970 to over 60 percent by the year 2000. Between 1970 and 1990, about 1,140 million persons were added to this working-age group, amounting to more than 1 billion in the developing countries. According to the population projections of the UN, between 1990 and 2010 the number of people in the working-age group will increase by 1,360 persons (specifically, by about 620 million in the 1990s, and 740 million in the first decade of the next century). Of the total increase, only 4.7 percent will be in the developed world, with more than 95 percent being in the developing countries—with their total increase equalling about 1,300 million people.

In the developing regions, the rate of increase of people in working-age groups will be the most rapid in the Middle East, South and Central America, and in certain African countries. In total numbers, the largest increment will take place in South Asia and China. According to available estimates in *World Population Prospects* (1989) and *Human Development Report* (1991, 1993) accounting for the increase in working-age groups, the level of unemployment, and the increasing participation of women, about 1 billion new jobs will have to be created within the next 10 years. This is a historically unprecedented task. It would justify coordinated policies and actions in order to increase employment. In the absence of appropriate measures, this employment issue could become a potential source of global instability.

Problems of Aging

The aging of the population is another aspect of the interrelations between demographic trends and employment. Aging reduces the proportion of working-age groups and of people belonging to the labor force. This factor reduces the pressure of job seekers on the society, and due to the extension of the average age and the human capabilities to work, presents a new kind of employment issue for the older part of the population. In countries where the contracting working-age groups represent a more serious problem, there is a push to increase productivity by innovation and by an accelerated mastery of new technology. This may impel certain countries to phase out and redeploy labor-intensive activities to other countries, concentrating instead on high, value-added production and services. Japan is a perfect example of this; there, rapid economic growth has been accompanied by declining fertility rates, causing a slowdown in the expansion of the labor force and a chronic shortage of labor. Similar patterns may be observed in other countries in Southeast Asia.

In the developing countries, the increasing number and proportion of people in the working-age group reduce demographic dependency ratios. This could be favorable from the perspective of economic and social development, but only on the condition that a sufficiently large number of new jobs are created. Aging, on the other hand, increases the dependency ratios and puts a greater burden on the working-age groups. The influence of the growing share of the older population increases the need for restructuring social expenditures, in order to concentrate on special health and other services needed by higher-age groups. There are already countries where more than half of the social and health expenditures is spent on such services.

Postulates of Sustainable Development

Employment issues on both the national and global level are also interconnected with the efforts for achieving environmentally sustainable development. For one, such development, requires appropriate social policies to moderate poverty. Relatively stable employment and income opportunities are, however, key components of long-term conditions for environmental sustainability, by reducing the incentive for migration into areas already environmentally strained and by facilitating the increase of public revenues for environment conservation. Moreover, the patterns of industrial and agricultural development, and the way natural resources are exploited, often ignore long-term environmental consequences, especially in the developing countries, for the achievement of short-term gains.

It has never been easy to find the appropriate balance between the goals of employment and environmental policies. While in many industrialized countries it has been understood that appropriate environmental management and the development of special services and industries have job-creating potentials, the trade-offs are not so clear in a number of important industries. In the majority of middle-level economies and the developing countries, the decision makers are giving greater priority to employment creation than to environmental considerations. The global level interrelations between employment and environmental sustainability are communicated through the patterns and conditions of trade and direct foreign investment. The debate about the North American Free Trade Agreement (NAFTA) in the United States revealed some of the de facto problems between stricter environmental rules in the United States and more permissive ones in Mexico.

The Uncertain Global Socioeconomic Perspectives

As it has been indicated by the above-mentioned problems, technological and structural changes and the slowdown of economic growth will increase tensions in the labor market in most of the industrialized countries, in Central and Eastern Europe, and in parts of the former Soviet Union. These areas will have to deal with the issues of employment (and unemployment) in different ways, including reducing working hours, instituting retraining programs, and parceling out part-time employment opportunities. The labor market, which had become acquainted to the high-growth syndrome of the postwar period—the full employment, the relatively many job openings that compensated for job losses connected with technological change, the positive conditions for both vertical mobility (upgrading the labor force), and horizontal mobility (moving in the direction of more productive sectors)—will find that under the new economic conditions of slower growth, they can only adjust at low speed. Europe will probably face more difficult and long-term problems than the United States, with its more flexible labor market. The U.S. market still offers employees a wide variety of working conditions, fringe benefits, and wages, but new problems are emerging. These include low job and income security, lack of health care, a deteriorating job quality, slow growth of incomes and increasing income inequality, high rates of job loss, and increasing structural unemployment.

According to the Economic Report of the President in 1994, in the United States more than 10 percent of all jobs disappear annually. However not all jobs lost create unemployment; people can sometimes find jobs at the same company or retire. Between 1981 and 1990, about 2 million full-time workers a year lost their jobs, spending an average of nearly 30 weeks unemployed. About one-third of them suffered more than 20 percent earning losses.

Excessive regulations as means of preserving employment and sustaining traditional work patterns can, of course, be extremely costly for the whole economy. They are resulting in the conservation of structural patterns that are losing their competitive position and comparative advantages. The "life-long" employment commitment of Japan is also endangered by the new economic realities; in fact, changes in the functioning of the labor markets are difficult in all the industrialized countries. While it has been generally recognized that greater scope be given to the play of market forces, a number of novel measures are needed for building up a new consensus among entrepreneurs, employees, and governments. This should include a radical improvement in the quality and scope of retraining, the improvement of mechanisms promoting intersectoral and interregional mobility, and a more efficient international coordination of policies related to the development and effective utilization of human resources.

The problems of employment are much more complex and difficult in the developing countries. The majority of the people (about 60 percent) in developing countries are employed in agriculture and in the low-productivity manufacturing and services, including the "informal sector." The informal sector is and will be for many years the largest employment area of last resort and one that, unfortunately, preserves poverty. The growing importance of the informal sector is also closely connected with the character of urbanization process resulting in shantytowns. The system basically serves the local population; its upgrading, from the point of view of productivity and income, depends to a large extent on an increase in the purchasing power of the people. Improving the traditional and the informal sectors further requires more stable and sustainable employment, and skill-intensive production.

Investment needs for creating new jobs in the modern industrial sectors of the economy are quite large in these countries. The range of gross investment per potential new worker varies between $1,090 in Bangladesh to $10,660 in Thailand (of course, the "modern" industrial sector of Bangladesh is a misnomer, as it lags significantly behind the technological modernity of Thailand's industrial sector). This industrial-employment situation stands in contrast to the historical patterns of developed countries, which were able to employ 40 percent of those entering the labor market in the last century. Today, the labor needs of industries using modern technologies are much more limited.

Various proposals suggest that the developing countries use more labor-intensive technologies within their modern sectors. This alternative, however, was rejected by those developing countries involved in modern industries. Some countries, for example China, have been able to combine modern technology and labor-intensive operations, achieving especially favorable results in employment creation.

Internationalization of the Labor Markets

In an interdependent world, especially in those countries dependent on foreign trade, national employment is directly related to changes in the external conditions of demand and supply and to international competition. The character of international trading regimes through national attitudes toward global trade policies is also influenced by employment problems. In this system, the capacity to adjust has become particularly pertinent, due to the fact that in the relatively liberal international trading system, the labor markets of different countries are more directly connected than in the past through transnational corporations, marketing, and distribution operations.

The interconnectedness of technology also influences changes in employment opportunities and occupational structures. The patterns of change in the most industrialized countries, the declining agricultural employment, the slow growth or gradual declining of employment in manufacturing, the increasing diversity of employment in services, the increase of skills, and the upgrading of employment structure could be observed in many countries. The speed of such developments is of course different, and variations occur even within industrialized countries, especially concerning the role of manufacturing and the patterns of changes in service-sector employment. All those structural changes are also related to the patterns of world trade. It is evident that the future and sustainability of the current, relatively liberal international trading system depends to a large extent on the success of developing new employment opportunities. Many of the trade-related direct foreign investments also have important employment-policy implications.

Employment issues, however, have been most directly globalized through those factors that influenced the functioning of labor markets and promoted their internationalization:

- international migration, which greatly concerns governments and people throughout the world,
- the globalization of employment through transnational corporations, as the result of their global sourcing and international integration of production,
- the labor market or labor legislation implications of regional integration.

The internationalization of labor markets requires, first of all, the liberalization of the international mobility of people, especially those in the working-age groups; second, the international convergence of labor legislation; and third, the increasing international standardization of education and training.

According to the abstract macroeconomic theory, in a well-functioning labor market, wages are determined by the balance of labor supply and demand. If a relatively scarce number of workers exists in one market, wages will be high; in case of relative abundance in another market, wages will be low. Migration represents an equilibrating mechanism. The consequences of the process would not only be the increasing international equalization of labor compensation, but the elimination of the relative advantages that employees gained in different countries from labor cost differences. Another result would be the disappearance of international differences in labor costs as incentives for direct foreign investments. Wage differences, however, are not providing either sufficient justifications or the only incentive for international migration; they are the result of a number of socioeconomic and political factors, including the constraints on labor force mobility.

The functioning of labor markets depends on institutions often at odds with one another. Some advanced, industrialized countries are highly unionized; in others, the role of trade unions is very limited. From among the industrialized countries, for example, the union coverage of the bargaining is about 18 percent in the United States, and 95 percent in Sweden. The role of government regulations in labor markets is also substantially different, as are labor conditions and incentives. In some countries, a larger proportion of remunerations depends on bonuses, while in others, wages are more important. Truly, a great variety exists in unemployment compensation programs, training and retraining mechanisms, and immigration regulations. Yet the single, most important factor in the internationalization of labor markets is international migration, especially the migration of people in the labor force.

Impacts of International Migration

International migration has, of course, other incentives than the search for employment opportunities. The movements of population have been important components and factors forming human history. Entire continents have been depopulated and repopulated, and historical waves of migration have occurred due to demographic reasons, changing climatic conditions, and political and economic pressures (or incentives). In the post-World War II period, the process of international migration had two separate components: one represented by dislocated peoples and refugees, the other by those who were economically motivated to improve their quality of life.

Modern history of international migration has usually been divided into four periods. In the first period, between the sixteenth and nineteenth centuries, the immigration patterns were connected with the process of colonization and the mercantilist economic growth in Europe, increasingly based on the raw materials from the colonies. The second period started with the post-Napoleonic war era and was characterized by the massive outflow of people from Europe to North America, certain countries of Latin America, Australia, and New Zealand. This period ended with World War I. In the third period, between the two world wars, international migration became extremely limited; strict immigration laws were introduced in all the traditional receiving countries. During World War II, there was a massive redeployment of people for slave labor; the hostilities also resulted in a large number of displaced persons. The fourth period started after World War II and can be characterized as the increasing globalization of international migration. At the early part of this period, most of the great population movements took place as the results of the political changes. Wars, revolutions, and upheavals resulted in tens of millions of temporary international refugees or permanent emigration in all continents.

There has also been a large increase in economically motivated migration throughout the world, the result of which has been the emergence of a transnational workforce in a number of countries beyond the traditional destination of emigrants. In Europe, Britain, France, Germany, Sweden, Switzerland, and the Netherlands became especially important target countries for this labor force. Saudi Arabia, Kuwait, and the United Arab Emirates also received millions of immigrant workers. In Africa, especially the Ivory Coast, Nigeria and South Africa became important centers of immigrants.

It is impossible, or at least it is very difficult, to predict future trends in international migration even for the next one or two decades. The process will be related on the one hand to demographic pressure, which is predictable for certain parts of the world, and on the other hand, to expected economic opportunities and employment. Demographic pressure is building for international migration, especially in the land belt south of the industrialized world (except, of course, Australia and New Zealand). North America will confront such pressures from Latin America, as will Europe from North Africa, and the Arab-Islamic hinterland and Russia from South Asia and China. It is quite possible that the disintegration of the Soviet Union will further result in a mass migration of people, perhaps of the Russians and other ethnic minorities residing in the new independent republics. Emigration in past decades temporarily eased the employment problems in certain southern European countries, but the time of the guest worker in West Europe is over. As the result of the changes in Eastern Europe, the list of countries from where political refugees are accepted has been redefined. In fact, the increase in public hostility may be as important in curbing immigration as are restrictive legislative measures. Immigration, however, will probably remain relatively high in the traditional receiving countries – the United States, Canada, and Australia.

Will emigration moderate the demographic pressure in the developing countries as it did in past history, especially in nineteenth-century Europe? The historical experiences of Europe in the field of mass emigration are irrelevant to developing countries today. Most of European emigrants went into a cultural environment not too dissimilar from their own. More importantly, the numbers were different. On the one hand, the demographic conditions in developing countries make emigration pressures much greater than they were in Europe's past. On the other hand, the needs of those countries receiving immigrants are relatively more limited, due to the character of technological and structural changes and to the increasingly knowledge-intensive character of the modern economy.

Economically motivated migration cannot be completely separated from the demographic pressures. Still, it has a number of specific aspects. First, in all regions of the world is a highly influential, well-organized, and internationally connected network of labor recruitment, which has developed into an important branch of the service industries. This industry is using all the possibilities offered by modern transportation and communication, making information on job opportunities widely available. Second, in spite of all the legal or political constraints on migration, domestic-labor shortages of certain countries not only encourage them to import people with needed skills, but may result in a greater level of tolerance for the presence of illegal, immigrant workers.

The relationship between the patterns of labor migration and economic development have distinctive patterns in different parts of the world. While during the post-World War II years, for example, the Asian countries were able to export less than 0.1 percent of their labor force increment, in the era of faster economic growth and aging population, the importance of migration may rapidly change. Taking into account current and projected disparities and increasing economic inequalities, it is more or less certain that the pressure for international migration will increase, becoming a key problem worldwide, especially between the developing and the industrialized countries, and between Central and Eastern Europe and West Europe.

If the development process is left to the spontaneity of socio-economic forces, people will be uprooted by poverty, and their migration may well become an important source of international and national conflicts, in addition to social violence. Thus, international migration will in the coming decades become a vital issue on the agenda of international, regional, and global organizations. There is a great probability that instead of an "iron curtain" separating the East from the West, there will now be a "golden curtain" drawn between North and South. Seen in one light, this will prove a controversial humanitarian issue, as the right of people to move and emigrate is understood as a universal human right. In another light, however, the industrial countries will have to protect their own labor markets, meaning measures for stricter regulations, quotas, and restrictions in obtaining citizenship, education, and/or property.

Another important aspect of international migration is the "brain drain," from the less- to more-developed countries. This migration from the developing countries will be "competing" in the future with the outflow of highly skilled professionals from Central and Eastern Europe and areas of the former Soviet Union. While it may become more difficult and selective, the skill level of emigrants is going to increase, due to changing demand patterns in the labor markets of the industrialized world.

The Role of Transnational Corporations

Transnational corporations (TNCs) have been important actors in the internationalization of the markets of goods and capital, yet their role has been much more limited. They influence, of course, the international demand for, and the career expectations of, a number of professional groups. They also have direct and indirect influence on the changes in global patterns of employment.

The investments of transnational corporations abroad usually increase the demand for skilled and professional labor in the host country. This demand, especially in the developing countries, is covered by the imports of people, not necessarily from the investing countries but from other regions. Most of the U.S., European, and Japanese firms recruit skilled, third-country nationals for managerial, supervisory, and technical jobs, especially when they cannot hire sufficiently qualified local workers. They often use their own nationals for training. Employment policies of the transnational corporations, are of course, primarily sector specific; within a given sector, they have declining flexibility in substituting capital with labor. They are also country specific in the sense that in labor-intensive operations, they seek low-cost and low-risk countries. Takeovers by transnational corporations may result in the decline in employment. The more recent experiences in some Eastern European countries proved that in most cases, when they took over the state-owned firms in the privatization process, they restructured, reduced, and did not increase employment. In technologically more-sophisticated operations, they increased the skill level while proving upgrading the labor force within their system. Because they are concentrated to high-technology sectors, which require higher skills, they have been and probably will be playing a key role in spreading new skill requirements, along with internationalizing skill and educational standards.

TNCs are efficient instruments by passing on skills to the local staff through personal contacts, on the job training, organized visits to other operations in their international system, and by formal training courses. The employee skill level in the firms owned by transnational corporations in most cases is higher than that of domestically owned firms, including public sector. This increases the compensation level of employees. It is not in the interest of TNCs to introduce a converging compensation level in their international system, because of the benefits from lower wages. They are, however, offering higher compensation than many of their local counterparts. Thus the international investments and especially the transnational corporations are contributing to the emergence of regional markets for skilled labor and professionals, which may result in the narrowing of the differences in their compensation. The competition of many governments for investments by transnational corporations may be also promoting the harmonization of employment policies.

Three factors, beyond the direct and indirect costs of labor, are vital for the transnational corporations. The first is the quality of the educational system and the structure of skills—to what extent researchers, engineers, and other qualified technical staff are available. The second factor is the transparency and flexibility of labor markets: labor legislation, unemployment insurance, retraining facilities, etc. The third factor is the degree of freedom of movement for the labor force, both entering and leaving the country.

Regional Integration of Labor Markets

While in almost all regions of the world cooperation institutions formulated some programs for employment and migration policies, they are mostly rudimentary and are strictly recommendations for national actions. They lack the common determination for collective measures. The European Economic Union is the only regional integration group that has coordinated policy directives in a number of areas. The action program of the Social Charter includes directives for employment and remuneration, on living and working conditions, freedom of movement, information, consultation and participation, equal treatment, health and safety, and the protection of children and youth. These directives, if implemented, may promote the emerging of a regionally integrated labor market. The directive on transnational posting of workers suggests that they are to enjoy the same terms and conditions as local workers in the host country.

The data for immigrants is incomplete because it does not include naturalized foreigners; it is, however, still a good indicator. In 1990, about 13 million persons, 4 percent of the total population were foreign residents; of the 13 million, 8 million came from outside the Community. According to those statistics, the proportion of foreigners was highest in Germany (about 16 percent). Between 1945 and 1989, the Federal Republic of Germany received about 15 million foreigners as refugees or guest workers, corresponding to about 25 percent of the population. The proportion of foreigners has been much lower in other member countries (i.e., in Spain, 0.7 percent). Immigration has been regulated so far on the basis of national legislation. The Maastricht treaty about the European Union provides common foundations for a European immigration policy, taking into account common goals and interests. It also recognizes the needs for a constant policy dialogue with countries that are the sources of immigration.

According to sporadic statistical data, in spite of certain converging trends in the long-term movement of labor costs, the differences in wage levels and social security benefits are still large. It is an important issue for future research, to what extent and by what mechanisms will those differences level off. Will there be a supranational synthesis of labor legislation?

An other important area where the integration process contributes to the internationalization of the labor market is the role of common or coordinated policies in increasing the quality of the labor force, including its educational and vocational skill levels and structure, as well as its capability to adjust in a flexible — though disciplined fashion — to changes in demand conditions and new technology.

The achieved level and the growing internationalization of labor markets require a greater degree of collective approaches to the emerging problems on the global level, in order to avoid some of the potential dangers. One should not forget that the accumulation of social dissatisfaction, and the frustration of hungry and unemployed millions, has played a substantial role in helping extremist regimes into power.

Human Resource Development Policy

There has been an important, international commitment of all nations, at least of all the members of the United Nations, which has been directly related not only to the employment issues but to general human welfare. Article 55 of the U.N. Charter states:

> With a view to the creation of conditions of stability and well-being which is necessary for peaceful and friendly relations among nations, based on respect for the principle of equal rights and self determination of peoples, the United Nations shall promote:
> a. higher standards of living, full employment, and conditions of economic and social progress and development....

Through the full employment pledge of the UN, employment and the development of human resources have become a global issue for the first time in history since World War II.

In fact, the issue can be construed in various developments in the past decades, not all of them positive. In many developing countries, the increase of highly qualified people resulted in an excess supply in the labor market, adding a new dimension to the unutilized or underutilized segments of the population. In the industrialized countries, the workers relationship to employer and income is changing rapidly, as are working patterns. Greater employment flexibility is demanded by many employers to secure business survival in an increasingly competitive world; this endangers opportunities for the individuals, and it may degrade employment conditions. Moreover, a new social judgment is required to define the proper balance between flexibility and employment security. In the developing countries, where rural employment opportunities will remain crucial and the role of the informal sector as a source of employment and income may even grow, new needs of human resource development and the efficient use of human resources raise questions as to how to keep the unemployed and underemployed off the streets.

The idea that those issues should be dealt with in national framework is shared by a number of governments, even though differences exist in the definition of their content and instruments. The "Social Charter" of the European Community has probably been the only comprehensive international document aimed at collective approaches to social policy issues. Even within the European Union, the views of the countries are still diverging in the interpretation and implementation of the Social Charter. On a global level, the differences are naturally even greater. Some of the approaches stress the role of entrepreneurship in the solution of those issues related to human development and employment, including the role of self-employment as an important component of human development tasks. It is also recognized, however, that the requirements achieving greater global security in the coming decades make human resource policies vital on both the national and international levels. The feasibility of international commitments and the availability of possible collective instruments of those policies remain highly debated issues.

Conclusion

The foregoing overview of topics indicate that employment and unemployment are extremely complex issues. They relate to a number of other processes in societies and are crucial for individuals by determining to a large extent their place, role, material welfare, quality of life, and future in the societies in which they live. While it is generally understood that in a dynamic economy the number of jobs created and destroyed every year may be large, the process can be a devastating psychological experience for an individual, and a disaster for a family. What is required is not only a comprehensive workforce policy at national level, as suggested by the 1994 Economic Report of the President of the United States (February 1994), but a thorough revision and restructuring of national policies in an international framework. It is not enough to return to the traditional, post-World War II approach to national full-employment policies. Full employment cannot be restored in the old ways, but on the condition that policy makers face up to the need for a profound restructuring of the system of production, work, and education and along with it, the rules of coordination of the macroeconomic structures.

The main challenges in the field of future employment developments on the supply side will be in the increase of the people in working-age groups, the growing participation of women, the influx of the surplus agricultural population to non-farming occupations, international migration, and the development of skills through formal and other forms of education. On the demand side, technological progress, rates of growth, and changing patterns of consumption and output will be the main determinants. Those and other challenges will impose historically unprecedented pressures on national government policies and international cooperation. The concrete manifestation of these efforts may be different around the world, but in the final analysis, the future of global stability depends on the character and efficiency of the responses.

Section 3

Entrepreneurship: A Youth Perspective for Employment

Ingunn Brandvoll

If you ask a young person today what is a main concern for the future, most would express anxiety about whether or not they will be able to find a meaningful job. While the youth of the 1970s worried about the threat of global political instability, young people today fear the future, because the prospects of getting a meaningful livelihood may be poorer than it has been in several decades.

Their concerns may be well-founded. Statistics show that the number of unemployed and underemployed continues to grow. In the Western European countries, the official unemployment rates have increased from an average of 5.4 percent in 1977 to a projected 11.4 percent in 1994 (8.5 percent if the rest of the Organization for Economic Cooperation and Development (OECD) countries are included). However, the situation from one country to another varies. A country like Spain has seen a sharp increase in the number of unemployed (from 5.2 percent in 1977 to an expected 24 percent in 1994).

For OECD countries, the number of unemployed has increased, particularly if one compares the current situation with the situation of the 1960s, which had unemployment rates between 2 and 3 percent. What would have been shocking unemployment levels in the 1960s and even 1970s are now considered normal. In the short term, it may even be considered "healthy" as the result of anti-inflation policies, a point which has been confirmed by statements from politicians like Norman Lamont. In 1991 he, as a chancellor of the exchequer, stated that unemployment was "a price worth paying to secure low inflation."

The growth, however, in the number of unemployed has been much more dramatic in Eastern European countries. Prior to 1990, the official unemployment figures of most Eastern European countries were below 2 percent. Today the average is 14 percent, a dramatic change for countries where the word unemployed was hardly ever used.

Even though the number of unemployed has grown rapidly in Eastern European countries as a consequence of the change from state-controlled to market economies, nothing beats the employment challenge of the poorest countries. It is in these countries that populations are growing the quickest. It is in these countries that young labor is most abundant. While the OECD and Eastern European countries are experiencing a population growth close to zero, the poorer countries have to satisfy the needs of populations growing at more than 2 percent annually. Their starting point is, in most cases, not the best, with unemployment and underemployment levels already exceeding 20 percent. Moreover, a job in the poorest countries means hard and potentially health-damaging work, for a salary that barely covers one's most pressing needs.

For the world as a whole, it is estimated that one-third of the labor force of approximately 2.2 billion is unemployed or underemployed. In 2050, the world population will be between 8 and 13 billion people, a substantial increase from the current level of 5.7 billion. The largest labor force growth will be in the poorer countries. In order to meet future demand for employment in these nations, it is estimated that 30 to 40 million new jobs will have to be created annually towards the year 2000.

With this background, employment is without doubt a major challenge both for the present and future. For youth, the issue of employment may be the difference between not having and having hope for the ensuing decades. Competition will undoubtedly be hard, not only for the most challenging and well-paid jobs, but for any job. Politicians, business people, public opinion, and youth in particular should therefore question: how can we today build a foundation that will ensure the present and next generation meaningful employment and a productive life?

Why is Employment a Key?

High unemployment levels directly affect young people, and their share of the percentage of unemployed often remains disproportionate relative to their share of the population. In Norway, for example, youth between the age of 20 to 24 years represent close to one-fourth of the total number of unemployed. In Britain, 34 percent of the unemployed between 20 and 24 years have been without work for more than a year. Many have not had a job since leaving school. With little or no work experience in a job market with an abundant supply of labor, older and more experienced workers are preferred.

Those unable to enter the job market find themselves not only shut out from a regular source of income, but also from the opportunity to develop professional skills and working know-how. No job may also mean a limited opportunity to develop personally and socially through the daily contact with workmates and colleagues, as a part of a team and an organization. The consequence for the individual may therefore be not only a lower living standard, but also limited social contact and a potential loss of self-respect and status. In addition, the younger the person, the more serious the long-term consequences may be both for the individual and society.

In some cases, this may mean potential self-destructiveness and/or destructiveness towards society. Crime, drug abuse, and racial conflict—particularly in urban areas—is high in many countries where the youth unemployment rate is increasing. Providing meaningful employment opportunities may prove a key solution to less crime and violence, racism and social conflict, and political and social apathy. It may also be the key to poverty alleviation, reduced population growth, and migration to already overpopulated cities.

The Challenge of Jobs Creation

The challenge is clear. The demand and need for new jobs is overwhelming, and will require innovative ideas and a strong ability to implement them. The whole concept of work will have to be rethought not only in terms of job content, but also in terms of distribution of work.

In order to create more job opportunities, politicians will be under pressure to take a stand in eight particular areas, which are or may be related to employment issues:

- Job content, including salary and employee benefits;
- Environmental concerns;
- Government priorities in fiscal and monetary policy;
- Economic incentives for labor intensive versus capital intensive sectors;
- Rural versus urban employment;
- Private sector versus public sector employment;
- Economic incentives for mall companies versus big companies;
- Trade and immigration policies.

At the Expense of Job Content?

For the largest part of the world's population, a job is first of all a source of income. To have an opportunity to develop professionally and personally is a secondary consideration, as the main goal is to be fortunate enough to have a job. The expression "meaningful employment" may therefore seem a bit irrelevant, taking into account the future employment challenge.

Most people agree that a job should not contradict human dignity, and that it should generate a sufficient salary to cover basic needs like food and housing. A job should also contribute to an enterprise's or institution's objective of either an economic or social nature.

However, as the demand for jobs increases, policy makers and trade unionists both in the rich and poor countries may find it increasingly difficult to implement and enforce regulations that protect workers' present rights and income levels, as well as unemployed welfare payments. They may also find it more difficult to defend the traditional concepts of a full-time job. Job sharing and demands for less strict regulation of part-time jobs are two possible solutions which are increasingly mentioned.

At the Expense of the Environment?

During the second half of the 1980s and 1990s, sustainable development became a fashionable word. Most people can agree that sustainable development should be an objective. The world's resources are limited, and so is the world's capacity to absorb pollution and waste. However, job creation is a result of economic activity—an activity that is bound to consume resources, cause pollution, and produce waste to a lesser or larger extent. Job creation, particularly in the nonservice sector, is difficult to imagine without some compromises at the expense of the environment. (It is first of all a question of keeping negative environmental effects to a minimum.) This compromise has become more obvious for the richer countries, as recession has to a certain extent changed people's priorities from environmental concerns to the fear of becoming unemployed.

While richer countries at least have some possibilities from which to choose, the main concern of poorer countries is and will continue to be, how to create a livelihood for its rapidly growing populations. Policy makers will therefore find it increasingly difficult to make unpopular decisions for the long-term benefit of the environment and society at the expense of jobs.

At the Expense of Other Government Priorities?

Employment creation is also a question of government priorities. During the second half of the 1980s and 1990s, the priority of the OECD-countries has been on reducing inflation. This objective has been met for most countries, but as illustrated by the Phillips curve,[1] at the expense of employment.

Many countries have found or will find themselves restricted in their economic policy, due to large government budget deficits and rapidly increasing debt burdens. As state debt increases, the priority shifts to reduce the debt and balance the budget. To do so, government spending is cut and/or government income is increased through taxes; both these measures will have a negative effect, at least in the short term, on employment. The ability to implement proactive employment policies in a situation with large budget deficits, are in other words, severely restricted.

However, with increasing unemployment, policy makers will be under pressure to implement strategies to reduce unemployment in the short term, sometimes at the expense of long-term fiscal or monetary priorities.

At the Expense of Capital-Intensive Industries?

Particularly during the 1960s and 1970s, many countries gave priority to the development of capital intensive industries. As a part of government policy, these industries, often heavy industries, were strongly subsidized and protected from competition. In order to finance and stimulate investment in capital intensive industries, more labor-intensive activities (meaning mostly the agricultural sector) were taxed. The result was a shift of capital and labor from the labor-intensive to the capital-intensive sector. In the long term, this contributed to increased migration to urban and industrial centers and higher unemployment levels overall.

With current and increasing unemployment levels, policy makers will hopefully be under pressure to encourage and favor investments in more labor-intensive industries, and to reduce taxes on labor. In the long-term, this may ensure higher overall employment and a more balanced relationship between the capital- and labor-intensive sectors.

At the Expense of Urban Employment?

As capital-intensive industries have been prioritized, urban employment has increased. Capital-intensive industries have also attracted additional services and investments in infrastructure. As cities often have the best base capital, technology-intensive industries tend to concentrate in and around urban areas. Both skilled and unskilled labor from the rural areas has migrated to the cities looking for a better livelihood. The result has been a countryside lagging behind in development, and urban areas facing increasing unemployment and underemployment problems.

As these urban unemployment and underemployment problems continue to increase, policy makers, particularly in poorer countries, will face greater pressure to create job opportunities—not only in urban areas, but in rural ones as well. Such a change in policy will hopefully contribute to reduced migration of labor to already overloaded cities.

At the Expense of the Public Sector?

While private-sector job creation has been low in the last decades, public-sector employment has boomed in many countries. In the European Economic Community (EEC), for example, more than half of the new jobs created during the period 1973 to 1991 were in the public sector. In the long term, the consequences for the private sector may be higher taxes and a possible brain drain to the public sector (depending on the relative difference in salaries between the two sectors).

As unemployment levels increase, the pressure on government leaders to expand public-sector employment will continue. However, higher unemployment levels will hopefully also stimulate a debate on how private sector employment can be increased, possibly at the expense of a further expansion of the public sector.

At the Expense of Larger Companies?

During the last decade, many larger companies and multinationals have found themselves suffering from reduced profit margins. As a consequence, cost-cutting measures have been implemented, which have affected thousands of employees and their jobs. Good examples are IBM and Phillips. Although larger domestic and foreign companies in many countries have enjoyed a privileged position, employment creation has been significantly greater in the smaller companies.

As unemployment levels increase, policy makers will hopefully be under pressure to stimulate the establishment of new enterprises and support growth in existing small-scale companies. However, this is not necessarily a question of either/or; rather, it is a question of developing and maintaining high activity levels in both sizes of organizations.

At the Expense of Richer Countries?

Jobs are not only a matter of competition between individuals, but also between countries. As unemployment levels in all countries—poor and rich—are increasing, the competition between countries to attract investments is becoming fierce. Politicians and businesspeople are becoming more concerned about their countries' comparative advantages, in areas such as labor costs.

An argument increasingly heard, although maybe not so bluntly, is that the poorer countries are stealing the "rich man's" jobs. What is often forgotten is that the richer countries have a greater ability to move into higher-value industries and services. Richer countries also have a strong self-interest in the economic growth of poorer countries. With growth, new markets will emerge, and political and social stability will be more easily secured. However, if the current unemployment levels in richer countries are not reduced, but continue to grow, more Western policy makers will face increasing pressure to implement protectionist modes of management in both trade and immigration.

The Entrepreneur: A Solution

The term entrepreneur is used here to describe an individual who is actively seeking to become, or who is already, self-employed through agricultural activities, small-scale industry, trade, or other types of small-scale services. An entrepreneur can operate both in the formal and the informal sector.

"Small Is Beautiful?"

Policy makers have traditionally focused on how to keep and provide new employment opportunities by creating the best possible conditions for existing large-scale industries and foreign investors. The recipe has often been tax incentives or even subsidies. All policies, which have been tailored particularly to suit larger companies, have, in certain cases, restricted the activities of domestic small industries and the agricultural sector.

The small and more entrepreneurial companies have often been "forgotten," although it is in these companies that potential for new employment opportunities are the greatest. In the United States, for example, eight out of 10 new jobs are created in small business. In poorer countries, the ratio even may be higher. *The World Development Report* (1989) estimates that the noncorporate sector, meaning small farmers, producers, tradespeople, and independent traders, accounts for 30 to 70 percent of the labor force in some poorer countries.

The entrepreneurial company is by nature local, more labor-intensive, and more people-oriented purely as a result of size. It is more dependent on its local community and its human resources than a larger company operating in several communities. This dependency can develop into a fruitful mutual relationship, particularly in small communities with few employment opportunities.

Entrepreneurship and Its Positive Effects

The positive effects of entrepreneurial growth, both for the individual and the society as a whole, can be many. Being self-employed means freedom for the individual to shape his or her future, and an opportunity for success and a higher income. If successful, it may mean increased status and self-respect.

For the local community, the successful entrepreneur will bring more job opportunities and economic growth. The establishment of one entrepreneur may even support two more. The start-up operation may also help improve the image of the local community, attracting additional investors and services. Moreover, new private investments are more likely to take place in a local economy already on the move. Additional economic activity may stimulate greater political and social involvement. As a result of his or her business, an entrepreneur may dedicate more time to understand local and national policy making. Finally, the successful entrepreneur may become a symbol for the rest of the community, a sign of hope and an ideal toward which to work.

Obstacles for the Entrepreneur

Although the entrepreneur may be desired, the obstacles he or she faces can be many. The access to capital, technology, contacts, and business know-how may be limited. In addition, structural aspects may create an environment that limits or even prevents the entrepreneur from implementing his or her initiative. Such aspects may be poor infrastructure, government regulations, society's attitude, and market and business structures.

In the richer countries, the trend in many markets is towards larger and more vertically and horizontally integrated companies; the aim is greater economies of scale and market control. For the entrepreneur, this trend may bring new opportunities in terms of new market niches and greater specialization, but it also results in more concerns and possible market barriers. Through mergers and acquisitions, the number of potential business partners (i.e., customers, suppliers, and distribution channels) are reduced. The consequence for the entrepreneur is a higher dependency on a limited pool of business partners, or in the worst case, a blocked market entry. Also, the more limited the pool become, the higher the financial risks for the entrepreneur. With fewer potential business partners, the more dependent the entrepreneur becomes on financial stability, market behavior, and long-term strategies of one, or only a few, business partners. A business partner, be it a customer, a distribution channel, or a supplier, may become so dominant that the entrepreneur's business is eventually controlled or marginalized.

The entrepreneur may also find it difficult to enter the market because of customers' requirements. Requirements like a consistent quality (for instance, an ISO-9000 quality-assurance system), top-notch service, and an ability to stay in the market for the long term are all elements that an entrepreneur will find difficult to fulfill, at least initially.

In poorer countries, entrepreneurs may also be restricted in their activities, due to market size (i.e., too few alternative customers, suppliers, and distribution channels). A large obstacle may be the negotiating power of suppliers (who may put prices so high that the entrepreneur become dependent on the supplier's expensive credit), or customers or distribution channels (which can dictate the price, product range, and market behavior).

Furthermore, within the poorest countries, an entrepreneur may also find it difficult to survive, because competition is too high. The problem is often too few business alternatives, (i.e., too few alternative ways for specialization), and the low purchasing power of the market (the customers are simply too poor to buy the goods offered). The result is, particularly in a recession, very low margins, and therefore no opportunity exists to save money and survive as an independent vendor.

Entrepreneurs are not equally appreciated in all societies. In Britain, for instance, less than one-third think entrepreneurs contribute a great deal to society.[2] Entrepreneurs may be wanted, but they are still treated with skepticism, because earning money and garnering success often create envy and suspicion. Being an entrepreneur is almost by definition being someone who is willing to be different from the rest, someone who is willing to take greater risks. This may prove difficult in societies where there is no culture for entrepreneurship. Here successful entrepreneurs may play a particularly important role; by behaving in an ethical and socially responsible manner, they may help improve the entrepreneurs' image in the society.

Moreover, government regulations may unintentionally discourage entrepreneurs. The number of formal procedures to set up a company are often too complicated, time consuming, and even costly, for an entrepreneur's patience and pocketbook. Government regulations may also be a direct barrier for an entrepreneur with an interest in investing in a particular industry or business that is protected from competition by law or heavy subsidies.

In order for the entrepreneur to set up and run a successful business, certain basic infrastructures may have to be in place. These include transport and telecommunication networks, clean water and sewage, and educational and financial structures. In poorer countries, weak infrastructure may be one of the greatest obstacles for an entrepreneur's establishment and growth. Equally important as the structural aspects is the entrepreneur's access to resources like capital, technology, contacts, and business know-how. The entrepreneur's access, however, is closely linked with such aspects as infrastructure, government legislation, society's attitude, and market and business structures.

Capital, Technology, and Contacts

Capital serves as one of the most important resources for the entrepreneur; at the same time, it may be one of the most difficult to obtain. In the initial phase, some start-up funds to buy raw materials and to produce and market the finished goods are needed until an income is generated. It is during this initial phase, which may last several years, that most entrepreneurs fail, often because of a lack of capital. As one's own financial resources may be small, the entrepreneur can choose to borrow money or find a business partner. To get a loan, some equity or guarantee is often required. If the entrepreneur is able to obtain a loan, repayment costs may be so high that the entrepreneur is discouraged from implementing his or her business idea.

The entrepreneur may also become discouraged or fail because he or she is not able to access the proper technology to produce goods in an efficient manner with the required quality. It may also be that he or she has no access to the necessary communication technologies to market the goods or services offered.

In order to be successful, the entrepreneur needs basic knowledge and understanding in several fields. First, he or she needs a perfect knowledge of the products or services being offered. This alone is far from sufficient; many entrepreneurs have a perfect knowledge of the product, because it is a result of his or her own innovative ideas. The problem centers on the entrepreneur's limited knowledge of the market (i.e., its needs and way of functioning), government regulations and support schemes, financial markets, and such administrative elements as financial control.

The importance of having the right contacts should not be underestimated. It is vital to have knowledge about potential customers, suppliers, distribution channels, financial sources, and government regulations and formalities; it is necessary to be able to access these players.

How to Build and Support Entrepreneurs

The importance of the above-described obstacles will differ from one society to another. However, the poorer societies will need to find solutions to several of the factors, as well as provide for more basic needs like infrastructure, start-up capital, basic education, and skills training. As the entrepreneur is local in nature, and needs may differ from one community to another, even within a city, the aim should be to stimulate initiatives locally, capitalizing on the entrepreneurs' innovative ideas and will to create.

Fostering Small Local Market Economies

A market economy is a prerequisite for fostering entrepreneurship — the more players in terms of potential customers and suppliers, alternative distribution channels, and financial sources, the more opportunities and choices for the entrepreneur. Also, the less government regulation in formal procedures for setting-up a company, the more likely it will be that the entrepreneur grabs the opportunity. A market economy is also more likely to foster a culture, which appreciates the efforts of the entrepreneur.

The government role in such an economy should be to control tendencies towards oligopoly and monopoly, and to monitor, together with the justice administration, the ethical aspects of market behavior in relation to environmental concerns.

The more impoverished the country and the less-developed the infrastructure and distribution channels, the more important it will be to stimulate a productive, but small in a geographic sense, local economy. The aim should be to create modest and relatively self-sufficient markets, where the entrepreneur is given as many opportunities as possible to choose and expand. In order to do so, the following policies should be implemented:

- Deregulation of local markets, meaning privatization of local monopolies.
- Enforcement of laws, which protect the rights of entrepreneurial and small-scale companies, including patent and other property rights, fair competition laws, and antimonopoly legislation.
- Encouragement of the establishment of alternative distribution channels, for instance through cooperatives, where small businesses will be the owners.
- Public investment in basic infrastructure, for example in local transport and storage systems.

Capital

Entrepreneurs' access to capital can additionally be improved by the establishment of venture capital funds. Parts of government pension funds can also be utilized for investment in small entrepreneurial companies with sound potential. Capital may also become more easily available if the growth of small and specialized banks are stimulated.

In poorer countries, informal and semiformal financing play a major role for providing entrepreneurs with capital. A survey from Niger (*World Development Report,* 1989) for example showed that informal credit accounted for 84 percent of total loans. In Sierra Leone, a survey on market women confirmed this picture; 30 percent of the market women got their initial start-up capital through loans, mostly from relatives and friends. Personal savings accounted for 27 percent, while 40 percent had inherited the business.

Capital can be stimulated by implementing the following policies:

- Stimulate the establishment of small, specialized banks through a cautious deregulation of financial markets;
- Establish schemes to support, advise, and encourage the establishment of informal and semiformal credit associations, for instance rotating

savings and credit associations[3] (which will stimulate both savings and lending);
- Introduce government-supported credit programs (i.e., provide relatively inexpensive loans as start-up capital for small businesses).

Education

An entrepreneur does not have to be a thoroughly educated person – in the academic sense. Research shows that in Norway, only 22 percent of the entrepreneurs had higher education; while 61 percent had spent 12 years or less in schools.

In poorer countries, the level of education is much lower. A survey conducted in Sierra Leone among 100 randomly chosen market women showed that only 2 percent had higher education; 26 percent had secondary education; 12 percent had primary education; and 59 percent boasted no education at all. Only 4 percent of the market women had some sort of formal training, such as accounting or bookkeeping.

The low figures for entrepreneurs with higher education may indicate that education in certain professions, such as engineering and business, which one would expect to benefit entrepreneurs, does not work that way. The reason may partly be found in current university curricula. Engineering and business students are educated and geared for working in large companies. American text books, written by academicians with experience and knowledge primarily about multinationals, are widely used, and entrepreneurship as a subject is barely ever introduced.

In order to bridge this gap, the following policies could be implemented:
- Entrepreneurship could be installed as a university subject, particularly for engineering and business students. (Perhaps even a degree in entrepreneurship could be established.)
- Educational programs on government regulations and support schemes, basic market law, finance and banking systems, bookkeeping, and financial control should be designed to suit the needs of local entrepreneurs.
- Literacy and basic mathematical (numerical) education could be provided, where necessary.

Entrepreneurs can feel isolated, and their opportunity to seek professional advice is often limited, principally because the entrepreneur by nature is someone who works on his or her own. Professional advice may prove financially too costly. In addition, there may not be many people to ask for help, or the entrepreneur may not know where to ask. But all is not lost. The establishment of local advisory boards as a simple, yet effective, measure could easily support local entrepreneurs. Such boards should be comprised of academicians, local prominent business people, and government officials.

Conclusion

Taking into consideration present unemployment levels in both rich and poor countries, in addition to current population growth rates, employment is indeed the main challenge of the future. It is the key to reduced crime, drug abuse, racial and social conflict, political and social apathy, and in the poorer countries, to poverty alleviation, reduced population growth, and migration to already overpopulated areas.

In order to help solve present and future employment problems, policies and priorities need to be reviewed, and the following list should be considered:

- More jobs need to be created in small-scale enterprises than in larger ones.

- Successful entrepreneurs can contribute to a positive growth effect, both in economic and social terms.

- Entrepreneurs have the best conditions for establishment and growth in a market economy, where there are many alternative customers, suppliers, distribution channels, and financial sources from which to choose.

- Capital, education, and advice are three key factors for developing successful entrepreneurial initiatives.

- NGOs can play a fundamental role in developing and providing programs for training and education on entrepreneurship and self-employment, conducting research on the needs and obstacles of local entrepreneurs, providing basic start-up capital, and in establishing local advisory boards to aid individual entrepreneurs.

Notes

1. The Phillips curve is based on the theorem that when Gross National Product (GNP) is higher relative to its potential, prices will increase; when GNP is lower relative to its potential, prices will decrease. In other words, in an economy where the production capacity, both capital and labor, is utilized to its fullest extent, inflation will occur, because there are no additional resources available in the short term.
2. *The Economist,* May 28, 1994, p. 76.
3. A rotating savings and credit association is normally formed by 6 to 40 people, with a chosen leader who periodically collects a given amount from each member. The collected money is then given in rotation to each member of the group.

Part 3

Enhancement of
Social Cohesion

The Social Question
in the 1990s
Louis Emmerij

The wheel has once again turned from an almost exclusive emphasis on economic growth to a more comprehensive set of economic and social objectives, including the reduction of poverty and the emancipation of women. It is amazing to observe this continuous swinging of the pendulum, with so little learned from past episodes. Experience should have taught that high rates of economic growth are necessary for achieving social objectives, such as increased productive employment, a reduction in poverty, high-quality education and health services, and a steady quality of life in urban centers.

Careful observation of the world economy should also have taught that the sustained, high rates of growth in East Asia did not bring about the full employment reached in the early 1970s (for example, in South Korea). On the contrary, focus on the full utilization of production factors and of labor was the key to high growth rates observed in the East Asian development model. Without the employment orientation of development policies, sustained rates in economic growth of 8 to 10 percent would not have been possible. The same phenomenon can now be observed in China. In short, the lesson to be drawn from experience is that the pattern of growth matters at least as much as the rate of growth.

Pattern of growth is determined by emphasizing certain economic sectors, population groups, and income groups over others. It is furthermore affected by the role assigned to the quality of a country's human resources, by assuring a regional balance leading to regional equity, and by giving people a say in their economic destiny.

All these points have been learned once since World War II's end. Growth, for example, has been reflected in the International Labor Organization (ILO) World Employment Program of the 1970s, and in the World Bank's endeavors under McNamara and Hollis Chenery, as summed up in the 1980 World Development Report. The lesson can be stated succinctly. If faster economic growth is essential to reduce absolute poverty and achieve social progress, the length of the transition period must be reasonably considered. It must be mature and acceptable. No one would deny that in the long run, economic growth is effective in tackling poverty and achieving social objectives, but change might take three to five generations.

During the 1980s, this lesson was all but forgotten. The world economic depression of the early 1980s, along with the international debt crisis beginning in 1982, resulted in the return to an economic paradigm of another age: "First Obtain Economic Growth and Everything Else will Follow." Gone was the lesson that a balanced and integrated set of economic, financial, and social policies was essential for obtaining not only growth, but also employment, a decent income, and access to education, health, and clean drinking water (in short, that essential needs are satisfied for everyone). Gone also was the conviction that an "economic growth first" policy would, as a matter of course, result in more poverty, more uneven income distribution, and eventually, in social unrest.

It is somewhat understandable that each generation, when confronted with an economic crisis, resorts to the old reflex of getting back to growth at "any price." And "any price"—now as in earlier times—means growing income disparities, fewer income earning opportunities, and less emphasis on "soft" social sectors, like education, health, and women.

Oneness of Economic and Social Goals

What is less understandable is that during the 1980s, the basic lesson of the previous two decades was forgotten—namely that the economic and the social were one, that they were complementary and mutually supporting, and that one without the other leads to disaster. Too much "social" without sufficient "economic" leads to bankruptcy and an end to growth. Too much "economic" without sufficient "social" leads to social unrest and an end to growth. How could informed decision makers still talk about "soft sectors" more than 20 years after the renaissance of the economics of education and health? For this rebirth showed that education and growth are investments in human capital, and hence, a prerequisite for economic growth, rather than a consumption good to be afforded only after a given level of economic achievement has been reached.

These lessons, based on experience, may have been put forward, but their influence was not far-reaching. Basically, the 1980s revived the old sequence that had proven wrong again and again: growth first, distribution later; stop inflation first, create employment later; buy now, pay later; free trade now, industrialize later.

The results of this decade can be seen everywhere. The employment problem has become universal (more than 11 percent open unemployment in the European Economic Community, or EEC); the maldevelopment of the city has led to unacceptable, global low levels of quality of life; educational quality is threatened, and health services need restructuring; social security and pension funds, where they exist, have become endangered species; political and economic refugees are coming in increasing numbers to Europe, an area still seen by people from the East and South as a haven of luxury, despite economic stagnation and rising unemployment. In short, never has it been more apt than today to say that "poverty anywhere is a threat to prosperity everywhere."

The perception of social cost was corroborated by increased poverty and by the appearance of the "new poor" (i.e., people who were not poor before, but whose income deteriorated to poverty levels). In a sense, being traditionally poor is unfortunate even if you are used to it, but having fallen into poverty for the first time is especially devastating. Lately, signs point to a deterioration in the employment situation, a decline in the quality of education, and a menaced quality of life in urban centers. These factors have resulted in a rise in open social unrest and a reappearance of the social question on the agendas of many countries.

Indeed, social reform is essential for the maintenance of political and social peace, which in turn is essential for long-term and sustained economic growth. Social reform must also be adapted periodically—it can never be defined by a status quo. In order to make this discussion more concrete, let us take the example of Costa Rica.

Costa Rica is situated in the midst of an unstable and volatile region. In spite of this, it has had an average, annual rate of economic growth of 5 percent (2.5 percent on a per capita basis) during the last half century. There can be little doubt that this exceptional performance is largely due to the foresight of the political and entrepreneurial class of the early century.

That class introduced a first Social Reform that had the following characteristics:

- Wide access to land, which made for "initial conditions" that assured a fairly equitable income distribution before and during the economic growth process (Costa Rica, therefore, is an illustration of the "redistribution-before-growth" thesis);
- Universal and free access to high-quality primary education leading to a sound human-resource base early on;
- Wide access to high-quality health services, which multiplied the quality of the human-resource base of the country.

These three factors comprised the first Social Reform, which was unique in its comprehensiveness and early timing. These social investments made for political and social stability in a highly unstable region, in addition to a healthy and productive labor force. In short, the reform set the foundation for a long period of sustained economic growth, first based on the export of coffee and bananas, later on a much more diversified production and export pattern.

Yet just as production and exports must be further diversified, so the social basis must be updated. The first Social Reform has served Costa Rica well, but it has run its course. Thus, it needs to be followed by a second Social Reform.

This second reform must be conceived in such a manner as to be the future basis of the next stage of economic growth and development. That stage will be orientated towards regional (the North American Free Trade Agreement, or NAFTA) and global markets of increasing sophistication. The weight of the traditional engine of growth—coffee and bananas—will diminish quickly. The new progressive market will be based on the export of services, such as tourism, computer programming, and medical services, and on agroindustrial products, like concentrated orange juice, flowers, and plants. However this will not be possible without the sustained interest of foreign investors, who have already proven interested in Costa Rica's political and social stability, its equitable societal nature, and its sound human-resource base.

The challenge before Costa Rica is how its country characteristics can be maintained, deepened, and updated. Therefore, the second Social Reform must have, as a minimum, the following components:

- San José and its surroundings threaten to becoming a sprawling, un-planned traffic-, crime-, and drug-ridden urban center of more than 3 million people over the next 25 years. Already the quality of life has diminished. Urban planning and a deconcentrated population policy are urgently needed if social peace there is to be maintained.

- Education, training, and retraining policies must be reformulated. The quality of primary education must be improved, the coverage of sec-ondary education extended, training and retraining programs sharpened, and the balance between university education and the rest of the edu-cational system reviewed. The same applies to the financing of higher education.

- The emphasis of health services must shift more to preventive care if costs are to be kept under control.

- The need for economic and geographic deconcentration has already been mentioned. The desirability of decentralization of decisionmaking and implementation structures is equally urgent.

This second Social Reform will enable the country to maintain social and political peace and to preserve an improved quality of its human-resource base. Such a concrete example has provided a clue to what must be understood by social reform. Let us now try to put this in more general terms.

Social Reform: What Is It?

First of all, social reform must be seen as complementary to the economic and financial reforms of the 1980s. An integrated economic, financial, and social strategy is required. It is no longer acceptable that the main thrust of development strategies be defined by economic considerations alone, and that only as an afterthought are certain social policies erected. The trend must be towards an integrated set of economic and social programs.

Second, social reform should be seen as a productive investment. Im-proving the quality of urban life, creating lucrative employment opportuni-ties, and spending dollars on high-quality education and health are not only consumption goods to be afforded once a certain level of income has been achieved. Rather, they are productive investments that are prerequisites for attaining certain levels of income.

Third, a problem has already been alluded to, namely that social reform is not necessarily having an impact on reform in fields such as education and health. Thus the repercussions lie more with quality than with quantity.

The renewed interest in both the social question and poverty is largely the result of growing recognition that a "social time bomb" was ticking beneath the financial and economic policies of the 1980s. The social price paid for because of these policies has led to unrest, caused by lack of remunerative employment opportunities, poor living conditions in cities and rural areas, and a lack of perspective and hope.

Social reform means, in the first instance, defining the four or five top priorities where qualitatively different policy action is required. In many countries, the top priorities that social reform must contain include:

- **Urban Policy:** Few countries have an urban policy on any comprehensive scale. Social unrest is in no small measure due to the extremely poor living conditions in cities, locales which illustrate the most extreme problems within individual countries. But city bias, or "urban bias," should not lead to an unbalanced rural–urban situation. An urban decentralization policy into the rural areas is essential, and a new look at rural development via "urban bias" will be required.

- **Employment Policies:** These must be economy-wide in scope. The full and productive utilization of the entire labor force is a precondition for achieving high and sustained rates of economic growth. Economy-wide, employment-maximizing efforts are not, and should not, be quick-fix solutions to poverty and social problems. Rather, they should be analyzed to provide the underlying economic basis for productivity improvement, income growth, and asset accumulation. Land reform must also be put on the official agenda again, because it will enhance the income of small farmers. Productivity within the urban–informal and rural–traditional sectors must be increased, in order to avoid the generalization of low productivity and low-wage employment. This will require an emphasis on appropriate technology within the sectors, and on linkages between these and the modern sector through such devises as subcontracting. The functioning of labor markets must be improved, while youth employment in the transitional adolescent years should be given special attention. Particular attention must also be given to the creation of *productive* employment.

- **Investment in Human Resources:** Special attention needs to be focused on the quality of education. This means, among other things, that the quality and motivation of teaching staff must be improved, and in turn implies looking at monetary and nonmonetary incentives and disincentives. Vocational, technical, and science education at all levels, as well as training and retraining—particularly when people are between school and work, or between jobs—must be given pride of place. The balance between basic education and higher education is becoming crucial.

In the health sector, a balance must be maintained between hospitals and preventive health care, with the allocation of resources switched to the latter.

- **Changing the Implementation Structure:** A social-reform policy along the above lines would remain an empty gesture as long as the implementation structures — administrative, budgetary, and institutional — remain in place. How to introduce policy changes to achieve top priorities is at least as important as what these policy objectives and top priorities need to be. Careful attention must, therefore, be given to: the question of centralization versus decentralization; questions such as the duties of the state versus the private sector and individual responsibility; and the role of actors such as Non-Governmental Organizations (NGOs) and religious institutions.

- **Social Security:** A modern society needs to have mechanisms and safety nets in place to deal with the old, the sick, the disabled, the unemployed, and victims of natural disasters. Quite a few countries have social security systems that often look good on paper; a closer inspection, however, shows serious inequities due to changing levels of inflation, severe financial problems, and benefits that are not always enforced. Another objective of social-reform policy must be to remodel social security systems, in order to increase their coverage and make them more equitable and efficient in administration and enforcement.

The correspondences between economic and social reforms are evident; in fact, the distinction between economic and social policies practically disappears given the intimate relationship between the two. Productive employment creation is both an economic and social objective. Indeed in any social reform, employment creation must be high on the list of priorities. At the same time, it is vital because full utilization of the country's labor force will boost both economic growth and development.

The same is true for policy action to increase output and productivity in the urban–informal and rural–traditional sectors. The relationship between the social objective of creating more and better income opportunities and the economic objective of achieving more balanced and widespread economic growth, is obvious.

Moreover, in the global markets that dominate the world economy of the 1990s, all countries must place more emphasis on innovation, science, and technology. This by definition implies more emphasis on human capital (i.e., on education and the quality of the human factor in general). But it also implies that priority must not only go to basic education. Indeed, if innovation, science, and technology are to be put at the heart of economic growth ("the goose that lays the golden egg"), then the creation of exceptional academic centers in education and research becomes equally important.

Finally, the way people live in the urban and rural centers (i.e., the quality of life) has important implications for labor-force productivity. Here again, the relationship between quantity and quality, and between economic and social reforms, stands out.

An integrated set of economic and social policies, as illustrated by previous example, will: produce both more equity and efficiency; improve the competitive edge of countries; and therefore provide the necessary balance to the financial and economic reforms of the 1980s.

Social Reform: How to Implement?

Past cases illustrate that money alone does not solve problems. On the contrary, generous resources unaccompanied by adequate fiscal control and distorted by partisan concerns can create distortions or "time bombs," which become evident when those resources diminish. Expenditures on traditional social areas can be relatively high in regional — indeed international — perspective, but the results can be poor and could rapidly turn worse. Very often, such a problem lies principally in the inappropriate and highly inefficient institutions that historically have channeled that money. Much of that problem, in turn, rests in the vested interests behind those structures. Challenging such vested interests at first may seem difficult, if not well-nigh impossible.

That is why it is vital to concentrate on how reform might happen. Often, on the question of what needs to be done, there is an important degree of internal consensus as to the goals which may or may not coincide with a country's priorities. The important matter is that quite often, a consensus exists as to objectives and what needs to be done in the social arena. However, those elements of consensus stop short when one enters into means rather than goals. Frequently, no agreement exists on, for example, the nature and degree of state support required to build an efficient social sector. There may not even be adequate information to evaluate how far different strategies for economic growth will generate employment.

State institutions appear so inefficient and distorted that they cannot be trusted on to execute policy decisions. This is why it is so important to reflect on the instances of positive change which are there, and of which there are many, not least of all at the local level (away from the heavy hand of central state ministries). The analysis and successful communication of such information at the community level can provide the basis for change, with careful learning from mistakes that inevitably occur. Social policy, however, is also about administrative efficiency. Unless institutions can translate preferences into the effective delivery of social services, aspirations will remain unfulfilled or even distorted.

In much of Latin America and elsewhere, social policy has been rather specifically focused. In fact, it has comprised the following four elements: the centralized public provision of health and education, and to some extent also, the public provision of low-income housing; the use of labor legislation to achieve social goals; the use of prices to redistribute income; and social security systems usually taken from the 1930s. Yet in the case of many countries, the state has failed to provide adequate access to health and education, let alone provide reasonable access to housing. Moreover, labor legislation has been undermined by partisan political practices and by a huge growth in the workforce not covered by any labor code. The price mechanism has proved insufficient in redistributing income, and the social security system is not only totally inadequate in its coverage, but very often bankrupt in practice.

Social policy, therefore, not only needs to be reformed, but often reformulated. As an integral part of that reform, concepts of its meaning and role need to be broadened. In synthesis, the whole institutional structure designed to redistribute wealth must be changed, both because it is failing in its original redistribution goal and because it must reflect the harsh reality of the need for economic austerity.

A main conclusion from this line of reasoning is that the responsibility for social reform does not lie exclusively with any single group or agent. The accountability for new and more productive relations between state and civil society rests in large part with the employer's associations, NGOs, neighborhood groups, and the like. This emphasis is important to counterbalance the power of particular vested interests in the implementation or blocking of institutional reform.

While the rethinking of models can be precipitated from below, as was the case in a number of countries, ultimately the entire process of reform has to involve the relaying and relating of these instances to the core, and the willingness of the center to respond to these reforms at the micro level. In each sector – be it education, health, or housing – the strong definition of norms from the center is top priority. However, it is one of our contentions that an incrementalist approach of building on small examples of success is a way, and possibly the only way, to make large themes manageable. Small examples can animate other local initiatives, which can learn from experience, both good and bad.

The point is that such strategies need to be routed in systematic investment in "institutional learning." This requires investment in resources to do the learning, to record the case histories, and to evaluate and then diffuse them.

Solid progress along these lines is central to the process of social reform. Examples abound where local communities have challenged and overcome the power of trade unions in the provision of basic services. There is reason to believe that there will be public support for determined government action which, with the correct inducements, could reform the way that the public-sector unions operate.

Conclusion

What is needed today is social reform that complements the economic and financial reforms already introduced in many countries, so that a balanced and integrated set of socioeconomic policies may be conceded. The economic policies introduced as of the 1980s paid particular emphasis to the modalities of implementation: private sector versus public sector; deregulation versus regulation; free trade versus protectionism. This emphasis on how matters must be implemented is of equal importance in the social sectors, as illustrated earlier in this section.

It is necessary to look at the implementation-cum-decision-making structure in a "vertical" and "horizontal" fashion. The vertical structure pertains to what must be decided centrally and what can best be handled by regions, municipalities, and communities. The horizontal structure is concerned with what must be done by the state (centralized or decentralized), what by the private sector, by NGOs, and what must be the responsibility of the individual.

A distinction must furthermore be made between those social expenditures that can be considered investments necessary for development on the one hand, and social expenditures that are more akin to consumption on the other. Big chunks of education and health care spending are investments in human capital. Employment creation by definition is essential for economic growth and development. Social security and unemployment insurance, where they exist, come close to consumption; yet even regarding these factors, by maintaining demand they avoid severe economic slumps.

In conclusion, "social development is economic development." Investments in people have among the highest economic returns of all possible spending directed to long-term economic development. Let us just hope that this lesson will not be forgotten in the future, as it has been in the past.

Chapter 1

The Challenge of
Social Integration

Section 1

Prospects for Global
Human Integration

Dankwart A. Rustow

Five thousand years ago human beings on this globe were divided into small communities of planters or animal herders across many separate continents. Then came various efforts at integration through regional empires, such as the Shang in China (16th to 11th centuries BC), the Romans along the Mediterranean (1st century BC to 4th century AD), Muslim Caliphs in the Near East (7th to 16th centuries), Mongols in Central Asia (13th to 15th centuries), and Aztecs and Incas in the Americas (14th to 16th centuries).

Full global integration has resulted only from the historic role assumed by Europe since the fifteenth century. The Portuguese sailed around Africa so as to break the Ottoman-Turkish monopoly on transit trade of spices and other goods from Asia. Columbus sailed westward from Spain so as to find a trade route that would bypass both Portuguese and Ottomans.

But as soon as the Portuguese landed in West Africa, they used their guns against the arrows of the local peoples and began the infamous practice of slavery. And when the Spaniards established themselves in the Western hemisphere, they destroyed the Aztec and Inca empires and introduced their own system of landlordism and serfdom. In the same pattern of competition other Western Europeans, such as the Dutch, British, and French, established their overseas colonies in Asia, the Americas, and Africa; and Czarist Russia on Europe's Eastern borders colonized all of Central and Northeast Asia.

By the eighteenth or nineteenth centuries, most of the habitable world from Alaska and Algeria to Argentina and Australia had been incorporated into those expanding European colonial empires. The exceptions were the Middle East (Ottoman Turkey, Iran, and Afghanistan) and East Asia (China, Japan, and Thailand). By the nineteenth century even Ottoman Turkey (from the Tanzimat, or "reform decree" of 1839) and Japan (since the accession of Emperor Meiji in 1867) began to emulate European patterns of technology and administration[1] following the ancient Roman maxim *fas est ab hoste doceri* ("you are fated to learn from your enemy"). Early in the twentieth century post-Czarist Russia under Lenin's leadership adopted a distorted version of Marxism; that Leninist example soon was followed by Mao Zedong in China (1927–1976) and later by leaders in European colonies or excolonies from Cuba to Angola and Vietnam.

Commerce and war, which provided the driving forces in this Eurocentric unification of the human globe, are, on the face of it, extreme opposites. Commerce involves the exchange of goods to mutual advantage — a positive-sum game; warfare is mutual slaughter — and hence, whoever wins, a negative-sum game. Yet there also are opposite aspects. Unregulated commerce makes the rich richer and the poor poorer, thereby leading easily to human inequality and exploitation; victory in war may establish a new political order that allows people to live peacefully within wider boundaries.

Global unification has been a dialectic process, in which the thesis of discovery and exchange, produces many antithetical results, such as human suffering and exploitation, and that the challenge for global humanity in the twenty-first century will be synthesize these competitive and often deadly forces into a peacefully united but dynamic and diversified human community.

Both commerce and warfare depend on communication and innovation. Successful trade requires a flow of information about potential exchanges and the transportation of goods. Victory in war largely depends on invention of new weapons and effective communication. Modern artillery enabled Ottoman Turks to win the siege of Byzantium in 1453, but by 1683 their communication system of relaying military commands on horseback from Istanbul to the gates of Vienna had overreached itself. And it was new technologies applied by Europeans — such as clocks and compasses aboard sailing ships and gunpowder used against bows and arrows — that enabled them first to "discover" the world and then to conquer most of it.

The Role of Technology

One of the bitter ironies of modern history is that many of the major technological inventions were applied first to warfare and then to peacful purposes. When Galileo Galilei (1564–1642), as a young academic in Padua, learned that a Dutchman had invented the telescope, he obtained an early sample that would let him conclusively prove the Copernican theory. But he first went to the rulers of Venice, recently involved in a major maritime battle with Ottoman Turkey, assuring them that this "spy-glass" would spot "sails and shipping...two hours before they were seen with the naked eye, steering full-sail into the harbour" — and his reward was promotion to a lifelong professorship.[2]

In the twentieth century, airplanes became important in World War I as fighters and became decisive in World War II as bombers, but only since the 1950s have they become a standard mode of civilian transportation. Similarly, atomic scientists in World War II and the early Cold War years concentrated on making A-bombs and H-bombs; and only decades after the destruction of Hiroshima and Nagasaki was atomic energy used to generate electricity. But here comes another of history's remarkable dialectic twists: with the Soviet Union having caught up with (and even surpassed) the Western powers in nuclear and space technology, both sides were afraid of mutual destruction. For the first time in history, the most advanced weaponry remained unused for (so far) half a century.

Why Europe?

Before exploring other aspects of this complex global dialectic, we must ask: Why was it Europe that unified the world? To answer that Europeans were more talented in science and technology would be arrogant and erroneous. Astronomy and agricultural technology were developed in Mesopotamia and Egypt when most of Europe was still populated by planters and herders. The heritage of classical Greek science and philosophy was kept alive mostly in the Middle East and rediscovered by the Europeans through new contacts with that region in the era of the Crusades (11th to 13th centuries) and Ottoman expansion (14th to 15th centuries). Similarly, the decimal system was passed on to Europe by the Arabs, who, in turn, had adapted it from India in the ninth century; it was not until 1576 that a Frenchman introduced decimal fractions.

Some of the most crucial modern technologies were developed in China many centuries before they appeared in Europe, including the compass in the third century, printing in the seventh century, and gunpowder in the eleventh century. Yet, significantly, China, having emerged early in human history as the largest empire and endowed with ample domestic resources, adopted a defensive strategy. Thus the Chinese built a "Great Wall" to protect themselves against nomadic invasions from Central Asia and, by the fifteenth century, forbade seaborne commerce so as to keep out subversive ideas from abroad. And China's technological inventions were carefully fitted into its own traditional framework — gunpowder for fireworks on holidays and printing for religious entertainment for the emperor.[3]

A more objective answer to the question "Why Europe?" would rely on some basic facts of geography, as well as on cultural and political history. A glance at the map tells us that Europe, among the habitable parts of the globe, has a uniquely diversified coastline, including peninsulas from the Balkans and Iberia to Scandinavia; off-shore islands such as Britain; and inland seas from the Black Sea and Mediterranean (literally "the sea in the midst of the lands") to the Baltic. All this meant that most regions of Europe were naturally differentiated and easily defensible, but also (in times when horses and sails were the best means of transport) easily accessible by land and sea.

Commerce and warfare were among the decisive factors in Europe's history. The ancient Greeks thrived on their commercial connections along the Middle Eastern and European shores of the Mediterranean, and their culture vastly benefited from those contacts, but their attempt to set up an empire from Macedonia to India under Alexander the Great (360–323 BC) quickly collapsed. The only successful imperial structure was set up by the Romans (1st century BC). Although imperial unity soon was destroyed through partition between rival emperors in Constantinople and Rome and Germanic invasions in the fourth century, the empire of Charlemagne (768–814) briefly reunited Western and Central Europe. Latin remained the common tongue of Europe's cultural–political elite of church and state until the sixteenth century, and of natural science well into the nineteenth century.

Europe's modern age was ushered in by a *cultural* revolution. Dante Alighieri (1265–1321) composed his poetry not in Latin but in his Florentine vernacular, thereby shaping the modern Italian language. Two centuries later Martin Luther (1483–1546) reasoned that since Jesus himself had been a man of the people, his message should be accessible to the common people of his own day. Luther's Bible translation, distributed by the newly crafted technique of book printing by movable type, became the landmark event in creating modern German. Dante's and Luther's precedents were widely followed throughout Europe and, by the eighteenth century, national languages had replaced Latin in most spheres of life. It might be said that this vernacular revolution adapted the geographic principles of unity and diversity to Europe's culture; and it was to have important, and at times contradictory, consequences.

The language revolution dissolved the unity that had been provided by Latin and ultimately divided Europe into separate nations. Those emerging nations found themselves in intense political conflict leading to ever more violent warfare, from the Hundred Years' War (1339–1453) between England and France and the Thirty Years War (1618–1648) that devastated much of Germany to the Napoleonic Wars (1796–1815) that engulfed most of Europe from Spain to Russia. The very multiplicity of nation-states also meant that a balance of power was periodically reestablished. The most successful military campaigns ultimately were fought not in Europe but to establish Europe's colonial dominion over other continents. Thus from 1914 to 1918 and again from 1939 to 1945, those European wars expanded into ferocious "World Wars."

The opposite effect of the same language revolution was that it bridged the social gap between rulers and subjects. In times of peace, it provided an ample base for exchange of cultural and even political ideas within Europe and beyond.

Nations, Ministates, and Empires

In the competition among modern European countries, geographic and cultural factors were highly influential. Some found themselves in locations inaccessible to foreign armed forces, such as England. In its island location, England has not faced foreign invaders since 1066. Switzerland and the Netherlands benefited from their difficult mountain or seacoast terrain in successfully fighting for independence from Habsburg rulers in distant Vienna and Madrid, respectively.

All three developed decentralized political systems. Great Britain from the seventeenth to the nineteenth centuries was ruled by a central government based on cooperation between king, lords, and elected representatives of a widening group of commoners; an independent judiciary; and decentralized local governments. Note, however, that although Britain's "United Kingdom" was originally based on the dynastic union of Protestant England and Scotland in 1603, its rule over Catholic Ireland until 1921 was, in fact, more of a colonial system.

Switzerland, since the original rebellion of its central portions against Austrian overlordship, expanded gradually into a broader association throughout the Western Alps—mostly of commercial cities dominating their rural hinterlands. After a period of intense conflict (1831–1848), however, a federal and democratic government was established among 22 cantons with four official languages.[4]

Britain, the Netherlands, and Switzerland all excelled in commerce and invention. The British became leaders in the natural and social sciences in the days of Isaac Newton, John Locke, and Adam Smith; they became the world's leading traders and industrialists in the eighteenth and nineteenth centuries. The Dutch invented the telescope and, since the late Middle Ages, were among Europe's leading traders. The Swiss profited from intense overland trade across the Alps, developing modern watches and centers of international banking. And their maritime locations allowed the British and Dutch the choice of staying out of European wars and concentrating instead on overseas trade and conquest. The Dutch established colonies from Nieuw Amsterdam (now New York) to South Africa and Indonesia; the British by the nineteenth century had the world's largest colonial empire.

Western and Northern Europe from Spain to Sweden developed in the modern age mostly as well-defined nation-states. The most centralized government among these was created by in France by the Bourbon monarchy (1589–1789), which established a comprehensive system of training for provincial administrators in the capital of Paris. By the eighteenth century, the country had emerged as the leading European power, and the Parisian *salons* were models for elegant society throughout Europe. (Note that the vocabulary for *haute couture* and *haute cuisine* in much of the Western world still is French-derived.)

But here comes another dialectic twist: As the American colonists rebelled against the imposition of a more centralized taxation system from London, the French government, for obvious geopolitical reasons (my enemy's enemy is my friend), supports the colonists. Yet the French government soon found that contacts with those republican forces by the Marquis de Lafayette in the colonies or by Benjamin Franklin and Thomas Jefferson as its representatives in Paris reinforced the demand for radical reform—and ultimately for the overthrow—of the French monarchy itself.[5]

By contrast to the northwest European pattern of nation-states, Italy and Germany until the mid-nineteenth century remained divided into petty states—from kingdoms, duchies, and bishoprics to principalities and free trading cities. Those political divisions set the stage not only for internal wars, but also for recurrent military invasions from outside. In Germany, a major attempt at liberal revolution in 1848–1849, centered on an elected parliament in Frankfurt, failed in part because those parliamentarians could not cope with the problem of whether or how to connect the Prussian Kingdom and Austro-Hungarian Empire with the community of smaller states from Holstein to Bavaria.[6] Both Italy and Germany were only forcibly unified by militant nationalists in 1861–1871, and, after brief interludes of constitutional government, became the first countries to lapse into fascism and Nazism.

Nonetheless, although the German and Italian ministate pattern continued, it provided a setting for great cultural creativity. Thus Galileo could move between Pisa in the Duchy of Tuscany (1589–1592, 1610–1633) and Padua in the Venetian Republic (1592–1610). At a time when French cultural life centered on the royal court and *salons* of Paris, the German composer Johann Sebastian Bach (1685–1750) found employment successively with the Duke of Weimar, the Prince of Anhalt, and in the trading city of Leipzig. Also, by another of history's dialectic twists, the ministate system provided Germany and Italy with vast pools of princely families suitable for royal marriage throughout Europe, thus reinforcing each country's international cultural connections.[7] Thus when the German elector George I of Hanover inherited the British throne, he brought to London his court composer Georg Friedrich Handel (1685–1759), whose style left its indelible imprint on English music.

Further to the East, the political pattern remained one of multiethnic empires. The Habsburg Austro-Hungarian realm included what later became Czechoslovakia and parts of Poland, Yugoslavia, and Romania—and, significantly, Hungary retained Latin as its official language. The Ottoman Turkish empire withdrew from Southeastern Europe after successive defeats (1683–1913) and national rebellions (for example, Serbia in 1804 and Greece in 1830), but at the time of its final defeat in World War I still included Turkish, Greek, Kurdish, and Armenian areas in Anatolia, as well as Arab provinces in Iraq, Syria, Lebanon, and Palestine.

In contrast to this dissolution of the Habsburg and Ottoman empires, the Czarist realm in the 1917 revolution was transformed into Lenin's Communist regime. Under Stalin after 1945, this Communist dictatorship established its dominion over Eastern and much of Central Europe, from Estonia to East Germany and Bulgaria. Even after Western decolonization in Asia and Africa, Russia itself survived as the largest European colonial empire from Bialystok to Vladivostok. Indeed, Communist central planning of the economy and a deliberate policy of ethnic "divide and rule" allowed few of the nominally sovereign member states of the "Union of Socialist Soviet Republic" to retain or develop any separate national identities. Under Mikhail Gorbachev (1985–1991) that USSR was, in 1991, nominally transformed into a "Commonwealth of Independent States"; yet whether the outcome will be fully independent states from Belarus to Kyrgyzstan, a genuinely regional association on the model of the European Community, or a reassertion of Russian imperialism over the "Near Abroad" still is very much an open question.

Diversity and Competition

The emergence of vernacular languages and national identities in Europe, by bridging the gap between the landed aristocracy and the common people, promoted the rise of a commercial bourgeoisie, European leadership in science and industry – and ultimately a political evolution toward democracy. The diversity of national cultures enriched the interchange of ideas within Europe. Thus the sonnet – a poetic form devised by Dante's disciple Francesco Petrarca – was adapted to other languages by poets from Shakespeare and Goethe to Elizabeth Browning and Rilke. Italian musical styles soon spread throughout Europe, and Italian words from *allegretto* to *concertante* became the core of musical vocabulary. But soon intellectual figures such as Johann Gottfried Herder (1744–1803) insisted that top-rate poetry could be composed in any language from Lappish to Latin,[8] and romantic poets of all nationalities and composers from Schubert and Chopin to Dvorak and Tchaikovsky began to draw on the rich resources of folk poetry and folk music. Also the expansion of Europe's wars and conquests across the globe provided opportunities for cultural contacts outside the European tradition; and some of its former colonies, notably the United States, Brazil, and India further contributed to this pattern of cultural diversification.

Similarly, political movements began to spread across Europe. Thus the example of the American and French Revolutions was followed by anti-monarchist revolutions from the Netherlands to Italy, although Napoleon's victorious armies soon converted those new republics into satrapies of his French empire.[9] Early in the nineteenth century the ideal of the nation-state had become so prevalent and infectious that it challenged the survival of the multiethnic Habsburg, Ottoman, and Czarist empires on Europe's Eastern fringe with nationalist movements from Serbia and Greece to Poland and Finland.

Competition among nations in Europe, and even their overseas expansion, added to freedom of movement, and hence of though. This was a major source of the Western revolution in science and technology from Newton's law of gravitation and invention of the calculus to Edison's light bulb (1887) and the invention of computers in the 1940s.

To cite some specific examples of the effect of Europe's political diversity and competition: When Columbus found no support for his westward sailing project in his native Italy, he peddled it in Lisbon and, ultimately, Madrid. But when, soon after Columbus' first voyage, the Spanish inquisition threatened to burn non-Christians at the stake, many Sephardic Jews, including the family of the philosopher Baruch Spinoza, resettled in the Netherlands, which had recently fought its war of independence against Spain. Other Spanish Jews were invited by the Ottoman Sultan to his multiethnic empire, where they helped make Istanbul and Salonica thriving commercial cities.

When the novelist Jean-Jacques Rousseau (1712–1778) found himself on the losing side in a political conflict in his home town of Geneva, he moved to Paris where he enjoyed great popularity with the ladies of the *salons* and helped inseminate some of the democratic ideas of the revolution of 1789. But when the philosopher Voltaire (1694–1778) was ostracized in France, he moved to England, then became an intellectual mentor of King Frederick II of Prussia, and ultimately settled near the Swiss city of Geneva. Later, when Prussian censorship banned the writings of the radical journalist Karl Marx, he moved to Paris, assembled his fellow Communists in Brussels, and earned a living as European correspondent for the *New York Daily Tribune*; and, when the political atmosphere in France shifted from the liberal revolution of 1848 to the imperial government of Napoleon III, Marx moved on to do his research in the vast library of London's British Museum.

Countries of overseas immigration—notably what became the United States—developed a very particular pattern of unity and diversity. Thus, in the seventeenth century, many of the Presbyterians, who had lost to Anglican royalists in England's bitter civil war (1640–1660), chose to join their coreligionists in Massachusetts (or "New" England). Soon new religious groups known as "Separatists" emerged and moved to different locations, including the Quakers in Pennsylvania. By the mid-nineteenth century, the United States had become the favorite destination of European emigrants— whether fleeing from Irish potato famine, defeat of liberals in the 1848 German revolution, pogroms in Eastern Europe, or, in the twentieth century, from fascist or Nazi dictatorships. Among those exiles were East European Jews who founded the film industry in Hollywood; men such as Enrico Fermi, Albert Einstein, Robert Oppenheimer, and John von Neumann who made decisive contributions to atomic science and computer technology; and musicians such as Arturo Toscanini, and Paul Hindemith. Toward the end of the twentieth century, even Japanese-born conductors, such as Seiji Ozawa, played major roles on the American concert stage.

But here, as one of the cruel dialectic features of modern history, it should be remembered that, while white Europeans voluntarily migrated across the Atlantic over the centuries, much of America's economy was based on the exploitation of African slaves in the cotton industry of the South. Indeed, one of those Southern slave owners was Thomas Jefferson, the author of the Declaration of Independence with its classic statement that "All men are created equal," and coauthor of both the French Declaration of Rights of Man and of the U.S. Bill of Rights.[10] And it was not until America's bloody Civil War that slavery was officially abolished, and not until the days of Martin Luther King, Jr. (1929–1968) that Afro-Americans have *begun* to move toward full equality.

Among the factors contributing to the diversification of Western culture are the growing sensitivity to human feelings and the increasing facility of communication. Operas developed as entertainment for royalty and nobility in seventeenth- and eighteenth-century Europe; yet both in Mozart's *Nozze di Figaro* and Rossini's *Il Barbiere di Siviglia* (as in the original play by Beaumarchais, 1775), it is the common barber rather than his aristocratic employer who is the moral hero. John Gay's *Beggar's Opera* (1728) mocked that aristocratic opera style. By the nineteenth century, operettas by Jacques Offenbach, Johann Strauss, and Gilbert and Sullivan further developed this humorous touch of classless humanity before their bourgeois audiences. Similarly, authors such as Charles Dickens, Emile Zola, and Fyodor Dostoyevsky (*The Idiot*, 1868) brought to their bourgeois readers human stories from the working class or from social outcasts. Jazz provided a form of self-expression for American Blacks late in the nineteenth century; by the 1930s became the rage in the United States and Europe. And the growing repertoire of popular dances in the Western world came to include French minuets, Austrian waltzes, Polish mazurkas, and South American tangos, rumbas, and chachas.

Meanwhile, contact with non-European cultures through such events as Napoleon's incursion into the Middle East or British rule over India and sponsorship of the Suez Canal stimulated poetry such as Goethe's *West-Östlicher Divan* (1814–1818) and Edward Fitzgerald's free adaptation of the eleventh-century Persian poet Omar Khayyam (1859) and operatic themes such as Verdi's *Aida* (1871). In the twentieth century, global trade and travel have stimulated such international fads as zen, yoga, and karate, and enriched our menus with such items as Turkish shish kebab, Japanese sushi, and kiwis from New Zealand.

In sum, whereas in classical Confucian, Islamic, or medieval Christian settings the aim was to achieve perfection within an unchanging, eternally valid tradition, the modern European or global artist responds to the audience's endless desire for stimulation and change. And of course all this potential of global cultural interchange and mass participation is vastly accelerated by the improved methods of communication. Travel has sped from sailboats to automobiles and jet planes; interchange of messages from horseback to telegraphs, telephones, and fax machines; visual art from painting to photography, movies, and television; and information exchange from printed books or newspapers to instant global news on the BBC or CNN.

From World Wars to the Global Community

In the continuing European, and later global, power struggle, those nations that achieved some combination of unity and diversity have tended to win in the long run. Great Britain had a more decentralized political system than France, and its colonial expansion was carried out through diverse methods such as emigration by dissidents or the commercial monopoly of the British East India Company. But when King George III tried to centralize the tax system and subdue rebellious North American settlers, their armed forces readily beat back the King's Hessian mercenaries. Similarly, the mercenary or feudal military forces that tried to squelch the French Revolution soon were beaten back by a democratically recruited army rallying to the slogan of "Allons enfants de la patrie...." And in the nineteenth and twentieth centuries, Britain prolonged the lifespan of its empire by promoting some colonies to "Dominions" joined in a "Commonwealth of Nations."

Until the eighteenth century, Sweden was the only European country with an effective conscription system; but after the wars of the French Revolution and Napoleon, conscription became the standard method of recruitment in most of Europe, greatly intensifying the violence and the level of casualties.[11] As Europe's colonialist expansion turned continental wars into World Wars, those conflicts were typically set off by aggressive monarchies or dictatorships (the Serbs and Austro-Hungarians in 1914, the Nazi Germans and Japanese in 1939/41), but won by the democratic allies with their greater popular involvement in government and their commitment to more open and competitive economies. And the same is true of the "Cold War," which involved Americans in an unwinnable war in Vietnam, and Soviets or Cubans in equally unwinnable wars in Afghanistan and Angola, but was ultimately won by the West because of the collapse of the inefficient Soviet command economy—leaving democracy, for the first time in history, as an ideology unchallenged in principle.

Democracy and Peace

As much of Europe after 1789 became involved in republican revolutions and counter-revolutionary wars, the German philosopher Immanuel Kant composed his essay *On Eternal Peace*. Yet after Napoleon's ultimate defeat, the peaceful order created by the Congress of Vienna (1815) relied on a carefully crafted balance of power among military monarchies; and modern technology made wars ever bloodier from the 1860s through both world wars. Still, political and intellectual leaders continued to wrestle with the problem of converting global wars into a new order of global peace. The Swedish engineer Alfred Nobel (1833–1896) invented dynamite, which soon was used not only for mining but for torpedoes, cannons, and bombs. But he left his large estate for the award of Nobel Prizes in the sciences, medicine, and literature—as well as for peace. And one of the first Nobel Peace Prizes was awarded in 1905 to his friend the Baroness Bertha von Suttner, an Austrian writer who in 1889 had published her provocatively titled novel *Die Waffen nieder (Lay Down Your Arms)*.

In 1918, Woodrow Wilson's "Fourteen Points" included a proposal for a League of Nations; but after the war, the Senate rejected U.S. membership in the new institution. Although the League established its headquarters at Geneva, it sponsored the conversion of former Ottoman dominions and German colonies into colonies of the victor powers under the figleaf of the "League of Nations Mandates." And when conflict broke out because of Italian aggression in Ethiopia (1935) and Hitler's annexation of Austria and parts of Czechoslovakia (1938), the League proved totally ineffective.

Drawing a lesson from Wilson's defeat by the U.S. Senate, Franklin D. Roosevelt insisted on preparing plans for international organization before the end of World War II. The Bretton Woods and Dumbarton Oaks conferences (July–August 1944) that created, respectively, the World Bank and IMF, and the United Nations. And as the colonial powers, exhausted from World War II, withdrew from Asia and Africa, membership in the UN rose from the original 51 to 126 (1969); and, following the dissolution of the Soviet Union and Yugoslavia, to as many as 178 (1992).

Nonetheless, the Bretton Woods institutions, located in Washington, DC, have continued to be controlled by the richest capitalist nations. And the UN itself, as an instrument of global peace, was soon paralyzed by vetoes in the Security Council. Above all, the Cold War brought not only a nuclear arms race and East–West wars in Korea and Vietnam, it also stimulated a massive competition of arms exports. these kindled regional wars among Israelis and Arabs, and civil wars from Nicaragua and El Salvador to Mozambique and Cambodia; they also made military coups the major threat to nascent democracies in the developing countries. After the end of the Cold War, with the loss of the restraints imposed by it, those massive arms supplies fueled ethnic warfare in post-Communist regions from Bosnia to the Caucasus and Central Asia and in African countries from Somalia to Rwanda.

Conclusion

While the UN and the Bretton Woods institutions remained limited in their effectiveness, the most successful post-World War II policy turned out to be the Marshall Plan. By insisting that U.S. aid to rebuild Europe's devastated industries be distributed by regional agreement, it encouraged a process of integration from the Coal and Steel Community (1952) to the European Economic Community (1957) of originally six and by 1986 as many as 12 members. Proceeding from customs union toward more complete economic integration, it became successively known as the European Community and the European Union, and by the mid-1990s countries such as Austria, Norway, Sweden, and Finland were eager to join, and former communist countries such as the Czech Republic, Poland, and Hungary to become associated with it.

Neutral and small countries have played a prominent role in this process of regional and global integration. Switzerland provided the headquarters for the League of Nations, the Netherlands for the World Court, and Belgium for the European Community. Norway and Sweden provided the first Secretary Generals of the UN, and countries such as Costa Rica and Norway played their crucial roles in settling the Nicaraguan civil war and moving the Israeli–Palestinian negotiations to a successful conclusion.

By the late 1980s, the collapse of Marxism (or rather pseudo-Marxism) had produced important global effects. It brought into the open lingering ethnic conflicts in the former Yugoslavia, the former Soviet Union, and Africa. But it conversely helped end civil wars from Nicaragua to Namibia; encouraged transitions to democracy and to outward-oriented economic policies in countries from South America to Africa and Asia; and promoted the constructive settlement of bitter disputes such as that between Blacks and Whites in South Africa and Israelis and Palestinians in the Middle East.

Within an ever more closely integrated world economy, there also is a growing tendency toward regional economic agreements. Thus by the 1990s, the United States, Canada, and Mexico joined in a North American Free Trade Agreement, and there were moves toward regional economic integration among Latin American countries such as Chile, Argentina, and Brazil. China, even after the cruelly repressive policies of the Tiananmen

Square massacre of 1989, continued to proceed toward economic liberalization and decentralization - perhaps because Deng Xiaoping or other leaders had reread a poignant passage in Marx's and Engels's *Communist Manifesto* of 1848: "The bourgeoisie, by the rapid improvement of all instruments of production, by the immensely facilitated means of communication, draws all...nations into civilization. The cheap prices of its commodities are the heavy artillery with which it batters down all Chinese walls....It compels all nations, on the pain of extinction, to adopt the bourgeois mode of production...[and] to become bourgeois themselves."

Similarly, the Israeli–Palestinian agreement crafted in Oslo and signed in Washington on September 13, 1993, devoted much space to the economic aspects of peace and prompted one journalist to recall a statement made by Yasir Arafat a decade earlier: "Oh, if only the Palestinians and the Jews unite. The resulting genius, the pooling of material and intellectual resources of our two people are enough to overcome the duplicity, selfishness and corruption of most Arab regimes."[12]

To consolidate these positive trends toward global economic and human integration, political leaders in the twenty-first century should encourage such trends as:

• The conversion of the conventional arms industries in the United States, Europe, and the former Communist countries to the production of civilian goods.

• The closer regional integration of the economies from the Pacific Region and South America to the Middle East, Africa, and Southeast Asia, perhaps by providing regional foreign aid on the model of the Marshall Plan.

• A restructuring of the UN in closer conjunction with its own economic institutions such as the World Bank and the IMF, and perhaps ultimately as a confederation of regional federations.

Those steps would seem, to this observer, the measures likeliest to achieve Kant's vision of "Eternal Peace" and Wilson's dream of making "the world safe for democracy." Above all, at a time when the demise of pseudo-Marxism in Moscow and Beijing allows us to rediscover Marx's materialist dialectic, it may help move us from the global thesis of commerce and interchange and its antithesis of warfare and exploitation to a constructive synthesis of unity and diversity within a classless global bourgeoisie.

Notes

1. See Robert E. Ward and D. A. Rustow (eds.), *Political Modernization in Japan and Turkey*. Princeton: Princeton University Press, 1964.

2. Quoted by Arthur Koestler, *The Sleepwalkers*. New York: Grosset & Dunlap, 1963, p. 364, who adds that this "was not the first and not the last time that pure research, that starved cur, snapped up a bone from the warlord's banquet."

3. For the dates of inventions cf. Bernard Grun, *The Timestables of History: A Horizontal Linkage of Peoples and Events*, 3d ed. New York: Simon and

Schuster, 1991; on the Chinese inventions and their limited applications see Daniel J. Boorstein, *The Discoverers*. New York: Random House, 1983, pp. 186ff.

4. These are German, French, Italian, and a fourth Romansch, spoken by a small minority of the country. Note that Swiss automobiles are marked by the sign "CH," for "Confederato Helvetica," which means "Swiss Federation" in Latin.

5. See Arendt Lijphardt, *The Politics of Accommodation: Pluralism and Democracy in the Netherlands*, 2d ed. Berkeley, CA, 1975.

6. Note that the poem that later became Germany's Anthem "Deutschland, Deutschland über alles" was composed in 1840 by Auguest Heinrich Hoffman Von Fallersleben, who later became a member of that liberal parliment. To him, "Germany above all else" meant not continental or world conquest, but rather superseding the many kingdoms and petty states of the time. By a courageous decision of President Theodor Heuss and Chancellor Konard Adenauer, the official anthem for the Federal Republic of Germany became Hoffman's second stanza: "Einigkeit und Recht und Freiheit" ("Unity, justice, and freedom").

7. Thus, by the nineteenth and early twentieth centuries, German- or Italian-descended dynasties, which included those of Este–Brunswick–Hanover, Oldenburg–Holstein, Saxony–Coburg, and Hohenzollern, ruled over monarchies from Britain to Greece and Romania and from Portugal to Norway and Russia. The only other competitor was France, branches of whose Capet–Bourbon dynasty, even after the French Revolution, ruled in parts of Italy (until 1859–1860) and in Spain (1700–1931, 1975–). Sweden's indigenous Vasa dynasty (1523–1654) was succeeded by a branch of the German Wittelsbach–Palatinate dynasty (1654–1818), which by adoption, was succeeded by the French Bernadotte family (1818–). Other than the Vasas, the Karadjordjevic dynasty of Serbia and Yugoslavia (1808–1945) were the only royal dynasty of modern Europe not of German, Italian, or French origin.

8. "Die lappäandische Sprache ist so gut wie die römische." In Bernard Suiphan (ed.), *Sämmtliche Werke*, Vol. 1. Berlin, 1877–1913, p. 162.

9. See R. R. Palmer, *The Age of Democratic Revolution: A Political History of Europe and America*, Vol. II. Princeton: Princeton University Press, 1964, Chapters 6–13.

10. For an account of those contradictory elements in Jefferson's life and his struggles to resolve them, see Fawn M. Brodie, *Thomas Jefferson: The Intimate History*. New York: Bantam Books, 1975, pp. 41ff.

11. For a survey of the evolution of modern wars see Quincy Wright's classic, *A Study of War*, 2d ed. Chicago: University of Chicago Press, 1965.

12. Yussef M. Ibrahim, "One of Arafat's Nine Lives Leads Him, Finally and Triumphantly, to the White House Lawn," *New York Times*, September 12, 1993, p. 12.

Section 2

The Social Impacts of Globalization and Marketization

Frances Stewart

Recent years have seen an acceleration in the globalization of the world economy, largely taking the form of an increased role for market forces and private capital among and within countries. At the same time, in many places poverty and inequality rose within the last 15 years. While globalization has created new enrichment opportunities for substantial areas and sections of society, it also has harshly affected—or completely left out—many others. Global and market forces destroy, rather than create, safety nets for those who are marginalized.

Indeed, a parallel exists within the history of the now-industrialized countries. First, the feudal and paternalistic support mechanisms provided by the pre-industrial social system (the extended family and the community) were broken down to allow the market to thrive. The dire poverty that emerged had clear economic and social costs. It led to new forms of protection of a legal and financial kind, eventually giving rise to the welfare state. In a cyclical process, the developed countries are presently dismantling their social protection to allow more room for the market, and once again, homelessness, crime, and poverty are re-emerging. Once again, the costs are proving to be economic as well as human.

The combination of growing market dominance, nationally and internationally, and the vapidity of social support systems means an urgent need exists for new emphasis on eliminating social and economic deprivation. This section briefly reviews some effects of globalization on deprivation and suggests international action to reinforce economic and social safety nets.

Impacts of Globalization

Globalization has involved goods, technology, labor, capital, and ideas. In recent years, a rising proportion of investment in developing countries has been accounted for by transnational companies (TNCs). During the latter part of the 1980s, direct foreign investment in developing countries rose by 17 percent per annum, accounting to around $70 billion in 1993. By the early 1980s, trade between the 350 largest TNCs amounted to an estimated 40 percent of global trade. Global sales of foreign affiliates in host countries are estimated to have grown by 15 percent per annum between 1985–1990, much faster than the growth of output. TNCs dominate international technology flows: for the United States, four-fifths of technology receipts are intra-firm; in Germany, that figure is over 90 percent. Even in more arms-length forms of technology transfer, the source of technology supply largely consists in the same multinationals that dominate direct foreign investment.

International trade has grown faster than production for many decades, partly due to reduced transport costs, and partly to trade liberalization. Export volume grew 1.6 times the rate of world output in the 1980s, 1.25 in the 1970s, and 1.4 in the 1960s. Despite restrictions, there continue to be increasing flows of migrants; rising cultural contacts; and increased dominance of the intellectual climate and policy-making by Western economic and political ideas. The International Monetary Fund (IMF) and the World Bank, in particular, have acquired massive influence over policy making in much of the developing world. They have used this power to promote further globalization, encouraging – and sometimes forcing – countries to open up their economies, to relax restrictions on inward and outward capital movements (and on trade and technology imports), and to reduce the role of the state while increasing that of the market.

Globalization of the world economy has provided opportunities for accelerated economic growth in some parts of the world. This is especially true for Asian economies, which have benefited from trading opportunities for manufacturing products; in fact, many have achieved impressive rates of economic growth and employment, and thus have reduced their poverty levels. However, over the last decade the economies of Africa, especially, and also of many Latin America nations have suffered from globalizing tendencies in terms of worsening commodity prices, unequal distribution of world-capital flows, and rising debt burdens. A significant number of countries have been unable to take advantage of increased opportunities for global trade – particularly for their manufactured products – due to of their weak manufacturing sectors, infrastructure, and human resources.

The global international economy does not distribute resources according to need, but to profitability. In the 1980s, low-income countries (which accounted for nearly three-fourths of the world's population) received less than 10 percent of the gross, private-capital flows. The expansion of world trade presented an opportunity for some developing countries – 12 had export growth rates of more than 10 percent per annum between 1980–1990. Eleven boasted rates between 5 and 10 percent. Over the same period, however, 21 countries experienced annual falls in exports.

The rapid rise in exports was concentrated among middle-income countries, while the falls in exports were concentrated among low-income countries (two-thirds of the falling export countries were in the low-income category). Commodity prices fell in an almost unprecedented way, with adverse effects on the developing countries that specialized on commodity exports: between 1980 and 1991, a weighted index of 33 commodities fell by almost 50 percent. More than half the exports of low- and middle-income countries are primary products, compared with 17 percent of the Organization for Economic Cooperation and Development (OECD) countries' exports, so that losses from the deterioration were concentrated among these countries, while the industrialized countries saw corresponding gains. By 1989–1991, the terms of trade loss on commodity exports from developing countries was around $50 to $55 billion, compared with the 1980 terms of trade, according to 1994 estimates of Maizels.

Negative Social Impacts of Marketization

Evidence of rising inequality and deprivation, associated with globalization and marketization, is to be seen in:

- Economic regress in many countries, with falling per capita incomes, investment rates, and consumption experienced in most African and Latin American nations in the 1980s. This regression continues in the 1990s for many African countries. For the 1980s as a whole, African per-capita income fell by about 15 percent; similar Latin American rates fell by about 10 percent.

- An acute slowdown (and sometimes decline) in the growth of formal-sector employment in these regions, and a rise in unemployment and in the proportion of the labor force employed in the informal sector. Industrial wage employment stagnated in Africa, while urban informal employment grew by nearly 7 percent per annum in the first half of the 1980s.

- Evidence of even less equitable income distribution and rising poverty rates in most Latin American countries. In Argentina, Brazil, Mexico, and Peru, income distribution became more inequitable throughout the 1980s. In Costa Rica, Chile, and Venezuela, severe worsening was followed by some improvement, with a net increase in inequality over the decade. Only in Colombia, which maintained positive growth in per capita incomes and underwent little stabilization and moderate adjustment policies, did income distribution improve. For the region as a whole, the proportion of households falling below the poverty line rose from 35 percent in 1980 to 39 percent in 1990, with a rise in the proportion of poor people from 41 to 46 percent.

- Evidence of rising poverty in Africa, and falling availability of food per individual. Evidence on changing poverty incidence in eight African countries shows rising poverty in seven of the eight. More than half of all Sub-Saharan African countries showed a decline in per capita food production between 1980–1989.

- Cuts in real expenditure per individual on education and health in nearly two-thirds of the countries in these two regions. This was the result of restraint on total government expenditure and the rising proportion taken by interest payments.

- Education indicators, which worsened in many countries (i.e., falling enrollment rates, numbers of pupils remaining in school, and attainments). From some of the country-based evidence, the deterioration in attendance and achievements was worst among the lowest income groups.

The fundamental problem is that the global market does not offer any automatic protection for the deprived. Indeed, by relating opportunities to ability and by cutting back on state interventions, it worsens the situation of the most vulnerable nations; at the same time, it offers improved opportunities for those countries/individuals with the capacity to exploit the market. In principle, those who benefit should be able to compensate those who lose. There is not, however, an adequate system of compensation either internationally or nationally.

Internationally, aid represents the sole system of compensatory transfers from rich countries to poor ones. These levels have become increasingly stagnant, and are, in any case, minute compared to the magnitude of the task. Moreover, such aid is badly distributed from an overall perspective, with most support going to the richest of the developing nations. Nor is there an adequate system of transfers from rich to poor within most countries.

The philosophy of the market encouraged cutbacks in international aid as well. Progressive taxes tend to be reduced to encourage effort and entrepreneurship, with a switch to flat-rate indirect taxation; there also occurs downward pressure on government expenditures in general, with particular emphasis on reducing food subsidies. Governments are encouraged to introduce user charges for public services, including social services. While in principle the poor are often intended to be exempt, in practice this often does not occur. Specific social funds introduced to provide a safety net during adjustment have typically been far too small to achieve substantial coverage of the poor, and they have usually been misdirected. Institutions that could possibly help protect particular groups (i.e., minimum-wage and labor legislation, and credit programs directed toward small enterprises) are discouraged as part of the attempt to eliminate economic distortions and market segmentation.

Safety Nets Measures

The continued advance of market and global forces makes it urgent to create safety nets at an international — as well as national — level. At best, where dynamic markets incorporate a growing proportion of the population and countries of the world, these safety nets may only be needed in exceptional circumstances. International safety nets are needed to:

- Improve resource flows to those impoverished countries that cannot gain access to private flows, through an increase in and redistribution of aid;

- Accelerate debt write-offs for the poorest countries;
- Develop a true "emergency fund" to finance relief during emergencies caused by natural and human-engineered catastrophes;
- Help support commodity prices by encouraging coordinated taxation of low-elasticity primary commodities.

Net financial costs of these changes could remain quite small, if flows of official finance to the countries with access to market-related flows were reduced or eliminated. In 1989, the richest 40 percent of developing countries received two-thirds of total aid. If only half of this were directed to the poorest 40 percent, their aid receipts would more than double. International taxation of common resources (such as those arising in the sea), of international financial transactions, and of transnational company profits — all of which generate huge incomes as a result of the activities of the global economy — could also act as a source of finance for international safety nets.

The most effective way of reaching the poor, however, is through national action to promote social goals. Many countries have introduced safety nets and achieved social goals on their own initiative with their own finances — take, for instance, Botswana and Costa Rica. Yet international support for social goals and domestic safety nets is needed more in those cases where national action is inadequate, especially when the international market and the community are already impinging on those domestic circumstances.

To date, the international system has approached the problem of promoting social goals in two ways. The first is through the conventions on human rights, in particular the 1976 *International Covenant on Economic, Social, and Cultural Rights,* which primarily focused on the sanction to food, health, shelter, education, and work. In addition, the General Assembly's *Declaration of the Right to Development* (1986) recognized development as a basic human right; major Western countries reinforced this notion in the 1993 Human Rights Conference at Vienna.

Second, the promotion of social goals has occurred through a series of internationally agreed targets. These include Universal Primary Education by 1980 (subsequently postponed to the year 2000); immunizing 80 percent of children by 1990; "health for all" by the year 2000; safe water and sanitation for all by 1990; and a series of goals for children for the year 2000, which were set at the World Summit for Children.[1]

Neither the human rights approach nor the internationally agreed-upon goals approach has proven effective, especially in the context of economic crisis. This was indicated by the fact that in the 1980s, many countries moved away from realizing the internationally acknowledged goal of human rights and decreased their records of achievement in some of the specified goals.

The problem with the human rights approach is that although rights may be globally accepted, they are not rigorously defined. The goals are furthermore not tied to a deadline, and their monitoring and enforcement mechanisms remain extremely weak. In 1986, an independent expert committee — the Committee on Economic, Social, and Cultural Rights — was established to clarify the norms contained in the Covenant on Economic and Social Rights, to expand the relevant information base, and to design a system of effective monitoring. Despite some progress in these areas, effective enforcement has not occurred.

In contrast, the internationally agreed-upon goals are dated and well defined. Yet they have not been translated into specific, national actions supported by mechanisms of enforcement. Many of the goals were not met by their deadline date, and in some cases, movement has turned away from their achievement. The United Nations International Children's Emergency Fund (UNICEF) has been one of the most successful agencies in promoting the goals set for children. To accomplish this, UNICEF follows up goal-setting with campaigns, financing, and national plans of action. Their realized goals are relatively cheap and require specific well-defined actions. This approach has not been tried for more ambitious goals, such as "the right to development," where it would certainly be less effective.

The international financial institutions have generally been more effective in achieving policy change in developing countries; they have used the financial needs of developing countries as a lever for achieving policy change. But the conditionality of the IMF and World Bank relates entirely to economic objectives — to such features as money supply, budget balance, exchange-rate changes, and trade liberalization. Social conditions are almost always ignored.

In recent years, the international financial institutions have acknowledged the objective of poverty reduction as important. Yet the policy package they insist on (which includes macrostabilization), the promotion of the role of markets, and the reduction of the role of the state, have not altered substantially. Their conditionality remains tied to conventional economic variables.

Integrated Approach

What social policy needs is to tie together the three mechanisms for achieving change. These are (a) the internationally agreed-upon Social and Economic Rights, which provide moral and legal justification for international and national action (but which at present are inadequately defined or enforced); (b) the "goals" approach, which if sensitively translated into national goals and national and international actions may help define the Social and Economic Rights and the changes needed to achieve them; and (c) the conditionality of the international financial institutions, which can finance and promote the achievement of social goals through policy dialogue, sector, and project loans.

The legitimacy and efficacy of any sort of conditionality is debatable. Whether the content of the policy change required is right or wrong, conditionality can be argued to represent unjustified outside intervention in what should be domestic-policy decisions. Moreover, many have noted that unless the policy changes are truly wanted by the government, they cannot be fully adopted or enforced. The legitimate role for outsiders is to offer advice, but not to insist upon it being followed where economic management and systems are concerned. However, the importance of the Human Rights Covenants is that in the areas covered, individuals have a moral claim on certain social and economic conditions, irrespective of where they live. These covenants can be viewed as providing more justification for outside intervention than the sort of monetary leverage associated with the international financial institutions. If, for example, people are starving— in clear violation of the Human Rights Covenants—this might override considerations of national sovereignty, just as the torture of citizens may do. Such considerations, however, would need to be tempered by respect for self-determination.

Conclusion

So long as economic conditionality is being enforced, confining conditionality to mainly macroeconomic issues, and omitting social and economic conditions as they affect citizens at the micro level, inevitably weakens governments' commitment to supporting economic and social rights, and combating social and private poverty.

As long as we have conditionality in policy making, social objectives should become at least as important as economic ones. The social agencies of the United Nations must help the international financial agencies to define goals and actions, to provide financial and technical support, and to monitor results. Discussions about country policies should involve not only Ministries of Finance and Central Banks, but also the social sector ministries. Countries' performances would then be monitored not simply in terms of economic variables, but also by their success in meeting social goals and realizing human rights. As time proceeds, the process would lead to the identification of more effective mechanisms for reducing poverty, including more poverty-related, macro-policy packages, as well as specific safety nets to protect the vulnerable from a hostile environment.

The most successful societies from both social and economic perspectives are those that respect the basic human rights—hence the need for international and national action to enforce these claims. At present, the realization of these rights is partially the random outcome of market forces. Thus, more systematic action is needed to ensure that human rights are furnished, at least at minimal levels and irrespective of the vagaries of the market.

Note

1. These goals come from different sources and were agreed at different dates. The 1980 education goal was agreed at UNESCO Conferences held in the 1960s; the water target and the immunization goal were part of the third development decade goals, agreed in 1980; the WHO Global Strategy for Health for All was initiated in the 1980s, and endorsed again at Talloires in 1988.

Section 3

Dangers of Slow Growth to Social Cohesion[1]

Leonard Silk

Slow growth of the world economy and rising unemployment in the indus-trialized world—along with the end of the Cold War, which once bound together the capitalist countries of North America, Europe, and Asia—have given new life to nationalism, regionalism, and protectionism in various quarters of the globe. Combating the persistence of slow growth must be a high priority for the leaders of the developed nations.

As they ponder remedies, the leaders of the industrialized nations start from a shaky base. In the United States, for example, the economy has experienced its slowest growth of the postwar period—an average of 1.2 percent per year during the last four years. Despite somewhat faster growth in the latter part of 1992, the U.S. economy is still hampered by deep structural problems and a global recession.

America's role in the new world economy has changed. Though still the largest national economy in the world, the United States is not the single dominant power it was at the end of World War II. The economic strength of Japan and other Pacific rim nations and of the European Union makes it unlikely that this nation will hold that position again.

The current global economic slowdown has been the most painful and protracted of the postwar era. The growth rate of the industrial countries has come down from 4.4 percent in 1988 to 3.3 percent in 1989, 2.6 percent in 1990, 0.9 percent in 1991, and 1.7 percent in 1992—too slow to keep pace with the growth of the labor force. Unemployment has risen above 10 percent in most of Europe and in Canada, and above seven percent in the United States.[2]

The combined growth rate of the "economies in transition"—the former Soviet Union and eastern Europe—fell from 4.5 percent in 1988 to 2.3 percent in 1989. It then went negative, plummeting by 5 percent in 1990, 15.9 percent in 1991, and 12 percent in 1992—a decline of one-third of total output in three years, a steeper decline than any country or combination of countries suffered in the Great Depression of the 1930s. Systemic collapse in the East has aggravated problems in the West—especially the huge influx of immigrants to Western Europe, a flood that may not yet have reached full tide.

The economic slowdown of the West did not begin with the collapse of the Soviet empire, the end of the financial boom of the 1980s, or the 1987 stock market crash. Rather it started two decades earlier with the beginning of a persistent decline in productivity, whether measured either by output per worker hour or total factor productivity.

The trend stands out in the data for the "big seven" members of the Organization for Economic Cooperation and Development: the United States, Japan, Germany, the United Kingdom, Italy, France, and Canada. The annual growth of U.S. gross domestic product per capita dropped from an average of 2 percent in 1955–1973 to 1.3 percent in 1973–1986. In the same two periods, Japan's per capita GDP growth fell from 8.8 percent to 3.3 percent, Germany's from 4.2 percent to 2 percent, and the combined rate of the other four members of the big seven from 3.8 percent to 1.7 percent. One may argue about the precise measures, but not about the overall downslide of productivity growth that has been going on for two decades.

This trend of slow productivity seems unlikely to change over the coming decade, since there is no reason to anticipate an upsurge of global savings and investment to make it happen. Indeed, there are signs of a global capital shortage. And, although one may expect a continuing flow of new technological developments, it is difficult to see this happening at a greater rate, and with a stronger industrial fallout, than during the past two decades, when the productivity slowdown occurred.

A modest recovery in the industrial countries took hold in 1994. Growth of the seven largest economies of the OECD is expected by World Bank economic forecasters to remain below potential, at 2.1 percent in 1994 and to rise to 3.1 percent in 1995. But this rate of growth seems too slow to reduce global unemployment significantly; indeed, unemployment may well drift higher, given the potential growth of the labor force and the fear of the monetary authorities that faster growth would overstrain both the available, trained labor force and existing industrial capacity. Modest further increases in interest rates in the United States, and only modest declines in European short-term interest rates, are likely to insure continuing slow economic growth.

Lingering Impact of Oil Shocks

What caused the productivity slowdown? Economists are still unsure. Their principal explanation, especially because of the timing, is the oil shocks of 1973 and 1979. Other leading suspects are an asserted greater rigidity of national economic systems, a fall off in the growth of new knowledge and technology, and tax systems (especially that of the United States) that favor consumption, discriminate against saving, and retard investment.[3]

Low savings and investment rates, it seems evident, have weakened

America's productivity growth and overall economic performance. In the 1980s, America's net national savings rate fell from about 8 percent of national income in the preceding three decades to less than 3 percent, because of large federal deficits and lower private savings. Proportionally the United States saves far less as a nation than any other major industrial country. In the past decade, America's net savings rate averaged about one-fifth that of Japan and about one-third that of Germany and the Group of Seven (G-7) as a whole. This shortage of savings has not only constrained American growth, but has also severely limited the capital the United States can supply to developing countries or the excommunist states struggling to build market economies and effective democracies.

The economic slowdown has deep political roots. The oil-price inflation of the 1970s and early 1980s was triggered by Arab states using oil as a weapon against Western importers following the 1973 Arab–Israeli war, and then by the Ayatollah Khomeini's Iranian revolution in 1979. These were what economists call exogenous shocks to the economic system.

But the oil shocks were also endogenous. They were linked to changing market conditions—that is, to growing Western dependence on Middle Eastern oil, to economic boom and worldwide commodity-price inflation kicked off by the escalation of the Vietnam War and the Johnson administrations' dilatory fiscal policy. President Johnson's unwillingness either to curb domestic spending by gutting Great Society programs or to demand a tax increase to finance the war—as well as his desire to push for economic growth—all helped prompt global inflation.

Excess fiscal and monetary stimulus on the part of other developed countries also contributed to the worldwide commodity boom. Inflation worsened the terms of trade of producers in developing countries and the Middle East, setting the stage for the first round of oil-price explosions. Rising oil prices fueled general inflation and forced the developed countries to adopt the tight monetary and fiscal policies that would in turn intensify the investment, productivity, and output slowdowns of the 1970s, 1980s, and 1990s.

In the 1980s the effect of the oil-price explosion on productivity growth gradually wore off; industrial nations, some faster than others, adjusted to higher oil prices, and the relative world oil price came down. Nevertheless the slow rate of productivity growth continued. Hence, the causes of continuing slow growth in the 1980s and early 1990s must lie elsewhere.

Deflating "Bubbles" Slowed Growth

Speculative fever gripped stock markets and real estate markets in the 1980s and caused a global wave of mergers and acquisitions. Rapid growth of the global financial markets and a "less government" political climate that reduced financial and antitrust supervision and regulation combined to produce "bubbles" in economies around the world. Lest the bubbles burst, governments and central banks decided to let air out of them. But, deflationary actions—not only by financial regulators but also private financial institutions themselves—aggravated the economic slowdown.

The fall of the Berlin Wall exacerbated the switch to counterinflationary measures in Germany. The high price paid by Chancellor Helmut Kohl to bring about quick unification—an exchange of West German marks for East German marks at an overpriced one-to-one rate and a transfer of capital to the East amount to about $100 billion a year—caused the German budget to swing from a moderate surplus in 1989 to a deficit equal to five percent of GDP in 1992. That set off inflation pressures and—still worse—inflationary fears.

To still the pressures and fears, the Bundesbank kept money tight and interest rates high while the rest of Europe was trying to fight recession. The result was to worsen the problem of slow growth in Europe and everywhere else. Bundesbank policy also intensified disequilibrium among currencies and political strains among European Community signatories of the Maastricht treaty, threatening European monetary and political integration and even the world trading system under the General Agreement on Tariffs and Trade.

Japan was also experiencing the worst economic and political tensions and anxieties since beginning its remarkable postwar recovery and long spell of high growth. Its financial bubble, build on inflated asset values, has been sharply deflated. Stock prices have fallen about 60 percent, and real estate prices, though they have already come down by about 20 percent, are regarded as very shaky. Scandals over political and business corruption have helped to undermine public confidence in the system. The Japanese establishment—including politicians, bureaucrats, and business leaders—now acknowledges that the country is in a genuine recession. Present strains, it warns, may last another five to seven years, and possibly a decade or more.

The fear is that the steep fall of security prices and land and other assets will have a long-lasting effect on Japanese banks and industries. One senior Japanese economist explained: "In the past the threats were like a broken leg—sharp, painful but specific—and it was clear what was needed to mend them. This downturn is more like a virus affecting the blood system—much more complex and pervasive."[4]

In its efforts to cure the disease, says Akio Mikuni, a leading Japanese financial analyst, the Ministry of Finance got caught in a dilemma: "If it allows the prices of land and equity to be set genuinely by market forces, asset prices would plummet and the capital cushion of Japan's banks wiped out. The Finance Ministry would have given up its most important tools right at the moment they would be needed for coping with a resultant first-order banking crisis."[5] For the time being, the Ministry of Finance has chosen to support the markets at deteriorated levels. Nevertheless, Mikuni believes that the ministry's actions are ultimately unsustainable. "The negative carrying costs of holding overpriced assets," he notes, "will continue to eat away not just at the stability of the financial sector but also at the profitability of manufacturing firms."

Other analysts, while conceding that Japan "has finally gone over the edge," believe that it will come back in a few years, stronger than ever. Japan, says Kenneth S. Courtis, strategist and senior economist for the Deutsche Bank Group in Asia, is "purging itself of the excesses of the

1980s, cleansing its economy, melting off the fat" it had accumulated ov
recent years. "By the mid-1990s," he contents, "once the economy
brought down again to its rock-hard competitive core, Japan will be pois‹
for another powerful leap ahead through to the end of the decade."[6]

Japan's future will depend not just on actions by the Ministry of I
nance, the Ministry of International Trade and Industry, or other agenci‹
banks, and businesses, but also on the policies of foreign governments a‹
developments in the world economy. Whichever crystal ball is right abo‹
Japan's economy, analysts, government officials, and central bankers agr‹
that this has not been a typical business-cycle recession, either in Japa‹
Europe, or the United States.

The Dangers of a New Depression

According to Alan Greenspan, "For the first time in a half century or mo‹
several industrial countries have been confronted at roughly the same tir‹
with asset-price deflation and the inevitable consequences."[7]

The last such asset deflation, credit crunch, and wave of bankruptci‹
followed the Great Crash of 1929. Fiscal, monetary, and trade poli‹
blunders helped to turn that earlier asset deflation into the Great Depressi‹
of the 1930s, which lasted a full decade – until the outbreak of World W
II.

Nowadays, reversing the celebrated maxim of George Santayana, ‹
believe or hope that those who remember the past are not condemned
repeat it. Yet it is already evident that the long period of slow growth, whi‹
some have called a "controlled depression," has produced revolutiona‹
consequences of its own. It helped to shatter the Soviet Empire. As t‹
British editor William Rees-Mogg has written: "A world economic crisis is
type of world revolution. It destroys old structures, economic and politic
The Soviet Union, with its rigid inability to adapt, was the first to fall befo‹
the full force of the storm. Such a crisis destroys well-meaning politicia‹
and promotes men of power.... It destroys respect for government,
people discover that their leaders cannot control events."[8]

The burst of optimism that greeted the downfall of Soviet communis‹
has given way to anxiety that years will pass before the new states
the East can become effective market economies and democracies – a‹
that some may not make it at all before dictatorship returns. The e‹
of the Cold War was expected to bring great benefits to people in ma‹
countries as resources were shifted from military to social programs. Th‹
far, however, the peace dividend only shows up in lost jobs and falli‹
incomes.

Theoretically there is no reason why this must be so; in a rational wor‹
the improved prospects for peace should have led to greater spendi‹
on consumer goods and productivity-raising investment. But that c
happen only if workers can be shifted to new jobs – and financial resourc‹
reallocated to create those jobs.

In the absence of such shifts of human and capital resources to expandi‹
civilian industries, there are strong economic pressures on arms-produci‹

nations to maintain high levels of military production and to sell weapons, both conventional and dual-use nuclear technology, wherever buyers can be found. Without a revival of national economies and the global economy, the production and proliferation of weapons will continue, creating more Iraqs, Yugoslavias, Somalias, and Rwandas—or worse.

Like the Great Depression, the current economic slump has fanned the fires of nationalist, ethnic, and religious hatred around the world. Economic hardship is not the only cause of these social and political pathologies, but it aggravates all of them, and in turn they feed back on economic development. They also undermine efforts to deal with such global problems as environmental pollution, the production and trafficking of drugs, crime, sickness, famine, AIDS, and other plagues.

Growth will not solve all those problems by itself. But economic growth—and growth alone—creates the additional resources that make it possible to achieve such fundamental goals as higher living standards, national and collective security, a healthier environment, and a more liberal and open economies and societies.

By the same token, slow economic growth, especially stemming from slow productivity growth, weakens social cohesion. Simply adding to inputs of labor and capital, without improving living standards or adding to economic and personal security, will cause fears about the future, for oneself and one's children, to heighten the competition of groups for access to jobs and land and shares of the national budget—or even lead to a breakup of the nation-state and civil war, as happened in former Yugoslavia. An even-worse ripping apart of social cohesion could occur in other states of Eastern Europe and the former Soviet Union, if greater economic progress is not achieved.

Reducing the Deficit to Promote Growth

What will it take to fuel the engines of world growth? The answer can be found in the lesson learned from the Great Depression: the developed countries need to pursue macroeconomic policies that will keep the world economy moving forward and keep world trade and investment flowing freely.

This means, first and foremost, that the United States and most other industrial countries must make efforts to increase savings and productive investment.[9] A higher rate of capital formation will serve not only their interests but also—through the global growth mechanism of expanded markets—promote the interests of the developing world. Asia's newly industrialized countries and the states of Eastern Europe and the former Soviet Union that are striving to modernize and build closer links with the world economy. Higher rates of capital formation in the developing and newly market-oriented economies are critical to their economic success and, in many cases, to their political viability.

The United States, still the largest and most important economy in the world, needs to play a constructive role in raising global capital formation. It can only do so if it eliminates its huge and still growing federal budget deficits. The Bush administration's final estimate of the U.S. budget deficit, which was $290 billion in fiscal year 1992, was revised upward to $305 billion by 1997, if present policies continue. That deficit is "structural" — meaning the bulk of it would still be there, even if the economy were operating at full capacity and full employment.

Repeated deficits have forced the United States to import capital from abroad in order to finance government activities and to help cover America's own investment needs. Instead of exporting capital to the developing world, with reciprocal benefits to its own exporting industries, the United States has been absorbing global capital, putting upward pressure on long-term interest rates and slowing its own and worldwide investment and growth.

America's deficits, both internal and external, could not have grown so large nor endured so long had it not been for the willingness of foreigners to invest in dollar assets. That willingness reflected the international role of the dollar and relative confidence in America's political stability and long-run growth potential. The United States must now move decisively to justify that confidence — or risk seeing it shattered.

Strengthening America's economic growth must be a top priority for the rest of the decade. Stronger growth will require eliminating the budget deficits that have undermined the nation's savings rate and long-term investment. Unless remedied, America's chronic and rising budget deficits and low national savings rate will act as a drag on its productivity growth and its ability to build any international cohesion on critical economic and political issues. Washington's budget deficits will also continue to limit its ability to deal with social problems at home.

U.S. economic policy should aim to raise the rate of national savings to at least its pre-1980 level of about 8 percent of national income, about 5 percentage points above its current level. When invested in plant and equipment, research and development or infrastructure, the additional savings would raise the annual growth rates of productivity back to its historical level of more than 2 percent per year, making possible a steady increase in living standards, a steady reduction in unemployment, and the accumulation of extra capital for meeting domestic and foreign needs.

Proposals by certain economists to get rid of the budget deficit problem by excluding outlays for capital goods from total government expenditures have little merit and might even aggravate problems with the nation's fiscal mismanagement. The idea of a government capital budget is not new. Proposals for a capital budget surfaced in response to public concern over the contribution of rising public expenditures to inflation during the Vietnam War, and they were rejected as likely further to confuse and distort the federal government's fiscal policy.[10] That conclusion still applies: use of a capital budget would seriously understand the government's current draft on the resources of the economy. Indeed, it was the overdraft on the nation's resources during Vietnam that broke the long spell of stable postwar economic growth and initiated the inflationary pressures and slow productivity growth that have dogged America and the world since.

In periods of inflationary pressure the appearance of a balanced budget, with capital expenditures excluded, would pose a political and psychological barrier to adequate taxation, even beyond the usual resistance present in Congress and the public. Those interest groups pressing for new spending would inevitably seek to stretch capital budget rules to get their proposals included as forms of investment, whether in physical, intellectual, or human capital, skirting the immediate impact that would normally be to increase the current deficit.

If the capital budget were limited to physical capital, it would be likely to distort decisions about allocation of resources, promoting the priority of investments for "brick and mortar" over programs for which future benefits could not readily be capitalized, such as health, public education, and child care, even when there was no accurate evidence that such a shift would be more beneficial to the nation.

Several foreign governments that previously used capital budgets subsequently abandoned them. In other countries, maintaining a semblance of capital budgets—the division of transactions "above the line" in the regular budget and "below the line" in the capital budget—became so arbitrary as to make the distinction meaningless. Even if a capital budget were desirable, it raises a formidable array of accounting problems and issues, such as how to count military hardware (which produces no incremental income year to year) and how to measure depreciation of government property.

Concerns about the distorting effects of a federal capital budget should not imply rejection of special tabulations and analyses of government spending of an investment nature. On the contrary, efforts to promote long-term productivity and overall economic growth could be served by careful analysis of the costs and benefits of proposed capital expenditures in future budget documents, without harm to the budget as a tool for furthering economic stability and growth. The Clinton administration should be encouraged to move in that direction. But it should bear in mind that the private sector requires at least as much attention as the public sector in its potential contributions to increasing investment in productivity-generating capital goods, research and development, and job training. A reduction of the structural budget deficit would augment private investment by increasing national savings. The long-term aim of fiscal policy should be not just to reduce the budget deficit but to achieve a structural budget surplus, including Social Security and other retirement accounts, of one to two percent of GDP over the coming decade.

Short-Term Growth versus Deficit Reduction

Achieving the nation's goal of stronger long-term growth must be accomplished in a way that is consistent with raising the level of economic activity in the short run, especially to increase employment. President Clinton has had to reconcile the apparent conflict between two types of economic advisers—the short-term fiscal stimulators versus the longer-term deficit eliminators.

If a solution to this dilemma is possible, it can be found in a unified program to encourage private and public investment: short-term stimulus and long-term progress toward eliminating the budget deficit should be offered and legislated as part of one package. The Congress must be persuaded to enact a program for gradually phasing in deficit-shrinking measures that would not interfere with the recovery or with the financing of public and private investments to spur national economic growth and to make each year's fiscal policy consistent with the longer-term program.

A program for recovery and steady growth should provide for deferring measures to get rid of the budget deficit if economic stagnation persists and the economy slides back into recession. But such deferrals should be only temporary until the economy recovers. Such a program is difficult to lay out firmly in advance and will require the closest cooperation between the administration and Congress to maintain flexibility without deserting its fundamental goals.

Stable growth will also require closer coordination between fiscal and monetary policy. In the past, some central bankers and economists have argued that the sole task of the Federal Reserve's monetary policy is to prevent inflation and to safeguard the value of the dollar. But in times when overcapacity and unemployment – and even deflation – are the main problems, the Federal Reserve has an obligation to aid economic recovery. The goals of reducing unemployment and preventing inflation are parallel, not irreconcilable, objectives.

Those objectives can best be achieved in existing circumstances by reducing the structural budget deficit, thereby making it possible for the Federal Reserve to maintain or increase the growth of the money supply and to bring interest rates down farther without fear of regenerating inflation. With industrial output at less than 80 percent of capacity and the unemployment rate above 7 percent, there is no reason for premature alarm about inflation. It was that kind of alarm that so inhibited monetary policy in the 1930s, worsening the depression and hampering the recovery. That was a time when reducing unemployment, not heading off a feared inflation, should have been the primary target of monetary policy. Although the present slump, except in Eastern Europe and the former Soviet Union, is not as severe as the Great Depression, monetary policy still needs to avoid focusing on the wrong problem at the wrong time.

Tighten G-7 Coordination

In this more closely integrated and stagnating world economy, it is the inadequate growth of the world money supply, not just the money supply of any single nation, that provokes the greatest concern. Collaboration among the three most important central banks and sources of international monetary reserves – the Federal Reserve, the Bundesbank, and the Bank of Japan – will be vital to curbing world inflation or deflation and achieving stronger and steadier world economic growth. Collaboration by nations and their central banks on monetary policy must be accompanied by efforts of national administrations and legislatures to coordinate fiscal policy, from which, as we have seen, monetary policy cannot be divorced.

There is no reason for not achieving greater fiscal and monetary cooperation, even among members of the "Group of three," which represents different national interests, different national cultures, and different regional constituencies. Such cooperation might most effectively be achieved within the framework of the G-7, where the other four members of the group could help to resolve disagreements among the three. Participation in the ongoing efforts to develop consistent fiscal and monetary policies to achieve common goals could also, within this context, be sought from representatives of the emerging regional organizations in Europe, North America, and Asia.

To become an effective policy coordinator, however, the G-7 needs to be more than a once-a-year "summit" of presidents and prime ministers, which has served as more of a photo opportunity than as a forum for analysis, debate, and decision making. The work of the G-7 must involve much more than drafting an annual communiqué phrased in its broad, if not altogether meaningless, generalities.

If the G-7 is to be transformed into a useful instrument for economic cooperation, it needs a secretariat, regular meetings of economic, financial, and political representatives, and more frequent ministerial meetings to prepare the way for decision making on the major issues. Its fundamental aim should be to strengthen the growth of the world economic system, on which all national economies increasingly depend.

In recognition of the likelihood of different conditions within national and regional economies at any given time, policies for systemic growth should not necessarily impose the same fiscal or monetary policies on all member countries at all times. Rather, the G-7 should aim at harmonizing national policies to achieve the common goal of systemic international growth.

International cooperation must also be sought in other multilateral and bilateral negotiations for reducing military spending to levels appropriate to the post-Cold War environment. Military expenditures need to be adjusted to meet changing national security requirements, competing private and public investment aims, and the goals of reducing budget deficits and increasing the world supply of savings and capital, crucial to the reconstruction and growth of the excommunist and developing countries.

The defense budget should not be treated by any nation, including the United States, as an employment-security or growth-stimulus program, with spending levels rationalized by misapplied economic arguments. It would be a tragically lost opportunity if America and other nations failed to transfer resources desperately needed for investment and growth from military uses because of incompetence or self-interested opposition to economic adjustment. Such a failure would not only waste resources but also create pressures for otherwise unnecessary tax increases. The excess military capacity, moreover, would continue to spur the proliferation of weapons, both convention and dual-use nuclear, thereby increasing threats to world peace and economic development.

Danger of Beggar-Thy-Neighbor Policies

The long-term problem made acute by economic globalization—and global slow growth, stagnating real output and income, overcapacity, and unemployment—is not just maintaining aggregate demand but also raising investment in activities that generate strong productivity growth and jobs. Increasing savings, per se, may not automatically raise the level of domestic investment sufficiency, although greater savings will help reduce interest rates and thereby encourage investment. In the integrated global economy, capital saved in one country can readily be invested either domestically or abroad; increasingly businesses and nations must create or acquire the capital, human skill, and technology they will need to meet international competition. The alternative—protectionism and an aggressive nationalism—would, as the world has learned over and over, endanger both peace and prosperity.

Every developed country has accepted, formally or de facto, the responsibility of employing macroeconomic policies to combat inflation and unemployment. But under varying economic and political pressures, countries weigh those objectives differently. Throughout most of the prewar postwar period, the need to contain and defeat Soviet communism went far to overcome political opportunism, the pressures of interest groups, and the inherent unpredictability of capitalist economic systems. As a result, the early postwar performance of the industrial nations was much better than in the years between the world wars.

But slow growth in the world economy now makes the danger of a reversion to beggar-thy-neighbor policies a real one.[11] Some see the three major economic powers—the United States, Germany, and Japan—riding in different directions and threatening to pull the world economy apart. But the interdependence resulting from economic integration has greatly reduced the effective autonomy of even large national economies. Nations have found that their policies are now less potent domestically, affect other countries more strongly, and produce sharp and often unwelcome changes in the trade and payments balances and exchange rates that link them with others.

Conclusion

In this changed world, cooperation among the major economies in policy making has become increasingly important. But there are no technical solutions to the economic problems the world is facing. What is most needed is the political will—the will of the United States, Germany, Japan, and other major industrial countries—to deal more effectively with their own problems and the will of all the major developed countries to work together for a common end.

The most important challenge for economic cooperation in the years ahead will be to keep the world economy growing at a vigorous and sustainable pace. With real economic growth, the serious problems of world debt, unbalanced trade, currency disequilibrium, and unemployment—as well as the social, ethnic, racial and nationalist tensions, and the violence to which they give rise—can be contained, and progress made toward their solutions.

The greatest change needed to preserve stability and nurture growth is for the world economy to become the focus of policy formulation. Despite the resistance of traditional national policies and interest-group pressures, the development of far-sighted fiscal, monetary, trade, and investment policies in the major industrial countries has become vital to the economic well-being of all nations.

Notes

1. Adapted from an article in *Foreign Affairs*, 72, no. 1 (1993).
2. Figures are taken from *World Economic Survey*. New York: United Nations, 1992, p. 1.
3. See articles by Zvi Griliches, Dale W. Jorgenson, Mancur Olson, and Michael J. Boskin in "Symposium on the Slowdown in Productivity Growth," *The Journal of Economic Perspectives*, (Fall 1988): 9–97; Martin Neil Baily and Robert J. Gordon, "The Productivity Slowdown, Measurement Issues, and the Explosion of Computer Power," *Brookings Papers on Economic Activity*, 1988, 347–431.
4. *Financial Times*, November 17, 1992.
5. Akio Mikuni, "The Collapse in Japanese Financial Markets," working paper for the Group of 30, Tokyo, September 1992.
6. K. S. Courtis, "Why Japan Will Come Back," *The International Economy*, September-October 1992, p. 1.
7. Alan Greenspan, testimony before the Committee on Banking, Housing and Urban Affairs, U.S. Senate, July 21, 1992.
8. *The London Observer*, September 7, 1992.
9. This section is based on "The United States in the New Global Economy: A Rallier of Nations," a statement by the Research and Policy Committee for Economic Development, of which the author was Project Director.
10. *Report of the President's Commission on Budget Concepts*. Washington, D.C.: U.S. Government Printing Office, October 1967, pp. 33–35.
11. See Jeffrey E. Garten, *A Cold Peace: America, Japan, Germany, and the Struggle for Supremacy*. New York: Twentieth Century Fund, Times Books, 1992.

Chapter 2

Learning from Experiences

Section 1

The Case of South Africa

Stef Coetzee, Elwil Beukes,
and Daniel Mokhosi

South Africa has recently concluded one of the most tragic periods of recent human history. The termination of apartheid could be viewed as one of the most important turning points of the twentieth century—an event as significant as the crumbling of the Berlin Wall and the peace initiative in the Middle East. South Africa's transition to democracy is symbolic and immensely important to those parts of the world still subjected to repressive rule and especially to a marginalized African continent desperately in need of stable democracy and sustainable patterns of development.

The events since the historically important April 1994 election afforded South Africa the opportunity to make a new beginning to solve the complex sociocultural, political, and developmental problems of the country. A climate of reconciliation, accommodation, and relative peaceful coexistence has dawned, and there are signs of a willingness among the new governing elite to grasp the complexity of the issues and trade-offs at stake.

However it will be no easy route to success. There are vexing underlying political, economic, social, and cultural causes for South Africa's development problematic and the heritage of the past is rather bleak. Moreover, the human development backlogs and imbalances are immense, given the country's higher middle-income status. To be successful will indeed require a paradigm shift that could give new content to the inner meaning of development. A new development paradigm should include participatory and inclusive forms of democracy, a human centered development approach aimed at creating new livelihoods and new forms of human security, a balancing act between sustained growth and equity, satisfying basic needs ensuring sustainability, and an appropriate institutional framework for development based on synergic partnerships between the state and the organs of a vibrant civil society.

Social Disintegration and Inequity in South Africa

Before discussing the impacts of social disintegration and measures to enhance social cohesion, justice, and inequity, it is appropriate to consider the multifaceted causes of social disintegration and inequity in South Africa. These causes include international and local political, economic, cultural, and social forces.

The causes of the present sociopolitical and development malaise date back to a period long before apartheid became officially institutionalized. After the "discovery" of South Africa by Vasco da Gama, the Cape was colonized by the Dutch and the British interchangeably, with the Dutch ruling for most of the eighteenth century and the British for most of the nineteenth century. Until independence in 1961, South Africa received powers for self-rule under the British monarchy.

During British and Dutch colonization, strong colonial influences had been exerted, and a pattern of development took shape that largely benefited the colonial powers. No attempt was made to involve the indigenous population in political decision making, and the development of the harbors and infrastructure was mainly aimed at promoting exports of natural resources to overseas markets. Racial separation was entrenched in the early history of the Cape, thereby laying the basis for an extended period of denial of political and basic human rights of the indigenous population.

Attempts by the African Native Council, the predecessor of the ANC, to mediate on behalf of the latter group after the formation of the Union of South Africa, were to no avail, both here and in England. This led to a long period of relative deprivation. The reaction of the black people to the denial of basic political and human rights between 1912 and 1958 was one of peaceful resistance. It was only ten years after apartheid was officially established that they turned to more revolutionary ways of combating political separation.

Despite losing the Anglo-Boer War against the British, the Afrikaners maintained a burning desire for freedom and self-rule. This desire was also inspired by fear of the aspirations of the growing number of black people in the country, which far outnumbered the white population. When the National Party took office in 1948, they therefore adopted a policy of separating the race groups, ensuring white hegemony over black subservience, in what became known worldwide as apartheid.

Three distinct phases of apartheid rule can be distinguished: separation; separate development (that is, the notion of "separate but equal"); and the neoapartheid phase when coloreds and Indians were coopted and most of the harsh measures of apartheid were reformed without relinquishing power.

During the separation phase (1948–1958), harsh measures were put on the statute book to separate the races. These included laws to separate residential areas of blacks and whites; to enforce separate amenities, schools, universities, and so on; to preserve job reservation for whites; and the implementation of influx control in what amounted to a total reconstruction of South African society. To protect whites against the inflow of blacks to urban areas, a comprehensive systems of influx control was adopted—the deeply hated dompas system. Black migratory workers were prevented from bringing their families to the cities and from owning property (land and houses) in the black townships. But most devastating of all these policies was the system of "Bantu Education," which was planned to restrict blacks to lower-level jobs, thereby severely affecting upward mobility in the labor market.

The above turn of events drew fierce criticism both locally and abroad. Finally the ANC embarked on a new revolutionary course of action, which included a more violent struggle to end apartheid. These pressures and the proposals of the Tomlinson Commission of Enquiry into the Socioeconomic Development of the Bantustans led to an attempt to provide apartheid with a more morally defensible position and "human face," namely separate development.

Under the leadership of Verwoerd, the basis for this policy was laid. Apartheid measures were kept intact, but they were supported by policies that turned the stream of people flocking to the cities back to the traditional "homeland" areas. The latter measures included both the so-called "border industry policy" to entice industrialists through incentives to the borders of the homelands (thus keeping white "capitalists" out) and later in the 1960s and 1970s programs to enhance the socioeconomic development of these areas. During the 1970s, the border industry policy was replaced by the Industrial Decentralization Policy, which allowed private business to invest directly in the homelands.

By the end of the 1970s, it was clear that the tide of people flocking to the cities had not turned around. The apartheid paradigm was under enormous pressures locally (especially after the 1976 uprising) and abroad. Botha, who succeeded Vorster, embarked on a new political program that could be called the neoapartheid phase. This program included a "Constellation of Southern African States" (never accepted by the African community of nations) and the replacement of the Decentralization Policy by the "Regional Industrial Development Policy." Botha also brought about limited political reforms that led to the establishment of the Three Chamber Parliament for whites, coloreds, and Indians. Blacks still had to exercise their political rights through the homeland system. The Three Chamber Parliament met unprecedented resistance from the black majority and resulted in the formation of the United Democratic Front, violence throughout the country, and eventually a state of emergency between 1985 and 1990.

In addition to the above reforms, the 1980s witnessed other important policy changes, including, most significantly, the abolition of influx control, a positive urbanization strategy, promotion of home ownership among blacks, establishment of Regional Service Councils to finance capital projects in urban areas, and black small business development. Although these changes were implemented, the other main tenets of apartheid remained intact. Behind the scenes deliberations between the government and Nelson Mandela did however commence in 1987, and people from big business and academics defied the official policies by talking and making contact with the ANC. This led to several rounds of discussions with the ANC before De Klerk's February 2, 1990 speech, which set the ball rolling towards the new South Africa.

In looking back on the past 46 years, there can be no doubt that apartheid as a political system had a most decisive effect on the human, social, and economic development of the country. Under apartheid, discrimination was entrenched — denying people their basic human dignity and severely limiting opportunities for upward mobility. Despondency, anger, frustration, and destructive behavior inevitably followed. Bantu education had a pronounced effect on the prospects for human development. Economic stagnation and an enormous flight of capital were experienced; poverty, unemployment, and inequality increased; South Africa became an extremely violent society; and in the early 1990s development projects came to a virtual standstill.

Economic Causes

The political economy of South Africa has been a codeterminant of its particular pattern of development. The most salient feature was the limited trickle-down effects that occurred between the late nineteenth and late twentieth centuries. With the advent of the new South Africa in 1990, 42 percent of the population (mostly black) is subjected to extreme poverty. Three economic causes of this predicament are discernible. They are international economic forces, the apartheid economy, and structural economic factors.

The international economy has had a marked effect on the pattern of development in South Africa. In the early phase, an export economy was promoted; harbors and infrastructure were developed mainly to serve the export markets rather than South Africa's domestic development. During the second phase, which began in the late nineteenth century with the discovery of diamonds and gold, the mining industry was developed with the aid of international capital and technology.[1]

Gold mining in the Witwatersrand led to a massive concentration of industry and financial services in Johannesburg and its environs and the instituting of a migratory labor system that separated workers from their families in South(ern) Africa. The low wages of mineworkers was another legacy of this development; it was not until the early 1970s, with the adoption of the Sullivan code, that the above situation was rectified. The discovery of gold therefore had a pronounced effect on the geographical economy of the country. By 1985 the eight major urban centers of the country produced 70 percent of GDP and the homeland areas only 6.0 percent.[2]

The apartheid economy reinforced some of the trends brought about by international economic forces and critical analysis often referred to the "unholy alliance" between capitalism and apartheid. Beginning in the 1960s, apartheid instigated a war economy that gave preference to "strategic projects" and import substitution at the cost of efficiency and equity and human development considerations. The laws of apartheid severely intervened in the economy and the upward mobility of labor. Thus the flow of factors of production and the spatial settlement pattern of the country were significantly affected by this attempt at social engineering. State intervention in the economy brought about by apartheid instigated South Africa's own variety of state capitalism.

The above factors and the long term decline of the international economy exerted a strong influence on the business cycle, and since the 1970s South Africa has experienced a period of economic decline. The latter trend was exacerbated by structural economic trends, including a shift from investment in manufacturing to investment in buildings and shopping centers as a hedge against inflation and the declining contribution of agriculture. In fact, both gross domestic savings and net domestic investment declined drastically during the 1980s. Economic growth has been severely dampened by shortages on the current account of the balance of payments, which was caused by financial sanctions that began in the mid-1980s. The authorities maintained high positive interest rates throughout the above period to combat the effects of inflation.

The consistent rise in unemployment since the 1970s and the decline in formal sector employment, even during short spells of economic upswing, is one of the most disturbing trends in the South African economy. The unemployment rate of between 20 to 30 percent has had a pronounced effect on poverty, inequality, and social disintegration, and South Africa has one of the highest Gini coefficients in the world. Inequality is further exacerbated by the concentration of the private ownership of wealth and property.

Social Causes of Disintegration

Political conflict, ethnic passions, the deep cycle of violence of the past decade, increasing criminality, the struggle for resources, economic stagnation, and poverty not only severely destabilized the fabric of society but at times threatened to tear it completely apart. These developments aggravated the already disrupted family life caused by migratory labor and the impact of political policies of the past. During the early 1990s violence became entrenched, with 14,146 people being killed between 1990 and 1994.

The long-term impact of apartheid, which led to the revolutionary climate of the 1970s and 1980s, combined with the effects of poverty, unemployment, and rapid urbanization during the 1980s, and the mushrooming of informal urban settlements and shack dwellers, created a new phenomenon—disrupted and marginalized families and communities, as well as a "lost generation" of young people who were instructed to put "liberation before education." Family structures crumbled under the weight of these developments, and the authority of parents, schoolmasters, and teachers was severely undermined. Violence became so entrenched that a whole generation of young people have known little else; some have already indicated that they are seriously considering the continuation of violent acts in the new South Africa. With the limited skills they possess they have not much else to contribute to society at present.

Culture and Ethnicity

South Africa's cultural mosaic is one of the strengths of the country, but simultaneously one of its most complex problems. During the apartheid era, ethnicity and racial division was entrenched with tragic consequences for the entire country. However, South Africa has eleven formally recognized languages and a large number of ethnic and minority groups that could prove to be very difficult to unite.

The simple existence of a pluralism of cultures and ethnic groups is something that South Africa shares with a multitude of other nations. Because of the early perception of Afrikaans-speaking whites that this pluralism, left to its own demographic and political dynamic, would seriously threaten their self-determination, its implications became the basic focus of policy making long before the challenges and issues of multiculturalism were significantly addressed elsewhere in the world.

It is not the mere fact that this important issue was addressed directly that created the difficult and sad history of South Africa in the twentieth century. The rest of the world now also recognizes that these issues cannot be swept under the carpet with pious but empty declarations of human solidarity, but have to be dealt with it in a constructive and complex way. The problem rather lies in the way it was done in South Africa. Instead of seeing pluralism as a beneficial form of diversity that could be harnessed for new and exciting forms of societal growth and development, it was seen from a zero-sum perspective. This meant that the majority of whites saw the realization of their cultural aspirations as inherently irreconcilable with that of other groups.

It is therefore too simple to blame the apartheid history of South Africa solely on the economic greed of whites, true though it may be as part of the country's history. The South African government, which since the 1930s has been influenced by romantic Germanic thinking (including its unsavory racist component), could not break through to a new vision of dealing politically with cultural pluralism. Instead, it retreated into a completely defensive and exclusivist approach that rode roughshod over the basic human rights and aspirations of the nonwhite majority. The bitter harvest of this approach is a deep and reciprocal suspicion between whites and blacks (and between Zulus and other black groups) of one another's true intentions, capacity for political and cultural tolerance, and willingness to accept the challenge of constructing a new form of multicultural society. The policies and tactics of the white Conservative Party and the mainly Zulu-based Inkatha Freedom Party today represent the main residual of the old way of thinking about cultural and ethnic diversity in South Africa.

Impacts of Social Disintegration and Inequity

South Africa on the eve of its first democratic multiparty election was a country in a state of severe political, economic, and social crisis. The apartheid regime experienced a legitimacy crisis; development actions came to a virtual standstill in the months before the election. "Third forces" formed strange alliances at the township level, civil disobedience was rife, criminality increased dramatically, and violence escalated to unprecedented levels. South Africa was cracking at the seams as the struggle for power and privilege reached a climax in the run up to the election. It was clear that a transition to a representative and legitimate political order was urgently required.

But what is the heritage of the past at this crucial turning point in history? A brief analysis shows that the postapartheid government has a formidable task ahead of it. All of its innovativeness and ingenuity will be required to win the "Second Liberation Struggle," that is to be freed from poverty, unemployment, and inequality. It is also clear that the new government lacks the capacity to tackle these problems on its own.

South Africa's human development profile shows that population growth is still very high in relation to the country's level of development (2.53 percent between 1985 and 1990). The Urban Foundation's demographic model predicts that the total population will rise to 46.6 million by the year 2000 and 59.7 million by 2010. Between 1980 and 2010 the black population is likely to rise from 21.1 to 46.5 million (that is, by 130 percent). Two-thirds of the black population were 27 years of age and younger in 1990.

The human development profile also shows a very skewed pattern. The profile of whites assumes the same level as in the countries of the developed North. But the situation of blacks assumes the character of the populations of developing countries. In 1993 South Africa ranked 85 out of 173 countries according to the UNDP's Human Development Index. Life expectancy at birth is 61.7, which is rather low for a medium human development country, but infant mortality is 55, which is comparatively high. The educational attainment index is also a low 1.59. Thirty percent of the adult population is illiterate. Approximately 4.6 million blacks are functionally illiterate. The pupil–teacher ratio of whites is 22:1 compared to 40:1 of blacks. In addition the housing backlog among blacks is some 1.4 million units and health services are vastly inadequate, especially in rural areas.

Access to public services in education, health, housing, pensions, and urban infrastructure all reflect significant interracial differences in favor of whites. In the PWV area, for example, nearly 70 percent of black households do not have direct access to water and about 50 percent live in nonpermanent structures. Only 29 percent and 13 percent of black households in urban and rural areas, respectively, have home electrification.

Social spending is 3.7 times higher in per capita terms on whites than on blacks; estimates of the cost of elimination of disparities between segments of the population regarding the social sectors show that the cost of parity at the 1986 white benefit level would imply an increase in social spending from 10.7 percent of GDP in 1986 to between 27.7 percent and 35.0 percent.[3] By 1992, government expenditure on education amounted to 20.7 percent of the total expenditure, leaving hardly any scope for upward adjustment. A redirection of funds will have to come from a reallocation of funds and whatever efficiency gains can be brought about.

The prospects for improved human development is hampered by South Africa's poverty profile. By 1990 some 17.1 million people (mostly black) have been living on income levels below the minimum subsistence level, and projections indicate that this may rise to 18.4 million by 1995. The percentage of people living under the breadline decreased from 50 percent in 1980 to 42 percent in 1990. However the absolute numbers below the line increased from 14.7 million in 1980 to 17.1 million in 1990. Of these, 6 million lived in urban and 11.1 million in rural areas. Poverty has marginalized a large number of families and people, aggravated socioeconomic backlogs, and simultaneously posed a serious threat to food security.[4]

The possibility of reducing the level of poverty is constrained by high levels of unemployment since the 1970s. Of the total population of 39.5 million in 1990, 13.4 million (or 33.92 percent) was economically active in 1990. In the latter year, 40.3 percent of the work force was "without a job" (approximately 20.15 percent unemployed and 20.15 percent in the informal sector) and 59.7 percent were employed in the formal sector of the economy. At least 350,000 persons enter the labor market every year, but from 1980 to 1990 only about 50,000 formal job opportunities were created. What is equally disturbing is the declining labor absorption capacity of the economy — from 73.6 percent for the period 1965 to 1970 to 12.5 percent from 1985 to 1990. Indications are that the latter figure may have declined to 7.0 percent in 1993. Since unemployment has constantly risen during the past two decades, despite some upswings in the business cycle, it is clear that unemployment has assumed structural characteristics.[5]

Unemployment and the concentration of wealth also have a very direct impact on the skewed income distribution and unequal development pattern. South Africa's Gini coefficient was 0.69 in 1990, while the ratios for agriculture and industry are both a high 0.82. Some 71.5 percent of income accrues to the richest 20 percent, 5.1 percent to the bottom 40.0 percent. The white share of personal wealth had been estimated to be over 80 percent in 1990. It should also be noted that land ownership is concentrated in the hands of whites. White farmers earn 78 percent of total gross agricultural income, but are only 26 percent of the total number of farmers. The 1.2 million subsistence farmers farm on 16 million hectares of farm land compared to 60,000 white farmers on 82 million hectares of farmland in South Africa.[6]

The creation of income and new opportunities has been jeopardized by the persistent decline in economic growth since the mid-1960s. In 1992, the GDP of South Africa was US $95,914m with an annual per capita income of US $2600. Annual average GDP growth rates of 5.7 percent, 3.8 percent, and 1.4 percent were recorded during the 1960s, 1970s, and 1980s respectively. The target growth rate to achieve full employment is 5.5 to 6.0 percent. By 1992 real GDP growth was -2.1 percent. Per capita income change for the above decades have been 2.9 percent, 0.7 percent, and -1.2 percent respectively.

The possibilities for sustainable patterns of economic growth are under threat from both increasing rural poverty and population pressure on rural land and a rapid rate of urbanization since the 1980s. In the rural areas there are very clear indications of overgrazing practices, soil erosion, and deforestation—in general, environmental degradation. In addition, poverty in rural areas is much more severe than in urban areas, and some 60 percent of blacks in these areas live under the minimum subsistence level. In the former homeland areas, some 82 percent of households were living in poverty in 1990. In the urban areas the mushrooming of urban informal settlements (the urbanization rate was 3.4 percent between 1980 and 1983 and 3.09 percent thereafter) have caused growing water pollution and mismanagement of land.

All of the above indicates a country with complex development problems and an economy with severe problems of both an efficiency as well as an equity nature and which is gravely underutilizing its productive resources. It is also, however, an economy blessed with a rich endowment of natural resources, a well-developed capacity for macroeconomic management, a modern technology and training capacity, an excellent physical and productive infrastructure in many areas, and a modern and diversified financial and legal system. South Africa has, in short, a semimodern and semi-industrialized economy with potential equaled nowhere in Africa. Unfortunately, there are also formidable structural and huge social development problems. The question is how its potential can be harnessed for the common good and the undeniable possibilities for derailment, stagnation, and even breakdown be kept at bay. Competitive advantages should be maintained, but it is crucial for a higher growth path to develop new competitive advantages in the future.

Challenges for the New South Africa

The new South Africa faces some daunting political, developmental, and economic challenges. To political economy analysts, a new paradigm is desperately needed. However, before the election, the forces militating against such a paradigm shift were overwhelming. Only after the election and the inauguration of the new president have the fortunes changed somewhat in favor of a stable transition to democracy. The question is whether this could bring about the broader paradigm shift that is needed to resolve social conflict and inequity. The initial response by the new government could provide the contours of an emerging new paradigm. However, quite a number of factors militate against the successful conclusion of such a paradigm shift.

A new development paradigm for South Africa will have to come to grips with the following challenges:

- A deeply divided society with latent ethnic passions that could quite easily arise if put under political pressure. Nation-building would not be easy to achieve under these circumstances.

- An extremely violent society in which some of the marginalized youth have, with the lack of alternative opportunities available, recommitted themselves to violence.

- Social disintegration — the disruption and break up of family life, breakdown of authority (both in society and families), the emergence of marginal people, civil disobedience, and street children.

- Human development challenges, including new strategies for affordable but effective education and training, health services, and housing. It is of particular importance that new forms of human security be brought about and that the new approach entails not only transfers to the poor, but create improved capacities and capabilities to empower people to take charge of their own destiny.

- A restructuring of the economy to provide the material basis for development.

- A more equitable development path to ensure a better distribution of the fruits of development.

- A development process that will take due cognizance of the importance of the relationship between people and the environment and that will adopt strategies to promote sustainable development.

- An institutional framework to support and enhance development, cast within a framework of basic human rights and promoting a process of local self-reliance and synergic partnerships between the state, the labor unions, the private sector, and civil society.

Response to the Actual Situation

Since the election, South Africa has witnessed a remarkable period of reconciliation, goodwill, and accommodation. Both the Inkatha Freedom Party and the National Party have pledged support for the implementation of the ANC's Reconstruction and Development Programme (RDP). Incumbent officials from the previous regime in growing numbers are cooperating enthusiastically with the new ministers of the ANC, and government has not retrenched white officials on a large scale. The policy of rapprochement has even been extended to include accommodation of the Afrikaner Right — a "Volkstaatraad" was officially established to consider alternative ways of giving effect to their ideal of a separate Afrikaner state and to negotiate their chosen option within the framework of the Interim Constitution.

The government has moved ahead cautiously in regard to changes to the economy and the bureaucracy. By reappointing the Governor of the Reserve Bank and the Minister of Finance of the previous government, strong signals regarding the economy have been sent to overseas markets. It is also common knowledge that a multiparty commitment was given to the IMF in 1993 that state expenditure would be kept in check. The government has announced the creation of 1,000 new posts in the public sector, a number that fell far short of expectations, but 11,000 previously "frozen" vacant posts were advertised. Only the financial markets responded negatively after President Mandela's first speech in Parliament, indicating a nervousness regarding the government's capacity to maintain financial discipline and to implement the RDP without raising taxes.

The RDP is based on six basic principles:

- An integrated and sustainable program.
- A people-driven process.
- Peace and security for all.
- Nation-building
- Linking reconstruction and development, as well as integrating growth, development, reconstruction, and redistribution.
- The democratization of South Africa.

The key programs of the RDP include:

- Meeting basic needs (e.g., jobs, land, housing, water, electricity, telecommunications, transport, a clean and healthy environment, nutrition, health care, and social welfare)
- Developing human resources.
- Building the economy.
- Democratizing state and society.
- The implementation of the RDP in a planned and coordinated way.

To achieve visibility with the RDP, government has set aside R2.5 billion; it will be allocated to the nine provinces for the first 100 days of the RDPs implementation. The total bill for the RDP remains a bone of contention. The ANC has put the total cost at an estimated R80 billion. A special RDP fund has been created and the above R2.5 billion serves to kick start the process as a basis to mobilize overseas funding. A few billion rands have been pledged by Western governments, but this is a totally insufficient amount.

The RDP is in broad keeping with the thrust of modern day development thinking, but has underestimated the importance of restructuring the economy to achieve sustained economic growth. It places more emphasis on measures to bring about a more equitable growth path than on achieving a higher level of growth. However, the National Economic Forum, a negotiating body including the state, labor, and business, has appointed a Task Team to integrate the RDP with the previous government's Normative Economic Model, which purported to be more market driven and growth oriented, accentuating the importance of financial discipline and "sound" economic policy.

Looked at in a comprehensive way, the successful implementation of the RDP would require

- An integration of short- and long-term plans.
- Politically acceptable prioritization of basic needs and human resource development targets.
- Balancing both human development and equity with economic growth.
- The promotion of both equitable and higher levels of sustained economic growth.
- Ensuring sustainability in a variety of dimensions.

- An appropriate institutional framework for development and a decentralization of the responsibility for implementing the RDP in the different provinces.
- A clear understanding of what government can and cannot do to accelerate development.

Enhancing or Strengthening Social Cohesion and Justice

There is no doubt of the enormity of the challenges and the need for a new development paradigm. The new policy line emerging in South Africa could, despite many complex problems militating against it, provide the opportunity for such a paradigm shift. The question is how the new unfolding approach should be implemented and harnessed to provide the basis for a new development policy. Below, we outline the framework for promoting social cohesion and justice in South Africa, taking into account the lessons of experience of other developing countries, particularly in the African context.

One of the fallacies regarding democracy is that it follows automatically from multiparty elections. Changing old habits and thinking requires more than a democratically designed constitution, however important constitutions may be. There are strong nationalist, commandist, traditional, and autocratic values stemming from South Africa and Africa's past that may not be easy to overcome.

Examples in Africa and elsewhere abound of a postcolonial leadership elite that has had an overriding concern with power for their own purposes, acquired by "capturing" the state. Those who captured the state "wanted to inherit it, instead of transforming it in accordance with nationalist aspirations."[7] The most disturbing feature of this quest for power is that those who acquire it no longer exert themselves for economic well-being, for this comes to them automatically with victory; those who have lost, have also lost their economic well-being. The unfortunate outcome of such a turn of events is the delinking of leadership from society (and especially the poor) whom they previously professed to serve.

In countries emerging from a long tradition of repression and discrimination, a stable transition to democracy will not be possible without a process of reconciliation between the former oppressor(s) and the new regime. Nowhere is this more applicable than in South Africa, where the ANC has won political power, through a landslide victory, and is legitimate in the eyes of the masses, but where the white minority controls the economic wealth, technology, financial infrastructure, and administrative skills. It presupposes a recognition on all sides that they are mutually dependent and will remain so. Synergy instead of conflict is the only meaningful way forward.

The calls by the new government for reconciliation augur well for the future, the simultaneous urge for a "Commission of the Truth" notwithstanding. These attempts at promoting reconciliation have been met by the amazing willingness of the white minority group to cooperate and participate in the application of the RDP. But given South Africa's history, it is a fragile peace that has to be nurtured and harnessed on the basis of a joint commitment to a common destiny to achieve lasting effects.

Divided societies like South Africa face the daunting task of bringing about both a representative and inclusive democracy. This is not easy to accomplish in a country where some people associate democracy with crude majoritarianism and others limit it to the boundaries of ethnonationalism. But representative democracy should not exclude the possibility of plural democracy—in fact, in a culturally plural society there should be a congruence of power and culture.

One of the burdens of democracy is the expectations that people have of what it can deliver independently of what would be required in terms of human effort. The poor are most vulnerable in this regard, even in a situation of majority rule. This is particularly applicable if the poor cherish the expectations that the state will materially improve their situation—and that it can do so almost immediately. The disillusionment is so much the greater if the poor find themselves marginalized again and discover that there are limits on what the state can deliver. Development therefore requires a vibrant civil society to counter attempts at concentrating power exclusively in the hands of the state, to make room for private initiative including NGOs, small business, grass-roots organizations, individuals, and households, and to activate and mobilize development action from below. This implies a willingness for far-reaching and effective decentralization bringing government much closer to people.

Reconstruction and Development

It is now a rallying cry in the international development community that ordinary people and their organized forms of living can undertake development themselves, according to their own needs and aspirations. Those from the outside can only assist by measures that enable and empower people to take charge of their own situation.

This approach implies that development is a process that owned and driven by the people themselves. The reconstruction of society that is mooted so resoundingly in South Africa has this idea at its core. It is nonetheless an idea with such far-reaching implications that its full implementation will take us into uncharted waters. The temptation is always present—partially fueled by the pressures of representative politics—for a government to attempt a quick fix of the situation by handing out goods and services. In addition to the question of available resources for such an approach, it flies in the face of a human-centered understanding of development. The choice is thus a difficult one, but it must be faced by the people of a new South Africa and its government. The indications are that this will not be an easy exercise.

The socioeconomic disparities and poverty in countries like South Africa calls for a renewed emphasis on addressing the basic needs of marginalized communities. Here it would be prudent to return to the original five core areas, namely clean drinking water, sewerage, nutrition, shelter, health, and education. In fact, it may even be necessary to prioritize within the basic needs basket and to initially concentrate on those areas that will be visible, cost effective, and provide the best economic spin-offs. It is also imperative where primary income is low that access to social services be improved through general and universal provision of rudimentary and accessible services. More complex but equally important is access to affordable food, water, energy, transport, and shelter. The second level entails schemes directed at specific groups and includes income support such as food subsidies or nutrition programs.

Economic stagnation in the developing countries and South Africa has not created the platform for human development and the satisfaction of basic needs. The poor are rendered even poorer by macroeconomic decline. Recent experience has, however, shown that it is all important what kind of growth takes place and who benefits from it.

To give direction to growth processes the obvious place to start is the basic needs of the poor. Instead of these needs remaining a goal to be striven for by the government, it actually indicates the range of opportunities for economic and other activity. Seen in this way, the process of their satisfaction becomes a large part of the engine of growth and development itself. In addition, the vexed issue of employment creation and income generation for the masses can be addressed, enabling communities to satisfy their own needs.

In South Africa the informal sector already has funds calculated at more than R10 billion per year circulating in it. The introduction of this pool and its concomitant range of economic activity into the formal economy presents a huge opportunity for invigorating the stagnant South African economy and creating new opportunities for the marginalized. But then those in economic power must make room for these small players instead of seeing them as a threat or a target for takeover. This applies particularly to financial institutions that have provided very limited access to their services to entrepreneurs from the poor.

But the resource base for human development is under threat from both rural underdevelopment and poverty and a rapid process of urbanization, with all its pathological manifestations. In the rural former homeland areas, poverty, a lack of economic opportunities, the pressure on land, and insufficient energy resources have had a direct bearing on soil erosion and deforestation. In the urban areas, the growth of the informal sector and squatter communities have exerted enormous pressures on South Africa's divided local government systems. Integrated urban and rural development policies, as well as population development programs, are required to address the underlying cause of environmental degradation.

New Forms of Human Security

The new South Africa has emerged from an extended period of conflict, violence, and disharmony, which has had a negative impact on development in South Africa and has also destabilized neighboring countries. Poverty, unemployment, inequality, discrimination, and resulting crime are daily realities that threaten the security and opportunities of almost half of

South Africa's people. For them life is under threat in a continuous an incipient way.

This situation indicates the need for new forms of human security. In direct physical sense, the police must become community oriented and the South African National Defence Force must become the custodian of peac rather than of war and destabilization. New forms of physical securit require a more humane society, where the security apparatus protect citizens from crime and violent acts, contributes to creating stability, an plays a supportive role in bringing about reconstruction and development The military infrastructure could be used to provide skills to marginalize youth, support public works programs in rural areas, and establish a peac corps that could undertake development work.

To pursue a policy of human security will, however, require a new way of defining development — to create a humane society and promot an equitable, human centered development process. It requires a vibran civil society and new partnerships between government and civil society It should enable and empower NGOs, grassroots organizations, privat business households, and individuals to actively participate in developmen planning and determining priorities. In short, development should not b done for people, but by people through local forms of self-reliance. Th institutional framework for development should include the promotion o private initiative and private economic activity as a vital component of free and democratic political order. Markets are essential for efficient an vigorous production, but they must be open and accessible to all, hav a flexible regulatory framework, and be supplemented by prudent socia policy action by government. Such a policy framework should particular! aim at promoting small and medium-sized enterprises that have come t play a very important role in successful developing economies.

Governance and Policy

Recent African history shows that, in most cases, governments were uncon nected to the rest of society, overburdened with expectations, and cream off by elite groups for their own benefit. Corruption and patronage wer rife, there was a general lack of development orientation, and that the stat was used to plan, direct, and control development actions. However, th state has become so overburdened in some areas that it has collapsed.

To create a truly "developmental state," the government should no attempt to provide all things, nor do everything. It should rather b supportive of human development and human security; it should enable facilitate, and empower people and the organs of civil society to improv capacities, mobilize resources, determine their own priorities, and tak charge of development actions. Development along these lines requires clear and definite framework of basic human rights.

Democratic governance entails a synergetic relationship between gov ernment and people. It can only fulfill the hopes and aspirations of peopl if it is undertaken in a participatory, accountable, and transparent manner This implies a new way of making and implementing policy in which organ of civil society become part of the full process and thus carry coresponsibilit for its success or failure.

In South Africa the transition to a new sociopolitical order also implies a difficult and at times painful transition and integration of the bureaucracy. This is particularly acute in the provinces where the old homelands are located. There, the bureaucratic structures must be integrated with those of the new provinces. Reorientation of all officials is required. Those from the old order must learn about the reconstruction and development framework of the new government; new officials must learn the principles of public administration and the functioning of government on all levels. Much emphasis will therefore have to be placed on development orientation and for capacity building during the coming years.

The integration and transition of the bureaucracy is no easy task. Especially during the first year of government, it may delay the implementation of policy. This could also undermine attempts at decentralizing government to the nine provinces, a process that is essentially for a vast country with such differences in concentration of economic activity and population.

South Africa and the New World Order

South Africa's return to the international community comes at a time when the world order has changed dramatically. Democratization and economic liberalization is in the ascendancy; there is an increasing trend towards globalization of financial markets. A second major trend is the transition to the information and technological era, in which organizations are increasingly based on expertise and the availability of information.

Within the above international context, South Africa must position itself for the future. With the abolition of sanctions, new markets are opening up, but markets are not as free and open as the Big Seven would have it be. Although markets in Africa are rapidly developing, African economies are crippled by economic stagnation. With the world economy turning from a resource base to an information base, South Africa's competitive advantages may not last — new competitive advantages will have to be developed and this will be difficult given the advantages that the Tigers of the East have built up.

International private investment is likely to return slowly to South Africa. Political stability, security, and a sound policy environment are prerequisites for securing private investment. Investors are likely to delay decisions until they have had the opportunity to monitor and analyze two or even three budgets of the new government.

If the international community's concern with the plight of the African continent is sincere, it has a huge stake in the successful transition of South Africa and the growth of its economy. Given all that we have learned from false starts and rural development, this will mean that support should be given for the right kind of growth. With the twenty-first century in view, an opportunity exists to use an African country with proven potential and to which the entire continent looks with great expectation, as a pioneer in new ways of development and development cooperation that can serve and bolster a whole continent.

In considering the possibilities for restoring justice and social cohesion to South Africa, two basic mind-sets need to be distinguished. The first — a linear response — attempts to improve the situation by roughly continuing the processes and patterns of the past but with a redirection and increase in the amount of public spending. It implies "more of the same" even if redirected. In practical terms, the inequalities and injuries of the past are addressed by trying to equalize the level and quality of social and other services provided by the government.

Many attempts are under way to calculate the cost of such an exercise. They clearly show that a linear extension and extrapolation of the present pattern of government expenditure, even in a scaled-down version, is not feasible. This does not mean that a sustained effort to improve the quality of life of South Africa's people is an exercise in futility. It simply indicates that such an objective cannot be obtained by merely "creating and spending additional funds." Given the deteriorating economic growth record of South Africa since the 1960s, particularly since 1980, and the accepted need for sustainable fiscal policy, the sources for such a rise in spending patently do not exist.

The problem with a linear approach is exacerbated by the issues surrounding affirmative action. Given that such action is entrenched in the interim constitution, it will raise expectations further, changing the perception about such action from a method into an entitlement. In addition, the slow nature of development and the process of redressing historical economic injustice is lost sight of when an official goal of parity is set. Incremental improvements in the situation are overlooked and perceptions of the intolerability of remaining differences become even more acute.

Thus there is no linear approach to the solution of the structural problems that South Africa has inherited. It follows that the "how" of future government spending and action is even more important than the "how much." It also places the huge task of effective and visionary leadership on the shoulders of the new government. Its task is to take the long-suffering majority of the population with them on the long journey of reconstruction and development by creating an understanding and support for a process that is owned and driven by the people and which will increase their self-reliance. It will be different from the past but holds out the promise of sustainable progress. But what then is the alternative to "more of the same?"

The second mind set can be called a "transformational" approach. In this approach, the complexities of modern societies and patterns of life are fully recognized, implying that we accept the interconnectedness of our actions. Development and fundamental change can only be grasped and tackled in a holistic fashion. Taken together, holism and complexity can create the temptation of a supereffort at macroscale social engineering. This will be a wholly inappropriate and nonfeasible reaction to the challenge. Instead the new leadership in South Africa should explore the exciting possibilities inherent in the following:

- Effective and empowering decentralization.
- Small but highly efficient central structures.
- Delegation in network organizations.
- Contracting out all nonessential production and services.

- Effective use of informatics and knowledge management systems.
- Access to lifelong training and capacity enhancement.
- Harnessing the positive energies of the young.

Conclusion

Unfolding events are auguring well for South Africa's future. A surprising degree of healthy pragmatism is evident in economic policy making. The biggest challenge lies in how the expectations and energy of the poor majority can be harnessed and channeled to work with the government and those with economic power in a synergistic fashion. It is here that the pursuit of a transformational instead of a linear approach to the issues will make the difference between success and failure. A promising start has been made, but it will need all the support and perseverance that can be mustered.

Notes

1. D. H. Houghton, *The South African Economy.* Cape Town: Oxford University Press, 1976.
2. S. F. Coetzee et al. *Regional Development in South Africa and the TBVC States.* Midrand: Development Bank of Southern Africa, 1985.
3. S. van den Berg, "Meeting the Aspirations of South Africa's Poor," *Human Rights Monitor,* 1990.
4. Elwil Beukes, "Restructuring the Economy of South Africa for Development: Trends and Options." Paper presented at the World Conference for International Development, Mexico city, April 6–9, 1994.
5. F. S. Barker, *The South African Labour Market: Critical Issues for Transition.* Pretoria: J. L. van Schaik, 1992.
6. M. McGrath and S. van den Berg, "Growth, Poverty and Redistribution Consultative Business Movement." Paper presented at the Internal Imperatives Workship, February 23, 1991.
7. Claude Ake, "The Legitimacy Crisis of the State." In David kennet and Tukumbi Lumuba-Kasongo, *Structural Adjustment and the Crisis in Africa: Economic and Political Perspectives.* New York: Edwin Mellen, 1992.

Section 2

Market Reforms and Women's Economic Status

Valentine M. Moghadam

The United Nations World Summit for Social Development will focus at tention on ways of addressing increasing worldwide poverty, unemploymen and societal disintegration. In this context, two sets of issues can be iden tified: the relationship between market reforms and social problems, an the implications of these problems for women's economic status and the productive and reproductive activities.

This section is a preliminary analysis of the immediate impact on wome of economic restructuring in two regions: Central and Eastern Europ (CEE) and Russia, on the one hand, and Vietnam and China on the othe It contains an implicit criticism of the poverty- and unemployment-inducin nature of the market reforms, and of their built-in gender bias, and fin some differences in discourses and policies pertaining to women and labor.

Some comparative observations on the subject can initially be made.

- All of the former socialist and communist countries are currently i transition. They have left a system of strict central planning marke by a predominant role for the Communist Party, full employment (i cluding high levels of female employment), and extensive social service to a one with a greater role for markets, less involvement of polit cal bodies and central authorities in economic decision making, risin unemployment, and shifting policies on social protection. There are of course, differences in the pace of the reforms, their social effect the capacities of the states, and the strength of nonstate institutior (markets as well as intermediate organizations of "civil society") amon the countries. This discussion, however, will pinpoint the difference between "the Asians" and "the Europeans."

- Central and Eastern Europe (CEE) and Russia have completely re jected the socialist/communist past, and their rush towards the mark system was done in a highly ideological manner. The high hopes of the early years, however, were dashed by economic recession, inflation, unemployment, and the rise of poverty. In contrast, China and Vietnam are moving more slowly, cautiously, and deliberately, with neither the "big bang/shock therapy" approach, nor the anticommunist crusade of Central and Eastern Europe. Although market reform in China and *doi moi* in Vietnam are both quite advanced, these reforms are considered to be within the socialist framework, rather than a negation of it. Furthermore, unlike CEE and Russia, where the former leaders have fallen into disrepute, the Chinese have not renounced their revolutionary history; in Vietnam, enormous respect for Ho Chi Minh and the experience of national liberation still lingers, even in the South. Continuity in China and Vietnam helps explain the differences in discourse on labor and women in the two regions.

- The early free marketeers of Eastern Europe anticipated unemployment, and in fact encouraged it.[1] In Vietnam, on the other hand, unemployment and underemployment are considered serious economic and social problems, and accelerated marketization is intended to reduce unemployment through economic growth. In China, collectivization rendered millions of peasants redundant, many of whom were subsequently absorbed into rural industries or migrated to the cities as cheap labor. The unemployment rate, at 2.3 percent in 1992, is not as high as in either Vietnam or the CEE countries (though it is closer to the official Russian rate of unemployment). Although CEE and Russia are more industrialized and urbanized than are China and Vietnam, growing involuntary unemployment is a major problem for both sets of transition economies.

- Unlike CEE planners and policy makers, who are totally blind—perhaps allergic—to gender issues, in Vietnam government documents evince a concern for women's welfare and are committed, at least rhetorically, to gender equality. The Chinese government is also, at least rhetorically, committed to women's equality, and it pushed hard to become the host of the 1995 Fourth World Conference on Women. Unlike the Central and Eastern European and former Soviet Union (FSU) region, the women's organizations in Vietnam and China are large and influential.

- CEE countries look towards the United States and Western Europe as models, while Vietnam and China look towards the East and Southeast-Asian newly industrialized economies (NIEs). While CEE countries and Russia are experiencing negative growth, China's growth rate in 1993—at 13 percent—was the highest in the world.

- In both regions, however, available evidence suggests that economic restructuring seems to be affecting women more adversely than men, and that unemployment rates are higher for women than for men. The new labor markets allow employers to discriminate on the basis of gender and age, leaving older women in particular at a distinct disadvantage. The new economic freedoms also allow employers to advertise openly for male workers only, citing the costs of maternity and child-care benefits as major factors in their choice of employees. (This is not yet a problem in Vietnam, however.)

With these preliminary observations, let us turn to the economic and employment situation of women in the CEE region and Russia.

Central and Eastern Europe and Russia

The discussion can be put into perspective by citing a passage from a recent United Nations International Children's Emergency Fund (UNICEF) report on economic crisis and the deterioration of social indicators in CEE:

> ...the economic and social reforms introduced since 1989 are facing severe problems of implementation and involve economic, social and political costs far greater than anticipated....initial hopes for rapid transformation and economic prosperity have quickly been tempered by a considerable and lasting decline in output, employment and incomes and by the worsening of many social indicators. The crisis is without doubt most pronounced in Eastern and South-Eastern Europe, where the spread of poverty, birth contraction, escalation of death rates, decline in school enrollments and an unstoppable crime wave have reached truly alarming proportions. Between 1989 and 1993, for instance, the crude death rate increased by 17 percent in Romania, by 12 percent in Bulgaria, by commensurate amounts in Albania and Ukraine and by 32 percent in Russia. In this country, the number of yearly deaths in 1993 exceeded that of 1989 by 547,000 units, a figure which more than anything else illustrates the gravity of the current crisis—a crisis which, in relative terms, appears even more acute than that recorded in Latin America and Africa during the 'lost decade' of the 1980s. Despite recent signs of recovery in several areas, Poland also suffered a considerable surge in poverty and death rates and a deterioration in other demographic and welfare indicators and is still in the grips of rising unemployment. After plummeting in the first and second years of reforms, social conditions stopped deteriorating in the better-off nations of Central Europe (Hungary, Slovakia and Czech Republic), where past achievements in some areas were protected despite difficult economic conditions. Only the Czech Republic, however, may slowly be returning to normal conditions.[2]

The report goes on to document the changes in social policies, such as those pertaining to family, children, and maternity leave. These policies, quite generous before, are now either eliminated or greatly reduced. In Russia's case, maternity leave was actually greatly extended, from 112 days to 140 days. But this was done to both discourage women from returning to the labor market and to reestablish women's family attachment.

A serious decline has also occurred in household incomes, and thus the quality of life. In Russia for example, fully 28 percent of wage earners receive salaries 50 percent below the average wage. Fifty million people—one-third of the Russian population—now live below the poverty line. More than half of the households headed by women have fallen into poverty, and the situation is particularly bad for pensioners.

The growth in the number of people living in poverty, along with the deterioration of real wages in an atmosphere of ever-rising prices, has indeed affected female-headed households. Although gender-disaggregated data is not available at present, it can be assumed that the well-being of women and children in households maintained by women alone has been adversely altered by recession and the loss of socialist-era subsidies. We do know, however, that working women have seen dramatic declines in their labor-force participation rates, and in their employment levels. The previously high participation rates of women (80 to 90 percent) dropped by five to 10 points during this period in formerly socialist countries. The drop in employment levels of working-age women was much larger than the participation rates in most countries. For instance, female employment rates declined to 66 percent from 93 percent in Bulgaria, to 70 to 62 percent from 82 percent in the Czech and Slovak Republics, to 66 from 78 percent in Hungary, and to 60 from 70 percent in Poland.

Women in the New Labor Markets

A recent UN report on the global economic situation of women observes: "Women generally continue to be the last to benefit from job expansion and the first to suffer from job contraction." In Eastern Europe, the introduction of economic reform and a competitive labor market has converged with traditional gender bias and a perception of women as relatively "expensive labor"—due to the generous benefits that women workers previously enjoyed. The result has been growing, involuntary unemployment and higher rates of unemployment for women than for men.

Of those registered unemployed in Romania in September 1990, 85 to 90 percent were women; today their unemployment rate is far higher than men's. In Poland, the proportion of unemployed women has grown steadily since 1990. By April 1992, this group constituted nearly 53 percent of the unemployed, as opposed to 45 percent of the workforce. According to one account, each time there are redundancies, perhaps 50 percent more women than men lose their jobs.

In the former German Democratic Republic (GDR), women's unemployment rates have risen much faster than men's. Between mid-1989 and mid-1991, they rose by 500 percent as compared with 300 percent for men. Women in the former GDR have twice as high an unemployment level as do the men. In Czechoslovakia, Bulgaria, and Albania, women represent about 60 percent of the unemployed. In the FSU, the share of women among those who lost employment in the period 1989–1991 was 60 percent. When the state bureaucracy was streamlined between 1985–1987, more than 80 percent of those laid off in the industrial sector were women, and more than half of them had higher education. Particularly vulnerable segments of the female population, like single mothers or mothers with several children, accounted for some 2.5 percent of the unemployed.

In Moscow in 1992, an alarming 80 percent of the unemployed were female. In 1992, estimated job losses in Eastern Germany were between 800,000 and 1 million. By 1993, the total number of Eastern Germans working had declined from 9.9 million in 1989 to about 5 million. In layoffs, gender stereotypes presume that men will suffer more from unemployment than women; once fired, however, it is much more difficult for women to find jobs. There are fewer reemployment opportunities, and fewer training or retraining programs for women. According to Regine Hildebrandt, the Social Democratic Party Minister for Labor, Welfare, Health, and Women in Brandenburg: "Women's unemployment, compared with men's unemployment, does not get the same attention."

A recent study on eastern Germany finds that as long-term unemployment worsens, a growing number of disillusioned claimants lose their entitlement to unemployment benefits and simply leaving the labor force. Furthermore, a marked trend exists towards sex-related, labor market segmentation, and women now account for two-thirds of the jobless. In the former GDR, 84 percent of women of working age were in the labor force (compared with 53 percent in the west). Now reaching more than 20 percent, official unemployment among women in the new federal states (i.e., eastern Germany) is almost double that of men. Women are also proportionately underrepresented in labor-market programs.

Small wonder that in Brandenburg, a textile-producing state in the east, a 1992 poll found that 82 percent of women surveyed believed that for them, things were worse than they had been before unification.

In every fifth family in eastern Germany, a child is cared for by a single parent. In the former GDR, single mothers enjoyed shorter hours, longer vacations, special protection against layoffs, and comprehensive childcare in day-care centers, kindergartens, and after-school programs. More and more of these parents now live on unemployment or welfare. One newspaper account quotes a 36-year-old single mother of two: "For people like me, reunification has brought nothing but disadvantages." After being laid off, she was offered a government-sponsored job working at a cemetery in Friedland, her hometown, but the woman later lost that job too. Her rent was about to increase, and the father of her two children—who was also unemployed—had stopped giving her money. At a time when day-care services are being cut back, made more expensive or privatized, some women can no longer afford it, and consequently cannot be employed.

In the former GDR, 9 out of 10 teachers were women. Following unification and restructuring, they were pushed out of the schools as ruthlessly as they were from jobs in factories and service industries. Almost one out of every four researchers at the Academy of Science of East Germany (which has since dissolved) was a woman. It has become increasingly difficult for these women to obtain one of the 2,000 government-sponsored jobs in this field. The same situation holds true for managers. Whereas in June 1990 there were 200,000 male executives in East Germany and 100,000 female executives, a report by the German Institute for Economic Research in

April 1992 showed that only 80,000 male managers were left, along with "hardly any women."

Gender stereotyping notwithstanding, little evidence depicts that Eastern European women wish to give up employment. A study carried out in Hungary in 1986 found that 77 percent of women questioned said that they would prefer to keep working, even if they were in a position to stay at home. Another study carried out in late 1990 showed that only 3 percent of East German women regarded housework as their preferred occupation, as compared with 25 percent in Western Germany. A Bulgarian study carried out in February 1991 showed that only 20 percent of women expressed a desire to stay at home. A Polish study carried out in the Lodz and Ostrow Wielkopolski areas in November and December 1991 showed that although men and women react similarly to news of their redundancy, women found it much harder to come to terms with their unemployment, due to their greater difficulty in finding alternative work. Once unemployed, men found it much easier to find even a casual job.

In Poland, the experience of unemployment has been particularly severe for single mothers. This group heads about 18 percent of families with dependent children. A recent study of more than 900 unemployed single mothers showed that 91 percent lived below the poverty line, while 52 percent had an income that reached about half of the poverty-line level. Most single mothers said they had no savings. One-third had managed to get some kind of casual work, though a further 29 percent said they had no chance of any work of this kind; unemployment had forced them to remove their children from nurseries and nursery schools, whose services had increased dramatically in cost. Only 6 percent of partners provided any help in caring or providing for their joint offspring. The overwhelming majority of these women (80 percent) said that unemployment had been an extremely painful experience, describing themselves as being "shattered," "appalled," "engulfed by a feeling of hopelessness," and full of "fear for their own future and that of their children."

Market Reforms in a Socialist Framework: China and Vietnam

In December 1978, the Chinese government that succeeded Chairman Mao Zedong started a series of experimental programs to adjust and reform the economy. The main objectives were to improve efficiency, productivity, and standards of living, and the methods were a more pervasive use of markets and increased use of material incentives. In the first stage of the reform, a "responsibility system" or "family contract system" was established to replace collective farming, increase productivity of the rural sector, and tie rewards to effort. Households were turned into tenant farmers contracting plots of land from the team (usually for as long as 15 years) in exchange for fulfilling production quotas and taxes. Although the reforms created a tremendous labor surplus problem, price reforms favored farmers and as a result, real per capita income of peasants and rural household consumption increased.

Following what it considered the success of rural reforms, the Chinese government turned its attention to the urban sector. The reforms called for the creation of markets for inputs and outputs, and instructed enterprise managers to stress cost efficiency—and therefore profits. The government also reduced control over industry, allowing for more competition and the deregulation of the previously restricted private and collective sector.

These reforms transformed the labor market, introducing labor mobility, flexibility, and segmentation under the "contract labor system." The state-run enterprises still have a large number of regular (permanent) workers, but there has been an exponential increase in the number of contract workers. By the end of 1992, 16 percent of workers were employed under fixed-term labor contracts, representing an increase of more than 50 percent from the previous year.

The labor contract spells out salary, bonuses, subsidies, and the individual worker's job requirements for a fixed-term of anywhere from six months to 10 years. The labor contract normally ties bonuses to individual, workshop, and enterprise performance. Labor-market reforms were carried out in tandem with the emergence of nonstate enterprises in industry, commerce, and services, along with the expansion of Special Economic Zones, coastal cities, and inland areas to attract direct foreign investment. Other plans within the framework of the "socialist market economy" include enterprise reform—closing outmoded factories, shedding redundant labor, discontinuing housing and unfunded pensions—as well as growth of the service sector and increased taxation.

China's rural and urban reforms have been widely hailed as a huge success. This is defined by China's extremely high economic-growth rates, expansion of rural industries (which have grown to employ over 100 million rural workers, according to a UNICEF study), its important role in global trade, its enormous increase in exports (most remarkably in textiles, clothing, and radios), and its attraction of significant foreign investment. Yet the impact on poverty, on labor standards, on female workers, and on gender relations has been mixed. Foreign-backed joint ventures tend to ignore existing labor codes: complaints of low wages, long hours, deplorable worker housing, the absence of unions, the use of child labor, and industrial accidents have increased in recent years.[3]

In the rural areas, the reforms not only created surplus labor, but in recent years, they seem to have contributed to a growth in rural poverty. Some have argued that inequalities have actually increased with reforms.

Although the official unemployment rate in China is under 3 percent, the unofficial international estimate is 5 percent, at a time when a social safety net is not in place. The response from labor has been increasingly militant, with many wildcat strikes and slowdowns, in addition to protests and demonstrations involving hundreds of thousands of unemployed and underemployed workers.

The prospects of the rural poor are worsened by the fact that basic education and health care are becoming less available than in the past. One Chinese official has conceded that 550 million rural women live in poverty, and unless they are helped, the numbers could rise. The shift from collective farming to household production also entailed a loss of wage-earning by women, resulting in a return to the traditional, sexual division of labor, and certain undesirable and patriarchal customs and social practices (i.e., boy preference, bride-buying, female feticide).

China's urban unemployed are estimated at 3.6 million. This represents about 2.3 percent of the urban workforce, much less (proportionately) than in the CEE region, but closer to Russia's official unemployment rate. And yet the gender-specific effects seem to be quite similar. Some have noted that the pre-reforms principle of "whatever a man can do, a woman can do" was reversed in the 1980s. Women have since been increasingly transferred to light industry and service trades, where physical requirements and cultural biases find them most appropriately allocated. Moreover, to deal with the labor surplus caused by rural–urban migration and the streamlining of state-owned enterprises, women have been encouraged to apply for extended leaves at 70 percent of their previous wage. In many cases, those who have reached the age of 40 are told to choose early retirement.

Discrimination against women has become overt. A study conducted in 1988 by the Institute of Women's Studies of the Chinese Academy of Managerial Sciences showed that almost 70 percent of the workforce made redundant by state-sector factories were women. Managers cite the cost of maternity leave and childcare in refusing to hire women, but many of them apparently also believe that men make better workers than women—even women with better qualifications—and can produce more goods.

Official policy calls for women to be treated equally with men in employment, but in every sector women are in the lower-paying, less prestigious jobs. The 1988 "Women's Protection Law" provides a minimum of three months' maternity leave and additional childcare benefits for women. The regulations, which do not affect rural workers, are designed to provide additional incentives to women workers of childbearing age to abide by family planning policies. However, as has occurred in the CEE region, the expense of these provisions to enterprises is widely believed to have increased discrimination against female workers. But in contrast to the situation of women's organizations in Russia and the CEE region, the All-China Women's Federation has an impact on policy and has protested the adverse effects of reforms on women, even though they are supportive of the general thrust of the reforms.

A 1990 study identifies three of the main problems Chinese women face in the context of economic reform. Evidence supports that: (1) Some units now discriminate against women, setting much higher standards for women than men when recruiting new employees. (2) Women account for the majority of those rejected by working groups within enterprises. (3) Most urban women now prefer to work in state-owned units, doing jobs with a lighter workload, secure welfare, and more flexible management policies. However, job opportunities in state-owned enterprises are becoming increasingly rare, as the economic reform program favors the expansion of self-employment and the private sector.

Doi Moi and Women in Vietnam

Vietnam's strategy of economic reform–which is called *doi moi*, literally "renovation"–was adopted in 1989. Doi moi measures include rural reforms; exchange-rate, fiscal, and interest-rate reforms; promotion of private sector growth; changes in foreign-trade regulations; and programs to minimize the "social costs" of economic reforms. Doi moi also continues the policies of the Second National Plan (1981–1985) and the framework of economic reforms adopted by the Sixth Communist Party Congress in December 1986. These changes promulgated a shift in emphasis from heavy to light industries, a partial deregulation of production activities by granting greater autonomy to individual enterprises, and a recognition of the need to promote an export-oriented manufacturing capacity, especially to Western and Southeast Asian markets.

Much of the impetus for the move to a market economy came out of the ruinous inflation experience of the 1980s, which slashed real incomes of many workers and most civil servants by more than 50 percent during 1985–1988. Concern over the precipitous decline in living standards confirmed the need to press forward to a market-led economy, but it also led the government to announce what it called a new "human strategy development policy," which involved a promise "to bring into full play the human factor" in Vietnam's development, by seeking to: ensure employment for all working people, especially for young people and those living in urban areas; ensure adequate real income for the working people; satisfy the people's educational and cultural development; and improve the country's health system.

Vietnam still remains a predominantly rural country, with 72 percent of the total, employed labor force of 30 million involved in agriculture, according to the 1989 Census. According to Professor Nguyen Quang Vinh of the Institute for Social Sciences in HCM City, the rural sector and agricultural production provide a mixed picture. Rice production is high, but "farmers do not have good living conditions, and the price for rice is very low compared with prices for industrial products." Rural–urban gaps and disparities are high in all social indicators. Vietnam is still 80 percent rural, and in some places, the level of urbanization is extremely low (such as the Mekong Delta, which is only 16 percent urban). One solution to some of the rural problems is to have a diversified rural economy, with mechanized farms and fruit orchards in addition to nonfarm activities, such as rural industries.

The percentage of the labor force involved in industrial production constitutes somewhat more than 11 percent. Nevertheless, doi moi emphasizes restructuring of the industrial sector through a drive to force state-owned enterprises to become profitable—much like the Chinese market-reform strategy. In 1989, there were about 12,000 state-owned enterprises in Vietnam; since the government's market reforms have taken hold, some 4,000 to 5,000 have closed their doors. Many of these companies had their subsidies cut by provincial authorities, others were too small or poorly managed to be competitive.

The government's encouragement of growth in the private sector since 1990 has led not only to the registration of many regular, privately-owned enterprises, but also to the explosion of sidewalk and other informal-sector activity, which is particularly evident in Ho Chi Minh City.

In 1989, Vietnam's workforce was estimated to be around 29 million, or about 45 percent of total population. Eighty percent were those of eligible age (16 and above). For women, the rate was around 47 percent, high in comparison with most other LDCs. The overall rate of unemployment as estimated by the 1989 census was around 5.8, or 13 percent for urban and 4 percent for rural areas. However the figures are probably underestimated, and unemployment is likely to increase as a result of redundancy rates in state enterprises. The census also reported a high rate of underemployment, or employment of less than six months.

The census further showed that in 1989, unemployment was higher for women than for men, in both rural and urban sectors. For the age groups 15 to 49, of the 1,375.8 people officially unemployed in urban areas, 56 percent was female. According to a recent government document, some 3.7 million persons were unemployed in 1992, and about 6.5 million were significantly underemployed. Even more serious was urban unemployment of 2.2 million persons in 1992.

One way the government is dealing with unemployment is by establishing training centers that provide courses from one to six months. In 1993, some 55 of these centers operated throughout Vietnam. Although priority is given to workers laid off from the state sector, the training courses are very popular with new labor-force entrants.

According to Vietnam's classification system of occupations and work-force by "material production" and "nonmaterial production," about 93 percent of the labor force was engaged in material production in 1991, while only 6 percent was engaged in various service sectors. Cooperatives were the predominant form of productive enterprise, accounting for about 55 percent of the workforce in 1989, compared with 15 percent for the state sector, and 30 percent for the private sector. With an estimated 350,000 new businesses registered between 1986 and 1991, private-sector activities have greatly increased. These employ less than 30 workers; only a handful of private companies have a workforce of above 1,000.

In 1989, state enterprises still accounted for one-third of industrial jobs — two-thirds in the construction sector, and 80 percent in forestry and lumber. In service sectors, such as science and education, more than 95 percent of workers were on the government payroll, and roughly 80 percent worked in finance, health, and other social services. The share of material output and employment under direct government control, however, is gradually being reduced, and the private sector is now the largest employer of workers engaged in material production.

The gender division of labor seems more evenly balanced than in most countries, developing and advanced alike. However, problems are antici-pated with increasing marketization. As private-sector jobs offering higher wages expand in Ho Chi Minh City, school drop-out rates may increase among teenage girls. This is already occurring, and is an appropriate area for government intervention. With the contraction of the state sector, the promotion of the private sector, and the rise of unemployment, the household has reemerged as a major unit of production. Persons employed in household production typically work long hours, and child labor is prevalent.

For the time being, however, the most pressing problem for women is unemployment, which remains higher for women than for men. It is the most difficult for young women who are newcomers to the labor market. Also, economic restructuring has led to the introduction of user fees in health care and hospitalization. Moreover, the six-month maternity leave of female workers is now being contested, with some government officials favoring four months.

To conclude, economic reform and its gender dimension in Vietnam is similar in some respects to the experience in China and the CEE region. Until the 1980s, the industrial policy of Vietnam put emphasis on heavy industries, resulting in an essentially import-substituting industrialization strategy. Later, the emphasis shifted in favor of light industries, especially for the establishment of an export-oriented manufacturing capacity. Economic reforms were introduced between 1981–1982, giving growth impetus to small and medium-scale industries, which were then put aside until 1986. One of the principal effects of the latter economic reforms was a significant liberalization of governmental industrial policy, with direct government controls over most state enterprises removed.

A major difference between Vietnam and the CEE region is that because a majority of workers in the industries that are being promoted for export — textiles, garments, food processing, and handicrafts — are female intensive in both the SOEs and the private and cooperative sectors. This then suggests a continuation of demand for female labor. On the other hand, discrimination against women workers may occur under a market economy, as employers seek to avoid the cost of benefits such as maternity leave and childcare, as has been occurring in East Central Europe, the Baltic states, Russia, and China. Not surprisingly, many current challenges and debates in Vietnam revolve around social policy, including maternity leave for women workers.

Yet a difference remains in how Vietnam is pursuing its market reforms, for the Vietnamese government is committed to the development of a labor-force adjustment strategy that involves the following elements:

- Financial support for labor-intensive projects to reduce the degree of unemployment;
- Encouraging foreign investors to invest in labor-intensive construction methods;
- Encouraging self-employment and the creation of small enterprises;
- Providing counseling on career requirements and opportunities;
- Establishing employment and training services;
- Implementing a social security or unemployment insurance system;
- Encouraging a gender-sensitive approach to employment;
- Establishing a new labor code.

Conclusion

This section has described and compared the approach to market reforms and the implications for women workers in two sets of cases: Russia and Central and Eastern Europe, and China and Vietnam. An important difference — and one with implications for discourses and legislation pertaining to women in the workforce — lies in the ideological underpinnings of the market reforms. Related to this, women's rights and women's organizations have a place in Chinese and Vietnamese society, and in official considerations. It is vital that the women's organizations and the NGOs in China and Vietnam continue to monitor the reforms for both their gender and overall social effects, and to continue involvement in top-level discussions and decision making on economic and social policies.

On the other hand, there are disconcerting similarities in the two sets of cases, derived from the inherent tendency of market reforms to accentuate existing vulnerabilities or create new ones. Social problems include rising inequalities, unemployment and underemployment, and poverty unalleviated by social protection. Moreover, market reforms have a built-in gender bias deriving from cultural constructions of gender and economic calculations. In the first instance, women are regarded as secondary earners, who should really be at home taking care of their husbands and children. In the second instance, they are regarded from a market point of view as "expensive labor," to be shed during times of cost cutting or restructuring. Thus occur higher rates of women's unemployment in both cases.

Notes

1. This assertion is based on statements made by CEE officials at a UNU/ WIDER conference on economic reforms and privatization, led by Jeffrey Sachs and Janos Kornai, in Helsinki in March 1990. It is supplemented by many published statements in which officials minimized the gravity of impending joblessness, and suggested that countries should "learn to live with unemployment." For specifics on the Polish case, see Mieczyslaw Kabaj, "The Evolving Labour Market in Poland in the Transformation Process." Paper prepared for the UNU/WIDER conference on *The Politics and Economics of Global Employment*, Helsinki, June 1994.

2. UNICEF, *Public Policy and Social Conditions: Central and Eastern Europe in Transition.* (Florence: International Child Development Centre, November, 1993), p. iii.

3. Marcus W. Brauchli and Joseph Kahn, "Workers in New China Often Find Hardship Tied to Opportunity," The Wall Street Journal (Europe), May 20-21, 1994, p. 1.

Section 3

Noneconomic Context of Japan's Economic Development

Masayuki Tadokoro

As the collapse of the Soviet and East European regimes amply reveals, the failure of the command economy as a model for development is now obvious. While the socialist model of state-led industrialization lost its appeal to developing countries, many of them began accepting a market-oriented approach for their development strategy. Even painful structural adjustments prescribed by the International Monetary Fund (IMF) are now more readily accepted. Thus, confidence in the market mechanism stands at a historically high level. Inspired by post-Cold War euphoria, author Francis Fukuyama refers to the "end of history," arguing that liberal democracy coupled with market economy represent the ultimate winner in the competition of ideals marking human history.

However, the transformation from a command economy to a market economy turned out to be far more difficult than first expected. A rapid and pervasive attempt for reform has destroyed a conventional order without establishing a new one. As situations in the former Soviet Union show, drastic economic reform can disintegrate a society, causing not only crime but radical political movements (including ultranationalism and even racism). This implies that a market economy needs some social infrastructure to serve human needs.

In rich countries, the plight of market economies is also striking. High levels of unemployment (particularly among young people), disintegration of social cohesion, the breakdown of the family, drug abuse, increasing juvenile crimes, and tensions between different ethnic groups are all problems in these nations. While the failure of command economy is undeniable, it does not follow that the other competitor in the game of the Cold War is the perfect winner. The market economy, in fact, falls far short of the final goal of human beings.

In contrast, recent economic development in East Asia appears far brighter. In China, while the authoritarian political regime still remains, economic liberalization since 1979 has been an enormous success. Other Asian countries have also been able to maintain high economic growth. They further moved significantly toward democratization and liberalization of political systems over the last decade or so. Most dramatic is the democratization of South Korea, but important progress has also been made in Taiwan and Singapore.

The Japanese Case

The Japanese economy, often regarded as a model for other East Asian economic development, so far seems relatively free from social problems widely shared by other rich countries. Japan's rapid growth, with limited social instability, has been an object of admiration and wonder throughout the world. Its unemployment rate is still fairly low, the distribution of income is one of the most equal in the world, social cohesion (including family life) has been preserved, and the crime rate has been declining from an already low level.

On the other hand, Japan's economic management has been under increasingly strong criticism from abroad. The so-called "Japan problem" is now a widely accepted concept in Western countries, particularly in the United States. Although it is a typical mercantilistic fallacy to view trade surpluses of one country as detrimental to another, Japan's continuous, huge trade surpluses are regarded as a symbol of idiosyncratic nature within the Japanese economic system. A widespread belief both in Western countries and in Japan itself supports that Japan's economy system is highly different from Western market economies and must be changed.

Thus important questions arise, such as whether Japan's economic system is really so unique that it is incompatible with the rest of the world? Whether the role played by the state in economies in Japan and other East Asian countries is different from the textbook-style free market model? This section focuses on the noneconomic elements of Japanese development pattern, particularly the role of the state. It argues that the state role in Japan has been largely conducive to Japan's economic success. But the positive position was possible under certain sociopolitical conditions, which are now rapidly disappearing.

Industrialization Process and the Social Contract

No matter how appealing the material affluence brought by industrialization, the process of economic development cannot be painless. Because economic development requires flexible mobilization of capital and of human resources, people are frequently subject to enormous uncertainty and instability brought about by dynamic market forces, while also being cut off from the protection that traditional communal societies offer. Rapid industrialization requires the reorganization of a traditional pattern of interests, so that capital and labor can be more flexibly mobilized. In other words, for modernization, reorganization of a whole society is necessary.

And of course, it would certainly meet strong resistance from groups that have strong, vested interests in the status quo. Thus, it would be hard to see rapid industrialization take place without a political structure allowing for a reshuffling of stakes.

The strong consensus for economic growth, shared by almost every group in modern Japan, was a great contributing factor in overcoming social and political conflicts arising from instability at the early stage of industrialization. The common feeling originated from a keen sense of national crisis, caused by an abrupt encounter with Western technology in the nineteenth century. Western political pressure—symbolized by four, American steel-made battleships that threatened the Japanese government in 1853—impressed upon the Japanese national psyche that unless Japan gained a means to counter advancing Western technology, the very independence of Japan would be lost.

In view of the fact that this period was the heyday of Western imperialism—with China falling under the control of Western powers—there was a perception that unless Japan caught up with the West in technology, its survival as a nation would be lost. Thus, technological "catch-up" and the building up of an industrial base became more than a matter of national welfare; it was a matter of national survival.

This strong, national consensus for industrialization became even more powerful after World War II. With the total devastation of the economy by a complete and humiliating defeat, economic reconstruction was a self-evident goal for all Japanese. In addition, the fresh memory of reckless prewar militarism made Japan's pursuit for national supremacy (through political–military means) totally impossible and unattractive. Thus, the consensus for economic growth was now associated with national prestige in the international community, becoming a nonmilitary means to pursue Japan's foreign policy. It also enabled the Japanese bureaucracy to play a large role in economic development. Many institutional features of the Japanese politicoeconomic system are, in fact, quite new. The heavy bureaucratic presence in Japan's economic life is largely connected with its experiences during the economic mobilization for war in the 1930s and 1940s.

The efforts to fight a war required the mobilization of limited production capacity for military purposes. Japanese prewar leaders attempted to improve productivity of manufacturing sectors by consolidating and centralizing production. The government encouraged concentration of heavy industries and tried to organize cartels through which they would control economic activities. Historians generally agree that Japanese economic mobilization during the war was a disaster, which contributed to the destruction of Japanese industrial capacity far more effectively than American strategic bombing. The failed attempt provided both first-hand experience and the institutional tools for the postwar economic bureaucracy.

After the war, the purpose of governmental economic intervention shifted from fighting a war to economic reconstruction. And the mode of intervention changed from unworkable direct control to indicative guidance. The large role played by the state in economic life, however, was maintained

Postwar Japanese political conditions were favorable for the bureau-cratic management of the national economy. Since Japan decided to leave the critical, military-strategic policy to the United States, widespread consensus maintained that the basic national goal for Japan was economic reconstruction and abstention from international power politics. Political climates surrounding the state bureaucracy were highly stable, particularly after 1955. Since the Liberal Democratic Party was always in power, pre-dictable conditions held that the state bureaucracy could pursue a long-term economic strategy. And while politicians were largely engaged in rewarding their constituencies (rather than formulating decisions on economic strat-egy), they did not try to intervene in the bureaucracy, as long as economic growth allowed them to reward their constituencies. Within this framework, the state bureaucracy was given a high level of autonomy and authority.

This setting can be perceived as a kind of social contract. The bureau-cracy, well-insulated from various social and political pressures, enjoyed wide discretion in action. This allowed the state to implement an eco-nomic strategy based on long-term considerations, rather than continuous responses to pressure from various special interests. Their power, however, has been far from limitless. Since their autonomy was based on a kind of contract, bureaucratic authority was circumscribed by general national con-sensus. As long as they were fulfilling the shared national goal, they could enjoy authority. But corruption and abuse of power by the bureaucracy—a likely result from such autonomy—would not have been tolerated and was, in fact, generally quite limited.

Redistribution Policy

Japanese industrial policy is well known among Western authors. Some argue that sectorial targeting exercised by the Ministry of International Trade and Industry (MITI) was the secret of Japan's postwar economic miracle. It is not as well known that many attempts by the MITI failed. Japan has failed to break into the commercial airplane industry despite considerable efforts and resources invested in the project. More recently, the fifth-generation computer project also fell short of success.

On the other hand, many of today's successful industries were not targets of governmental help. Judging from the distribution pattern of governmental credits, neither the automobile industry nor electronics were given subsidized loans. Financial resources controlled by the government were largely directed toward declining sectors, such as coal mining, agri-culture, and fishing. The Japanese automobile industry, one of the most competitive in the world, was never given strong support from the MITI because the industry did not look promising, given the expected competi-tion from the "Big Three" car companies in the United States. Thus, the performances of Japanese industrial policy are far more mixed than many Westerners presume.

However, what definitely deserves attention is the fact that strong redistribution policies were coupled with Japanese economic strategies. Subsidization of the agricultural sector in the postwar period is a good example. Since the last century, as industrialization continued, the agricultural sector was so badly squeezed that peasants often had to "sell" their young daughters as prostitutes. In addition, rapid industrialization caused outflows of population from rural areas to urban areas, which damaged the traditional pattern of social order. Given the plight of the peasants, it is not surprising that the hard-hit rural areas in the 1930s became a hot bed for Japan's prewar ultranationalism and militarism.

It is in this context that the Ministry of Agriculture developed a highly paternalistic attitude towards the sector it was administering. The ministry tended to view its mission as protecting vulnerable peasants and farmers from wild and merciless capitalism. Bureaucrats in the ministry, therefore, even examined the possibility of land reform before it later materialized under the U.S. occupation after World War II.

The paternalistic attitudes continued after land reform. Newly created, small-scale farmers could never be as productive as large foreign producers. They, therefore, have enjoyed constant governmental subsidization in the form of price support. It is important to note, however, the generous subsidization did not stop a rapid and constant outflow of labor forces from the agricultural sector into the industrial sector. On the contrary, Japan experienced one of the most rapid shifts in labor force from the primary to manufacturing sector, which is now quickly moving into the service sector. The protection offered by the government could alleviate the painful adjustment process, but it did not reverse the general trend of the market forces.

International Environments

There is no doubt that international trade played an important role in Japan's modern economic growth. However, difficulties associated with trade also date back from an early stage of Japan's industrialization. Its growing industrial capacity and increased exports, particularly its textile exports to Asia before World War II, created trade frictions with established industrial powers, particularly Britain. The resulting anti-Japanese sentiment became even stronger in the shrinking market after the Great Depression. Japan was under constant charge of low-wage dumping, social dumping, and the manipulation of exchange rates.

Japan's postwar return to the international economy was not easy either. While it lost its traditional markets in China, its access to international markets encountered strong resistance from war-devastated European countries. The difficulty is well symbolized by the fact that Japan's accession to the General Agreement on Tariffs and Trade (GATT) was delayed until as late as 1955, due to the resistance of Britain, whose declining textile industry voiced strong objection to competition with Japan in the Asian market.

Nevertheless, Japan's amazing success in the world market after the 1960s was helped by the U.S. policy to integrate it into the international economy. This policy was largely motivated by the desire to make Japan a strong ally for fighting the Cold War. A constant worry focused on the possibility that Japan might be attracted to the Communist camp in order to gain access to the Chinese market. While the Cold War gave rise to strong military confrontation in East Asia, including two actual wars in Vietnam and Korea, it was a blessing for Japan's international trade. In addition, the difficulties caused by growing Japanese presence in the world market were mitigated by high growth in Western economies throughout the 1960s.

Thus, the favorable international environment surrounding Japan's economy in the postwar era cannot be overemphasized. The United States tried to promote Japan's economic growth by giving her access to the world market, including its own. This was far more effective in promoting Japan's economic growth than pumping aid into Japan's economy. The market access motivated the Japanese to improve their productivity, which left far more lasting and profound impacts on the nation's economy. No matter how effective Japanese bureaucracy might be, unless Japanese private industries were strongly motivated to meet the challenge of international competition, such a national "miracle" would not have occurred.

Technological Innovation

The importance of technological innovation is also obvious in Japan's economic development. The strong Japanese desire to introduce new technology from abroad marks a sharp contrast with its efforts not to depend on capital imports. Access to international financial markets by Japanese business corporations was strictly controlled, and direct foreign investment played a very limited role, due to strong control imposed by the government. In contrast, the Japanese government actively promoted the introduction of advanced technology from abroad.

For example, the MITI allocated a large part of Japan's very limited foreign-exchange reserves for introducing promising technology from outside the country. The MITI also gave tax breaks and soft loans to research and development projects. The benefit of the introduction of foreign technology is obvious; it represents one of the most important advantages for a late starter. By introducing technology from abroad, a late starter could save in both investments and time to improve its productivity.

But why was postwar Japan particularly successful in promoting its technology? It seems likely that the postwar environment was favorable for Japan's attempt to advance technologically. The nature of postwar technological development was more of maturation in existing scientific knowledge than revolutionary scientific breakthroughs. Automobiles, radios, and televisions were not revolutionary technological advances when Japan started manufacturing these products. But as the demand for these goods expanded—through an improved production process and through constant efforts for streamlining the production lines—Japan could dramatically strengthen its industrial competitiveness.

This condition was convenient for Japan in several ways. First, since the historical phase of technological development was one of maturation, rather than the shift of basic paradigm, it was relatively easy for a late starter to catch up. Second, it was relatively simple for the Japanese government to pick a technologically promising industry. Because of the nature of development at that time, tangible economic returns could be expected with relatively high certainty from the introduction of new technology. Third, the Japanese educational system, whose merits lie mostly in elementary and secondary education, was suitable for adopting and improving new technology of foreign origins. While the Japanese education system so far has failed to produce many Nobel laureates, it has been extremely successful in creating a large pool of technicians and workers who are ready to absorb newly introduced technology from abroad.

The Postwar Japanese Politicoeconomic System

As we have seen, the role played by the state in Japan was both important and generally consistent with market forces. The resulting postwar, Japanese politicoeconomic system was never a command economy. Many statistics suggest that direct state presence in Japanese economy is one of the smallest among industrial countries. For example, in 1987 Japanese governmental spending is only 16.8 percent in terms of the total GNP while comparable figures are 23.9 percent for the US, 31.5 percent for the UK, 40.2 percent for Italy. The level of nationalization in industries is also lower than France, Italy and Britain.

In terms of government spending, Japan's fiscal spending has always been one of the lowest among industrialized countries. The number of bureaucractic institutions has also remained small. Unlike popular perception, government subsidization has been largely concentrated on redistribution for declining sectors, rather than on the promotion of competitive industries.

In addition, the Japanese economy has been characterized by strong elements of competition among many producers. Most of its strong products, such as automobiles, machine tools, and home electronics, have larger numbers of manufacturers than in Western economies. In particular, Japan's machine-tool industry was led by medium- and small-scale producers engaged in constant and fierce competition. In fact, small-scale businesses have accounted for a larger share of economic activity than any other industrial economy. These examples cast strong doubt on the simplistic image of Japan as a state-led economic development model.

Nevertheless, the close relations between the state and business indicate that the Japanese development process was very different from the liberal economic model. State intervention into the market economy took place to support uncompetitive sectors for the purpose of redistribution of income. It also intervened to promote industries by inducing them to improve competitiveness through various administrative instruments, including administrative guidance, tax breaks, and organizing joint-research projects.

For bureaucratic representatives, the expansion of the sector they were administering was in their organizational interest, as well as in the national interest. By strengthening their clients, bureaucrats could expand their organizations. It would mean more budget, more posts, and higher prestige for their department. Besides, the clients would reward them by offering lucrative postretirement jobs to bureaucrats.

The role of political parties, however, should not be underestimated. They certainly did not work out detailed strategy for the economic development. Yet they worked as agents for various interest groups to bring as much fruit of the expanding economy as possible to their constituencies. Thus, the ruling conservative party secured support of farmers by subsidizing them. The Socialist party bargained hard to ensure pay raises for organized labor in the public sector. These policies obviously cost tax money, but with the economy growing at a pace of more than 10 percent a year, it was relatively easy to accommodate various demands from various sectors at the same time. Thus, subsidization and protection were mostly applied to the inefficient sectors. The strong lobbies in Japan have not necessarily been big businesses, but rather have been well-organized sectors like farmers, fishermen, and tightly organized trade unions.

This type of redistribution policy is not what standard economic theory would prescribe. Because subsidizing inefficient sectors would distort the price mechanism, standard economic theory would call for income support, such as unemployment benefits and job training for the unemployed. The sociopolitical costs of massive unemployment from agricultural sectors, however, would have been overwhelming. A huge number of hard-hit farmers, even if they were financially supported, would have lost self-esteem and a strong motivation to work. The local community would have totally disintegrated, destabilizing social order and political stability.

The whole system, of course, was not designed by a small number of bureaucrats; it was a product of trial and error. However it is undeniable that the system worked wonderfully while reproducing itself. The competitive industries took full advantage of world economic growth, as well as favorable business environments at home. Uncompetitive sectors were handsomely subsidized through various means. Though this did not halt a rapid shift of labor forces from declining sectors to ascending sectors, sociopolitical stability was maintained. Bureaucracy, while promoting the interests of their clients, could also satisfy its organizational interests.

Thus, postwar, Japanese politicoeconomic system was characterized by close interrelations between state and society. Though it certainly was not a state-dominant system (because of the tightly knitted networks between private and public sectors), the whole method was replete with state presence. At the same time, within a well-managed framework set by public authorities, strong competition has existed among private enterprises.

Yet the Japanese system can never continue infinite expansion. Both internal and external tensions are becoming increasingly noticeable. Tensions are deeprooted and structural in nature, because they are related to basic and irreversible changes surrounding the Japanese politicoeconomic system.

Changing Basic Conditions and Growing Tensions

Postwar Japanese economic success evidently improved the standard of living for the Japanese; the improvement, however, was not as impressive as its national statistics suggest. Despite the fact that Japan is now the world's second-largest economy, the everyday lives of its citizens are hugely dominated by work, and their personal lives are still poor. In other words, they have sacrificed amenity of their personal lives for the sake of future productivity. Relatively small current spending, short holidays, and modest housing were tolerated for the dynamic growth of the Japanese economy. Today, this is inevitably perceived to be increasingly illegitimate, as well as an irrational sacrifice for a vast majority of the Japanese whose per capita Gross National Product (GNP) is now even larger that of the United States.

From an international viewpoint, economic growth is becoming an unattractive national goal for Japan. Its success certainly gave it a higher political status in the world, but it is creating increasingly serious international criticism, rather than respect. As Japanese hear voices calling for "containing Japan," and when their financial contribution to the multilateral efforts during the Persian Gulf war was looked down upon as "checkbook diplomacy," they naturally wonder if further economic growth is the proper international role for Japan.

The affluent society resulting from postwar economic success caused irreversible societal changes. While materialism does not motivate people per se, the desire for many different values is attractive. The enormous variety of people' wants cannot simply be satisfied by a choice of state bureaucracy. For example, so-called "life-time employment" made sense for both employee and employer when Japan was poor. For employees, the merit was obvious: the long-term certainty of a job, albeit gained at the expense of the inflexibility of their lifestyle. While the risks and costs involved in changing jobs were big, even their personal lives could be easily dominated by their employers. However, trading one's lifestyle for job security is becoming an unattractive choice for increasing numbers of younger-generation Japanese. This is evidently a result of decreasing risk and cost of unemployment in Japan, resulting from the affluence brought to the Japanese by postwar economic success.

Thus, economic growth is no longer the unquestionable supreme national goal. As a result of the emergence of an affluent society in Japan, the politicoeconomic system designed to maximize productivity can no longer enjoy strong support. Increasingly, people are becoming more and more reluctant to swap the amenity of their personal lives for the sake of an obsolete national goal.

Systemic Immobility

The changed preferences of the Japanese people do not directly translate into changed economic performances of the entire system. The well-established system outlives national needs. The redistribution system, which was constructive in protecting groups vulnerable to the rapid changes associated with industrialization and in limiting the gap between the rich and poor, has inevitably created vested interests in the system.

Japanese agricultural labor dropped from 40 percent of the total workforce in 1960 to only 6.5 percent in 1990. Additionally, a great many of these 6.5 percent are part-time farmers, who receive more income from nonagricultural engagement. Despite its reduced importance, tight protection for this inefficient sector continues. The Agricultural Coop, which enjoyed many privileges, has steadily expanded its scale, now employing as many as 300,000 people while the number of full-time farm households has fallen to only 460,000.

Public investment projects administered by the government are another sound example of an obsolete policy. The distribution pattern of public works has been fixed for a long time, giving a large portion of funds to fishing ports and agricultural infrastructure while the increasing needs of the urban population—like sewage and public parks—are not met by a corresponding increase in the share of resource allocations. The reason is that every public-investment project is associated with vested interests among the bureaucracy, politicians, and various interest groups.

Curtailing the obsolete regulations and protection is admittedly very difficult, since the large presence of the state in the private economy gives strong opportunities for politicians to work as brokers of interests. Organized interests in Japan, like everywhere else in the world, reward politicians with political funds and votes in exchange for continued protection in their vested interests. Those among the bureaucracy who remain outside the interest network are put in handicapped positions.

Thus, it is becoming more and more noticeable that the postwar Japanese politicoeconomic system is degenerating into the immobile system of vested interests, coupled with structural political corruptions. The state intervention into economic life no longer looks like a legitimate national policy. Under such a condition, the social contract between state bureaucracy and people cannot be maintained. The authority and autonomy of the elite are coming under growing, popular resentment.

Changing International Conditions

The redistribution policy was never designed to exclude foreigners. It generally works, however, against new entrants into the market, including competitors from abroad. Small mom-and-pop shops in Tokyo streets are fairly wellprotected by regulations against large retail shops, including foreign-owned chain stores. The price support for Japanese rice farmers also shuts out foreign producers from the Japanese market; these measures have been working against both Japanese consumers and foreign producers. As we have already seen, Japanese consumers no longer see suppressing consumption as a legitimate policy. Moreover, the system is increasingly intolerable for foreign competitors, and it is causing economic friction between Japan and other industrialized countries.

When Japan was a relatively small economy, such a protective measure could be easily treated as a trivial deviation from the norm. But when Japanese products flood international markets—forcing uncompetitive foreign producers out—Japan's policy to protect their uncompetitive sectors cannot fail to look like an excessive double standard.

Of course, protective measure exist in every country. And indeed, the level of nontariff trade barriers in the Japanese market is difficult to measure. While many Japanese authors cannot help having an impression that Western allegation over the closed nature of Japanese markets is exaggerated, it is inevitable that the Japanese will receive stronger attention on its misbehavior from abroad, as the Japanese economic presence in the world becomes greater.

More importantly, the end of the Cold War has changed the basic conditions surrounding the Japanese economy. The United States has lost motivation to accommodate competition from Japan in international markets, for reasons of national security. It is true that trade frictions have always existed between Japan and Western countries. The tensions, however, were controlled by the strong U.S. desire to maintain a vital security alliance with Japan. Without an immediate and noticeable military threat, economic interests gain larger voices in politics and become increasingly important factors in international relations.

The increasing tension surrounding economic relations with Western countries is intensified by the perceived decline of American and European economies. A rising power always faces difficulties in getting into the established pattern of existing international order. Many Japanese economic practices that did not attract attention when the nation was economically small are now viewed with growing suspicion. In part due to Japan's non-Western origin, international environments are getting ever more hostile to the existing Japanese system.

Completed Catch-Up Process

Although industrial targeting — coupled with redistribution policy — has been generally successful, it admittedly was a difficult task. As pointed out earlier, not all targeted industries were successful, and many important Japanese industries did not receive strong government support. Nevertheless, it is true that the MITI made a vigorous effort, at least up until the mid-1960s, to foster strategic industries.

The criteria the MITI used to select target industries are two-fold, being based on technological and income-elasticity criteria. An industry with strong possibility for technological innovation would have a better chance for high productivity in the future. An industry that produces goods with high-income elasticity would also enjoy an expanded market.

But the problem is that predicting future technological innovation was possible only because Japan was catching up with advanced economies in the West. By introducing and improving Western technology, one could foresee with a reasonable level of accuracy the future possibility of technological development. Yet what does one do when there is nobody to catch up with? This is the question Japan now faces.

With Japan's technological catch-up complete, it has now to lead, rather than catch-up with, industries abroad. Once you are in position to lead, the state is far less effective in finding a promising field. Innovation happens rather randomly out of individual initiatives. The failure of the recent state-concerted effort to develop the so-called "fifth generation computer" is indicative of this. State-led efforts have become less and less workable. Rather it is quite possible that the existing system is hindering dynamic and innovative adjustment of Japanese development through obsolete regulations and controls.

Conclusion

While one can easily agree that strong discipline of market forces must be coupled with redistribution policy, strong state intervention is also a risky endeavor. Close exchanges between private and public sectors can quickly slip into a rigid and corrupt mechanism for protecting vested interests. Here lies a dilemma between the merits of impersonal market mechanism and a need for state intervention to alleviate excessive pains caused by market forces. Between the market and the state, there is no categorically correct answer, because both can fail.

In postwar Japan, several factors allowed the state to play generally positive roles and prevented the state bureaucracy from degenerating into a corrupt protector of vested interests. There existed general, sociopolitical acknowledgement of the goal the bureaucracy should pursue. Their role was well defined within the framework of a social contract, which helped secure the impartiality of bureaucracy. But as the postwar Japanese politicoeconomic system was a product of a certain set of historical conditions, the system is now rapidly changing in response to the alterations in these conditions. As a mature economy with a large international presence, Japan has to further deregulate and liberalize its economic growth. It has to find its own way to solve problems shared by other rich countries.

Thus, Japan's system does not offer the future model for the affluent world. When Japan was small, it could be accommodated. But the world's second-largest economy, characterized by industrial targeting and active redistribution policy, is inconsistent with the interests of the rest of the globe. More importantly, the Japanese system is no longer attractive for the Japanese themselves.

For many developing countries, however, the Japanese model could be an attractive one to follow. Protecting vulnerable people from excessively painful market forces is obviously essential for human needs. On the other hand, strong state intervention into economies can only create political corruption and systemic immobility, unless a mechanism exists to check the behavior of the bureaucracy. State bureaucracy can never be impartial and honest on its own; it is only broader politicoeconomic contexts that allow it to play positive and effective roles in a national economy. Thus, East Asian developmentalist models characterized by active state bureaucracies cannot simply be applied to other developing countries. There must be sociopolitical conditions and a mechanism to encourage the positive role of the state bureaucracy, while at the same time limiting abuse and corruption of its power.

There is a lesson to be learned for developed countries as well. As postwar Japan's experiences show, exposure to the international market has far stronger impacts on the economies of the developing world. Accommodating rapidly developing economies into the international market requires a painful adjustment at home for industrialized countries. It is doubtful if rich countries with high unemployment rates can welcome stronger competition from abroad by giving up uncompetitive industries, and allowing the shift of labor force from the losing industry to a new sector.

We are already seeing ominous symptoms. Some rich countries are starting to blame cheap labor in the developing world as social dumping. The criticism is particularly familiar for the Japanese, since they were subject to the same charge when they tried to penetrate into the world market. Whether or not forcing higher standards of labor conditions on developing countries is a matter of human rights or hypocritical protectionism, the improvement of labor conditions cannot be helped by impoverishing already poor economies.

The responsibility of industrialized countries, therefore, is both crucial and difficult. On one hand, they have to resist temptation for protectionism. While accommodating the industrial catch-up of developing countries by forcing painful adjustment on themselves, they have to acquiesce aggressive developmentalist strategy of poor countries.

Japan's role in this context is clear. As the second-largest economy and the largest creditor in the world, it has to absorb imports from the developing world. As a relatively new and the first non-Western member of the global "rich men's club" (with fresh memories of difficulties during its own modernization), nothing is more suitable for Japan than actively encouraging the incorporation of economically developing countries into the world. Admittedly, this remains a difficult task; however the alternative — enjoying isolated prosperity in the midst of poverty and misery for a huge number of people — is not only ugly, but also impossible.

Chapter 3

Measures for the Enhancement of Social Cohesion

Section 1

Globalization and Social Integration

Dharam Ghai and
Cynthia Hewitt de Alcántara

"Social integration" is a broad and ambiguous term, variously understood by different people. To some, it is a positive goal, implying the promotion of well ordered and harmonious relations at all levels of society. To others, increasing integration has a negative connotation, conjuring up the image of an unwanted imposition of uniformity. For a third group, the term implies neither a positive nor a negative state. It is simply an invitation to analyze the established patterns of human relations and values that tie people to one another in any given time and place, defining the parameters of their life chances.

This section adopts the latter approach. Patterns and processes of integration are phenomena to be studied, not goals to be attained. Accepting such a premise makes it easier to explore the underlying causes of growing violence, deepening inequality, and lack of solidarity throughout much of the world.

Bases of Integration

No one goes through life alone. All of us are created within, and influenced by, networks of social relations that provide our identity and establish a framework for our actions. We pursue goals within a structure of institutions ranging from our families or households, clans, or neighborhoods or communities (where we seek primary support and protection), to the schools, associations, street gangs, or video parlors (in which we are trained); and the smallholdings, plantations, factories, sweatshops, stores, and offices (in which we work). On a more general level, our opportunities are affected by larger political and economic structures, ranging from tribal councils or municipal governments to the nation-state, and from nonmonetary exchange relations among friends to the international financial system.

As soon as it is remembered that it is virtually impossible for any human being anywhere to survive entirely on his/her own, it becomes obvious that terms like exclusion, inclusion, disintegration, and integration must be used carefully. Neither exclusion nor disintegration can ever be absolute; therefore one must not fall into the trap of supposing that the roots of our current social dilemma can be clarified by relying on simple dichotomies between exclusion and inclusion, or disintegration and integration.

Setting the Stage for Social Integration

Patterns of social integration are shaped by dominant trends in politics, economics, culture, and technology. In this respect, the context for social integration has changed radically over the past two decades. Of the many important and far-reaching changes that have taken place, six are especially pertinent.

Democracy and Individual Freedom

In the realm of politics, the most remarkable change has been the collapse of communism in Eastern Europe and the former Soviet Union, and the progressive replacement of one-party, military and authoritarian regimes by multiparty systems in many parts of the world. This opens up new possibilities for participation and creates opportunities for the flourishing of a wide range of voluntary associations and interest groups.

Such organizations may widen and deepen bonds of solidarity and citizenship. But they may also become focal points for the accentuation of ancient rivalries and the creation of new divisions along territorial or cultural lines. This is particularly likely when a sudden collapse of authoritarian regimes reveals a void in institutions and values.

It is perhaps important to point out that the interest in greater individual freedom, which is currently sweeping the world, is not always a positive force for democracy. It certainly may be so when emphasis is placed on asserting the worth of every human being and proclaiming the right of each person to express his or her opinions. But freedom can be sought for a number of reasons that have little to do with political representation or tolerance. A great many people are, for example, currently engaged in a search for the freedom to make money or to define personal lifestyles. Extreme individualism can be associated with intolerance and disrespect for the rights of others.

Market Forces

The turn toward liberal democracy and the search for individual freedom have been preceded or accompanied by a worldwide shift in favor of market forces and private enterprise in the management and organization of the economy. The origins of this latest burst in economic liberalization may be traced to the crisis experienced by industrialized countries in the aftermath of the sharp increases in oil prices of the 1970s; but the new doctrine has since attracted an ever-increasing number of adherents in countries around the world, including the communist regimes of East and Southeast Asia.

This dramatic shift in policy is manifested in such changes as the steady retreat of the state from intervention in the economy, the phasing out of administrative and quantitative controls as tools of economic management, price liberalization and deregulation of utilities and services, privatization, reduction of budget deficits, control of inflation, and more generally in stabilization and structural adjustment policies and programs.

Increasing reliance on and liberalization of markets has profoundly altered the economic and political context for social integration. It has contributed to major changes in the configuration of power relations among different social groups and countries. For instance, it seems clear that the organized working class has been greatly weakened, while transnational enterprises, owners of capital, and some managerial and professional groups have been significantly strengthened.

Economic liberalization has unleashed fierce competition nationally and internationally. Although this has often led to gains in static efficiency in resource use, in the short to medium run at least, it has also driven down wages and contributed to increases in unemployment, poverty, and inequalities, and thus to accentuation of economic insecurity. Such problems have been exacerbated by the elimination or reduction of subsidies on goods and services of mass consumption, by substitution of indirect for direct taxes, and by cuts in social services and welfare benefits.

Economic Integration

Economic liberalization has removed impediments to the worldwide expansion of trade in goods and services. At the same time, innovations in technology, communications, and transport have provided fresh stimulus for capital, enterprise, technology, and skills to move across national frontiers.

The worldwide scope of these financial markets—which have recently expanded to include "emerging" markets in a number of Asian, Eastern European, and Latin American countries—combined with the unprecedented volume of current investment in them increases the danger of sudden instability within the global economy. The destinies of people from all walks of life are linked as never before through such highly interdependent investment networks. Transnational enterprises are the predominant actors in the continuing process of global economic integration, controlling almost 75 percent of all world trade in commodities, manufactured goods, and services. Obviously, the power of transnational corporations in the market significantly reduces the degree to which globalization can be easily equated with the creation of "free" or "competitive" markets, and increases the likelihood that liberalization will be associated with managed competition. While globalization provides some countries and regions with opportunities for accelerated growth, it may worsen the performance of others through flight of capital, skills, and enterprise, and competition from stronger economies.

Production Systems and Labor Markets

Changes in production systems and labor markets are also profoundly affecting patterns of social integration around the world. In manufacturing production, for example, the importance of raw materials and unskilled labor appears to be declining, while that of skills and knowledge is increasing in a wide range of economic activities. Because the availability of cheap labor has underwritten the comparative advantage of many developing countries in their efforts to attract foreign direct investment, longer term trends favoring highly trained personnel over the unskilled will present difficulties for many developing economies.

In addition, technological progress and organizational reform appear to be weakening the relationship between expansion of output and growth of employment. Industrial employment is thus likely to shrink. This is a qualitative change of the first order in the structure of opportunity of most societies around the globe.

All of these trends will worsen the existing trend toward an increase in part-time, informal, and insecure jobs, involving a growing number of women workers.

Technological Change

Rapid technological change—especially in electronics, communications, transport, and biotechnology—is one of the key features of the contemporary world. Its effects are evident everywhere, in the invention of new products and services, methods of management, and organization of production. Technological breakthroughs transform work relations, destroy existing jobs and create new ones, and alter patterns of consumption and leisure activity. They have drastically reduced the importance of distance in economic activity and made global communication both relatively inexpensive and virtually instantaneous. Thus they affect the distribution of power among different social groups, between governments and civil society, and among states.

The Media Revolution and Global Consumerism

The sixth major force for change can be found in the impact of the media on culture, social relations, and institutions. Recent years have witnessed an extraordinary expansion in the reach and influence of the media. While the written word and press have acquired increasing importance, the really revolutionary developments have taken place in television and video. The images and messages transmitted through these media influence the thinking, behavior, and values of hundreds of millions of people.

The revolution in mass communications, which encourages the creation of a global culture, has great potential for promoting understanding and solidarity, and enhancing knowledge throughout the world. In its present form, it also has an awesome capacity to exalt consumerism. This can represent a serious challenge to traditional values. Furthermore, the instant and widespread transmission of news, especially of a sensational and dramatic nature, seems to encourage some people to emulate these exploits in order to obtain publicity or to achieve other objectives through violent means.

Exclusion and Inclusion

The incorporation of very large numbers of people around the world into a global culture — holding out the promise of participation in an affluent consumer society and the exercise of greater individual freedom — occurs during a period when developments in the world economy in fact profoundly restrict the life chances of many.   The picture of wealth and leisure transmitted by mass media thus frequently stands in harsh contrast to a real world of increasing deprivation. This contradictory process of simultaneous inclusion (in the realm of the imagination) and marginalization (in day-to-day material terms) must be highlighted when considering the grave social problems of our times.

At the same time, the ability of governments to provide social services and compensatory support has been severely curtailed, both out of economic necessity and as the result of a growing perception that the size of the public sector should be significantly reduced. In the industrialized countries, the reduction in social benefits has been stimulated by increasing budget deficits, themselves a consequence of slow growth and high levels of unemployment, as well as by the revolt of taxpayers against tax increases and by a feeling that existing programs of social support for those without work may encourage chronic unemployment.

The crisis is most acute in Central and Eastern European countries, whose people have been faced with overnight collapse of a system of full employment and a range of comprehensive social benefits, as well as by sharp reductions in living standards. In developing countries, stabilization and structural adjustment have required implementing policies which tend — at least in the short to medium term — to worsen under- and unemployment, reduce wages, limit the range and quality of social services, and eliminate or cut subsidies on goods and services of mass consumption.

Ironically, the impoverishment of increasing numbers of people through-out the world — and often their growing inability to meet even the most basic requirements for food, water, shelter, education, and medical attention — occurs during a period when the incomes of the very rich have risen markedly.

This noteworthy process of polarization can also be observed among regions. While growth in some areas of Asia has been remarkable over the past two decades, most African countries lag further and further behind in the sharpening competition to capture a portion of the world's wealth.

As opportunity is concentrated in certain regions and countries and in particular economic sectors, one of the most obvious responses on the part of those threatened with exclusion or marginalization is to migrate, whether within countries or abroad. And over the past few decades this has become a central element in the livelihood strategy of millions.

Migration, like the revolution in communications technology, both integrates and divides. For the well educated, or relatively affluent, migration is simply a means to improve life chances: to obtain a better job, to enjoy more personal freedom or a different style of life. Receiving countries or cities generally welcome the transfer of wealth and knowledge inherent in this kind of immigration, although it signifies a loss for the societies and economies left behind.

Larger-scale migration by poorer people can imply greater impoverishment and disruption of existing forms of social organization in communities and regions of origin of migrants, particularly when most able-bodied members of households depart, leaving the young and the old to cope as best they can. Nevertheless the potential for improving the level of living of migrants' families is also considerable, as remittances are sent home and invested. Some migrants get ahead, and some find departure from their place of origin a form of liberation from oppressive obligations. In all too many instances, however, migration remains a harsh necessity − a last resort involving privation and not infrequently the danger of physical harm.

In major receiving countries, international migration creates enormous problems of social integration and cultural adaptation that are currently at the center of the policy debate. The juxtaposition of people who often share neither a common language nor a common religion, and who have very different customs, makes unusual demands on human tolerance and understanding. The arrival of large numbers of foreigners also creates unusual strains on existing social services and local economies.

Changing Values, Behavior, and Institutions

All of these developments − advancing globalization accompanied by the strengthening of relatively unregulated world market forces, deepening polarization and immiseration, a revolution in communications and transport, new aspirations for greater individual freedom − are associated with deeper changes in the most basic institutions of society. These involve both modification of existing bonds and patterns of behavior, and the creation of new forms of interaction and obligation. Although this is obviously a very complex subject, some underlying currents of social change will be explored below.

Adaptation and Modification of Family Structures

Families in different parts of the world vary so markedly in composition and function that it is impossible to make a simple statement about developments within them. In many parts of the industrialized world, traditional nuclear families, composed of two parents and their children, are declining in importance, as single-parent households increase in number. Rising divorce rates, as well as the growing number of children born to unmarried parents, can be taken to indicate a "disintegration of the [traditional nuclear] family."

In the industrial world, single-parent households, most often headed by women, are usually the poorest. This, as many analysts have noted, is because there is only one adult income earner, because women tend to receive lower wages than men, and because their double burden of child care and work outside the home leaves them less time for the latter.

This is also the case in areas of the developing world in which two-parent families (often extended to include grandparents, aunts, and uncles) are the ideal. Nevertheless it is important to note that self-contained two-parent families are not the norm in many parts of the world, where women and children may traditionally live with the former's extended family, or with other wives and children of a common father. There is no direct link between female-headed households and poverty under these conditions.

Longer working hours at lower pay, more frequent periods of unemployment, and other trends associated with economic retrenchment and changing production practices are placing an enormous burden on low-income households throughout the world. They are also weakening the capacity of families, whatever their composition, to care for their young. Under contemporary conditions, every able-bodied family member must often work, and this increasingly includes children. Although such a trend can be called "disintegration," it should probably more aptly be labeled "degradation": households may stay together, but under such difficult circumstances that the quality of interpersonal relations deteriorates markedly.

Permanent migration of some members of a household does, of course, promote disintegration of the family in many areas of the developing world. So does temporary migration, when virtually all able-bodied adults must make a living somewhere else, leaving grandparents to take care of children, as is increasingly the case in rural areas hard hit by economic crisis and adjustment. Yet heroic efforts are made by millions of migrants to keep their families together, and their departure in search of work is in fact often the central element in a strategy to provide for the continuity of their households.

A final, tragic element in the disintegration of households in some parts of the world at the end of the twentieth century is civil strife. The indiscriminate killing of civilian populations that characterizes wars like those in Cambodia, Rwanda, or Somalia decimates families and leaves a legacy of millions of widows, widowers, and orphans.

The Weakening of Communities and Neighborhoods

Globalization reduces the importance of social bonds based upon residence or place of work, and creates new relations which do not depend upon "groundedness" or "place." In developed and newly industrialized countries, for example, where informatics increasingly dominate the workplace, the life chances of people begin to depend less on their daily interaction with fellow workers than on management of distant relations through computers.

At the same time, the credo of extreme individualism that gained favor among many during the 1970s and 1980s has made it publicly acceptable — and perhaps even fashionable — for large numbers of people to renounce responsibility for the welfare of others. If the free market, driven by individual interests, is accorded supremacy in strategies to promote development, then it becomes harder to justify a call for sacrifices to be made by individuals, in the name of the common good. Stunning examples of the socially destructive character of extreme individualism can now be found in the former socialist world, where the collapse of an egalitarian ideology has created an opening for daring, and sometimes violent, attempts on the part of new "entrepreneurs" to appropriate the property of neighbors and coworkers.

Deepening poverty and associated migratory trends also pose serious challenges to community solidarity in the majority of developing world and former socialist countries, as well as in China. Agrarian communities, which have provided the primary framework for local level cooperation in developing countries, are being torn apart by contradictory forces associated with globalization and recession.

A further element of stress that poses a sharp challenge to existing mechanisms of social solidarity—whether traditional institutions or modern programs—in both urban and rural settings is, of course, the accommodation of refugees. In an age marked by a growing flood of people fleeing violence and persecution, local communities must often make extraordinary efforts to provide for the uprooted. The fragile resource base of poor rural areas can be strained to the breaking point by the massive influx of refugees, and the local labor market forced into dangerous surplus. As in the towns and cities of the developed countries, the degree to which cultural differences can be accommodated within the existing structure of social relations is also problematic.

Changes in Civil Society

"Civil society" is an extremely ambiguous term. In many cases, it is used as a catchword that is difficult to distinguish from "society" itself. Here it will refer to the network of associations and interest groups formed to accomplish certain goals, further certain causes, or defend particular interests outside the structure of political institutions directly associated with the state.

Until recently, in countries characterized by one-party rule, the kind of independent association necessary to constitute a civil society was generally proscribed. Over large areas of the world, people therefore pursued their interests through channels controlled by the government. This situation is changing markedly, as steps are taken to replace authoritarian regimes with nominally democratic political systems. There is thus a new opening for citizens' initiatives in situations of transition to democracy, whether in China, Eastern Europe, the former Soviet Union, or the developing nations. And such initiatives are being encouraged by the international development community, which is currently committed to strengthening what have become known as "nongovernmental organizations" through channeling an increasing proportion of available funds for aid and relief to that sector.

Since it is a truism that neither democracy nor development can be achieved without effective organization of people to pursue common intercsts, the awakening of civil society in many parts of the world is a heartening sign. Nevertheless some cautionary words would seem in order.

First, it should be remembered that under authoritarian regimes, the kinds of associations that permit a certain limited expression of independent identity are often based upon religious or ethnic loyalties. This "civil society," although truncated, may be better developed than any secular or nonethnic alternative when the transition to democracy begins; it should therefore not be surprising that exclusionary and messianic forms of organization can gain prominence in this context.

Groups may be formed to defend some very unsavory interests. At the same time, organizations that spring up to defend very worthy causes may prove totally ineffective. Both observations suggest that the apparent burgeoning of private associations is not a sufficient indicator of progress. The strengthening of civil society must be based not only on organizing drive, but more importantly on the broadening and deepening of a kind of "civic culture," which presupposes adherence to certain universal values and acceptance of workable rules for the adjudication of interests and the protection of the weak.

Furthermore, the effective exercise of citizens' initiatives presupposes the existence of a functioning governmental structure based on law. And government in turn depends upon a relatively stable and widely accepted political system. These obvious points become less obvious when seen from the perspective of societies totally shattered by civil war or engaged in a revolutionary change of regime.

Governance and Social Integration

The combination of institutions, laws, procedures, and norms, which allows people to express their concerns and fight for their interests within a predictable and relatively equitable context, forms the basis of good governance. Efficient administration of public resources is an additional element in this definition. Contemporary concern with exclusion and social disintegration reflects not only the perception that structures of governance in the developing world are failing to provide a minimally acceptable framework for processing the demands of most people, but also that the political and administrative systems of the industrial nations are increasingly unable to live up to the expectations of their citizens.

Part of the problem is obviously ethical; part is most certainly structural. Corruption scandals have rocked a great many governments in the past few years. The situation is greatly complicated by the interpenetration of leading business groups of different countries. The development of transnational enterprises over the past four decades has created conditions in which national boundaries became increasingly irrelevant for giant conglomerates. These developments divide established interest groups, creating new alliances among subgroups with particularistic links to the international economy. National labor movements, for example, suffer new forms of division. Business groups split into opposing factions based upon differing access to international markets. Political parties, which have aggregated interests in relatively stable patterns over a number of years in many countries, are therefore increasingly likely to confront the threat of fragmentation, instability and ineffectiveness.

In a great many industrialized and developing countries, economic crisis and adjustment have simultaneously promoted a deep reduction in government expenditure on administration, regulation, and the provision of general services, ranging from health and education to the maintenance of roads and other vital infrastructure. Especially in the developing countries, as well as countries of Eastern Europe and the former Soviet Union, the quality of public administration and social services has often dropped markedly, as staff is laid off and salaries cut. Once again, this reinforces a public perception of incompetence on the part of the state. When services are subsequently privatized, this may improve their efficiency. Nevertheless the introduction of fees simultaneously reduces the coverage of the programs involved and sharply lessens access to them on the part of low-income families.

The progressive segmentation of social services is in fact related to an important change of direction in social welfare policy. Over wide areas of the world, the very idea that governments have the obligation to ensure a certain minimum level of welfare for all citizens is being challenged on both economic and ideological grounds.

For many people — particularly in Africa, Eastern Europe, Latin America, and the former Soviet Union — the existing state is becoming increasingly less relevant to the satisfaction of their everyday needs. The explosion of the informal sector, under the impact of economic crisis and restructuring, is one of the clearest symptoms of this trend. Growing numbers of people provide for themselves without contributing through taxes to the maintenance of public services or receiving the protection and benefits that have been stipulated in national laws.

The question of how the rapidly growing informal sector is being — or can be — integrated into new political coalitions, so that the interests of the many groups within it can be effectively represented in widely based and relatively stable structures of governance, is an important and difficult one. The extraordinary heterogeneity of this "sector," as well as the often semi-illicit nature of activities within it, constitutes difficult terrain for the construction of political pacts within national political systems which are democratic, or engaged in a transition to democracy.

Over a significant part of the world today, the struggle to create relatively more democratic political systems and to defend elemental human rights is being undermined by the growing strength of criminal organizations. In countries from Colombia to Thailand, from Pakistan to Russia, the resources which can be marshalled by these syndicates rival or surpass those of governments themselves. In the specific case of the drug trade, which is said to control the second most important commodity in international commerce (after petroleum), the revenue recycled by drug syndicates determines the viability of a number of national economies; and the political fate of some governments depends to a considerable degree on negotiations with such interests.

In summary, then, developments in the global economy and society are posing increasingly complex problems for political and administrative institutions at both local and national levels. Some of these problems must be addressed at least in part through institutional innovation at the international level.

Social Integration in Multiethnic Societies

Many of the problems discussed above are magnified and distorted within the context of multiethnic societies. Most countries in the world are of course to some degree multiethnic: they contain a number of groups distinguished by differences of language, religion, tribe, and/or race. Nevertheless the historical processes creating ethnic difference, as well as the challenges posed to public policy by the latter, vary greatly by country and region. In consequence, some have been more successful than others in attempting to forge tolerant and just societies.

Western Europe

Despite the fact that the unified nation-state was forged in Europe, most states on the continent comprise many different ethnic groups brought together by conquest, colonial expansion, and migration. The countries of Western Europe, in particular, are currently faced with two major ethnic problems: the older problem of accommodating the demands of "nationalities," such as the Basques, Britons, Catalans, Flemish, Irish, Walloons, and so forth; and the newer problem posed by postwar immigrants, first from developing countries and currently from countries of Central and Eastern Europe.

Most countries have been able to accommodate the older problem, although it continues to pose challenges in some cases, such as Northern Ireland and Belgium, and to emerge in new contexts, like that of the Lombardy League in Italy. The consolidation and expansion of the European Union both stimulates regional nationalisms and provides a framework for their accommodation. The presence of newer minorities, however, constitutes a much more serious policy challenge in Western Europe. The rise of far right parties on the strength of their anti-immigrant slogans, as well as a growing wave of violence and harassment directed against minorities in several West European countries in recent years, represent a dramatic manifestation of underlying tensions and policy ambiguities.

The presence of migrants from Asia and Africa is a legacy of the colonial empires of European powers. Small numbers of these immigrants, already resident in Western Europe in the early postwar years, were swollen by waves of new arrivals in the 1960s and early 1970s, drawn by booming economies and labor shortages in the region. There was, however, a virtual cessation of immigration from developing countries following the first oil shock and the accompanying economic slump. Recession and unemployment in the 1990s have led to a further intensification of restrictions on immigration throughout Western Europe.

Governments of Western European countries have developed at least four different approaches to dealing with ethnic problems: separation, toleration, cultural pluralism, and assimilation. Separation, exemplified by the German experience, is based on the policy of treating migrants as temporary workers who will at some stage return to their countries of origin. Residence is therefore tied to work permits and employers assume responsibility for provision of hostels and other forms of accommodation. The approach of the United Kingdom, in contrast, is characterized by toleration. Integration is defined as equal opportunity, accompanied by cultural diversity, in an atmosphere of mutual tolerance. Equal opportunities are promoted through enforceable antidiscrimination legislation rather than through the creation of positive programs to benefit ethnic minorities.

The Netherlands and Sweden have been the leading proponents of cultural pluralism. Although during an earlier period migrants in the Netherlands had been treated as guest workers, as in Germany, the Dutch government assumed the responsibility in the 1980s to help minorities preserve, develop, and express their cultural identity. At the same time, alarm over continuing marginalization of minorities has encouraged the Dutch to shift the focus of policy toward combating deprivation. In recent years, there seems also to have been a subtle shift in French policy towards encouragement of cultural pluralism, despite the fact that in the 1960s and 1970s, the emphasis in France had been on assimilation of ethnic minorities to national culture or repatriation to the country of origin.

It is evident that, while considerable progress has been made in ensuring a relatively secure legal status, as well as de jure equal treatment in such areas as housing, employment, and education for most immigrants in Western Europe, no line of policy has proved totally effective in removing socioeconomic barriers to upward mobility. Approaches adopted by governments have evolved and have become more flexible, but clearly the factors responsible for the continuing subordinate socioeconomic status of ethnic minorities are stubborn and complex.

Central and Eastern Europe

The historical experience of Central and Eastern Europe has been radically different from that of Western Europe in at least two respects. First, most of the people in this region have been accustomed to live in states that were specifically defined as multinational and multicultural. This was the case not only under the Austro-Hungarian, Ottoman, and Russian empires, but also after the break-up of these empires in the aftermath of World War I. Most of the new "nation-states" — particularly the Soviet Union and Yugoslavia, but also in varying degrees Czechoslovakia, Hungary, and Romania — continued in the interwar period to display characteristics of sharp ethnic and cultural diversity.

The second distinguishing feature of the Eastern and Central European experience is of course that the population of this region lived under communism for periods ranging from four to seven decades. Communist states displayed an ambivalent attitude toward the question of "nationalities." On the one hand, ethnic inequalities and other culturally defined differences were attributed to the operation of the capitalist system. It was assumed that with the establishment of socialism such differences would disappear. Indeed the dominance of the working class and the achievement of economic equality were supposed to deal a mortal blow to the ethnic problem. On the other hand, some versions of communist doctrine insisted on the principle of the sovereignty of nationalities and their voluntary association in a commonwealth of republics or multinational federations. Reality, however, seldom conformed to these ideals. In practically all communist states for most of the time, while superficial expressions of national identity were tolerated and indeed encouraged, power was highly concentrated in the central committees and politburos of communist parties. In some countries, systematic efforts were made to erase all markers of ethnic identity.

The collapse of communism has been followed by a veritable explosion of ethnic conflict. The eruption of ethnic violence is perhaps most attributable to the situation created by the sudden collapse of the communist system. The abrupt disintegration of the latter created a formal institutional vacuum. With the discrediting of the communist party, which constituted the center of political and social organization, there were few institutions that could provide a viable and legitimate basis for any kind of organized activity. In this respect, a fatal weakness of the system was the paucity of autonomous institutions of civil society. At the same time, there was widespread rejection of the values associated with communism. Furthermore, this institutional and moral crisis coincided with a profound economic crisis, which produced a massive decline in living standards and the collapse of the social security system. Under the circumstances, it is understandable that people turned to ethnicity in their search for security and identity, and that leaders succeeded in exploiting cultural differences for political ends.

The English-Speaking New World

The industrial countries of the English-speaking New World share many of the problems of Western Europe with regard to integration of ethnic minorities. Unlike Western Europe, however, the former were created as immigrant countries of relatively recent origin. Their societies have been formed through the interaction of people of European origin, on the one hand, and indigenous minorities, descendants of slaves or indentured workers, and new immigrants from the developing countries, on the other.

The experience of the United States with the integration of ethnic minorities is especially revealing. First, it illustrates with dramatic force the bitter legacy of large-scale slavery, whose consequences are still to be found in many areas of national life. Second, it can provide insights on the impact of a de facto apartheid system, which functioned for nearly a century. The South African experiment with apartheid was merely a more formalized and ruthless version of the American model. Third, over the past four decades beginning with the struggle over civil rights, the United States has probably made a more systematic effort than any other country to come to terms with the ethnic dimensions of social integration. Fourth, the country continues to keep its doors open, even if on a modest scale, to immigrants from developing countries at a time when many other doors are closed.

Thus, in terms of diversity and size of ethnic groups, the United States is without parallel. In a certain sense, its experience can be considered the first large-scale effort in human history to create a truly global society on national soil.

The most interesting aspect of the experience of industrialized New World countries is to be found in the unusually wide range of policies and programs designed to remove discrimination and create equality of opportunities for ethnic minorities. These include establishment of autonomous territories for indigenous people, restitution of their rights to lands and natural resources, a battery of legislation to combat all forms of ethnic discrimination, wide-ranging programs of affirmative action, strong promotion of cultural pluralism, as well as the sensitization of the media, educational institutions, the police, the judiciary, and the bureaucracy to the ethnic dimensions of social integration. The activism of the English-speaking New World in this domain stands in sharp contrast to the timidity of the Western European stance.

Latin America

The clash of cultures began earlier in Latin America than in most of the English-speaking New World and involved larger numbers of people. The core of the Spanish empire in the New World was in fact built in the sixteenth century on the ruins of well-developed Indian civilizations in Mesoamerica and the Andean region, whose peoples were conquered and eventually integrated into multiethnic societies.

In contrast, the Portuguese New World, southern Central America, and the Southern cone of Spanish South America did not contain great Indian empires and were settled largely by European immigrants (supplemented, especially in the case of Brazil, by slaves). Relatively primitive or isolated groups of native people in these regions were exterminated in the course of military campaigns, much like those undertaken in the United States, or managed to find refuge in the vastness of the Amazon. With the notable exception of these campaigns, racism and other forms of ethnic conflict were muted by a relatively less exclusive definition of lines between cultures in Latin America (when compared to the English-speaking New World) and by centuries of intermarriage among Europeans, Indians, and Africans. Slavery was abolished in Spanish America during the early nineteenth century, although it lasted in Brazil until 1888.

The major lines of social conflict in Latin America have been drawn more frequently along class than along ethnic lines. Nevertheless there are significant areas of Mesoamerica and the Andean region in which the large pre-Columbian indigenous population was gradually pushed into marginal rural areas and dominated by large landowners, mining companies, moneylenders, and/or political bosses of both Indian and non-Indian background. Resentment against exploitation, which was only partially based upon ethnic identity, contributed to revolution in Bolivia and Mexico, and to a number of Indian uprisings in other Andean and Central American countries. Unlike indigenous populations in the English-speaking New World, those in Latin America have not fought for territorial separateness. They have, however, demanded recognition of their rights to hold communal land and to preserve their local customs, as well as assurances of economic and political equality within the wider society. Ethnically based violence has been limited to certain regions, such as Ecuador, Guatemala, southern Mexico, and Peru, and has usually taken the form of sustained, low-level conflict. On occasion, however, this has given way to encounters on a large scale.

Despite the reality of a violent conquest and later of everyday discrimination against indigenous minorities, Latin America has witnessed many enlightened attempts to promote and protect Indian culture and livelihood. Progressive elements within the Catholic Church wrestled with questions of cultural difference as early as the sixteenth century. During the early twentieth century, Mexico and Peru were once again sites of pathbreaking efforts to integrate Indian peoples into national societies without destroying their cultures. Perhaps the greatest stumbling block to promoting the well-being of indigenous peoples in Latin America is the deficient development of institutions that protect human rights for all citizens of the region and permit the development of democracy.

Asia and Africa

Unlike Latin America, the boundaries of most Asian and African countries are relatively recent colonial creations. Typically the colonial authorities grouped together a diverse collection of neighboring ethnic groups into territories that subsequently became independent states. The ethnic mosaic was further enriched by immigrants from other parts of the colonial empire. The primary challenge faced by governments under these circumstances was to create a sense of national identity and unity among their diverse ethnic groups and to promote economic development and improve living standards of the people.

At the time of independence in the mid-twentieth century or later, few leaders had given much thought to the complex issues raised in the course of creating national identity and integration. Special constitutional arrangements were made on the eve of independence in some countries, such as Fiji and Malaysia, where indigenous people felt threatened by immigrant communities. Similarly, a few countries (such as India and Lebanon) devised power-sharing and territorial arrangements in response to ethnic problems. More generally, however, there was a tendency to opt for strong states, centralization of power, and suppression of ethnic claims. The expression of ethnic identity was generally frowned upon, and tribalism (and its variants) became a term of opprobrium.

In contrast to the sporadic violence seen in Western Europe and the New World, ethnic tensions are a pervasive reality in most African and

Asian countries. The incidence of violent conflicts appears to have increased significantly since the early 1970s. The heritage from the colonial era continues to cast a long shadow on ethnic relations in many countries. Since separate communal residential areas, schools, hospitals, and social and cultural organizations were a common feature in many colonies, social and economic distance among different ethnic communities was often systematically maintained. In several countries colonial policy also tended to promote or intensify specialization of occupation along ethnic lines, as well as regional or ethnic economic inequalities.

Violent ethnic conflict is by no means inevitable or universal in African and Asian countries. Several multicultural and multiethnic states (including Cameroon, Mauritius, Tanzania, Zambia, and Zimbabwe in Africa and Malaysia, Singapore, and Thailand in Asia) have succeeded in achieving peaceful accommodation of tensions inherent in all such societies. There are no doubt many features specific to these countries that account for their relatively favorable experiences. But some of the lessons they have learned are of wider relevance.

Accommodating Ethnic Tensions

Although any realistic attempt to deal effectively with ethnic tension must be firmly grounded in the historical experience and current situation of a particular country, certain kinds of policies are likely to promote accommodation in a wide range of situations.

For example, it is obvious that the existence of a rule of law, respect for fundamental human rights, and an independent judiciary are essential in mitigating minorities' fears that they will be victimized and discriminated against. At the same time, broad-based and sustained economic growth creates a feeling of general well-being and security, and gives governments access to resources that can be used to meet some of the demands of aggrieved ethnic groups. On the other hand, economic crisis, mass poverty, and high levels of unemployment are breeding grounds for tensions that can be manipulated by ethnic entrepreneurs who capitalize on a generalized state of insecurity.

The experiences of countries as diverse as Belgium, India, Lebanon, Malaysia, Nigeria, and Switzerland illustrate the fact that systems of government characterized by power-sharing arrangements between the center and the regions, as well as among different ethnic groups, can be effective in easing ethnic tensions over critical periods. Electoral systems can also be tailored to the specific ethnic structures and problems of individual countries, so that they guarantee a place for minority ethnic groups. The extremely original and imaginative arrangements recently hammered out in South Africa over a long period of intensive discussions among contending ethnic groups highlight the central importance of developing innovative institutional mechanisms for relieving ethnic tensions.

A dense network of advocacy groups, concerned with humanitarian questions and human rights as well as with social welfare and development, is another central element in the search for new approaches and solutions to ethnic conflict. These institutions have no doubt contributed to the reduction of ethnic discrimination and bias in Western Europe and the New World, and they are now beginning to do so in Latin America. In contrast, the absence or weakness of such a web of autonomous institutions has been an important factor in the failure to find peaceful means for accommodating ethnic conflict in many countries in Central and Eastern Europe, Africa, and Asia.

Finally greater attention must be paid to the important role that education can play in promoting understanding and tolerance in multicultural societies. This should go hand in hand with tough policies and actions directed against those who seek for various reasons to stir up ethnic hatred and to indulge in acts of ethnic harassment and violence.

Conclusion

It is perhaps useful to place current patterns and processes of social integration in historical perspective before looking toward the future.

We live at a time when the vast majority of people around the world are being integrated into a single global economy and culture, organized around the principles of individualism, liberal democracy, and faith in the market. This is a revolutionary development, comparable in its scope to the Industrial Revolution of the late eighteenth and early nineteenth centuries, and in many ways a logical extension of that process.

Mass migration accompanied the Industrial Revolution, just as it marks our contemporary world. And ethnic conflict erupted in the nineteenth and early twentieth century, just as it does today. Throughout the past century, many were required to build new identities, as certain categories of occupation and certain localities or regions were degraded or made irrelevant by the rapidly changing economy. Again, however, migration and the juxtaposition of cultures occur at present with a speed and depth not possible in a less technologically advanced era. The sheer numbers of people affected today are much larger than a century or more ago. The scale of the current process of social reorganization is planetary.

The new order created over the course of the last century to cope with the deeply divisive effects of the Industrial Revolution rested in many parts of the world on citizenship, nationality, and class. In a growing number of settings, individuals were eventually perceived to have rights, and these rights were protected by new forms of social organization, including trade unions and other interest associations, political parties, courts, and so forth. The modern state became the guarantor of political and economic rights and provided the framework for collective identity across wide areas of the world. An attempt was made under colonialism to transplant it into new territories.

Current developments within the global economy and society, however, tend increasingly to undermine the efficacy of states. In some instances, they create incentives for their fragmentation or dissolution. Unregulated markets can destroy social compacts, as notions of solidarity and the concept of citizens' rights are subject to the strains inherent in all-out competition.

Uncritical adherence to consumerism has a similar effect. In consequence, many of the modern structures of representation and accountability, which emerged as an outgrowth of social conflict and accommodation in industrial or newly industrializing democracies, are being severely challenged.

At the same time, of course, the current process of rapid economic and social change creates new opportunities for personal freedom and choice in many settings traditionally characterized by rigid social stratification and/or the authoritarian or dictatorial exercise of power. The problem faced in these situations is how to create new institutions that satisfy the basic economic and political needs of most people, during a period when so great a degree of influence on local conditions is in fact exerted by forces far beyond local control.

There is at present a striking incongruence between patterns of social integration, that bind people around the world more closely together than ever before, on the one hand, and the frailty of existing mechanisms for subjecting global processes to regulation and channeling them toward the promotion of human welfare, on the other. Although the nation-state increasingly fulfilled this function in the aftermath of the Industrial Revolution, it cannot be expected to assume primary or sole responsibility for doing so in the new global context.

A number of challenges thus emerge that have only partial corollaries in earlier periods. How, for example, can the international community control the centripetal, polarizing effects of global markets — sustained by information technologies which permit virtually instantaneous communication — without returning to a kind of protectionism that stifles possibilities for growth in developing countries as well as Northern economies?

How can new bases of solidarity be created during a period when capital is almost infinitely mobile and labor is much more mobile than it has ever been before? And how can the clash of values and cultures be minimized, and elements of a common culture constructed, in a world that grows smaller and more densely interconnected with each passing day?

How can new forms of livelihood and standards of personal worth be created in a context characterized by secular decline in the need for human labor? And how can the current trend toward socioeconomic and political marginalization of growing numbers of people be reversed?

Finally, how can we deal with the unprecedented degree of environmental degradation generated by current patterns of resource use, as well as with the equally unprecedented opportunities created by modern technology for conflict to degenerate into violence, and for violence to expand over wide areas.

Confronting these challenges will require institutional reform at many levels of society and within many different spheres of daily life. It will also require a conscious shift of values. The international context assumes greater importance in this endeavor than ever before — not because it is possible to design universal solutions, uniformly applied around the world, but because global forces have created inescapable common problems of worldwide scope. The concept of an "international community" is no longer a simple ideal. It is a fact of life.

Section 2

Lessons from Social Safety Nets and Adjustment in Developing Countries[1]

Jessica Vivian

It has long been acknowledged that structural adjustment measures entail significant social costs, at least in the short term, and that these costs are likely to have their severest impact on the poorest sectors of society. Even those who believe that adjustment measures will ultimately be in the best interest of the poor acknowledge the "frictional" difficulties of the transition period, and it is generally accepted that the poorest groups suffer disproportionately because of their vulnerability and lack of economic flexibility.

Concern with the social costs of adjustment increased in the late 1980s, with the publication of empirical studies documenting the impact of adjustment measures, as well as increased popular opposition to such key adjustment-related policies as devaluation and reductions in consumer subsidies.[2] The response among international agencies has been, on the one hand, at least some willingness to acknowledge the possible advantages of more gradual adjustment programs, as well as a professed interest in amending the standard adjustment package to match countries' particular social conditions. On the other hand, in many countries a range of compensatory measures have been introduced which are meant to mitigate the social costs of adjustment. These social adjustment packages—or, as they are commonly called, "social safety nets"[3]—usually involve both targeted social services and benefits, and various types of project-based "social funds."

This section examines social policies and safety nets in the context of economic restructuring in developing countries.[4]

Social Policies and Compensatory Programs

Adjustment measures are meant to change the structure of the economy. They will necessarily have distributional effects, and thus by definition will create winners and losers. The problem is compounded by the phenomenon of "exit before entry" as enterprises hurt by adjustment exit the economy before enterprises benefiting from adjustment enter it.[5] Thus the losses from adjustment normally precede the gains. But who will comprise the winning and losing groups from adjustment in any particular country is not immediately clear without local social and economic analysis. The adjustment model is strictly agnostic about how real wages will change, as well as welfare effects on households more generally. Factors determining the impact of adjustment at the household level include, among other things, what is produced and consumed, whether labor is bought or sold, and characteristics of existing markets and access to them.

Although the early adjustment models were able to predict social impacts, they did not foresee how socially and politically disruptive the "human face" dimensions of adjustment were to be. The decline in real per capita household income in adjusting countries, especially in Africa and Latin America, as well as the greatly increased incidence of poverty, was both striking and well documented by the late 1980s. Although the argument was made that in the absence of robust counterfactuals such changes could not be attributed to adjustment measures — they could also be linked to the economic crisis that necessitated adjustment, and might have been worse without adjustment — by the late 1980s the lending institutions had acknowledged the fact that early adjustment packages had paid insufficient attention to the social dimensions of adjustment. Thus in 1987 the World Bank's Operational Guidelines were amended to require analysis of the impact of adjustment programs on the poor and attention to measures to alleviate their negative effects.[6]

This increased attention — at least in the public discourse — to the social dimensions of adjustment coincided with something of a shift in emphasis regarding the overall purpose of the adjustment package. While in the early 1980s adjustment policies tended to be justified quite simply with the argument that external deficits were unsustainable and countries must live within their means,[7] by the late 1980s there was more emphasis on adjustment as a precondition for what became described as the ultimate goal of poverty alleviation.[8] The argument became focused on the contention that poverty could not be addressed without economic growth, and that structural adjustment was the most efficient way to return to a sustainable growth path. Adjustment was thus portrayed not merely as a matter of fiscal responsibility, but also as the best solution to the long-term problem of poverty. The analogy used was that of crossing a desert: it is a difficult trek, but a better condition would be reached on the other side.[9]

However, it was not a priori clear from the adjustment model that the poor would benefit from the increased growth that was supposed to come with adjustment.[10] At about the same time that interest grew in exploring the implications of this fact, calculations made of the economic benefits attributable to a healthy and well-trained workforce helped to generate concern that "human capital" not be allowed to "depreciate" during the adjustment period. Together, these two concerns implied an increased willingness to mitigate the social costs of adjustment — an acknowledgment that some groups would need special help to "cross the desert." But it was still maintained that the social costs must be addressed within the overall constraints of adjustment measures—otherwise the pain would simply be prolonged.

An obvious answer to the dilemma of the need to increase social support while reducing overall expenditure was targeting—the allocation of expenditures to those groups most in need and most likely to benefit from them. Proposed targeting took two forms: first, the reallocation of existing social expenditure in order to increase efficiency and equity (e.g., shifting funds from secondary to primary schooling, from curative to preventative health care, and generally from urban to rural sectors); second, the creation of supplementary programs designed specifically to reach the poor and those directly affected by adjustment (e.g., public works programs, infrastructure development, nutrition interventions, unemployment compensation and retraining initiatives, and credit and other support for microenterprise development). The first type of targeting—expenditure shifting—was seen as a way to correct the tendency for better-off groups to capture the bulk of social expenditure, and thus to greatly increase welfare benefits within a budget constraint. The second type of targeting—restricting additional interventions to particular groups—was considered the only feasible way to administer compensatory measures within the terms of the adjustment package.

Targeting, in fact, was embraced so enthusiastically, and was portrayed as such an ideal solution to the social problems of adjustment, that some writers considered it necessary to warn that targeting should not be considered a panacea: "the real world is not quite so straightforward. There are good reasons why this best of all possible worlds is not available to policy makers in developing countries, and hard decisions will have to be made that weigh up the costs and the benefits of targeting."[11] Indeed, it is clear that it is politically much more feasible to implement targeted programs that are additive in nature—especially when such compensatory programs receive external financial support—than those which seek to reduce resource allocation to privileged groups.

Aside from acknowledging the possible political difficulties in implementing targeted measures, it should be noted that the distributional effects of targeted policies—when they are implemented, as they must be, in the real world—are not as unambiguously positive as the theoretical models would suggest. "Universal policies are regressive when they do not adequately take into account certain characteristics of the recipients, or as a result of the regressive nature of their funding or of other factors such as inefficiency." On the other hand, "selectiveness is regressive—regardless of the concrete performance of some programs—when it is part of a strategy of dismantling policies which have had a significant progressive impact.[12]

It is important, in other words, to distinguish the *effectiveness* of untargeted interventions from their *efficiency*. For example, untargeted food subsidies in both Brazil and Egypt in the early 1980s transferred more, in absolute terms, to the rich than the poor. However, in Brazil the percentage increase to the real income of the poor was eight times that of the rich, while in Egypt the subsidies increased the real income of the poor by 17 percent, and the real income of the rich by three percent. The possibility of such a tradeoff between efficiency and effectiveness implies that interventions that are effective in reaching the poor "should not be reduced or eliminated unless and until alternative means of reaching the poor are firmly in place."[13]

Concern with poverty and equity was not the only—or at times even the primary—rationale behind the development of social safety nets in the context of economic restructuring, however. By the mid-1980s, internal political opposition to adjustment measures coming from both poor and middle-class groups had threatened the successful and full implementation of adjustment programs in a number of countries and interest was raised in finding ways to overcome this opposition. In any event, the lending institutions relaxed their emphasis on firm, swift, and undiluted adjustment packages where it became clear that adjustment would not be sustained in the face of political opposition. At this point, they became more supportive of measures meant to address the social costs of adjustment. As an official of the IMF put it: "in essence, the underlying rationale [of social safety nets] was the necessity to buttress the social and political acceptance of the adjustment effort."[14] The creation of the first formal social fund, that of Bolivia, was influenced by a World Bank consultant who was a politician, and who helped convince the Bank of the political importance of highly visible action to address social issues if the package of economic measures was to have a chance of implementation.[15]

This political concern is reflected in the fact that often the first and most emphasized goal of safety nets is assistance to retrenched workers, especially public sector employees, who are both visible and relatively vocal victims of adjustment. Of the 28 adjustment packages examined in one study, 16 contained specific measures for the newly unemployed;[16] of the remainder, no retrenchments were foreseen in seven cases–thus in only five of the 28 cases were retrenchments expected but not addressed by the program. In 21 safety nets in developing countries, 12 are described as being targeted to the new poor, an additional six are targeted to both the new and the old poor, and only three (Chile, Venezuela, and Zambia) are described as being targeted to only the old poor.

More recently, a third goal has been connected with social safety nets, and specifically with social funds, that centers on institutional reform and the creation of social infrastructure. The idea that is evolving is that the approach to social provisioning taken by social fund schemes— which commonly involves decentralization, including recipients in soliciting, designing, and contributing to interventions, and, in short, making the process of social service provisioning more "participatory"—will have two impacts.

First, it will reinforce and increase the viability of more narrow targeting of social expenditures by creating incentives for self-selection; the participation or labor requirement of most social fund projects means that better-off groups are less likely to attempt to capture the benefits. At the same time, the fact that beneficiaries are seen to be making a contribution helps to reduce the resentment of other groups, who become more inclined to view the recipients of social expenditure as "deserving."

Second, and more importantly if more vaguely defined, the process through which social funds are implemented is seen as promoting equitable and democratic development processes. Because social fund projects often require some sort of group organization, it is believed that they will help to strengthen civil society, to create new constituencies and support for new leaders, and in the process will restructure power relations, and give previously excluded groups a means and an opportunity to participate in a meaningful way. In short, social funds are seen as a training ground in the democratic process.

There is an implicit assumption that these three goals—poverty alleviation, increasing the political acceptability of adjustment, and institutional reform—are mutually compatible, and that safety net programs—in the right circumstances, and if properly designed, and so forth—can be expected to achieve all three. However, there are often incompatibilities among these three objectives. Most obviously, emphasis on the political function of safety nets has been demonstrated to reduce success in poverty alleviation in at least several cases. The picture is further complicated by several other factors. These three goals are based on incompatible assumptions about the nature of the state and civil society; priorities of national governments and external donors may not coincide; and the actual impact of the safety net scheme may have little relation to any of its stated goals. The remainder of this section takes a closer look at safety net schemes in developing countries: the different models and their assumptions, their observable characteristics and trends, and their impacts.

Types of Safety Nets

Social safety nets have been variously conceptualized and categorized in the last several years.[17] Here, the category "safety net" is used to cover a variety of mechanisms implemented in conjunction with structural adjustment measures, and designed to address either structural or transitional poverty and unemployment, to reduce the impact of adjustment measures on certain groups, or to create or improve both social and physical infrastructure. Emergency funds, compensatory funds, employment funds, and social investment funds are various types of safety nets, although there are not always clear boundaries between these schemes. The terms are in themselves quite fluid, each country's program is conceived of somewhat differently, and the newer ones are often explicit hybrids of earlier approaches that are thus difficult to categorize.

The concept of social safety nets is not new—early "poor relief" laws were often described as safety nets, while public works programs have a long history in both developed and developing countries. The term has more recently been explicitly linked to adjustment, and in this context has taken on a particular connotation. Most adjustment-related safety net programs are meant to supplement the activities of existing ministries and agencies unable to address the direct or indirect social costs of adjustment.

The functions of safety nets are to fill gaps, target the poor, directly address adjustment costs, and explore and experiment with more efficient approaches to poverty alleviation.

Safety nets often represent a significant departure from other governmental organizational structures and procedures. Typically, the umbrella agency is a "social fund," set up as an intermediary agency, which does not directly implement projects, but rather solicits project proposals and evaluates them, and finances and monitors projects carried out by private contractors or self-help groups. The staff associated with the social fund is often much better paid other civil servants, and may be paid directly from external funding sources. Sometimes the program is given significantly greater infrastructural support than that enjoyed by other governmental departments, including communications equipment, computers, and tailored computer programming.

Safety net programs undertake a wide range of activities. The most common element is employment creation, which may involve both public works, especially infrastructure development, and private sector job creation. The latter is carried out at a much higher cost per job created than the former, but it is now felt that the benefits will be more sustainable, and the trend is toward this type of employment program. Training or retraining is provided to the unemployed, and credit and technical assistance is given to the informal sector and to small farmers. Social infrastructure may also be funded independently of public works programs. In many Latin American countries, for instance, schools, roads, and clinics are constructed by private contractors, with employment generation being a secondary consideration. Safety net programs are also commonly responsible for the delivery of certain social services, including nutrition supplements to targeted groups, primary health care and immunization drives, and literacy campaigns. Many safety nets also contain a compensatory element meant to reduce the direct impact of adjustment on certain groups. In Zimbabwe, for instance, exemptions from health and education cost recovery measures are paid out of the social fund on a means-tested basis, and grants are given to the urban poor to compensate for reductions in consumer subsidies.

The targeting of safety net benefits takes a variety of forms. It may be carried out by region (for instance, the northern regions of Ghana, certain low-income urban neighborhoods in Mexico), by easily identifiable vulnerable group (children, mothers, elderly, widows, for example), or by a more formal means test associated with registration procedures for subsidized food or for education or medical services. But there is most interest in designing self-targeting mechanisms which reduce the incentives of the nontarget groups to claim benefits. Such mechanisms may involve switching subsidies to inferior commodities (such as coarse or yellow maize meal or other less-preferred food), they often include work requirements (as in the food-for-work model), and they may involve imposing inconveniences, time costs, and stigma on the beneficiaries (such as lengthy queues). Deliberately poor product quality in particular has long been associated with the targeting of food programs, but the same idea is now being applied to the services associated with social investment funds, including daycare programs, housing, water, and sanitation services. Self-targeting is valued because it reduces administration costs and the likelihood that nontarget groups will benefit, and it may also reduce the opposition of nontargeted groups to the scheme. However, it does involve opportunity costs for the targeted group, particularly in the case of work requirements, and it may reduce the percentage of the target group reached by the program.

One of the most important distinctions to be made between types of safety nets concerns the process by which projects are selected, designed, and prioritized. The traditional model of centrally based decision making is still found in some cases, but generally there is an effort to make the safety net participatory, or "demand based." This term refers to a process by which groups or communities submit proposals for project funding to the social fund, and then assume a certain amount of responsibility for implementing the project. This "participatory" aspect of safety net schemes is credited with a variety of advantages. It helps to ensure that projects are really desired by their beneficiaries, it encourages local organization as well as local conceptualization and prioritization of needs, and it creates self-targeting incentives. The demand-based approach does have certain limitations, however. It requires an exclusively project-based approach, it has difficulty in reaching the poorest or otherwise traditionally excluded groups, and true participation is not always easy to achieve. The advantages and limitations of the demand-based approach are discussed in more detail below.

Characteristics of Safety Nets

There is a wide variety of ways in which safety nets are conceptualized, planned, and implemented. The safety net model is evolving in response to experiences and experiments, and thus generalizations should be made with caution. However, there do appear to be some common characteristics and trends in safety net schemes in developing countries.

External Funding

With the exception of Mexico, safety net and social fund schemes are heavily externally funded. In Africa, the proportion of external funding ranges from 78 to 100 percent; in Latin America, from 43 to 95 percent, excluding Mexico. The remaining costs are met primarily from government. This may include in-kind contributions. Beneficiary contributions are low, ranging from zero to nine percent in Africa and from zero to 24 percent in Latin America. In the case of Mexico, external donors are not involved. The financing comes in large part from the sale of public sector enterprises, but also involves reallocation from other items in the national budget, including regular social expenditures.[18]

External funding for safety net programs raises questions of autonomy and sustainability. There is concern in some countries that governments are losing control over their social policy to external bodies, as they previously lost control of their economic policies. In addition, external funding increases uncertainty about the future of the program, which may easily fall victim to changing donor priorities. Internal funding, on the other hand, raises questions of opportunity costs and politics. Funds spent on the program would otherwise have been allocated elsewhere, and efficiency may be adversely affected by political considerations. In addition, the question of sustainability remains if, as is the case with Mexico, a large part of the funding comes from the privatization or other one-time sources of revenue generation.

Project-Based Activities

With the exception of certain compensatory measures, the majority of safety net activities take the form of discrete projects, which in some cases may displace traditional program-oriented social services. The desire to increase efficiency by cutting through bureaucratic red tape and increasing reliance on the private and nongovernmental sectors implies working through projects rather than programs, because programs, if they are to be comprehensive, require an extensive organizational structure not usually found outside of government. In addition, donors explicitly see a project framework as a way to maximize control over the safety net scheme, and particularly the activities of the generally untested nongovernmental sector.

The project approach, as has been long pointed out in the development literature, has a number of inherent limitations. These include difficulty in reaching certain groups, pockets of impact rather than broad coverage, and a tendency for duplication and lack of coordination to reduce inefficiency.

The original rationale behind the use of the project approach in safety nets schemes was that they are by definition transitional measures, meant not to replace more standard social policies but rather to supplement them through the difficult adjustment period. Thus safety nets were not initially intended to alleviate poverty or unemployment, but rather to prevent further declines until such time as adjustment-led growth rationale made them unnecessary. However, in many countries this rationale has been superseded by events. Not only are safety nets now expected to tackle both transitional and structural poverty and unemployment, but in many cases they are seen as medium- to long-term policy shifts, rather than as temporary emergency measures.

Slow Beginning

Although the early safety nets, designed as emergency measures, were funded and launched relatively quickly, more recent programs often face long delays between the proposal and implementation stages. To some extent, this seems to be a function of donor conditionalities. The programs with the fewest donors, and which are granted the greatest autonomy, begin most rapidly, while those with many donors, especially when donor funds are tied to specific projects, experience delays of months or even years.

Emphasis on Visibility

Safety net programs tend to be heavily advertised, both to domestic and international audiences. Indeed, visibility is often an explicit criterion in project selection.

This emphasis on visibility derives from the use of safety nets as political instruments, intended to convince the public (as well as international critics) that the social costs of adjustment can be successfully managed, and that the current government is serious about doing so. The extent to which this political objective is acknowledged varies with the country, the speaker, and the audience addressed, but it seemed to be common to virtually all safety net programs.

In principle, this political objective can be compatible with the more commonly mentioned objectives of poverty alleviation, employment generation, and social development, especially if the government depends on a broad-based constituency for support. It can even be argued that, by using safety net programs to broaden their political support, governments can create a virtuous circle whereby the poor gain power and help to maintain progressive government policies. However, in practice there are often trade-offs to be made between these two goals. Most obviously, the visibility criterion means that speed and rhetoric are valued over long-term impact.

Male Bias

Although safety nets usually rely on the notion of "vulnerable groups" for much of their targeting, and although it is generally acknowledged that women suffer disproportionately from the effects of adjustment, the primary direct beneficiaries of safety net activities are men. Women do benefit from some of the compensatory components of safety nets, particularly nutrition interventions, but, where data are available, they indicate that women are clearly disadvantaged especially in the employment generation component of social funds.

Reaching the Affected Population

Although the data are incomplete, the total impact of safety net schemes varies widely. In part, this is the result of funding levels, which range from an initial budget of about US $10 million in Zimbabwe to 80 million in Ghana, more than 600 million in Egypt, about 100 million in Honduras, 300 million in Bolivia, and 2 to 3 billion in Mexico.[19]

Employment creation is usually presented as one of the central purposes of nearly all safety net programs. Because it is also relative easy to measure, it is often accepted as an indicator of performance. The data indicate that employment programs have measurable impacts that benefit thousands of people, but the impact seems less significant when compared with the scale of the unemployment problem.

Reaching the Poorest

The metaphor of a "safety net" implies an ability to prevent every person from falling below a certain level or standard of living. However, adjustment-related safety net schemes have experienced significant obstacles to directly reaching the poorest groups in society. There appear to be three primary reasons for this difficulty. First, the emphasis on the project approach, especially demand-based projects, presents a number of obstacles to participation by the poorest people. These types of projects involve writing proposals and soliciting estimates. In some cases, they require such technical expertise as producing blueprints or engineering assessments. NGOs, which often carry out these activities when independent or government coordination is limited, tend to concentrate their activities in urban areas and have a limited reach into the poorest and most remote communities.

Second, in a number of cases, political considerations led to a loss of targeting focus on the poorest. In particular, an urban bias was evident in many countries, especially where an emphasis on visibility was strong.

Third, in many safety net activities, opportunity costs present barriers to participation by the poor. In the case of demand-based projects, the poor are faced not only with the need to work around existing local power structures in the organizational phase, but also with the need for a significant time investment before benefits are received or even committed. Often, it is the poorest who can least afford this time commitment.

Long-Term Tendency of Programs

Safety net programs were originally sold to donors as short-term emergency measures, with a strictly limited life span. They were meant to provide a bridge between crisis and reactivation. They were not intended by their original designers to solve the problems of poverty or unemployment; it was expected that adjustment would address these problems. They were merely meant to be palliative measures, making it easier for some people (not necessarily those most directly affected by adjustment) to make it through the transition period. However, quite soon they came to be embraced, particularly by donors, as a way to mitigate the social costs of adjustment. Soon after that, their mandate was stretched to include not only transitional but also structural social problems. In particular, it was hoped that they would be able to provide examples of more efficient and equitable methods of social service provisioning, and even that they would stimulate the creation of institutional forms and relations that would strengthen civil society and provide the basis for more equitable development trends. In the process, the stipulation that safety nets remain strictly temporary measures was largely abandoned. The country studies indicate that safety nets are increasingly seen as part of a longer-term strategy of social and bureaucratic restructuring.

One reason for this trend toward institutionalizing what was originally meant to be a temporary measure is that the period of time during which "frictional" difficulties from adjustment are experienced has proved to be longer than expected. What were thought to be transitional problems sometimes emerged as structural ones, especially where the distributional effects of adjustment were regressive. If adjustment is a process of crossing a desert, not only is the desert wider than had been predicted, but its boundary is unclear and the trek has left some people far behind.

A second reason that safety nets have tended to linger beyond their original termination date hinges on their utility as political instruments. Governments that have won political capital from the program will be reluctant to dismantle it as long as it remains popular.

The trend toward institutionalizing the safety net approach is an important one, because it means that these programs must now be assessed on an entirely new basis. When safety nets are short-term emergency measures, strictly complementary to existing social programs, and especially when they do not represent significant opportunity costs, whatever benefits they can provide are welcome extras. When, however, the safety net approach becomes incorporated into long-term development strategy and provides a model for alternative forms of social service provisioning, it becomes imperative to assess its long-term social impacts more carefully.

Assessment of Safety Nets

As noted, safety net programs in developing countries have been variously credited with making progress toward three separate goals: alleviation of poverty and unemployment (both frictional and structural), defusing social and political opposition to structural adjustment measures, and spurring a process of institutional reform involving a strengthening of civil society and leading ultimately to more meaningful democratization. The first thing to be observed in assessing progress toward these disparate goals is that they entail various contradictory perceptions of the roles and responsibilities of the different actors involved. On the one hand, the state is ostensibly given the responsibility for establishing, directing, and setting the priorities for the safety net program—a model that implies a basically benevolent state. The explicit use of safety nets as means to attract support for government policies also implies that the state is taking a leading and positive role in setting the social policy agenda.

On the other hand, lending institutions and donors actually have a great deal of control over both the implementation of safety net schemes and the national economic and social policy agenda. When such external controls are portrayed as being applied in the interests of the poor, the implication is that the donors are allied with "the people" against the state. This is a model of a benevolent "metastate," comprising donors and the national and international "development community" through whom they work; it is best able to act in the interests of the poor. At the same time, although this model implies an extremely centralized decision making process, it also calls for grassroots organization, empowerment, and participation in decision making. Implicitly or explicitly, it assumes that such participation will be compatible with the externally determined policy priorities.

The situation is further confused by the various rationales and priorities that governments and lending institutions offer—both publicly and privately—for safety net programs. Especially in the case of lending institutions, it seems clear that the political function of safety nets is considered central. However, this may not be acknowledged by all audiences. Groups most directly affected by adjustment—often middle-class retrenchees—are often assured that the safety net is meant to mitigate the social impact of adjustment. The safety net's benefits to the poorest, on the other hand, are more likely to be stressed in the external development community.

Any assessment of the performance of safety nets, therefore, must be accompanied by the disclaimer that the expressed objectives of existing programs may not always correspond to their actual priorities. Thus, there is conceivably a difference between the actual performance of existing schemes and the potential accomplishments that such schemes may have, if their actual priorities were to be reformulated in line with their stated goals.

Poverty

Safety nets are generally described both as a way of addressing the direct social costs of adjustment and alleviating poverty in that context. All of the programs target the poor, but some stress adjustment-caused poverty (the new poor), while others emphasize preexisting poverty (the old poor). On the face of it, if only a fraction of those in need are reached, and further, if there are impediments to reaching the poorest, safety nets are not successful in directly alleviating either frictional or structural poverty.

Indeed, although safety nets are often described as mechanisms for poverty alleviation, it is seldom claimed that they have actually made a significant impact on the overall problem of poverty. Most obviously, the extreme spatial patchiness of the impact is evident in many programs. To some extent, this is a matter of the scale of the programs; it is clear that the massively funded programs have made much more impact than those that are basically token efforts. However, the lack of a significant impact on poverty is also the result of the widespread structural nature of poverty in developing countries and the inherent limitations of the project approach.

Even if existing adjustment-related safety nets cannot be said to directly alleviate poverty on a substantial scale, two questions remain. Do they nevertheless have direct benefits that justify their costs? Do they have indirect effects that may multiply their impacts?

If the performance of safety nets are judged against the overall scale of development problems, they are obviously insufficient, but this is just as obviously an unfair standard. In fact, hundreds of thousands of individuals have been touched directly by such schemes. In addition, at least the most effective programs have measurable indirect effects because of the relatively large amounts of money they inject into the economy; this money is spread relatively well, at least geographically.

It seems reasonable to assume that the effects of social funds on poverty and on inequality are positive as far as they go, at least to the extent that they imply limited financial and institutional opportunity costs. Whether they go far enough to justify the program and whether better alternatives are available needs to be considered on a case-by-case basis.

The Political Viability of Adjustment

Even a cursory examination of safety net programs in developing countries makes clear that the primary rationale of most programs is based on creating support for adjustment measures. There are two intended audiences here. Most obviously, there is the national one, which is of immediate concern to the survival of country-level adjustment measures. But there is clearly also an international target audience. The safety nets are meant to assuage the doubts of certain agencies, organizations, and academics that the short-term costs of adjustment might not be worth its long-term benefits. IMF and World Bank representatives invariably make use of safety nets in international fora, citing them as an indication that although the social dimensions of adjustment had been previously neglected, the problem is now really being addressed. The question becomes: If this is a public relations exercise, how successful is it?

Evidence of the political impacts of safety net programs is somewhat mixed, with some programs being clearly more persuasive than others. Political success depends to some extent on the actual impact of the program, but another important variable is the extent to which safety nets are perceived to be a political instrument.

Social Sector Restructuring

The social sector reform proposals of which safety nets are a part emphasize a system of provision that is decentralized and that often involves NGOs or the commercial private sector rather than relying exclusively on traditional government channels. However, this decentralization is combined with a maintenance of central control over policy making, priority setting, and monitoring. A system of "managed" competition is set up to increase both efficiency and accountability, as competing providers are assumed to have more incentive than government bodies to respond to policy priorities. The central objective of these reforms is to stimulate institutional change that will impact on the perennial problems of bureaucratic inefficiency and corruption.

This type of social sector reform proposal constitutes an attempt to link the neoliberal, market-based model of social provisioning to the formerly "alternative" approaches of participation and empowerment in a kind of "neoliberal populism." This is an interesting concept. It implies that safety nets are not merely short-term palliatives, to be judged against the number of projects they have completed, but should rather be seen as part of a process of long-term social restructuring, which will end with a more equitable distribution of power in society. There are, however, a number of obstacles to the realization of this scenario. First, governments cannot afford to implement unpopular social programs on top of unpopular economic programs. Thus, depending on distributional patterns in society, the agenda of the social reforms favoring the poor may fall victim to the usual concessions to existing power groups. The prevalence of a strong male bias in these programs is one indication that they make little attempt to touch the more entrenched societal structures. Furthermore, the stress on ensuring that beneficiaries are "deserving" of the interventions – by being willing to work, for instance, or consuming inferior commodities – suggests that power relations remain unchanged.

The social sector reform model, which sees safety nets as an instrument of progressive social change, is problematic in its generalized assumptions about processes of institutional change. Echoing the earlier literature on NGOs, the model envisions the creation of a decentralized, responsive network of social service providers, a "thickening web" of grassroots organizations that are transparent, cooperative, and stably funded, and that are able to bring new services to the poorest and most isolated communities previously excluded from government activities. However, another possible outcome of this decentralized approach is a limited patchwork of superficial interventions, their effectiveness impaired by duplication, lack of coordination, and various kinds of bias.

In addition, the costs of safety nets and social sector restructuring more generally must be counted not only in financial terms, but also in institutional terms. The process implies a dismantling of certain institutions, in the hope that they will be supplanted by better ones. This hope may not always be realistic.

Conclusion

Ultimately, what one thinks of compensatory mechanisms such as safety nets depends largely on what one thinks of adjustment. Those who see adjustment as a necessary precondition for both economic and social progress and believe that it is really in the best interest of society as a whole, will see safety nets as political necessities and will try to make sure that they have as little distortionary impact on the adjustment process as possible. This is something of a paradox. The schemes distribute additional revenues without increased exports. They create low-productivity employment, and they prolong exactly the pattern of creation and distribution of income that adjustment tries to modify.

Those who see adjustment as unavoidable – who believe that "there is no alternative" – see safety nets at least as a way of mitigating some of the social hardships of the transition period and, at best, as a way to help develop new forms of social relations that promote the establishment of democratic processes in the long run. Their objective becomes to design the most useful programs possible within the overall constraints of adjustment.

Those who believe that the social costs of adjustment indicate a need to reexamine the standard approach are more inclined to see social funds as a "smokescreen." Structural adjustment measures are likely to create enclave development and to reinforce structural poverty rather than reduce it in the long run. The safety net package is completely unable to mitigate these effects; it can have little bearing on the outcome of the process and is essentially extraneous to the debate on adjustment.

It is, in fact, difficult to find fault with an intervention that brings a large amount of foreign funds into a poor country, distributes these funds relatively well, and, at least, in some cases, has measurable multiplier effects. However, a set of caveats are in order. First, such programs are not an answer either to the social costs of adjustment or to poverty in the context of adjustment. They should not provide an excuse for not taking seriously the question of how to refine adjustment programs to make them more sensitive to the needs and vulnerabilities of the poor. Safety nets have been portrayed at times as the answer to the social costs of adjustment. This, they clearly are not, and this fact implies that other options, including modifications to adjustment programs, should be considered in situations where social costs are high.

Second, the institutional development hoped for as an outcome of the demand-based social fund approach should not be assumed. The fallacy of a "fiat lux" approach to institutional change should be avoided. Even "participatory" social funds will have uncertain social outcomes, and they may serve to block other channels of social organization.

Third, social sector reform models must be assessed in terms of their overall social efficiency and effectiveness as well as their impact on social development. Social policies have long-term effects on social divisions and social structures, and if safety nets become institutionalized as an alternative model of social service provisioning, a long-term question is raised. What will be the legacy of the neoliberal approach to social service provisioning? Will it promote or retard progress toward social development and positive forms of social integration? These questions must be addressed on the basis of a much better understanding of the dynamics of institutional change than is currently available in most countries.

Notes

1. This article appears in full as UNRISD Occasional Paper for the World Summit for Social Development, No. 1, July 1994, Geneva: UNRISD. It has been edited by UNDP for this book. This version appears by kind permission of the United Nations Research Institute for Social Development.

2. See G. Cornia, R. Jolly, and F. Stewart, eds. *Adjustment with a Human Face: Protecting the Vulnerable and Promoting Growth*. Oxford: Clarendon Press, 1987.

3. The term "safety net" is also used to describe new social packages in countries in transition to market economies; this section only considers safety nets in developing countries.

4. Safety net programs examined for this section include those of Honduras, Mexico, Nicaragua, Egypt, Ghana, Zimbabwe, and India. Social funds in Bolivia, Chile, El Salvador, Peru, Senegal, and Zambia were also covered, as were social policies in China, Hong Kong, Papua New Guinea. In addition, a review of existing literature was undertaken.

5. See Omotunde E. G. Johnson, "Managing Adjustment Costs, Political Authority, and the Implementation of Adjustment Programs, with Special

Reference to African Countries." World Development 22 no. 3:399–411.

6. See Helena Ribe and Soniya Carvalho, "World Bank Treatment of the Social Impact of Adjustment Programs." World Bank Policy, Research and External Affairs Working Paper 521. Washington D.C.: The World Bank, 1990.

7. See Wanda Tseng, "The Effects of Adjustment." Finance and Development 21 no. 4 (1984): 2–5.

8. See Ngee-Choon Chia, Sadek M. Wahba, and John Whalley, "A General Equilibrium-Based Social Policy Model for Côte d'Ivoire." World Bank Poverty and Social Policy Series, Policy Analysis Paper No. 2. Washington D.C.: The World Bank, 1992.

9. See Lionel Demery and Tony Addison, *The Alleviation of Poverty Under Structural Adjustment.* Washington, D.C.: The World Bank, 1987. The Word Bank may now be retreating somewhat from this position linking adjustment measures directly with poverty alleviation: a 1994 Bank publication cautions that adjustment "cannot work miracles in reducing poverty or ensuring sustained equitable growth."

10. Paul Glewwe and Dennis de Tray, "The Poor in Latin America during Adjustment: A Case Study of Peru." *Economic Development and Cultural Change* 40 no. 1 (1991): 27–54.

11. Timothy Besley and Ravi Kanbur, "The Principles of Targeting." In V. Balasubramanuam, ed. *Current Issues in Development Economics.* New York: St. Martin's Press, 1990.

12. Ana Sojo, "Nature and Selectiveness of Social Policy." *CEPAL Review* No 41.

13. Ribe and Carvalho, "World Bank Treatment of the Social Impact of Adjustment Programs."

14. George Kopits, "Toward a Cost-Effective Social Security System." In *The Implications for Social Security of Structural Adjustment Policies.* Geneva: International Social Security Association Studies and Research No. 34, 1993.

15. Katherine Marshall, "Genesis and Early Debates." In Steen Jorgensen, Margaret Grosh, and Mark Schacter, *Bolivia's Answer to Poverty, Economic Crisis, and Adjustment: The Emergency Social Fund.* World Bank Regional and Sectoral Studies. Washington D.C.: The World Bank, 1992.

16. Ribe and Carvalho, "World Bank Treatment of the Social Impact of Adjustment Programs."

17. For instance, UNCTAD uses the term "safety net" to encompass three categories of activities, termed "social action programmes," "emergency social funds," and "social investment funds" (UNCTAD, 1994:4). The World Bank, on the other hand, tends to use "social action program" as an umbrella term.

18. UNCTAD, 1994:4.

19. UNCTAD, 1994:4, and ILO Interdepartmental Project on Structural Adjustment, "Structural change and adjustment in Zimbabwe." ILO Interdepartmental Project on Structural Adjustment Occasional Paper 16. Geneva: ILO, 1993.

Section 3

Philosophy and Global Social Development

Philip Allott

It may seem strange to suggest that philosophy could play a significant part in global social development, but it would be good if it were true. Philosophy is an infinitely renewable – and inexpensive – resource.

The social structures of the human world are products of the human mind. Whatever the physiological and biological predispositions reflected in them and whatever the accidents of human history that have caused them, actual social systems are complex structures of ideas within human consciousness.

The result is two serious consequences:

- We bear responsibility for social systems. We cannot pretend that they are natural features of the human habitat.
- That which consciousness has made consciousness can change.

Three Autonomic Systems

There are three features of the global social situation at the end of the twentieth century that pose a great challenge to philosophy:

- The spread of liberal democracy as a complex of ideas and as a way of organizing public-realm social power;
- The spread of capitalism as a complex of ideas and as a way of organizing economic power; and
- The ever-increasing power of science and engineering, applying ideas to transform the conditions of human life.

These three phenomena share a common characteristic that has profound consequences for the future course of global social development. They act, in two respects, as autonomic systems. Each seems to be controlled by an invisible hand that is not itself subject to control by human consciousness, and each contains its own set of fundamental values that, at least for participants in the system, seem to offer a self-contained and self-sufficient basis for legitimizing the systems and for evaluating their performance. Humanity has created systems within human consciousness whose tendency is to assume power over human consciousness.

Those who participate in liberal democracy believe that its fundamental systematic principles (freedom, consent, representation, and legality) are capable of generating social outcomes that are naturally good. Those who participate in capitalism believe that its fundamental systematic principles (competitive market-behavior, the self-adjusting propensity of markets, and the residual place of public interest in relation to private interest) are capable of generating social outcomes that are naturally good. Those who participate in science and engineering believe that its fundamental systematic principles (the uniformity of nature, performance objectivity, and the teleological imperative of the possible) are capable of generating outcomes that are morally and socially neutral. The social application of those outcomes (added social value, as it were) is a matter for democracy and capitalism.

Effects of the Autonomic Systems

The disempowering effect of these phenomena is most apparent in their effect on three other, rather more ancient, phenomena of human consciousness — individuality, sociality, and spirituality. The individual human being, as a unique self-judging moral agent, becomes a theoretical presupposition and a systematic residue of the autonomic social systems. Morality, that is to say, shared rationalizing consciousness of the human striving to do good and avoid evil, becomes a diffuse systematic macroeffect. Society, as the shared enterprise of human self-identifying and human self-perfecting, is overwhelmed by a phenomenon known as the state, that is, the hypothetical, but reified and personified, system of the autonomic systems. All that surpasses the individual and society, metaphysically and morally — the material, the nonmaterial — is coopted by the systems (as an aspect of public power or as a commodity) or is treated as an extrasystemic irrelevance.

Another significant side effect is the elimination of the ideal as a prime motivating force of social change. Although they were themselves the product of thousands of years of human self-surpassing struggle, the three autonomic systems are now coming to be seen as the end points of human social development or, at least, as capable of organizing all remaining possibilities of that development.

The spectacular achievements of democracy, capitalism, and science and engineering seem to prove the unlimited potentiality of the systems — the efficient harnessing of vast social energies, the improvement of material conditions for all humans, and the mastery of the human race over the physical world, including the physical aspects of human existence. There seems to be no limit to the world-transforming power of the autonomic social systems. They seem to have internalized the ideal.

The extraordinary consequence of these developments is that humanity's future is now liable to be nothing other than the net outcome of the three autonomic systems of democracy, capitalism, and science and engineering. Humanity will become the product-for-the-time-being of systems that are beyond the control of human consciousness. We will have to want to be that which we find that we have become.

The Role of the Philosopher

All the above incidentally define the role of the philosopher in the face of such developments. The function of the ideal in human history has been as a standing negation of the actual. The good, truth, beauty, and, above all, justice have served to orientate human consciousness, precisely by suggesting that the actual is never the ideal and that beyond the actual there is always the potential. Democracy, capitalism, and science and engineering would, in such a view, themselves be liable to be surpassed through further human effort. There is no reason at all to believe that they exhaust human potentiality.

The philosopher may insist that the acts of the collective will of democracy are liable to be evil, at least as often as the acts of individual human beings. Democracy can generate a form of mass consciousness that is capable of high levels of fantasy and irrationality and which is readily manipulated.

The philosopher may insist that capitalism is no more liable to generate the outcomes that are best for society in general, let alone for all human beings, than would any collection of self-interested human beings. Capitalism is not necessarily a system of justice, even if it can be remarkably efficient at processing overwhelmingly complex economic data. Like democracy, capitalism modifies fundamental aspects of human consciousness, including human desire, so that our wants are what the system can provide, and our wants become our needs.

The philosopher may insist that the products of science and engineering, products of a supposedly innocent exploration of the possible, also modify consciousness in fundamental ways, propagating more or less subliminally a particular world view of the most general kind, modifying our conceptions of the good life, of health and happiness, and of humanity's potentiality. The human animal is following a new kind of evolutionary development, adapting to changes in the human habitat which are the product of human ingenuity.

But the task of the retranscendentalizing philosopher is made immeasurably more difficult by two other aspects of the actual global social situation: the decline of Western philosophy and the globalization of social phenomena.

It so happens that philosophy in the Western, or European, tradition has, over the last 150 years, worked hard to prove its own transcendental incapacity. Since ideas are merely words, and ideas about ideas are merely more words, then surely there is no conceivable way in which human consciousness can claim to rise above itself, let alone to prescribe rules for itself. Such a view has led many modern philosophers to the conclusion that philosophy can do nothing but clarify mental puzzles and articulate instrumental choices.

Since the autonomic systems discussed above are themselves constructs of ideas in human consciousness, such a view leads to an ultimate self-disabling and self-abnegation in the face of the vastly powerful works of human social consciousness. Western philosophy, having done so much to cause the social phenomena of the contemporary world, has more or less withdrawn from intellectual responsibility for their further development.

Over the same period of time, the disabling of general philosophy has been accompanied and assisted by a sort of triumphal naturalism in the human sciences. Through the work of a vast new priest class in the universities, there has been a profound naturalizing of human phenomena, a naturalizing that is also dehumanizing. A methodological assumption has become a new antimetaphysical metaphysics. Human phenomena have been detached from human values and human responsibility. The study of things human has become a sort of human entomology.

Global Potential of the Autonomic Social Systems

The result is that the human world comes to be seen, not as a world of good and evil, of justice and injustice, but as a world of problems—war, the arms trade, the terms of trade, global warming, desertification, famine, teenage pregnancies, inner-city crime, poverty, illiteracy, AIDS, torture, political corruption, child labor, and child prostitution. All such familiar, almost tedious, phenomena are seen as natural by-products of social processes. All being well, and resources permitting, they will be dealt with pragmatically and systematically. No doubt, there will be an unending succession of other problems of the same intrinsic nature. So it will be for the whole of humanity's foreseeable future. The mysterious and profound challenge of human existence has become a set of pending administrative tasks.

Over the same 150 years, the autonomic social systems have been reproducing themselves at the global level. The state-system has generated a vast global public realm of intergovernmental agencies, politically and legally unaccountable to the people, spending vast sums of money provided ultimately by the taxpayers of the world. In due course, no doubt, a global democratic system will legitimize, dehumanize, and naturalize the global public realm. Already worldwide media of communication are beginning to generate the sort of crude international mass consciousness that is appropriate for crude democratic reprocessing.

Capitalism revealed its global potentiality in its earliest days. Soon the whole human world will be locked into an autonomic system of supercapitalism, and all human beings will become its more and more efficiently programmed dual-use component parts, as workers and consumers. The originators of the scientific revolution already saw the essentially global character of natural science (Francis Bacon's "invisible college" of scientists), and the Industrial Revolution made possible the globalization of science-based engineering.

The invisible global forum of a nascent global democracy, the invisible global marketplace of a relentless global capitalism, the invisible global laboratory of wonder-working global science and engineering; these are the places where humanity as a whole will find its self-made but unchosen future.

Realizing Human Potentiality

The ultimate task of global social development is to find a way to construct a global mental superstructure that can rise above all such social phenomena and can enable humanity to judge its own works and choose its own future. It will be an all-encompassing manifestation of the human spirit. All cultures and creeds will participate in its endless reforming. No voice will be systematically excluded.

The initial systematic principles of the new superstructure of humanity's self-consciousness might include the following:

- Humanity recognizes itself as a society, the society of all societies and of the whole human race.

- Social systems are means not ends. They are means for the never ending self-creating and self-perfecting of the human species, as one species among many in a shared world, one presence among many in a limitless universe.

- Humanity's high values determine the purposes and judge the performance of individuals and their social systems.

- Humanity's high values may take new forms or they may be re-affirmations of ancient values, such as those of love, friendship, fellow-feeling, justice, the moral responsibility of each human being for all human beings, rationality, spirituality, the unique and equal value of every single human being.

It takes only a moment to recollect humanity's potentiality. It is a change of consciousness that could transform fundamentally the development of humanity's actuality.

The disempowering, dehumanizing, detranscendentalizing effects on global social consciousness of the autonomic social systems inhibit us from striving to go beyond the actual, from seeking radically new forms of social, moral, and even metaphysical consciousness, from imagining radically new forms of social organization. They mean also that the scandals and the evils of the actual global social situation are seen as incidental systematic effects which can, in principle and in due course, be overcome systematically by appropriate action within the systems of democracy, capitalism, and science and engineering.

It so happens that, in addition to all the material, social, and moral problems that the human world faces at the end of the twentieth century, one problem is a sort of self-inflicted wound. It is the self-disabling of philosophy in what is called the "Western" or "European" tradition (even if the roots of that tradition are really much wider and more complex than those adjectives suggest). So-called Western philosophy has played a major part in the making of the existing social systems of the world. But, during the last 150 years, it has developed in two ways that hinder it from doing all that it can to contribute to further global social development.

These intellectual developments have unfortunately coincided with dramatic social developments that seem to make more than ever necessary the most efficient possible use of the reasoning capacity of the human mind: the vast increase in world population, the vast increase in the complexity of social organization, in the energy levels of advanced societies, in the power of government systems and in the power of economic operators.

Part 4

Building Blocks of Security for People

Ensuring Peace in a Changing World

Üner Kırdar

We are on the threshold of a new millennium. In just six short years the twentieth century will be over, bringing to a close an era that witnessed two worldwide armed conflicts and one political war that divided the world for almost fifty years. Together these three conflicts deeply affected the course and destiny of humanity.

After the devastation of World War I, the League of Nations proved ineffective in preventing another such conflict. During World War II alone, military casualties exceeded 14 million, with over 45 million wounded and millions of civilians either killed or missing. As a result, nations lost almost two generations of their youth. The Cold War, in its own way, was equally as crushing and wasteful. In the more than 120 minor conflicts that were caused or exacerbated by the superpower rivalry, almost twenty-two million people were killed. Millions of people lived in an environment of oppression and tyranny, while valuable resources that could have improved human life were squandered on the arms race. Among the lessons of World War II is that political stability is dependent on economic and social development and on the fulfillment of human needs. A new international organization was needed that had a different vision than did the League for ensuring international security. The Charter of the United Nations shows us that the organizations founders took heed of the lessons of World War II.

Thus, when the UN was established on October 24, 1945, its Charter was formulated to be explicitly based on the notion that international peace can only be ensured if people's security is guaranteed for all. One of its major goals is to foster peace by promoting social progress and better standards of living in an environment of freedom.

The end of the Cold War has provided us with an new opportunity to apply this lesson and fulfill the objectives of the UN Charter. This section examines the extent to which we have succeeded in taking advantage of this opportunity. How far we have come in the five years since the Cold War ended in fulfilling the objectives of the Charter? Will we be able to use what we have learned from history to ensure that we do not repeat our mistakes? Are we better prepared now as we approach the twenty-first century to handle the challenges that face us?

This section argues that international peace in the coming century can only be ensured if we make a serious effort to fulfill the objectives of the UN Charter. To achieve this, we must recognize, as the Charter does, that international security has many components. It involves not only political but also people's security, and the two are indivisible. In maintaining international peace and security, the well-being of people is as important as national political security. The world cannot become a secure place unless people's security can be ensured in their homes, in their jobs, and in their communities. A better and more peaceful world, as foreseen and inspired by the UN Charter, requires higher standards of living, full employment, and social progress.[1] This requires wisdom, leadership, commitment, and most importantly, vision.

Political Changes in the 1990s

The world entered the 1990s with unprecedented hopes, as profound changes in politics, economics, demographics, technology, and ethics were happening. It was the beginning of a new era. The dimension of these changes and the opportunities they offered were unprecedented in modern history. Among them were the disappearance of ideological confrontations and barriers. These changes opened new horizons for individuals to achieve their aspirations for a better and more prosperous life, free from tyranny and oppression.

The world has the potential to become a much safer place, as superpower rivalry has disappeared and the threat of nuclear conflict has diminished. Democracy, political pluralism, market forces, and private enterprise have become the fundamental institutions of society, likely to shape the world's future. If these changes are properly chartered and specific policies and actions are adopted, the world could be well prepared for the new century. People's fears could be converted to hopes and threats to opportunities, resulting in an environment of world peace and economic and social prosperity. Otherwise, there may be cause for more stagnation, more economic and social disparity, more disillusionment, and more political, social, and ethnic conflict.

The Emerging New Order

The world we have known is receding into history. A new world is emerging, strangely shaped and formless, yet rapidly coming into focus. Familiar landmarks are changing before we can adjust our thinking. At present, the world presents a "Janus face" — on one side the face of "hope" and, on the other, the face of "fear."

In some parts of the world, entire societies have risen to levels of great affluence. Yet millions of people continue to live in poverty, endure hunger, remain jobless, suffer from preventable diseases, and experience social conflicts. Some developing countries have coped with change in an impressive manner. Unfortunately, most have not. They have experienced a decline in growth rates and living standards and have suffered from even greater poverty than before.

Many hopeful developments on the political scene resulted from the end of the Cold War. Other positive signs include the resolution of several national and regional conflicts in Cambodia, Central America, and Namibia; the end of apartheid in South Africa; and the evolving peace process in the Middle East. Progress toward disarmament, significant curtailments in military spending, and the convergence of views among many nations on effective approaches to economic and social development are additional sources of hope.

However, for most of the world's population the prognosis is not positive. The proliferation of all types of weapons continues; threats of war and terrorism are increasing; and racism, divisive nationalism, and religious and ethnic antagonism are becoming the most destructive forces working against peace and security, both within countries and between them. Millions of new refugees and displaced persons are migrating within and beyond national boundaries. Dangerous and destructive conflicts are exploding in several parts of the world, including Angola, Somalia, Rwanda, Burundi, Bosnia and Herzegovina, and parts of the former Soviet Union, such as Georgia and Azerbajian. People who are striving to build a new and freer way of life — whether in Eastern or Central Europe or in the former Soviet Union — are facing enormous hardships and mounting disappointments. For many, living standards are falling; jobs are nonexistent; and poverty, corruption, and crime are widespread. In former Eastern bloc countries, communists who were ousted from office only a few years ago are being reelected, indicating the extent to which people are disillusioned. The "old guards," although more committed to reform than their predecessors, are in many instances back in power.

Developing World

The end of the Cold War and the resultant new world political balance are rendering the developing world politically powerless and less relevant. In the view of some, their previous "usefulness" has now ended, and there is little value in taking any real interest in their fate. Africa is the best example of this apathy. No one seems to be concerned with its fate. This crisis-torn region has become a continent of famine, human deprivation, massacres, ethnic cleansing, and mass movements of refugees and displaced persons. For instance, it is estimated that in Somalia, as a result of the full-scale civil conflict, more than 500,000 people died from war or starvation. One million more became homeless. In Liberia, at least 20,000 have been killed and hundreds of thousands have been uprooted in a civil war. More recently in Rwanda, the majority Hutu tribe, which is estimated at approximately

3 million people, in an effort at ethnic cleansing killed more than 200,000 of the minority Tutsi tribe of 1.5 million. Similar killings took place in Burundi, Mali, Chad, Senegal, Togo, Uganda, Mauritania, Nigeria, Kenya, Zaïre, Angola, and South Africa. According to the *New York Times* on May 21, 1994, in Sub-Saharan Africa, where 600 million people live, there are more than 6 million refugees. Internally displaced persons total about 16 million, or three-fifths of the world's total.

New Conditionalities

Human rights and democratization are now often portrayed as political conditionalities to be implemented without any qualification. Promoting democracy before economic and social development is a new policy guideline. However, the experiences of Spain and Portugal in Europe and Japan, South Korea, Taiwan, and Singapore in Asia have shown that when a reasonable level of economic growth and capital formation have been ensured, it creates both a working and a middle-class that have a vested interest in a democratic system and stability.

The revolutions in Eastern and Central Europe and the former Soviet Union were triggered mostly by economic and social failures. Similarly, in parts of Asia and Africa economic deprivations and famine are promoting anarchy and warlord rivalry. History should make us wary of separating economic and social well-being from political freedom. The reverse is equally valid. Most crimes against humanity, including the genocide and mass starvation of the twentieth century, stemmed from such separations. Political and economic freedom are indivisible. There cannot be democracy without development, nor can there be development without democracy.[2]

The Cases of Bosnia and Rwanda

A tragedy unprecedented in fifty years has been occurring in the middle of Europe for more than two years. In Bosnia and Herzegovina, millions of Muslims have been the victims of Serbian atrocities in a program of ethnic cleansing. Old men and little children have been machine-gunned and thousands of women are gang-raped. With the arms embargo imposed on them, the Bosnians are defenseless against these acts of aggression and genocide. Unlike the situation in Kuwait, where the Western industrialized nations quickly and decisively punished Iraq for its aggression, world leaders are still arguing over whether to lift the arms embargo in Bosnia or to launch air strikes against the aggressors' military targets.

In his recent, thought-provoking book *Out of Control: Global Turmoil on the Eve of the 21st Century* and also in an OP-ED article in the *New York Times* on April 22, 1993, Zbigniew Brzezinski, national security adviser during the Carter Administration, illustrates how the emphatic Western pledge of "Never Again" does not apply for Bosnia. He notes that half a century after the Holocaust—in fact, on the fiftieth anniversary of the last gasp of the Warsaw Ghetto—one national leader after another proclaimed that the civilized world could never again tolerate genocide. Reflecting on current events in Bosnia, Brzezinski asks, "Is this a true proclamation of moral imperative?   Or merely a pompous affirmation of hypocrisy?" He challenges the views that the never again principle should apply only to "novel conflicts" and not to "the ones which have historical roots". Similarly, the United States should not become militarily involved in the cases of human rights abuses, if "national security interests" are not also threatened.

A similar policy approach has been adopted vis-à-vis the ongoing slaughter of thousands of innocent Rwandans. The former colonial powers are reluctant to participate in UN efforts to stop the mass massacre. As in the case of United States policy toward Bosnia, the Europeans do not have an imminent "national interest" for intervening again in Africa. In the British newspaper *The Guardian*, columnist Simon Hoggart offers this explanation for the Europeans' reluctance to react forcefully to the innocent killings: "Rwandans are thousands of miles away. Nobody you know has ever been on holiday to Rwanda!...And Rwandans don't look like the Europeans. They have even less clout than Bosnian Muslims...." An opposition member of the British Parliament challenged this European reluctance and asked, "Is there one law applicable to Kuwait and another for black Africans and Muslims Bosnians?"   Although public outrage is growing, the cold calculation of "national interest" is again outweighing humanitarian impulses. Realpolitik wins again.

Governance

There is a noticeable multipolarity, at present, in global leadership and decision making; regionalism is increasing vis-à-vis globalism. The leadership of the industrialized world is divided among America, Europe, and Japan, at a time when the need for joint leadership has never been greater.

Unfortunately, Western societies are turning inward instead of looking outward.   Instead of formulating forward-looking policies to meet the challenges of the new century, today's leaders are guided by the results of media polls.   In addition, most Western countries are suffering from institutional defects. Their governments are finding it difficult to convince their own populations of the need for such adjustments and sacrifices as budgetary reductions and trade deficits.

For example, the U.S. national debt rose from $735 billion in 1981 to more than $3 trillion by 1992 — more than half of the countries' whole economy. The annual interest is more than $200 billion, which exceeds total federal spendings for education, science and technology, law enforcement, transportation, and housing.

Finally, the international community is dumping the most intractable problems of the changing world on the UN, without contributing the funds necessary for their solution.

Economic and Social Changes in the 1990s

Revolutionary changes are also occurring on the world economic and social scenes.   Marketization and privatization of the economy are now worldwide phenomena.   Because of rapid advances in the technology of communications and information, traditional notions of borders are being eliminated. The world economy is in the process of being integrated into a single market, especially in the areas of trade, finances, and services. Since the end of the Cold War, this process has dramatically hastened. This globalization process affects every corner of the world. However, the advantages and disadvantages depend mostly on the level and structure of each country's economic activities.

In his recent report *An Agenda for Development*, the Secretary-General of the UN, Boutros Boutros-Ghali, emphasized that economic and social development will provide the most secure basis for peace and security. The lack of development contributes to international tension, confrontation, and conflicts. Economic growth is the engine of development. It is not sufficient, however, to pursue economic growth for its own sake. Growth should power higher standards of living, full employment, and social progress.

According to Boutros-Ghali, peace, economy, environment, societal justice, and democracy are integral parts of a whole:

- Without peace, human energies cannot be productively employed.
- Without economic growth, there can be no sustained, broad-based improvement in material well-being.
- Without protection of the environment, the basis of human survival will be eroded.
- Without societal justice, mounting inequalities will threaten social cohesion.
- Without political participation in freedom, development will remain fragile and perpetually at risk.[3]

These pertinent elements constitute the broad framework of an agenda for development. In the context of this section, however, four specific subjects deserve special consideration: population explosion, unemployment, increasing poverty, and social disintegration.

Population Explosion

The demographic trends for the year 2000 and its critical impact on human development and economic growth are fairly predictable: future population growth will take place mainly in the developing countries. By the beginning of the twenty-first century, the increasing number of people living in poverty and in need of adequate food, better education, health, and shelter may generate even stronger pressures for policy changes that will achieve rapid social progress.

At present, the world population is 5.7 billion people; 80 percent of this total (i.e., 4.5 billion) live in developing countries and 20 percent, i.e., 1.2 billion, in industrialized countries. It is projected that by the year 2000, the world population will reach 6.25 billion and by 2025, a minimum of 8.5 billion. Of this increase of 3.5 billion, or 95 percent, will live in the developing countries.

The impact of this increase will vary considerably among and within regions, but Africa and Asia will be the most affected. Africa's population is expected to increase by 225 million during the 1990s—more than the total population of that continent in 1950. By the year 2025, its population will triple from the present 550 million to 1.6 billion. In Asia, particularly South Asia, the increase will also be enormous. By the year 2000, Asia will have almost 600 million more people to feed, clothe, house, employ, educate, and keep healthy; by 2025, that number will have tripled, adding almost another 1.8 billion. The Latin American population will nearly double, from 374 million to 780 million. In contrast, in the industrialized countries, population growth will come to a standstill; in some of them, it will be negative.

Another alarming concern is the rapid increase of urban populations in developing countries caused by mass migration from rural areas to the large metropolitan centers. By the year 2000, the number of cities with more than 5 million inhabitants is expected to reach 48, of which 37 will be in the developing countries. Because of resources constraints, most of these megacities may become unmanageable and uninhabitable. All of this will cause new social problems, including disintegrating families, tens of millions of new street children, growing urban poverty, and environmental degradation.

At present, there is a striking contrast between the age structure of the populations of developed and developing countries. In the future, all the net growth in the world population of the 20-to-40 age group will take place in the developing countries. By the beginning of the next century, the industrialized countries will have nearly 15 million fewer people in that age group. The workforce will continue to age—producing a much larger number of older workers. Rapidly growing numbers of older and retired persons will require increased expenditures for health, welfare, and social security.

Normally, the process of aging has a considerable impact on the size and structure of the labor force, affecting the capacity and willingness to innovate and to respond to technological change. It may, therefore, have major implications for future economic growth. Young people can acquire new skills and adapt intellectually and socially to the required changes faster than older people.

In the developing countries, at least one million new jobs—more than the current number of jobs in all industrialized countries—will have to be created by the year 2000 just to accommodate new entrants into the labor forces. With the present high unemployment rates, it seems almost impossible to meet such a challenge.

In this context, however, it should be remembered that in the 1960s a similar situation, but on a much smaller scale, existed in the industrialized countries. The largest segment of the population was young and, in most parts of the industrialized world, youth was in ferment. There was a seething pool of discontent among young people as they approached maturity without satisfactory work opportunities and hopes for a reasonable living. Their activities prompted national and international action for a new social concern and sense of responsibility, and for improvements in the well-being of young people. If a similar course of action is not taken immediately, the world will probably see a recurrence of this revolt by young people, but on a much larger and more dangerous scale. This time it will occur in the developing world as a result of frustration, disappointment, and lack of satisfactory work opportunities.

The dynamics that trigger social revolutions are not sudden; they usually build up over time. True political wisdom is, therefore, to respond as early as possible to the needs and frustrations of people.

Employment

Employment has multiple dimensions in people's lives. It is not merely an economic means to generate financial resources. Far more important, it gives people a sense of dignity and integrates them into their society.

The painful experiences of the Great Depression, as well as the economic causes of World War II, convinced the founders of the UN that "full employment" was one of the main pillars of international peace, stability, and well-being. Its members, therefore, pledged themselves to take both joint and separate action to achieve this goal. Today, however, this objective seems to be forgotten. It has progressively disappeared from the agenda of the UN.

Jobless growth is a new, but common, phenomenon. The elimination of jobs and massive layoffs are considered effective measures to ensure competitiveness in the global markets. Among the richest countries, therefore, structural unemployment has reached its highest points. During the 1950s and 1960s, an unemployment rate of 3 to 4 percent was considered normal in the industrialized countries. Today, this figure exceeds 12 percent. Current policy makers are not only becoming reconciled to low paying jobs, but also to high rates of unemployment.

In a classical economy, voluntary unemployment was a temporary phenomenon that would be reduced by natural market forces. This does not apply with today's market rules. In the United States, for example, permanent jobs losses as a percentage of total unemployment has reached 45 percent per annum. According to the new philosophy, if you can fire workers without affecting production and sales, you can reduce costs and increase profits. New technological advancements make possible for companies to produce more with fewer workers. Thus, companies are increasing their gains by reducing their labor forces.

This growing impact of job cutting is evident in national economic statistics. Wages are falling as a percentage of national incomes, while corporate profits are rising. Recently, for example, General Electric reduced its workforce from 400,000 to 230,000. During the same period, sales tripled. The same is true for other profitable companies, such as Procter and Gamble, AT&T, Johnson and Johnson, and IBM.[4]

In the industrialized countries, most new jobs are in the service sector, including banking, tourism, insurance, retailing, health care, and restaurants. Job cutting is now occurring mainly in manufacturing and mining, as it did in agriculture at the beginning of the twentieth century. At that time, the mechanization of farming forced many farmers to migrate to urban areas to find new jobs in the industrial sector.

The link between "full employment" and "rising inflation" is creating a new international concern. Current policy makers believe that if people work more, they may spend more money. This, in turn, may cause higher inflation. Therefore, a trade-off must be made between "job growth" and "low inflation." In other words, a choice has to be made between "putting people back to work" or "keeping prices under control." In the view of market-oriented economists and policy makers, safeguarding the value of currencies and low interests rates is more important than job security and economic growth. As a consequence, in the new economic literature, the term of "full employment" is replaced by "cut of the fat" or "job shedding!"

To the developing world, with its expanding unemployment problem, the powerful role of the corporate world in the globalization of the world economy and in the channeling of capital, according to its own policies and priorities, becomes more apparent. Although capital and goods are moving freely among countries, the same freedom does not exist for the labor force. Instead, strict regulations govern the movements of workers. In addition, as soon as developing countries learn to produce something that is labor intensive, restrictions are applied to those very products.

In the industrialized countries, the largest part of GNP consists of new jobs in the modern service sector. Developing countries are not yet fully aware of this structural change in the world economy, nor are they paying enough attention to the training of their human resources to be supported by the new technologies. Technological change is the real basis of the new economic and transnational corporate power. In the short run, many developing countries are not equipped to compete with industrialized countries because of lack of skill, technological knowledge, and resources. They are increasingly falling behind and from the outset are condemned to be marginalized.

Poverty

Increasing polarization in living conditions is another common trend, both within and between nations. Growing disparities, sharp differences in incomes and living standards, and unequal distribution of wealth and access to resources are the visible symptoms of increasing poverty in all societies.

For example, look at the United States, which enjoys one of the highest living standards in the world. The real GDP per capita still ranks first, but for the past two decades incomes—both in real and in purchasing-power terms—have eroded. More American households now need two income earners to produce even modest gains in family income. The wages and benefits given to the young and less educated workers have fallen enough to push some into poverty. Average national income (GDP), which increased annually by almost 5 percent during the 1960s, has dropped to approximately 0.5 percent in the 1990s. Similarly, average yearly median family income, which was rising by 3.2 percent in the 1960s, has declined by 2 to 4 percent in the 1990s. The number of poor people increased from 1.2 million to 36.9 million in 1992, which is three times the overall growth rate of the population. This is the highest poverty rate since 1983. The overall number of poor Americans rose by 3.3 percent in 1992, while the total population increased 1.1 percent. It is mostly poor children who suffer from extreme poverty. During 1992, 47 percent of all poor children under the age of 18 lived in households where incomes were less than half of the official poverty level.[5]

These recent poverty data on the United States reflect the general trend evident in many other countries. The rich clearly get richer, while the poor get poorer — or, at best, run in place. The expectation that each generation will live better than the previous one no longer seems to be true.

Social Values and Disintegration

A noticeable trend shows that the social fabric of most countries — rich and poor — are weakening. As a result, several nation-states are beginning to disintegrate socially.

One may start by citing the growing alienation from established social values. At present, a highly materialistic global culture is developing. Emphasis on "competition" is overshadowing the older and essential habits of "sharing" and "cooperation." The pursuit of happiness is more and more defined in terms of money and patterns of consumption.

In addition, increasing polarization is taking place in different nations because of ethnic, tribal, religious, and cultural differences. The rise of nationalistic and separatist movements is causing national disintegration. Other factors include discrimination against minority and disadvantaged groups; unequal treatment of women; and increases in single-headed families, maladjusted and poorly educated children, juvenile delinquents, street children, crime, drug addiction, and disease. As indicated by the 1994 UNDP *Human Development Report*, these problems are not isolated events confined within national borders.[6] For many people, the greatest sources of anxiety to their own personal security are the increasing numbers of today's violent crimes, drugs and juvenile delinquencies.

In the United States in 1992, 14 million crimes were reported to the police. The economic toll of these crimes is estimated at $425 billion annually. In the second half of the 1980s, the murder rate in Italy and Portugal doubled; in Germany it tripled. During the same period, drug-related crimes roughly doubled in Denmark and Norway, and increased more than thirtyfold in Japan. Brazil, where more than 200,000 children spend their lives on the streets begging, stealing, trafficking in drugs, a minimum of four children are murdered every day — the killing of minors increased by 40 percent during 1993 alone.[7]

Another trend in many countries is the disintegration of family structure. The number of single-parent households in the United States, which was marginal in the 1960s and 1970s, has grown remarkably. Estimates project that by the end of this century, only 40 percent of new families will be of the traditional type; 60 percent will be single-parent families.[8] In marriages contracted between 1987 and 1991, the percentage of divorces is more than 58 percent in Finland, 49 percent in Denmark, and 48 percent in the United States and Sweden. Births outside of marriage, between 1985 and 1992 have increased by 52 percent in Sweden, 47 percent in Denmark, 34 percent in Norway, 32 percent in France, and 27 percent in the United States.[9] In developing countries, the disintegration of the family is taking place mainly because of rapid urbanization, migration, and increasing economic difficulties and poverty. The weakening of family links is reflected by increases in the school dropout rate, juvenile delinquency, drug addiction, and homicide.

Global social peace is thus challenged by new assertions of discrimination and exclusion and by acts of terrorism and civil conflicts that undermine the recent evolution and peaceful changes of the democratic process.[10]

Conclusion

All societies today are affected by increasing poverty, unemployment, and social disintegration. However, this situation could become a plus. In this area, unlike many hard-core development issues, all countries — developing, industrialized, and transition — share a common interest. Therefore, at least a hope exists of creating a feeling of solidarity among people in the North, South, and East. Much depends on the farsightedness of world leaders, who need to better understand that security is not only political, but also human.

The idea of helping the economically weak is not new. In national communities, such as ancient Rome, the concept of aiding the poor appear was regarded as a moral obligation. The advent of Christianity and Islam strengthened that moral obligation by giving it a religious basis. Finally, the concept acquired the form of a legal obligation. In modern states, it is now an essential and legally imposed duty, enforced through the mechanism of taxation, for the rich members of the community to help the poor to raise their standard of living.

In the international sphere, however, this concept does not have the same status. Although international assistance has sometimes been driven by idealism, generosity, and international solidarity, it has more often been influenced by political motivations, ideological confrontations, and commercial self-interest.

With the end of the Cold War, support for this cause is eroding. Development, as an objective, has been pushed aside. Adjustment is becoming the key word and the main economic concern. In addition, the signs of so-called aid fatigue are becoming more politically apparent every day.

Perceptions play a leading role in shaping world politics and economy. This was particularly evident during the post war period, as global development challenges and cooperation gained a special dynamism. In this sense, this period was unique. With a feeling of satisfaction, developed countries entertained a sense of confidence, as well as commitment, to meeting future global development needs. Indeed, the late President Kennedy committed himself, in his inaugural speech, not only to the people of his own country, but also to the cause of the developing world.

This type of world leadership, with its perception of interdependence among the nations, must be revived. Every country has to ensure adequate growth and development not only for its own sake, but also for the world community at large.

We are at a crossroad. If the necessary vision, wisdom, farsightedness, leadership, and commitment prevails, the foundations for a better world as foreseen and inspired by the UN Charter, can be laid down for the next century. All nations, rich and poor, large and small, can prosper in that environment assured of peace, human security, and dignity.

During the Cold War, the UN was rendered powerless to deal with many crises because the rivalry between the superpowers paralyzed the organization and its members. Two years ago, Secretary-General Boutros Boutros-Ghali, stated that the end of the Cold War had given the UN a second chance to create the world described in the Charter.[11]

To do so, we must change the prevailing concept of security. Although the concept of peace is easy to understand, international security is a more complex issue. During the Cold War, security was viewed from a political perspective and was shaped by the potential for armed conflict between East and West. For too long, security has been equated with the threats to national borders. States sought arms, as the primary means to protect their security. With the end of the Cold War, the need to change this concept has become urgent. Recent events, as in Somalia, the former Yugoslavia, and Rwanda, indicate that future conflicts may often occur within, rather than between, nations. Their origin may lie in growing socioeconomic disparities and deprivation. The slaughtering in Bosnia, Somalia, and Rwanda proves that potential threats to security are increasingly threats to human survival. It is therefore imperative that we give equal importance to people's security as to national political security. The security of people in their homes and in their jobs, as well as freedom from want, must indeed become the central concerns of the twenty-first century.

When one reads the following appraisal from the report of U.S. Secretary of State Hull to President Truman on the results of the San Francisco Conference of June 1945, one deems to praise warmly the farsightedness of the founders of the United Nations, especially with respect to the concept of security:

> "The battle of peace has to be fought on two fronts. The first is the security front where victory spells freedom from fear. The second is the economic and social front where victory means freedom from want. Only victory on both fronts can assure the world of an enduring peace. If the United Nations cooperate effectively toward an expanding world economy, better living conditions for all men and women, and closer understanding among peoples, they will have gone far toward eliminating in advance the causes of another world war a generation hence. If they fail, there will be instead widespread depressions and economic warfare which would fatally undermine the world organization. No provision that can be written into the Charter will enable the Security Council to make the world secure from war if men and women have no security in their homes and their jobs."[12] (emphasis added)

The above makes fascinating reading at a time when we are once again rediscovering the complexity of defining the concept of security. From above it is clear that the architects of the United Nations have given equal weight to people's security and political security.

The main argument of this section is, therefore, the necessity of returning back to the basic aims and objectives of the Charter of the United Nations, as foreseen by its founders, and to implement them vigorously with new energy and commitment.

To meet the challenges of the twenty-first century we must be inspired by the farsightedness of the UN Charter provisions. We can no longer fight the battle of tomorrow with the weapons of the Cold War period. The preamble of the Charter starts with the words "We the people." We must, therefore, put people at the center of all our concerns for the future. Our ultimate objective must be people first and the improvement of their conditions. Our future policies must aim to be responsive to the social and economic needs of people and to reduce their poverty and misery. We must better use the people's capacities and capabilities. We must encourage the release of human energies in accordance with people's aspirations.

Notes

1. United Nations Charter, Article 55.
2. See Üner Kırdar and Leonard Silk (eds.), *A World Fit for People*. New York: New York University Press, 1994, p. xv.
3. Boutros Boutros-Ghali, *An Agenda for Development*, Report of the Secretary-General, UN Doc. A/48/935, dated May 6, 1994, pp. 4-10. See also the United Nations Charter, Article 55.
4. See "Strong Companies Join Trend to Eliminate Jobs," *New York Times*, July 26, 1993; "Job Extinction Evolving into a Fact of Life in US," *New York Times*, March 22, 1994.
5. See "The Economy: Problems," *New York Times*, February 14, 1993; "Poverty in US," *New York Times*, October 5, 1993.
6. *Human Development Report 1994*. New York: Oxford University Press 1994, p. 3.
7. *Human Development Report 1994*, p. 3.
8. Üner Kırdar, "Policies and Strategies for Human Development: Recent Record." In Khadija Haq and Üner Kırdar (eds.), *Managing Human Development*. North–South Roundtable, Islamabad, Pakistan, 1988. UN Sales E.88.III.BL.
9. *Human Development Report 1994*, p. 186.
10. Boutros Boutros-Ghali, *An Agenda for Peace*, Report of the Secretary-General, United Nations Publication, 1992, p. 6.
11. Boutros Boutros-Ghali, *Agenda for Peace*.
12. Report to the President on the Results of the San Francisco Conference by the Secretary of State, Department of State, Publication 2343, 1945.

Chapter 1

From Political to People's Security

Section 1

The Changing Concept of Security

Flora Lewis

Suspension of the ideological confrontation that was central to the Cold War has brought an evolution of the international vocabulary, more slowly than the political change but moving perhaps with less friction. "Security" meant the defense of states, their territory, their system, and their institutions. Now it is coming to mean much more than what military and police power can protect. The meaning of "human rights" was harshly contested. To the West, it meant essentially political and civil rights of the individual, free speech and assembly, due process, the complex of guarantees that democracies are expected to assure. To the East, ideologically speaking, it meant economic and social guarantees, food, shelter, employment, access to health care, with all the emphasis on society as a collective whose will (as expressed by the regime in power) was not to be challenged by personal demands or nonconformist opinion.

Human Security

Now there is a subtle, and still far from clearly explained, fusion of these concepts with the emerging phrase "human security," which is coming to mean not only what is absolutely essential to people for survival, but all those aspirations that come naturally — for material well-being, for dignity, for opportunity, and for community. It is a very broad concept, perhaps utopian, but compelling, and despite all the differences that culture, history, and circumstance impose, obviously a universal yearning. It implies protection against many more dangers and sources of distress than mere "security"; it even implies protection against protection in the sense of freeing people from dependency and enabling them to take charge of their lives.

This is a very big order, and nobody will be able to say exactly what it should comprise for others, let alone be able to donate it. So the idea must be approached with due modesty, a willingness to listen to what various groups of people and people in different parts of the world most want and feel able to achieve if conditions can be made favorable, a willingness to sort out the long list of needs and goals and address those where practical measures can achieve results. It is true that all the many diverse, and sometimes apparently contradictory, factors that make up "human security" are linked. Changes in one area may have consequences on others that were not foreseen or intended. But it is also true that such a great transformation cannot be effected all at once, however powerful or magical the desire. The needed effort must be undertaken step by step. Even if unimaginably vast resources were available, people cannot change as fast as technology now does. It would be too painful. Too much they consider precious would risk being lost. Putting everything on the wish list at once, with equal urgency, risks achieving nothing but disillusion, frustration, and destructive anger.

Sustainable Development

This is what underlies the idea of "sustainable development." It means taking care that one big project which may be highly desirable in itself does not create other highly undesirable consequences, as when a new industry destroys the environment, or a huge cash crop, whose market may not always be assured, leads people to a situation where they can no longer feed themselves. It also, and perhaps even more important, means building a chain, so that the rewards of each step become the basis for the next, a self-propelling production of the wherewithal to produce better and more, to learn more, to be more capable. There are going to be mistakes. That must be taken as a given. So "sustainable development" also has to mean paying attention as you go along, not being too proud or too smug to admit when what seemed good ideas are not working and a change in direction, even a step backward, has to be made.

Many parts of the world are suffering now from the wreckage of grandiose plans that consumed enormous wealth and effort, efforts that could have been fruitful if constant correctives had been applied as the need became visible. This has been particularly true of tightly planned societies. But whatever the system there are always human faults that have to be taken into account. Plans are needed, theories are needed, or things do not get done. But continued attention to results with a readiness to make adjustments is also needed if failure is not to be dramatic.

Nor should it be assumed that just because they are capable of reason, people are always going to be rational; that just because they are capable of kind and noble action, people are going to be saints; that just because they want a better life, a better world, people are going to dedicate themselves to that alone.

One of the strengths of democracy is that it recognizes human failings and tries to balance them out, in part by providing for everybody in the society to participate, in part by limiting even the power of the majority to override basic guarantees and offering the minority the possibility of becoming the majority if it has sufficiently convincing arguments. Social harmony must be understood as finding ways to resolve the conflicts of interest and attitude in a peaceable, civic spirit, not as eliminating them. There will always be disputes. Change itself, which is the essence of development, helps some and hurts others at any given moment; that necessarily produces disagreements. Human beings are both individual and social animals. Neglecting either side of that duality is destructive. As the French poet Paul Valery has warned, two great dangers always threaten the world — order and disorder. Excess in either direction is destructive.

Successes and Failures

In the last quarter of a century, some societies have fared very well in raising living standards, providing education and the cultivation of skills, slowing population growth to manageable numbers, and thereby achieving sustainable development. Some have failed miserably. Because the most impressive examples of the first group are in Asia and the most distressing of the second are in Africa, there have been attempts to explain the difference by differences in culture and history. No doubt these are factors, but they are not a satisfactory explanation. If these were the only factors involved, the conclusion would have to be that a substantial part of humanity is hopeless, doomed to perpetual despair. There really has not been adequate study and understanding of these unexpected patterns.

Colonialism is an excuse for their existence, not an explanation. Different imperial regimes treated subject peoples differently, but the patterns tend to be regional rather than consistent with the different habits and methods of the former masters, whether British, French, Belgian, Portuguese, or Russian. Nor do strong historical cultural achievements give sufficient account of why there is success in one place and failure in another. Islamic societies have as much past glory on which to build confidence as those inspired by Confucianism, but they have not as good a current record for development and modernizing. And there are striking differences in results within the large regional groupings. Given our incapacity as yet to figure out why, with the reliable assurance of predictability that theories on the laws of nature provide, it is better to proceed case by case, experimentally and pragmatically, rather than try to stretch hunches and ideological biases to fit all. That Procrustean bed approach has made for some disasters. We should try to avoid it.

Democracy and Development

Nonetheless, the current debate on the utility of the "Western model," which usually means the role of the state and the desirability of democracy with individual freedoms, is also an obfuscation that substitutes political convenience for applicable knowledge. The objections come either from those who already have power and want to keep it without challenge, or in cases of acute disorder and collapse where the natural revulsion for such an extreme drives desperate and panicky people to the opposite one.

Malaysia's Dr. Mahathir bin Mohammad asserts "Asiatude," some inherent characteristic of Asians that assures better progress under strong, authoritarian government. This makes a more democratic organization of their societies unapplicable, even downright pernicious. Like the rulers in Beijing and elsewhere who for their own reasons are less vocal or articulate, he denounces support from abroad for domestic dissidents on the grounds of human rights as an unwarranted, unjustifiable interference in the sovereign affairs of these states.

We have no way of knowing what the bulk of the people living under these regimes really think, since they have no safe way of expressing their feelings. We do know from history and contemporary examples that keeping such a tight lid on societies, especially when they inevitably become aware of rapid change in the rest of the world, is a recipe for dangerous upheaval. The explosion usually comes only after a little opening has occurred, but sooner or later that cannot be prevented. Beyond a certain basic level, economic development is blocked without some opening, and stagnation, even deterioration, sets in.

But sudden collapse of existing excessive constraints by no means assures a self-regulating, better functioning society. If old hatreds and grievances have merely been suppressed, not healed in reconciliation with new habits of voluntary cooperation, they can burst force with renewed and even murderous power. Europe is now experiencing this two-directional tug of war — toward integration to amass the ability to deal with problems too big for any existing single state to handle on its own and toward fragmentation, separatism, and ethnic conflict. It takes gradual development of tolerance and mental habits of accommodation, which cannot be imposed by command, to channel these impulses toward fruitful, not destructive, energies. There is nothing peculiarly European about this double strain. It has come after a millennium of terrible conflict and several millennia of population movements, wave upon wave depositing sediments of a large variety of genetic and cultural mixtures. "Ethnic purity" is built mainly on myth, and the myths have good and bad purposes. They can mobilize people for large tasks, provide the comfort and warmth of a community beyond one's immediate surroundings, give a sense of solidity and continuity to confront the eternal bewilderment of life and death. They can also be used to create a power base for the unscrupulous, to blind people to the faults and vanities of their leaders, to distract them from normal pursuits, and to harness them to enterprises of no service to themselves.

Democracy and Social Consensus

Europe's turbulent history is not so different from other parts of the world; its western half has just recently managed to transcend it better than some others. There are few truly homogeneous countries. Both the mixtures and the myth making exist practically everywhere. That is why the need for mechanisms to undertake change peacefully, in "social harmony," is universal.

It is as false to define democracy as a western idea, a social technique uniquely suited to societies based on European cultures, as it would be to classify gunpowder as a purely Chinese artifact. True, democracy sprouted in the West; the Chinese invented gunpowder. But the origins do not define the utility of these inventions. The difference between democracy and social consensus, which is a long and deep tradition of many Asian and African societies, is that democracy can provide a method of avoiding conflict when consensus breaks down or is too hard to achieve because internal differences become strident and abrasive. This situation is likely to grow and intensify in the modern world because change has become so rapid and differences have become so noticeable with economic and communications globalization. Therefore, the need for a mechanism to hasten consensus and provide an alternative basis for decision making that is accepted as fully legitimate is all the greater. So far, we have not stumbled on anything that performs the chore anywhere near so well and so regularly as democracy. It does not guarantee good decisions, by any means. It does make sure bad decisions can be rectified when people become aware of their effects, instead of allowing the consequences to pile up and rot and ferment until only heroic measures can clear them away.

Democracy and Decentralization of Decision Making

The practice of democracy does tend to limit the power of the state, enough to make it quite distasteful to autocrats. For one thing, there are certain kinds of decisions affecting their immediate, everyday lives that people can make and want to make locally. They see no need for far away representatives, however legitimately chosen, to make an overall rule that may not suit local circumstances. Therefore, democracy favors decentralization of certain powers. For another thing, democracy gives people the sense of their right to participate in even the biggest decisions, and therefore to resent delegating what they consider too much to central authority. People do not always trouble to make use of that right. There has been a fairly dramatic decline in the proportion of the electorate actually going to the polls in many of the established democracies over the last half century. But it reflects not a desire to leave more power to the state, to increase its authority, but rather an increased suspicion and even resentment of how it is seen to use its power. They feel they already have too little control, not too much.

Democracy, the State, and People

It is not easy for individuals to make decisions for the long-term when their most urgently felt needs and desires are the most immediate. And it is not easy for them to discern and grasp which of the sacrifices asked of them in order to promote constructive change are really necessary and likely to be rewarding and which are unnecessary or likely to be pernicious. So the state has an added role in countries where development must be spurred. The state must not only keep order, but look ahead, educating and explaining to people where they are going. "Failed states" make development and practically every other constructive activity impossible. People can live without a state, as they more or less did in primitive societies or on the frontier during America's westward expansion, but then they cannot do much more than they can achieve with their own resources.

Larger-scale undertakings require more organization, and modernizing and modern societies are so complex that they require a firm internal structure to keep functioning at all. A delicate balance is needed between the state's ability to make and impose decisions and the room left to individuals to fuel and make use of their energy. Just where the balance should lie must be determined case by case, with experiment and adjustment to fit each specific set of circumstances. There can be no general rule, but there must be an underlying principle that leaves it to the individuals as a polity to decide stage by stage whether the balance is appropriate. Where the state has all power and where the state cannot act at all are examples of Valéry's twin order–disorder menaces of disaster.

Conclusion

So the conclusion must be not to draw too many, or anyway, too rigid conclusions. International peace and security does depend on spreading satisfaction and tolerable conditions of life. Egregiously proliferating humanity leaves practically no room that can be barricaded against the miserable.

There is a moral imperative for human solidarity, but even if it is not accepted there are economic, social, and political imperatives that make it indispensable. Development is essential so that those left behind can make a decent start on catching up with those who have prospered and go on to fashion their own prosperity in the form and manner they choose. But development, in a society as in an individual person, has its own mysterious rhythms and pulses. They must be respected.

Section 2

People: Builders of Peace

Princess Basma Bint Talal

I come from a region that has generated great ideas and noble principles, yet it has rarely enjoyed comprehensive peace. Therefore, people of that region especially appreciate the theme of this book, which is a manifestation of the common will of the international community, represented by the United Nations, to enhance the role of people in building peace and benefiting from its fruits.

Traditionally, nations and governments have engaged in military preparedness. However, as we approach the twenty-first century, the UN is appropriately shifting the emphasis to peace and development preparedness by engaging the peoples of the world in preparing an Agenda for People.

The UN Charter starts with "We the Peoples." It proclaims that its major objectives include the maintenance of peace and security and the promotion of economic development. Recent events have vividly shown the interdependence of this triad. There can be no lasting peace without development, development cannot become a reality without security and stability, and "people" are and should always be at the center of all concerns. To achieve these goals, governments must adopt the correct priorities for their sustainable human development policies.

Priorities for a Sustainable Human Development Policy

Sustainable human development means an economy and a society in which people live in balance and harmony with nature and its resources. Their actions, in totality, should not, in the long run, jeopardize this balance. This is not an idealistic slogan, but an achievable objective in most developing countries if certain policies and strategies are adopted. There are, however, four prerequisites for achieving this goal: the eradication of illiteracy through free and compulsory education; improving the status of women;

a balance between human needs and resources; and the elimination of poverty to reinforce the dignity of people.

The Eradication of Illiteracy

Only a literate population can attain sustainable human development. Today, one-third of the developing world is illiterate, so are one-half of its women. Eradication of illiteracy, particularly among the young, through free and compulsory schooling is essential for any meaningful human development objective.

Financial aid, although limited, is available, but it is not distributed in equitably among people, nations, and competing projects. Expensive infrastructural projects receive the lion's share of investment and development aid—not because of the prestigious nature of such projects, but because they allow donor countries to export their products and services.

Thus, power stations, telecommunications, and weapons are favored over schools. High education is encouraged at the expense of primary education. Such policies, which have been implemented for decades, do not lead to sustainable human development. How can illiterate and uneducated people efficiently run and maintain sophisticated systems and machinery? How can a sophisticated infrastructure be built without developing the foundations of basic education? To attain sustainable human development, eradication of illiteracy and basic education for the grass roots are essential.

The Status of Women

Sustainable human development requires the equal participation of both genders. However, in most developing nations, women still lag behind men in education and employment opportunities. As a result, illiteracy is still common, and the role of women in the development process is marginalized. This disparity handicaps the development process, because education begins in the home. Healthy and educated mothers provide improved care and better opportunities for their children. A clean national environment starts with a clean and healthy home environment. The two are complementary.

Respect for human rights is an integral part of sustainable human development. Nowhere is that respect more essential than it is for women. Women's rights to equal opportunities and enhancement of their abilities is necessary for sustainable human development. Without it, development remains partial, as in the case of most developing countries.

Human Needs and Resources

The third priority for sustainable human development is to balance social needs with those of national security. Neglect of social and human developmental needs is often the root cause of extremism, civil tensions, and the eventual weakening of the social fabric.

In this decade of major political transition, we must narrow the gap between the rich and the poor, the literate and the illiterate, abundance and scarcity; and last but not least, the opportunities available to men and women. Children, the future assets of the world, must not be robbed of their childhood by child labor, terror, and a lack of elementary education.

If the ghastly examples of Rwanda, Somalia, Haiti, and other nations that have experienced internal social disasters are not enough to open our eyes, the disastrous consequences of social tensions will engulf us without mercy. What limited resources that exist must be wisely shared between social and security needs.

Nations must also realize the extent and limitations of their resources, including natural resources. Such limitations pose both economic and demographic constraints on development. An Arab proverb states, "stretch your legs only to the extent of your bed." The emerging balance must accommodate nature's resources, such as agricultural land and water, with such factors as habit and demand. If this does not happen the environment will be strained.

Economic development is dictated by the ability of nations to finance and service their investments. Overambitious investments can only be sustained by large borrowing and that only to a limited extent. At the same time, these factors can hamper the development process. Technology and good management help to stretch the usefulness and enhance the efficiency of limited resources. Technology, in most instances, is not cheap and must be compatible with ecological needs. Sustainable human development requires a balance among population, nature, development, and resources.

The Eradication of Poverty

The eradication of poverty, which is necessary to reinforce the dignity of people, should be the focus of all efforts. Labor and dignity go hand in hand. This is why the right to work should be an inalienable right of all individuals. Toward this end, cooperation among government, nongovernment, and regional bodies, as well as with the UN and its agencies, should be strengthened and deepened.

Social integration, and therefore social harmony, can only be achieved if the problems of poverty and unemployment are addressed. Future efforts to achieve peace – to replace destruction with construction and violence with stability – should not be thwarted because of poverty and underdevelopment.

The New Role of Nongovernmental Organizations

For many years now, nongovernmental organizations (NGOs) have been working to achieve the goals and priorities of sustainable human development. Thus, although development should be human-centered and broad-based, with equal opportunities for men and women, it should also achieve a balance with nature and a balance between the imperatives of modernity and tradition. The goal is the full and free participation of ordinary men and women in making decisions that affect all aspects of their lives, whether political, social, economic, or cultural.

Quietly and consistently, NGOs have been playing a role in alleviating poverty and unemployment; that role should now be expanded. Because of their direct contact with the grass roots, because they are voluntary organizations, and, more importantly, because many of the governments in the developing world need help in mobilizing societal resources and public opinion, the NGOs are well placed to assist in achieving sustainable human development. NGOs can be a major catalyst for change, for improvement within communities and among people, and in building consensus from the bottom up, which is needed for any venture to succeed.

The direct link between NGOs and the grass roots gives these organizations a realistic insight into the problems and needs that have to be tackled. They are, therefore, best suited to identify early warning signals that can help prevent problems and avoid crisis management. Throughout the world, NGOs have played a crucial part in rebuilding society. They are always ready to assist governmental efforts in organizing humanitarian assistance, promoting the role of women, rehabilitating the disabled, and promoting grass roots development. The role of NGOs, which has always been to respond to the immediate needs of people, has become an integral part of national developmental processes.

With this mind, the role of NGOs should be imaginatively expanded. As the main channels through which new approaches, ideas, and solutions are implemented, NGOs need the support of the international community and other international organizations. They are a vital link between politicians and decision makers, as well as the translators of policies and abstract theories into concrete actions and solutions.

Peace and People

The world community has a special and urgent responsibility to encourage the peace in the Middle East by ensuring that development efforts will be directed toward social integration and the eradication of poverty and unemployment. The Middle East has faced a number of challenging situations; the wars of the past have created a unique culture. Now, efforts toward a genuine peace in the Middle East are underway. If such efforts succeed, the people of the region need not worry about their future and children can grow up in a peaceful environment.

The problems and challenges of the Middle East are no different from those in many developing countries: the imbalance between natural resources and population growth remains unsolved, the introduction and transfer of appropriate technologies are still at their early stages, and significant institutional and structural changes are required. But what is unique about the region is the peace process currently taking place, for it requires not only a change of attitudes, but also the creation of common interests through regional and bilateral cooperation.

If development is the road to peace, it should be people centered. As His Majesty King Hussein stated in his address before the joint session of the U.S. Congress in July 1993, "It should never be forgotten that peace resides ultimately not in the hands of governments but in the hands of the people. For unless peace can be made real to the men, women and children of the Middle East, the best efforts of negotiators will come to nought."

The Middle East needs a new educational approach that will eventually create a cultural framework that enhances peace. This must not be the sole responsibility of governments of the region. Significant support from the world community is required during this sensitive period of transition.

Regional conflicts in the Middle East have created great imbalances by forcing population movements and creating rapid, but uneven, growth. Leaders are trying to alleviate these unhealthy conditions, while simultaneously building peace. Conditions in this region did not develop in a vacuum; the Middle East is at the crossroads between Europe, Asia, and Africa. Thus peace will not only benefit the countries directly involved, but will transcend its boundaries to the world at large. The social integration that will be the focus of the 1995 World Summit for Social Development will be greatly enhanced by an immediate economic rebuilding program in the Middle East.

Conclusion

The sense of oneness among peoples is being enhanced by the growing awareness of the challenges facing humanity. It is the people who can help meet these challenges, by contributing to their solutions and by pragmatically implementing whatever action plans are created by the international community. Government efforts are not enough; success requires the participation of men and women at the community and village levels.

No single or magical formula exists. Circumstances change among different people and in different geographical locations. National interests bias actions to suit local circumstances. There are however certain common denominators. The main impetus should be targeted along these four fronts: eradication of illiteracy; improving the status of women; a right development balance; and successful social integration by addressing the problems of poverty and unemployment.

In the Middle East, my generation has not been able to lead the normal life of a people at peace. It is important that we maximize this historical moment, during which the atmosphere is imbued with hope and promise. Although much remains to be done, we look with great anticipation toward an era of peace, in which the people can be both the facilitators and beneficiaries.

In an increasingly materialistic world, our priorities surely become more clearly defined when we recall that we are the recipients of the three great Abrahamic religions. Each, in its own way, stresses that pure values and true justice must be the foundations of social solidarity, in whose folds competition aims at leaving room for excellence rather than the fulfillment of selfish instincts. Social peace within as well as peace among nations is more than the absence of violence. Peace is a positive force. In the Middle East, we hope it becomes a way of life.

Section 3

Toward Global Human Security

Federico Mayor

The lifting of the global nuclear threat has freed us to focus on the comparable threats to human security presented by poverty, which is linked to massive overpopulation and pollution; uncontrolled migration; extremism of all kinds; and violence rooted in ignorance and deprivation. Poverty, like war, kills. Many situations can be remedied, but not death. Poverty in many cases means misery in the slums, and this exclusion can lead to radicalization and even to aggression.

Development is a total human process encompassing all aspects of human existence, and it is a right due to all human beings in their diversity. Greater emphasis on the social and cultural dimensions of development than has hitherto been the case is essential.

War Against Poverty and Oppression

Is it feasible to build peace in the minds of people in order to prevent conflicts, alleviate poverty, and ensure — through education — mastery of their own destinies? The answer is yes. We must act with this conviction, with the awareness that the "forecasts" of the past ten years have been proven wrong. The "pragmatists" can manage reality, but not reform it. Could we have anticipated ten years ago that 60 percent of the world's population, then under the shadow of oppression, would today be engaged on the long march to democratization? And what of Cambodia, Namibia, South Africa, Mozambique, San Salvador, and the Middle East? Let us pay tribute to those who have been outstanding in demonstrating that the "linear-minded" were wrong, are still wrong, and that many things that now appear impossible will be possible in the future if approached with imagination and solidarity.

Current ethnic conflicts are not the result of freedom, but of oppression. There are so many positive examples of intercultural peaceful coexistence! Ethnic conflicts do not arise in long-established democracies, but in long-established dictatorships. There is an urgent and compelling need to tackle the interlinked problems of global human security at their sources, to equip ourselves with international policies and mechanisms that respect every individual's rights. If opportunity does not go to poverty, then poverty will go to opportunity. Getting this message across is our best chance of galvanizing all concerned into action.

A Global Human Security Strategy

What should be our strategy for improving global human security in the interests of present and future generations? As matters stand, we are prepared for other kinds of threats. We are prepared to cope with the past, but we are unprepared to react rapidly and effectively to present threats. Some steps can and should be taken immediately.

Military conflict clearly remains a major threat to human security—and development—in many parts of the world. The devising of early warning mechanisms could go some way toward preventing such conflicts. The existence of regional forces for immediate action could avoid the vicious circles of correct diagnosis and belated treatment.

Other measures include external debt reduction or complete revision. We cannot expect "social serenity" in countries that pay two-thirds of their oil revenues, for example, in interest on their external debt. Investment must include human resource formation, as investment without human resource development does not lead to progressive national self-reliance.

The main emphasis must be, however, on enhancing global human security through medium- and long-term measures aimed at promoting that "social progress and better standards of life in larger freedom," which, together with peace and justice, is the supreme goal of the United Nations as defined in its Charter. Such emphasis on the long-term is indispensable to the gradual consolidation of a culture of peace. However, long-term strategies cannot be implemented by short-term governments. Therefore, on some crucial issues, state pacts or agreements of all parties are necessary, since we cannot expect sustainable development to result from unsustainable governance.

Endogenous capacity building, through permanent, diversified, and open learning systems, must be at the heart of any agenda for sustainable human development. This means that everyone has access to education—a goal that will only be achieved by radical changes. Such education would offer new empowerment to girls and women, employ all the resources of modern technology to "reach the unreachable"; vary its forms and methods to respond to diverse social needs; and provide opportunities for the continuous upgrading and extension of knowledge. It is the key to unlocking the creative potential of every individual and to tackling the problem of underdevelopment at its source.

The latest step in the "Education for All" process was the meeting in New Delhi in December 1993 of leaders of the world's nine most populous countries, which include 72 percent of the world's illiterate population and more than 50 percent of the world's total population. This meeting adopted an educational plan specifically focusing on girls and women—a key factor in the moderation of population growth, the development of human resources, and the alleviation of poverty. On this occasion, the Prime Minister of India set an example by announcing an increase from 3.6 percent to 6 percent in the amount of GNP to be devoted to education. New Delhi represents a turning point because, when upstream preoccupations, the setting of national budget priorities, and a commitment to long-term action converge on this scale, there is a real possibility of curbing population growth and increasing the availability of new human resources.

Endogenous capacity building implies educational investment and development at all levels. It also implies increased international cooperation for the rapid transfer and sharing of knowledge through new partnerships and networking arrangements. Parliaments have a vital role to play in this new approach to education in a democratic society.

Education cannot achieve the desired social transformations without changes in the wider employment and international trade contexts. New links must be forged between the worlds of education, training, and work. Efforts must be made to promote an "enterprise culture," to create new kinds of jobs, such as "ecojobs," which answer the growing municipal need for recycling water, dealing with waste products, and applying necessary fertilizers. We also need to favor labor-intensive approaches to work and to envisage work-sharing arrangements. At the international level, alternative patterns of assistance to developing countries and new financial and trade relationships need to be established.

Particular emphasis should be placed on improving the conditions of life in rural areas, where so many people live, but from which so many are being driven in desperation to swell the marginalized populations of the large cities. The only answer is rural development. Again, the key is education—particularly for girls and women—and the provision of social services. Other valuable measures would include the development of credit machinery for rural areas, incentives for microindustries, the promotion of artisanal and cultural tourism, the peacetime use of military facilities, and the ability to deal effectively with emergencies.

Values and Culture

Education, in its fullest dimension, must also be concerned with values. To improve the prospects for global human security, we must refashion educational content and teacher training to promote human rights and democracy, forge attitudes of tolerance and nonviolence, foster respect for the natural environment, facilitate multicultural living, and encourage attitudes of "earth patriotism" that are essential if the world's culturally diverse people are to live together successfully.

Citizenship depends on participation, particularly at the municipal level. As a citizen, each person should reassert: "I participate, therefore I exist." Democracy is the best guarantee for global security.

Culture is rooted in everyday behavior. Democratic behavior is the foundation for a peaceful in diversity. The UN stands for the united nations, not the "uniform nations." Nations are different, but should united around the fundamental values of democracy. A radical reform of the UN is now indispensable and requires that the Security Council deal with all matters of global security and adapt its composition accordingly.

In this respect, we need to emphasize those essential values that can be shared by the various cultures—justice, freedom of expression, and equity—and to avoid imposing Western models on cultures of a different complexion or at a different stage of development. The desirable diversity of cultures dictates that each country have its own paradigm of development. Languages are the soul of cultures and therefore multilingual education is also a way to promote tolerance. Democratic governments, respect for human rights, tolerance, justice, equity, and freedom of expression are the surest ways to regulate political, cultural, economic, social, and ethnic tensions.

Peace Building versus Peacekeeping

All the measures mentioned above may be thought of as preventive in nature. Prevention is certainly better than cure. But we are in a Catch-22 situation: prevention, being largely invisible, fails to attract funds, which are ironically relatively easily found for relief and peacekeeping activities. Until peace building receives the same or more attention, until we learn the importance of the "management of the intangible" (including all those sociocultural factors that are the source of such tension and uncertainty in the world today), global human security will prove elusive. Here, the media must play an essential role by making the visible the invisible and mobilizing a commitment to peace and tolerance throughout the world.

The difficult, but essential, questions are: How are we to move from a culture of war to a culture of peace? How are we to overcome the inevitable problems of inertia, deeply ingrained attitudes, and formidable vested interests in order to construct the defenses of peace in the minds of people? Although conscious of the enormous political, social, cultural, and psychological complexities of the issue, UNESCO has placed the promotion of a culture of peace at the center of its programs.

Conclusion

All the proposals to promote global peace and development will be unsuccessful unless the flow of capital and talent reverses itself to reduce the gap between rich and poor nations. We can wait until disaster strikes or make the moral and imaginative leap that will enable this process to begin. To admit the inadmissible today can help to bring about the irreversible tomorrow.

The image of Leonardo da Vinci comes to mind here: when a boat is threatened with shipwreck, any difference between those on board is abolished. They all become passengers, eager to cooperate to ensure their common survival. In the end, this universal sentiment is probably the best guarantee of the security of present and future generations. It remains for us to work together to avoid the threat of disaster.

Security does not mean a lack of human tension, just as nonviolence does not mean docility. The necessary breakthroughs will emerge only from passion, compassion, and a common belief that human beings are "equal and free" and a common determination that they shall be.

Chapter 2

Putting People First

Section 1

New Imperatives of Human Security

Mahbub ul Haq

We are entering a new era of human security, where the entire concept of security will change dramatically. Security will be interpreted as:

- Security of people, not just security of territory.
- Security of individuals, not just security of their nations.
- Security through development, not security through arms.
- Security of all people everywhere–in their homes, in their jobs, in their streets, in their communities, in their environments.

And yet another perception will change. Human security will be regarded as universal, global, and indivisible. The same speed that has brought many modern products and services to our doorsteps has also brought much human misery to our backyards.

If we imagine for a moment that every drug that quietly kills, every disease that silently travels, every form of pollution that roams the globe, every act of terrorism that destroys life senselessly–just imagine for a moment that they all carried a national label of origin, much as traded goods do–then we shall realize with sudden shock that concerns for human security are more globalized today than even global trade.

Borderless Poverty and Disease

A second perception will change. We shall realize that poverty cannot be stopped at national borders. Poor people may be stopped, but not the tragic consequences of their poverty. They travel without a passport, and they travel in unpleasant forms. Drugs, AIDS, pollution, and terrorism stop at no national frontier. They can strike with devastating speed in any corner of the world. In fact, when people travel, they bring much dynamism and creativity with them. When only their poverty travels, it brings nothing but human misery.

One more perception will change. We shall begin to recognize that it is easier, more humane, and less costly to deal with the new issues of human security upstream rather than downstream. Did it make any sense to incur a staggering cost of $240 billion in the last decade for HIV/AIDS when even a fraction of that amount invested intelligently in primary health care and family planning education may have prevented such a fast spread of this deadly disease? Is it a great tribute to international diplomacy to spend $2 billion in a single year on soldiers in Somalia to deliver humanitarian assistance when such an amount invested much earlier in increased domestic food production may have averted the final human tragedy–not for one year but for a long time to come? Is it a reflection of human ingenuity that we are willing to spend hundreds of billions of dollars on drug prevention and rehabilitation, but not even a small part of that amount on alternative livelihoods for poor nations from where drugs may originate?

The Five Pillars of a Human World Order

We need to fashion a new concept of human security that is reflected in the lives of people, not in the weapons of countries. From the emerging concept of human security, there flow many hopeful insights and policy prescriptions. Human security can also serve as the new basis for a Human World Order. This would require at least five determined steps.

Sustainable Human Development

The first step is to seek a new concept of development. There must be a search for models of development that enhance human life, not marginalize it; that treat GNP growth as a means, not as an end; that distribute income equitably, not concentrate it; that replenish natural resources for future generations, not destroy them; that encourage grassroots participation in the events and processes that shape people's lives.

The issue is not growth per se, but its character and distribution. Those who postulate a fundamental conflict between economic growth and sustainable human development do no service to the poor nations. To address poverty, economic growth is not an option: it is an imperative. But what type of growth? And who participates in it? And who derives the benefits? These are the real issues. To benefit the masses, growth opportunities must be equitably distributed, as well as sustainable from one generation to the next. The concept of sustainable human development is fairly simple: it is based on equal access to development opportunities for present and future generations. But such a simple statement does scant justice to its far-reaching policy implications.

The heart of this concept is equity–within and between generations. But it is equity in opportunities, not necessarily in results. What people do with their opportunities is their own concern, but they should not be denied an equal opportunity to develop their human capabilities. The purpose of development is thus to enlarge people's choices—income being only one of those choices, not the sum total of human life. Such equity, however, requires many structural reforms: better distribution of productive assets, including land and credit; open access to market opportunities; a conducive policy environment for job creation; and social safety nets for those who are bypassed by the markets.

The emerging concern with sustainability takes this dialogue a step further. Development opportunities must be provided not only to present generations but to future generations as well. This does not mean protecting every form of natural capital or every resource or every species. If more efficient substitutes are available, they must be used. What must be protected is human life. We must never forget that it is human life that is the most threatened species on this earth. Whether it is economic growth or whether it is environmental protection, these are only means—the real end is human welfare. What must be sustained for the next generation is the capacity to enjoy the same level of well-being that our own generation possesses.

The concept of sustainable development focuses attention not only on the future but also on the present. There would be something distinctly odd worrying about the yet unborn generations if the present generations are poor and wretched. There would be something clearly immoral about sustaining the present levels of poverty. Development patterns that perpetuate today's inequities are neither sustainable nor worth sustaining. Indeed, global sustainability without global justice is an elusive dream. Again, the policy implications are profound. A major restructuring of the world's income and consumption patterns—especially a fundamental change in the current lifestyles of the rich nations—may be a necessary precondition for any viable strategy of sustainable human development.

In the last analysis, the ethical and philosophic foundation of the new development paradigm lies in acknowledging the universalism of life claims. No newborn child should be denied development opportunities merely because that child happens to be born in the "wrong class," or in the "wrong country," or to be of the "wrong sex." For people, the purpose of development must be to increase their options, to equalize their opportunities, to enable them to enter the market competition on an equal footing. This is the real essence of sustainable human development strategies.

There is an increasing consensus on this new paradigm of development. Our next real challenge is an operational one: it is to translate this message of equality of opportunity in the formulation of national development policies, in the dialogue on development cooperation, and in the actual workings of the international institutions.

From Arms to Human Security

A second step is needed to move from arms security to human security and to use the emerging peace dividend to finance the lengthening social agenda of humankind. The Cold War is not over yet. The job is only half done. We have phased out the Cold War in East–West relations, but we have forgotten to phase it out in the developing countries. No leader from the developing countries ever participated in the disarmament talks at Geneva; it was entirely an East–West affair.

Is it not time that we ask the leaders of the developing countries:

- Why do they insist on spending two or three times as much on arms as on the education and health of their people?

- Why do they have twenty times more soldiers than doctors today?

- How can they find the resources for air-conditioned jeeps for their military generals when they lack even windowless schoolrooms for their children?

And is it not time that we ask the leaders of the rich nations to stop the continuing arithmetic of death and destruction in the developing countries, where 22 million have died in more than 120 conflicts during the so-called "peaceful transition" since the World War II? Should they not fix a concrete timetable, say the next three years, within which they undertake to:

- Close down all existing military bases.

- Convert all existing military aid into economic aid.

- Stop the existing arms shipment of over $35 billion a year to make huge profits from poor nations that cannot even feed their people.

- Eliminate subsidies to arms exporters and retrain their workers for jobs in civilian industries?

Our next challenge is to curtail the huge arms spending of $130 billion a year in the poor nations and to invest this money instead in the welfare of their people. Those big powers that launched the Cold War have a moral obligation now to defuse global tensions, to build new alliances for peace, and to help developing countries make a smooth transition from arms security to human security.

Let us also not give up on the peace dividend. It is a fact that global military expenditures have begun to decline for the first time in our lifetime. It is a fact that, between 1987 and 1992, global military expenditures have fallen and yielded a cumulative peace dividend of $500 billion. Where has this peace dividend gone? Why is it not available for the neglected social agenda held over from the days when societies were accumulating arms and their people were praying that the arms race would stop?

In the rich nations, the current preoccupation is with balancing budgets. But would it take a new genius to discover how to balance the financial budgets without unbalancing human lives? Why should rich societies find it impossible to provide resources for their unvaccinated children or for their homeless people or for their decaying cities in an era of such rapidly falling military expenditures?

In the poor nations, unfortunately, the decline in military spending is still slow and hesitant. In fact, military expenditures are still going up in two of the poorest regions of the world—Sub-Saharan Africa and South Asia. Obviously, the poverty of their people is no barrier to the affluence of their armies. Even a freeze on current military spending levels in the developing countries will release sufficient resources to take care of their essential human agendas.

In Sub-Saharan Africa, its military spending to GNP ratio increased from 0.7 percent in 1960 to 3.5 percent in 1990 — a fivefold increase at a time when its countries were cutting down social spending in the name of structural adjustment. In South Asia, India and Pakistan spend $18 billion a year on defense even though they contain the largest number of the poorest people in the world. From 1988 to 1992, India and Pakistan imported twice as many arms as Saudi Arabia, which is twenty times richer.

It is time for one final push, to ensure that arms security is replaced by human security — particularly in the poor lands where the cost of every new jet fighter equals the cost of educating one million children.

A New North–South Partnership

The third step relates to a new partnership between the North and the South — one based on justice, not on charity; on an equitable sharing of global market opportunities, not on aid; on two-way compacts, not on one-way transfers; and on mutual cooperation, not on unilateral conditionality or confrontation.

Foreign aid has often dominated North–South relations in the post-World War II era, even though this aid was often marginal and misdirected. Just consider one sobering comparison. Rich nations channel an average of 15 percent of their GNP to their own 100 million people below a poverty line of around $5000 a year. The same nations earmark only 0.3 percent of their GNP for poor nations which contain 1.3 billion poor people below an income level of $300 a year. What a telling contrast between national and international social safety nets! And yet a public perception persists in the rich nations that their aid money could be better employed at home. The rich nations hardly recognize that even if all their aid stopped today, it would increase their domestic social safety nets from 15 percent of GNP to merely 15.3 percent — perhaps not the most handsome bargain in history. It is not just the marginal role of aid, but its distribution that matters. Aid carries today all the scars of the Cold War era. It was often given to strategic allies rather than to poor nations. Just consider the link of aid with the oft-repeated objective of eliminating global poverty. Only one-third of ODA is earmarked for the ten countries containing two-thirds of the world's absolute poor. Twice as much ODA per capita is given to the top 40 percent income group in the world as to the bottom 40 percent. Egypt receives $280 per poor person; India receives only $7. Only less than 7 percent of bilateral ODA is directed towards human priority concerns — that is, primary health care, basic education, safe drinking water, nutrition programs, and family planning services.

We must consider yet another dimension of aid. Most of it was directed to strategic allies in the Cold War, to many authoritarian regimes, to many high military spenders. Even today, two-and-a-half times as much per capita ODA goes to high military spenders as to low military spenders.

Even today, strategic allies get preference over poor nations. For example, El Salvador receives 16 times as much U.S. ODA per poor person as does Bangladesh, even though Bangladesh is five times poorer.

The final irony is that although aid transfers so few resources to the developing world, denial of global market opportunities takes away several times more through trade protection, immigration barriers, and an increasing debt burden. According to the 1992 *Human Development Report*, such global losses are about ten times the aid that poor nations receive.

It is time to restore our perspective. What is crucial for poor nations is an equitable access to global market opportunities, not charity. What we must battle for today is a removal of trade barriers, particularly on textiles and agriculture, which would yield at least $100 billion a year in additional exports. What we must insist on today is a compensation package from rich nations for imposing immigration controls, since free labor flows were supposed to be an essential component of a liberal international economic system that would equalize global opportunities. What we must negotiate today is a price market in global environmental resources that would oblige the rich nations to pay their due share for the overuse of our common heritage: they may end up paying as much as 5 percent of their GNP according to some recent studies on tradable environmental permits. This is not aid. This is not charity. This is merely taking the logic of the market place back to the rich nations.

For too long, we have missed the real essence of a new system of development cooperation between rich and poor nations. When we should have sought participation in markets, we sought exemption from these market rules. When we should have constructed a comprehensive design of relations between the North and the South — including all flows of trade, labor, investment, and technology — we got hopelessly stuck on the 0.7 percent aid target. When we should have sought fair rules for international competition, we kept counting our diminishing aid dollars.

It is time to advance from a charitable aid relationship to a more respectable development relationship. It is time to build a new design of development cooperation between the North and the South, which enables the poor nations to gain a more equitable access to global market opportunities. We must also create a new mechanism to facilitate payments by one country to another for services rendered. These are mutually beneficial services, which by their very nature cannot be mediated by markets. Examples include payments for environmental services, control of narcotic drugs, and control of contagious diseases. We must, at the same time, create a new mechanism to facilitate compensation for damages when one country inflicts an economic injury on another. Compensation can be thought of as fines payable by countries that depart from internationally agreed rules of good conduct. Some of the examples may include encouragement of the brain drain from poor nations, restrictions on the migration of low-skilled labor, and trade restrictions on exports from poor countries. These compensations are in a sense voluntary; they can be avoided by refraining from engaging in objectionable behavior. Aid will have only a marginal role in this new design of development cooperation — as a global social safety net for the very poorest nations and, hopefully, as a more predictable and obligatory commitment by the rich nations. Aid is needed to address some of the darkest aspects of poverty but it must be far better targeted than in the past.

We need, therefore, a much broader design of development cooperation than just aid—a design that draws new strength from our domestic reforms in the South, that recognizes that real human security in the North will ultimately depend on an investment in reducing global poverty, and that secures an equitable access to global market opportunities for all people all over the globe.

New Forms of Global Governance

A fourth step in the search for a Human World Order is to fashion a new framework of global governance. Global markets or automatic mechanisms cannot achieve justice for all nations or all people. Global institutions are necessary to set rules, to monitor "global goods" and "global bads," and to redress widening disparities. Paradoxically, these global institutions are weakening precisely at the time that global interdependence is increasing. All global institutions desperately need both strengthening and reform.

Take, for instance, the Bretton Woods institutions. What should worry us is not their seeming arrogance, but their growing irrelevance. They are no longer institutions of global governance; they are now institutions to direct economic management in the developing world.

The writ of the IMF runs only in developing countries, which are responsible for a mere 10 percent of global liquidity. G-7, not IMF, influences the global monetary system today. The rich nations hold their breath for the pronouncements of Alan Greenspan, not of Michel Camdessus.

The World Bank has a limited role in recycling global surpluses. It collects more debts each year than the resources it lends to the developing world. It is private capital markets which recycle resources, but three-fourths of those go to about ten better off developing countries in East Asia and Latin America. The other countries wait for a World Bank intervention that never materializes on a scale that was originally envisaged.

The GATT jurisdiction was excluded till recently from most of the important items of international trade: textiles, tropical products, agricultural commodities, services, and labor and investment flows. And the GATT stands strangely silent on the sidelines as the United States and Japan get ready to launch a disastrous trade war.

The United Nations never became the strongest pillar of human development that it was supposed to be. To be frank, most donors always preferred the one-dollar-one-vote governance pattern of the Bretton Woods institutions to one-country-one-vote governance of the UN. So UN development programs never got the support they really deserved. Limited financing led to diminished efficiency, and diminished efficiency became the justification for even more limited financing. What are our real options today? Bashing international institutions is a tempting option. But it is a self-defeating one at a time when global governance is already so weak.

Instead, we must form alliances for change within these institutions as well as with their governance. Our goal should be reform, not demolition. We must convince these institutions to focus more on human development strategies, to formulate adjustment programs that place much greater burdens on the rich than on the poor and that balance budgets without unbalancing the lives of the people, and to evolve governance patterns which give a much greater voice to the poor nations.

We can draw up all sorts of scenarios for the global economic and financial institutions of the twenty-first century, but one thing is certain. As distances shrink and we become a global village, we are likely to witness a similar evolution at the global level as we did at the national level in the last century. That is why we should start giving serious thought to the possible structure for a world central bank, a global taxation system, a world trading organization, an international investment trust, and even a world treasury. Some of us may not live to see all these global developments, but we are completely confident that our grandchildren surely will. So let us at least begin with the rough architecture of these global institutions.

In fact, it is simply amazing how little intellectual ferment we have today regarding a new structure of global governance. Out of the rubble of the World War II, there emerged the UN, the Bretton Woods institutions, the Marshall Plan for the reconstruction of Europe, the faint blueprints of a European Economic Community, and many more hopeful institutions. John Maynard Keynes and Jean Monnet were preparing the rough architecture of the global institutions of the future, even as bombs were still raining on their cities. But today, when we have seen some unprecedented change in the global environment—from the fall of the Berlin wall to the end of apartheid in South Africa—our sources of creativity are curiously passive regarding the future shape of global governance. It is time to begin designing the global institutions of the twenty-first century.

Whatever shape this new architecture takes, it is increasingly essential to set up an Economic Security Council in the UN—as the highest decision making forum—to deal with threats to global human security and to agree on necessary actions. Such a Council must deal with all issues confronting humanity—from food security to environmental security, from global poverty to jobless growth, from international migration to drug trafficking. While its total membership should be kept small and manageable, it should represent all world constituencies and carry no country veto. It should oversee the policy direction of all international and regional institutions. It must be serviced by the ablest professional staff, formulating enlightened policy options on economic and social dilemmas facing humankind. In fact, it is impossible to think of a democratic global governance for the next century without the evolution of such an Economic Security Council, in one form or another.

Toward a Global Civil Society

The fifth and final step that the imperatives of human security force upon us is the inevitable evolution of a global civil society. Future changes will not depend exclusively on governments. They will come primarily from the actions of people at the grassroots—people who are often far ahead of their governments. People will hold their leaders increasingly accountable for their actions.

The forces of democratic change have swept across the world in the last decade. In one country after another, people are standing up to their authoritarian regimes and bending them to the popular will. The nation-states are under much pressure today. The age of people may have finally arrived.

This new momentum for change carries both dangers and opportunities. There are dangers of anarchy and social disintegration if people are denied their legitimate economic and political rights. But there is also a unique opportunity to build together a new global civilization at this particular hinge of history.

In poor nations, a realistic process of change has already begun. These nations are opening up their economies, carrying out many painful structural adjustments, and passing through a rapid phase of democratic change. They no longer blame the North for all their troubles. They are beginning to recognize that the real battle of poverty will be fought and won in the South itself. They seek justice, not charity.

Unfortunately, at a time of such a profound change in human affairs, the North is choosing to become somewhat passive, cautious, conservative and almost reactionary—fearing that it may lose some of its previous privileges.

Consider the recent evidence:

- While the poor nations are beginning to open up their economies, the rich nations are beginning to close theirs.

- While the poor nations are undergoing a structural adjustment at such a low level of income, the rich nations are resisting any such adjustment in their own lifestyles.

- While the rich nations preach democracy to the poor nations, they resist such democracy in international institutions and in global governance.

- While the rich nations rightly condemn corruption in poor lands, they fail to discipline their own multinationals which offer bribes or their banks which gladly accept corrupt money and make a handsome profit on it.

- While the rich nations have started advocating reduced military spending to developing nations, they have quietly turned around and increased subsidies to their own arms exporters.

Conclusion

A new partnership between North and South will also demand a new ethics of mutual responsibility and mutual respect. The North does not realize yet that, through its constant advocacy, it may have unleashed forces of change that will not only change other nations but also its own lifestyle. In particular, democracy is rarely so obliging as to stop at national borders. Its vast sweep will change global governance in the twenty-first century. The real choice is either to accept the evolution of such a global civil society and to speed up its arrival — or to resist it in the name of old-fashioned power balances and to plunge the world into utter confusion.

These five steps can lead towards a new Human World Order. A unique opportunity to build such an order will come at the time of the World Summit for Social Development in March 1995 in Copenhagen. The Social Summit will review the progress made by humanity in the last fifty years and the new architecture of peace and development for the next fifty years. This is the time to fashion a new concept of sustainable human development, to take concrete steps to capture the peace dividend, to design a new structure of international development cooperation, to initiate some work on the architecture of a new global governance, and to speed up the evolution of a global civil society and a human world order.

Section 2

Prerequisites of an Agenda for People

Wangari Maathai

In 1945 many people of the world were hardly included in the statement "We the peoples of the United Nations," because they were still colonies of the victorious allies who were meeting in San Francisco. Since then, and despite gallant efforts by the UN to decolonize the world, many people, especially in Africa, are still out of the picture economically, politically, and culturally. They can hardly be said to be free from fear and want. Today, the threat is mostly internal. Not only is the quality of life rapidly falling, but indicators show they are being marginalized and denied "the dignity and worth of a human person."

With the end of the Cold War, people speak of the emerging "one world." A few examples of regional economic blocks, such as the European Union, the North American Free Trade Agreement, and the globalization of markets by transnational corporations, may fit into this generalized portrait. But many states, such as the countries of the former Soviet Union, Yugoslavia, and Africa, are experiencing fragmentation and disintegration.

In 1945 the UN committed itself to economic development. Resources were allocated to its various organs to help eliminate poverty and improve the quality of life of all peoples. Why, then, have development expectations not been realized in many parts of the world? Why, particularly, not in African countries? Why are so many people, still living in such squalor? Clearly, bottlenecks impede the efforts made at both the local and international levels. These bottlenecks keep the majority of poor people on the backstage of the international political agenda. Probably, none of them are new, but they must be addressed if "A New Global Agenda for People" is to be drawn. Peace and security are prerequisites for development.

All people want peace and an acceptable quality of life. Because many African states have hardly every enjoyed peace and internal security, the agenda for development has been stalled. The rivalry between the superpowers for strategic African states precipitated some of the most devastating internal wars. Human and material resources were directed towards destruction rather than towards development. Because of this rivalry, leaders who were unpopular with their citizens were supported by the superpowers; the world stood by and watched as these dictators massacred their own citizens with guns purchased by the funds that were intended to help the people. These leaders acquired huge supplies of arms and built up massive armies, police forces, and networks of secret service officers to spy on their own citizens. Citizens became prisoners in their own country. This preoccupation with internal security and political survival sacrificed the development agenda for decades. The national warfare machinery be dismantled, so that people can feel free to think, move, write, express themselves, and advance private initiatives for human development.

Empowerment of the People

Compounding the problems are centuries of cultural adulteration through religious and mental indoctrination. Political and economic domination and exploitation have so disengaged the people that they suffer from what can be termed as the "Messiah Syndrome." This is a state of mind in which people search for anyone or anything that promises to save them from their predicament. Thus, the people idolize political and religious leaders as "messiahs," who are expected to deliver them into a better life.

Once people surrender their political and economic power to these idols, they submit to the sycophantism and opportunism that drives them further into a state of helplessness. Nevertheless, their leaders encourage this and relish the adoration. Together the rulers and the ruled nurture and sustain irresponsible governance characterized by authoritarianism, nonaccountability, corruption, and naked opportunism. In the face of such political conditions and realities, the majority of people and the agenda for development and long-term investment in humans are ignored.

Fortunately, citizen groups are challenging this tendency. These groups are pushing for the emergence of a strong civil society that can pressure governments and aid agencies by demanding development models that put people first. The voices of these NGOs should be heard more often and at more effective fora both nationally and internationally.

International Cooperation

Despite public statements to the contrary, there is little willingness on the part of the international community to support genuine, mutually-supportive, and cooperative solidarity for poor people. It is not as if the causes and symptoms of underdevelopment and deprivation are unknown. They are discussed with a myriad of words in books, magazines, evaluation reports, and development plans, many of which are written by experts from the same international community. So why do national and international development agencies prefer to spend huge resources in curative social welfare programs (for example, famine relief, food aid, refugee camps, peace keeping forces, and humanitarian missions) rather than use these resources for preventive and sustainable human development programs? Why is the rich and developed world unwilling to adopt levels of production and consumption that would provide all people of the world with a development model that is environmentally sustainable and morally just?

At the heart of this debate are national and regional political and economic interests, as well as the concepts of equity, human rights, and natural justice. No world will ever be without injustice, inequalities, and violations of human rights; such evils exist. Yet, without global guidelines and rules of law for all, unilateral decisions by the economically and politically powerful threaten the peace and security of many in this world.

National Capacity Building

Even if effective cooperation at the international level existed, national capacity would still be underdeveloped. Leaders have not created the enabling environment for such development. This would include institution building; the creation of infrastructure; development of a vibrant civil society; expansion of the private sector and entrepreneurship; and the creation of development agencies. The political will is still not there. African leaders, for example, have tended to take advantage of their people's state of disempowerment and debilitating poverty to rule them with an iron fist. They have been dictatorial, divisive, manipulative, and opportunistic. In short, they lack political vision. For them, the impoverishment of their people is an asset that enables them to retain political power and authority over their people and the enormous resources entrusted to them by their citizens. Some leaders have even managed to destroy what little development the colonial governments had produced. It is, therefore, no surprise that some Africans openly admit that they were better off as subjects of colonial governments than under the oppressive governance of their own leaders.

Anticorruption

In some developing countries, leaders are suspected of appropriating large sums advanced for the development of their people and stashing them in secret bank accounts within donor countries. If, for example, African leaders returned such sums to the rightful owners and made them available for development, the continent would not be in need of loans and foreign aid.

Why does the international community, which knows that these funds are stolen, fail to respond to these crimes? If it is a crime to kill half a million people in Rwanda why is it not a crime to steal millions from national treasuries and indirectly cause the death of millions? And why are the donor nations, which are cooperating by hiding such funds, protected by global public opinion?

There is a need for an international code of moral responsibility or global ethic so that such crimes are recognized as a threat to international peace and security. Leaders who steal from their people and violate their rights should be denied entry into the UN and regional political bodies. International cooperation should benefit poor people in general, and not reward the greedy, corrupt, and nonaccountable ruling elites and their supporters.

Market Rules

During the colonial period, markets and development projects were provided raw materials to stimulate industrial production in the mother countries. These markets were controlled by colonial administrators and African collaborators who were given special powers through such rules as the oppressive Chiefs Act. Although many countries have achieved political independence, the economic markets of the developing countries are still geared to supply mainly stimulants (such as, coffee, tea, and cocoa) and luxury delicacies (such as, nuts, beans, tropical fruits, and flowers) to the developed economies. Local economies are unable to compete or withstand the shock waves produced by international cooperation and global markets.

Unless good governance is fully achieved and people assume control of their resources and economies, it is difficult to see how any development model would generate wealth for them. Certainly, international investments are important and open markets are desired, but unless people are put at the center of all concerns by their governments, development initiatives will be deficient. International aid cannot be a substitute for a vibrant, creative, and free civil society that is backed by a responsible and accountable national governance.

Traditional Wisdom and Culture

All people have a traditional culture, knowledge, wisdom, and set of values. These have evolved over thousands of years and have been passed from one generation to the next. This accumulated heritage sustains communities in times of peace, insecurity, birth, life, and death. It is an antennae into the unknown future, and the reference point into the past. Although some people have invented the art of reading and writing and have been able to record this in books and the arts, others pass it exclusively through oral instructions, stories, ceremonies, and customs.

People who are robbed of this heritage during occupation, enslavement, and colonization, become disoriented and disempowered. They lose self-respect, self-confidence, and the capacity for independent decision making. They may escape into religious fanaticism and intolerance. Their society experiences a breakdown of the social fabric, as street children, alcoholism, and drug abuse rise. They are hit by epidemics and other social ills. These problems are largely a result of centuries of adulteration of their cultural and religious values.

For this reason, many opt for some form of escapism — often through religion, drugs, or crime. African societies have suffered and continue to suffer this form of adulteration. Unless they are regain traditional culture and values, the agenda for people will never trickle down to the masses of poor people.

Governance

All people want to see the rule of justice, equity, transparency, responsibility, and accountability in their societies. They want a decent life, with an opportunity to feed, shelter, and clothe their families. They do not seek to dominate nor to marginalize each other, but to create a civil society that holds leaders accountable and ensures security for all people. Millions of Africans are striving for this type of governance. However, many political systems in Africa are inherently undemocratic and oppressive; they are part of a colonial legacy whose main objective was plunder national resources. To achieve this, the colonial powers disempowered the people, destroyed any creative energy, and misruled. People were denied the freedom to think and speak effectively, inform themselves, move freely within their countries, and use their creative abilities. Every aspect of life was controlled. A culture of fear and silence replaced a dynamic and vibrant culture.

After independence, many African leaders retained that oppressive colonial structure of governance; they used it ruthlessly when political grievances and instability began to emerge as a result of deepening poverty. Corruption, dishonesty, nonaccountability, nepotism, and incompetence were tolerated and even encouraged. To sustain such a system, resources intended for development purposes were and are diverted to purchase guns and support huge armed forces, secret intelligence networks, and police forces.

A responsible, open, and democratic government does not need weapons and armed forces to maintain its power. It needs to meet the basic needs of its citizens. And that is an essential element of the new global agenda.

Combating Poverty, Poor Health, and Hunger

Good health is essential for a sustained, creative, and productive life. If millions of people never have enough to eat and are suffering from parasitic infestations and diseases associated with malnutrition and poor sanitation, development is bound to stagnate. Poverty, poor health, and sustained hunger become a vicious cycle of misery and want.

Notwithstanding statements at international conferences and round tables of development agencies about agriculture, food security, farming techniques, and preventive medicine, adequate attention is given only to export crops, such as coffee, tea, and flowers.

Of course, food has become a political weapon, as leaders keep the key to the national granaries, dispose of the food when their own people need it, and subsequently appeal for food from the international community. National agricultural policies discourage local farmers and opt for cheap food in the international community.

In general, African governments give a low priority to agriculture and food production. Most of the available food is produced by women, who also carry much of the burden for work done in the rural areas and in the family. But women's work receives low priority, prestige, and compensation. Only a government that cares about its people will protect its citizens from using food as a political bargaining chip. Only an informed strong civil society will persuade its government not to sacrifice local farmers at the altar of international food politics.

Literacy

Illiteracy is one of the most important obstacles to development. The older generation of people, many of whom are illiterate, tend to overvalue education and the ability to read and write. They give too much trust to those with these skills, while undervaluing themselves. This puts many citizens at the mercy of literate people and the state controlled media. In many countries, national radio and television, which are the main means of communication, are intended for public education, but unfortunately are used by many leaders for political propaganda and personal aggrandizement. To change this requires a democratic and accountable government, with effective checks and balances to prevent the misuse of political power.

Enhancing Communication

When they achieved independence, many African nations decided to adopted a foreign language as their official language. Although only a small number of people speak and write these languages fluently, job opportunities are linked with these skills. Thus, even people who have been exposed only minimally to these languages in primary and secondary schools, feign competence in them.

Particularly in a continent where illiteracy is very high, communication technologies are few and far apart, and transport is still slow and inadequate, the need to use a foreign language marginalizes a majority of the indigenous populations. In fact, people of average intelligence often communicate so incompetently that they are often misunderstood.

This inability of many countries to communicate effectively with themselves needs to be recognized as a major obstacle to development. This is especially at true at a time when communication technology is bypassing them, thereby further marginalizing them in the process of globalization. This inability disempowers people, minimizes self-confidence, and destroys creative energy, while encouraging dependency a fear of decision making. It also minimizes indigenous knowledge and expertise.

Ethnic Cohesion

Ethnic consciousness has resurfaced in many parts of the world, rekindled by politicians who need it for political survival in civil society reacts to the injustices and oppressive governance that have nurtured poverty and discontent. Politicized ethnic consciousness would be disruptive to any country, but this is particularly true in nations where ethnic communities were arbitrarily clustered together. Still, it is not usually national ethnic entities who advocate separateness; it is rather their leaders who are arousing ethnic nationalism as a way of retaining political and economic power.

Environmental Sustainability

Among the many causes of world-wide environmental degradation, underdevelopment, and poverty are desertification, droughts, soil loss, destruction of forests and grassland, loss of biodiversity, and pollution. The symptoms, which are devastating, include pollution, drought, environmental refugees, internal ethnic conflict, and widespread poverty.

Many governments give only lip service to environmental concerns. They appear to make commitments at the international level and then follow a completely different policy at the national level. Otherwise, forests would not be encroached upon, open spaces in urban centers would be protected, and national parks, wildlife, and other sources of biodiversity would be safe.

Conclusion

These are but few of the bottlenecks that stall the development of people. They exist because those of us with the power to remove them are not really interested in doing so. Is there a global ethic that can embrace them? The millions who are affected by these bottlenecks do not pray for mercy and charity. They only yearn for justice and equity, liberty, and mutual respect. The less fortunate too have a right to live and die with human dignity. For them, freedom from fear and want is a source of pride, inspiration, and hope. These values give them the strength to fight existing injustices and meet future challenges. Helping them would make all of our lives richer, more meaningful, and more human.

Section 3

The Role of Women in a Changing World

Yung-Chung Kim

The twentieth century has been one of overwhelming advancement for people – an era of sweeping change and transformation. Globalization in the areas of telecommunications and transportation and the migration of people are further breaking down any remaining isolation in the world. Information, ideas, and capital have already become borderless, moving internationally with ease and speed. Yet, ironically, the same era has produced an increase in the extent and intensity of poverty. Seventy-five percent of he world's people do not share in the good living of this century. Within this context, we should be concerned with the entire process of change – political, economic, cultural, technological, and ecological – which has complex and far-reaching consequences.

Today, women throughout the world share common concerns for justice, peace, and development in an environment where violence and dehumanization are prevalent. In building a better world, women will certainly have a major role to play, whether by creating new attitudes in their children or by contributing to the promotion of sustainable human development.

Equity Concerns

The world is currently preoccupied with industrialization and development. Although industrialization has brought improved technology and higher living standards, economic growth does not automatically lead to increased opportunities for all people, which should be the ultimate purpose of development. Contradictions have already manifested themselves in the uneven processes of change both domestically and internationally. Studies undertaken in various parts of the world show that certain groups may reap a disproportionate share of the benefits of development; others become its victims, inducing an ever-widening gap between rich and poor, rural and urban populations, women and men, and the better and less educated. The economic systems of most developing countries are embedded in a rationale of free competition based on capitalism, whereby they are led to consider increases in production and profit as the sole objective. This aggravates existing economic disparities and social inequalities. Such a concentration of wealth deprives the majority of people of their equitable share in national resources and creates tensions within a society.

Development has bypassed large segments of the rural and urban population, particularly working women. In Korea, despite an impressive increase in overall production, the agricultural sector has lagged behind in both facilities and income. Because of a decline in the male agricultural labor force as a result of growing urban migration, there has been a sharp rise in the number of rural women working in agriculture. This change should have resulted in improved economic and social status for rural women, but, in fact, they have fewer opportunities than men to claim the advantages promised by an industrialized economy. Rural education has been designed primarily for men; little attention has been given to the need to train rural women, even though they are playing an increasingly important role in the rural economy. Women's labor thus remains largely unskilled and less valued than male labor.

Although both men and women may become victims of development, women suffer from more handicaps because of family obligations that make them less mobile than men, their traditional occupational choices, their lack of education and training, and sex discrimination in recruitment. In most countries, a much larger percentage of women than men is engaged in traditional occupations, which are precisely those that are being eliminated by technology. Although women comprise 42 percent of the workforce, they are found in the least developed sectors of the economy and still bear the main responsibility for home and family care. The real goals of sustainable development, such as social justice, self-reliance, and growth of the total person are yet to be realized.

The Changing Role of Women

The rapid changes in economic and social structures marked a shift in the roles of women. For centuries, in most societies, women have been confined to the jobs of child rearing and homemaking. In Korea, women's participation in socioeconomic activities has been restricted by traditional customs stemming mainly from Confucian ethics. From their early childhood, girls have been taught to limit their concerns and interests to the home and family. Today, the process of industrialization and urbanization has brought about concomitant changes in the pattern of family life and women's roles. These developments are impacting women directly, presenting new problems as well as opportunities. Some notable changes include prolonged life expectancy, smaller families, and leisure for middle-income housewives. Thanks to ever-expanding educational opportunities, an increasing number of women are receiving a high-school education, while the ratio of women in college has reached 26 percent. With advances in medical technology and improved nutrition, the average life span has increased. As a result of a vigorous family planning program that is an integral part of the government's economic development plan, the population growth rate declined dramatically from 2.9 percent per year in the 1960s to 0.97 percent today. The need to balance population and economic growth has made family planning a crucial issue, and appropriate policy measures have been successfully carried out by the Planned Parenthood Federation in conjunction with government and nongovernment organizations. As a result, childbearing and rearing now occupy a smaller portion of women's lives, while labor-saving devices have relieved them of time-consuming domestic chores.

As a result of such changes, women are beginning to find alternatives for meaningful living and fruitful uses for their potential. With steady industrial growth, employment opportunities are increasing, although jobs for women college graduates are still limited. They are eager to work and, if possible, to move into various jobs formerly monopolized by men. The trend is for marriage not to be a barrier that keeps women from working. With the current reemphasis on fertility, married women, too, have new alternatives. They may take routine jobs, continue their education, embark on new training programs, and do volunteer work. Women's roles have indeed become diversified as family patterns have changed.

One encouraging sign is that attitudes toward women working outside the home are changing, especially in countries where economic growth is rapid and labor shortages severe. The traditional role expectations of spouses are also changing into one of equal partnership. The issues are not merely education and opportunity, but the right for a woman to realize her individual potential. To met such a need, the government and private sector must make united efforts to provide more child care facilities.

Questions relating to the family and work roles for women are being publicly debated in many countries. Findings emphasize the need for external sources of support for working mothers. If the family is to enhance its quality of life while continuing its function to bear and rear children, the institutional solutions must be found to ease the pressure on parents. This is an important policy issue.

Participation in Decision Making

As in many countries in the Asia-Pacific region, Korea is undergoing far-reaching transitions that are opening the way for unseating authoritarianism and ushering in a new era of democratization. This restoration of democracy is largely the result of popular pressure. The legitimacy of the democratic system of government will be determined by its progress in building broad-based popular support. The success of an elected government, therefore, largely depends on bringing women into the political arena.

Obviously, Korean women are enjoying de jure equality. In response to the demands and pressures of women's groups in conjunction with the United Nation's Decade for Women, some noteworthy legislative and institutional achievements have been made. These include the signing and ratification of the Convention on the Elimination of All Forms of Discrimination against Women; the founding of the Korean Women's Development Institute, which deals exclusively with women's issues on a national level; the establishment of the National Committee on Women's Policies under the authority of the Prime Minister's office; the enactment of the Equal Employment Opportunity Act; the Family Law revision; and the establishment of the Ministry of Political Affairs in charge of women's affairs at the national government level.

Despite of these legal measures, women's de facto status has made little progress. Women face both formal and informal barriers to full and equal participation in society. They are conspicuously absent from decision-making bodies in general and serious underrepresented in positions of political leadership in particular. They need to learn how to organize effectively to advance their interests.

Korean women have an obvious concern with peace and unification, but how are they going to be able to participate in the mechanisms of peacemaking and peacekeeping? Women play an important role in the production processes, but few are involved in the decisions that determine the financial and resource development of their nation? This complex issue is the priority concern for Korean women.

After the installation of a new civilian government in 1993, women's visibility improved. Three women ministers and one woman vice-minister were appointed simultaneously—an unprecedented event in Korea. As a result of the Equal Employment Act, the number of women in government service has increased considerable, thereby opening up the possibility of promotion to higher decision-making posts.

Equal partnership between men and women is critical to national development and global survival. Men as well as women stand to benefit from this development.

The Environment and Development

Many of the changes taking place must be assessed not only in terms of community interest, but from a global perspective. The problems of resources, pollution, and population, for example, are global in nature. Conservation of the environment and natural resources is closely linked to sustainable development. In developing countries, women have been successful environmental managers. They are aware of the importance of ecosystems, of preserving natural resources, and of energy efficiency. In developed countries, women have become involved in "green" parties and other activist groups. They recognize that environmental degradation is closely linked to the issues of poverty, consumption, and population growth.

Few women, however, have had the opportunities, training, or financial resources to carry out such action at higher levels of decision making. In policy formulation and designing development programs, attention should be given to the level of participation of women and the impact should programs will have on their lives and status.

Conclusion

As society continues to change, there are increasingly alternatives to consider and choices to make. The future does not spring from a wish; it grows out of the past and present. Much of it is shaped by individuals, the family, and the community. It is not enough to adapt to the changes; one must transform them into qualitative changes.

People must find a model for growth that can serve us all. Economic expansion is no longer the only measure of development. Even economists know that economic development must involve fundamental transformation—a total process of change in all aspects of human life. There is a new understanding of the interdependence of nations and the need to work together in resolving the development problem. We often divide the world into the "developed" and the "developing" countries, as if a nation had to pass through one stage to reach the other. In fact, development is two sides of the same coin. The interests of developed and developing countries can no longer be isolated from one another. The well-being of the international community depends on the well-being of its component parts. It is essential, therefore, that new ways of living demonstrate a concern for the equitable distribution and responsible use of resources.

The redistribution of wealth and resources will not come without a struggle. Transformation of the economic and social structures requires new value systems than run counter to the existing establishment. We must reexamine the basic assumptions and goals of affluent consumer societies. We should challenge people to take action that will help humanize oppressive power structures so that they will promote a new paradigm of development.

Section 4

Hopes and Fears of Youth

Miguel de Paladella and Maria Figueroa

Young people and children are the promise for the future. However, investments in youth today have become one of the most critical issues to be recognized by the international community in order to safeguard and improve our common future.

The present period of globalization and interdependence, as well as the collapse of political and societal models, has resulted in growing uncertainty and risk. This is creating an expensive confusion among young people. In the face of daily exposés on growing global poverty and unemployment, widening disparities of income and opportunity, and degradation of the environment—all of which constitute a tremendous danger to the security of the future—youth must take action.

Yet the obstacles to such mobilization seem insurmountable, as young people suffer disproportionately from the results of world instability and conflict. Youth represent more than 30 percent of the world's total population, with the larger number of them living in lesser-developed nations. They are among the first to suffer the deprivations of illiteracy, unemployment, lack of access of markets and capital, human rights abuses, and disease; still they are not adequately capable of redressing these threats to their personal security and daily lives. As the situation of youth deteriorates, it is not without ramifications for the rest of the population.

The world enters a historic period of transition lead by the end of the Cold War, but can its youth realize and act on the opportunity and hope that such a transition presents?

The Fears

In the 1990s, global development has not always served the needs of the people. It has not adequately redressed the dramatic increase in the disparity of income both within and between countries. Conditions such as poverty, unemployment, and social disintegration are visible in all communities—from a small village to the large industrial metropolis. The number of young people living below the poverty line has never been greater than it is today. Of particular importance is the increasing reliance on the informal sector as the only means to provide a sustainable livelihood, income, and skill development. It is estimated that in South Africa more than 80 percent of youth are employed in the informal sector, with very little possibility for continuing education, training, and eventual absorption into the formal job sector.

The 1994 Worldwatch Institute's State of the World Report presents a detailed picture of environmental deterioration and the limitation of the Earth's "carrying capacity." The pace and scope of environmental degradation has been increasing exponentially in recent decades. Based on the current world population, consumption patterns, and technology, the habitat cannot sustain indefinitely human alterations of the environment. The resource base of the planet is declining and is insufficient to sustain both our present pattern of economic development and the life support systems on which we depend.

The traditional concept of the "Third World" disappeared with the collapse of the Soviet model of communism and the tearing down of the Berlin Wall. No longer can the phrase retain relevance as the juxtaposition between the "First" and "Second" worlds. The meaning of the cliché must be adjusted to an international reality that has always existed, but has only recently become more prominent. Economic, social, political, and cultural deprivations, in their many forms, still plague us. Although the foci of such problems problems may vary in appearance or circumstances, the fundamental roots that cause these conditions are the same. Many loci of inadequacy and dissatisfaction culminate in a global impact. International concern should focus on the global divide between the centers of power and the marginalized, wherever they may be—in the South, North, East, or West. The uniqueness of our period is that the same problems that have characterized "developing nations" now have expanded to hit the cores of those societies that define themselves as "developed."

Yet if poverty and deprivation constitute threats to security, it is the symptoms of these threats that face us daily—the hunger, the violence, the disease. And when these symptoms themselves turn to causes we find ourselves creating piecemeal strategies to alleviate the surface and not the source of the problem. The imperative is to recognize the root causes of such threats. The challenge is to address them.

Hopes for the Future

Despite the deterioration of living conditions for an increasingly marginalized group, the world economy is experiencing a revolution. Spectacular advances in microelectronics, computers, telecommunications, biochemistry, and engineering and new energy sources, materials, and technologies have transformed global patterns of production, trade, organization, and management.

Technological progress is providing people with unprecedented opportunities for global dialogue and sharing of information, ideas, and projects. Communication systems, which speed the process of globalization, offer a new range of possibilities for increasing human knowledge. Trade and financial flows have achieved an enormous global magnitude and will develop further as a result of the institutionalization of major international agreements, such as the recently concluded Uruguay Round.

The current distinction between developing and developed countries is based on the degree of information and knowledge much more than on the factors of industrialization or income generation. The evolving dissemination and application of knowledge, with its unprecedented scope, will be the determining factor in providing a new range of opportunities for people. This has created the conditions for the most impressive revolution — the emergence of an active, moral, and value-driven civil society.

This progress also has a human dimension. Literacy has increased in developing countries from an average of 30 percent in 1960 to 60 percent today. Primary and secondary education has been significantly expanded. There is an emerging generation with knowledge and a higher capacity for decision making.

During the Cold War, fear and insecurity were felt because of the danger of military confrontation. The tension between the two blocs were in the minds of people everywhere and at the root of many conflicts. The majority of people perceived that little could be done to lessen this insecurity; decision making and the capacity for change were concentrated in the hands of a few political leaders. At that time, people's movements and voluntary organizations were still an exception.

The alleviation of superpower rivalry changed this perception drastically. Problems came closer to home — more invisible but also more insidious. Military conflilcts between nations and the prospect of nuclear confrontation no longer seem to threaten human security to the same extent as formerly perceived. Rather, joblessness, poverty, crime and delinquency, drugs, terrorism, marginalization, and lack of access to markets are threats in all parts of the world. The globalization process is bringing these issues to all corners of the planet. No country today can claim that all of its citizens are secure.

As a result, the number of nongovernmental organizations and people's movements has increased in all countries at the local, national, and international levels. Many citizens have reacted by organizing themselves in an effort to better their lives and those of others by promoting individual and social conditions and human development.

People use these movements and organizations as a vehicle to express their needs and aspirations concerning justice, solidarity, equity, freedom, and peace. Even more importantly, they contribute to the solutions to problems, looking at new ways and methods of coping with challenges and issues in a creative and participative framework. Most of them have implemented projects much more efficiently and effectively than have the public and private sectors.

The Opportunity for Cooperation

If there is an opportunity today for youth, it is the capacity for dialogue with other young people all over the world. The occasion for self-awakening is unique and provides an immense capacity for action. Redesigning our future is feasible if we properly utilize the means at our disposal.

Although opinion leaders, the United Nations system, and other institutions and relevant NGOs require the participation of all sectors of civil society, young people feel totally excluded or lack a sense of contribution to their communities. On the one hand, youth lacks trust in itself, in its capacity to change. On the other, youth has found enormous obstacles in the path of participation.

Chapter 25 of Agenda 21 reads, "It is imperative that youth from all parts of the world participate actively in all relevant levels of decision-making processes because it affects their lives today and has implications for their futures." This "imperative" is more present in rhetoric than in action, and there is little sign to date to indicate that all actors, governments, the business community, institutions, NGOs, and even young people themselves are prepared to face the implications for their activities and working methods.

However, the ability to mobilize resources, energy, and idealism, which are the intellectual contribution of fresh insights, and the unique perspectives of young people are critical factors for societal change. With some inspiration, stimulation, and development of their capabilities, youth can efficiently contribute to the processes of change and reform.

It would be wrong not to recognize the increasing number of impressive youth initiatives, too numerous to mention in detail. However, projects such as the mobilization of university students in Colombia, Peru, and Mexico to work in rural areas or the efforts of members of city youth volunteer corps who work are having an effect on the lives of people who may have fallen between the cracks of traditional development plans.

Youth can no longer accept and play the role of observer, but must take the lead in solving the issues that compromise human survival, such as ecological degradation, war and militarization, human rights violations, economic inequality, and injustice. The myopic approaches of the present can no longer be accepted by young people, who must be awakened to their rights and responsibilities. We must create a new vision among youth and provide mechanisms for participation in decision making.

Youth's Part in Sustainable Human Development

Awareness creation is easier among young people and it is of crucial importance. It requires continuity, participation, and experience. Only through these can understanding be ensured.

Education is the means for constructing peace in the minds of people. It is the means for real development. Education should prepare people to face future challenges as well as develop the ability to deal with present obstacles in a creative way. The young must learn to anticipate the future while maintaining a strong sense of reality—to develop a vision for the future instead of worrying about it.

Young people must learn to anticipate and prepare for change, to solve more of their problems through dialogue and communication rather than violence and conflict, and to generate creative alternatives for mutual gain. But this process requires activism. Young people should move proactively toward achieving their aspirations. NGOs that accept young members or, even better, youth NGOs are the best way to utilize young people's energy and to develop curiosity and understanding. The presence of young people in processes and fora are key factors for this process.

The emerging global village needs responsible citizens, with a strong sense of ethics, capable of anticipating and adapting to uncertainty and constant change, curious about the world, and tolerant of cultural diversity. In the final analysis, world citizens have to develop a sense of ownership of humanity. Young people should be given the opportunity to develop this vision.

To do this, current channels for youth participation and development must be challenged. The participation of young people in decision-making processes is still an exception in many countries. This responsibility belongs to the business sector, institutions, organizations, and the government. Every company, department, and NGO should initiate reforms that institutionalize opportunities for youth in all fields.

Real participation requires radical changes in attitudes and thinking. The opinions of young people have not been taken into account, even though they represent a real basis for debate and reform. The following are possible changes:

- Participation of young people as speakers in opening debates.
- Involvement of young people in national missions representing the country in the intergovernmental sector.
- Involvement in program evaluation.
- Student involvement in decision making in educational and governmental institutions.
- Easier access for young people to communications and the media.
- Promotion of youth mobility, training and skill development, and efforts at encouraging entrepreneurship.

Conclusion

The progress made in the last decades does not ensure a minimum degree of security to all citizens of the world. How is it possible that we exchange US $1 trillion a day, but are unable to feed the 34,000 children who die every day because of malnutrition and disease? How is it possible that we have on-line teleconferencing between two continents via satellite, but have one billion illiterate people? What good are communication capabilities if young people have no access to them?

People must forget the obsolete way of viewing the world, where the North represented opportunity and the South misery. This dichotomy has been transformed. There are opportunities in the South, and there are miseries in the North. Globalization has created the breakthrough that gives people broader opportunities to react and change, wherever they are. The ability for young people to achieve results through direct action is greater than ever before. One must accept that in the present, the best and the worst exist side by side; the highest expectations are accompanied by terrible risks. To change is an ethical imperative for youth, as it means the security of all people in the present and future.

Chapter 3

Strengthening International Cooperation

Section 1

Rethinking Development: A New Challenge for International Development Organizations

Keith A. Bezanson

During most of the postwar period, while the ideological duel of the Cold War was conducted, North–South relations have been grounded in an inspiring, publicly funded experiment in international development. All evidence suggests that the experiment is drawing to a rapid close. The funding base, stagnant in real terms for more than a decade, is now beginning to erode in nominal terms as well.

This situation has generated anxiety and alarm in poor countries, especially in Africa, where words like abandonment and betrayal are used to describe what is taking place. Development organizations—bilateral, multilateral, and nongovernmental—have been investing heavily in demonstrating that "development works." Such demonstrations, their authors hope, will galvanize public and political will in industrialized countries for increased allocations of public funds for international development.

Thus, a growing literature tries to demonstrate that economic development is working. The World Bank, for example, devoted its entire 1991 World Development Report (WDR) to this purpose. With few exceptions, the case being made by development organizations rests on the following points:

- Average incomes in developing countries have doubled over the past three decades, increasing faster than in the United States, the United Kingdom, or Japan;
- People in developing countries now live some 10 years longer on average than in 1960—twice the gain the United States could achieve by eliminating both cancer and heart disease; and
- The rate of infant deaths has nearly been cut in half, child death rates have plummeted, and immunization rates have soared.

The case is valid, and the frequency and sophistication of its presentation are increasing. Its influence, however, is limited. It may be reducing the erosion rate of public finances for development, but it is certainly not stopping or reversing the trend.

Nor, in my view, will it. The problem lies not in the validity of the argument, but in the argument itself. Bluntly stated, it is the wrong argument. The case that development organizations are making rests, implicitly and explicitly, on four broad propositions:

- The declining commitment to publicly funded, international development results from the global, which is part of the normal economic cycle. Matters will "return to normal" once the recession is over.

- Development has been and remains a "North–South" issue. The poverty of the South can be eliminated by transferring the "surplus" of the North.

- The state is the appropriate instrument of intermediation between North and South in redistributing the economic "surplus."

- The task of development remains what it has been over the past five decades—to achieve, in the span of one generation, the standards of living that the rich nations of the West achieved in three or four generations.

However noble the underlying intent, some of these propositions are completely wrong, and none account for the dramatically changed context of current development efforts. That context calls for the fundamental reexamination of the meaning of development and progress.

The New Context for Development

The visions of plenty and happiness, which for decades guided the efforts of less fortunate nations to catch up, have become hazy and blurred. Development, in theory and in practice, has rested on and been measured against the material standards of living of the rich nations of the West. Today, however, those very Western standards are being questioned because of their negative environmental consequences and because they were defined in primarily material terms. The social, cultural, and spiritual dimensions of human development were ignored. The rise of religious fundamentalism and fierce ethnic rivalries throughout the world indicate the extent to which these neglected, nonmaterial dimensions of development have reemerged, and have acquired a disruptive and even pathological character.

Most of the postwar intellectual architecture of development has derived from economics. "Development economics," a new area of economic specialization starting in the 1950s, held that under the right conditions, development was linear, measurable, predictable, and subject to the universal treatment of economic theory.

Much of this architecture, we now know, requires fundamental rethinking, which must take place at a time of unprecedented turmoil and change in practically all aspects of human activity. Most notably, the international order that prevailed for five decades collapsed by the early 1990s; nations and individuals are now facing the uncertainties and instabilities that accompany the difficult transition to a new, and as yet undefined, world order.

International security and political concerns, once processed through the relatively stable, bipolar system of East–West confrontation, have acquired a much more complex and unpredictable character. The world economy is experiencing profound transformations, mainly as a result of shifts in trade patterns, the globalization of financial markets, the changes in the nature of work, and the impact of technological advances, all of which challenge established economic practices and confound the search for models and strategies.

Accelerated social and cultural changes have turned upside down the time-honored and cherished assumptions that underpinned the social order in many parts of the world, and particularly in developing regions and former socialist countries. The complex web of human values and interpersonal relations that keeps communities together has been subjected to unprecedented strains; in some instances, it has broken down completely.

But it is in our capacity to generate and utilize the knowledge that has brought about these profound changes. Scientific and technological advances will be the main determinants of the paths that much of the world community will take in the new millennium. As a consequence, those with access to the products of scientific and technological research – as well as the ability to understand, absorb, and apply them – will exert an ever-increasing influence in the conduct of human affairs. Moreover, the astonishing pace of advances in science and technology during the last few decades has been accompanied by pronounced and abysmal differences in the capacities of nations to generate and utilize this knowledge. Thus, many nations will be severely limited in the pursuit of their own developmental objectives, whichever form they take. Left unchecked, this phenomenon could create a new global apartheid that will apply both among nations and within individual societies.

All these changes configure a completely new situation. This, in turn, is embedded in an even larger framework: our very understanding of the essence of humanness is evolving. New discoveries are forcing us to revise our ideas about humanity and its place in the order of things, as well as our conception of what human beings are, can be, and will be. We are beginning to internalize the interrelationship between human beings and the physical world, acknowledging that we cannot act with impunity by destroying the environment, trusting blindly the regenerative capacities of ecosystems. This is a radical shift from eighteenth- and nineteenth-century perception; human beings are now viewed as stewards of a precious heritage that must be protected and passed on to future generations.

Advances in information technology are additionally creating new levels of reality—such as virtual reality and cyberspace—that lie between the tangible world, which has always been with us, and the world of abstract concepts, which the Greeks developed at least 2,500 years ago. Communications technologies are not only creating new modes of human interaction, they are altering what we mean by experience, privacy, individuality, cultural identity, and governance.

People have a newfound capacity for consciously altering the direction of human evolution and for overcoming the limitations of an individual's biological and genetic composition. The possibility of managing evolution carries moral responsibilities for which regulations must be established. Human beings are responsible for their biological, as well as cultural, future. In addition, advances in expert systems and robotics are forcing us to reconsider the functional attributes of human beings. As artifacts and mechanical constructions have an increasing impact on the way we live, the idea of "coevolution" between humans and machines is emerging.

All of this suggests that, as the new millennium approaches, humanity is in the midst of a bewildering transition towards something that cannot be clearly visualized. Such momentous changes are accompanied by profound fears of the unknown, by a low tolerance for uncertainty, by a desire to escape from real or imagined threats, and by a crippling sense of helplessness. A retreat to what is perceived as safe, known, and familiar emerges as a response, usually expressed in the form of nostalgia for certainties of the past, and a return to primal loyalties. But our human condition is changing, and history tells us that it is not possible to go back.

As our turbulent world stumbles forward, rethinking the concepts of development and progress has become an urgent task. As the scientist Albert Einstein stated many years ago: "We cannot solve the problems we have created with the same thinking that created them."

Rethinking Development

A new world order is changing the traditional North–South axis that divided wealth and poverty. Indeed, the very term "North–South" is fast becoming a serious impediment to any understanding of development. A more accurate formulation in our emerging reality is a geographically heterogeneous "included–excluded" axis, where the included is growing. For example, the South, particularly in Asia, is experiencing an expansion in manufacturing. Unfortunately, the excluded is also expanding, as a higher percentage move North.

Development thinking—indeed its very language—will have to be modified. This will not be easy. To quote the renowned economist John Maynard Keynes: "The difficulty lies not in new ideas, but escaping from old ones." This is complicated by the fact that we have grown accustomed to political and business leaders addressing themselves only to limited manifestations of our present crisis. Unlike previous crises of economic depression or warfare, this one has not generated its own language. We continue to use the language of development, but we have enriched it with the most reactionary principles of neoclassical economics. The result is that most development discourse continues to speak of unlimited economic growth and expansion in the face of social and ecological collapse. Development may become dangerously incoherent; unless changed, its language will be judged as disjointed with our historical reality.

It may be instructive to pause for a moment and recall a time when the world, staggered and bewildered by forces of tidal change, approached a new century. Thomas Paine (1737–1809), renowned in England, France, and America as the protagonist of the Rights of Man, looked about his world. What he saw was a planet in disarray; the French Revolution; the rise of the Reign of Terror; the American Revolution; Europe on the verge of the Napoleonic Wars; demagogues rising up throughout the world; the breakdown of government; people homeless as a result of the Industrial Revolution; individuals whose social, economic, and cultural roots had disappeared, who were no longer rural and had no place in urban society; high degrees of violence and criminality; and the beginning of the breakdown of the Church.

Thomas Paine stood back from this frightening landscape and wrote: "We have it in our power to begin the world all over again. A situation similar to the present hath not appeared since the days of Noah until now." Paine's words would, of course, be hyperbole were it not for the fact he was right. The very nature of society, of government, of the relationship of the individual to the collectivity was being transformed, as were patterns of values, attitudes, and beliefs. The result was the progress and development of the last 200 years.

The diagnosis of a problem is usually much easier than its prognosis. Certainly, the dangers today are greater than they were for Paine. We have a heavier legacy and a shorter time in which to fix things. Yet just as the Chinese ideogram for "crisis" is two symbols—one for danger and one for opportunity—development thinking must look beyond the dangers and seek out the opportunities. There is no roadmap to redefining development, but there are three significant clusters of opportunity that represent good starting points.

Global Interdependence

The first is the trend towards increasing recognition and acceptance of global interdependence. To say this may appear naive, to ignore completely the current reality of ever-increasing economic globalization with its unprecedented competition. Yet in parallel with that globalization, the ideological battles of the past are being replaced by the search for a more pragmatic partnership between market efficiency and social compassion. The growing force of the environmental threat and of the imperative of common survival on this fragile planet reminds humanity that we are all in this together.

Although this thinking is far from new, the idea of global interdependence, dangerously slow in taking root, is finding a place in the public mind. The United Nations Conference on Environment and Development, the Earth Summit at Rio, was evidence of this. Of the 182 participating nations, 105 were represented by their heads of government. Also in attendance from all parts of the world and as major new players in international negotiations were Non-Governmental Organizations (NGOs), women's organizations, young people, and representatives of indigenous movements. Yes, there were different agendas. Yes, some came saying "the problem is in developing countries where population is growing too fast." Yes, some argued that "the villains are industrialized countries where consumption is out of control." But, equally true is the fact that they came, and that in some modest way initial building blocks were laid for a global framework. Conventions on carbon-gas emissions and biodiversity were signed. Statements on forestry principles were promulgated. "Agenda 21" was announced as a global action plan, though one that was much watered down because it was in the end what it had to be: an intergovernmental consensus document. But for whatever its defects, "Agenda 21" is a global action plan that assumes interdependence.

Another element of the recognition of interdependence can be found in the debates within countries and communities on security, which is no longer defined in the Cold War sense of protection from nuclear attack. Security entails a much more complex view of how a lifestyle – be it national or individual – depends on factors far removed from direct control, but over which some influence is desirable. Security for the Northern hemisphere is seen increasingly in terms of what happens to the rainforests of the Amazon or the drylands of Africa. Certainly, we do not understand all the linkages, but awareness and concern are growing.

The security debate is not limited to environmental concerns. It includes education, health, food, employment, and culture. This is natural, for we are beginning to see that future conflicts will occur more among people than nations. If we succeed in redefining security in this way, we may be able to take advantage of the only opportunity that history has given us to reduce military expenditures. In the past five years, global military expenditure has been reduced by some $250 billion. This has never before happened in our lifetime. This is a peace dividend, and we should not be fooled into thinking it is only an illusion. Military spending, which has increased annually for more than 40 years, has decreased by 3 percent each year over the past six years.

This notion of interdependence is revolutionary; it requires not merely a change to some of our thoughts, but a change in actual mindset. We might begin with a change in language. Language is not mere detail; it hampers or facilitates our ability to look at a new set of relations and concepts that may be better adapted to the future. A characteristic of the current global transformation is that the landscape is changing even as we attempt to understand and analyze it. A second characteristic is that our concepts, and the language we use to express them, are increasingly inadequate, or even erroneous.

Interdependence is a concept of enormous complexity; its comprehension requires fresh thinking. Although we know how to describe and explain it, we can easily overlook the fact that describing and explaining do not amount to understanding. The former has to do with knowledge, which is the stuff of science; the latter has to do with meaning, the stuff of enlightenment. Moreover, the theory and practice of economics and development will be changed profoundly by an understanding of interdependence, and much of the current language will not fit into an interdependence paradigm. Terms like "Third World," "North–South," or even "developing countries" suggest homogeneous groups that no longer exist in simple definition. Indeed, we have long known that labels obscure as much as they elucidate; thus change in language – and in mindset – is necessary.

Rise of Local Initiatives

A second opportunity involves the rise of local initiatives as people and communities around the world demand more control over their lives. The rate of technological and economic change has far outstripped the rate of social innovation, or even the power of governments to keep up. This, of course, again challenges us to rethink what we mean by "development." Can the international development community bury the mindset that development is something done to and for people? Can effective conceptual frameworks and models be generated to move us beyond simple macroeconomic formulations and a growing dependence on a globalized marketplace to arbitrate development? Can strategic planning approaches, which help build social capital and which are conducive to community ownership, be constructed around the rise of local initiatives? In development, many of the actors—both donor and government organizations—have lost sight of these factors. In some cases, people have lost sight of them too. We desire a clean environment, but it is someone else's responsibility to provide it.

The evidence of community initiative and the seizing of local control is growing worldwide. This is driven in part by sheer necessity, by the declining capacity of the nation-state to distribute social goods, and by the basic drive for survival. But it is happening. There are elements of social innovation, or reclaiming control, that give cause for optimism. The importance of social capital as the engine of development is underscored in an elaborate study by Robert Putnam, which demonstrates that the quality of social organizations in the community is a precondition to economic growth.

> Historical reviews in Italy suggest that communities did not become civil because they were rich, but rather became rich because they were civic.... The social capital represented by networks of civic engagements seems to be a precondition for economic development and effective government. A society that relies on generalized reciprocity and mutual assistance is more effective than a competitive, distrustful society. The network helps to overcome anonymity, cultivates reputation and builds trust of others through communication and interaction. Successful collaboration in one activity builds social capital connections and trust for other activities. The social capital is built from an investment of the time and caring of individuals: it does not deplete the public treasury.

For much of the past 40 years, development has been cloaked in the pretence that it was value free or value neutral. Nothing was further from the truth. The foundation stone of development thought and practice was the dominant socioeconomic paradigm of the industrial North, emphasizing individualism, technology, consumption, personal wealth, and the inadvertent neglect of the social fabric of the community. Values and culture were factors that, for the most part, simply "got in the way"; they were dealt with as incidentals, as "externalities" to the development model. The rethinking of development must deal with this and not merely with how to "enhance" and "refine" our approach.

Knowledge of Innovation

A third opportunity cluster lies in the growing realization of the importance of knowledge and innovation. Not only are we in the midst of global transformation based on knowledge, but we require improved knowledge overall to respond to the conditions defining the crisis in which we find ourselves. This demand for knowledge about how to do things better has never been more pronounced. The quest for innovation is accelerating, and is evident at both macro- and microlevels.

At the macrolevel, we are emerging from a major ideological battle about the issues of the market and state. One of the myths that characterized the battle was that the market could do it all. Yet any reading of history tells us that the very qualities of aggressiveness, daring, and greed that make markets work also cause them to fail. That same reading of history tells us that a strong state is needed to deal with market failure, or better still, to prevent the more severe dislocations by preventing market failure. History notwithstanding, we still hear strident claims that socialism is dead, and that the market has triumphed. Capitalism has shown its vitality, but we must ensure that the victory is not a victory of personal greed. If socialism as an ideology is vanquished, let us ensure that it is not also the death of all social objectives. Of course, the efficiency of the marketplace is needed; however, the creative energies of capitalism must be blended with the social objectives of equity and human development.

Robert Heilbroner in his 1992 essay "Twenty-First Century Capitalism" looks to the future and reflects on the possible nature of an innovative, economic-social blend:

> If I were to hazard a description of the capitalisms most likely to succeed, I would think they would be those characterized by a high degree of political pragmatism, a low index of ideological fervor, a well-developed civil service, and a tradition of public cohesion. All successful capitalisms, I further believe, will find ways to assure labor of security of employment and income, management of the right to restructure tasks for efficiency's sake, and government of its legitimate role as a coordinator of national growth....

The call for appropriate innovation at the macrolevel is as yet largely unheeded. Globalization is the current watchword. We all compete for each others internal markets, and in so doing, we continue to dismantle what Heilbroner refers to as the "legitimate" role of government as coordinator of national growth. If development is to be rethought and viewed as a credible approach to the crisis, it will have to help formulate appropriate innovations in this area. For it is here—in the pragmatic combination of efficiency and equity—that the viability of future models of development will be found.

At the microlevel, technological innovation also has a role to play — if not as the all-powerful fixer–at least the essential helper. We know that technology has been a driving factor in all cases of rapid economic growth. This proved as true for the United States in the nineteenth century and Japan in the nineteenth and early twentieth centuries, as it has been for South Korea, Taiwan, or Singapore over the past few years. Entirely new technologies open fantastic new opportunities. Ongoing adaptation, enrichment, and innovation to technologies, however, is the key to sustained economic growth. Development thinking must move beyond the simplistic, macroeconomic formulations on which it has depended for so many years. Development institutions must discover approaches that stimulate appropriate technological innovations.

Conclusion

This section has tried to demonstrate why international development organizations will be increasingly ignored and marginalized unless they move quickly beyond their current and limiting preoccupation with demonstrating their own effectiveness. Development itself must be rethought — and rethought urgently — to take account of the principal features of change in the global context, of the profound and wrenching transformations that the world is undergoing.

Building on the recognition of interdependence will require an international, institutional framework that is more effective and more robust than what we now have. The present set of institutions and mechanisms is inadequate for dealing with the changes that have already taken place in our world, much less those yet to come. There will clearly be much discussion of reform to the UN framework as the organization approaches its 50th anniversary.

People will expect and demand a more direct role in their own development, and in the international, regional, and national institutions undertaking development. NGOs are going to play a bigger role in the United Nations, either directly or through such parallel, but influential, channels as occurred at Rio. More experimentation and use will be made of inclusive means of consultation and consensus building. Social innovation, or building on our social capital, must invigorate our communities and interactions.

The quest for innovation presents enormous challenges to development organizations and knowledge-based institutions. A global partnership must be built by strengthening the capacity of developing countries to participate in the creation and application of knowledge for development. Knowledge can only be used by those who "appropriate" it, and this requires capacity.

The twenty-first century may be a time when human knowledge supports a new vision of global sustainable and equitable development. International development organizations should heed the words of Harvey Brooks, distinguished scientist and professor emeritus of Harvard University. In a recent lecture, he stated: "We find ourselves at a unique moment in human history on the planet...a time not only of unprecedented problems but also unprecedented opportunities.... We are thus in a time of transition—a transition leading either towards catastrophe and social disintegration or towards a sustainably growing world society...."

That positive transition necessitates leadership. The world's international development community should be an important part of this, and for that to happen, the community must rethink what it is, and remake what it does. This will involve the controversy that goes with the dismantling of conventional wisdoms, along with the high risks that accompany real leadership. Only in this manner can development signal a much-needed hope for a sustainable and equitable future.

Section 2

A New Framework for
Development Cooperation

Keith Griffin and
Terry McKinley

With the end of the Cold War, we have an opportunity to replace the ideological competition that dominated international relations for nearly half a century by a new spirit of solidarity and cooperation. The world is no longer divided between East and West, and we must not let it become divided again along a new fault line separating North from South. Instead of viewing international relations in terms of conflicts between states, the problems of the globe should be seen in the round – as problems confronting all of us as people, and not as citizens of states. Indeed the actions of states frequently are the source of global problems, and adequate solutions to global problems may require that the actions of states be regulated by rules circumscribing acceptable international behavior.

Our framework seeks, whenever possible, to be based on the mutual interests of people. States as such have no interests; only people or groups of people have interests – and group interests increasingly transcend national boundaries. Thus in creating a framework for development cooperation, people must be kept sharply in focus. We look for positive-sum games where all players benefit or, failing that, for solutions where everyone potentially could gain if compensation were paid to the losers. Of course even if everyone gains, conflicts over the division of gains might occur, but at least such conflicts can in principle be resolved without making anyone absolutely worse off. This approach gives high priority to policies that accelerate growth or that result in greater efficiency in the use of the world's resources. Often this means extending the market mechanism to new areas (the migration of labor and exports from poor countries) or devising market-like mechanisms to cope with new problems (global environmental issues and the disposal of nuclear weapons). Because policies that promote mutual interests do not necessarily also promote human development, reduce global poverty, or contribute to other desired objectives, more is needed – namely, policies that seek to achieve justice or equity.

For this reason, another equally prominent theme of this section is equity: the need to provide a global safety net to combat severe poverty in the poorest countries, and a need for the rich to compensate the poor when discriminatory actions of the former injure those who are weak and vulnerable. These ideas of equity, solidarity, and community are commonplace in nation-states and should be extended people everywhere. Hunger, disease, and misery are becoming no more acceptable "abroad" than they are at "home" and, indeed, as our horizons widen, the distinction between home and abroad becomes blurred. It is no longer an oxymoron to speak of a global community. Similarly, just as discrimination within a state is not tolerated, and those who discriminate are liable for damages, so too discrimination by states against others should not be permissible, and those who discriminate should be required to pay compensation.

A Global Balance Sheet

Let us begin by summarizing international flows of capital and labor, and the factor payments associated with these flows. To do this, we constructed a rather crude global balance sheet. The goal is to determine whether the operation of international capital and labor markets benefit developing countries. To the extent that they do not, appropriate corrective measures can be taken.

The world is divided into four groups of countries. Group A countries are the 31 countries with a real per capita GDP of $10,000 or more (in purchasing power parity terms). The lowest income countries, Group C, are the 51 developing countries with a real per capita GDP of $1500 or less. In between, there are the Group B countries, which are divided in two groups: B1 consists of 31 countries with a real per capita income between $10,000 and $4,000; B2 consists of 44 countries with a real per capita income between $4,000 and $1,500. The 15 republics of the former Soviet Union are excluded from these calculations because of lack of data. All of them, however, would have fallen into Group B.

We then compare the population of the "world" and real GDP in 1990. The total population is 4.9 billion and real GDP is $23,538 billion. At one extreme, the Group A countries account for 16.5 percent of the total population, but receive 62.1 percent of total real income. At the other extreme, the Group C countries account for 32.3 percent of the total population, but receive only 6.6 percent of total real income. The Group B countries fall in the middle.[1]

Long-Term Capital Flows

Consider the overall estimates of resource flows associated with long-term movements of capital across international boundaries. The significance of these resource transfers can perhaps best be understood as an expression of a percentage of real GDP. In 1990, the outflow of resources associated with movements of long-term capital was equivalent to 1.12 percent of the real GDP of the Group B1 countries; in the Group B2 countries it was much lower, that is, 0.14 percent; it rose to 0.31 percent in the Group C countries.[2]

A negative resource transfer does not imply that the market for long-term capital is impoverishing the developing countries, but it does indicate that current inflows of capital are more than offset by an outflow of service payments on previous capital. This net outflow reduces the resources available for current expenditure, including expenditure on investment in physical and human capital. Thus, it lowers the potential rate of growth and the future standard of living. A positive resource transfer, in contrast, increases the level of current expenditure and raises the potential rate of growth. Seen in this light, net resource transfers are one measure of the distribution of current gains from international transactions. The negative transfers from the developing countries indicate that they enjoy the smaller share of the benefits from global capital movements. Given that they are much poorer than the Group A countries, negative transfers from the Group B and C countries accentuate global inequalities in the distribution of income. These market forces, in other words, are part of the mechanism for the international transmission of inequality.

Capital Flight

Capital flight from developing countries constitutes an outflow of resources generated domestically that otherwise could be used to finance investment and human development and promote faster economic growth. It thus exacerbates the negative net resource transfers resulting from the such inflows of capital as commercial loans and foreign direct investment and helps to perpetuate underdevelopment.

World Bank calculations indicate that capital flight increased sharply beginning in 1977 and reached a peak in 1988. Our estimates of capital flight in 1990 indicate that the problem remains serious, particularly in the Group C countries.[3] Although our estimates represent only rough orders of magnitude, they appear to be broadly consistent with the estimates of recorded capital flows and we believe they represent the reality of capital movements in the global economy.

The richest developing countries (Group B1) experienced a flight of capital in 1990 of approximately $11.2 billion. This outflow was equivalent to 0.35 percent of their real GDP. Not all countries, of course, suffered from capital flight; there were large outflows in Argentina, Brazil, Hungary, and Poland, and significant inflows of repatriated capital in Chile, Malaysia, Portugal, and Mexico. In the Group B2 countries, the pattern was far from uniform, with many countries having large inflows and others equally large outflows, but for the group as a whole there was a small net inflow of about $0.6 billion. Repatriated capital was 0.02 percent of their real GDP. The largest net inflow in the Group B2 countries was in Thailand, followed by Egypt and Botswana. There were significant outflows of capital in Algeria, the Philippines, and Pakistan.

Capital flight was most prominent in the Group C countries, that is, in the poorest of the developing countries. In 1990 the outflow was approximately $18.9 billion or 1.22 percent of their real GDP. Moreover, capital flight appears to have affected almost all of the countries in Group

C and hence was a fairly general phenomenon. Some of the hardest hit countries in the group were Angola, India, Bangladesh, Nigeria, Côte d'Ivoire, Senegal, and the Sudan.

Again, as with recorded flows of capital, flight capital responds to market forces. Capital flight should not be viewed as an aberration—a reflection of political instability, risk of nationalization, and inappropriate macroeconomic policies—but as a normal feature of the world economy. Unfortunately this feature operates to the disadvantage of developing countries, particularly to the disadvantage of the poorest developing countries, but this is a fact of global economic life and not a random occurrence that can be disregarded.

Migration and Worker Remittances

International flows of capital are biased against developing countries in general and largely bypass the poorest countries, those in Group C. The net transfer of resources actually is negative. This raises the question whether flows of income arising from the operation of the international labor market offset or reinforce the income flows originating in capital markets. To answer this question, we examined the international flow of worker remittances in developing countries for 1990. Groups B1 and B2 have much larger gross receipts than Group C. Total receipts for the three groups of countries were about $35.4 billion, or well above the $22.5 billion they received in the form of direct foreign investment. Payments by the Group B1 and C countries were quite large and equivalent to 26.8 and 31.6 percent, respectively, of the gross receipts of workers remittances.[4]

Net receipts in the Group B1 countries were $11.2 billion. Four countries, however, accounted for 105 percent of the total, the rest on balance paying out more than they received in remittances. The four countries are Portugal, Greece, Turkey (which benefit from their association with the European Community), and Mexico (which benefits from proximity to the United States). The Group B2 countries received somewhat more than the Group B1 countries, namely, $15.6 billion. Once again, however, net receipts were concentrated among a small number of countries: Morocco, Egypt, Pakistan, Yemen, and the Philippines accounted for 76 percent of the total.

The poorest countries, Group C, received only $2.6 billion of remittances net of payments. This was equivalent to only 0.17 percent of the real GDP of the Group, or less than half the amount received by the Group B1 (0.35 percent) and B2 countries (0.37 percent). In the case of the Group C countries, India and Bangladesh accounted for 105 percent of total workers remittances, implying that other members of the group paid out more than they received. The small inflow of remittances into the Group C countries as a whole did not compensate for the negative resource transfer arising from capital market transactions, which was equivalent to 0.31 percent of their real GDP. This underlines the point that the Group C countries are on the margin of the global economy and have a strong case for special attention in the form of grants of foreign aid.

A New Basis for Financing Aid

Given that international markets are not very successful in channeling resources to developing countries and indeed often drain resources out of the poor countries, official development assistance should be used to compensate for these market forces.

A Progressive International Income Tax

There is widespread disappointment, to use the World Bank's own words, that "aid has done much less than might have been hoped to reduce poverty."[5] This prolonged disappointment has undermined the support of humane internationalists in the developed countries for foreign aid programs. The basis for aid will have to be reconstructed if the support for aid is not to wither away. Yet the moral case for the people of rich countries to help those in poor countries remains intact.[6] Those who are prosperous do have a moral obligation to assist those who live in poverty. Thus there is a prima facie case for a transfer of resources from rich countries to poor.

One issue that needs to be resolved is the amount of aid provided and the way it is financed.[7] At present, official development assistance is financed by what can be described as a system of voluntary taxation of rich countries. In a rational world, the burden of aid "taxation" would be expected to fall most lightly on donor countries with the lowest per capita income and gradually rise as per capita income increases. That is, one would expect the "tax rates" to be progressive. Yet if one compares GNP per capita of the 18 major OECD donor countries with each country's aid burden as measured by the percentage of GNP allocated to official development assistance, one discovers that the aid burden is randomly distributed among donors.

A strictly proportional aid burden would be less inequitable than the present randomly distributed burden, but it would not correspond to what most people would regard as fair. The present system in which three very rich countries (the United States, Japan, and Switzerland) contribute less than the average percentage is utterly indefensible, but it would be almost as difficult to justify a system that requires Ireland (with a per capita income of $9,550) to pay as much as Switzerland (with a per capita income of $32,680).

When creating a new framework for development cooperation, the objective should be to end the present system where aid contributions are voluntary, the aid burden is distributed randomly and inequitably, and the flows of aid are unpredictable because they are subject to annual appropriations by national parliaments. Instead the world should move to a system where contributions to the aid effort are obligatory, the burden is distributed progressively, and the annual flows are predictable. In short, what is needed is a progressive international income tax on rich countries administered by an international authority such as the United Nations. The tax receipts would constitute the foundation for an international development fund.

The design of such a scheme could be very simple and easy to implement. We present one scheme to illustrate how it might work. The first issue that must be resolved is which countries would be liable to an international tax. We suggest that the cut-off point be a real GDP per capita in 1990 (expressed in US dollars of purchasing power parity) of $10,000. The 31 countries with a real income higher than $10,000 — our Group A countries previously identified — would be liable to the tax; those with an income less than $10,000 per capita would be exempt.

The second issue is the rate of taxation. The tax schedule should be progressive in order to take into account differences in real income among the donor countries; it should also be simple in order to avoid disputes over tax liabilities that turn on alternative estimates of a country's GDP. We suggest that there be only three tax rates and that the tax base be a country's gross domestic product as conventionally measured, that is, not adjusted for purchasing power parity. Specifically, a tax rate of 0.375 percent would be applied in countries with a real GDP per capita (in PPP terms) greater than $16,000. Sixteen countries, from Norway to the United States, fall into this category. Next, a tax rate of 0.25 percent would be applied in countries with a real income between $12,000 and $16,000. This category includes eight countries, from New Zealand to Italy. Finally, a tax rate of 0.20 percent would be applied in countries with a real income between $10,001 and $11,999. This category includes seven countries, from Ireland to Spain.

Application of these rates of taxation implies that some countries would contribute less foreign aid than they do at present, notably the Nordic countries, France, and the Netherlands. Others would contribute more than they do at present, notably the United States and Austria. Still others would join the club of donors for the first time, such as Singapore, Hong Kong, and the Bahamas. Those countries that wished to contribute more to the aid effort than required by their tax obligation would of course be free to do so. They could either make voluntary contributions to the international development fund or they could supplement the multilateral program with a bilateral program.

This scheme produces a tax yield of nearly $56.8 billion, excluding Brunei for which data are not available. This is only slightly more than the $55.6 billion contributed by the OECD countries in 1990. Moreover, all of the aid would be in the form of grants and none of the grants would be tied in any way. Hence the real value of the aid under an international tax financed scheme undoubtedly would be considerably higher to the recipients than the value of the present mixture of loans, export credits, surplus commodities, and so on.

Disbursements under a Negative International Income Tax

Once the question is resolved of how to finance foreign aid under a new framework for development cooperation, attention can be turned to a second issue, namely, the criteria of eligibility to receive development assistance. If foreign aid is to enjoy the support of the public in donor countries, the criteria used to select recipient countries must be clear and fair. That is far from the situation at present. Indeed we now have an extreme case where Ireland is an aid donor and Israel a large aid recipient, yet Israel's per capita income is higher than Ireland's. Such a situation obviously could not be allowed to continue if aid were to be financed through a system of international taxation administered by the United Nations.

What is needed is an internationally agreed cut-off point so that only those countries below the critical point would be eligible for foreign assistance. The dividing line could be either absolute or relative. One possibility would be to make a real per capita income (in PPP terms) of, say, $1,500 in 1990 the cut-off point, which would include the 51 countries in Group C.

The total population of the 51 countries eligible under this criterion is just over 1.5 billion persons. If the entire international development fund of $56.8 billion were divided equally among the eligible recipients, the average aid allocation per person would be about $37.87. We suggest, however, that it would be more equitable to allocate more than average to the poorest countries and less than average to those who are not quite so poor. The poorest 27 countries, with a real (PPP) income per head of less than $900, would be allocated $50 per head of foreign aid. This group of countries, from Zaïre to Bangladesh, contains 385.4 million people and merits special assistance. The second group contains 24 countries with a real income per capita between $900 and $1,500. This group, from the Gambia to Nicaragua, contains nearly 1,182 million people. The aid allocation to this group is $30 per head.

Such a system of grants, a negative international income tax, could become a powerful mechanism for ameliorating and ultimately eliminating world poverty. Much would depend however on the policies of the governments of recipient countries. Under the global transfer program we recommend, aid would be concentrated where it is most needed. The amount of aid per head of the population would be large enough to have a significant impact on the well-being of people. And the amount of aid received, expressed as a percentage of GDP, would make it possible, if it is used wisely, to accelerate markedly the rate of growth in the recipient countries. The two largest countries in group of 51, Bangladesh and India, would benefit enormously under this aid disbursement scheme. Bangladesh, for example, currently receives aid equivalent to about 9.5 percent of its GDP; under the negative income tax aid inflows would be equivalent to 23.3 percent of its GDP, and all of the aid would of course be in the form of grants. Aid to India is only about 0.6 percent of its GDP; under this scheme it would rise to 10 percent. Some countries would lose, such as Zambia and Ghana, because their entitlements under a negative income tax would be less than the amount of foreign aid they now receive. And of course those countries that now receive aid but are not included in our group of the 51 poorest countries would cease to receive foreign aid under our scheme. Countries such as Argentina, Malaysia, Tunisia, and Botswana would not be eligible for assistance from the international development fund. The limited resources available for international transfer payments would be channeled to countries with the lowest real incomes.

Payment for Services Rendered

Quite apart from resource transfers to provide a global safety net, there is potentially a large number of intergovernmental transactions that would be of mutual interest to the contracting parties. Where these transactions involve more than two countries, it may be advantageous if the same multilateral institution that administers the international development fund also assumes responsibility for collecting and disbursing funds and monitoring contract compliance as part of a second window of operations.

The purpose of this second window is to maintain a clear separation between foreign assistance proper and payments to countries for services rendered. There is a category of transactions, mostly between rich countries and poor, where the motivation is not humanitarian interests but self-interest. These transactions are perfectly legitimate, in fact beneficial; they are of a market-type but are not mediated by markets; and they are likely to increase in future. But they are not foreign aid and should not be confused with foreign aid; they are payments for services rendered.

Examples are:

- Environmental programs in developing countries that are partly or even primarily of benefit to developed countries.

- Programs to destroy nuclear weapons and reduce the risks of radiation to countries downwind of nuclear facilities.

- Programs in developing countries to reduce the supply of narcotic drugs exported to developed countries, such as crop substitution projects.

- Public health measures in developing countries designed to prevent the spread of the AIDS epidemic or other communicable diseases.

One might also include:

- Financial support for programs to convert armaments factories to civilian purposes as a way of reducing exports of military equipment and thereby contributing to global peace.

- Programs to control international terrorism and transnational crime.

- Measures to improve the health and economic and social position of women as ways to reduce the rate of growth of the world's population.

- Negotiations over the joint financing and management of natural resources which cross national boundaries, such as coastal fisheries and river systems.

- The management of the global commons, such as Antarctica, the oceans, and outer space. If one looks ahead there are many possibilities, although it would be sensible to begin modestly and allow the machinery for negotiation to evolve naturally in the light of experience.

The central point is that if the developed countries wish the remaining tropical forests to be preserved in order to prevent global warming and maintain biodiversity, then it is reasonable that they should bear part of the costs of preservation. Their portion of the costs should reflect the portion of benefits that accrue to them. Similarly, if the developed countries wish to discourage the use of CFCs in developing countries in order to reduce the rate of depletion of the ozone layer in the upper atmosphere, then they should compensate the developing countries for net social benefits foregone, either by making cash payments, providing substitute technology, or helping to finance the development of alternative technologies. Economic and technological globalization generate "externalities" and "free rider" problems, particularly but not exclusively for the environment. As a result, no one has an incentive to contribute to the solution although it is in the interests of all that a solution be found. The purpose of the second window is to provide a mechanism whereby mutually beneficial transactions can be arranged, the transfer of funds facilitated, and the results monitored.

The same principles apply in other areas of mutual interest between developed and developing countries. For example, just as it makes sense for the entry visas of international passengers to be checked at the point of departure rather than at the point of arrival, so too it pays developed countries to support public health programs in developing countries and thereby prevent the spread to them of communicable diseases. It is cheaper to vaccinate the entire population of developing countries against smallpox than it is to police permanently the borders of developed countries; it is cheaper to clean up the water supply in cholera-prone countries than to prevent contaminated food from being loaded on to airplanes. Of course, in many cases the developing countries should be spending money on such things as public health measures and clean water supplies regardless of possible external benefits. It is in the self-interest of their people to do so. We are here concerned only with those cases where consideration of external benefits makes the difference in the overall evaluation of a project or program.

Compensation for Damages

The point of origin for a new framework for international economic cooperation is a liberal, market-oriented global economic regime. The rules of the game of such a regime should permit the unimpeded flow worldwide of goods and services, technology, capital, and labor. Departures from this regime can on occasion be justified, but departures should not be arbitrary, and no country should be allowed to ignore the rules with impunity. The rules, after all, are intended to make it possible for everyone to share in global opportunities. Under a liberal regime this implies that commodity markets, capital markets, and labor markets should be allowed to operate freely.

The intellectual basis for a liberal economy is the demonstration that apart from exceptional circumstances both parties to a transaction benefit. The benefits may be unequally distributed, but both parties gain. It follows from this that when one party refuses to engage in potentially beneficial transactions with another, that party harms both itself and its potential trading partner.

One would perhaps not be unduly concerned if an economic agent (a firm or an individual) were to inflict harm upon itself by failing to engage in beneficial economic activity. One might react with pity, puzzlement, or irritation, but one is unlikely to respond by offering charity. When one agent injures another, however, our attitudes are likely to change. Indeed in many countries discrimination against workers (on the basis of race, religion, and gender) is illegal, as is discrimination against particular groups of borrowers or businesses owned or managed by particular groups of persons. The injured party may take the offender to court and claim substantial damages. There is a remedy in law.

The time may have come to review the situation and consider whether, within a new framework for economic cooperation, some provision can be made to compensate countries for damages inflicted upon them by other countries. The discussion below assumes that compensation would be payable only in cases where rich countries injure the very poorest countries, that is, when Group A countries inflict damage on Group C countries. We illustrate how a system of compensation might work by considering the international migration of low-skilled labor.

The international labor market is segmented. Professional, technical, and highly skilled labor are relatively free to move. In some countries, this gives rise to a brain drain. On the other hand, the mobility of low-skilled labor is severely restricted by immigration controls, not only in the Group A countries but in many other countries as well. This deprives millions of poor people of an opportunity to improve their livelihood.

Both the sending and receiving countries benefit from a free global labor market. The receiving countries are able to augment their human capital, increase the level of output and incomes, and accelerate the rate of growth. The economic boom in Western Europe in the 1960s and the explosive growth in the oil-producing states of the Middle East were made possible by large flows of immigrant labor. Contrary to popular perceptions, immigration stimulates expansion and prosperity rather than depresses it. The main economic disadvantage is that large inflows of low-skilled labor dampen wages at the bottom of the scale. This tends to increase inequality in the national distribution of income, while of course reducing it internationally.

Within the receiving country, the wage rate for low-skilled labor falls. There is a redistribution of income from the low skilled to the rest of the population (highly skilled labor, professional and managerial workers, and property owners). Because in a market economy the remuneration of the low skilled will be less than the average, the initial effect of immigration will be to transfer income from the poor to the rich within the receiving country. That is, unless suitable policy measures are adopted by the government, the distribution of income will become more unequal. This explains why many workers in developed countries are hostile to large-scale immigration. Potentially, however, everyone in the receiving country could be better off and hence policy makers should concentrate not on keeping foreign workers out but on introducing policies which ensure that income is equitably distributed.

The analysis so far, moreover, has considered only the immediate impact effects of migration. The dynamic effects lead to additional gains for both the migrants and the local population. These dynamic effects arise from investments in human and physical capital that are made possible by the original increase in total income. The local population is likely to save and invest part of their additional income (DBE). This will increase the stock of capital and raise the productivity of labor. More important, migrants are known for their entrepreneurial propensities, their thriftiness, and the emphasis they place on education and training.

This analysis assumes all workers are able to find employment. Some challenge this assumption; it is frequently argued that in periods of high unemployment, immigration accentuates the problem of joblessness. In fact, little evidence supports this, because most immigrants enter low-wage occupations that are not attractive to the indigenous population and few become openly unemployed. Moreover, in practice the inflow of immigrant workers is small in relation to the size of the total labor force. Hence, even if migrant workers were to displace some indigenous workers and add to unemployment, the quantitative effect on the aggregate rate of unemployment would be marginal. In any case, the solution to unemployment is not to restrict the international mobility of labor, but to adopt macroeconomic policies that encourage employment, investment, and growth.

The benefits to the sending countries are considerable. Not only do the migrant workers benefit directly from the higher incomes earned abroad, but those left behind also benefit from remittances sent home. If restrictions on the international migration of low-skilled labor were reduced, there is no doubt that remittances would increase sharply, further reducing the relative significance of aid.

Obstacles to the mobility of labor erected in the developed countries harm the developing countries. The extent of the damage depends on two things. First, it depends on the difference between what the migrant would earn in the rest of the world if free to migrate and what the migrant earns in his/her country of origin. Second, the amount of damage depends on the extent to which barriers to immigration actually succeed in reducing the flow of migration.

Conclusion

The present framework for development cooperation has little to recommend it. Perhaps the most that can be said in its favor is that it has outlasted the era of the Cold War. The system is inequitable, arbitrary, inefficient, and ineffective; it ought to be overhauled. In its stead, we have proposed a new system of cooperation based on three principles. First, foreign aid should be used to construct a global safety net funded by a progressive international income tax on the GNP per capita of rich countries. Disbursements to the poorest countries should be automatic, along the lines of a negative international income tax. Second, machinery should be created, in cases of global market failures, for intergovernmental negotiations of transactions that are mutually beneficial. Provision should also be made for monitoring contract compliance and collecting and disbursing funds. Payments to poor countries for services rendered by them for the benefit of rich countries should be separated from foreign aid transfers. Third, when rich countries violate the rules of a global, liberal economic order and inflict harm on poor countries, the rich countries should be liable for damages. That is, compensation should be paid when norms of a competitive international market economy are disregarded and this results both in global inefficiency and a worsening of the global distribution of income.

Notes

1. UNDP, *Human Development Report 1992*. New York: Oxford University Press, 1992; World Bank, *World Development Report 1992*. New York: Oxford University Press, 1992.
2. World Bank, *World Tables 1993*. Baltimore: Johns Hopkins University Press, 1993.
3. Our calculations are based on essentially the same methodology as that used by the World Bank. That is, capital flight is estimated as a residual from the balance of payments statistics, namely as the positive difference between the sources of external finance (foreign direct investment and external borrowing) and the uses of this finance (to cover the current account deficit and finance an increase in reserves). This implies a rather broad measure of capital flight, including both recorded and unrecorded flows, and hence our measure of capital flight overlaps to some extent with our earlier calculations of overall capital flows. In order to maintain consistency we relied as much as possible on statistics from the World Bank, *World Debt Tables 1992-93*. Washington, D.C., 1992, and where necessary we incorporated statistics from the International Monetary Fund, *Balance of Payments Statistics Yearbook 1992*. Washington, D.C., 1992.
4. International Monetary Fund, *Balance of Payments Statistics Yearbook 1992*. Washington, D.C., 1992.
5. World Bank, *World Development Report 1990*. New York: Oxford University Press, 1990, p. 127.
6. The moral case for providing foreign aid is discussed at length in Roger C. Riddell, *Foreign Aid Reconsidered*. Baltimore: Johns Hopkins University Press for the Overseas Development Institute, 1987, Part I, Chapters 1–7.
7. See Keith Griffin and Azizur Rahman Khan, *Globalization and the Developing World*. Geneva: United Nations Research Institute for Social Development, 1992, pp. 33–36.

Section 3

The Need for a Balance Between Economic Efficiency and Justice

Nemir Kırdar

This section addresses the issue of economic efficiency in the context of the emerging global economy, setting the issue against the backdrop of deep and growing poverty in the developing countries and then looking at the opportunities offered by the economic and technological transformations that are sweeping us into a new era and the dawn of the global village. Then, a way forward will be proposed—by sketching a vision of a new interventionist world order that sees as its task the establishment of economic efficiency and social justice. These are the very building blocks of peace, security, and prosperity in a world where for too many there is only war, terror, and poverty. In creating a new approach, especially the one proposed in this section, there are formidable political challenges.

Drawing the Line Between Economic Efficiency and Social Justice

The debate on economic efficiency and social justice is clear. The issue is not either or, but a mixture of the two. It is about getting the balance right. If a political system establishes economic efficiency as its only priority—the creation of wealth above the equal distribution of wealth—then you produce a system of winners and losers. Eventually, the cost of sustaining or excluding the losers becomes too great. Either the system shifts itself back—through the creation of welfare structures—as in many Western democracies in this century, or the balance is forced back either by revolution or a regime of terror.

Similarly, an overconcentration on social justice becomes self-defeating. If too much is taken away in tax, if the burden of social welfare becomes too great, then the effects of the wealth-creating sector become destructive. Social justice depends on a strong and dynamic economy to sustain it.

There is never a perfect balance between economic efficiency and social justice—societies move back and forth between the two within the defined parameters of liberal democracies. The question is always over where you draw the line—how much economic efficiency or how little justice. In the Western world, the democracies function in order to settle the dispute—at least for three or four years, until again a collective decision is taken where the people want to draw the line. In essence, this has been the issue that has driven the historic battles between left and right.

But the battle never ends, because human nature does allow any balance to be maintained. We always want what we do not have. If we concentrate on economic efficiency, we soon begin to desire social justice—the grass is always greener on the other side of the fence. This cyclical alternation between economic efficiency and social justice is the dynamic that drives our societies. The objective of democracies is to find a framework within which an acceptable disequilibrium between economic efficiency and social justice is tolerated?

But we need to look beyond this relatively cozy world and begin to consider the balance between social justice and economic efficiency in the developing world. This debate is only possible from a position of democratic and economic modernization. The question is how to achieve a process of modernization?

The Three Worlds

In examining the world at large, we can divide the countries into three broad categories:

- The industrialized nations that enjoy higher standards of living and democracy and which are in a race against time to achieve still greater technological advancements.

- Nations that have not reached the standards of the first category, but are on the right track—aiming to achieve similar objectives. They are in the process of democratization, moving toward prosperity through free enterprise and the market economy. Although some countries in this category may well be advanced, others are still lagging behind. However, they are, at least, progressing in the right direction.

- Nations that are not on the right track or that are following too slow a pace to achieve any meaningful progress and where, therefore, talk of where to draw the line between economic efficiency and social justice is meaningless.

One normally can find fundamental reasons that have restrained the progress of some of the nations in the third category:

- Some of these countries are experiencing a population explosion that exceeds any feasible economic progress.

- Other nations suffer from bad government, dictatorial rule, totalitarianism, and corruption. They are ruled by fear and terror.

- Some are subject to natural disasters and/or a lack of resources. Indeed, some do not have any of the prerequisites to be an independent country with a viable self-sustaining economy.

There are other countries, still, that have not been able to liberate themselves from ancient prejudices and destructive practices. They would go to any extreme to fight an ideological war to conquer and destroy. For example, religious and ethnic fundamentalism is gathering strength in different parts of the world as a result of such dogma. Such countries presently find it impossible to achieve any kind of balance between economic efficiency and social justice. For some, neither are remotely possible. Others lurch from one extreme to another.

This section is addressed to those privileged nations in the first category that have a responsibility to themselves to see that the world in which we live is in relative peace and that no major outbreaks will endanger their own well-being. Indeed, it is for the ultimate security and stability of their own privileged nations that they need to be concerned with the rest of the world.

The industrialized countries should not meet among themselves to discuss only their own employment and economic growth rate. They need to be concerned with the vast and alarming unemployment and poverty throughout the rest of the globe.

It is estimated that 1 billion people will be out of a job in the year 2025. Can the world afford to wait for this to happen? The problems are lack of equity; lack of opportunity for hundreds of millions of individuals to achieve a minimum standard of acceptable living conditions; and lack of human rights. All these will lead to severe unrest and disorder. Take Africa as an example. Excluding South Africa, the 1991 GNP of all countries south of the Sahara, with a total population of 600 million, was the GNP as that of Belgium, which has a population of only 10 million. Of the world's 20 poorest countries, 18 are African. They are getting poorer still. Per capita GNP declined by 2 percent a year through the 1980s. Africa's share of world trade has fallen below 4 percent and is now closer to 2 percent.

In the Middle East, countries spend $60 billion a year on armaments, while 17 out of 22 Arab states, for example, have a declining GNP. In the next 20 years, at current growth rates, the population of many Arab countries will double.

Over the next 50 years, the earth's population of 5.5 billion is expected to increase to 9 billion. The worst part is that 95 percent of this population increase will be in the poorest regions of the world, where governments are not effective and the social structure is in disorder.

Meanwhile, the environment is at risk through ozone depletion, deforestation, and global warming. Never have there been so many challenges.

The New Opportunities

Yet, never have there been so many opportunities in a world of technology where digitalization and the fiber optic revolution open the world to everyone. We cannot, and should not, try to build the future in the image of it.

Two revolutions are sweeping our world—the consequences of which we are only just beginning to appreciate. More change will be packed into the next 20 years than the last 200. The global village becomes ever closer. Distance is increasingly no barrier. The world is shrinking as fast as we can lay fiber optic cable between all of us around the globe. Our lives are becoming increasingly interlocked. There are no local problems, because the ripples soon fan out and affect the rest of us. It is no longer a case of "them" and "us"—only us.

The new interdependency that characterizes this new global economy is evident first in the global capital markets where deregulation—itself the product of vast technological changes—has brought, round the clock, financial world markets in which the daily flows of foreign exchange are already almost twice the monthly flow of actual trade.

Second, this new interdependence can be seen in the global sourcing of companies; not just commodities and raw materials, but production itself. The information technology revolution has created the age of transcontinental rather than simply the multinational company, where a car can be designed in Japan, made in Germany, the United States, and France, and assembled absolutely anywhere.

The consequences of this new interdependence are staggering. First, it eliminates any lingering idea that economic policy can remain a matter solely for national governments acting according to outdated principles of national sovereignty. True national sovereignty must now be sought within the new realities.

Second, globalization and the ability to shift resources from one continent to another increasingly means that it is the skills of a nation's workforce that are the determinant of its economic success. In a global economy where techniques and capital are more mobile than ever, and markets are truly international, ultimate success depends on the skills and talents of people. If those skills and talents are not allowed to develop to the full, then economic development will prove elusive.

The effects are already being felt. The nature of the developing world has changed enormously. The South is no longer homogeneous. Some nations have enjoyed rapid growth. By 2010, the Pacific Rim economies could be bigger than those of Europe or America—a level of unprecedented economic development built on global economic interdependence. Meanwhile, other nations have floundered because of overpopulation, ethnic wars, or totalitarianism.

How are we responding to this interdependent global economy?

Instead of taking on responsibility for the world economy at large, we are witnessing a clear tendency for the world's major industrialized nations to coalesce into distinct trading and financial blocks—blocks we are retreating into rather than building from.

As our capacity to act has grown, because of this emerging interdependence, our willingness to act has diminished. Each country is preoccupied with what is happening in its own backyard. Some nations are even beginning to blame the developing world—it is their problem and probably their fault, the argument goes.

If the planet is only habitable for the few, it will end up uninhabitable altogether. To concern ourselves with the rest of the world is in our self-interest. If we allow the continued creation of a global underclass by excluding whole areas of the globe from growth, then we simply invite on ourselves the plague and terror of AIDS, drug trafficking, and environmental disaster, let alone the exclusion of half of our potential markets or labor force.

As economies become more interdependent, we require institutions that measure up to the emerging realities of the global economy. People are coming to understand the need for systematic and continuous rather than ad-hoc international cooperation. The real challenge is to make sure that our mechanisms for international cooperation measure up to international reality.

The global economy and the information technology revolution mean that there is no excuse to be backward as long as the developed world gives every opportunity to the developing world to fulfill its potential. These revolutions offer the developing world a choice—an opportunity to catch up with the rest of the world.

What Should Be Done?

It is a world out of control, but a world ripe for possibilities for universal progress. The gap between what is and what could be has never been closer—it is up to all of us to ensure the gap is bridged.

For the past 40 years, the world has been polarized between the West, which alternated between different levels of economic efficiency and social justice, and the East. This polarization denied such a debate. The consequence was that if one of the two parties wanted to do something useful for all humanities, the other would try and undo it. Now, for the first time in 40 years, we have an opportunity to act rationally in order to ensure a better and more secure world for our children.

Some advocate that it should be the responsibility of a world body, perhaps the United Nations and the World Bank combined, to deal with the huge obstacles that curtail the ability of a nation to transform itself into a healthy, modern, and prosperous statehood. However, this world body needs to be reorganized and restructured in order to fulfill the expanded role that we are advocated.

The "New World Order" will require a renewed international body that has the will and capability to take decisive and effective action. The UN should be redefined to ensure equity, prosperity, and human rights in every corner of the globe.

The people of each developing nation should be given the right to decide. They can opt for the process or economic and political modernization or they can decide against it. They must, however, accept the consequences of either decision. If they want meaningful help, then they must play by the rules. The third tier countries should be expected to follow a strict regime.

The new UN should have the capacity to monitor and control progress in the developing world. It should also have the authority to step in and engage directly in the removal of whatever obstacle is holding back a certain country. During the Gulf War, the UN proved it could, with determined leadership, solve real problems. Bosnia, sadly, shows this is not always the case. The lesson is that the role of the UN should not depend on transitory factors, such as the strength of political leadership, but on the ongoing moral and institutional framework.

Today, the developing countries are estimated to be spending 200 pounds sterling on arms procurement and military expenditure. this should go instead to skill and human resource development. That means the North should stop all arms sales to the South. There should also be an end to environmental destruction and exploitation of labor. The North must provide moral leadership. The North must assume its responsibilities.

A New Global Contract

President François Mitterrand has recently proposed a "Development Contract" between North and South. According to him, what we need is a unified view on development just as we have a single global view on the environment, which emerged at the Rio Earth Summit.

If aid is to be meaningful, then it has to work both ways. It is a question of rights and responsibilities, and a recognition of mutual self-interest. The North has a responsibility to assist the development of the South. In return, it should expect the adoption of an acceptable economic and social contract that is based on a new set of equitable, ethical, and moral international values. Mitterrand has said "Development aid must become more than a means to help poor countries respect their financial obligations. It must be a means to help bolster respect for social and moral contracts within societies and within the world community."

If there is no development, then there will be no lasting domestic peace in those countries torn by strife. In the midst of poverty, war, terror, and overpopulation, it is impossible to establish basic human rights and efficient economic capacity. The South needs to be convinced that it is impossible to have economic prosperity without democratic efficiency.

On all this, the North must provide material and moral guidance. That means not just financial assistance, but leadership by example. If we condemn the existence of an underclass in the developing countries, then we must eliminate the underclass in our society. We must show that economic efficiency and social justice only work when they operate together.

Conclusion

In the emerging global economy, there is a relentless drive for greater efficiency. No one is owed a living. There are winners and there are losers. What we offer is not an end of all the problems, but the creation of more level playing field within which more of the world's population can prosper. People need to solve their own problems, to learn by their mistakes, but they needs the material and moral means to start on the road to economic and political modernization and to begin to make their own decisions about the mix of economic efficiency and social justice.

However, the international community must help the developing world achieve these goals for themselves. It is up to the countries with the means to provide the opportunity. It is up to the countries in need to seize it. And it is up to the new world body to see that both interact most effectively.

Section 4

Political Mobilization, Civic Spirit

Mats Karlsson

Political mobilization is the link—too often the missing link—between prescribing and achieving change. In the past, we have seen significant conceptual progress. The Palme Commission introduced "common security," the Brundtland Commission "unsustainable development." With "human development," the UNDP is helping again to put people first. "Governance" came to be used more and more in an attempt to at last deal with political issues.

We have also seen progress in defining agendas and plans of action. Agenda 21 of the Earth Summit is the paramount one. We now have the Secretary-General's Agenda for Peace and Development. New, relevant ones are prepared for upcoming United Nation's summits and conferences, and by independent groups, such as the Commission on Global Governance.

No doubt these endeavors to conceptualize and influence mark progress in understanding, probably in broad-based commitment, too. Real progress is, of course, only measured by real change. And everybody's frustration is how to actually achieve it. Why, then, do so many of these programs and action plans end with the only too obvious remark that realization depends on "political will"—thus stopping short of dealing with that missing link, political mobilization?

Political Mobilization

Try to analyze "political will," "political capacity" is probably the most useful inroad. So, trying to understand nations' capacities, one will look for:

- Institutions; wide range of institutional capacity, government, political set-up, civil society.
- Interests: conflicting and common.

- Individuals: their commitment, their propensity to take common responsibility.

These analyses will reveal the constraints for each country, reflecting its history, or rather histories, as the case most often is. With globalization occurring, unevenly but incredibly rapidly, countries are being put under increased pressures, more often than not exacerbating constraints. This is happening while people in most countries also experience increased unemployment, insecurity, and alienation. This limits political possibilities even more.

So, politicians are forced on to the edge of a knife. They have to move between the danger of international involvement in a way that does not command domestic support and in turn is not sustainable on the one hand, and the danger of focusing on domestic issues in a way that does not correspond to the challenges of the deepening interdependencies, which is also not sustainable, on the other.

To take an example from Sweden, a country with at least some evidence of broader popular consciousness of international issues. Here, political leaders, sharing the conviction of the benefits of membership in the European Union, face strong resistance in popular opinion. Many of those who argue against Swedish membership in the EU think of themselves as convinced internationalists.

What should be called "common sovereignty" again and again proves to be difficult to accept. Sweden and the EU is about an evolving regional cooperation, but countries are now facing unavoidable global issues. Sovereignty will increasingly have to be pooled on a global level, if there is going to be any sovereignty left for anybody. The emerging global society has only begun to acquire its political instruments. So, if we want to analyze global society, we must look at global political capacity.

"Political capacity" is actually a too-limited concept as well. For the purposes of getting at that elusive "political will," it tends to focus too much on constraints. What we want, of course, is to expand, to build that capacity, to get at the political driving forces of change.

It is by now clear, five years and more into the post-Cold War period, that global political capacity is not being built in any way commensurate with the challenges of increased interdependence.

This is not happening among governments. Leave the UN aside for a moment and look at the G-7, the closest we come to a group of world leaders actually meeting and claiming to have a decision making mandate on both economically and politically acute issues. It is pitiful to see the flurry of media coverage as this periodical July summit constantly bears mice. Even without issues like legitimacy and representation, it is obvious that the G-7 mechanism, with any institutional base, is wholly unsuitable to the task of leadership today.

And take the EU, which actually is an example of real progress in international regional governance in the past years, and the recent debacle in choosing its new president. We may well see this lack of responsible political leadership ignite a destructive rivalry of nations and institutions, when instead we could have had the positive competition and balances among nations and institutions that the EU governance form actually makes possible.

Civic Spirit

Today's crisis is a crisis of leadership as much as anything else. We cannot expect the revival of multilateralism, the expansion of regional or global political capacity to come from above. We must look below, but is it coming?

The great expansion in numbers, membership, and activity of NGOs in recent years — their greater involvement in international affairs, the greater acceptance of them in governmental and intergovernmental frameworks — does have revolutionary potential. Of that we can be certain. But can it be realized; can it turn into that missing link of global political mobilization?

First, we must distinguish between NGOs and NGOs. They come in all kinds. Some are limited, one-issue, marginal groups, with less than adequate accountability — adequate from the aspect of being that missing link.

It is time to get rid of the term "nongovernmental organizations." What we need is another term that evokes the idea of independent, democratic organizations committed to assuming responsibility, working to expand the political capabilities of nations and peoples. They are the responsible actors of civil society, working to expand the capabilities of governments as well. We need a better term than simply "nongovernmental." The term "civic organizations" is better suited.

Among the many kinds of civic organizations are political parties. Many listings of NGOs fail to mention political parties. Yet parties certainly do belong. Some do from time to time take on governmental powers, but precisely this makes them such an important part of civic life. We need good government.

Political parties are crucial to democratic culture. Yet, for many committed persons, in other civic organizations — young people, people in careers — it is a very big step to get involved in a political party. This is a subject deserving of its own complicated analysis. But if we want living democratic cultures, we must recognize that we also need living parties. This is a truly global issue, affecting the South, the new democracies of Central and Eastern Europe, and the West. Suffice it to mention one extreme European example, the political crisis in Italy, its critical implications augmented by the media dimensions of the Berlusconi phenomenon.

We must take care that responsible political mobilization in nations again finds a footing, a resonance, a legitimacy. And it also needs to reach out beyond borders. With a global society emerging, we need to see political movements stretch across borders. This even though all political movements are far behind in shaping the language and the organizations that can create that global civil mobilizations.

When the civic movement in Sweden worked to achieve democracy, it took almost 25 years from the formation of the Social Democratic

Party until there was universal suffrage. The labor movement, which was the strongest force in a movement comprising liberals, some churches, temperance movements, independent intellectuals, and others, took up a slogan that had great impact—"Do your duty! Demand your right!" Civic responsibility and civic rights went together. And it carried political weight. The synthesis concept was "civic spirit."

That is what we need now—a global civic spirit.

When the many agendas for the future are written, there should be a word or two on global mobilization.

Conclusion

Both at national and global levels, there will be neither political change in harmony nor change without conflict. The key, of course, is to make that conflict a civilized one.

To turn a phrase of former French President, Giscard d'Estaing, "France has to be governed from the center." This implied universal relevance. But we need to make sure that the political struggle is a struggle about the center, in nations and in the wider world.

Ideas and interests will differ. Political struggle is legitimate. We must not pretend that there is or will be conflict-free change or that there is an easy consensus emerging without alternatives. We must just not give room to extremes.

As we move toward a global neighborhood, we will surely need the civic formats to make the political struggles at home and with others civilized ones.

Chapter 4

The Role of the United Nations

Section 1

What Role for the United Nations in World Economic and Social Development?

Benjamin Bassin

This section examines the possible functions of the United Nations' system —
in particular, the central economic and social decision making organs — in
the environment supposed to prevail in the twenty-first century. It focuses
entirely on the institutional aspects of the problem, leaving aside the
administrative, managerial, and structural aspects which are often central
to similar essays. This is done partly in the interest of readability, but mainly
because the position of the UN in the universe of international decision
making seems an issue of more primary importance than the questions of
funding, staffing, and command structure. Important, even vital, as these
questions are, they will be meaningless if we do not know whether we are
designing the future government of the planet or only a loose assemblage
of intergovernment talkshops. Furthermore, a clear sense of purpose is
essential for the kind of institutional self-respect that is a condition *sine
qua non* for any large-scale reform of structures and policies. Only if the
UN system knows what is expected of it, what its purpose is, can reforms
be successful.

Concert of Nations or Rule of Law?

The history of multilateral diplomacy in modern times can be divided into
three phases. The first began with the Congress of Vienna in 1814 out
of which the Concert of Nations arose. The second began with President
Wilson and the Paris Peace Conference of 1919. The third phase is, of
course, the present one, inaugurated with the Atlantic Charter of 1941 and
the San Francisco Conference of 1945.

The Concert of Nations represents clearly what one could call the
"aristocratic" principle of international relations. It is based on a balance
of power and interests among the Great Powers, those possessing the means

to force their will on any opponent if need be. It is "realpolitik" in its most essential form, assuming a Hobbesian view of the world *(bellum omnium contra omnes)* where only strength counts. The weak either submit or succumb.

The Wilsonian concept was a revolt against this attitude. It envisaged an international community of nations under rule of law, instead of the alliance of victors against the vanquished foreseen by the British and the French at the end of World War I. Wilson assumed the existence of a community of free nations, whose peoples would use public opinion to pressure their leaders. These leaders, in turn, would conclude "open agreements, openly arrived at," instead of the secret diplomacy of alliances and counteralliances of the nineteenth century. Subsequent events proved that many Wilsonian principles were suspended in a void and therefore not practicable, but they were nevertheless a turning point in thinking about international relations and an inspiration to millions. If the balance-of-power structure of the Concert of Nations could be said to represent the "aristocratic" rule, the Wilsonian concept incorporated definite "democratic" elements. In the latter form, multilateralism forms an alternative to bilateral arrangements, which enhance the leverage of the powerful over the weak. Multilateralism in its Wilsonian form implies that small and weak states have a voice in international affairs, without the patronage of a Great Power.

The United Nations thus has two sets of antecedents. The drafters of the Charter seem to have chosen some elements of each. The centerpiece of the mechanism created in San Francisco, the Security Council, is a descendant of the Concert of Nations, a "directoire" of the mighty, each of whom was given the right of veto as a symbol of their Great Power status. The General Assembly is a Wilsonian structure, a "planetary town meeting" conducting diplomacy and open to pressures of world opinion. But the General Assembly cannot make decisions binding on the member states; its only power is the power of persuasion. Thus, the Charter can be said to lean towards "realpolitik," while maintaining the forms and mechanisms of "democracy" and the rule of law.

The Charter is, however, a product of a long tradition of Western political philosophy that goes back to Kantian humanism, the French Enlightenment, and seventeenth-century empiricism. It is the heir of the same ancestors as modern liberal democracy. Against that background, the "aristocratic" features of the Charter could be seen as an exception to the rule, as an inevitable but temporary concession to present-day reality. The spirit of the Charter is Wilsonian, resting of a community of nations under the rule of law, rather than on balance of power among the strong. With this in mind, one could perhaps formulate a strategic principle for the organizational development of the UN system. While it has to continue to accommodate the interests of the Great Powers, its long-term development objectives should conform to the liberal, humanist ideals of the Charter.

The nations of the world cannot form a community, as they cannot manifest the "volonté générale" that, according to Rousseau, constitutes the nation as a political entity. That might invalidate the Wilsonian idea of an international community under the rule of law, were it not for the testimony of the last two centuries that the "volonté générale" has been a much needed prop of totalitarian societies, whereas in truly democratic states, it has remained a purely mythical concept.

Does Multilateralism Have a Future?

Descending from the lofty heights of abstract ideas into the daily grind of international relations, one is faced with some awkward questions about the "democratic" manner of dealing with international issues. Why would the Great Powers, having other means at their disposal, consent to deliberate their often vital interests with smaller states, not to mention the other actors on the international scene? All through its existence, multilateralism in general and the UN in particular have been criticized and underrated on this account. The realist critique has argued that multilateralism will fail because Great Powers wish to pursue their national interests in bilateral bargaining, immune from the scrutiny of others. The leveling impulse of multilateralism simply does not fit the hierarchical power configuration of the international system. The neoliberal critique addresses itself to the universalist tendency of multilateralism, pointing out the difficulty of cooperating in groups of large membership. This argument is of particular relevance to the UN system, with a membership of 184 states, each having one vote in the General Assembly.

One convincing answer lies not in idealism or exalted principles, but in sound self-interest. The logic of interdependence is creating situations where the industrialized countries can no longer allow the developing countries a "free ride" by excluding them from their limited clubs and gatherings.

Miles Kahler has analyzed three sets of recent multilateral negotiations: the UNCLOS III, the Uruguay Round (before its final conclusion), and the negotiations on the ozone layer (the Vienna Convention and the Montreal Protocol). He concludes that "bargains limited to great powers were less valuable because of the large number of free riders. To obtain the cooperation of less powerful states, it was necessary to negotiate not only the substance of a new bargain but also new modes of governance, incorporating large numbers of participants and their interests."[1]

Smaller industrialized countries and a growing number of developing countries have come to see multilateral institutions, however imperfect, as preferable to a world of resurgent bilateralism. Kahler points out that in issue areas such as international monetary affairs and macroeconomic policy coordination, "minilateralism" is likely to continue because the collaboration of lesser economic powers is neither necessary nor desirable. It is perhaps not unreasonable to assume that, over time, the logic of interdependence would force a change in this respect.

To illustrate Kahler's thesis, one could mention two instances where the "free rider" problem plays a central role. One is the trade-and-environment complex that will certainly be one of the primary problems in international economic negotiations in this decade and beyond. The other is the question of labor standards and their impact on international competitiveness, also bound to be felt more acutely in a more interdependent world. In addition, one could note that if the still rather vague suggestions of various forms of international taxation for internationalist purposes (such as the "Tobin tax" on currency transactions) become subject of serious negotiation, they are likely to stand or fall on the issue of "free riders."

In assessing the future of multilateralism, we must not allow ourselves to be too much inhibited by past experience which, as far as the UN is concerned, falls almost entirely in the period of the Cold War.

The end of the Cold War has removed many obstacles that for more than four decades prevented multilateral fora, not least the UN, from addressing economic and social problems seriously or from perceiving them correctly. On the contrary, there was a real incentive to reduce economic and social issues to the status of weapons in the ideological war. Now the UN can embark on economic and social debates without the risk of turning them into "beauty contests" between ideologies. This ought to give new impetus to member states to use the UN for such debates. The World Summit for Social Development can be seen as an indication of this.

Harlan Cleveland has compiled a list of the common factors that according to him have accounted for successful multilateral cooperation.[2] One may differ with his views on some points, but his conclusions are certainly worth noting:

- There is a consensus on desirable outcomes.
- No one loses ("win–win" situation).
- Sovereignty is pooled (that is, nations use their sovereign rights together to avoid losing them separately).
- Cooperation is stimulated by a mixture of fears and hopes.
- Nongovernmental actors play a key role.
- Cooperation is carried out in flexible, decentralized systems, aided by modern information technology.
- In the case of developing countries, preference is given to educated, local talent.

This list provides valuable clues for the survival and strengthening of multilateralism in the economic and social spheres. On the whole, well-defined economic and technological issues of the kind debated in, for instance, ICAO, IMO, UPU, ITU, or WIPU, seem to fall more easily into Cleveland's categories than do macroeconomic or humanitarian issues.

A New International Agenda and People

The UN has from its inception been, and still predominantly is, an organization for collective security. The initial justification for including economic and social affairs into its mandate was precisely their linkage with security, as Roosevelt and Churchill suggested in the Atlantic Charter.

The definition of security is changing as a result of the changed world situation. Major powers are programming into their strategic planning more economic, social, humanitarian, and cultural aspects. Not only well-intentioned idealists, but presumably hard-headed strategic planners have noted the "new international agenda" of socioeconomic problems that no country can solve on its own. Readers of the "Annual Report to the President and Congress, January 1994" of the U.S. Department of Defense, of the French "Livre Blanc sur la Défence 1994," of the German "Weissbuch 1994" or the British "Defence White Paper" of 1992 will find these new concerns discussed at some length. The term "human security," denoting a widening of the concept of security beyond the traditional strategic–military security of the state and into the area of the security of the individual human being, is gaining currency. It is important to note that this "human security" is, in the final analysis, nothing but the "new international agenda" seen from the point of view of the individual. For once, the concerns of the strategic planners in ministries of defense coincide with those of the people on the street.

No international institution, except for the UN, has the breadth and universality of mandate to consider the entire spectrum of security in its new definition. Other institutions either lack the security policy element (Bretton Woods institutions or the World Trade Organization) or the global geographic extent (NATO, EU, and CSCE). There is no real alternative to the UN if interlinkages between peace and development are to be examined jointly from a global perspective, as the logic of interdependence would dictate. How exactly such an examination would be arranged in the UN goes beyond the scope of this essay. Suffice it to say that the present work on the structure and working methods of the Security Council has a bearing on the issue. The UNCED in Rio in 1992 and the World Summit on Social Development in Copenhagen in 1995 provide much of the substance for the debate on "human security."

The United Nations: A Regime among Regimes

Those who work in and around the UN system seem to suffer from an understandable but singularly persistent myopia that prevents them from seeing the world much beyond their organization or, at best, the UN system. They tend to overlook the fact that the UN is but a part—and probably not the most important part—of what might be loosely called "international governance." Roberts and Kingsbury point out that the "roles of the UN must not be seen in isolation from other aspects of international relations. Part of the genius of the Charter order is precisely the integration of the UN into the wider structure of the international system."[3]

Perhaps this simply but profound truth would be simpler to remember if the structure of the Charter would not be so reminiscent of a world government, with the Security Council and Secretary General as the executive arm, the General Assembly as the legislature, and the International Court of Justice as the judiciary. Even if one includes the "immediate family" of the Bretton Woods institutions and the soon-to-be-born WTO, one fails to see the UN in the context of the new international system for deliberation and negotiation that is slowly taking shape to respond to the needs of the twenty-first century. That system will in all likelihood be built on organizations already in existence, as it is perhaps easier to get acceptance for modification of existing institutions than for setting up new ones. Thus the G-7 (or, as it seems, G-8), the OECD, various regional organizations like the EU and NAFTA, are searching for new roles and new mandates and, in some case, for new legitimacy as well. In addition, there are innumerable international (but not necessarily intergovernmental) political, economic, legal, technical, and other regimes, with or without an organization attached to them. It is in this setting that the UN must find its place or face decline.

Here, an international regime means any governing arrangement by states or other international actors to coordinate their expectations or organize aspects of international behavior in various issue areas. A regime comprises a normative element (principles, norms, and rules), a state practice (decision-making procedures), and organizational roles. Evidently, regimes are not a thing of the future but the dominant feature in today's international relations, dealing with an enormous range of subjects. From the point of view of our subject, it is interesting to note that regimes providing for monitoring compliance or enforcing rules are usually ones to have an organizational component.

International governance in the twenty-first century would consist of regimes, mostly with less than universal membership. A number of them would be UN inspired or otherwise related. Many of them would exist as a set of standards, norms, or rules, without any organization. Keohane and Nye, echoing the neoliberal critique of multilateralism, summarize the outlook as follows: "A crazy quilt of international regimes is likely to arise, each with somewhat different membership. Better some roughness around the edges, however, than a vacuum at the center. Poorly coordinated coalitions, working effectively on various issues, are in general preferable to universalist negotiations, permanently deadlocked by a diverse membership."[4]

The picture evoked by this forecast is a far cry from the well-ordered design of the UN Charter. At first sight, it seems a negation of the Charter view of international relations—incoherent, potentially contradictory, and lacking an overall vision. It seems to be a house of cards compared to the Greek temple of the Charter which, after all, stands on the philosophic tradition of Locke and Montesquieu. A closer look indicates that this need not be the case. Kratochwil and Ruggie assure us that "the robustness of international regimes has little to do with how coherent they remain—how coherent is the U.S. Constitution?—but depends on the extent to which evolving and even diverging practices of actors express principled reasoning and shared understandings."[5]

As we shall see, it is precisely "principled reasoning and shared understandings" that ought to be the most important product of UN intergovernmental bodies. Furthermore, the point of reference should not be the intentions of the drafters of the Charter in 1945, but the realities of today. From that point of view, the difference between the "crazy quilt" of regimes and the actual structure of the UN system is not very significant.

An unkind observer has compared the growth and structure of the UN system to a coral reef that could also serve as a metaphor of the international nonsystem of regimes.

Economic and Social Functions of the UN

We have established that:

- Although the UN is an inheritor of the Concert of Nations, its basic calling is "democratic" and it ought to aspire toward the concept of an international community under the rule of law.

- The concept of multilateralism in international economic and social relations is ever more relevant as interdependence increases and underlines the security aspects of economic and social issues.

- The UN must be viewed in the context of the new forms of international governance being generated after the end of the Cold War.

Now, we must approach the question of the functions of the UN in international economic and social deliberation and decision making.

Clearly, the function cannot be a legislative one, in the narrow sense of the word. Reliance on the declaratory impact of resolutions passed by large majorities in ECOSOC or the General Assembly (New International Economic Order, Charter of Economic Rights and Duties of States, and so on) turned out to be an illusion in the late 1970s and early 1980s. The hortatory effects of resolutions by central UN economic and social policy-making organs have been minimal because, as Wilensky has pointed out: "They have been hammered out in debate by serious and dedicated middle-rank officials of foreign ministries in ECOSOC and the Second Committee of the General Assembly—officials with absolutely no influence on economic policies of their countries. Insofar as the texts have been scrutinized in the capitals it is to ensure that they included nothing new that might be contrary to existing policy. They have not been read by the economic ministers of either developing or industrialized countries who have more practical matters with which to concern themselves."[6]

Can the UN, under these circumstances (which Wilensky attributes to the muddled thinking on the part of the drafters of the Charter) play a useful role? The answer seems to be "yes, in the larger context of international governance."

The first and foremost role of the UN would be to provide a forum for debates and decisions lending (or denying, as the case may be) legitimacy of ideas, doctrines, and decisions produced in various international fora on economic and social issues. This is the realm where, according to Conor Cruise O'Brien, politics, drama, and religion meet.[7] The ODA target, the concept of "common heritage of mankind," the rejection of colonialism are examples of such doctrines and ideas. There are numerous examples of the same in the sphere of political affairs, particularly in disarmament. It has been suggested that conclusions reached in a limited forum, patterned after the Cancún Conference of 1981 (G-5 and a selected number of developing countries) could be submitted to the General Assembly. Another variant of the same theme could be a G-7 "post-Conference dialogue" (practiced for many years by ASEAN summits), the results of which would be submitted to scrutiny in the UN. This would combine the "aristocratic" and "democratic" principles and give policies a much stronger legitimacy than could ever be reached through either the G-7 or the UN alone. It would come a step closer to the objective of enabling "the smallest and least considerable [of the UN's] members to feel themselves part of the world community."[8] Against this background of the ongoing search of international legitimacy by the G-7 and what has been said above about interdependence and the "free rider" problem, such a role for the UN could be attainable.

Closely linked to the first function is the UN's potential in shaping the international agenda, facilitating and conditioning the articulation of new policy demands.[9] Keohane and Nye, writing from the U.S. point of view, have expressed this as follows: "In today's world, universal international organizations are more valuable as sounding boards than as decision-making bodies. If the United States listens carefully, but not naively, these organizations may tell something about the intensity of, and shifts in, others' views. These forums do not influence the agenda of world politics. They may legitimate important decisions made elsewhere.... But only rarely are the universal international organizations likely to provide the world with instruments for collective action."[10] The role of the UN in bringing the environmental issue to the forefront of international consciousness is a case in point. It remains to be seen whether the UN can repeat this feat, in respect to the issues of social development.

The UN and its agencies have an important role, each in their respective areas of specialization, as proclaimers of international rules, norms, and standards. The creation, approval, promulgation, monitoring, and enforcement of international rules, norms, and standards from the most exalted principles of sovereign equality and human rights to the mundane regulations on issuance of postage stamps or standardizing geographic place names, is a central function of the UN as a regime among many other regimes. In fact, the Nordic UN Project pointed out the weakening of the normative role of the specialized agencies at the expense of the intellectually less taxing but politically and morally more rewarding operational activities.[11]

The functions of the UN as a channel for economic and technical assistance to developing countries and, in the apt phrase of Brian Urquhat, as the "world's police force and humanitarian rescue service," in other words, all that is subsumed under the apellation "operational activities" are being recast after the end of the Cold War. It is likely that these functions remain important for the UN system, but in the economic and social sphere may perhaps not attain the degree of importance they had in the 1970s and 1980s.

If one looks beyond the present functions of the UN into the Utopian future, one should not overlook the UN's potential to exercise intellectual influence, "a leadership through ideas, vision, and initiative."[12] For this to be possible, some fundamental changes must take place in the secretariats of the UN system, in the relations of the UN system with other centers of influence in the world. The structure, organization, and management (not least personnel management) of the secretariats would have to be completely reformed – for there is no shortage of thoughtful and far-sighted prescriptions for this – and, above all, the secretariats would have to gain a sense of purpose so many of them seem to have lost. The rising standards of management and professional quality would be preconditions for an increased intellectual freedom, a degree of political independence, without which a leadership role would be inconceivable.

Recently, much has been written about an "economic and social security council," which would be set up within the UN system. The proponents of this idea have not been very clear on the exact workings of the council. In light of the functions enumerated above, it tends to increase rather than dispel the confusion. Economic and social problems seldom lend themselves to a treatment analogous to that given to political problems in the Security Council. Using Article 65 of the Charter, for instance, to bring economic issues to the Security Council would be likely to result in politicizing them and bring about a series of deadlocks. It is not conceivable to bring macroeconomic policies of a single member country to a vote in an intergovernmental body. Nor could labor policies in developing countries or issues of social disintegration be simplified to the extent of being resolved by vote. Were it possible to find subjects amenable to treatment in such a council, its decisions could not bind member states without a deep-going revision of the Charter, which for the time being seems almost unimaginable. Without such binding force, the new "economic security council" would be just another version of ECOSOC, the inefficiency of which has been a concern for the UN since the early 1950s. The new council might have a chance were it established outside the UN, reinforced by major developing countries, allowing their conclusions to be debated in the UN, presumably in the General Assembly.

The Role of Nonstate Actors

In one respect, the world seems to have taken a long step toward the Wilsonian ideals. President Wilson personally seems to have had an almost mystic faith in "the people" as a counterweight to sovereign governments. Although the Charter of the UN starts with "We the Peoples of the United Nations determined," it seems that the founders had not much time for "the people." O'Brien has pointed out the irony of the famous opening lines: " 'We' were not the people, but Roosevelt (later Truman), Churchill and Stalin; the nations were not really united – as General de Gaulle was later to emphasize – and the peoples, so far from being 'determined,' were not even consulted."[13]

However, at present, all this seems to be changing. The sovereign state's role in the economic and social sphere is diminishing in relation to the role of impersonal, nonterritorial forces such as the international capital markets and international business more generally as well as what is broadly known as the "civil society." NGOs have also achieved a new status in intergovernmental bodies, as evidenced by developments before and during UNCED. The use of the "civil society" and more particularly the NGOs as "watchdogs" in monitoring compliance of governments with commitments undertaken in UN fora seems to many a foregone conclusion regardless of the somewhat unclear legal basis for such an arrangement. The "public diplomacy" of which President Wilson spoke is coming true in ways he hardly imagined. This goes hand in hand with the fact that the dichotomy of "foreign" and "domestic" is rapidly losing its traditional importance. The UN, an organization of sovereign nation-states, cannot remain unaffected by the fragmentation of economic and social decision making power.

The UN thus needs to incorporate into its institutional design some expedient for meaningful communication with the bearers of these new decision making structures, the international business community and the "civil society." The present procedures where NGOs are allowed in "on sufferance" or for mainly ceremonial reasons are inadequate. With the business community, the UN has even more tenuous links. The problem of selectivity looms large. To illustrate the depth of reforms needed (although not to endorse the suggestions as such), we might recall the proposal of Marc Nerfin a decade ago of setting up three parallel Assemblies, one for states ("The Prince Chamber"), one for economic power ("The Merchant Chamber"), and one for civil society ("The Citizen Chamber").[14] As an intermediate step, as a bridge from the exclusive domination of the UN processes by governments to the full involvement of the "new actors" on the international scene, one could envisage the kind of Parliamentary Assembly suggested by a recent report of the Rajiv Gandhi Foundation.[15]

Subsidiarity and the UN System

Apart from Chapter VIII, dealing with regional security arrangements, the UN Charter does not deal with the question of regional organizations or of taking decisions at a lower than global level. The regional economic commissions are not Charter bodies. The agendas of ECOSOC and the Second and Third Committees of the General Assembly are full of items which by any logic could and should have been debated or resolved at the regional or subregional level before being brought to a global forum. In operational activities, some progress has been made in delegating decisions closer to "the field," but this is not reflected in other activities of the UN. For a variety of reasons, the regional economic commissions have not established themselves as a "second tier" of the UN economic and social structure. In some instances, they have assumed rather specialized roles; in others, their activities seem rather marginal to the overall economic and social development of their respective regions.

Another aspect that highlights the need for subsidiarity in developmental issues in the increasing differentiation of member states reflected in the emergence of regional economic groupings. NAFTA, ASEAN, APEC, SADC, SARECC, MERCOSUR, and so forth—not to speak about the European Union which is *sui generis*—are potential "dialogue partners" of the UN and its regional bodies. If the UN system is unable to tap their creative energies or to make a contribution to their deliberations, through its own regional or subregional machinery, it might imply another step toward the marginalization of the UN.

Ideally, the reform of the regional structures of the UN could consist of:

- A reconsideration of the geographic extent of the mandate of the UN economic commissions in order to make them correspond better to economic and political realities rather than geographic divisions.

- A reshaping of the substance of the mandates of regional commissions, with a view to greater comprehensiveness and priority to policy-related work.

- A thorough administrative, managerial, and structural overhaul of the present machinery.

The end product might well be a larger number of regional commissions with a smaller geographic extent but with a more universal mandate, veering toward regional or subregional "mini-UNs." Over time, this network of commissions could develop into a veritable two-tier system, in which the Charter organs would deal primarily with global concerns and with those regional issues referred to them by the commissions.

Conclusion

With the end of the Cold War, the definition of security is broadening. Increasingly, socioeconomic and humanitarian problems, which could not be solved through bilateral negotiations, are included in the "New International Agenda." "People" problems are gradually becoming the concerns of national strategic planners. Thus, widening of the security concept beyond the traditional strategic–military security of state into the security of individual human beings is gaining a new importance. Under these circumstances, there is no real alternative to the UN, if the issues related to security in its new definition — in other words, the interlinkages between peace and development — are to be considered from a global perspective.

However, to succeed in this fresh quest, the UN must adapt itself to the new forms of international governance generated after the end of the Cold War, and needs *inter alia* to incorporate into its institutional design a better way to communicate with the "new actors" on the international scene.

Notes

1. Miles Kahler, "Multilateralism with Small and Large Numbers," *International Organisation*, 46, no. 3 (1992): pp. 681, 707.
2. Harland Cleveland, *Birth of a New World*. San Francisco, 1993, pp. 44–55.
3. Adam Roberts and Benedict Kingsbury (eds.), *United Nations, Divided World*, 2d ed. Oxford: Oxford University Press, 1993, p. 48.
4. Robert O. Keohane and Joseph S. Nye, Jr., "Two Cheers for Multilateralism," *Foreign Policy*, 60 (Fall 1985): 159.

5. Frederick Kratochwil and John G. Ruggie, "International Organisation: A State of the Art of the Art of the State," *International Organisation*, 40 no. 4 (1986): 771.
6. In Roberts and Kingsbury, *United Nations, Divided World*, p. 459.
7. Conor Cruise O'Brien, *United Nations: Sacred Drama*. London, 1966.
8. Roberts and Kingsbury, *United Nations, Divided World*, p. 80.
9. Roberts and Kingsbury, *United Nations, Divided World*, p. 50.
10. Keohane and Nye, "Two Cheers for Multilateralism," p. 155.
11. *The United Nations in Development*. Stockholm, 1991, pp. 61–67.
12. John P. Renninger, "Improving the United Nations System," *Journal of Development Planning*, 17 (1987): 86–111.
13. O'Brien, *United Nations, Sacred Drama*, p. 10.
14. Marc Nerfin, "The United Nations: The Next 40 Years," *IFDA Dossier*, 45(1985): 2.
15. "Reform of the United Nations," Rajiv Gandhi Foundation, New Delhi, April 8-10, 1994, 9–10.

Section 2

The United Nations' Socioeconomic Mission

Benjamin Rivlin

"The process of revitalizing the work of the United Nations in the economic and social fields must be put back on track." So wrote Secretary-General Boutros Boutros-Ghali in his 1993 annual report. He went on "I appeal to Member States to do all they can to that end."

As the UN nears its fiftieth anniversary, the economic and social issues that had long commanded its attention have receded from center stage. Today, the organization is preoccupied with peacekeeping operations. Largely as a consequence of the end of the Cold War, the Security Council had become the hub of the UN, a marked contrast to the earlier domination of the organization by the General Assembly. This shift from one UN principal organ to another indicates a change in organizational priorities from dealing with the longer-term underlying causes of disequilibrium to coping with immediate conflicts and human devastation.

New Concept of Security

Not too long ago, the Security Council was concerned with those very issues that are now being neglected. At its January 1992 summit meeting, the Security Council affirmed the affinity between international security and worldwide economic and social conditions, a central principle of the UN Charter as enunciated in the preamble, in Article 1's statement of purposes and principles, and in Chapters IX and X, which established machinery and procedures to implement these precepts.

When the membership of the UN changed following decolonization, the organization's conception of economic and social rights became the central focus of the political process in the General Assembly. The new majority in the Assembly was preponderantly a group of underdeveloped, poor, and economically deprived states, subsumed under the rubrics of the "South" or "Third World." Using its political strength in the General Assembly, the South instigated a proliferation of UN units, programs, committees, and conferences to further its interests in the economic and social sectors. Dissatisfied with the progress of its agenda, the South stimulated the creation of the post of Director-General, second to the Secretary-General in the UN Secretariat hierarchy, to coordinate socioeconomic activities. These included the adoption of the New International Economic Order (NIEO) resolution, the establishment of the United Nations Conference on Trade and Development (UNCTAD) and the creation of the United Nations Development Programme. The North reacted by using its financial power to limit the expansion of these operations. The stage was thus set for the North–South confrontation that persists to this day.

The resurgence of economic liberalism following the collapse of the Soviet Union and the fading of the Cold War greatly enfeebled the position of the South in the General Assembly. Not only had it lost the bolstering support of the Soviet-dominated Eastern Bloc, but the changing international economic climate, particularly among the increasingly prosperous East and South Asian states, undermined the rationale of a coherent Third World.

This setback put socioeconomic issues on the back burner, but did not eliminate gnawing and destabilizing economic and social challenges from the world. One has but to look at the UNDP's annual *Human Development Report*, the World Bank's *World Development Report*, the IMF's *World Economic Outlook*, and the UN's *World Economic Survey* to be reminded that the world is beset with serious economic and social problems. Moreover, recent demands for UN peacekeeping operations clearly manifest the linkage between social and economic malaise and international peace and security, as heralded in the Charter.

The issue before us is whether the organized international community — notably the UN system — be brought to the point where it can address these underlying socioeconomic causes of tension and instability in the world? Can policies that promote international cooperation and economic development, while at the same time protecting the environment, be promulgated through the help of the UN and its affiliated agencies? Can the promise to promote conditions of economic and social advancement proclaimed in the Charter and reaffirmed by the summit Security Council be fulfilled? Can instruments for cooperative action be enhanced to meet the challenges of global interdependence? To answer these questions, we must look at the UN system machinery and techniques in the social and economic spheres.

The Multilateral Tracks

Concern for the globalized international economy is the domain of institutionalized multilateralism, that is, the UN system, which includes the Bretton Woods institutions (the IMF and the World Bank), the G-7, and the General Agreement on Tariffs and Trade (GATT), which is to be succeeded on July 1, 1995, by the World Trade Organization (WTO).

Given the Charter's provisions, the UN system certainly does have a major, but certainly not an exclusive, responsibility in the area. The international economy is being increasingly reshaped by private activity into an integrated systemic whole. This globalization of economic activities necessitates multilateral state attention, coordinated decision making in global economic management. It should be noted that the leading manifestation of economic multilateral cooperation takes place outside the UN system, namely the G-7 and GATT. Because the economies of the G-7 dominate the world economy, their impact is pervasive; but, the G-7 has not yet shown appropriate concern for how their decisions impact on the non-G-7 world. Their main focus is on short-term adjustments among industrial countries. The impending shift from GATT to the WTO signals the intent to broaden the scope of international trade policy and dispute settlement to include the developing as well as the industrialized world.[1]

A basic point that should be stressed is that the UN is not a monolithic institution. First, there is the division between the central organs and the dispersed specialized Agencies. Of greater importance, however, is the gulf between the UN, particularly ECOSOC, and the Bretton Woods institutions.

Clearly, the UN Charter's original intent was to give ECOSOC a major role in the process of achieving greater coherence in global socioeconomic policy making. The Charter mandated ECOSOC in Articles 57, 60, and 63 to coordinate the activities of the specialized agencies by entering into "relationship agreements," by consultation, and by making recommendations to the agencies, the General Assembly and the member states.

It is generally recognized that ECOSOC's efforts have not been successful. From the very outset, there were built-in obstacles to effective coordination by ECOSOC. First, each specialized agency—not only the World Bank and the IMF—were established as separate entities with their own charters, distinctive membership, budgets and financing, governing body and system of governance, and executive head. Second, insofar as the Bretton Woods institutions are concerned, their structure— notably the weighted voting power vested in the industrialized countries—and the agreements reached between them and the UN deliberately distanced them from the UN majority. Third, in many instances, the specialized agencies tend to resist ECOSOC coordination as "wastefully formalistic." Fourth, effective coordination is in large part dependent on governments whose follow through on the rhetoric of economic coordination is woefully weak. Former Secretary-General Javier Pérez de Cuéllar underscored this point, writing "Coordination would certainly be facilitated if Member States would ensure the consistency of their positions in the relevant intergovernmental bodies of the United Nations System."[2] Representatives of governments to the specialized agencies frequently take positions at variance with what their colleagues express in other agencies or at the UN. Governments, even of older industrialized countries, often fail to coordinate the positions their representatives take in different UN agencies. The Secretary-General also reminded us of a basic reality of international organization—that international agreements (that is, policies adopted in international organs) are enforced and implemented through domestic agencies.

The UN system is not a centralized system. Each of the specialized agencies was created independently; some, such as the ILO, the FAO, ICAO, the World Bank, and the IMF, predate the establishment of the UN itself. We may decry their autonomous behavior and the absence of a hierarchical structure to ensure consistency in the development of an economic and social program to meet the challenges posed by this increasingly interdependent world. This is the reality. Although conventional wisdom holds that ECOSOC and the UN do not fill this need, the record of nearly a half-century shows a degree of achievement in this area. Clearly, the UN General Assembly and ECOSOC have not had any formal coordinating role vis-à-vis Bank or Fund activities. But over the years, UN debates, resolutions, and reports have focused the attention of the Bretton Woods institutions on poorer and less developed countries. This resulted in the establishment of the International Development Association (IDA) and the International Finance Corporation (IFC).

The World Bank or the International Bank for Reconstruction and Development (IRBD), as it is officially called, lends money to states. In its own words, "the IBRD's decision to lend must be based on economic considerations alone."[3] Perhaps, this guiding principle explains why many developing countries view the Bank with such suspicion. What is rational to an economist could be a disaster politically and socially. As part of the UN-negotiated El Salvador Peace Accords, steps designed to eliminate the underlying causes that led to the conflict were instituted by the UN family of agencies. Close observers of the El Salvador scene note that "the UN and...the IMF and the World Bank are overseeing separate, simultaneous processes in El Salvador which are nearly on collision course." The UN is "playing a central role in ensuring that far-reaching political and institutional reforms agreed in the negotiations are carried out," while the IMF and World Bank input "consists of the implementation of a rigorous economic stabilization and structural adjustment program."[4]

The programs for developing countries of the World Bank and of its sister Bretton Woods agency, the IMF, have been criticized from the right as "a welfare check to the Third World," while from the left they have been labeled as "the spearhead of neo-imperialism." As one might expect, the reality falls somewhere in between these two characterizations. One point that must be borne in mind is the heterogeneity within the developing countries. Certainly, they do not all face bleak economic prospects; there is a group of developing countries with quite favorable prospects. But, by and large, economic conditions within the developing world deteriorated during the past decade. The World Bank and the IMF, as key institutions of the contemporary international economic order, have been attacked for the stringent conditions they attach to their programs in developing countries, the secrecy in which they operate, and the lack of accountability of their staffs. Within the UN community, as a result of UNICEF's emphasis on attaching a human face to conditionality and structural adjustments, key aspects of IMF policy towards developing countries has been modified.

The Matter of State Sovereignty

Decisions reached in international organizations are basically policy recommendations that may or may not be accepted by each sovereign state. Thus, such decisions lack the authoritative quality of governmental decisions within states.[5] The point to stress is that the "international community" and even the "UN" itself are largely euphemisms for the individual sovereign states of the world, ostensibly acting together. A case in point is the UN Commission on Sustainable Development (UNCSD), which was established following the awesome and inspiring 1992 Rio Conference on Environment and Development to monitor international efforts to protect the environment. This commission reported in May 1994 that "the international community was failing to provide the money and the know-how needed to foster environmentally benign development in poor countries and that rich countries should do more to restrict harmful consumption by their citizens."[6] A strong commitment by sovereign states to work toward implementing the goals of the Rio conference was not evident in the UNCSD session. An NGO observer from the Philippines noted: "This is becoming another United Nations talking shop. The ministers of economy and development who really count are not involved." The UNCSD meeting chairman, German Minister of Environment Klaus Töpfer, echoed the view "that by themselves environment ministers could do little to save a threatened world by the efforts of more powerful branches of government to promote industry, exports and jobs."

To assume that sovereignty reigns supreme in all matters of concern to the international community other than those covered by the Security Council's overriding authority under Chapter VII of the Charter, is a failure to recognize some basic realities about the international political system. Politics among states leads to intervention in the political system of a state by another state, or a group of states, or an international organization, usually through diplomacy which has been termed "formalized intervention." Penetrations into the sovereign domain of states are evident daily in the economic and social realm, ranging from the decisions of the Bretton Woods agencies to those of the UN Commission on Human Rights. Theoretically, sovereign states are hermetically sealed units. In reality, no one state is totally self-subsistent. This does not mean that the international community has effective machinery for managing the ever-increasing interdependence of the world, that is, the global agenda. States are resistant to outside penetration. Some are strong enough to withstand this pressure; others are so weak that they are almost totally at its mercy. No state is involved in this process willingly, which is another way of saying what Pérez de Cuéllar said above. Moreover, the transnational corporations and the instantaneous operations of financial and equity markets have taken a large part of the world economy out of the control of individual states. Efforts to deal with the global agenda internationally must first confront the reluctant participation of many member states.

Coordinating the dispersed and fragmented agencies of the UN system in the economic and social area is often perceived as a futile exercise — fighting the war that cannot be won. In face of a world economy that is in need of some coherent form of collective management, the UN, in particular its central structures, appears singularly ill-equipped, hopelessly under financed and unduly fragmented. Numerous calls for reforming the system have been advanced, from Inspector Maurice Bertrand of the Joint Inspection Unit, the Group of 18, UNA-USA's *Successor Vision*, a South Commission Report, a Nordic Perspective, and the like. The common thread among the proposed reforms is improved and strengthened multilateral governance through the creation of an "Economic Security Council" or of "an International Development Council." Although improvements can be made in the existing machinery and some duplication of effort eliminated, this kind of tinkering can not produce lasting and effective changes.   Only the international community can formulate meaningful policies for global economic and social management. Progress towards these goals requires a willingness on the part of the major economic players in particular to work within the framework of multilateral institutions, which, by the nature of the task, will impinge on national sovereignty.

What the UN Can and Cannot Do

The UN is not a world government. It has neither the authority nor the resources to deal with all global problems.   Nor can it be expected to create a blueprint to coordinate all world activity in the socioeconomic sector. The role of the UN and most multilateral institutions is a restricted one. Its function is to identify problems and suggest policies to be taken by governments. We must remember that the current framework for global economic interdependence is a patchwork affair.   In some instances we have international agencies with operational authority (for example, the IMF, World Bank, and UNDP), but most multilateral agencies can at best monitor the current and prospective state of world economic and social situations, informing the world community about them, and propose possible national and multilateral policies. Thus, an assessment of the capacities and capabilities of the organized international community to meet the intricate challenge of contributing to world security in the socioeconomic sector must conclude that the multilateral machinery is no stronger or weaker than the commitment of the member states. The most basic of all questions is what role the states are prepared to give to the organs of the UN. It is not primarily a matter of reform and reorganization, as many have suggested. Rather, as the Nordic Report argued, its "effectiveness and organization can only be judged against what the UN is supposed, mandated or expected to do."[7]

To deal with this problem, the General Assembly at its 47th session in 1992 asked the Secretary-General to submit *An Agenda for Development,* which would be a companion to his *An Agenda for Peace,* prepared at the behest of the Security Council.   The Secretary-General was asked to specifically include his views on substantive priorities in the economic and social fields.[8] The difficulties inherent in dealing with this subject are apparent by the fact that the report has not yet been completed.   In contrast, Boutros-Ghali was able to produce *An Agenda for Peace* within six months of the Security Council's request.

Conclusion

Despite these two formidable obstacles—reliance on the member states to carry out international policy decisions and the Byzantine-like structure of the UN system with its built-in sectoral biases—the UN's fifty-year record is by no means entirely negative. The world of the 1990s is very different from that of the UN's founder. With all their shortcomings, UN programs and agencies for economic development and social advancement, such as UNDP, the Commission on Human Rights, the High Commissioner for Refugees, UNICEF, the International Atomic Energy Agency, the Commission for Sustainable Development, and the Commission on the Status of Women, represent important accomplishments. As Ralph Bunche declared in 1942 as he and others were working on plans for organizing the postwar world, the "real objective" of international organizations, "must be the good life for all the people—peace, bread, a house, adequate clothing, education, good health and above all, the right to walk with dignity on the world's great boulevards."[9]

Perhaps the most important contribution has been consciousness raising—drawing the attention of governments, nongovernmental organizations, and individuals to the socioeconomic facts of life, providing authoritative knowledge about the issues, and setting goals for betterment of the human condition. It may be that the UN's reaching out beyond states to nongovernmental sectors may prove to be the most effective means of putting the UN's socioeconomic mission on track. Governments on their own seem sluggish and defensive in responding to the international community's call for action. As a general rule, governments respond to pressure from within their societies rather than to exogenous policy proposals coming from the UN. With the movement towards democratic polities taking off in the world, nongovernmental organizations play an increasingly significant role in generating support for implementing policies promoted by the UN and for cooperative approaches to dealing with global problems.

Notes

1. See Andreas F. Lowenfeld, "Remedies along with Rights," *American Journal of International Law*, July 1994.
2. Javier Pérez de Cuéllar, "Foreword" to *Coordination Questions: Annual Overview Report of the Administrative Committee for Coordination for 1989*, April 5, 1990, p. 5. E/1990/18
3. *The World Bank Annual Report 1992.* Washington, D.C., p. 4. The identical wording appears in previous annual reports.
4. Alvaro de Soto and Graciana del Castillo, "Obstacles to Peacebuilding," *Foreign Policy*, No. 4 (1994): 70.
5. There is, of course, the notable exception to the sacrosanct supremacy of the sovereign state in the UN Charter's enforcement provisions of Article

2(7) and Chapter VII.

6. Paul Lewis, "Panel Finds Lag in Saving Environment: Financing of Goals Set at Rio Faulted," *New York Times*, May 29, 1994, p. 13.

7. *The United Nations in Development.* Stockholm, 1991, p. 33.

8. UN A Res. 47/181.

9. Institute of Pacific Relations, 8th Conference, Mont Tremblant, Canada. Secretariat Document 15, December 12, 1942.

Section 3

The United Nations and
a New Approach to
International Cooperation

Inge Kaul

Poverty and human deprivation in developing countries have ceased to be issues of only national concern, just as they have ceased to be simply issues of moral concern about socioeconomic inequity and injustice. They have become an issue of global human security. Poverty adversely impacts the environment and global climatic conditions, while socioeconomic disparity is a powerful push factor behind the rising tide of international migration. In addition, the present conflicts in Bosnia, Haiti, Rwanda, Somalia, and elsewhere show that ethnic and political tensions within countries can have worldwide repercussions.

As a result, concepts of security are changing fast. As outlined, for example, in *An Agenda for Peace* of the Secretary-General of the United Nations, improving social justice, eradicating poverty, and fostering more participatory and sustainable development now form key elements of the strategies for preventive diplomacy and for keeping, making, and building peace. The concept of security today includes territorial security and human security.

Although the need for a social pillar in global peace efforts is recognized, the question is whether the international community possesses policy instruments that will allow it to redress effectively the developmental trends that today put human security at risk. Are there global policies for tackling poverty, for reducing human deprivation and disparity among people, rich and poor, rural and urban, or among ethnic groups and nations?

One policy instrument that immediately comes to mind is official development assistance (ODA). But, what does ODA at present contribute to alleviating poverty and closing North–South development gaps? How could it be made a more effective instrument of global human security? And how could interested policy makers mobilize the necessary political support for a change in the present ODA system in favor of human development? These are the questions which will be examined in this section.

Only if international cooperation for development succeeds in meeting the needs of human security will the present UN peace initiatives become more than short-term crisis management and containment efforts. Approaches need to be two pronged, embracing both peacekeeping operations and social policy initiatives. Territorial security should increasingly be promoted through human security, and social policy initiatives should increasingly help prevent the need for the deployment of UN forces, whether it is for peacekeeping or peacemaking.

Poverty Focus

Despite all donor policy statements that one of ODA's main purposes, if not the main purpose, is to help poor nations and poor people, this is not what ODA does today. ODA at present lacks a clear focus on poverty. Aid statistics are quite clear on this point:

• Three-fourths of the world's poor people live in ten developing countries, which receive only about one-fourth of total ODA.

• Egypt receives $370 per poor person, Swaziland $124, Mali $99, Rwanda $22, and India $4. There is no clear link between ODA and the recipient country's GNP per capita.

• Only about 6.5 percent of total bilateral ODA from 1988 to 1990 was, on average, allocated to human development priority concerns, such as basic education, primary health care, nutrition support, rural water and sanitation. In the case of multilateral aid, it was 11 percent.

• It does not seem to matter much what countries do with their own resources: high military spenders get as much reward from ODA as low military spenders and almost twice as much as moderate military spenders.

• What developing countries receive in ODA on the one hand—$54 billion from DAC countries in 1990—is taken away on the other, for example by external debt servicing which claimed $140 billion in the same year.

It could be argued that ODA need not directly focus on the poor to alleviate poverty, but that it might accomplish this goal by promoting a country's overall economic growth. However, studies of ODA's impact on the economic growth of recipient countries have not demonstrated many positive results. Some even question whether such an impact exists at all.

The lack of effectiveness of such aid is attributed to two main causes. One is the modest size of ODA. In 1991, ODA amounted to about 2 percent of the developing countries' combined GNP. In terms of the donor countries' GNP, it stood at about 0.3 percent, falling considerably short of the agreed upon international target of 0.7 percent. Some research even indicated that although these amounts are modest and positive results are difficult to trace, aid may even have had some adverse effects on the economies of developing countries. ODA may have discouraged domestic savings and resource mobilization, and it may also have exacerbated consumption of capital-intensive imports and capital flight. Thus, it is rather unlikely that

ODA has had any significant impact on poverty or the closing of intra- or intercountry gaps in human development through a trickle-down effect of economic growth.

Why has ODA failed to make a significant contribution to poverty alleviation and human development? After all, some of the objectives involved would have been attainable even within the rather limited aid resources that were available. For example, according to estimates of the *Human Development Report 1991*, the achievement of basic education for all by the year 2000 would imply additional spending per year of about $5 billion. Estimates prepared by UNDP, UNFPA, UNICEF, and other agencies show that financing a more comprehensive set of poverty alleviation measures, including for example, basic education, primary health care, nutrition support, sanitation, and family planning services, would require additional annual spending of approximately $20 to 40 billion.

The reason ODA has not focused more on such "doable" tasks is that ODA allocations have been affected, and distorted, by a number of political and economic considerations. ODA as an instrument of development, and especially as an instrument of global human development, has not been given much of a real, systematic chance in the past.

The Four Scars

The literature on aid effectiveness is voluminous, with much attention devoted to the design and management of aid programs and projects. Complicated machineries have been set up to ensure ever tighter monitoring and evaluation. Yet, aid effectiveness has not really changed. This is not surprising, because technical problems were not what made aid go wrong during the past four decades. Rather, aid was affected by the political, military, and ideological divide between East and West and the divide between North and South. These global divides inflicted four major scars on ODA.

The Cold War Scar

The beginnings of ODA date back to the beginning of the Cold War during the post-World War II days of the late 1940s. Until the late 1980s, ODA served, in large measure, as an instrument for forging political alliances along the East–West divide. Among the first major assistance efforts was the Marshall Plan, which immediately after World War II benefited such strategically important countries as Germany. Other aid programs in politically and militarily critical areas included those for the Republic of Korea, and later South Vietnam and the South and Central American region. East–West bloc building continued as an increasing number of developing countries won their independence in the 1950s and 1960s. As late as in 1990, three-fourths of total bilateral US aid went to only five countries: Egypt, Israel, Honduras, Nicaragua, and the Philippines. These countries are certainly not the poorest of the poor.

The fact that ODA has often been allocated to actual and potential crisis areas no doubt helps explain the above-mentioned connection between military spending and aid.

The Ethnocentrism Scar

ODA is mainly a resource flow from rich to poor countries, and especially from North to South. In the North, the Western industrialized countries have contributed the largest amount of aid. The share of DAC countries in total ODA, for example, was about 90 percent in 1990. However, it must be stressed that the aid statistics of the formerly centrally planned economies may not adequately reflect what may have been the actual amount of aid given. This is partly because they considered aid as gesture of solidarity to which they did not want to attach a monetary value. In addition, their aid statistics showed modest financial amounts because of the often highly subsidized cost of some of the aid services rendered, especially those in the social sector.

In composition and content, much of ODA has consisted of what so-called richer countries were seen to be richer in—capital and advanced technology, including both equipment and expertise. ODA has been aimed at transferring what was perceived to be abundant in the North and lacking in the South. Hence, it has reflected more the development conditions in the donor countries than the development conditions and needs in the recipient countries.

Yet, only a tiny fraction of ODA flows into the priority areas of human development, including the formation of human capabilities. This has not only hampered more balanced development in developing countries, but impeded the absorption of ODA. Neglecting investment in human development perpetuates the lack of qualified national personnel who could act as counterparts of external assistance experts and assume progressive responsibility for aid management and implementation. In spite of four decades of development assistance, Africa today has more foreign experts that ever before and Tanzania pays three times as much for foreign expert advice than for its whole civil service.

The State/Public Sector Scar

Most aid has been moving from (donor) government to (recipient) government. A major change—and a step in a new direction—is that Northern nongovernmental organizations (NGOs) today channel some $5 billion in aid funds to the South. This is about one-tenth of ODA and as much as the International Development Assistance (ODA) facility of the World Bank has to offer. And note that the former provide grants and the latter loans.

The close government-to-government connection in the present ODA system is no doubt linked to the political and military context in which ODA has been embedded since its inception. But another factor is that past development models have accorded a strong role to the state as promoter and provider of development. This was reflected in the considerable expansion of the public sector in developing countries that took place until the mid-1980s, to which ODA no doubt provided major inputs, helping to set up and strengthen national ministries and public enterprises. Many of these efforts were necessary, justified, and in line with the preoccupation with nation-building and national sovereignty that prevailed in the developing countries at that time. However, the consequence has been a strong development and aid emphasis on central government, with only meager resources for subnational and local levels. As a result, only small amounts of aid have directly benefited people.

The Country-Focus Scar

Closely linked to the foregoing is that in the past, ODA has been allocated to countries rather than for development challenges. It is a difficult and perhaps even impossible to figure out from the present DAC aid statistics what development assistance has done for children, for women, or to combat malnutrition, eradicate illiteracy, or protect the environment. But, there is no doubt that recent years have seen an increased resource flow into areas of relevance to sustainable human development. A number of thematic accounts now exist in bilateral and multilateral aid agencies. Examples from the sphere of multilateral aid would include the Global Environment Facility (GEF), the United Nations Population Fund (UNFPA) and the United Nations Fund for Women (UNIFEM).

Besides only marginally targeting the priority concerns of human development, ODA remains based on the notion that global development results from the sum total of national development experiences. But this no longer holds true: the globalization of both developmental "goods," such as trade and information, and developmental "bads," such as poverty and environmental degradation, have changed the situation. Today global development requires national action (including at subnational and local level) as well as global action. And in both cases, financial support is needed.

A New Approach

A basic restructuring of ODA is not only necessary, but possible. The disappearance of the East–West divide has removed many of the factors that caused the former political distortions. Moreover, experience has changed development thinking and strategies. More attention is now being given to country specificity, people, and free enterprise. Factors that led to ODA's ethnocentrism and state/public sector focus have been removed. Growing recognition of the need to complement national development action with global development action has opened up new avenues for action.

The restructuring of ODA in support of the new development challenges the world is facing should, therefore, not be delayed any further. To hesitate would risk letting aid fatigue settle in. It could also weaken the present

ODA system beyond repair. This section suggests a ten-point agenda for restructuring ODA.

1. ODA's objectives must be set right. If there is agreement that the main challenge of future development is lack of human security, then ODA must be allowed to focus on this objective, within the framework of a longer-term strategy for sustainable human development. This implies that ODA be given an opportunity to address on a priority basis such issues as:

- The population explosion;

- Poverty and socioeconomic disparity, including lack of food security and threats to human survival stemming from such factors as preventable childhood diseases or HIV/AIDS;

- International migration, employment creation, and better sharing of existing work opportunities;

- Lack of political participation, ethnic conflict, and civil strife;

- Drug trafficking and abuse, and other issues of social disintegration and weakening of the social fabric;

- Environmental degradation; and

- Nuclear proliferation.

These problems must be tackled urgently if major developmental and political disasters are to be avoided. They must become priorities for a global policy that emphasizes new priorities for development finance. To match policy priorities and finance priorities systematically, and to give aid a chance to be successful, it would be desirable to provide wherever possible and feasible, estimates of needed investments and the required development finance. Aid targets should be established not in terms of the GNP of donor countries, but in terms of the development needs aid is expected to meet.

2. ODA must be placed into a broader, improved context of international cooperation for development. ODA alone cannot meet all the challenges. If it were to do so, its size would need to be increased several times — and there is little likelihood for that to be politically feasible. Moreover, ODA may often not even be the right means to bring about change. For example, improved international trade conditions or an increased flow of foreign direct investment (FDI) to developing countries can probably do much more for employment creation than any external assistance effort. Therefore, to succeed, ODA must be complemented by improvements in other areas of international cooperation for development. Examples would include further trade liberalization, especially the opening up of the markets of industrial countries to goods and services from developing countries; improved flows of FDI; improved access of developing countries to development finance and technology; and structural adjustment in the North. Unless these changes occur, ODA will continue to fight an uphill battle — and in many instances a futile one.

3. ODA must pursue a two-pronged strategy. It must help the national development of the poorest countries and it must support the attainment of

global objectives of human security and sustainable development. Just as social safety nets within the national context are a last resort—an exception rather than the rule—so should ODA be used only for countries that cannot cope on their own and would not be able to benefit much from improvements in the functioning of international markets. This would be the case in many of the poorest countries. Just consider the countries of Sub-Saharan Africa. While world trade has expanded considerably in the last years, Africa's share declined from 3.8 to 1 percent between 1970 and 1989. Clearly, an international social safety net is needed. One part of ODA should be allocated to this purpose.

Just as national government spending and public policies and programs act not only as a social safety net but as an enabling framework for development and private initiative, ODA should seek to create an international framework of incentives and help ensure that global development challenges are actually tackled. The countries to be involved in such global development initiatives should be those that can make a significant contribution—irrespective of their level of income or other criteria that play a role in today's system of ODA allocations.

For example, in the case of population growth, some ten countries will contribute half of the total growth that the 1990s are likely to witness. They are the ones that matter when it comes to tackling the problem of population pressure. But, China, which is included in this list of countries, has already achieved significant progress in reducing population growth. Its fertility rate in 1991 was 2.3—only 40 percent of what it was in 1960. By contrast, that of India in 1991 was 6.0—as high as it was in 1960. The international community would probably want to have a policy dialogue on possibilities for further development change with countries such as India rather than those such as China.

Similarly, one could identify countries that really matter in respect to other global challenges—whether they be migration, environment, or nuclear proliferation. Global ODA must focus on these countries, regardless of whether they are rich or poor in income. This also holds true for tackling poverty. An ODA focus on the poorest (low-income) countries, as suggested above, can only partially address the problem. In addition, global ODA would have to be used for tackling poverty in other countries, which may not be the poorest in terms of income but nevertheless have large pockets of poverty. India or Brazil are cases in point.

4. ODA must be people oriented. Both parts of ODA—its global part and its national part—must be geared more towards improving the lives of people than overall conditions in countries. The latter will happen as a result of the former, as a result of more participatory development. But experience has shown that improving country conditions does not necessarily help to improve people's lives.

ODA must, therefore, follow the shift in perspective that is now marking development thinking. People have to be put first. Development should be development by people—that is, it should be participatory; and it should be development of people—that is, investment in human capital; and it should be for people, that is, ultimately leading to widening the range of people's choices.

A people-centered approach to development cooperation would have several implications. First, more ODA must be invested in enabling people to help themselves — in building basic human capabilities. If this does not happen, participatory development will continue to be a distant goal. Second, more aid must be made available to people, not just to governments. One way of achieving this could be through increased support to credit schemes for the poor.

When considering support for participatory development, it would also be important to focus clearly on the two main aspects of development by people: (1) people should be involved in development through, for example, employment and work; and (2) people should take part in the decision making on development. Both aspects must come together, if participatory development is really to work.

5. ODA must recognize that political development is an integral part of development. In the past, development has often been equated with economic growth and social progress. Although heavily influenced by politics, development strategies have given little attention to political development. Most programs and projects aimed at national capacity building in support of democratization and the guarantee of human rights are of very recent origin, and so far, limited to a relatively small number of countries.

This will have to change. As countries embark on more participatory development strategies, they realize that political freedom requires political development in the same way as economic growth requires economic development. Policy formulation, skills, management capacity, and technical know-how all need strengthening. ODA must equip itself to provide support to political development and pursue a constructive approach, helping countries to extricate themselves from the political conditions which have, at times, prompted donors to impose political conditionality. Halting aid resource flows temporarily because of unsatisfactory political, social, or economic conditions in the host country can never be more than a tactical measure in the process of policy dialogue and negotiating change. It is not a developmental measure. And it often punishes the people of the country concerned twice: by lack of political freedom as well as by loss of external development support. A much more constructive approach is to clearly direct resources towards improving the overall political conditions.

6. ODA must facilitate development cooperation rather than overextend itself into implementing development cooperation. This means that the role of the state in international development cooperation will have to change. Development assistance should become less a government-to-government relationship. It should increasingly involve the private sector, NGOs, and people themselves. Also, ODA resources should not only be found within government budgets; and governments should not necessarily be the executing agencies of aid programs and projects. All development actors must be involved. This requires a search for new assistance modalities and a greater use of ODA for incentive purposes — making human development happen rather than doing development for people.

7. ODA must be in the mutual interest of all countries. The problem

with ODA in this respect is not so much that it is not in the mutual interest of all countries, but that it is often not seen as being so. The rich countries still feel that they just give; the poorer countries feel that they just take. There is a problem of perception on both sides.

Development in the North cannot succeed in isolation—surrounded as it is at present by a sea of poverty, deprivation, despair, economic collapse, political tension, civil strife, and war. Socioeconomic disparity has become so acute that it is only through more evenly spread development—not through new immigration laws or strengthened border police—that current tensions can be defused and development brought back into balance. Industrial countries, therefore, do have a self-interest in the development of developing countries, and one should probably include in this category today's economies in transition. They do have a self-interest in trade liberalization, resolving the debt crisis, and strengthening aid effectiveness.

But because developing countries have an even greater interest in their development and as great an interest in tackling global challenges as industrial countries, they must also contribute to facilitating future international cooperation. To create strengthened political will and support in the North for international cooperation, they could, for example, clearly demonstrate their firm commitment to avoiding, to the fullest extent possible, unproductive, wasteful expenditures. They could demonstrate their commitment by reducing military expenditures and increasing social spending as well as domestic savings.

8. ODA must take the form of human development compacts. The proposed new system of international development cooperation requires that aid be less charity and more business—a "trade in services." Three types of compacts between the cooperating parties would be required.

First, there would need to be cooperation agreements between the poorest countries and the international community. The poorest countries would offer to improve their human development levels and state precise objectives and targets for poverty eradication, investing in people, domestic resource mobilization, and public spending. The international community would indicate the amount and type of its support: the price it would be willing to pay for the poorest countries' offer to help free the world from the scorch of poverty.

Second, there would have to be agreements between the international community and the countries that would offer contributions to tackling various global challenges. However, such offers are likely to be forthcoming only if the "price" is right. The international community cannot realistically expect that the modest amount of ODA available at present could "buy" the whole package of required policy changes.

It will therefore be all the more important to combine ODA with an improved international economic environment and enhanced international market opportunities for developing countries. Thus, the third type of compact would have to ensure that improvements in the international economic system are indeed complemented by progress in meeting national human development objectives and targets. For example, there could be and agreement within the framework of GATT to lower trade barriers in a particular market in return for a commitment from governments to increase social spending on human development priorities to a defined level. Future development cooperation—if it is to be true cooperation—must be a balanced quid pro quo.

To adopt a more business-like approach to international development cooperation, agreements between the different parties concerned must be marked by clearly stated commitments and responsibilities—agreed-on objectives and targets that lend themselves to monitoring and hence facilitate transparency and accountability.

9. ODA must be prepared for emergencies. Development is not necessarily a process of gradual change. The last decade in particular witnessed an increasing number of disasters and emergencies—natural, economic, social and political. This trend is likely to continue as the world community as a whole and individual countries struggle to find a new balance between a number of opposing and conflicting forces, between increasing globalization of development and growing demand for decentralization and people's self-determination, between the rising expectations of a rapidly growing world population and the requirements of environmentally sound development.

Responding to emergencies must therefore become a strengthened focus of ODA. This will require an integrated, adequately funded multilateral approach. This policy conclusion is conveyed loud and clearly by the recent experiences with emergency aid in Somalia.

10. A new approach to ODA needs new institutional mechanisms. If future ODA is indeed to be more focused, more targeted, more business rather than charity, a two-way rather than a one-way process, then it will require new institutional arrangements. It will require greater emphasis on multilateralism, global policy making, and joint policy action. There is a need for strengthened global governance.

Whatever institutional arrangement one were to choose—new or existing—the guiding principle should be to place future UN multilateral peace efforts on the twin strong pillars of political security and human security and to have appropriate negotiating and decision making force for both.

Building Political Alliances for Change

Changing the existing international framework of development cooperation along the lines proposed above will be a complex process. It is likely do meet with political opposition and concern among both today's donors and recipients and the rather elaborate institutional machinery established to administer the present ODA system. But, it will also have its political proponents among those policy makers who realize that without more participatory development there cannot be sustainable human development, peace, and security; that change must come; and that it might be better to facilitate this change than to obstruct it and to risk political, economic, and social crises with unforeseeable consequences. These policy makers will, no doubt, be able to find broad-based political support among the growing number of people both in the South and North who are affected by loss of personal security—food security, job security, environmental security, and social and political security.

Making International Fora More Representative

People's representatives—especially parliamentarians—will have a critical role to play in initiating the debate on a new approach to international development cooperation and helping to build necessary political alliances for change. To make reform happen, parliamentarians will have to become more involved in global governance, in particular in UN human security matters. They will have to realize that many of the changes in national development today require more than national policy making. More and more issues have an international dimension and will require global policy action. Although the nation-state and national policy making are still important, the growing interdependence among countries necessitates growing global policy making. Democracy should not be expected to stop at national borders. International policy making should also be representative and marked by accountability. People's representatives will have to become involved, especially where the issues concern ensuring human security through more participatory development.

Similarly, international fora will, in future, have to allow for greater participation of, and consultation with, the other main development actors, notably nongovernmental organizations (NGOs) and the business community. Global policy making must catch up with the political change that has in the recent past occurred at national and subnational levels, especially the emergence of a much more active civil society.

Conclusion

Today one often hears that aid fatigue exists in donor countries and that politicians feel that their voters would not approve of more development aid. This reaction in large measure reflects the prevailing but mistaken public notion of aid as charity, as money that is being given without direct benefit to the donors. A lot of public awareness building will be needed to achieve the strengthened public support required for sustainable human development. Policy makers will not gain from shying away from such awareness-building campaigns. Without a new framework for international development cooperation, fewer and fewer of their national policy measures will work. Policy makers in the South will, for example, find that employment generation is curtailed by international trade barriers that limit the expansion of production in the South. And policy makers in the North will find that if economic opportunities are not allowed to travel to people, than people will travel to economic opportunities. Police forces cannot stem the tide of international migration, and they cannot halt environmental degradation. Only global human development can. Mobilizing public support for a more targeted, business-like type of international cooperation will benefit people, their representatives, and policy makers, both in the North and South.

In light of the above, it might be desirable for donor governments to reserve a certain amount of their aid—let us say, 3 percent—to prepare public opinion for the new post-Cold War realities and the increased interdependence between North and South.

The year 1995 will offer important opportunities for real progress toward enhanced human security and international cooperation. It will be the year in which the World Social Summit will be held in Copenhagen, Denmark. And it will be the year in which the UN will celebrate its fiftieth anniversary. Action is urgent if these opportunities are not to be missed. The future of the world and its people is not just a matter of destiny; in large measure it is a matter of the right policy choice—of putting people at the center.

Chapter 5

Toward a
Summit for People

Section 1

From Stockholm to Rio
to the
Twenty-First Century

Maurice F. Strong

In the stream of history and human progress, the two decades from 1972 to 1992 are but a ripple. Yet we know that ripples cause waves, and historians may yet come to regard this twenty-year period as a watershed era – the beginning of the Environmental Renaissance. At either end of the two-decade span are the United Nations Conference on the Human Environment in Stockholm in 1972 and the United Nations Conference on Environment and Development in Rio in 1992. Although many significant ecological events occurred in the intervening years, these two world assemblies define the period in which the global community confronted its destiny in an unprecedented manner. It now remains to engage and shape that destiny, to nurture the promise of the renaissance into the reality of a more secure, more equitable, and more sustainable future for the twenty-first century and beyond.

The Stockholm Conference illuminated the dark side of industrial and economic progress. It laid bare the human consequences of our wasteful patterns of production and consumption, and affirmed humanity's "solemn responsibility to protect and improve the environment for present and future generations." The Stockholm proceedings and the resultant Declaration on the Human Environment, endorsed by 113 nations, first put the environment issue on the world agenda.

The Earth Summit at Rio twenty years later moved the issue into the center of economic policy and decision making in virtually every sector of economic life. UNCED was a remarkable political event by any standard. In conference preparation and participation, both UNCED and the accompanying "peoples summit" had unprecedented broad involvement of governments, organizations, and people. The presence of more than twice the number of media representatives than had ever before been accredited to a world conference ensured that people everywhere were aware of what was happening in Rio and were alerted to its importance.

Understandably, much attention was focused on areas of controversy and disagreement. In the final analysis, however, leaders from some 180 countries reached agreement on the most comprehensive and far-reaching set of measures ever approved by the nations of the world. Despite some significant shortcomings and disappointments, the Rio Declaration and Agenda 21 provide the framework and essential elements for a new global partnership that can start us onto the path towards a more secure and sustainable future. The fact that these measures were agreed upon at the highest possible political level gives them unique political authority.

Lessons from the Stockholm to Rio Era

Although it is too early to assess fully the response to Rio, it is useful to reflect on the lessons learned from the Stockholm-to-Rio era, the prospects for the realization of new hopes that it engendered, and the new directions it set for our common future.

The decision of the UN General Assembly to hold the Earth Summit in Rio followed the World Commission on Environment and Development, which was chaired by Prime Minister Gro Harlem Brundtland of Norway. The main theme of its landmark report, Our Common Future, issued in 1987, was the relationship between economic development and the condition of the environment. It made clear that although a great deal of progress had been made toward environmental improvements in particular instances since 1972, overall, the planet's environment had deteriorated and major environmental risks, such as ozone depletion and global warming, had increased significantly. Indeed, some of these threats had been unknown or barely recognized at Stockholm. In compelling terms the Brundtland Commission documented the case for sustainable development—the full integration of environmental and economic development as the only sound means of ensuring both our environmental and economic futures.

The evolution of the environment as an important public issue in the 1970s was accompanied by the establishment of environmental agencies and ministries by virtually all governments. Although some, like the U.S. Environmental Protection Agency, were given formidable powers, these were primarily in the areas of review and regulation. Environmental agencies and ministries had little influence on economic policy or the policies and practices of the major sectoral agencies, the activities of which are the principal sources of environmental impacts. The result was in many cases a disproportionate reliance on regulation. We are now experiencing, and in some cases are already exceeding, the practical limits of regulation. Regulation is necessary, of course, but experience has demonstrated that its effects can be limited, and sometimes counterproductive, if not accompanied by changes in economic and fiscal policies that provide positive incentives for environmentally sound and sustainable economic development.

Environment–Development Relationship

Although progress was made in many individual areas after Stockholm, it had little effect on environment–development relationships in the policies and practices of governments and industry. Even more ominous was the fact that the underlying conditions driving the risks to the human future that had been perceived at Stockholm did not fundamentally change in the two decades that separated Stockholm from Rio. During that time, approximately 1.7 billion people were added to the Earth's population, almost the same as the total population of the planet at the beginning of the century, and most of this growth took place in developing countries. Despite recessions, the global economy more than doubled, but most of the growth accrued to the already rich industrialized countries. During the same time the environment and natural resources of developing countries deteriorated at an alarming rate.

One did not need to be a scientist or a statistician to know this; the extent and nature of environmental degradation and its tragic human consequences are evident everywhere. The cities of the developing countries, growing at rates never before experienced, were now among the world's most polluted, many of them headed for environmental and social breakdown. The appalling destruction of natural resources, loss of forest cover, erosion and degradation of soils, and deterioration of supplies and quality of water were and still are visible throughout the developing world. Economic losses in agriculture, fisheries, and tourism are tragically manifested in diminished livelihoods for already impoverished and struggling people. This forbidding drama is unfolding throughout the developing world, threatening a massive human ecotragedy beyond any ever witnessed, the grim portents of which can be seen in the recurring famines and grievous civil strife in Africa.

The pressures of population growth have historically been mitigated by migration, but today all the habitable places are within the boundaries of nation-states, most of which are closing their borders to newcomers. Large-scale migration is no longer a solution to overpopulation or to accommodating refugees from conflict and economic crises. Yet the pressures for migration are increasing, and countries with living space and stable economies are inevitably going to have vast numbers of impoverished or dispossessed people knocking at their doors.

Unfortunately, there few signs that the underlying conditions that have produced the current crisis are changing. Developing countries face these challenges at a time when their already serious handicaps and disadvantages are increasing. As industrialized societies move toward more sustainable patterns of production and consumption, there will be a relative decline in the need for some of the key raw materials and commodities on which the economies of developing countries depend so heavily. In a world economy in which knowledge applied through technology, marketing, design, and sophisticated management systems has become the principal source of added value and competitive advantage, developing countries face the prospect that their disadvantages could well deepen.

In addition, the countries of the former Soviet Union and Eastern and Central Europe, in which the failures of centrally planned economies were accompanied by some of the worst environmental devastation anywhere, are now trying to make the transition to market economies. It is important that they do this on an environmentally sound and sustainable basis.

We cannot divorce the gathering crisis of the developing world and the degeneration of Eastern European economies from the West's economic and security interests and moral responsibilities. After all, the modern industrial civilization has produced this dilemma, however inadvertently. It continues to monopolize its benefits while people in the developing world must share, and indeed bear disproportionately, the global risks for which the West is so largely responsible. As the twenty-first century approaches, the cooperation of developing countries is needed to bring these risks under control and to build a secure and sustainable global society. This cannot be done without a much more equitable sharing of both the responsibilities and the benefits of industrial civilization.   Industrialized countries have an obligation to reduce the environmental impacts of their own economic activities and leave "space" for developing countries to fulfill their developmental needs and aspirations.

Prospects for Agenda 21

What then are the prospects for implementing the principles contained in the Rio Declaration and the action program incorporated in Agenda 21? The short-term signs are mixed. Governments have understandably tended to lapse back to business as usual, particularly in light of the immediate and pressing political and economic concerns that preoccupy virtually all administrations.   In particular, the large-scale commitments of new and additional financial resources required for implementing Agenda 21 are proving difficult to obtain.

The 1993 meeting of the Development Committee of the World Bank, which is the annual World Bank meeting, the negotiations on the International Development Association (IDA) replenishment, and the meeting of Parties to the Montreal Protocol all demonstrated the deepening reluctance of major donors to commit new funding. A number have announced further reductions in development assistance programs.   In this atmosphere, the agreement on refurbishment of the Global Environmental Facility constitutes a welcome achievement, but it did not come easily. Furthermore, a resurgent parochialism in most industrialized societies erodes the political commitment to the environment at home and prospects for increased foreign assistance.

It would not be realistic to expect the fundamental changes in the existing order that were called for at Rio to emerge quickly or easily from the current political situation. However, there is reason to hope that the Earth Summit has laid the foundations for the changes in public attitudes and the political mind-set that are necessary to achieve the transition to sustainable development in the long term.

There have, however, been some positive developments in addition to the agreement on renewal of the Global Environmental Facility. The UN Commission on Sustainable Development has been established as the forum for continuing governmental consultation and cooperation in following up and implementing the agreements reached at Rio.   And a High-Level Advisory Board has been set up to advise the UN Secretary-General on

Agenda 21 implementation issues. The United States has reestablished its leadership in respect to the issues on which it was so reluctant at Rio. In addition to signing the Biological Diversity Convention, agreeing on targets and timetables for reduction of greenhouse gas emissions, which it was not prepared to do under the Climate Change Convention, it has established a new Presidential Commission on Sustainable Development. Japan has enacted a Basic Environment Law. Other countries, including China, are developing their own national "Agenda 21" in response to Rio's Agenda 21.

The most exciting and promising post-Rio developments are occurring outside of governments, where there has been a virtual explosion of activities and initiatives on the part of grass-roots organizations, citizens groups, and key sectors of society. People returning from or inspired by Rio are determined to translate its basic themes into direct responses to Agenda 21. Engineers and architects, through their international bodies, have committed to sustainable development and cooperative programs designed to support implementation of Agenda 21 in their sectors. The Business Council for Sustainable Development, which made such an important contribution at Rio with its report, *Changing Course,* has been reconstituted with a commitment to continuing leadership in effecting the change of course it called for at the Earth Summit. And the International Chamber of Commerce has brought together a similarly impressive group of business leaders in its World Industry Council for the Environment. Many of the world's cities are establishing their Agenda 21 under the aegis of the International Council of Local Environmental Initiatives. And similar initiatives are proliferating at the community and sector levels in every region of the world.

It seems clear that UNCED has produced a broad and growing constituency throughout the world that is committed to fulfilling the hopes and expectations engendered in Rio. This will infuse the political process with new energies, which can provide the basis for changes in the political mindset that are needed to make the transition to a sustainable future. The momentum generated by Rio must be maintained if the global partnership required to forge a new world order is to be realized.

The main elements of this global partnership are a new economic regime, a new security regime, a new legal regime, and a new multilateral system.

A New Economic Regime

The economic system that has produced unprecedented levels of growth and prosperity for the societies of the industrialized world has also produced severe imbalances and disparities, which are simply not compatible with a secure and sustainable world order. The concentration of population growth and poverty in developing countries and of economic growth in industrialized countries is a recipe for deepening conflict and disorder, as seen in Somalia and Rwanda. At a time when cooperation within and among societies has never been more imperative, divisions are becoming more entrenched. There is a real risk of a growing rich–poor conflict both within and among nations.

A new global partnership would not be viable without a new economic regime. Dr. Stephan Schmidheiny and forty-eight chief executive officers of the world's leading corporations, who formed the Business Council for Sustainable Development, made it clear that what is required is a veritable ecoindustrial revolution. This new industrial revolution would be driven by the full integration of the environment into economic life. Hence, it would involve reshaping the entire industrial system. Efficient use of materials and energy, as well as efficiency in eliminating, recycling, and disposing of waste would be the keys to both environmental and economic success. Far from being a drag on the economy, the transition to environmentally sound and sustainable development offers the prospect of revitalizing economies and opening up an exciting new era of opportunity for innovation and creativity.

In most countries, the fiscal system provides tax incentives and subsidies to meet a variety of political and public policy objectives usually unrelated to environmental considerations. Many of these "perverse subsidies" have become deeply entrenched and difficult to change. Agricultural subsidies are a prime example. Many of these, in addition to their economic cost and the distortions they create in the market economy, also provide incentives for environmentally unsound economic practices. This is even more true in the energy field, where public spending on exploration incentives and depletion allowances far outweigh any financial rewards for increasing energy efficiency. One of the most important things governments must do is to extensively review and reorient the system of incentives and penalties that motivate the economic behavior of corporations and individuals to ensure that it provides positive incentives for environmentally sound and sustainable behavior.

It is fully in accord with market economy principles that each product or transaction should internalize the costs to which it gives rise, including environmental costs. When products are priced on a basis that does not include the environmental costs incurred in producing or disposing of them, these costs are not negated; they are simply added to the environmental deficit, which must eventually be met, and usually at far greater cost. Attaching monetary value to the natural processes that sustain life itself and to abstract terms like "cultural values" and "leisure" is not easy. But when the vast majority of environmentally destructive practices are justified by economic evaluations that do not take into account the depreciation of natural capital, these practices clearly need to be revised and means found to account for and to internalize environmental costs. Decision makers must be provided with information about the true cost of their intended actions. The Earth Summit recommended that all governments adopt new methods of presenting their national accounts so as to reflect environmental costs and benefits and to institute measures that will lead to internalizing environmental costs in all economic transactions.

Internalizing environmental costs has special implications for international trade. When the industrialized world imports products from developing countries at costs that do not reflect the destruction of natural capital, it exacts an environmental subsidy from them, which impoverishes their resource base and contributes to global environmental deterioration. Yet when industrialized countries unilaterally impose restrictions on imports from developing countries to meet their own requirements, they inflict immediate and often critical damage on the vulnerable economies of developing countries. These double standards can only be resolved by international agreements that respect the interests of all parties and protect the integrity of the global environment.

All of this adds up to profound changes within national economies. These must be accompanied by equally far-reaching changes in the system of arrangements that guide the world economy, particularly with regard to developing countries. For the poor and the weak, interdependence is not an unmitigated blessing. In many cases it exacerbates their vulnerabilities. A new economic regime must lend support to developing countries by facilitating their access to additional flows of financial resources, both private and official, and to industrialized countries' markets and technology.

Of the estimated $625 billion per year that developing countries will require for the full implementation of Agenda 21 provisions, 80 percent, or $500 billion, must come from redeployment of their own internal resources. Of the additional $125 billion per year, approximately $55 billion may be available from existing Official Development Assistance (ODA), leaving a gap of some $70 billion. Under today's conditions these funds will not be easy to come by. Certainly it is unrealistic to expect this funding in the form of more "foreign aid" in traditional terms, although it would be conceivable if industrialized countries met the internationally accepted target of .7 percent of GDP for ODA. Nevertheless, as an indispensable investment in environmental security, it is in the interest of industrialized countries to ensure that these needs are met.

Despite the need of developing countries for concessional financing, they would prefer to earn their way through fair and open access to industrialized countries' markets for their exports. The recent round of GATT negotiations produced some significant improvements in trade conditions for developing countries. However, GATT still falls far short of providing the open access that would relieve developing countries from dependence on development assistance and, at the same time, benefit consumers in industrialized countries. Unfortunately, current tendencies in industrialized countries seem to be running in the other direction, in favor of more protectionism.

A number of proposals have been made over the years for some form of international taxation, including taxes on international trade or energy, or fees for the use of the international commons by aircraft and ships. To date, governments have been unwilling to yield taxing power to any international authority. However, the combination of the substantial resources required for global environmental security and governments' reluctance to help by adding to already overstretched budgets may soon make such taxes possible. Indeed, at some point, they are inevitable. In the first instance they may come about through the designation of a portion of nationally levied taxes, like a carbon tax.

A New Security Regime

Economic interdependence both requires and contributes to world peace and security. However, as the proliferation of ethnic and regional conflicts since the end of the Cold War demonstrates, the end of the era of superpower conflict has not produced a peaceful and secure world. What is now needed is a system of international security guarantees for nations and minorities based on clear enforcement criteria, under UN auspices, with prior commitment by UN members states to the means of enforcing such guarantees.

The validity and effectiveness of such a system requires that it be enforced uniformly. Selective enforcement, however useful it may be in particular cases — such as that of Iraq's occupation of Kuwait — will be neither a sufficient deterrent to offenders nor a sufficiently reliable reassurance for small nations and vulnerable peoples. The system of guarantees must carry the full commitment of the major world powers to ensure its consistent and dependable enforcement.

A new security regime must also embody a commitment to environmental security and the redeployment of some of the resources presently directly to military security — human skills, research and development capacities, and financial resources. People and nations have always been willing to give priority to allocating resources required for ensuring their security. The evidence presented at the Earth Summit makes it clear that the entire human family today faces risks to its security caused by excessive impacts on the Earth's environment and life systems that are beyond anything ever faced from conventional military threats.

A New Legal Regime

A new legal regime must be based essentially on the extension into international life of the rule of law, together with reliable mechanisms for accountability and enforcement that provide the basis for the effective functioning of national societies. The world is a long way from this today. UNCED defined many of the needs for the continued development of international law, including the strengthening of existing instruments and agreements on new ones. However, even this would be only a short step toward establishing an effective international legal regime.

The conventions on climate change and biodiversity, despite their deficiencies, represent significant accomplishments, provided that they are followed up by vigorous and continuing efforts to strengthen them while ensuring their full acceptance, ratification, and implementation. United States agreement to the Convention on Climate Change came at the cost of specific targets and timetables, to which most other nations were prepared to agree. But the unwillingness of the United States to agree to the Convention on Biodiversity did not prevent others, including some of its closest allies, from signing it. Both conventions were signed by representatives of more than 150 nations at Rio, and in the end, under the new Clinton Administration, the United States also signed the Convention on Biodiversity.

The actual convening of UNCED and the decision to have the climate change and biodiversity conventions signed at the conference provided the impetus necessary to reach agreement on difficult and complex issues within the two years allowed by the preparatory process. However, some of the toughest issues remain to be resolved.

The agreement at Rio to initiate negotiations on a convention on desertification was an encouraging step forward, particularly for developing countries. However, the hard-won agreement on forestry principles was not accompanied by agreement to begin the further process of negotiating a convention.

Since Stockholm, there has been a significant increase in the number and range of new international legal instruments negotiated, covering issues from regional seas to endangered species, from toxic wastes to ocean dumping. Unfortunately, there has not been equivalent progress in implementing and enforcing these agreements.

The whole process of negotiation has placed severe strains on the capacities of many countries, particularly developing countries, which are likely to hinder further progress in new negotiations and implementation. This underscores the importance of the capacity-building provisions of Agenda 21, because developing countries will be increasingly reluctant and unable to participate fully in international environment and development cooperation unless they are able to strengthen their scientific, technological, professional, and institutional capacities. It is clearly in the interest of industrialized countries to help developing countries strengthen these capacities.

The Rio Declaration and Agenda 21 are major new examples of "soft law," based on political agreement rather than on legally binding instruments. Although not legally binding, they provide a basis for voluntary cooperation, which enables the action process to proceed expeditiously and paves the way for the negotiation of binding agreements. Although these cannot serve as long-term substitutes for enforceable legal measures, their value should not be minimized. After all, until there is an effective and enforceable legal regime at the international level, political commitment is the primary basis for cooperative action in negotiating and enforcing legal instruments.

The International Court of Justice offers another possible basis for legal reform. In recent times there have been signs of an increasing propensity to accord the International Court of Justice a more important role in the enforcement of environmental law. There have even been proposals to give it mandatory jurisdiction in some areas. Rio did not provide concrete progress towards realizing their prospect, but it should help give it accelerated impetus.

Two other developments offer hope for change. Measures that permit victims of environmental damage originating outside of their countries to have access to the courts of the source country are particularly promising and innovative legal devices. So is the growing acceptance of the "polluter-pays" principle and principles of responsibility, information, and participation. Although in many cases they were expressed in the Rio Declaration in conditional terms, they nevertheless provide a potentially powerful basis for progress towards establishing a new international legal regime. One of the key priorities in the period ahead must be to work for their broad acceptance and application.

A New Multilateral System

A particularly important principle of governance provides that all functions be carried out at the level closest to the people affected – this is the level at which such functions can be carried out most effectively. Even with the application of this principle, more and more functions will have to be performed at the international level. In many cases, if not most, the international role will be to provide the context and framework for national, local, and sectoral actions.

The UN, together with its agencies and organizations, provides the framework for carrying out those functions requiring global cooperation. Although there is now a greater appreciation of its usefulness, it is still the newest, least understood, and least supported of the various levels of governance. The UN's approaching fiftieth anniversary presents a unique opportunity, as well as an imperative need, to strengthen and revitalize the UN as the centerpiece for a new world order.

An a priori need in this respect is resolution of its current financial crisis, caused primarily by a number of nations, including the United States, not meeting their obligations to pay their share of assessed dues. The UN, unlike other levels of governance, has neither taxing nor borrowing powers. It will ultimately need both. In the meantime, the dues of member states, which are after all treaty commitments, should be treated as due and payable at the first of each year with interest accruing from that date. The UN should have the right to borrow against these obligations. There is precedent for this in the World Bank's borrowing very large sums of money against the security of the unpaid capital guaranteed by its members governments.

Great importance should be attached to provisions in the mandate and modalities for the new Sustainable Development Commission for monitoring, review, and accountability with respect to the financing of Agenda 21. If there is no clear link between financial commitments and programming, the entire Agenda 21 review process could be reduced to a meaningless charade. Already they are some signs of attempts to weaken the mandates and capacities of the Commission and its secretariat. Future governmental decisions regarding these institutional measures will be an important test of the strength of the commitments made at Rio. The Commission also provides a positive opportunity for substantial strengthening of the UN's role in the environmental and developmental fields.

One dimension with respect to these institutional issues is the provision to be made for participation by nongovernmental organizations and constituencies. The successes achieved at Rio were greatly due to the high degree of public awareness and unprecedented levels of participation by nongovernmental organizations and citizen groups. It is of vital importance that people build on this experience and provide broader channels for participation and for private–public partnerships—locally, nationally, and internationally.

UNCED made it clear that the future of the planet and its people cannot be left in the hands of political leaders. Although their role is important, their involvement is not sufficient. On the whole, the agreements reached at Rio represent an important launching pad for the new global partnership that is the key to our common future. But the major concern is the depth of commitment that underlies their agreements. At a time in history when the world hungers for leadership, there is all too little evidence of it.

The dynamics of the political process today tend to reward those who are responsive to the current public mood. In a very real sense, leadership must come from the people, which means that focusing continuing attention on the issues that shape the future and ensure that people have access to reliable, objective information so that they can take positions on those issues and reflect them in their own actions and through the political process.

UNCED has also made clear that there must be a much closer linkage between science and decision making. More knowledge is needed, of course, but the most urgent priority is the dissemination and application of existing knowledge. This means making it available to those who need it at the times and in the forms in which they can use it to guide their decisions and actions.

The world is confronting new challenges of almost baffling complexity at a time of crisis in governance. Even the strongest and most successful industrialized nations are reaching the limits of what their governments can do to deal effectively with these issues. Necessity, more than ideology, is driving a reduction in the role of all governments and increasing the reliance on the private sector. In addition, responsibilities are moving both downstream to state and local governments and upstream to the international level. For developing countries, this experience is especially traumatic because governments have played a dominant role in unifying and shaping their societies. Yet in many, if not most, developing countries today, the capacity to govern and the governmental institutions themselves have seriously deteriorated. For the most part, this has not been offset by a sufficient development of private sector capacities.

The engagement of unprecedented numbers of nongovernmental organizations in preparation for UNCED and at Rio provides the basis for continuing and deepening citizen concern and action on issues that individuals perceive as critical to their own futures. UNCED produced an explosion of awareness about these issues in all parts of the world. We should be encouraged by evidence that those who participated in this process have gone back to their own communities and organizations committed to ensuring the implementation of Agenda 21. As a result of UNCED, the networks that link these people and organizations together have been strengthened, and many new alliances have been formed. To facilitate this process, the Earth Council has been established to foster the development of an informed, aware, and concerned global constituency, thus ensuring a continuing focus on the issues addressed at Rio and a coordinated effort for the implementation of its results. A secretariat has been established in

San José, Costa Rica, in response to Costa Rica's offer to host the Earth Council's headquarters.

Conclusion

The Earth Summit provided an exciting vision of a new and more hopeful future as the twenty-first century approaches. It established the direction for the path toward that future. Only time will tell if this vision will be a deceptive mirage or the dawning of a new era of sustainable peace, harmony, and progress for the peoples of the earth. There is still time to change, but no time to lose.

Inertia is as powerful a force in human affairs as it is in the physical world. Even as change is discussed, we continue along the same path toward a future in which civilization will be unsustainable. Every year, every day, every hour that we continue along this path reduces the prospect of "changing course" peacefully and successfully. Many claim that it is not realistic to call for fundamental change in times of economic difficulty, but experience suggests that it is precisely at such times that change is possible, even inevitable. Far better to manage a process of willful, constructive change than to be engulfed by the tumultuous and uncontrolled changes that will occur people continue along the present path.

Stockholm and the Earth Summit and all the other initiatives of the Environmental Renaissance of 1972 to 1994 provided the basis for a constructive process of change; only people can provide the political will required to effect it, acting through their own professions, in their own communities and organizations, and through the political process at all levels of government. Rio prescribed no quick or easy fix for the perils that confront our planet, but it did point the way through those perils to a more hopeful and promising future for the entire human community.

Section 2

The Challenge of Empowering People

Nafis Sadik

This book discusses and proposes tangible recommendations for ending poverty and securing the well-being of each individual in all countries, now and in the future. Until the end of the Cold War, the greatest perceived risk to universal well-being was nuclear war between continents. This has apparently been removed, but as it recedes hostilities have appeared on our own doorsteps. Some 29 million people have been killed in local or civil wars in the last 50 years. Expenditure on arms is 5 percent of total world income.

During the second part of the twentieth century, the world's wealth has increased many times over, but it is overwhelmingly in the hands of less than 20 percent of the world's people. The income of the richest fifth may be 15 to 20 times that of the poorest fifth, and its share of the world's wealth even greater.

In response to famine and emergency, we are willing to help strangers, even in far distant countries, but we are apparently less willing to explore and deal with the causes of hunger and conflict, even among close neighbors.

The end of the Cold War apparently removed the security rationale for development assistance; the economic rationale has been weakened by its perceived failure in many countries to spur economic take-off. At the same time, successfully industrializing countries are perceived to be competing for markets with the industrialized nations.

The picture is clouded further by the apparent surge in numbers of people crossing international boundaries in search of a better life, or escaping threats to life itself. In Europe and North America, there is less sympathy and more opposition to immigrants than at any time since 1945.

The Need for Commitment

Yet, the need for an understanding and commitment to development is greater than ever before. At present, some 1 billion people live in poverty and some 800 million people are malnourished. The same numbers as those of almost four decades ago. The number of refugees is 20 million and rising daily. The numbers of poor people in the poorest parts of the world are rising faster than ever before; average annual population growth during this decade is 95 million a year, nearly all of it in today's developing countries, and over half in the Indian subcontinent and Africa, the poorest regions of the world.

The world's resources are still sufficient to support all the world's people, but it may not always be so. Poverty, on the scale it exists today, damages the environment by sheer weight of numbers. At the same time, development can also damage the environment. Five countries, namely China, India, Indonesia, Brazil, and Mexico, together account for more than half the world's population and a small but growing share of the world's GNP. The economies of these countries are growing at a minimum of 5 percent a year. They aspire to the same levels of affluence as Western Europe, Japan, or the United States. This is a perfectly legitimate aspiration, but if they succeed without dramatic changes in the technologies they use, the results could be catastrophic for the global environment. Their success will turn, quite literally, to ashes.

Challenge and Opportunity

The challenge, in a word, has never been greater. It is the same as ever — to defeat poverty and injustice. But it is also more diverse than ever. In a new and uncertain world, it may seem more difficult than ever.

The opportunity, however, is also greater than ever. Collectively, we have at our disposal not only more knowledge and experience but better technology; not only more technical resources but better awareness of how to use them; not only wealth but wisdom.

Let us look briefly at the issues before us:

- Economic growth has lifted millions into prosperity, but the poorest countries and the poorest groups have been left behind. There is a growing gap between rich and poor, within and between countries; among the poor there is a disproportionate number of women and children.

- Despite all efforts, the numbers of illiterate and the numbers of the poor are unchanged from twenty years ago.

- The biggest-ever cohorts of young people are moving into the workforce, but employment creation has not kept up.

- The environmental cost of population and economic growth has been huge and is increasing.

- There are more people and their numbers are growing faster than ever before.

In the past, the tendency has been to assume that these questions would be answered by economic development. Now we face a dilemma. We have learned that poverty increases inequities and imbalances between people and nations, and that economic development by itself will not correct them. In recent years, we have also had to face the phenomenon of economic growth without commensurate increases in employment, so that in developing countries fewer and fewer of the increasing numbers of young people who are coming into the cities are able to find work. At the same time, in the industrialized countries, social systems are cracking under the strain of heavy unemployment and an increasing number of elderly people. Both developing and industrialized countries are subject to increasing threats to public order and peaceful existence, apparently independent of overall economic conditions.

A Direct Approach

Through the discontinuities and contradictions of economic growth, we have learned that countries must address the issue of poverty and powerlessness directly, and that this can be done even in the absence of additional resources. We have learned, for example, that investing in reproductive health and family planning, education, and literacy programs for women is possible even in relatively poor societies. We have learned that the payoff is so important that this investment cannot be deferred. We have also learned that benefits can be immediate, real, and tangible, such as lower infant mortality as a result of better family planning or lower health expenditure from a reduction in unsafe abortions.

We have also learned these issues must be addressed directly, because economic development depends on it. We have learned in fact that social development is the key to economic development, rather than the other way round, and that putting individuals at the center of the development process is the key to social development.

Reversing Convention

Conventional wisdom has, in fact, been reversed: better health care and education are the way to economic prosperity, not its byproduct; equal access to the benefits of social development is the basis, not the result of, successful programs; women are the actors and the instigators of social and economic change rather than obstacles in its path; establishing individual choices and the ability to choose is not a luxury but a necessity.

We are asserting, in short, that individual empowerment is a condition — not a consequence — of national development.

Investing in Empowerment

Investing in empowerment is like any other kind of investment — it offers a tangible return in the form of individuals, families, and communities that are better equipped to meet the challenges of the modern world. It is not a short-term investment; over the long term, it will put economic development on a firm footing. Because it implies a degree of equity in and among nations and between generations, investing in empowerment also offers the prospect of sustainable economic growth.

Success is not guaranteed. The approach to economic and social development has so far been biased heavily towards the economic side. The terms in which success is measured are equally heavily weighted on the economic side. Social development is still seen as a desirable offshoot rather than an essential precondition of economic success. The contribution of women in particular is consistently underreported and undervalued.

Building Blocks of Empowerment

During the 1970s, the UN convened, on an ad hoc basis, a series of world conferences on a range of issues, including the environment, population, food, human settlements, advancement of women, and desertification. These conferences made available to the international community a wealth of policy inputs. However, these sectoral initiatives have resulted in both an excessive diffusion of responsibility and a loss of coherence. At present, there is wide realization within the UN system of the need for an integrated approach and more effective pooling of the results of existing work.

The Secretary-General has recommended that the recent series of major UN conferences on social and economic development should draw strength from the outcomes of the preceding conferences. The 1994 International Conference on Population and Development, held in Cairo, has been a major building block in the challenge of empowering people. Its Plan of Action has direct relevance to the World Summit for Social Development, to take place in Copenhagen in 1995. Thus the recommendations of the two must be integrated to assist the UN's family system to translate recommendations into a series of concrete and multidimensional actions.

The Cairo Programme of Action is a very comprehensive document. All sixteen chapters focus on one central goal – the improvement of the quality of life of all people, in particular the eradication of poverty, the need for sustained economic growth, the creation of productive jobs, and the empowerment and advancement of women. The document acknowledges that efforts to slow population growth, to reduce poverty, to achieve economic progress, to empower people, and to increase environmental protection are mutually reinforcing. It also recognizes that there can be no sustainable human development, without the full and equal participation of women in all aspects of development. Thus, the empowerment of women, for the first time, has become an explicit cornerstone in the formulation and implementation of both national and international policies. Education is seen as one of the most important means of empowering people in order to participate fully in the development process.

Conclusion

Today, the international community is in a unique position to confront the single but diversified challenge of empowering individuals and ending poverty. Most governments and nongovernmental organizations are cognizant of the prerequisites of securing peace and development in our lifetime. They know that they have to commit themselves to a human-centered approach to development and that development must be based on the well-being of the individual. They are also aware of the importance of good governance, including the ability of government to deliver the services that empowerment implies.

The role of NGOs as intermediaries between governments and the governed and the new concept of the "civil society" in which the public, their representatives in parliamentary, professional and community organizations, religious groups, and the private sector produce outcomes that would be impossible if each group worked separately.

The series of major UN conferences that started in 1992 with UNCED and was followed by the International Conference on Population and Development, the Social Summit, the Women's Conference, and HABITAT II, reinforce the connection between economic and social development, linking issues of governance and social justice. Through these conferences and working from different perspectives, the international community can develop approaches to global questions, such as harnessing the great social power of multinational corporations in an economically diverse world, and bringing them into partnership with national organizations. It can propose bold solutions to thorny questions such as immigration; suggesting ways in which the dependency burdens of industrialized countries could be relieved by the large proportions of working-age people in developing countries, to the benefit of both.

The world faces the great challenge of empowering people by defeating poverty. Certainly, the different aspects of this challenge vary between countries and within countries. Our response must be similarly varied, and adapted to local and national circumstances.

Section 3

Civil Society and Social Development

Juan Somavia

We need a more humane world. If this message is to come from somewhere, it must come from the United Nations. With all its complications, contradictions, and difficulties, the UN is still the only place in which governments and civil society—private business, nongovernmental organizations, labor unions, churches, political parties, and people's movements—can come together and collectively decide to move forward in certain definite directions.

The directions of the past simply cannot continue as the course for the future. This is an era in which the forces of exclusion, isolation, and discrimination result in tremendous insecurity—evidenced in poverty, unemployment, and social disintegration. We cannot go on talking about human rights, democracy, and the marvels of the open economy unless we acknowledge that side by side with dramatic change, we are generating great levels of exclusion. These express themselves, first and foremost, in enormous levels of poverty, along with crime, violence, drug abuse, and ongoing environmental degradation in countries, rich and poor.

The World Summit for Social Development offers a unique opportunity for governments and people to discuss together the challenges of today and to chart the course for tomorrow. Within the series of UN summits and conferences, the World Social Summit is but one gathering in a now two-decades old series. Yet it is different—because of its stress on intersectoral analysis of problems and the search for integrated solutions in which people are truly coequal actors with governments in carrying out and implementing action plans for change.

Whereas past UN meetings have focused on a single issue in all of its complex dimensions—for example, the environment, population, education, or human rights—the Summit aims to integrate the contemporary problems of poverty, unemployment, and social integration by using a paradigm that equates values with empirical evidence. It is a UN meeting, in which the assessments, experiences, hopes, and plans of people themselves are central to the process of crafting not only a declaration of political commitment on the part of heads of state, but also a Program of Action for finding solutions.

The Summit aims to bring the complex problem of humanism — of considering issues in terms of people, not purely in terms of structures — to the negotiating table at the UN; to the Ministry of Foreign Affairs in innumerable capitals; to meetings of municipal authorities in cities and towns throughout the world; and to people, within their workplaces, neighborhoods, and homes. We live in a world in which the need to bridge the public and private, state and market, local and global dimensions of our shared reality has never been greater.

Heretofore, nations and people were fundamentally separated by the ideological, political, and attendant economic dichotomies of the Cold War. With its passing, one great chasm — between East and West — was closed. With it went the multiple fissures that grew in its wake, which were the sources of many internal and external conflicts throughout the world. Today, the sources of conflict in the world are multipolar and multicausal. Some were camouflaged in the Cold War years and have only now surged to the fore; others, as age-old as the conflict between haves and have-nots, or between extremists and relativists, have reemerged with a vengeance. All of us, policy makers and publics alike, rich and poor, old and young, consequently suffer the insecurity and instability of change. It is our interdependence which binds us — as it always has, in birth and death, and always will.

The growth of an ever-increasingly global marketplace is another feature of the current landscape. Within it, the values of competitiveness and efficiency have begun to outgrow the specific, natural spaces and limits that they have traditionally held. Competitiveness and efficiency, as well as the changing technical knowledge and social customs they have begotten — seemingly indispensable to progress — evolved so rapidly that we often failed to realize that no matter how rapidly these shifts take place, one thing remains constant: the nature of human relations.

The nature of a relationship in a family, the nature of the relationship in educating children, the nature of the relationship in a couple, the nature of the relationship in work, the nature of one's response to the types of things that mark old age — these do not really change fundamentally from epoch to epoch. Indeed, people seemingly overwhelmed by sociopolitical and geoeconomic change are nonetheless very clear about the nature of problems that directly affect them, their families, and their communities. The world-weary citizen is more often than not a surprisingly decisive voter; throughout the world, politics seem increasingly local and driven, in great measure, by concern over the economics of human security.

The challenge of putting economics at the service of the needs of human beings is thus at the heart of the Summit's agenda. The Summit is about breaking with the past characterization of economics as a dry, dismal science, divorced from human experience and lived out among widget makers in the splendid isolation of graphs and derivations. It is about understanding the fundamental link between economic growth and social development—namely, that the two are interdependent and promote each other. Broad-based sustainable economic growth is a prerequisite for social development, while social development is a necessary foundation for equitable and sustained economic expansion. To that end, patterns of growth are as important as rates of growth.

If the Summit is truly to have relevance in the lives of those people on whom it ostensibly focuses, heads of state, in partnership with key actors in civil society (chief among them, leaders in business and the labor movement), must affirm that in the long run, the most productive policies and investments are those that promote equality of opportunity by empowering people to make full use of their own capacities and resources. This, in turn, means taking action to staunch the waste of human resources and the ineffectiveness of market functioning so evident in Africa, the least-developed countries, and countries in transition. It means enlarging market access for countries in a rapidly changing global trade arena and increasing the access of people within countries to both domestic and international markets.

It also means reexamining the nature of employment (that is, the fundamental nature of work) even in the wealthiest countries, where rates of unemployment remain stubbornly high. Therein, an inexcusable number of women, young people, and older persons—among them, many late-career workers and resourceful volunteers of all ages—are "underutilized" (not to mention, unfulfilled) given the constraints of economic systems in which narrow patterns of economic growth progressively marginalize them.

The Summit is thus about the empowerment of people as members of civil society and as economic actors; it is about enabling people to satisfy basic human needs while at the same time taking responsibility for their own lives and for the well-being of their communities, based on values of personal dignity, mutual respect, and unity in diversity. It is about securing safety while at the same time releasing the positive forces of creativity and full human potential. The Summit's greatest contribution will, in the end, be measured by the degree to which it serves as a catalyst for enabling people to determine the directions their societies will take in the twenty-first century.

Notably, the World Summit for Social Development marks the first time that heads of state will come together to discuss, in an integrated manner, the daily problems of ordinary people throughout the world. It is a first step, and we must make that first step as ambitious as possible. At the Summit's heart is a collective commitment on the part of heads of state, in the name of the people they represent, to eliminate the most extreme forms of poverty.

Obviously, one does not wish poverty away—no matter how rich or poor the region, country, or community. Yet by beginning with a commitment to eliminate the most extreme forms of poverty, on a date to be set by each country and in a manner carried out in accordance with the policy priorities in those countries (notably, with the assurance of the international community to support countries, as necessary, and the commitment of those nations to steward their resources effectively), the UN system will have the chance to act as a catalyst in this process. At the same time, people will have a concrete benchmark against which to measure their leaders' political commitment to bettering the quality of human life and progress.

In this regard, it is critical to remember that the most extreme forms of poverty cannot be eradicated through resource allocation alone. If so, we would have achieved this goal long ago; there is plenty of money to do so. Rather, this goal is achieved by the empowerment and organization of people at the local level — people who are able to produce processes that truly change the lives of themselves and others at that level. In committing to eliminate the most extreme forms of poverty, heads of state at the Summit can actually take the bold step of saying: We commit ourselves to the goal of eradicating poverty in the world, through decisive national actions and international cooperation, as a moral, political, and economic imperative of humankind.

Implicitly, governments acknowledge herein that "it is up to each of us to organize ourselves, in order to have the discussions, to have the debates, to produce the ideas, to think together how it is that we will address poverty as a common national problem, not just a problem of income distribution between rich and poor within and among nations."

Activism at the local level will be essential to achieve this goal; despite the complexity and enormity of a world in which intersectoral problems, intrastate conflicts, and international markets are the norm, individual people are nonetheless at the center of all action — individuals, with their own hopes, frustrations, dreams, and values.

Conclusion

The World Summit for Social Development is thus about placing the security of people at the center of the UN agenda, not just in the context of the Summit, but in statecraft and international relations, in discussions of global economic decision making, resources management, and rule making. The Summit offers the UN an opportunity to play a role similar to that it played in shepherding the drafting of the Universal Declaration of Human Rights; in approving the Resolution on Decolonization; and in taking the decisions necessary to pave the way for the end of apartheid. The Summit could not come at a more fitting moment than the fiftieth anniversary of the UN. Let us meet the challenge of realizing its promise together.

An Agenda for People

Üner Kırdar and Leonard Silk

We have arrived at the end of a long collaborative survey. We have seen that despite the many advances over the past fifty years in the quest for empowering people, there is still a large unfinished agenda to be fulfilled. We have examined both in our overview chapter and in the sections of the book why global poverty is worsening, unemployment is on the rise, and societies are disintegrating.

What conclusions are we to draw from this retrospective? What are the prospects for the future?

Perhaps the most important conclusion that emerges is that there is an urgent need for a renaissance in development thinking. True development requires a balance between economic growth targets and social goals. Without this balance, long-term development cannot occur, and progress in meeting social goals will never be sustained. The international community must renew its commitment to the original goals of the United Nations—building people's security. No provision of the United Nations Charter will enable the organization to make the world a secure place if people have no security in their homes and their jobs, and no freedom to express their opinions, wants, and desires. Therefore, development efforts should be people centered. They should generate not only economic growth but distribute its benefits equitably. They should regenerate the environment, instead of destroying it. The should empower people rather than marginalizing them. They should enlarge people's choices and their opportunities. Governments, international organizations, and all other new actors in the international community must contribute to achieving these goals.

The World Summit for Social Development which will take place in Copenhagen in March 1995 provides a unique opportunity to achieve these objectives. All world leaders must join forces to formulate an urgently needed agenda for curing some of the world's major social ills.

In order to assist them in this momentous and urgent task, the participants of the Stockholm Roundtable and the contributors to this book submit here below a series of recommendations:

- The goal of the Summit should be to initiate the preparation of fresh designs for national and global social contracts that will help achieve acceptable standards of human dignity and well-being. At the national level, this could mean a renewal of the contract between the state and the people, putting people, especially poor people, first. At the international level, this could mean a renewed commitment to key goals of the United Nations charter: higher standards of living, full employment, social progress, and political and personal freedom.

- The Summit should be used as an opportunity to reconsider the roles of the state and the market and the traditional ideas of social safety nets.

- Delegates to the Summit should strive for an "Agenda for People" and a new declaration of human responsibilities, not just a declaration of human rights. They should also strive for a new system for monitoring progress in maintaining these responsibilities.

- Delegates to the Summit should forge a compact in which nations agree to prepare their own strategies to reduce poverty. These strategies should empower people and increase opportunities for productive employment. The nationally developed strategies should become the basis for assistance from aid donors.

- Delegates should recognize the role of civil society and the media in empowering people.

- People should have access to certain types of information as a tool for social change. This information includes national statistics on military spending and the arms trade and details about World Bank-International Monetary Fund lending.

- Delegates at the summit should note the need for an "early-warning system" to identify potential cases of social disintegration. But such a system will be worthless unless the international community can agree on how to respond to the system's alarms. The international community must replace the present system of ad hoc interventions with a standard, universal system for intervention.

- Delegates must appeal to the world community to shift mindless investments in arms to judicious investments in people.

- Structural adjustment programs must be changed so they protect people's security. Social spending should be the last thing to be cut. Subsidies for the rich should be cut before subsidies for the poor. Delegates to the Summit should call for a new "social contract" and endorse the idea of "human adjustment loans" by international financial institutions to protect the poor during periods of economic transition.

- Delegates must also recognize the need for structural adjustment in the industrialized countries.

- The new form of "social contract" should be based not on donor edict but on a genuine dialogue between governments and citizens' groups, the Bretton Woods institutions, aid donors, and United Nations agencies. The dialogue could result in taxing windfall winners from structural adjustment programs and owners of undeveloped land and in reducing military expenditures. The funds generated could be used to maintain and improve the poor's access to health, education, clean water, and other social services.

- Safety nets that address areas of health, education, unemployment, falling incomes, and other personal tragedies should be an integral part of social policy.

- The poor must gain access to fair and effective justice systems, and regulations that penalize the poor should be abolished.

- Women's access to basic education, skills training, health care, nutrition services, family planning, "productive resources," and markets should be expanded.

- Assets and security of tenure should be redistributed. This includes rural land reform and urban land security for the poor and fair and equal rights for women.

- Governments should decentralize many activities and introduce mechanisms to increase accountability to the poor. Governments should also strengthen structures of civil society to aid participation by the poor in national policy decisions.

- The international community should establish and enforce global environmental and social standards for transnational corporations.

- Governments and multilateral creditors should relieve countries' debt burdens.

Institutional, professional and personal changes are essential in achieving the goal of "putting poor people first." The following recommendations for change will help meet that goal.

- *Institutional changes.* Development organizations need a culture of participatory management if they are to successfully promote shared and fair development policies. Information must flow freely among all actors. To mount an effective attack on poverty, multilateral institutions need to reduce competition, increase collaboration, and devote resources to areas where they have a comparative advantage.

- *Professional changes.* Putting poor people first requires an overhaul of professional ethics and actions. Development experts must learn from poor people and base actions on the special needs and circumstances of each community.

• *Personal changes.* Putting poor people first entails changes in individuals' values, behavior, and attitudes. People who have traditionally been in positions of authority must become listeners and learners.

Expansion of Productive Employment

• All governments should commit themselves to full utilization of human resources. Full employment should be the central goal of all economic and social policy. Social integration and the eradication of poverty depend on the expansion of productive and remunerative work, including wage employment, self-employment, and employment in cooperative enterprises.

• Governments should explore all alternatives for ensuring full employment with macroeconomic stability. This means that full employment takes precedence as an objective in policy formulation.

• Countries need an international economic "enabling environment" to attain goals for expanding productive employment. The main elements for creating this environment include:

  • A pledge by industrial countries to coordinate macroeconomic policies to ensure a minimum overall growth rate of between 3 and 3.5 percent.

  • A dismantling of protectionist policies in both developed and developing countries.

  • Exclusive allocation of official development assistance to the poorest countries that demonstrate effective use of resources and economic growth with social and gender equity.

  • A reduction in the debt burden of the developing countries, especially the poorest ones. This should include forgiveness of officially held debt.

  • Trade reform in developing countries to promote international commerce and boost trade and investment among developing countries.

  • A small tax on international capital movement to help reduce fluctuations in exchange rates stemming from speculative capital movement. The proceeds could fund environmental protection, increased development assistance, and debt reduction.

• Investment should rise to promote higher growth in developed and developing countries. Investment must be backed by a high rate of domestic savings. The goal is to have job creating growth. A system for reaching this goal includes the following.

  • A foreign trade regime that adopts careful support for infant industries but avoids overvaluation of exchange rates, discrimination against imports, and dependence on import quotas.

  • A pricing system that provides reasonable indicators of scarcities and is free of arbitrary controls.

  • An economic environment that encourages foreign investment.

- Special actions to help Sub-Saharan Africa. These actions include building up human capital, improving food production and distribution, establishing a base for export earnings, and diversifying economies.

- Governments should intervene in labor markets only to make them more efficient and responsive to the needs of the economy. Workers should have access to social protection, and everyone should have access to basic education. Governments should emphasize higher education that is of high quality and provides students with technical skills to aid countries' science-led sustainable development. And, all governments must guarantee certain human rights, such as the protection of children by making child labor unnecessary and illegal, creating freedom from forced labor, and allowing unrestricted organization of workers. Minimum-wage laws that do not overprice labor should be put in place.

- Government policies must be designed to unleash people's creativity and energy and enable them to become self-employed or entrepreneurs. This means the following.

  - Increased access to education.

  - Access to such resources as land and credit.

  - Reduction in regulations that impede entrepreneurship.

  - Improved infrastructure, particularly that which enables the working poor and small-scale entrepreneurs to raise their productivity and earnings.

  - Improved access by the agricultural sector to productive resources. This sector will have to absorb a significant proportion of the growing labor force. Improved access by the working poor to land would also help boost employment and labor productivity.

Enhancement of Social Integration

- In most cases, the initiative for reform must come from within countries, but must receive international support. In Africa, for example, some countries require a national and regional "shock" to restructure economies, diversify exports, increase savings and investment rates, and lower fertility rates.

- There are cases where an outside initiative must come first, but this shock should be accompanied whenever possible by national action. This has been the case, for instance, in Central America.

- In some cases, there should be a political shock rather than an economic one. And, external and internal changes must be realized simultaneously. One illustration is the Israeli–Palestinian issue. Another is the dissolution of the former Soviet Union.

- The management of expectations and pluralism is crucial. This is particularly applicable wherever expectations have been suppressed for a long time, as in South Africa. The only viable option in such a case is to set clear intermediate targets. These must be met at any price, so that the people experience progress toward the realization of their expectations and continue to support reforms.

- The most fundamental change must come from the heart and the mind. We must become more tolerant and respectful, show more solidarity with one another, and halt violence. Respect for human rights, freedom of expression and association, and true justice are the cornerstones of stable societies.
- Countries must develop or procure the skills to manage complex economic and political problems. Care must be taken in hiring foreign experts, who must be highly sensitive and observant.
- Promoting a flourishing civil society will help guarantee democracy and citizens' social and economic rights.
- Institutional reforms at the grassroots, national, and international levels are needed to respond to today's complex and overwhelming social problems.
- Discrimination against women must stop. This discrimination is morally wrong but is also a waste of resources.
- Governments should use public policies to promote solidarity and tolerance in multicultural societies. These policies include devolution of power, electoral reforms, and respect for different cultures, languages, and religions.
- Everyone needs to join forces to nurture an ethos and culture of world citizenship. Educational institutions, media, and individuals all have responsibilities to expand our moral horizons to include values of solidarity, tolerance, and partnership.
- Sometimes harmony may not lead to change. Conflict can therefore be an impetus for positive change.

International Reforms

- The World Summit for Social Development should give the Secretary-General of the United Nations a mandate to set up a blue-ribbon commission to establish a framework for development in the twenty-first century. The commission should review the potential for redirecting aid toward specific global objectives, changing the motivations and levels of future assistance and broadening the scope of development cooperation to include trade, investment, technology, and labor. Meanwhile, the international community should consider new methods for raising funds (e.g., an international currency transaction tax, environmental permits, and taxes on the arms trade) and for restructuring the United Nations in social and economic areas.
- The United Nations needs a high-level decision-making body to handle issues of social and economic security. Some possibilities include restructuring ECOSOC or creating an Economic Security Council. The

Bretton Woods institutions should work under the direction of one of these new social and economic security bodies.

- The World Summit for Social Development should set up a small (maximum 20-member) advisory group to permanently monitor global progress on social development. The group's annual report should cover progress by governments, transnationals, non-governmental organizations, and other institutions.

- The summit should endorse a 20:20 global compact described in the Overview as a first step in a comprehensive attack on global poverty.

Conclusion

In sum, without specific proposals an agenda for empowering people would be vacuous. The preceding suggestions have been advanced as a starting point. However, it is the role of governments and people, working together, to flesh out the agendas that will steadily reduce impoverishment and to implement these into effective action and change.

Contributors

Cynthia Hewitt de Alcántara, United Nations Research Institute for Social Development (UNRISD), Geneva.

Philip Allott, Professor, Trinity College, University of Cambridge, United Kingdom.

Benjamin Bassin, Ambassador, Ministry of Foreign Affairs, Helsinki.

Elwil Beukes, Professor, Department of Economics, University of the Orange Free State, South Africa.

Keith A. Bezanson, President, International Development Research Centre, Ottawa.

Ingunn Brandvoll, Sales Manager, Peterson Moss A/S, Norway.

Deborah Brautigam, Professor, Department of Economics, Program on Economic and Political Development, School of International and Public Affairs, American University, Washington, D.C.

Donald Brown, Deputy Vice President, International Fund for Agricultural Development.

Margaret Catley-Carlson, President, The Population Council, New York; and former Deputy Minister of Health and Welfare of Canada.

Robert Chambers, Professor, The Institute of Development Studies, University of Sussex, United Kingdom.

Stef Coetzee, Vice Principal, Research and Development, Potchefstroomse Universiteit for Higher Christian Education, South Africa.

Dag Ehrenpreis, Chief Economist, Swedish International Development Agency, Stockholm.

Louis Emmerij, Special Adviser to the President, Inter-American Development Bank, Washington, D.C.; and former president, OECD Development Centre.

Maria Figueroa, Research Assistant, United Nations Development Programme.

Dharam Ghai, Director, United Nations Research Institute for Social Development (UNRISD), Geneva.

Vladimir Gimpelson, Visiting Scholar, Russian Research Center, Center for International Affairs, Harvard University; and Head of Department, Institute of World Economy and International Relations, the Russian Academy of Sciences.

Keith Griffin, Chair, Department of Economics, University of California, Riverside.

Khadija Haq, Executive Director, North-South Roundtable, New York; and Senior Adviser on Education, United Nations International Children's Emergency Fund.

Mahbub ul Haq, Special Adviser to the Administrator, United Nations Development Programme, New York; and former Minister of Finance and Planning, Pakistan.

Vali Jamal, Senior Research Economist, International Labour Organization, Geneva.

Mats Karlsson, Under Secretary-General for Development Co-operation, Ministry of Foreign Affairs, Sweden.

Inge Kaul, Director, Office of Development Studies, United Nations Development Programme, New York.

Azizur Rahman Khan, Professor, Department of Economics, University of California.

Yung-Chung Kim, Vice-President, The Republic of Korea National Red Cross.

Nemir Kırdar, President and Chief Executive Officer, Investcorp International, Bahrain.

Lawrence R. Klein, Nobel Laureate, Professor, Department of Economics and Finance, University of Pennsylvania, Philadelphia.

Arvo Kuddo, Research Fellow, World Institute for Development Economics Research (WIDER), Helsinki; and former Minister of Labor of Estonia.

John Langmore, Minister of Parliament, Canberra.

Flora Lewis, Senior Columnist, The New York Times, Paris.

Wangari Maathai, Professor and Co-ordinator, The Green Belt Movement, Nairobi.

Federico Mayor, Director-General, United Nations Educational, Scientific, and Cultural Organization, Paris.

Terry McKinley, Department of Economics, University of California, Riverside.

Robert S. McNamara, Former President of the World Bank, Washington, D.C.

Valentine M. Moghadam, Senior Research Fellow, UNU/WIDER, Helsinki.

Daniel Mokhosi, OFS Strategic Unit, University of the Orange Free State, South Africa.

Wally N'Dow, Secretary General of the United Nations Conference for Human Settlements (HABITAT II), Nairobi.

Miguel de Paladella, Vice President, External Relations, AIESEC International.

Anthony W. Pereira, Professor, Department of Political Science, New School for Social Research, New York.

Maria de Lourdes Pintasilgo, President of the Independent Commission on Population and Quality of Life; President of the Board of the World Institute for Development Economics Research (WIDER), Helsinki; and former Prime Minister of Portugal

Gustav Ranis, Professor, Department of Economics, Economic Growth Center, Yale University, New Haven.

Benjamin Rivlin, Director, Ralph Bunche Institute on the United Nations, City University of New York, New York.

Dankwart A. Rustow, Distinguished Professor of Political Science and Sociology, City University of New York, New York.

Nafis Sadik, Executive Director, UNFPA, Secretary-General 1994 International Conference on Population and Development, New York.

Mihály Simai, Director, United Nations University/World Institute for Development Economics Research (WIDER), Helsinki.

Juan Somavia, Permanent Representative of Chile to the United Nations; Chairman, World Summit for Social Development, New York.

Frances Stewart, International Development Centre, Oxford University, United Kingdom.

Maurice F. Strong, former Secretary-General, United Nations Conference on Environment and Development, Canada.

Masayuki Tadokoro, Associate Professor, Department of International Relations, Himeiji-Dokkoyo University, Japan.

Princess Basma Bint Talal, The Queen Alia Jordan Social Welfare Fund, Jordan.

Carl Tham, Minister of Education of Sweden, Stockholm.

David Turnham, Development Centre, OECD, Paris.

Jessica Vivian, United Nations Research Institute for Social Development (UNRISD), Geneva.

Yue Chim Richard Wong, Hong Kong Centre for Economic Research and School of Economics and Finance, University of Hong Kong.

About the Editors

Üner Kırdar is a Senior Adviser to the UNDP Administrator. Born in Turkey on 1 January 1933, he graduated from the Faculty of Law, Istanbul, undertook postgraduate studies at the London School of Economics, and received his Ph.D. from Jesus College, University of Cambridge, England.

Dr. Kırdar has served the United Nations system in various capacities, including Secretary of the Preparatory Committee and United Nations Conference on Human Settlements (1974–1976), Secretary of the Group of Experts on the Structure of the United Nations System (1975), and a Senior Officer for Inter-Agency Affairs in the Office of the United Nations Secretary-General (1972–1977). He was Director of the Division of External Relations and Secretary to the Governing Council Secretariat of UNDP from 1980 to 1981. He has been the main architect of the UNDP Development Study Programme and has organized several seminars, roundtable meetings, lectures, and discussion groups attended by high-level national and international policy makers.

He has also held senior positions in the Ministry of Foreign Affairs, Turkey, including Director for International Economic Organizations and Deputy Permanent Representative of Turkey to the United Nations Office at Geneva.

Dr. Kırdar is the author of the book *Structure of UN Economic Aid to Underdeveloped Countries* (1966; 1968). He is a coeditor and contributor to other books, including *Human Development: The Neglected Dimension* (1986); *Human Development, Adjustment and Growth* (1987); *Managing Human Development* (1988); *Development and People* (1989);*Equality of Opportunity Within and Among Nations* (1977); "Human Resources Development: Challenge for the '80s," *Crisis of the '80s* (1983); "Impact of IMF Conditionality on Human Conditions," *Adjustment with Growth* (1984); *The Lingering Debt Crisis* (1985); *Change: threat or Opportunity?* (five volumes, 1991); and *A World Fit for People* (1994). He has also contributed numerous articles to professional books and journals.

Leonard Silk is Senior Research Fellow of the Ralph Bunche Institute on the United Nations at the Graduate School of the City University of New York and Distinguished Professor of Economics at Pace University. From 1970 to 1992, he was the Economics Columnist of *The New York Times* and has served as a member of the Editorial Board of that newspaper.

Prior to joining *The New York Times,* Dr. Silk was a Senior Fellow at the Brookings Institution and Chairman of the Editorial Board of *Business Week* magazine.

Born in Philadelphia on 15 May 1918, he graduated from the University of Wisconsin at Madison and received his Ph.D. in economics from Duke University in Durham, North Carolina.

He served in the U.S. Army Air Forces (1942–1945). For the U.S. Army, he covered the founding conference of the United Nations in San Francisco. He was Assistant Commissioner of the U.S. Mission to the North Atlantic Treaty Organization and other regional organization in Paris (1951–1955). He has been a member of Presidential commissions of Labor–Management Relations and Budget Concepts, of the President's Task Force on the War Against Poverty, and of the Research Advisory Board of the Committee for Economic Development.

Dr. Silk has been Ford Distinguished Research Professor at the Graduate School of Industrial Administration of Carnegie–Mellon University, Marsh Professor at the University of Michigan, and Poynter Fellow of Yale University. He has received honorary degrees from the University of Wisconsin, Duke University, Southern Methodist University, Haverford College, and several other institutions.

Dr. Silk is the author of *Sweden Plans for Better Housing, The Research Revolution, Forecasting Business Trends, Contemporary Economics, The Economists, Ethics and Profits, The American Establishment, Economics in Plain English,* and *Economics in the Real World,* as well as coeditor of *A World Fit for People.*